Proceedings

International Conference on Virtual Systems and MultiMedia

Proceedings

International Conference on Virtual Systems and MultiMedia VSMM '97

September 10–12, 1997

Geneva, Switzerland

Organized by

University of Geneva (MIRALab-CUI)

Sponsored by

International Society on Virtual Systems and MultiMedia (VSMM)
University of Geneva (MIRALab-CUI)

In cooperation with

Computer Graphics Society (CGS)
International Federation for Information Processing (IFIP), WG 5.10

Hosted by

International Telecommunication Union (ITU)

IEEE COMPUTER SOCIETY

Los Alamitos, California

Washington • Brussels • Tokyo

IEEE Computer Society Order Number PR08150
ISBN 0-8186-8150-0
ISBN 0-8186-8152-7 (microfiche ISBN)
IEEE Order Plan Catalog Number 97TB100182
Library of Congress 97-80069

Additional copies may be ordered from:

IEEE Computer Society
Customer Service Center
10662 Los Vaqueros Circle
P.O. Box 3014
Los Alamitos, CA 90720-1314
Tel: + 1-714-821-8380
Fax: + 1-714-821-4641
E-mail: cs.books@computer.org

IEEE Service Center
445 Hoes Lane
P.O. Box 1331
Piscataway, NJ 08855-1331
Tel: + 1-908-981-1393
Fax: + 1-908-981-9667
mis.custserv@computer.org

IEEE Computer Society
13, Avenue de l'Aquilon
B-1200 Brussels
BELGIUM
Tel: + 32-2-770-2198
Fax: + 32-2-770-8505
euro.ofc@computer.org

IEEE Computer Society
Ooshima Building
2-19-1 Minami-Aoyama
Minato-ku, Tokyo 107
JAPAN
Tel: + 81-3-3408-3118
Fax: + 81-3-3408-3553
tokyo.ofc@computer.org

Editorial production by Penny Storms
Cover art production by Alex Torres
Printed in the United States of America by The Printing House

IEEE
COMPUTER
SOCIETY

IEEE

Table of Contents

Preface

VSMM 1997 is the third annual conference of the Society of Virtual Systems and Multimedia (VSMM), founded in 1995 in Japan by Professor Ojika.

VSMM took place in the PALEXPO exhibition complex in Geneva, Switzerland and was organized by the University of Geneva (MIRALab-CUI). The conference formed part of TELECOM Interactive 1997, together with a number of other events focusing on interactive media and telecommunications.

Unique aspects of VSMM 1997:

- Participants sampled the other events featured at TELECOM Interactive, such as the exhibition, lectures for more general audiences, interactive demonstrations and displays, and the 1997 Computer Animation Film Festival.
- The presentations at VSMM were through panels and discussions only. Researchers discussed the significance of their research results with the others at the same session, instead of having the full contents of each paper read out one after another.

The February call for full papers for VSMM 1997 attracted 74 submissions. Each paper was reviewed by three members of the International Program Committee.

The conference was highlighted by four invited speakers and, based on the review process, we selected 23 full papers and 6 two-page abstracts. The members of the program committee deserve special acknowledgment for reviewing the papers in time for us to publish this volume simultaneously with the conference. We would like to thank Dr. Laurent Moccozet and Dr. Prem Kalra for their efficient collaboration in organizing the conference, and Penny Storms of IEEE for expeditiously making these proceedings available in time.

Nadia Magnenat Thalmann
General Chair, Program Co-Chair
MIRALab, University of Geneva

Conference Committees

General Conference Committee

Honorary Committee Chair

Thomas B. Sheridan, *MIT, USA*

General Committee Chair

Nadia Magnenat Thalmann, *University of Geneva, Switzerland*

General Committee Vice-Chairs

Scott S. Fisher, *Telepresence Research, USA*
Hiroshi Harashima, *University of Tokyo, Japan*
Robert J. Stone, *VR Solutions, UK*

International Program Committee

Program Committee Chairs

Nadia Magnenat Thalmann, *University of Geneva, Switzerland (Europe)*
Takeo Ojika, *Gifu University, Japan (Asia)*
David Zeltzer, *David Sarnoff Research Center, USA (America)*

Program Committee Members

Massimo Bergamasco, *Scuola Superiore S. Anna, Italy*
Tat-Seng Chua, *National Univ. of Singapore, Singapore*
Rae A. Earnshaw, *Univ. of Bradford, UK*
Ole Henrik Ellestad, *Norsk Regnesentral, Norway*
Jose L. Encarnacao, *Fraunhofer-Institut fuer Graphische Datenverarbeitung, Germany*
Scott S. Fisher, *Telepresence Research Corp., USA*
Eddy Flerackers, *Limburg Univ. Center, Belgium*
Jean-Guy Fontaine, *Lab. de Robotique de Paris, France*
Mark W. Green, *Univ. Alberta, Canada*
Charles Grimsdale, *Director of Division Ltd, UK*
Hiroshi Harashima, *Univ. of Tokyo, Japan*
Michitaka Hirose, *Univ. of Tokyo, Japan*
Young Whan Kim, *Korean Telecom, South Korea*
Tohru Ifukube, *Hokkaido Univ., Japan*
Takeo Kanade, *Carnegie Mellon Univ., USA*
Stanislav Klimenko, *In. for High Energy Physics, Russia*
Myron Krueger, *Artificial Reality Corp., USA*
Tosiyasu L. Kunii, *LDAT, Japan*
Nadia Magnenat Thalmann, *Univ. of Geneva, Switzerland*
Hermann Maurer, *Univ. of Graz, Austria*
Makoto Nonaka, *President of FISA, USA*
Junji Nomura, *Matsusita Electric Works LTD, Japan*
Setsuo Ohsuga, *Waseda Univ., Japan*
Takeo Ojika, *Gifu Univ., Japan*
Alex Pentland, *MediaLab MIT, USA*
Werner Purgathofer, *Vienna Univ. of Tech., Austria*
Larry Rosenblum, *Naval Research Laboratory, USA*
Joachim Sauter, *ART+COM, Germany*
Hans-Peter Seidel, *Erlangen Univ., Germany*
Luis Serra National, *Univ. of Singapore, Singapore*
Sung Yong Shin, *KAIST, South Korea*
Vaclav Skala, *Univ. of W. Bohemia, Czech Republic*
Mel Slater, *Univ. College London, UK*
Martin Sperka, *Slovak Univ. of Tech., Slovakia*
Robert J. Stone, *VR Solutions Ltd, UK*
Yasuhito Suenaga, *Nagoya Univ., Japan*
Susumu Tachi, *Univ. of Tokyo, Japan*
Zesheng Tang, *Tsinghua Univ., China*
Demetri Terzopoulos, *Univ. of Toronto, Canada*
Daniel Thalmann, *Swiss Fed. In. of Tech., Switzerland*
Hal Thwaites, *Concordia Univ., Canada*
Junichiro Toriwaki, *Nagoya Univ., Japan*
Jiaxin Wang, *Univ. of Tsinghua, China*
Kaye Wohn, *KAIST, South Korea*
Franz-Heinrich Wolter, *Univ. of Hannover, Germany*
Kazuhiko Yamamoto, *Gifu Univ., Gifu, Japan*
David Zeltzer, *David Sarnoff Research Center, USA*

Collaborative Virtual Environments

TRADE: A Transatlantic Research And Development Environment

José L. Encarnação[1], Stefan Noll[1], Michael R. Macedonia[2],
Ammo Goettsch[2], Norbert Schiffner[1], Andreas. Graeff[1]

[1] Fraunhofer Institute for Computer Graphics,
Rundeturmstraße 6
D-64283 Darmstadt, Germany
Fax: +49 6151 155 430
jle@igd.fhg.de

[2] Fraunhofer Center for Research in Computer Graphics,
321 South Main Street, Suite 2,
Providence, RI 02903 USA
Fax: +1 401 453 0444
mmacedon@crcg.edu

Abstract

The universal advancement of network and graphics technology, new business models, and global infrastructure development are transforming the solitary, platform-centric 3D computing model. With the availability of global information highways, 3D graphical intercontinental collaboration will become a part of our daily work routine.

Our organisations, the Fraunhofer Institute for Computer Graphics (IGD) in Germany and the Fraunhofer Center for Research in Computer Graphics (CRCG) in the United States, are looking ahead into a new age of telecommunication and cooperation by establishing a transcontinental computer graphics research effort and a proposed G-7 testbed. We are studying how 3D computer graphics and virtual environments can aid global collaborative work. [1]

We have focused our research efforts on determining how computer networks can transform the distributed workplace into a shared environment, allowing real-time interaction among people and processes without regard to their locations. Our research is part of a long-term project - the Transatlantic Research and Development Environment (TRADE).

Background and Rationale

To the ever increasing competition in practically all industries, it is vital for businesses to effectively and rapidly design, prototype, and manufacture new products to meet the demands of a world where business has no borders. The challenges of the global marketplace result in new requirements which can be summarised as follows:

- reduced product cycle times;
- reduced costs;
- improved quality and customer service;
- adaptability to changing markets;
- development of new business, security and organisational models.

Until recently, only large companies were concerned by these issues because of the inherent communication and personnel costs associated with running global enterprises. However, Small and Medium Enterprises (SMEs) are encountering both the challenges and opportunities of the world market because new technologies and infrastructure are making every business a global enterprise..

The project „Transatlantic Research And Development Environment" (TRADE) addresses these challenges by developing an environment for collaborative product development and integrated supply chain management over transatlantic ATM and ISDN networks. TRADE demonstrates the benefits of using such an environment for companies that want to exploit their resources effectively world wide.

Global Imperatives

Recent surveys show that many manufactures have manifold business relations all over the world and that they have to be internationally competitive. However, problems have arisen from this trend. For example, companies must be able to synchronise and allocate resources dynamically across a wide range of cultures and practices in each country. Distributed companies typically keep the design and engineering centres in their home country, while manufacturing is established in another foreign country. Design changes are sometimes made without being communicated in a timely manner to the subsidiary because of differences in technical standards and paper-based communication.

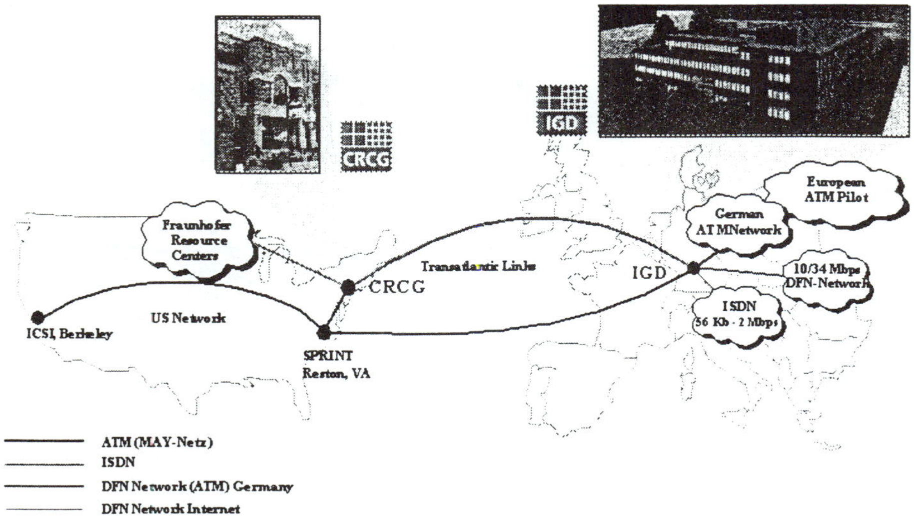

Picture 1: TRADE Network - Transcontinental ATM Testbed of TRADE

Technological Imperatives

The cost-of-entry to the world of advanced technology has been reduced considerably costs for world-wide communication are decreasing rapidly. Fiber-optic links, low-earth-orbit satellites, and digital broadcast techniques are enabling the wide spread use of voice and data network. Low cost personal computers have reshaped productivity in the United States. Over 90% of US office workers now use a personal computer. This trend is now extending into manufacturing with the arrival of low-cost CAD software and rapid prototyping techniques such as stereo lithography. Consequently, SMEs are now able to extend their presence and participate in the global marketplace over international networks.

Network technology and infrastructure are constantly progressing with the growth of the Internet and the increasing competition in the telecommunication industry. This has already led to substantial decreases in costs in the United States - a trend which is expected to follow in Germany.

Another important development in network technology is the Intranet and Extranets. Intranet is the descriptive term for the implementation of Internet technologies using Internet standards within an enterprise. Extranets connect corporate Intranets with clients and partners. Their implementation delivers the information of an organisation to each individual desktop with minimal cost, time, and effort. Extranets will emerge in1998 to become a major influence on the relationships between companies and clients in global trade.

TRADE

The Fraunhofer Institute for Computer Graphics (IGD) in Darmstadt, Germany and the Centre for Research in Computer Graphics (CRCG) in Providence, USA, have developed the Transatlantic Research and Development Environment (TRADE) project and its related network (TradeNet). The TRADE project establishes world-wide laboratory among project members. The objective of the TRADE project is to create and provide the knowledge to build affordable, accessible and suitable technology and interfaces for a „Global Market Place" environment. The project also examines the technological basis and appropriate services for users. The results will be combined with an analysis of critical application areas such as the management of ever-expanding supply chains and enabling tools for small and medium-sized business. This will allow SMEs to synchronise their operations and extend their presence, as they will have to compete with firms not only in the home country but also across borders.

The TRADE project uses an ATM network between Darmstadt, Germany and Providence, Rhode Island (Picture 1). Operationally, we establish a permanent virtual channel (PVC) to Providence. The connection of the Fraunhofer-IGD to the pilot ATM network uses the facilities of the Metropolitan Area Network DArmstadt, (MANDA). MANDA uses the ATM protocol for connecting various research institutes in the area of Darmstadt. One of the institutes connected to the MANDA ring is the Technologiezentrum Darmstadt, which has direct ATM access to the pilot ATM network.

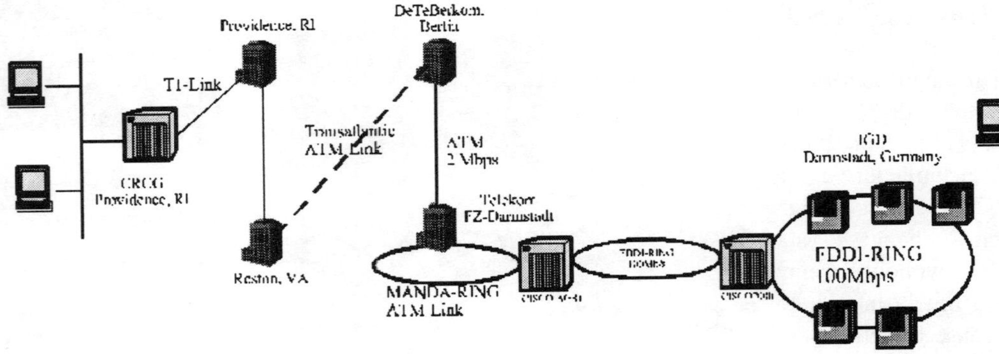

Picture 2: ATM connection between Fraunhofer-IGD in Germany and Fraunhofer-CRCG in the United States

The nodes of the pilot ATM network are traversed in the following order: from the Fraunhofer-IGD by way of an FDDI ring to the MANDA CISCO router which provides access to the MANDA ring and thus to the Technologiezentrum Darmstadt; from there by way of the ATM network of the Deutsche Telekom to DeTeBerkom in Berlin; from Berlin by way of a direct CANTAT3 link to Reston, Virginia, USA; and finally, from Reston by way of a leased link to Providence, Rhode Island, USA. The ATM protocol is then converted into a T1 link and fed into the CISCO router of our partner, the Center for Research in Computer Graphics (CRCG) in Providence. Picture 2 illustrates this communication.

Picture 3: Virtual Conference Room

The Transatlantic Research and Development Environment (TRADE) with its network lets us

- establish an intercontinental distributed testbed for gaining operational experience and management practice
- identify key research and development topics for global virtual environments (VEs)
- define and select experiments that use the benefits of 3D environments and high-speed digital networks
- obtain measurements and performance results and overall system evaluations
- develop global VEs for research and development, industrial and commercial applications

Virtual Collaborative Environments (VCE)

The use of techniques like 3D graphics, 3D sound, 3D interaction and haptic feedback make a multidimensional form of telecommunication possible that allows the simultaneous addressing of the three main perception senses of human individuals. These advanced forms of telecommunication make it possible to transform distributed workplaces into shared virtual environments. Scenarios can be tailored to the particular needs of an application or user. Possible applications range from simple distributed multimedia visualisation of scientific data in standard 3D data formats to technologically very costly distributed VR environments for teleconferences (e.g. Picture 2) and simulators. [2]

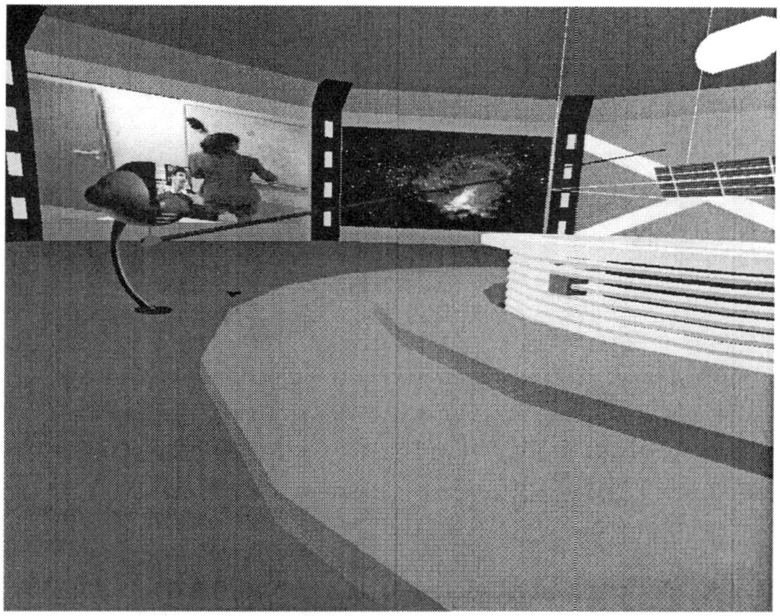

Picture 4: Virtual Emergency Task Force (VETAF) ACM '97 Expo in San Jose, California, USA

Virtual Emergency Task Force (VETAF) and Virtual Showroom

The next two scenarios presented here are those used in demonstrating TRADE at the ACM '97 Expo in San Jose, California and at the G7 exhibition in Bonn, Germany. They show the function of transatlantic ATM and ISDN networks in the future.

Both demonstrations present the idea of a fast exchange of knowledge and man-power with advanced computer technology. In the VETAF scenario, a group of experts located throughout the world meets to discuss a global crisis in a virtual environment specially designed to support their cooperation, whereas the Virtual Showroom is mainly intended to demonstrate how virtual environments can be used in advertising and presentation.

In both scenarios the setting is a virtual room with a 3D-model of the object of interest suspended in the middle (Picture 4&5). The 3D-model in the virtual environment has different levels of detail and can be edited or replaced by other objects (supported formats include VRML, 3DS, NFF). It is possible to map additional data into the model.

On the walls are projections of blueprints, diagrams and video-recordings from other participants in the virtual environment or - in the VETAF scenario - of rescue teams on location. The virtual projection-walls are used for projections of static data (diagrams, blueprints, video records), integration of standard Microsoft Windows applications (PowerPoint, Word) or as distributed whiteboards.

The people in the virtual environment are represented by movable figures called "avatars". Avatars are graphical representations of the participants; they have video-textured faces and business cards for identification. Their position and orientation is related to the current location of the specific participant in the scene.

Users get a stereoscopic impression of the virtual environment via shutter-glasses and large scale projections or via a head-mounted-display. The level of immersion depends on the application. While shutter-glasses and large scale projections fully satisfy the requirements for standard office and conference applications, full immersive virtual reality (e.g. simulators or walks through virtual buildings) require head-mounted displays.

All participants can talk to each other with full duplex spatial sound. A chat capability makes it possible to connect to other participants on low bandwidth networks. The VETAF system is not designed to allow users to examine every detail of the environment and so it uses constrained moving modes to make navigation through the scene easier. A person uses a 3D mouse to move through the environment and to select between multiple moving modes. To select and move an object in the virtual environment, participants can use the mouse to guide his distributed pointer, a light-ray to the target.

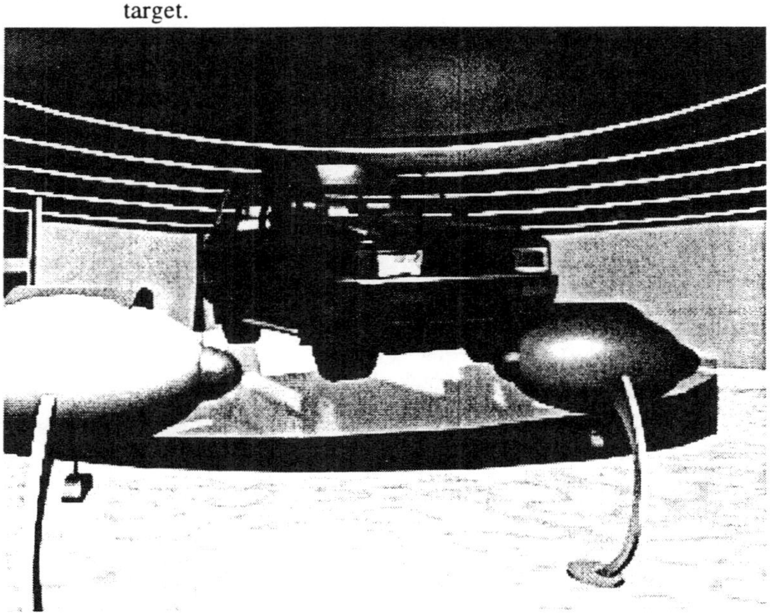

Picture 5: Virtual Showroom, G7 Exhibition 1997 in Bonn, Germany

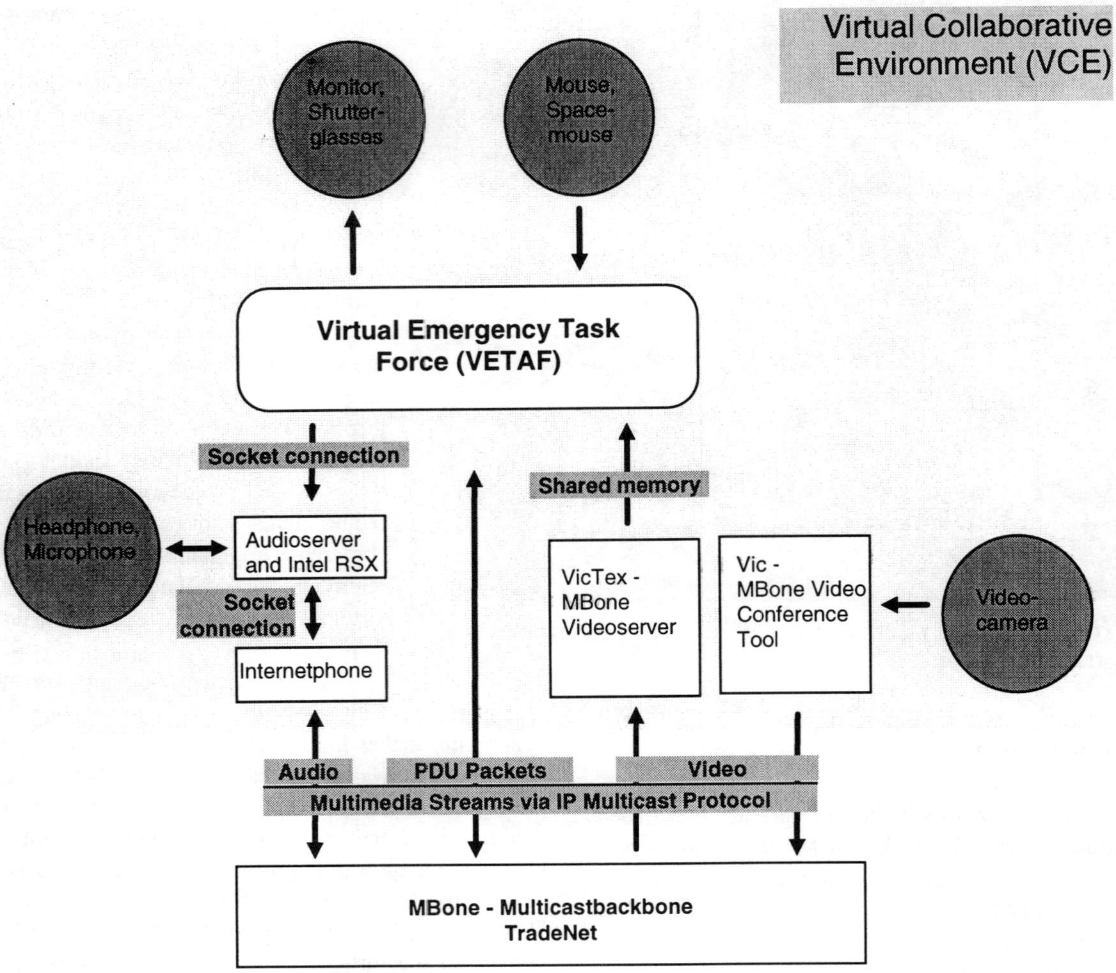

Picture 6: VETAF Architecture

Technical realisation

The whole VETAF environment is separated into two components - the main VETAF application and three MBone tools for audio and video communication. [3]

The main VETAF application is realised with WorldToolKit® R6 a portable, cross-platform software development system for building high-performance, real-time, integrated 3D applications. VETAF renders the virtual environment and handles the input/output devices (e.g. 3D SpaceMouse, monitor, shutter glasses). Any transformation or movement of entities in the environment is sent as protocol-data-unit (PDU) packets to every other participant. The communication between the multiple participants is based on the IP multicast protocol.

For video and audio communication in the virtual environment we use the standard MBone tools Vic/VicTex and NetPhone together with the RSX API from Intel for spatial sound experience. [4]

Vic is a multicast video conferencing application developed by the Network Research Group at the Lawrence Berkeley National Laboratory in collaboration with the University of California, Berkeley. Vic takes a signal from the video device and sends it to a designated multicast address. VicTex is a modification of the standard Vic application developed by Fraunhofer CRCG in Providence. Instead of viewing the video data in a window VicTex writes the video stream into a shared memory area from where the VETAF application can load and use it as a video-texture in the virtual environment.

Class	Example Data	Requirements
Renderer	Synchronization between renderers	Lowest latency
Agent	Communication between agents	Guaranteed delivery, flexibility
Simulation	Distributed shared world state updates	Low latency, variable QoS
Device	Input/Output device events	Low latency, LAN use only
Live Media	Video textures, live audio	Internet conferencing quality

Table 1: Classes of Data

The spatial sound audio server is a development of the Fraunhofer IGD in Darmstadt and based on client-server architecture. Different audio sources (e.g. InternetPhone, Mediaplayer) can be related to objects in the virtual scene. These audio sources are connected as clients to the audio server which renders these audio signals depending on the position and orientation of each source in the virtual scene. The VETAF application transmits this position and orientation data via a socket connection to the audio-server.

Future work

Current research at Fraunhofer IGD and Fraunhofer CRCG includes work on a general architecture for VCE applications. This architecture is intended to support current applications such as VETAF as well as research in the areas of distributed simulation, agents in VE, and networking for large scale virtual environments.

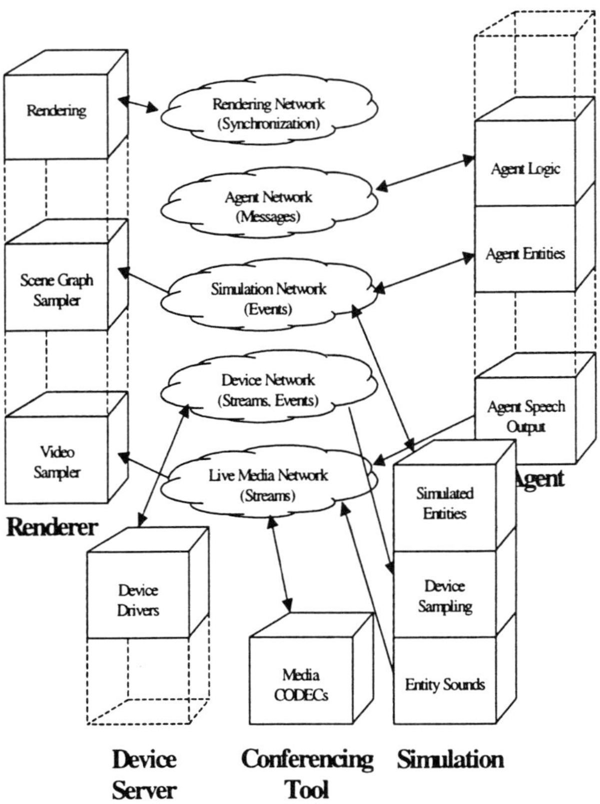

Picture 7: VCE Archtitecture

Multiple Network Model

The architecture outlined here is based on the observation that different VCE components have very different networking and synchronization requirements. Past attempts at mapping these disparate requirements to a single networking protocol have failed to produce solutions scalable to wide-area, general purpose networks. However, protocols currently exist to implement most, if not all, of these components individually. We have identified five classes of networked data which must be supported in order to provide a general purpose VCE architecture. These classes are shown in Table 1.

The architecture is based on assigning each class of data its own network. Potentially, several of these virtual networks can be implemented using the same network transport protocol. However, at this time, we anticipate using a different protocol for each class.

Each component of a VCE is allowed to participate in any set of these networks. The networks do not form a protocol stack, but rather parallel communication channels with different characteristics. Picture 7 shows an example set of components connected by the five networks. In the figure, each vertical cylinder represents a component. These components can be implemented as separate processes running on a set of networked computers. Components become clients of the various networks through a protocol-independent application programing interface (API) represented by the five clouds in Picture 7.

The different „Networks" present a shared data abstraction to the components, which is accessed through a well defined API. Communication between components is permitted only in so far as multiple components can access the same objects in the shared data. The use of an API for inter-component communication allows local communication as well as remote communication in a transparent manner. When multiple components are operating on the same node in the physical network, then their communication can be via shared memory rather than network packets. In the trivial case, a monolithic high-performance VE application running on a single machine can be assembled from reusable, networkable components. In this case, only shared memory communication would take place, providing a clean separation between components without generating network traffic.

The API presented by each network is based on asynchronous sampling of the states of the objects that occupy the given network. Since components sample the various networks asynchronously, they can operate in a decoupled manner. Decoupled operation implies that components can operate independently of other components. This is an important characteristic of any VE design, because it allows rendering components to operate at a constant frame rate, independently of the current update rate of simulation components. The well-defined inter-component communication mechanism also allows different components to run on different processors, when available. In such a case, parallelization and pipelining of rendering, simulation, agent operation and device handling is possible.

CONCLUSION

The Fraunhofer IGD and CRCG are focusing their research efforts on determining how computer networks can help transform the workplace into a shared environment, allowing real-time interaction between people regardless of their location.

IGD and CRCG have successfully demonstrated a distributed virtual environment in which participants can collaborate and interact with live voice, video, text, modelling and imagery. This application has proven to be an effective environment for collaboration among research partners even when participants have been separated by great distances. During the G7 meeting in Bonn 1997, delegates were able to witness and participate in a demonstration of this application between Bonn, Darmstadt, Germany and Providence, USA. As a result, TradeNet was selected by the delegates to be officially designated as an international testbed pilot project for the development of electronic commerce. Electronic commerce is an ongoing policy working group about one of the major activities on the G7. Formally called the Global Marketplace for Small and Medium enterprises, the group is developing underlying policy recommendations for facilitation of global electronic commerce, especially for small and medium enterprises.

Current research includes work on a general architecture for applications in virtual collaborative environments. This architecture supports current applications as well as research in the areas of distributed simulation, agents in virtual environments, and networking for large scale virtual environments.

References

[1] Rix, S. Haas, and J Teixeira, eds., Virtual Prototyping: Virtual Environment and the Product Design Process, Chapman Hall, New York 1995.

[2] Brutzman, „Graphics Internetworking: Bottlenecks and Breakthroughs, „Digital Illusions, C. Dodsworth, ed., Addison Wesley, Reading, Mass., !996.

[3] Macedonia and D. Brutzman, „MBone Provides Audio and Video Across the Internet", Computer, Apr. 1994, Vol. 27, No. 4, pp. 30-36

[4] McCanne, S., and Jacobson, V., vic: A Flexible Framework for Packet Video. ACM, Multimedia '95, November 1995, San Francisco, CA, pp. 511-522

Collaborative CyberMirage: A Shared Cyberspace with Mixed Reality

S. Uchiyama*†, A. Katayama*†, A. Kumagai*, H. Tamura*†, T. Naemura**, M. Kaneko**††, and H.Harashima**

*Media Technology Laboratory, Canon Inc.
(† Currently with Mixed Reality Systems Lab. Inc.)
*890-12 Kashimada, Saiwai-ku, Kawasaki-shi 211
{uchiyama,katayama,kumagai,tamura}@mr-system.co.jp
FAX: +81-45-411-8110

**Faculty of Engineering, The University of Tokyo
(†† Currently with KDD R&D Lab.)
**7-3-1 Hongo, Bunkyo-ku, Tokyo 113
{naemura,kaneko,hiro}@hc.t.u-tokyo.ac.jp
FAX: +81-3-5800-5797

Abstract

This paper describes a virtual reality system called "Collaborative CyberMirage", which makes it possible to share photo-realistic virtual environment between multiple points. This system was developed to realize a virtual shopping environment, and although this system is expected to be used through the Internet in a near future, it is based on equipments and networks available now. This paper states about the technics required for virtual shopping, then about the structure of this system, and finally about the methods used to develop it. This system is a largely improved version of the former single-user CyberMirage. In both system, the cyberspace is made by combining image-based data and geometric models to realize superior photo-reality.

1. Introduction

The Internet and WWW browsing tools greatly increased the possibility of a person to collect and broadcast multimedia information. Now, various social activities such as shopping, trading, education and volunteer activities are held through the Internet and Intranets.

Many technologies like casting of live video, building up of 3D space using VRML (Virtual Reality Modeling Language), etc. are being developed to make the 'cyberspace' given by the Internet even more visual and more attractive.

A next required improvement is a method to make possible to people share and experience the cyberspace at realtime, as well as to improve the photo-reality of this space.

Several CSCW (Computer Supported Cooperative Work) and networkd virtual reality systems in which you can share 3D space are already introduced [1]-[8]. In these systems, one can move around the space and manipulate the objects inside it. Nevertheless, they are regretfully poor in photo-reality because they used conventional computer graphics techniques based on geometric models that imposes limits to render the objects in realtime.

Presently, the image-based rendering technology which depicts virtual environment using images captured from the real world attracts many people's interests [9][10]. The previous CyberMirage [11] system was already based on merging of both image-based rendering technology and VRML. This previous system consisted of a dedicated viewer and sample data, and they can be accessed by everyone through the Web [12][13]. A user (only one) can enjoy walking through a virtual mall where various photo-realistic goods are displayed by downloading the viewer and the sample data

The Collaborative CyberMirage introduced through this paper a largely improved version of the former CyberMirage to make possible for several people to jack-in and co-experience the shared cyberspace while making conversation at realtime. This system is developed using equipments and networks available now, and many efforts are made to provide photo-realism with users and to reduce waiting time.

The following sections describe the structure and methods used to realize this system.

2. Outline of the Collaborative CyberMirage

2.1 Requirements for Cybershopping

The basic objectives of the Collaborative CyberMirage are as follows.

- To make it possible for multiple remote users to experience the same cyberspace simultaneously.
- To realize realtime interaction such as walking through the space and manipulating the objects inside.
- To realize realtime voice communication

The system has been developed based on a model of cybershopping in a virtual mall, which was also used in the former single user version of CyberMirage. During the development of this system, requirements like the following were found:

- Multiple users can go into a shop separately and can walk around viewing the displayed goods. Users can look inside the shop from its point of view and can recognize his/her companion as an avatar.
- Users can verbally communicate with each other and can call a clerk (real person) if necessary.
- Customers can be in their home, or some other place, far away from the shop, where they can get into the Internet while the clerk is in his/her shop. This is a pragmatic requirement so that a clerk in a real shop can also take care of customers in the virtual shop.
- Users can select goods that are not displayed, i.e. goods which data are not stored in the client computer, from a catalogue menu. Then the data of the goods not displayed are transmitted from the shop computer if the virtual shop is open.
- A clerk can select goods from a inventory menu and present them to the virtual customers on his/her own decision.
- Users can move and rotate goods inside the cyberspace to view them from different points of view. This operation is granted to a single customer or a clerk at a time by making it exclusive to one user.

2.2 System Configuration

Although modern computers have great processing

0-8186-8150-0/97 $10.00

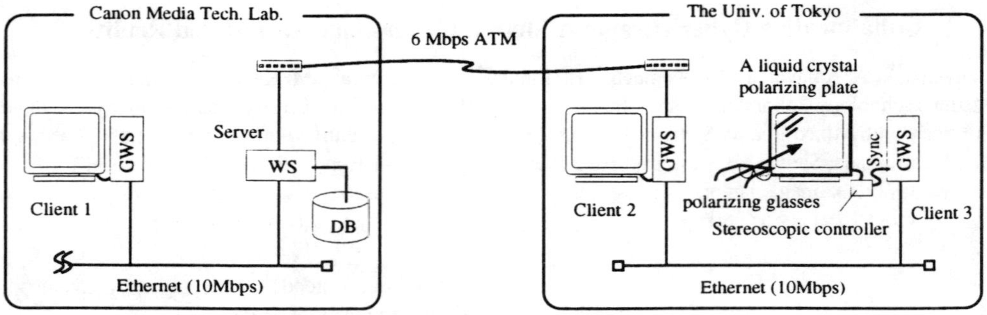

Fig. 1 System configuration

power, it is beyond their power to depict all the objects inside the virtual environment using the image-based data. Therefore, we have decided to describe the environmental portion of the space such as walls and display shelves using geometric-model data and only the goods which are of most interest are described using image-based data.

The main hardware of the system consists of Graphic Workstations (GWS) which generates the views of the cyberspace on its screen, display monitors, a network connecting several remote equipments, and voice communication equipment. Refer to fig. 1 for the structure diagram of this system.

[Graphic Workstations (GWS)]

The developed system can accommodate three users (two customers and a clerk) in the cyberspace. Therefore, three GWSs (SGI's Indigo2 Maximum IMPACT) are connected to the system. As the system requires vast amount of memory, 320 MB of main memory is installed in each workstation.

Another SGI Indigo2 Maximum IMPACT is used to manage the cyberspace, and works as the server as described in section **4**.

[Network]

Since the cyberspace generated by this system requires vast amount of data, the system uses closed network environment having broader band width than the ordinary Internet.

The present system has two customer workstations at The University of Tokyo and other two workstations for a clerk and the server are placed at Canon Media Tech. Lab. These two sites are separated by some tens of kilometers.

Workstations at each site are connected to a local Ethernet network (10 Mbps) into which other computers are connected for local activities. The two sites (LANs) are IP connected with a 6 Mbps dedicated line (ATM) provided from NTT for this experiment.

[Display Monitor]

A stereoscopic display for 3D images is used in one of the workstations. The display is made by placing a liquid crystal polarizing plate (circular polarizing system) in front of the SGI standard monitor screen. It requires polarizing glasses to view the stereoscopic 3D pictures. SGI standard monitors are used for the other workstations. Other stereoscopic displays can also be used since the data structure of our virtual environment is independent from the display equipment.

[Voice Communication]

Each workstation in this system uses external microphone and built-in speaker to perform realtime voice communication and users can communicate with each other through these audio equipments even when they are viewing the cyberspace. A special software is used to provide voice communication.

3. Getting Virtual Environment Data

The Collaborative CyberMirage system uses the same virtual environment data used by the former single user version of CyberMirage. The virtual environment data consists of geometric model data to describe walls, display shelves and other fixed objects, and ray-space data [14] to describe goods.

3.1 Ray-Space Data Acquisition System

The ray-space data is obtained from images captured from real objects. The equipments and method to acquire the ray-space data are as follows.

[Image Capturing]

Images of a subject must be taken from various directions to obtain the ray-space data. The data used by this system can express horizontal parallax but not vertical parallax. Images of the subject are taken from all angles against its horizontal circumference.

The image capturing equipment consists of a turntable, a CCD camera, a controlling computer and a blue backscreen (fig. 2). The turntable can be rotated within 0.5 degree accuracy. It is placed before the blue backscreen and the camera is set at the opposite side so

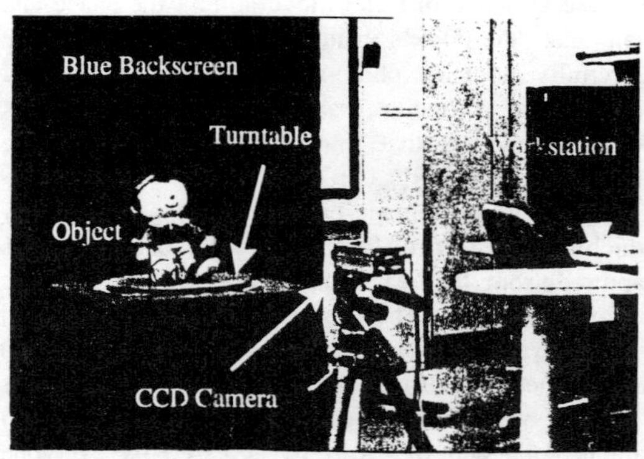

Fig. 2 Image capturing system

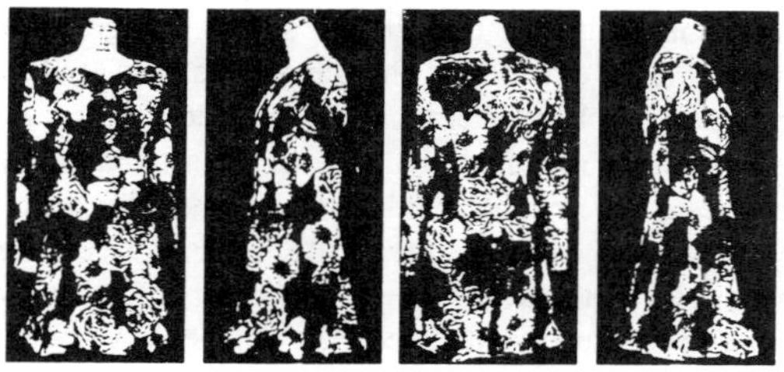

Fig. 3 Captured images of a dress

that the light axis of the lens intersects the rotation axis of the turntable in right angle.

Images are taken by placing a subject onto the turntable. The quality of the reconstructed image from the ray-space data depends on the number of images taken from the subject and the spatial resolution of each image. It is necessary to consider an adequate quality of the reconstructed image when capturing the images of the subject.

In this system the images are taken from 120 points for a single subject. The size of each image is set so that it has enough spatial resolution. For example, the dress shown in fig. 3 was taken by setting image resolution to 261*513 pixels and its data size became to about 64 MB.

[Obtaining the Ray-Space Data]

We extract the image data of the subject from the background by using a popular chroma-key technique. The extracted object data are converted into the ray-space data using the method shown in [11].

Since the raw data can be quite large and they should be compressed in actual data transmission and storage. The first compression reduces the size of the data shown in fig. 3 to about 30 MB [15]. The compressed data is re-compressed using gzip technique to about 9 MB when it is transmitted or saved into a disk.

3.2 Rendering the Virtual Environment

Fixed objects inside the shop in the virtual mall such as walls and display shelves are generated from geometry data. They are modeled separately from the goods data (ray-space data) and are described by VRML.

These two types of data were merged using the method described in [11], and a virtual environment with some shops with goods were rendered. This is a kind of expansion of VRML to describe and mix geometry data and ray-space data.

4. Sharing Virtual Environment

Users that come into the virtual environment can walk-through the space and can manipulate objects inside the space. If multiple users come into the space, each user interacts with the environment independently from other users. However, the virtual environment observed from various different remote places must be a single entity presented in the same way to all the users in order to make them experience the same environment simultaneously. Besides, it is also desirable that one user can see others activities.

To realize this environment, a mechanism is required to share the same virtual environment. This section describes the mechanism and data structures necessary to share the virtual space and the method used to manage the dynamically changing data. It is also shown how several users can share the same environment simultaneously.

4.1 Client/Server

Users must transmit information about the virtual environment between each other in order to share the same virtual space. There are several methods to exchange virtual space information, and the method adopted in this work is to transmit parameters such as positions and orientation of objects and users, because this method requires minimal data transmission.

The transmission method used in our system is client/server method. In this system, a viewer works as the client to show the scenery of the user inside the virtual space. The number of clients will be the same as the number of participants. The server works as a centralized manager for the virtual environment which handles the client parameters described above. The client/server system adopted in this work minimizes the transmission paths, and the number of paths required for n participants are only n. Considering a system where the clients are connected to each other, the number of transmission paths would be $n(n-1)/2$.

In order to actually share the same virtual environment, transmission of the parameter changes is not sufficient, since the data of the environment itself must reside in each user's computer and they must also be transmitted. Therefore, the server also works as the manager of the database of the virtual environment data.

4.2 Data Structure

The data of the shared virtual environment can be divided in the data used to construct the virtual environment and the data necessary during the communication between server and clients. The structures of these data are as follows.

4.2.1 Representation of Virtual Space

Our system adopts tree structure, which is the data structure of the VRML, to describe a virtual space. For example, the virtual space shown in fig. 4 (a) is expressed by the tree structure shown in fig. 4 (b). The virtual space expressed by this tree structure can be altered by changing the structure of the tree as well as the components of the tree.

This system has functions that let the user manipulate objects inside of the virtual space. These manipulable objects are described by partial trees of the entire tree structure. Each partial tree expresses a meaningful "group" or "entity" in the space. These partial trees can be placed to be shown in the virtual space or can be stored separately from the virtual space. In order to make it possible to manipulate objects in the virtual space, the tree structure of the environment has special branches, which we call modifiable branches. These modifiable branches are used when the system operates on objects, like when a partial tree expressing an object is added to the space. Also, the search for the object being manipulated can be restricted to the modifiable branches, avoiding the waste of time when looking at the entire tree structure.

Modifiable branches to manipulate objects in the virtual space is one important characteristic of the tree structure adopted by our system.

4.2.2 Dynamic Information

Everytime a user operates his/her viewer (client), the configuration inside the virtual space changes. To manage these alterations, the server has also a data structure to track the alterations in the space.

This data structure is a linear list of information of the objects to be manipulated, and is not the same as the tree structure used to represent the virtual space. The server and clients use an object serial number to identify each object to be manipulated. The number is uniquely

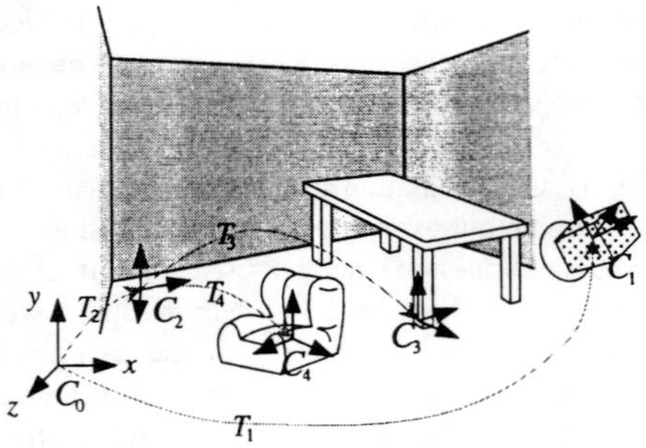

(a) Virtual space including a table and a couch

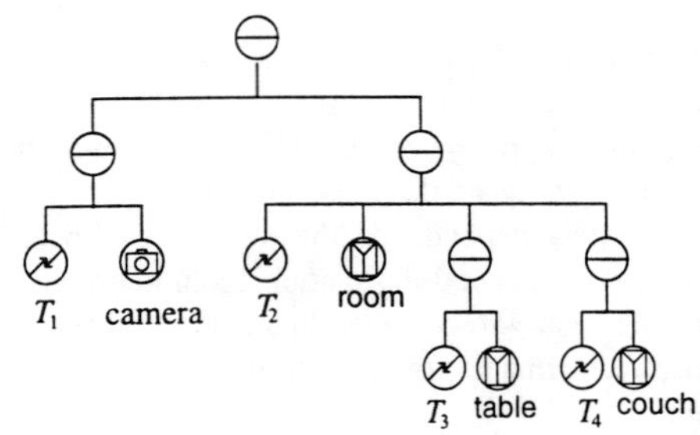

(b) Tree structure of (a)

Fig.4 Representation of virtual space

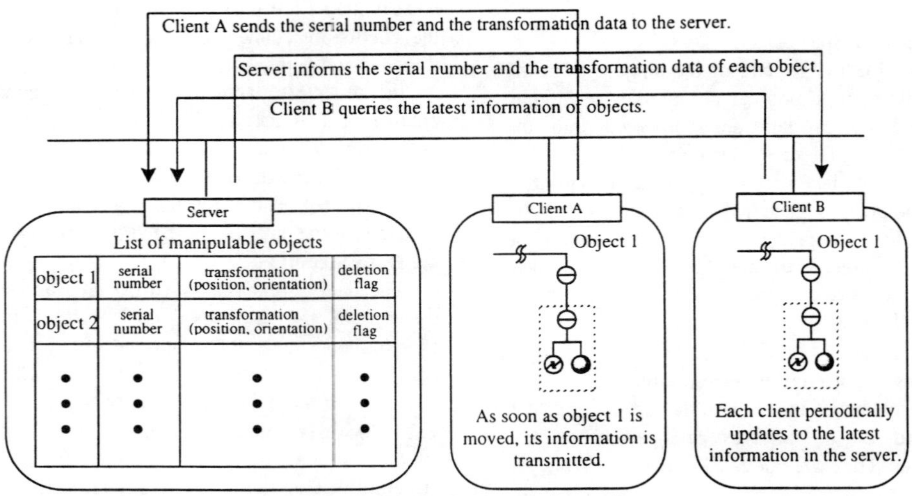

(a) Management of altered information

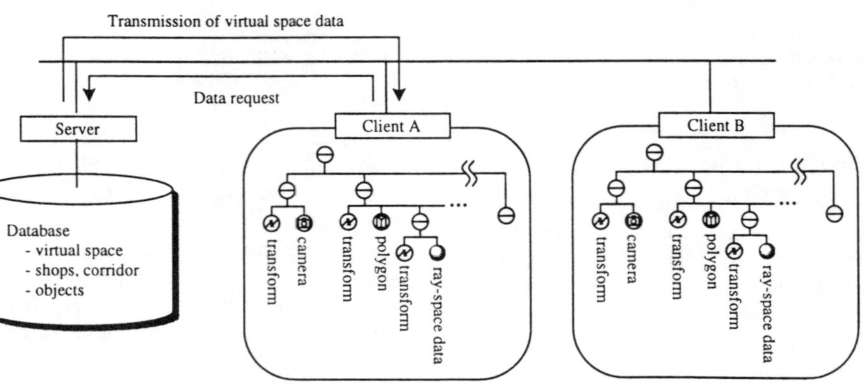

(b) Server as a database of virtual space

Fig 5 Concept of the management of virtual space

set to each object. An object in the server is recognized as the same object in the client when the objects have the same object serial number. In this way, an object expressed by a partial tree in the server is related to one object in the object list kept by every client.

Fig. 5 (a) shows the concept of this object list in the server. As shown in the figure, each item in the list has informations about an object such as name, object serial number, position, coordinate transformation data showing orientation, deletion flag, etc.

4.3 Management of Shared Virtual Space

Our system uses the following methods in order to keep consistency of the environment when the virtual space is modified by users (fig. 5).

(a) Each client can modify the virtual space independently from other clients. The modification is made by altering the tree structure of the virtual space shown in **4.2.1** (More precisely, a client modifies the partial trees below the modifiable branches).

(b) Everytime an object is manipulated by a client, as in (a), the object information changes is transmitted to the server. The server receives that information, selects the corresponding object from the list and updates its information.

(c) Each client periodically queries the server about modification information in order to update its environment according to the modification made by other clients. The server sends the modification information about the requested object (information placed in the object list) to the client. Then the client modifies the data of the tree structure of the virtual space stored in its own computer according to the information sent from the server.

(d) When the client first joint the virtual space, it has not data about it. Thus the server keeps a database to provide the necessary data to generate the virtual space in the client computers. When the client requests the data, and the server sends the necessary data from the database to the client. Clients request

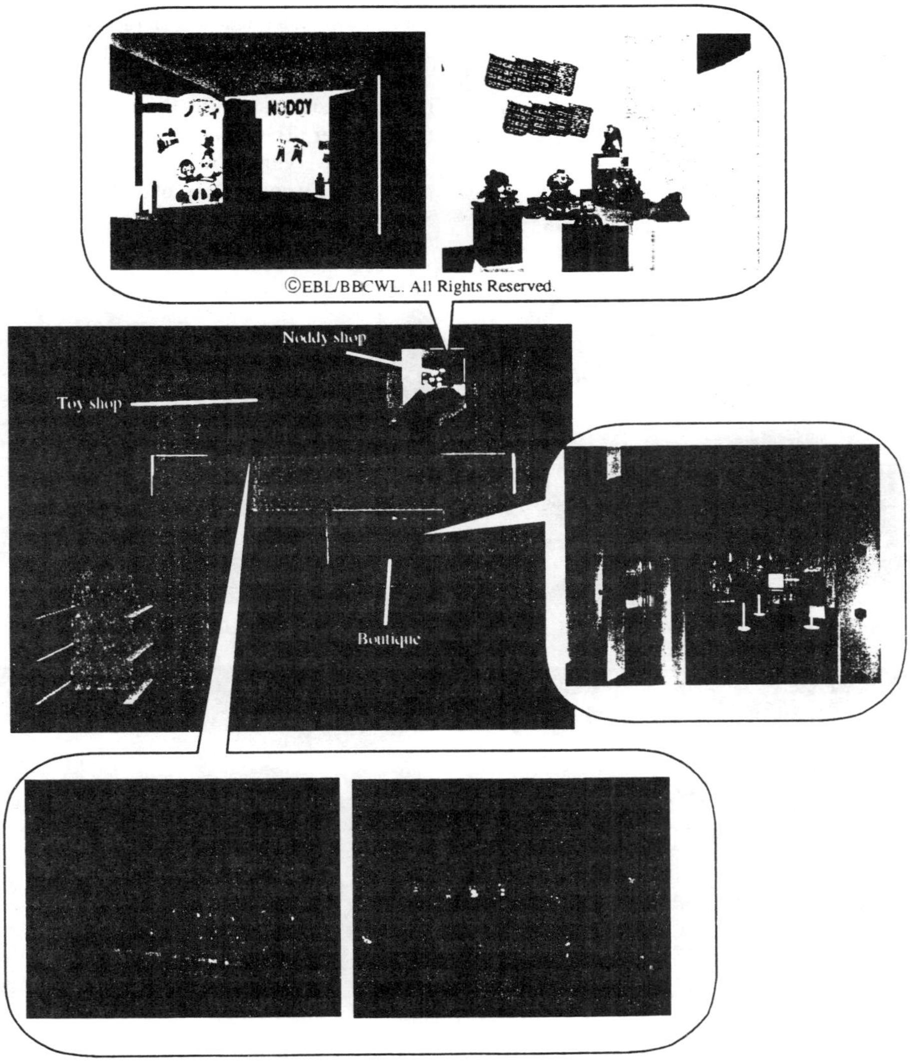

Fig. 6 Virtual space built by our system

the virtual space data when they construct the environment for the first time as well as when they need to add some objects which are not in the space.

In this way, the consistency of the virtual space between each client is kept through the communication centralized by the server, using this client/server method. Section **5** brings more information about these processes, and describes more concretely the processes used to add, delete, move and rotate objects.

4.4 Example of a Shared Space View

Fig. 6 shows a virtual space built by mixing ray-space data with geometry data. Fig. 7 shows an example of a view of an boutique shown in fig. 6, which shared by three users. Each client, as a participant in the virtual space, has its existence and movement expressed by avatars in the space. Fig. 7 (a) is a bird's-eye view of the space. Fig. 7 (b) through (d) are respectively the views from the viewpoints of clients 1 through 3. As shown in the figures, each client can view the same space from different points.

5. Interaction with the Shared Space

Each participant can interact with the shared virtual space. The interaction includes free walk-through the space, manipulation of objects in the space, addition of an object into the space, deletion or replacement of an existing object. These interactions are necessary to perform the operations done by the customers and the clerk described in section **2**.

This section describes the interactions with the shared space, and in special describes the communication mechanism between the server and clients.

5.1 Walk-Through

Each client can join the virtual space as a participant using the viewer, and walk-through the space using it. The walk-through function is implemented so that the viewpoint of the viewer is moved and rotated according to the mouse movement. Each client can walk-through the space independently from other participants. Participants are represented by avatars when they enter the virtual space as if they actually exist in the space. Thus, participants can observe other participants' activities. The following processes are performed to implement this functionality, and they are required to keep the environment consistency as shown in the section **4**.

[Informing the Viewpoint of a Client to the Server]

In this system, each client informs its viewpoint data to the server. In this work, the viewpoint data is the coordinate transformation data and is grouped as a data set consisting of translation, rotation and rotation center. The coordinate transformation data is based on the world coordinates and can uniquely state the position and the orientation of the viewpoint.

Since the informing process is performed everytime the client mouse is moved, this data is continuously sent to the server. The server updates its data of the client viewpoint everytime it receives them.

[Getting Viewpoint Data of Other Clients from the Server]

Each client queries the server about the viewpoint

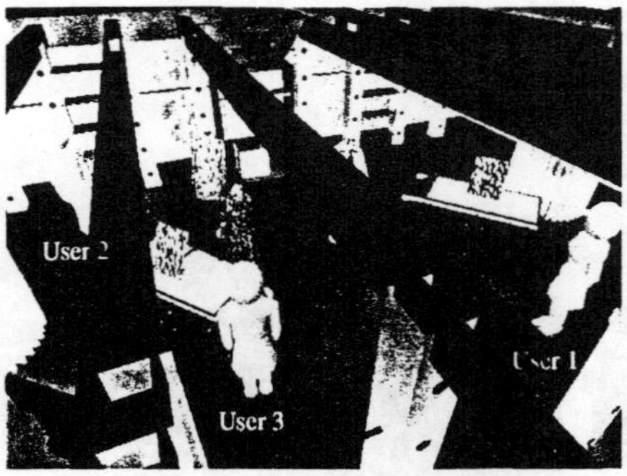

(a) Bird's-eye view of the virtual space

(b) User1's view

(c) User2's view

(d) User3's view

Fig. 7 Examples of rendered images of shared space

data of other clients periodically (every 200 milliseconds) and the server sends back the viewpoint data of the requested client. These data are used by the client to update the position and the orientation of the avatar of the corresponding participant.

Through this process, movements of other participants are displayed in the viewer of the client.

5.2 Moving and Rotating Objects

Each participant can freely "grasp and move" objects in the virtual space. This operation is done in two steps; to select an object and then to move it. A participant first selects an object he/she wants to move by clicking it. Then the manipulator shown in fig. 8 (b) is displayed around the object selected. The object is moved when the participant drugs this manipulator with a mouse (fig. 9 and 10). Objects that can be grasped are limited to those previously designated. It is necessary to designate in advance an object as movable in the partial tree of that object.

Each participant can freely grasp and move objects independently from other participants. However, one participant can operate only one object at a time. Also, multiple participants cannot operate on the same object at the same time. These restrictions are required to keep consistency of the space in the same way as described in **5.1**. These restrictions are implemented in the following way.

[Object Selection]

Each client informs the serial number of the selected object to the server when it selects an object. The server receiving the information sets the number of the informing client into the selection privilege field of the object as long as no other client number is set already. In this way, the server exclusively controls the object selection and prevents multiple clients from selecting the same object at the same time.

[Informing the Object Movement and Rotation from a Client to the Server]

A client sends the transformation information to the server when it moves or rotates an object. This notification is made everytime a mouse event is generated to manipulate an object. Since the mouse is almost always manipulated, the notification is made continuously. The server updates its coordinate transformation data of the object when it receives this notification.

[Informing Object Movement and Rotation from the Server]

Clients periodically (every 200 milliseconds) query about the positions and orientations of all the objects below all the modifiable branches of its virtual space. The server sends the transformation information according to the received serial numbers of the objects being queried, and the client receiving the response from the server changes the information of the objects below the modifiable branches of its virtual space.

Through these processes, operations made by other participants are reflected on the view of the client's viewer.

5.3 Adding, Deleting, and Replacing Objects

Participants can add an object into the virtual space, delete an existing object from the space or replace an existing object with another object.

5.3.1 Adding an Object

Participants can add an object into the virtual space provided that the object to be added is registered in the database of the server. The participants can see a list of all objects registered in the database. Our system opens a popup window with images of typical objects which can be added to the space when a participant clicks on the addition button on the viewer (fig. 11). When a participant clicks on an object in the popup window to select it, the object is added to the space. The processes performed at this time are as follows.

[Object Addition Notification from a Client to the Server]

When a client instructs to add an object, the serial number of the selected object is sent to the server, and the server adds it to the list described in **4.2.2** as a new object.

[Object Addition Notification from the Server]

Clients periodically (every 2 seconds) query the server if a new object was added to the virtual space, and if a new object was added to the object list, the server informs its serial number. Clients receiving the serial number add the object to a modifiable branch of their tree structure. Since the actual data of the object is placed in the database of the server, clients read them

(a) Before selection (b) A manipulator appears after selection.

Fig. 8 Selection of an object

Fig. 9 Translation of the object selected in fig. 8 (b)

Fig. 10 Translation and rotation of the object selected in fig. 8 (b)

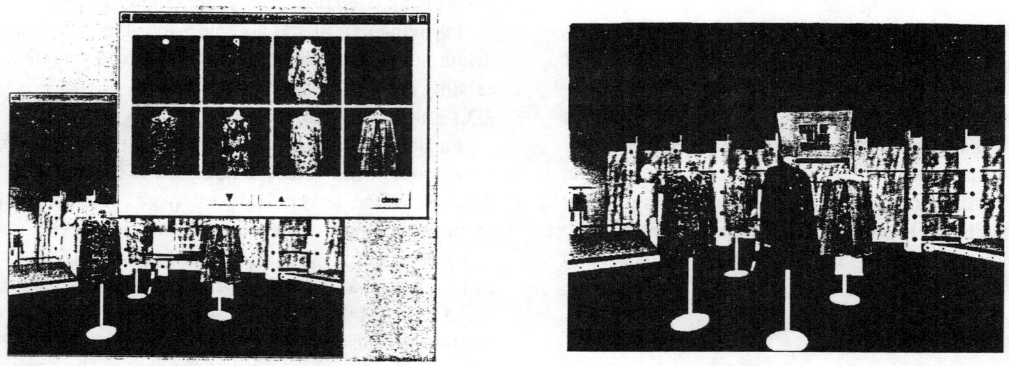

(a) Popup window to add an object (b) Suits added to virtual space

Fig. 11 Objects addition to virtual space

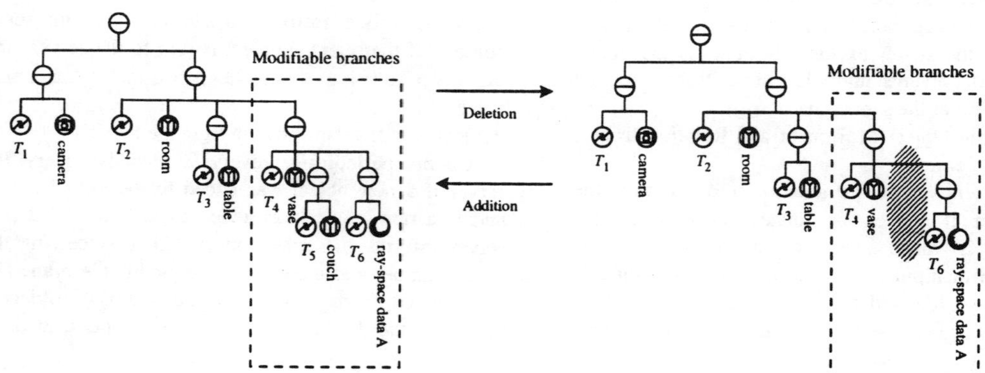

Fig. 12 Alteration of tree structure when adding/deleting objects

from that database to set up the partial tree of the object (fig. 12).

Through these processes, an object added by other participants is reflected on the view of the client's viewer.

[Setting the Placement of an Object]

If the partial tree of an added object describes its initial position, the client adds this partial tree with this initial position in a modifiable branch and informs the resulting transformation to the server. This notification is performed as described in **5.2.**

However, if the initial position is not stated in the partial tree, the client adds the object in front of the participant who added the object. In this process, the object is set two meters apart from the viewpoint of the client and the resulting transformation is informed to the server in as described in **5.2.** The object is placed in front of the participant to keep it from losing the sight of the added object.

5.3.2 Deleting an Object

Participants can delete an existing object from the virtual space provided that the object is placed under a modifiable branch in the tree structure of the client. A participant must click the object to delete to select it and then click the deletion button on the viewer (fig. 13).

[Object Selection]

Participants can select an object in the same way they select an object as described in **5.2.**

[Object Deletion Notification from a Client to the Server]

When a participant instructs to delete an object, the client deletes the partial tree of the corresponding object and then informs the serial number of the deleted object to the server. The server receiving this notification sets a deletion flag in the item in the object list.

[Object Deletion Notification from the Server]

Clients periodically (every 200 milliseconds) query the server if an object was deleted from the virtual space. This query is done at the same time a client queries about object transformation. If a client finds an object with the deletion flag set, the client deletes the partial tree of the object from its tree structure. Through these processes, an object deleted by other participants is reflected on the view of the client's viewer.

5.3.3 Replacing an Object

Participants can replace an existing modifiable object in the virtual space with another object. This operation is performed by deleting an object as described in **5.3.2** and then adding an object as described in **5.3.1**. This operation is performed when a participant instructs to add an object while another object is selected. The selected object is deleted and then the specified object is added. The added object is placed at the same position of the deleted object (fig. 14 and 15).

6. Concluding Remarks and Discussion

We have developed the Collaborative CyberMirage system using the technologies described in sections 3 through 5. Three shops are presently implemented, one boutique and two toy shops. In each shop, goods which are difficult to be represented by geometric model are displayed using ray-space data. We introduced this system to visitors on the open day of the laboratory.

The crucial problem of this system is the amount of data. The size of the object data depends not on the complexity of the object, but on the physical size of the object and the required spatial resolution of the image in the viewer. The size of the raw data for the dress shown in fig. 3 is about 64 MB and 57 MB for the doll shown in fig. 8 (b). They are about 9 MB and 3.2 MB even when compressed. It is required 20 to 60 seconds for on demand transmission from the warehouse to a customer, decompression and loading data. In a real situation, it would be natural to wait for the clerk go into the warehouse to seek an object, but it may seem a long waiting time for the user accustomed to work on computers displays. How to reduce this waiting time using more sophisticated compression schemes is another research theme.

On the other hand, there was little complain about the manipulation of the displayed objects. We think it is because people who experienced our system expected the poor operationability performance normal on virtual environments, in contrast to real objects which people can take and freely see in details. Therefore, it seems that the method described in this paper to manipulate the objects is enough for people who visits a cyberspace.

In this implementation of our system, objects can only be rotated horizontally. It is impossible to rotate goods vertically because there is no data to express the vertical parallax of goods. Theoretically, we can

Fig. 13 Deletion of the object selected in fig. 8 (b)

(a) Selection of an object

(b) Replacement

Fig. 14 Replacement of objects

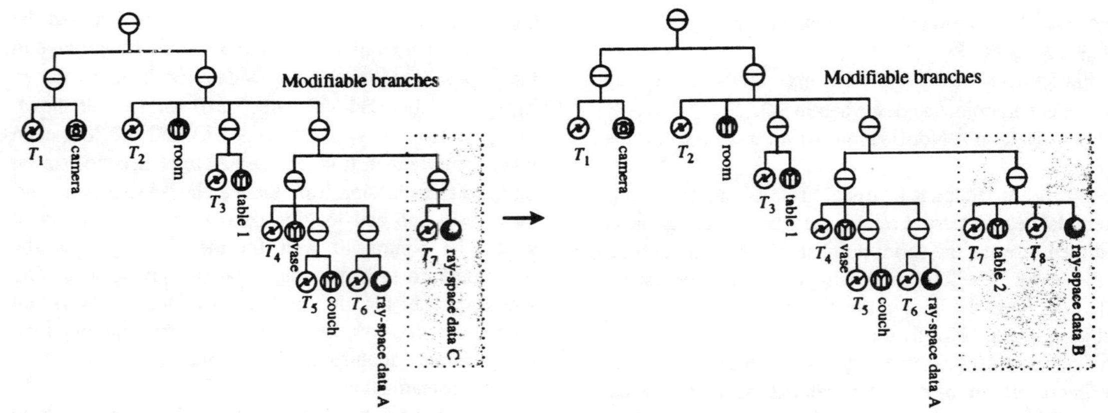

Fig. 15 Alteration of tree structure when replacing the objects

introduce vertical parallax to objects, however, if we do so, the amount of data that is the biggest bottle neck of our system will increase drastically.

Instead of introducing vertical parallax to objects, it is more desirable to apply the ray-space data method not only to the objects, but also to the environment portion such as walls, shelves and sights seen through windows. How to implement it and with which combination of geometry based rendering and image based rendering, is our next work.

References

[1] M. Sohlenkamp and G. Chwelos, "Integrating communication, cooperation, and awareness: The DIVA virtual office environment," Proc. ACM CSCW'94, pp.331-343, 1994.

[2] L.E.Fahlen, et.al., "A space based model for user interaction in shared synthetic environment," Proc. ACM CHI'93, pp.43-48, 1993.

[3] S. Benford, C. Brown, G. Reynard, and C. Greenhalgh, "Shared spaces: Transportation, artificiality, and spatiality," Proc. ACM CSCW'96, pp.77-86, 1996.

[4] S.Sugawara, et. al., "Interspace: Networked virtual world for visual communication," IEICE Transaction on Information and Systems, Vol. EE77-D, No.12, pp.1344-1349, 1994.

[5] W. Broll, "Distributed virtual reality for everyone - a framework for networked VR on the Internet," Proc. IEEE VRAIS'97, pp.121-128, 1997.

[6] J.W.Barrus, R.C.Waters, and D.B.Anderson, "Locales and beacons: efficient and precise support for large multi-user virtual environmets," Proc. IEEE VRAIS'96, pp.204-213, 1996.

[7] T.A.Funkhouser, "RING: A client-server system for multi-user virtual environments," Proc. ACM SIGGRAPH 95, pp.85-92,1995.

[8] M.R.Macedonia, M.J.Zyda, D.R.Pratt, D.P.Brutzman, and P.T.Barham, "Exploiting reality with multicast groups: a network architecture for large-scale virtual environments," Proc. IEEE VRAIS'95, pp.2-108, 1995.

[9] M. Levoy and P. Hanrahan,"Light field rendering," Proc. ACM SIGGRAPH 96, pp.31-42, 1996.

[10] S. J. Gortler, R. Grzeszczuk, R. Szeliski and M. F. Cohen,"The Lumigraph," ibid., pp.43-54, 1996.

[11] S. Uchiyama, A. Katayama, H. Tamura, T. Naemura, M. Kaneko, and H. Harashima, "Building a cyber-space by mixing real data based on ray-space theory with computer graphics model," Proc. 3D Image Conference '96, pp.13-18, 1996 (in Japanese).

[12]http://www.x-zone.canon.co.jp/CyberMirage/index-e.html

[13]http://www.hc.t.u-tokyo.ac.jp/3D/CyberMirage/index-e.html

[14] T. Naemura, T. Yanagisawa, M. Kaneko, and H. Harashima,"Efficient projection of ray space for a ray based description of 3-D real world," Technical Report of IEICE, IE95-119, pp.49-56, 1995 (in Japanese).

[15] A. Katayama, S. Uchiyama, M. Shibata, H. Tamura, T. Naemura, M. Kaneko, and H. Harashima,"A study on ray-space data compression for mixed reality," Proc. IMPS'96, pp.9-10, 1996 (in Japanese).

MPEG-4 for Networked Collaborative Virtual Environments

Igor Pandzic[1], Tolga Capin[2],
Nadia Magnenat-Thalmann[1], Daniel Thalmann[2]

[1] MIRALab - CUI
University of Geneva
24 rue du Général-Dufour
CH1211 Geneva 4, Switzerland
{Igor.Pandzic,Nadia.Thalmann}@cui.unige.ch
http://miralabwww.unige.ch/

[2] Computer Graphics Laboratory
Swiss Federal Institute of Technology (EPFL)
CH1015 Lausanne, Switzerland
{capin, thalmann}@lig.di.epfl.ch
http://ligwww.epfl.ch/

Abstract

MPEG is traditionally committed to coding and compression of audio-visual data from natural sources. However, the emerging MPEG-4 standard aims not only at multiple natural audio-visual objects composing the scene, but also synthetic audio and video to be integrated with the natural. It will also allow more interaction with both synthetic and natural objects.

Networked Collaborative Virtual Environments (NCVE) have a wide range of different requirements on networking. This paper analyzes how these requirements could potentially be met by MPEG-4 and shows that MPEG-4 tools could be extremely useful for development of such environments.

Keywords: Networked Collaborative Virtual Environments, MPEG-4

Introduction

Networked Collaborative Virtual Environments (NCVEs) are systems that allow multiple geographically distant users to evolve in a common virtual environment. The users themselves are represented within the environment using a graphical embodiment. An example of such an environment is shown in figure 1.

The user can evolve within the environment and interact with it. All events that have an impact on the environment are transmitted to other sites so that all environments can be updated and kept consistent, giving the impression for the users of being in the same, unique environment. The users become a part of the environment, embodied by a graphical representation that should ideally be human-like.

All users' actions, movements, facial expressions, changes in appearance etc. are transmitted to all participating sites in the simulation, enabling the interaction between the users.

The need to maintain environment/user state coherent on multiple networked sites generates an extensive set of requirements on the networking part - various data types to be transmitted, each with different requirements and priorities.

0-8186-8150-0/97 $10.00 © 1997 IEEE

Moving Pictures Expert Group (MPEG) is currently working on the new MPEG-4 standard, scheduled to become International Standard in November 1996. In a world where audio-visual data is increasingly stored, transferred and manipulated digitally, MPEG-4 sets its objectives beyond "plain" compression. Instead of regarding video as a sequence of frames with fixed shape and size and with attached audio information, the video scene is regarded as a set of dynamic objects. Thus the background of the scene might be one object, a moving car another, the sound of the engine the third etc. The objects are spatially and temporally independent and therefore can be stored, transferred and manipulated independently. The composition of the final scene is done at the decoder, potentially allowing great manipulation freedom to the consumer of the data.

Figure 1: An example session of a Networked Collaborative Virtual Environment

Video and audio acquired by recording from the real world is called natural. In addition to the natural objects, MPEG-4 aims to enable integration of synthetic objects within the scene. Synthetic, computer generated graphics and sounds are being produced and used in ever increasing quantities and it is the role of the Synthetic/Natural Hybrid Coding (SNHC) group of MPEG to integrate the coding of these objects with the natural data. Current work of SNHC concentrates on Face and Body Animation, Generic Object Coding, Media Integration of Text and Graphics and Synthetic Audio.

Currently there are four groups that work on producing MPEG-4 standards: Systems, Audio, Video and SNHC. The standard will finally consist of Systems, Audio and Video parts, and the specifications produced by SNHC will be integrated in either Audio or Video.

The Systems layer supports demultiplexing of multiple bitstreams, buffer management, time identification, scene composition and terminal configuration.

MPEG-4 video provides technologies for efficient storage, transmission and manipulation of video data in multimedia environments. The key areas addressed are efficient representation, error resilience over broad range of media, coding of arbitrarily shaped video objects, alpha map coding.

MPEG-4 Audio standardizes the coding of natural audio at bitrates ranging from 2 Kbit/sec to 64 bits/sec, addressing different bitrate ranges with appropriate coding technologies.

Synthetic/Natural Hybrid Coding (SNHC) deals with coding of synthetic audio and visual data. SNHC is described in detail in following sections.

In this paper we analyze how MPEG-4 tools could be applied to meet the requirements of Networked Collaborative Virtual Environment (NCVE) systems. The following section presents the networking requirements of NCVEs, focusing on the types of network traffic encountered in NCVE systems. After that we attempt to match these requirements to tools that will be available in MPEG-4. Conclusions are presented at the end.

The analysis of NCVE systems is based on several existing systems [Barrus96, Carlsson93, Macedonia94, Ohya95, Singh95] and in particular on the Virtual Life Network (VLNET) system [Capin97, Pandzic97]. The analysis of MPEG-4 tools is based on various MPEG documents [MPEG-N1361, MPEG-N1365, MPEG-N1545] and related papers [Koenen97, Doenges97], and in particular on the MPEG-4 Requirements definition [MPEG-N1595].

Networking requirements of NCVE systems

Networking for Collaborative Virtual Environments can be thought of in a simplified manner as represented in figure 2.

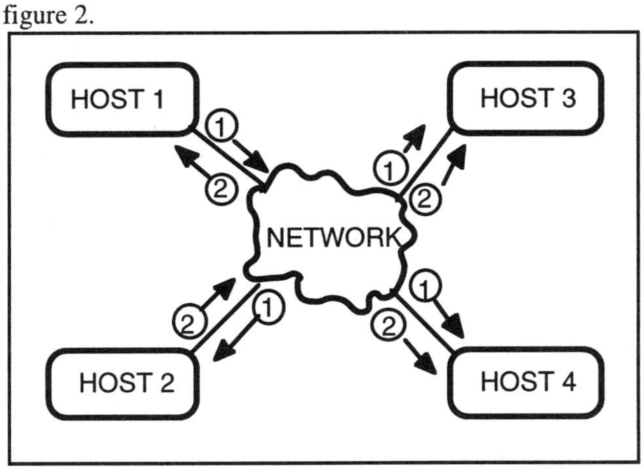

Figure 2: Simplified View of Networking for Collaborative Virtual Environments

All updates from any host are passed through the network (represented by the cloud in the figure) to all other hosts in form of bitstreams (bullets in the figure). The requirements on networking can now be divided in two categories: network topology (what is in the cloud?) and bitstream content (what is in the bullets?).

We treat these two issues separately in the following two subsections.

Network topologies for NCVE systems

The basic requirement for the network topology for an NCVE system is simple: when one host sends a message to the network, all other hosts should receive it. This is easy enough to do with a client-server or peer-to-peer approach if the number of participants is small. Unfortunately, if a system must support more then a few users, scalability becomes an important and potentially difficult issue. More sophisticated solutions have to be sought with multicasting, networks of multiple servers or hybrid approaches [Funkhouser96]. Usually, not all data needs to be transmitted to all participants, e.g. if two users are standing back to back or if they are in different (virtual) rooms, there is no need to communicate facial expressions between them since they don't see each other anyway. These "as-needed" data transfers can be achieved using an intelligent server to do data filtering or using dynamic multicast groups, to name two common examples.

Bitstream contents

Regardless of the network topology we analyze various data types that are transmitted through the network in NCVE systems. Figure 3 presents an overview of all data types usually encountered. Current systems usually support only a subset of the data types presented here.

Download. The main need for download arises when a new user joins a NCVE session. At this moment the complete description of the Virtual Environment has to be downloaded to the new user. This includes 3D objects structured in a scene hierarchy, textures and possibly behaviors in form of scripts or programs. The new user also has to download the embodiment descriptions of all users and send his own to everyone. The embodiment might be a simple geometrical object, but in a more sophisticated system it should be a body and face description in a form that allows later animation of both body and face.

Downloads are not restricted to the session establishment phase, they can also occur anytime during the session if new objects are introduced in the scene - they have to be distributed.

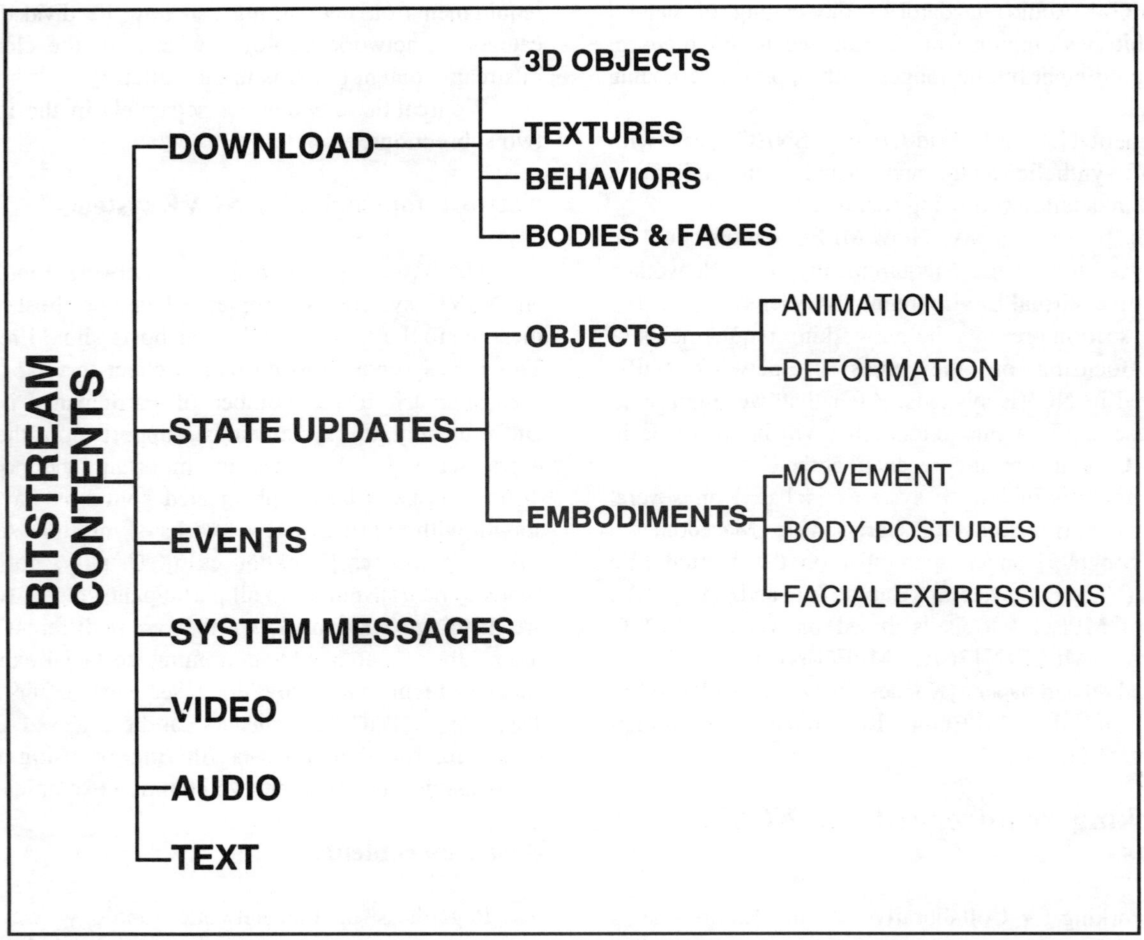

Figure 3: Bitstream contents breakdown for NCVE systems

State updates. All state changes for both the environment itself and the users' embodiments as special part of the environment have to be propagated through the network.

For the objects in the environment, this commonly involves the change of position/orientation, i.e. animation of rigid objects. In non-networked VEs objects are often deformed and not only animated rigidly. Free deformation of objects is not commonly supported in NCVE systems because of increased bandwidth needs - all displaced vertices have to be updated. It is however a very desirable feature to be included in NCVE systems.

For user embodiments, state updates also involve basic movement, and in the case of simple, rigid embodiments this is enough. For articulated, human-like embodiments means must be provided to communicate body postures and facial expressions to allow the simulation of natural body movements and actions.

Events. These are typically short messages about events happening in the environment. The basic difference from state updates is that a state message makes all previous state messages for the same object obsolete (e.g. a new position of the object makes all previous positions obsolete) [Kessler96], which is not the case with event messages. An event is sent only once and can influence the environment state potentially for a long time. Therefore the security of event messages must be higher then for state updates.
System Messages. These messages are used typically during session establishment and log-off. Their security is essential because errors can cause serious malfunction of the system.

Video. Video can be streamed and texture-mapped on any object in the environment producing real-time video textures. This can be used in different ways for various applications. Examples include virtual video presentations, facial texture mapping for facial communication

[Pandzic96] and mixing of real and virtual worlds for augmented reality applications or virtual studios.

The requirements on the video quality may vary from application to application.

Audio. The most common use of audio in NCVEs is for speech communication. However, synthetic 3D sound can also be an important part of a Virtual Environment.

Text. The most common use of text is for text-based chat between users. There are however more exciting ways to use it. Autonomous Virtual Humans with built-in AI decision-making algorithms can also be participants in NCVEs [Capin 97, Noser 96]. The best way to communicate orders/questions/dialogues to them is through text, and that is also the easiest way for them to respond. Speech recognition and Text-to-Speech (TTS) systems (possibly coupled with facial animation for lip sync) can be used to interface naturally with the users.

How MPEG-4 tools fit NCVE requirements

Based on the requirements laid out in the previous section and MPEG-related documentation [MPEG-N1361, MPEG-N1365, MPEG-N1545, MPEG-N1595, Koenen97, Doenges97] we study how MPEG-4 tools can be deployed to solve the problems of NCVE.

As for the network topologies, the solutions are out of scope of MPEG which mostly concentrates on bitstream contents. It is however worthwhile noting that an MPEG-4 system will be capable of receiving objects from up to 8 different sources, a fact to be considered when planning network topologies for particular applications [MPEG-N1595].

In the following subsections we study various components of bitstream contents with respect to MPEG-4.

Download

The MPEG-4 standard shall provide the means to download and store audio, video and synthetic objects [MPEG-N1595]. Furthermore, progressive transmission based on scalable coding techniques will be supported.

MPEG-4 will support a VRML-like 3D geometry hierarchy with all attributes, as well as behavior data. It will provide means for efficient compression of 3D meshes. Efficient still texture coding will be supported, as well as spatial- and quality- scalable coding to fit available bandwidth and rendering capabilities.

MPEG-4 will support body and face objects. Using Body Definition Parameters (BDPs) and Face Definition Parameters (FDPs) [MPEG-N1365, MPEG-N1545] it is possible to define body and face representation. BAPs and FAPs are scalable, offering a wide choice of tradeoffs between definition quality and bandwidth required. In case of absence of FDPs and/or BDPs generic bodies and faces can be used.

State updates

MPEG-4 supports scaling, rotation and translation of any video object (natural or synthetic, i.e. 3D objects included) about any axis in 2D or 3D space [MPEG-N1595]. Changes in audio objects localization are supported.

As for deformable 3D objects, at the time of writing this paper the need was recognized in MPEG to support efficient coding of object deformations, though this specification was not yet included in the documents.

MPEG-4 will support efficient coding of face and body animation. The parameters are defined to express body postures and facial expressions in an efficient manner and independently of a particular face/body model. These parameters are compressed to obtain very small bitrates (e.g. approx. 2 Kbit/sec for facial expressions).

Events and system messages

These messages are specific to a particular NCVE system and as such are not explicitly covered by MPEG-4.

Video

Video is a traditional part of MPEG and the video tools are mature and extensive. MPEG-4 Video will support all types of pixel-based video with high compression efficiency. Tools will be provided to achieve error resilient video streams over a variety of networks with possibly severe error conditions, including low-bitrate networks [MPEG-N1595]. Scalability in terms of content and spatial and temporal quality will be supported. Various delay modes, including low delay modes for real-time communication will be supported. MPEG-4 tools are optimized for the following bitrate ranges: < 64 Kbit/sec (low), 64 - 384 Kbit/sec (intermediate) and 384 Kbit/sec - 1.8 Mbit/sec (high). Various video formats will be supported.

Audio

MPEG-4 will support following types of audio content: high quality audio (> 15 KHz), intermediate quality audio (<15 KHz), wideband speech (50 Hz - 7 KHz), narrowband speech (50 Hz - 3.6 KHz) and intelligible speech (300 Hz - 3.4 KHz) [MPEG-N1595]. Tools will be provided to achieve error resilient audio streams, including support for low bitrate applications. In particular, speech coding compression will support intelligible speech at 2 Kbit/sec. A number of audio formats, as defined by sampling frequency, amplitude resolution, quantizer characteristics and number of channels will be supported.

Text

Simple text is not explicitly supported by MPEG-4. However, there will be tools for Text-to-Speech functionality [MPEG-N1595] which requires at least simple text, and possibly auxiliary information such as phoneme duration, amplitude of each phoneme etc. Capability to synchronize TTS output with facial animation system visualizing the pronunciation will be supported.

Integration

For NCVE systems it is not only important to support all the data types described in previous sections, but also to achieve an orderly integration of all data types with respect to relative priorities and synchronization.

MPEG-4 shall support dynamic multiplexing of all objects [MPEG-N1595]. Means will be provided to identify relative importance of parts of coded audio-visual information with at least 32 levels of priority. Synchronization between all objects is supported, with specified maximal differential delays (e.g. between two video objects or between an audio and a video object).

Conclusions

We have analyzed the networking requirements of Networked Collaborative Virtual Environments, and how MPEG-4 tools can be used to fulfill these requirements.

The building of network topology, session establishment/destruction and system-particular message passing are out of MPEG-4 scope and should be dealt with on another level. However, most of the data types that are important for NCVE systems will be very well supported by MPEG-4 tools (video, audio, 3D objects, textures, bodies, faces). On top of this, MPEG-4 will offer reliable multiplexing, mechanisms for establishing priorities among data, as well as synchronization. We believe that MPEG-4 tools should play an important role in building future Networked Collaborative Virtual Environment systems.

Acknowledgments

This research is partly financed by "Le Programme Prioritaire en Telecommunications de Fonds National Suisse de la Recherche Scientifique" and the ACTS project VIDAS.

References

[Barrus96] Barrus J. W., Waters R. C., Anderson D. B., "Locales and Beacons: Efficient and Precise Support For Large Multi-User Virtual Environments", Proceedings of IEEE VRAIS, 1996.

[Capin97] Capin T.K., Pandzic I.S., Noser H., Magnenat Thalmann N., Thalmann D., "Virtual Human Representation and Communication in VLNET Networked Virtual Environments", *IEEE Computer Graphics and Applications, Special Issue on Multimedia Highways*, March-April 1997.

[Carlsson93] Carlsson C., Hagsand O., "DIVE - a Multi-User Virtual Reality System", *Proceedings of IEEE VRAIS '93*, Seattle, Washington, 1993.

[Doenges97] Doenges, P.K., Capin, T.K., Lavagetto, F., Ostermann, J., Pandzic, I.S., Petajan, E.D., "MPEG-4: Audio/Video & Synthetic Graphics/Audio for Mixed Media", *Image Communication Journal, Special Issue on MPEG-4*, Vol.9, No. 4, May 1997. (to appear)

[Funkhouser96] Funkhouser T.A., "Network Topologies for Scalable Multi-User Virtual Environments, *Proceedings of IEEE VRAIS '96*, 1996

[Kessler96] Kessler G.D., Hodges E.F., "A Networked Communication Protocol for Distributed Virtual Environment Systems", *Proceedings of IEEE VRAIS '96*, 1996

[Koenen97] Koenen R., Pereira F., Chiariglione L., "MPEG-4: Context and Objectives", *Image Communication Journal, Special Issue on MPEG-4*, Vol. 9, No. 4, May 1997 (to appear)

[Macedonia94] Macedonia M.R., Zyda M.J., Pratt D.R., Barham P.T., Zestwitz, "NPSNET: A Network Software Architecture for Large-Scale Virtual Environments", *Presence: Teleoperators and Virtual Environments*, Vol. 3, No. 4, 1994.

[Noser96] Noser H., Pandzic I.S., Capin T.K., Magnenat Thalmann N., Thalmann D., "Playing Games through the Virtual Life Network", *Proceedings of Artificial Life V*, Nara, Japan, 1996.

[MPEG-N1316] Doenges P., Jordan F., Pandzic I.S., "SNHC Application Objectives and Requirements", ISO/IEC JTC1/SC29/WG11 N1316, MPEG96/July 1996.

[MPEG-N1365] Petajan E., Pandzic I.S., Capin T.K., Ho P.H., Pockaj R., Tao H., Chen H., Shen J., Chaut P.E., Osterman J., "Face and body definition and animation parameters", ISO/IEC JTC1/SC29/WG11 N1365, MPEG96/October 1996.

[MPEG-N1545] "SNHC Verification Model Version 3.0", SNHC, ISO/IEC JTC1/SC29/WG11 N1545, MPEG97/February 1997.

[MPEG-N1595] "MPEG-4 Requirements version 2", ISO/IEC JTC1/SC29/WG11 N1545, MPEG97/February 1997.

[Ohya95] Ohya J., Kitamura Y., Kishino F., Terashima N., "Virtual Space Teleconferencing: Real-Time Reproduction of 3D Human Images", *Journal of Visual Communication and Image Representation*, Vol. 6, No. 1, pp. 1-25, 1995.

[Pandzic96] Pandzic I.S., Capin T.K., Magnenat Thalmann N., Thalmann D., "Towards Natural Communication in Networked Collaborative Virtual Environments", *Proceedings FIVE 96* , Pisa, Italy, 1996.

[Pandzic97] Pandzic I.S., Capin T.K., Lee E., Magnenat Thalmann N., Thalmann D., "A flexible architecture for

Virtual Humans in Networked Collaborative Virtual Environments", *Proceedings Eurographics 97* (to appear)
[Singh95] Singh G., Serra L., Png W., Wong A., Ng H., "BrickNet: Sharing Object Behaviors on the Net", *Proceedings of IEEE VRAIS '95*, 1995.

Collaborative Virtual Environments, Real-Time Video And Networking

Samuli Pekkola Mike Robinson
Department of Computer Science
The University of Jyväskylä
P.O.Box 35, 40351 Jyväskylä, FINLAND
E-mail: pejysa@cc.jyu.fi, mike@cs.jyu.fi

Abstract:

Two real life workplaces, a Studio and an Office are described. Both have Virtual and Mixed Reality counterparts. Issues of work process and social interaction taken from CSCW are utilised to understand the functionalities that virtual studios and offices need to provide. It is broadly concluded that different media (documents, audio, video, VR) all have different strengths and weaknesses, and each may be appropriate for different purposes in different contexts. Offices and Studios are best extended into virtuality by a mix of media (Mixed Realities) with a VR interface. The integration of video into VR environments presents the greatest technical difficulties, and some of these are considered from the viewpoints of computational load and networking. It is concluded that an optimal solution would be to provide separate network architectures for real-time interactive VR and video.

Introduction

Many different multi-actor virtual environments have been built and investigated during the last decade. For example MASSIVE (Greenhalgh and Benford 1995) and DIVE (Carlsson and Hagsand 1993), Rubberrocks (Codella, Jalili et al. 1992), NPSNet (Zyda, Pratt et al. 1993), and even Multi-User-Dungeons (MUDS). Virtual Reality Modeling Language (VRML, 1996) also offers a simple way to build virtual environments, even if the functionality is limited when it comes to real time interaction between users. User interaction with objects or with other users is better supported in e.g. MASSIVE or DIVE, members of the class of VR systems known as Collaborative Virtual Environments, or CVE's[1]. The Work reported here concentrates on CVE's that support, or have the potential to support multi-modal interactions between users, and between users and objects. Moreover, we note that face-to-face, real time audio/video interaction, as well as more traditional file and document handling have an important role in office and other work. We therefore try to support this in our applications and designs, seeing VR as both a natural interface, and an integrating application for other media. In other words, VR has an important role, both technically and from users' perspectives, in accessing and utilising *Mixed Realities*.

The first section of the paper introduces two real world environments: the Telematic Studio here in Jyväskylä, and a "typical" entrepreneurial office as characterised by ongoing work in CSCW (e.g. (Salvador 1997)) and specifically by the TeleLEI Project (Robinson and Hinrichs 1997). In both cases, we are in process of building a VR mirror world, as a first step to full Mixed Reality Studio and Office applications. Both projects encounter issues of real life working practice (social) and technological issues.

The second section of the paper considers social and work practice issues in the different contexts of the Studio and Office. The Telematic Studio, from the outset, had one foot in virtuality, as one of its main uses is for video-conferencing. By contrast, the Office, as we conceive it, is routine and mundane, and often has only tenuous or basic telematic facilities. Overlaid on this is an account of uses of a very rudimentary Virtual Office: the BSCW shared workspace (BSCW 1997). These accounts of working practice are used to inform the design of VR mirror worlds, and their integration in Mixed Reality applications.

The third section discusses some technical issues that arise in the construction of a VR Studio and Office. In particular, we discuss problems and some solutions to questions of networking, and of integration of real-time "live" video into a VR environment;

[1] CVE: a distributed multi-user virtual reality system, some features of which include: networking based on multicasting; support for the extended spatial model of interaction, including third parties, regions and abstractions; multiple users communicating via a combination of 3D graphics, real-time packet audio and text; extensible object oriented (class-based) developers API. (http://www.crg.cs.nott.ac.uk/crg/Research/crgshare/)

0-8186-8150-0/97 $10.00 © 1997 IEEE

and issues arising for VR when users have a simultaneous video presence in multiple locations.

The last section draws on existing work, and the social and technical considerations, to outline some promising development paths for VR and Mixed Reality applications.

Real and virtual environments

This section will focus two different virtual reality environments; a conference or meeting room, and a virtual office. Both environments have their own usages and functions, but communication and user interaction are important issues in both worlds. Exchanges of documentation, text messages, audio and video are all media which play a huge role in communication and interaction between different virtual reality environments and the real world. These aspects and especially the need for video channels are central to the designs of the virtual office and virtual conference room.

Figure 1: A local Studio mobile camera design session.

The first environment, a 15x 10m. telematic Studio, was opened in Jyväskylä, Finland, in May 1996 to support teaching and research on cooperative work and communication. The Studio is equipped with full audio-visual and teleconferencing facilities. These include: 3 large (2m x 2m) screens for video, computer monitor, TV, slide, or document camera projections; 3 video conference systems (for ISDN, and Internet over ATM); desk-set Pentium PC's and free standing SGI's; and electronic whiteboard. Unusually, the desks (each containing up to 3 consoles, and able to seat from 3 to 9 people) can be repositioned as required. The Studio can be used for work, meetings, or playful activities. It is comfortable for up to 50 people, but not over-solemn for a few (See Fig. 1).

Various commercial and other external organisations in addition to the university use the Studio. It is instructive to contrast the different usages, and the different configurations of technology and communication arrangements both local and remote. For instance, one group of executives were concerned to define formal arrangements for Finnish EU programs. They used a circular seating arrangement (usually considered "informal"); a facilitated and strongly proceduralised set of discussion conventions; and GroupSystems software with desktop input and large screen projection. Another local group of graphic designers needed to compare developing work and techniques with a similar group in Helsinki. They used a theatre seating arrangement (usually considered "formal"); free discussion; and the PictureTel videoconferencing system with large screen projection. Other groups use e.g. Lotus Notes or TeamWare. While point to point videoconferencing is common, it is not unusual to have multi-point conferencing.

In recent months, the Studio team has been reconstructing the Studio in virtual reality, using DIVE (1997) as a development platform. The long term research is to develop a Virtual Telematic Studio, where all the real-world equipment is available as well as additional tools specific to VR. Research on uses of the VR studio, especially in comparison with the RL Studio use, is one objective. Another, possibly more innovative, is to explore the Mixed Reality aspects and usages with some participants in the RL Studio and others in VR Studio(s), all utilising the "same" equipment, where the RL/VR interface will be seamless. At least, "seamlessness" is our hope and ambition, given working solutions to some of the technical and social issues to be discussed in the following sections.

The second environment is the "typical" entrepreneurial office. This has 3 levels of embodiment. The first is the office(s) of small companies, as found in Europe, Japan, North and South America, and probably elsewhere. This will be described in more detail in the next section. It suffices to say here that two aspects of office work and technology caught our attention. The first was identified by (Reder and Schwab 1990) as "channel switching". The notion of communication chain was operationally defined as a sequence of distinct interactions between the same individuals on a given task. A channel switch was a change within a communication chain from e.g. face-to-face to phone, fax, or email. The authors observed:

> "When the chain length is only two communicative events, nearly 50% of the chains involve a channel switch; as the chains progressively lengthen the percentage having a channel switch steadily increases, rising to 80% in chains of 4 links." (ibid. p. 310)

The second aspect of office work was theoretically identified by Hollan and Stornetta (1992) in a paper that also has important general implications for VR and Mixed Reality Applications. "Beyond Being There" argued that simulating face-to-face copresence was the objective of most tele-application designers: to produce environments that were as close as possible to "being there". This does not parallel experience. A phone call or an email is often better, more effective, or more appropriate than a visit to another's office or a conversation. The authors argue that each medium has its own affordances, and that mere approximation to face-to-face is a bad design objective, and does not mirror experience.

Both the virtual Studio and virtual Office are being constructed with user driven channel switching to the most appropriate medium in mind — whether or not the medium approximates to "being there". The technical focus of the last section is switching in and out of, and between multiple networked video links from inside the Mixed Reality Office.

The "typical" RL office with Internet links can already utilise a simple virtual office e.g. Alta Vista Forum (Forum 1997) or the GMD BSCW (1997) These share much functionality, and we will illustrate our argument with reference to BSCW where we have more experience. BSCW functionalities include rudimentary awareness of others in the form of change histories of files and folders. Currently they do not include features which would enable members to know who is in the office at the same time — which we will argue is a precondition for VR or video/audio interaction. Other features of BSCW (Fig. 2) , which would also need to carried over to a Mixed Reality Virtual Office (MR.VO) are:

1. structured sets of files and facilities accessible by multiple people via telematic network, regardless of location
2. permission structures for accessing and editing files
3. change histories of objects and awareness of ongoing changes
4. tailorable interfaces and ability to change file structures
5. ability to attach comment, post notes, and send email
6. member lists, and ability to invite new members, and remove existing members
7. multi-language support
8. independence of hardware and software platforms.

Mixed Reality Virtual Offices (MR.VO) do not yet exist. In addition to the functionalities of BSCW, an MR.VO needs to offer three specifiable general features, whose social underpinnings will be examined further in the section on Social & Work Practice Issues.

"Awareness": availability of information on who is "in the office" at any given time. This is simply not available in BSCW, but would be a natural part of a VR interface — since the presence of avatars stands

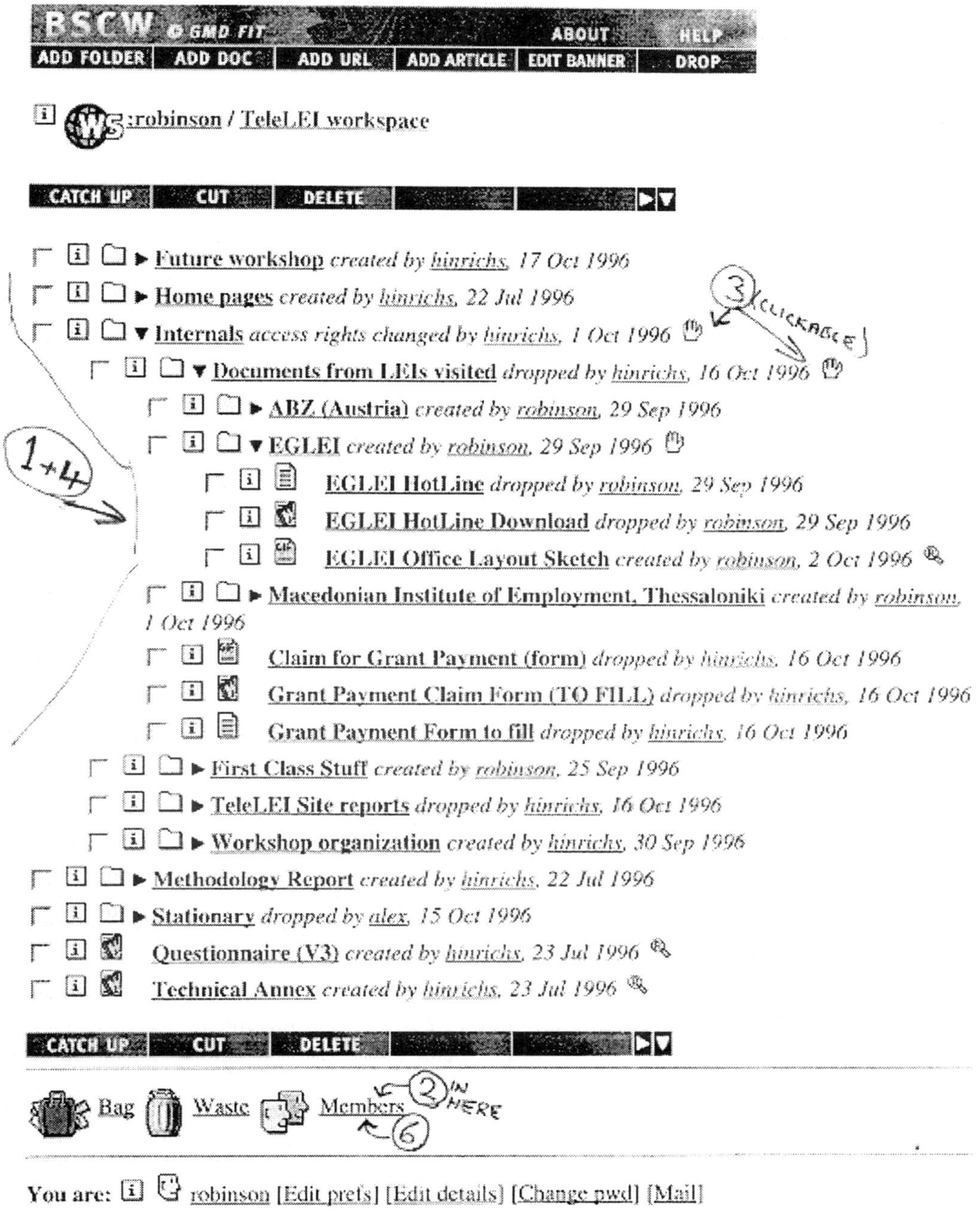

Figure 2: A BSCW Virtual Office as used by members of the TeleLEI Project (Robinson and Hinrichs 1997) from several European countries *(annotated by functions in list above).*

for the presence of people[2].

- Multi-way Interactive Video, Audio[3], and Text[4]: the ability to open one of more of these channels

2 It would not be difficult to add 'awareness' to BSCW e.g. an icon bar in which icons or mini-pictures of active present members are coloured; inactive present members are greyed; and members not present are not shown. This would be desirable when a MR.VO is entered via different software (text, BSCW) from different locations. This raises issues of scalability, heterogeneity of clients, downward compatibility, and graceful degradation (e.g discussed in Star and Ruhleder (1994); also a 2D interface is provided to DIVE (Carlsson and Hagsand 1993)) all of which we are considering, but are outside the scope of the current paper.

3 In the context of the TeleLEI Project, audio was prioritised for implementation over video, since it is more generally available e.g. Onlive! Talker (http://www.onlive.com), and a main

with one or more other people who are "in the office" at the same time.

- VR Interface to all other modalities, from file handling to multiple video interactivity. There is a strong case to be made that VR is the natural successor to the wimps interface in the late '90's. Its underlying spatial model can offer "natural" user-configured layout of, and access to applications and communications facilities. It has a potential for unrivaled movement (as we argue in this paper) between real and virtual regions, between and within multiple locations, and between and within multiple media. Mixed Reality VR realises many of the ambitions expressed by Harraway (1985).

Social And Work Practice Issues

This section will consider three categories of research, mainly from CSCW, that need to inform the design of VR and MR systems: *direct* awareness and interaction; *indirect* awareness and interaction; cooperation and collaboration.

Issues of direct awareness of, and interaction with others

Eye contact and facial expressions: The meanings and importance of eye-contact has been extensively discussed over a long period e.g. (Bales 1951). O'Hair et al. (1995) examine the social significance when e.g. a speaker looking into the eyes gives a different impression to gazing at her socks. Also speakers' and listeners' faces express different meanings. Littlejohn (1996) shows that positive (e.g. smiling) and negative (e.g. frowning) faces invoke different feelings, and the listener takes meaning from facial expression as well as speech, while the talker receives information on the receptiveness of her audience from faces. Altogether non-verbal communication has great influence in human-human interaction. Facial expression and especially eye contact are technically difficult and cumbersome to reproduce in VR. Augmenting VR with video overlay or window seems a simpler and more natural solution. However, in this area, it is the view of the authors, in agreement with Nardi (1993), that the importance of "talking heads" video is overrated.

Gestures: Video conferences differ significantly from normal conversations. Heath and Luff (1993) show that body movements and small gestures are hard or even impossible to transmit between participants.

> A speaker will attempt to produce a description and during the course of its production use gesture to gain a visually attentive recipient. The gesture becomes increasingly exaggerated and meets with no response, the description reveals linguistic difficulties and it may even be abandoned.
>
> (Heath & Luff. op. cit. p.839)

We have observed similar troubles in videoconferencing. Some are due to self-consciousness, some to technical issues such as delays, desynchronisation of video and audio, and quality of service. Much is undoubtedly due to the nature of the medium, as for instance when pointing fails because the object is out of camera, or a person in a different "place" to different participants (Buxton 1993).

The situation is different in the CVE sector of VR. Since body suits, hand trackers, etc. are generally not used, there are no naturalistic gestures. There are, however, a limited number of gestures that can be consciously reproduced (by keyboard actions), such as waving, pointing, standing on one's head, lying down, turning towards/away from. Pointing is relatively unproblematic, and as Bowers et al. (1996) point out, fine grained distinctions (such as between "turning away from" and "looking round") are unproblematically made by VR participants. There is of course a trade-off between the number of possible gestures, and the complexity of managing them.

It is a moot point whether instrumented reproduction of gesture, eye movement, heart rate (for embarrassment, anger, etc.) would be an enhancement to VR if transmitted to the avatar. The authors are inclined to the view that video or meters (for heart rate, etc.) are better treated as auxiliary displays to the VR proper. This would be a further dimension of MR, rather than strict VR. It can also be noted that e.g. heart rate, or GSR meters would add a dimension of bodily intimacy to MR interactions that are not available in face to face interaction. For such reasons, for some interactions, MR rather than RL might be the medium of choice.

Issues of indirect awareness of, and interaction with others

The majority of ethnographic workplace studies in CSCW over the last decade show that indirect awareness of the presence and activities of coworkers is a *sine qua non* of collaboration. Participants are aware

---

need of the office in this research was for *cheap* audio interaction.

[4] Text "chat" is not a poor alternative to audio or video connections. There are occasions when text is better than audio — for instance when people have different mother languages and little speaking practice in the language being used. An existing example of a good quality Internet Text Chat with graphics application is WhitePineBoard (http://www.cu-seeme.com)

of the activities of others without making any special extra effort, and this provides essential context and resources for their own work. We propose that the most effective and efficient means of achieving indirect awareness is via a VR interface. It is effective because the information in immediately given (does not have to be "opened" or "searched for"), and its resolution is instantly user-recalibrable (one can turn towards others, or approach closer to them for a better view). It is efficient because technically, unlike video, it requires little bandwidth.

Munro (1996) has shown that a major defect of current videoconferencing systems is lack of indirect awareness. Since managers are only likely to be available and in their office 18% of the time, the probability of two managers "connecting" is around 3% — and of 3 or more spontaneous connections vanishingly small. For this reason (amongst others) such systems fall into disuse. Munro suggests adding an asynchronous capacity, e.g. answering machines (with which we agree): we also suggest that ongoing VR awareness of others would go a long way towards dissolving the difficulty. Another notorious difficulty with video connection is that users get stuck with fixed views of the other person or environment, and are unable to overcome this by exercising camera control (Dourish 1993; Gaver, Sellen et al. 1993) — although fascinating work has been done with remote mobile robots (Kuzuoka, Kosuge et al. 1994).

"Gaze awareness" (as opposed to eye contact) is another aspect of indirect awareness. Broadly it means being able to see where the other is looking, and what she is looking at. This can be achieved with a complex video arrangement (Ishii, Kobayashi et al. 1992). Gaze awareness is fairly naturally supported in VR (e.g. the availability of "focus" information to all parties)

"Peripheral awareness" has been extensively explored by Heath & Luff (1991) and Heath et al. (1993). They show the environments as diverse as a London Underground Control Room, and a Stock Exchange Dealing Floor both depend for their competences, coordinations, and effectiveness on "overhearing" and "out of the corner of the eye" awareness of others. Video, per se, does not seem good at supporting this since it does not provide 360° awareness. An interesting hybrid alternative would be a (360°) VR environment with video windows set in it.

"Implicit communication" is where changes made to an artefact inform others about the state/status of a workprocess (Sørgaard 1988; Robinson 1993). A good example is in Air Traffic Control where a set of "flight strips" (showing current information on planes in the skies) are stored/displayed in a large rack that can be seen by all controllers. Pushing a flight strip out of symmetry with the others can indicate a problem with that particular flight. A simple action by one controller on a "common artefact" has the effect (implicit communication) of informing the others. (Bentley, Hughes et al. 1992). In this case we conjecture that sometimes it would be appropriate to reproduce the "common artefact" in the VR, in others it would be better (technically or socially) to provide a video view of it.

Issues of cooperation and collaboration

We have seen in the above section that the non-procedural aspects of work practice (Suchman 1983; Suchman 1987), such as peripheral awareness and implicit communication, can largely be supported by a combination of interactive VR, video, and audio. There are also many occasions when direct work on documents needs to be done. Video and VR are rarely the most appropriate medium for this work (although they can provide its context) hence we should add text, graphics, and document handling to the above constellation of media that constitute the field of work.

Another aspect of collaboration is detailed by Nardi et al. (1993) in an excellent account of the coordinations between surgeons, anaesthetists, neurophysiologists, nurses, and many others in complex micro-neurosurgical operations. Here all participants benefit in different ways for different activities from a video picture of the "field of work" — in this case an on-line picture of the inside of the patient's brain or spinal cord. While this is a rather dramatic example, it illustrates a commonplace — namely that all participants need access to the ongoing fields of work, which they use to inform their own (role specific) activities, and to keep them coordinated with the activities of others. In addition, consider the following quotes:

> **Neurophysiologist**: In fact, the audio is better over the network than it is in the operating theatre because you can't hear what the surgeons are saying in the operating room......

and

> **Neurophysiologist:** In that case I heard the technician say something to the surgeon that I didn't agree with..... [He] said there was a change in the response. There wasn't.
> Interviewer: ..... So what did you do, you called?

> **Neurophysiologist**: Called right away..... Told the surgeon there was no change.
>
> (ibid. p. 332)

Here we see an example of a virtual medium (network audio) which is better than "being there". We also see, in the second quote, an excellent example of "channel switching" as a natural part of interaction. A more developed conceptualisation of "channel switching" is found in Bowers et al. (1995) and Bowers et al. (1996). The authors observe that the "management of multiple worlds" is a major accomplishment of both ordinary and virtual working practices.

> Each participant is then simultaneously operating in several 'worlds' — some real, some virtual, some local, some nearby, and some distant .... the alignment of these worlds is practically managed during the real-time of the meeting (p. 386)

and

> We see ordinary interactional competences (methods for managing turn taking, displaying attentiveness and orienting bodies, using another means if one fails) deployed .... In all this the virtual world is but one domain and the management of multiple arenas appears in many ways a normal and unexceptional task and in that sense mundane — which is not to say it requires no skill, indeed quite the reverse. (p. 389)
>
> (Bowers, O'Brian et al. 1996)

We would like to add the *mundane but skilled management of multiple media* to the management of multiple worlds in definitions of our virtual, mixed reality Studio and Offices. That concludes our brief exploration of the work process and social issues of virtual and mixed reality, and brings us to some of the technical problems of implementation.

Technical issues

In the context of two new virtual environments (MR.VO and the Virtual Studio), and of some CSCW findings on work process, video, and VR, we will now concentrate on some technical issues. We discuss some ways of incorporating video-images and ensuing problems which have to be resolved before building virtual environments with real-time video.

Spatial model and awareness of video

Benford and Fahlen introduced a spatial model (Benford and Fahlén 1993) in 1993, which several VR applications (e.g DIVE, MASSIVE) use as an interaction model. The principle is to manage conversation among large groups by dividing communication between members (and objects) to smaller functional parts. Any interaction between objects occurs through some *medium* (audio, video, text or even object specified interfaces) which will be chosen by negotiations between interacting objects. Actual interaction takes place when any of objects' *auras* collide (there is one aura for one medium). Aura is therefore a subspace which bounds the presence of an object within a given medium. Once aura is used to determine the potential for object interaction, *focus* and *nimbus* control the level of awareness of the object. Focus is the your level of awareness of other objects and nimbus is the level at which others are aware of you.

Heath and Luff (1991) show the importance of awareness of co-workers where several people work together. The awareness of video *objects* is useful in VR, even if the video itself is not fully open. The user has a visual focus on other objects and other users' embodiments as well as on the video objects. To handle these two related but different image sources, it is useful to create different auras for the graphical image sources (embodiments and objects) and the video objects. This partitioning ensures that it is relative easy to manage different types of situation as well as to support the VR environment with live-video on computers with different local resources (e.g MASSIVE is supported by powerful machines (SGI's) or basic terminals (Greenhalgh and Benford 1995)). By changing the level of focus and nimbus, the virtual environment is more transportable to different platforms and more suited to different users' unequal needs.

Showing the video

Showing video clips on-screen is quite complicated. Conservative, existing video conference systems show each video channel in a separate window. This has a lot of advantages: it is relative easy to built; easy to use; and does not demand a lot of CPU. Systems like Mbone (Macedonia and Brutzman 1994), CU-SeeMe (Dorcey 1995), ProShare (ProShare 1997) or InPerson (InPerson 1997) are based on point-to-point connections, or broadcasting information from one location to many receivers. Because the number of open connections are limited it is easy to see all participants on a screen at the same time. But what happens when there are ten participants? Or twenty? Or a hundred? There is no theoretical limit to the number of simultaneous users in CVEs such as a Virtual Studio or Virtual Office — or at least the number of users is much greater than traditional computer video conference systems allow. Limits on the graphical performance of the computer and monitor will soon be reached, because the number of video windows is directly related to the number of participants. There must be some other way to handle this situation.

One possible solution is to show all the video clips as texture maps. A video image is inserted as the face of the avatar, making the appearance of the VR embodiments more 'realistic' (e.g VLNET (Thalmann et al. 1996)). By doing this, there is no additional windows to confuse the user, but showing many live texture maps demands a lot from the computer. Participants can turn around and move anywhere at any speed i.e the distance to others and the angles of their faces can change very fast. To calculate these placing and positions of the texture maps is quite hard, so the amount of the CPU required is great. Again the limits of graphical performance will soon be reached.

If video images are inserted as texture maps on faces of the avatars, a second (or even third) camera could be used to show the facial profile, or even the back of the head. Each avatar has two (three? four?) live texture maps and the amount of CPU required per user will be doubled or worse. To decrease that, the profile/back of the head could be ready-made static texture map, or even a standard blockie-type surface. The CPU requirement could also be decreased by checking the gaze of the avatar the user is focusing to. If 'it' is gazing in a direction where his face cannot be seen, it won't be drawn.

The Spatial model (Benford and Fahlén 1993) looks like a good choice for managing the video object (i.e the object which shows the video texture map). By controlling the nimbus of a video object and the focus of an observer, CPU load can be decreased. If the environment is crowded by the users, the sizes of members' video focuses and the nimbuses with respect to video objects must be reduced. In the opposite case, with few users or few video objects, the size of focus and nimbus could be increased. Also the *shape* of the nimbus of the video object is very important for saving CPU. For instance a texture mapped video object could have a cone shaped nimbus while the user has a cone shaped video focus. The calculation to find out where these auras collide and the amount of needed CPU are relative easy compared to the calculations needed to draw the video image.

Arikawa et. al. (1996) introduce an idea for controlling the level of details (LoD) of the live video. More detail is shown if an object is close the observer, and the LoD goes down as the distance between the video and the user increases. When the video object is distant, only a grey screen will be seen. This idea is basically the same as calculating the focus and nimbus of the objects if the auras are sphere shaped. The Spatial model adds some new features to LoD e.g. the direction of the video surface of an object is considered as well as the direction of the user's gaze. If the focus and the nimbus are cone shaped, LoD of the video depends on the position of the video object in the field of vision of the user and the direction of the video object related to the user. Thus the LoD is at its best when the video is in the middle of the user's field of vision and user is facing directly towards it.

If the VR environment is a conference room environment (or Virtual Studio) it may be enough to show only one texture map on a wall. This built-in window shows only the talker or it could be a window between the reality and VR as Arikawa et al. (1996) show. But now other problems arise e.g if the number of simultanous users increases, user embodiments may stand in front of each other, blocking their fields of vision.

As already noted, texture maps require much more CPU and video windows much screen space. These limitations are not serious when the number of simultaneous users is limited to a few, but when contemplating collaborative virtual environments with a hundred or more simultanuous users the restrictions are significant. Some way needs to be found of combining the benefits without the disadvantages of both methods. One possibility is to let the user choose which images are shown, by letting her either control the focus (when all available video sources are shown) or choose the incoming video screen by clicking the desired image. Dynamic systems should also control the nimbus of the video source automatically depending on the amount of traffic.

Network structures and the amount of traffic

Distributed virtual environments are, as the name indicates, distributed — the members of the VR environment can be physically located anywhere around the globe. Long distances between users, different needs of communication media (audio, video, text), and different VR applications set many requirements both for the network structure and for the transmission channel between its terminals. For example single user VR applications (e.g. VRML, (1996), etc.) have different network needs to multi-user CVEs. The size of the video image packets is greater than the size of audio packets and the amount of the traffic in the network varies over a wide range.

The choice of network structure for the desired VR application is important for minimizing the traffic. Traditional client-server architecture is suitable for applications with only a few simultanous users. For example VRML uses regular www-standards for locating the server and the client as well as for creating the world. Rubber-rocks (Codella et al. 1992) and HyCLASS (Kawanobe et al. 1996) use distributed client-server architecture i.e the clients exchange information with each other through the server (see Fig.3).

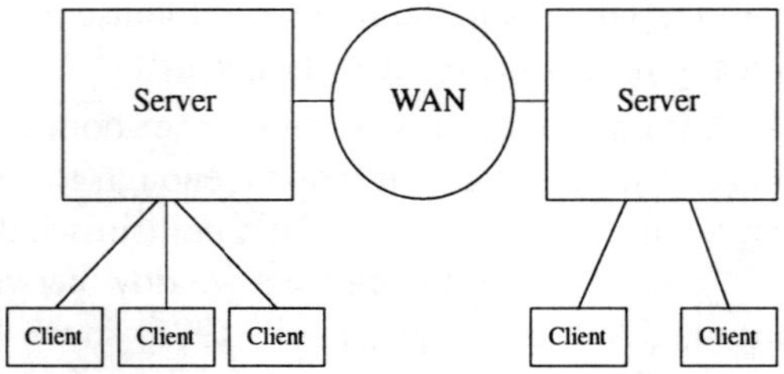

Figure 3: A distributed client-server architecture with 2 servers and 5 clients.

Mbone (Casner 1993) has more advanced client-server architecture where the servers are able to communicate with each other through tunnels. DIVE (Carlsson & Hagsand 1993) and MASSIVE (Greenhalgh & Benford 1995) are claimed to be more intelligent by basing themselves on a peer-to-peer scheme i.e there is no central server, but each process of the world has a complete copy of the world database. The exchange of the information occurs by distributing it among the processes (see Fig.4) (Benford et al. 1995).

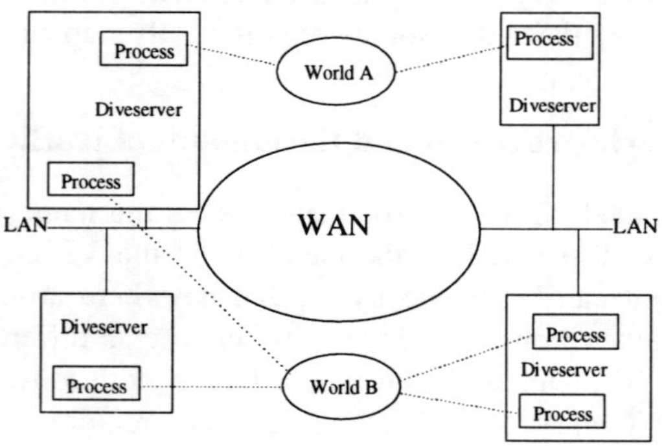

Figure 4: Peer-to-peer scheme without a central server.

Currently video conferences are accomplished either by point-to-point connection (in systems like CU-SeeMe (Dorcey 1995)), or by broadcasting the video to multiple different destinations (like MBone). Neither of those distribution models is the best one for the distributed virtual environments. Brutzman (1997) shows the problems of the MBone system but these limitations also apply to other server-client architectures. Clearly there is a bottleneck in the server, because all the traffic has to pass one particular point. If the number of packets increases (from increasing numbers of simultaneous users or the growing packet size) the server will run out of capacity and go down. In non-server based systems (DIVE) this problem doesn't occur, but other problems appear. The benefits of the multicasting can be lost, because the system works on peer-to-peer scheme and the packets have to be sent one by one to the desired destination. This increases the total number of packets in the network and new bottlenecks appear (e.g the local server, the gateway to the outer world).

The amount of traffic is highly dependent on the way how clients (or peers) communicate with each other and how they create a VR environment. All the VR systems discussed so far load the environmental information when the user joins. Later, when she moves around or interacts with others, the VR systems just update their databases either from the server (e.g NPSNet (Zyda et al. 1993)) or from the other peers (e.g DIVE, MASSIVE or HyCLASS). This is very economical way to minimize traffic, since the world is relative stable and its landscape information would demand a lot of bandwidth (specially if complicated or filled by many texture maps).

When the user moves or interacts with other users or objects in VR, information has be exchanged between terminals. This produces some problems, because the sizes of the supplied packets depends on the media used and the application. For example a MASSIVE peer could transmit 5.2kbps (packet size appr. 2kbit) while NPSNet server could process appr. 30kbps (packet size of 142bit) (Zyda et al. 1993; Greenhalgh & Benford 1995). The video data transmission speed varies from 64kbps up to 2Mbps depending on the standard used and the quality of the picture (MBone uses 128kbps) (International Telecommunication Union 1993; Macedonia & Brutzman 1994). Besides the speed of transmission, the type of transmission is also significant. In VR movements and/or interaction does not occur all the time (and data packets are not sent) while video and audio sources produce more or less continuous semi-constant (i.e the size of the packet varies within a certain range) streams of data packets. This leads to an important note that larger packets tend to be transmitted continuously (using much bandwidth), while small packets (reflecting comparatively infrequent VR events) are much lighter for the network performance.

The differences in the data packets (size and frequency of production) in various medias set unequal requirements to the network architecture. A server based application *can* manage hundreds of simultaneous users (Kawanobe et al. 1996) as well as distributed systems (Greenhalgh & Benford 1995) if only light-weight-media (interaction, movements, audio) are used. When the number of users is great and the video is used, problems arise such as the client being overwhelmed with the video data. CU-SeeMe VR (Han & Smith 1996) can handle 10-20 simultaneous users, but this number could be extended by clever network architecture and multicast solutions.

Each communication channel has its own benefits and disadvantages, but what are the best solutions for multiple media. To combine all the benefits in one global structure, as a universal system, creates new problems (the size of the structure is huge, it is extremely hard to implement, etc.). A different solution is to use one channel for each medium i.e interaction data and video both use their own network architectures. The disadvantages are still there, but they only effect the current medium. If one channel becomes overwhelmed or the server crashes, it doesn't have any influence to the other media or their usability. Another useful aspect is portability i.e if the local terminal does not support video, it is unneccessary to reserve such resources from the computer or network.

Conclusion

Two real life workplaces, a Studio and an Office have been described, along with their Virtual and Mixed Reality counterparts. Issues of work process and social interaction taken from CSCW were utilised to understand the functionalities that virtual studios and offices need to provide. It is broadly concluded that different media (documents, audio, video, VR) all have different strengths and weaknesses, and each may be appropriate for different purposes in different contexts. Offices and Studios are best *extended into virtuality* by a mix of media (Mixed Realities) with a VR interface. The integration of video into VR environments presents the greatest technical difficulties, and some of these were considered from the viewpoints of computational load and networking. We conclude that an optimal solution would be to provide separate network architectures for real-time interactive VR and video.

Acknowledgements

Thanks to Mikko Jäkälä for his help in non-verbal communication and Kimmo Wideroos for his great ideas when showing the video images.

References

Arikawa, Masatoshi, Akira Amano, Kaori Maeda, Reiji Aibara, Shinji Shimojo, Yasuaki Nakamura, Kaduo Hirakiet al. (1996). QoS Management for Live Videos in Networked Virtual Spaces. Virtual Systems and Multimedia VSMM96, Gifu, Japan.

Bales, R.F (1951). "Channels of Communication in Small Groups." American Sociological Review(15): 461-467.

Benford, Steve, John Bowers, Lennart Fahlen, E., Chris Greenhalgh, John Mariani and Tom Rodden (1995). "Networked Virtual Reality and Cooperative Work." Presence **4**(4): 364-386.

Benford, Steve and Lennart Fahlén (1993). A Spatial Model of Interaction in Large Virtual Environments. Proceedings of the Third European Conference on Computer Supported Cooperative Work - ECSCW'93. 13-17 Sept. Milan, Italy. G. de Michelis, C. Simone and K. Schmidt. Dordrecht, Kluwer Academic Publishers: 109-124.

Bentley, R., J. A. Hughes, D. Randall, T. Rodden, P. Sawyer, D. Shapiro and I. Sommerville (1992). Ethnographically-Informed Systems Design for Air Traffic Control. Proceedings of ACM CSCW'92 Conference on Computer-Supported Cooperative Work: 123-129.

Bowers, John, Graham Button and Wes Sharrock (1995). Workflow from within and without: Technology and cooperative work on the print industry shopfloor. Proceedings of the Fourth European Conference on Computer Supported Cooperative Work - ECSCW'95. 10-14 Sept. Stockholm, Sweden. H. Marmolin, Y. Sunblad and K. Schmidt. Dordrecht, Kluwer Academic Publishers.

Bowers, John, Jon O'Brian and James Pycock (1996). Practically Accomplishing Immersion: Cooperation in and for Virtual Environments. Proceedings of the ACM 1996 Conference on Computer Supported Cooperative Work. M. S. Ackerman. NY, ACM: 380-389.

Bowers, John, James Pycock and Jon O'Brian (1996). Talk and Embodiment in Collaborative Virtual Environments. Proceedings of CHI '96, Vancouver, Canada, NY, ACM Press.

Brutzman, Don, Ed. (1997). Graphics Internetworking: Bottlenecks and Breakthroughs. To appear in Digital Illusions. Reading, MA, Addison-Wesley.

BSCW (1997). Basic Support for Cooperative Work Homepage. http://bscw.gmd.de/.

Buxton, William, A.S. (1993). Telepresence: Integrating Shared Task and Person Spaces. Readings in Groupware and Computer Supported Cooperative Work: Assisting human-human collaboration. R. M. Baecker. San Mateo, CA, US, Morgan Kaufmann: 816-822.

Carlsson, C. and O. Hagsand (1993). "DIVE — A platform for multi-user virtual environments." Computer & Graphics **17**(6): 663-669.

Casner, Steve (1993). Frequently Asked Questions (FAQ) on Multicast Backbone (MBone), http://www.mediadesign.co.at/newmedia/more/mbone-faq.html.

Codella, Christopher, Reza Jalili, Lawrence Koved, J Bryan Lewis, Daniel T Ling, James S Lipscomb, David A Rabenhorstet al. (1992). Interactive Simulation in a Multi-Person Virtual Environment. CHI'92, ACM Press.

DIVE (1997). The DIVE Homepage, http://www.sics.se/dive/.

Dorcey, Tim (1995). "CU-SeeMe DeskTop VideoConference Software." Connexious **9th**(3rd).

Dourish, Paul (1993). Culture and Control in a Media Space. Proceedings of the Third European Conference on Computer Supported Cooperative Work - ECSCW'93. 13-17 Sept. Milan, Italy. G. de Michelis, C. Simone and K. Schmidt. Dordrecht, Kluwer Academic Publishers: 1251138.

Forum, Alta Vista (1997). Homepage, http://altavista.software.digital.com/forum/showcase/index.htm.

Gaver, W., A Sellen, C. Heath and P. Luff (1993). One is not enough: multiple views in a media space. Proc. INTERCHI '93, Amsterdam, 22-29 April, ACM.

Greenhalgh, Chris and Steve Benford (1995). "MASSIVE: A Virtual Reality System for Tele-conferencing." ACM Transactions on Computer Human Interaction (TOCHI) **2nd**(1): 239-261.

Han, Jefferson and Brian Smith (1996). CU-SeeMe VR: Immersive Desktop Teleconferencing. ACM Multimedia '96, Boston, MA, ACM.

Harraway, Donna (1985). "A Manifesto for Cyborgs: Science, Technology, and Socialist Feminism in the 1980's." Socialist Review **80**: 65-107.

Heath, Christian, Marina Jirotka, Paul Luff and Jon Hindmarsh (1993). Unpacking Collaboration: The Interactional Organisation of Trading in a City Dealing Room. Proceedings of the Third European Conference on Computer Supported Cooperative Work - ECSCW'93. 13-17 Sept. Milan, Italy. G. de Michelis, C. Simone and K. Schmidt. Dordrecht, Kluwer Academic Publishers.

Heath, Christian and Paul Luff (1991). Collaborative Activity and Technological Design: Task Coordination in London Underground Control Rooms. ECSCW '91. Proceedings of the Second European Conference on Computer-Supported Cooperative Work. L. Bannon, M. Robinson and K. Schmidt. Amsterdam, Kluwer Academic Publishers: 65-80.

Heath, Christian and Paul Luff (1993). Disembodied Contact: Communication through Video in a Multi-Media Office Environment. Readings in Groupware and Computer Supported Cooperative Work: Assisting human-human collaboration. R. M. Baecker. San Mateo, CA, US, Morgan Kaufmann.

Hollan, J. and S. Stornetta (1992). Beyond being there. CHI '92: Striking a Balance, Monteray, CA., ACM.

InPerson (1997). InPerson 2.2, Silicon Graphics, http://www.sgi.com/Products/software/InPerson/ipintro.html.

International Telecommunication Union (1993). Recommendation H.261 (3/93) - Video codec for audiovisual services at p*64kbit/s. Switzerland, ITU.

Ishii, Hiroshi, Minoru Kobayashi and Jonathan Grudin (1992). Integration of Inter-Personal Space and Shared Workspace: ClearBoard Design and Experiments. Proceedings of ACM CSCW'92 Conference on Computer-Supported Cooperative Work: 33-42.

Kawanobe, Akihisa, Susumu Kakuta, Yasuhisa Kato and Katsumi Hosoya (1996). The Proposal for the Management Method of Session and Status in a Shared Space. Virtual Systems and Multimedia VSMM96, Gifu, Japan.

Kuzuoka, Hideaki, Toshio Kosuge and Masatomo Tanaka (1994). GestureCam: A Video Communication System for Remote Collaboration. CSCW 94: Transcending Boundaries, Chapel Hill, North Carolina, USA, ACM.

Littlejohn, Stephen W (1996). Theories of Human Communication. Belmont, CA, Wadsworth Publishing Company.

Macedonia, Michael R and Donald P Brutzman (1994). "MBone Provides Audio and Video Across the Internet." IEEE Computer: 30-36.

Munro, Alan (1996). Multimedia Support for Distributed Research Initiatives: Final Report, Centre for Requirements and Foundations, Oxford University Computing Laboratory, Parks Road, Oxford, OX1 3QD, England.

Nardi, B., H. Schwartz, A. Kuchinsky, R. Leichner, S. Whittaker and R. Sclabassi (1993). Turning Away from Talking Heads: The Use of Video-as-Data in Neurosurgery. Proc. INTERCHI '93, Amsterdam, 22-29 April, ACM.

O'Hair, Dan, Gustav W Friedrich, John M Wiemann and Mary O Wiemann (1995). Competent Communication. NY, St. Martin's Press.

ProShare (1997). Intel ProShare Production, http://cs.intel.com/Intel/networking_and_communications/proshare_products/threads.htm.

Reder, Stephen and Robert G. Schwab (1990). The temporal structure of cooperative activity. CSCW 90, Proceedings of the Conference on Computer-Supported Cooperative Work, Los Angeles, CA, October 7-10, 1990. New York, ACM Press: 303-316.

Robinson, Mike (1993). Design for unanticipated use .... ECSCW '93 (3rd. European Conference on Computer Supported Cooperative Work), Milan, Italy, Kluwer.

Robinson, Mike and Elke Hinrichs (1997). Study on the supporting telecommunications services and applications for networks of local employment initiatives (TeleLEI Project): Final Report. Sankt Augustin, Germany, GMD, Institute for Applied Information Technology (FIT), D 53754.

Salvador, Tony & Bly, Sarah (1997). Supporting the flow of information through constellations of interaction. Proceedings ECSCW'97. Amsterdam, Kluwer (forthcoming).

Sørgaard, Pål (1988). Object Oriented Programming and Computerised Shared Material. Second European Conference on Object Oriented Programming (ECOOP '88), Springer Verlag, Heidelberg.

Star, Susan, Leigh and Karen Ruhleder (1994). Steps towards an Ecology of Infrastructure. CSCW '94, Chapel Hill, N. Carolina, USA, ACM.

Suchman, Lucy (1987). Plans and situated actions. The problem of human-machine communication. Cambridge, Cambridge University Press.

Suchman, Lucy A. (1983). "Office Procedures as Practical Action: Models of Work and System Design." TOIS **1**(4): 320-328.

Thallman, Daniel, Christian Babski, Tolga Capin, Nadia Magnant Thalmann and Igor Sunday Pandzic (1996). "Sharing VLNET Worlds on the Web." Compugraphics'96 Marne-le-Vallee, France.

VRML (1996). The Virtual Reality Modeling Language Specification: Version 2.0, http://vag.vrml.org/VRML2.0/FINAL/.

Zyda, Michael J, David R Pratt, John S Falby, Chuck Lombardo and Kristen M Kelleher (1993). "The Software Required for the Computer Generation of Virtual Environments." Presence **2nd**(2nd): 130-140.

A Virtual Office Environment for Home Office Worker Based on 3D Virtual Space

Shinkuro Honda, Hironari Tomioka, Takaaki Kimura,
Takaharu Ohsawa, Kenichi Okada and Yutaka Matsushita
Department of Instrumentation Engineering, Keio University
3-14-1 Hiyoshi, Kouhoku-ku, Yokohama, 223, Japan
Tel: +81-45-563-1141, Fax: +81-45-562-7625
E-mail: {honda,tomioka,kimura,oosawa,okada,on}@myo.inst.keio.ac.jp

Abstract

In this paper, we describe a system that provides a "work-at-home" environment based on a virtual shared room built on a 3D graphics workstation. We realize "Awareness Space" on the system to avoid the tradeoff between providing facility of informal communication and keeping one's workspace from others' awareness information. Also, this system provides the feeling of their presence at virtual office by using "around view" and "sound effect".

keyword – Virtual Office, Informal Communication, Personal Space, Presence, Awareness Space, Concentration

1 INTRODUCTION

Recent technological advances made it possible to cooperate or communicate among distributed members by using audio, video and other media. Moreover, these technologies enable us to have a home office environment. In addition to supporting cooperative work and formal communication such as a video conferencing system[5][6], much attention is focused on the research of informal communication[1] and providing awareness information.

Our purpose is providing other members' awareness information at a home office and finding a solution about the tradeoff between providing awareness information and securing personal space.

An advantage of home office is as following: decreasing population of large cities, economizing high cost office space, and giving a chance to the people who are not able to work outside. Nevertheless, the disadvantages of home office includes problems such as burden from less communication, and an excludance from society. To avoid these problems, the home office system should support informal communication. Therefore, we have realized home office system which enables the home office workers to go to an office in 3D virtual space and work with his/her colleagues. The system provides a virtual shared room as a space for working and communicating. Also, the awareness of other members were provided as a trigger for the communication[9].

The environment which workers can plunge into the work largely affect work efficiency. This is a very important factor to an office environment. For example, it might bother workers, if too much awareness information had been given[10]. In this system, we have defined "Awareness Space" to make possible the coexistence of informal communication and work space where workers can concentrate.

In this paper, we explain the features of our work, which realizes "Awareness Space" to avoid the tradeoff between supporting informal communication and securing personal space, and which provides the feeling of their presence at virtual office by using "Around View" and "Sound Effect".

2 RELATED WORK

Montage[8] aims to provide a sence of teleproximity. The system uses video to help collaborators find opportune times to interact with each other. It uses momentary, reciprocal glances among networked workstations to make it easy to peek into someone's office. It is one example of considering one's privacy.

Portholes[9] supports awareness across distance. A data network provides a shared database of image information that is regularly updated and available at all sites. Initial experiences of the system in use demonstrate that Portholes supports shared awareness where helping to build a "sense of community". Portholes supports informal communication by providing video and audio to all the members, not only single member, so the user can feel work with his/her colleagues.

DIVA[2] is a vitual office environment which supports communication, cooperation, and awareness in both the synchronous and asynchronous modes. DIVA was integrated into a simple and intuitive interface which may be viewed as a replacement for standard graphical user interface desktop. DIVA is modeled after standard office, abstracting elements of physical offices required to support collaborative work, in order to utilize the experience that people have acquired through years of shared work in real offices.

VENUS[3] aims to support communication (especially, informal communication) among distributed collaborating colleagues realizing a new awareness

0-8186-8150-0/97 $10.00 © 1997 IEEE

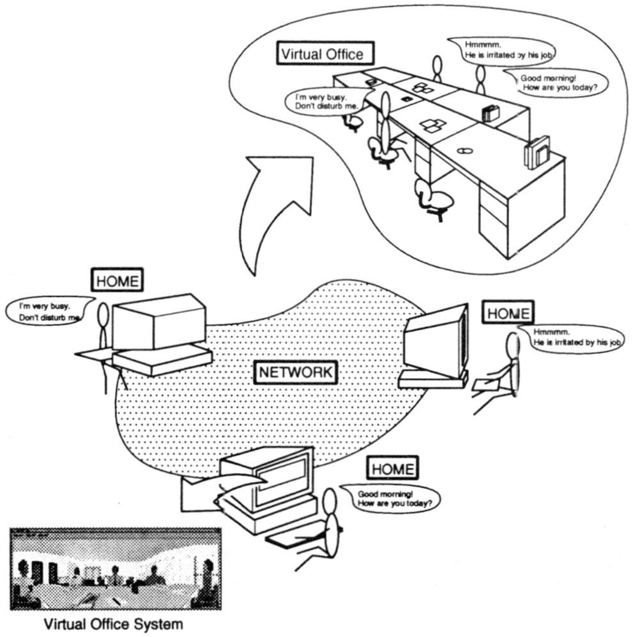

Figure 1: The Concept of Virtual Office

concept "Interest Awareness". VENUS supports two new aspects of awareness support, information-sharing triggerd awareness and activity triggerd awareness. Two metaphors are proposed for awareness support. In VENUS, co-workers can obtain communication opportunities triggerd by natural activities amond workspaces.

There are some examples of using 3D virtual spaces. Mainly they are used as a place for providing a communication.

FreeWalk[4] is a desktop meeting environment to support informal communication and which provides a 3D community common where everyboby can meet and can behave just as they do in real life. Each participant is represented as a pyramid of 3D polygons on which his/her live video is mapped, and can move freely.

Massive[7] allows multiple users to communicate using arbitrary combinations of audio, graphics, and text media over local and wide area networks. Communication is controlled by a so-called spatial model of interaction so that one user's perception of another user is sensitive to their relative positions and orientations. In this system, the awareness of others is controlled by observing the object's focus and nimbus. Each object's aura defines the total region within which it interacts.

3 SCHEME OF A VIRTUAL OFFICE ENVIRONMENT

In our system, we use the 3D virtual space to simulate office, and simulate that the workers go there. Compared with existing conference systems or communication systems, this office system also considers about worker's personal job when user is not communicating with others. In real office, the workers are able to sense the existence of his/her colleagues while working personally and recognize the occurrences in realtime manner. But actually, home office worker can not feel such things by using existing systems. Our system provides virtual office on the network, and they can go there, exchange greetings, feel atmosphere, and do their work. Figure1 shows the concept of our system. Every worker is in his/her own home, and has workstation for personal work and for office system. They connect to server which provides virtual office environment to go to work and come together virtually. This system enables the user to receive the other colleagues' awareness information and supports communication while they are in the virtual office.

At first, this paper describes how to realize the environment that is mentioned above. Secondly, how to keep one's personal space from these awareness information. Section4 explains the way of transmitting awareness in detail. We propose two techniques "Around View" and "Sound Effect" in this section. Section5 describes "Awareness Space" for the solution of the tradeoff between keeping home worker's personal space and providing awareness. Implementation of the system is described in Section6, evaluation of our system is shown in Section7, and we conclude this paper in Section8.

4 THE WAY OF TRANSMITTING AWARENESS IN DETAIL

We usually feel other members' awareness such as actions and gaze. For this reason, we are able to feel the atmosphere or tension of the real workplace. This also triggers the occurrence of informal communication. In general, simple audio and video transmission have used to provide other's awareness, but compared to the real world office, these are not enough to transmit other members' awareness in detail.

To realize members' awareness which is similar to the real office, we provide interfaces called "Around View" and "Sound Effect".

4.1 Around View

Former method of viewing 3D virtual workspace could not specify what the next person was doing[7]. But in real world, one is able to recognize if the person next to him/her sits down or stands up without looking. This is because the field of view of human being extends to more than 180 degrees.

If the interface can view more than 180 degrees, the user has no need of turning his virtual body to communicate with next person. This looks very strange in the point of view of other virtual members, since human usually communicate by looking each other's face. Human can clearly recognize the colors and the shapes only about 60 degrees in front. We cannot clearly see the angles more than that, but are adopted more to the movement of objects.

Therefore we have implemented the interface called "Around View" which is based on the field of view of real human. To be more detail, it has a field of view of 180 degrees. But only the middle 60 degrees is shown clearly, and the rest is shown vague gradually as it moves away from the middle.

Figure 2: Office View

Figure2 shows the office view. The office view is divided into five regions. The center region(Region1) shows the office view in detail using huge polygons(about 50000). Users can recognize other members' face and other objects in the office clearly. Perspective is set 86 degrees because the larger fields of view introduce serious perspective distortion. Region2 and 3 are around view that is made of less polygons(about 10000). Perspective of each region is 60 degrees(Figure3). Around views are mosaicked to express only the movement of members. In this way, this system realize the field of view more than 180 degrees. This view realizes seamless office adjusting each region to appropriate width. By using Around View,

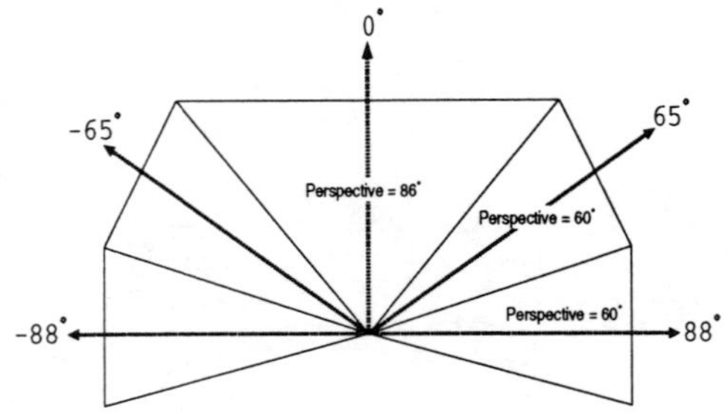

Figure 3: Realization of the Wide Field of View

the user recognizes the movement and the awareness of the next person, and, of course, the detail of the person in front. So, if the user wants to see the specific person, he/she has to turn his/her virtual body around just like in real world. By this action, other members can notice what the user is looking at.

4.2 Sound Effect

In the real world, we can not only see but also can hear the awareness information. The examples of the awareness information of sound are divided into two types. One type is the sound made by human itself, such as the voice or sneeze. The other is the sound made by human movement, such as footstep, the sound of door opening or closing. If we think of this virtual office system, the former could be heard from audio communication, but the latter could not be heard. So, we provide the sound effect which corresponds to each member's action. The type of sound effect we used are as follows:

- The sound of footsteps.
- The sound chair makes.
- The sound door makes.
- The noise of the office.

By hearing these sounds(excluding office noise), the user can sense other members' action. And the office noise were added to give a reality that the user really works in office.

5 AWARENESS SPACE

5.1 The Concept of Awareness Space

In good Japanese offices, you should have your own space to work at provided that you can feel the sorroundings. But the tradeoff exists between the facility of communication and keeping one's personal space from other members' awareness information. To avoid the unlimited flow of other members' awareness information, we have defined the notion of "Awareness Space", and solved the tradeoff problem explained above. "Awareness Space" is defined as the circled area centering the user in 3D virtual space. User can sense others' awareness information who is in the circle(see Figure4). The user can receive the sound information, the movement information from the sound effect, or the realtime video information of the member who had entered the user's awareness space.

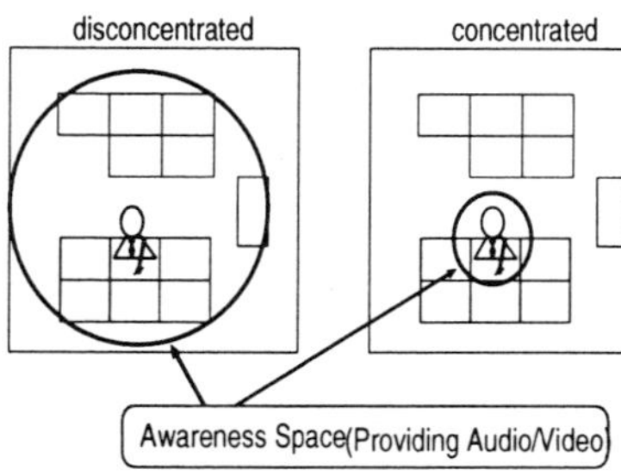

Figure 4: Awareness Space

In our system, the awareness space is provided with 3 levels. The volume of the other members' voice and sound effect and the mosaic of around view are changed in accordance with the level of awareness space. Figure5 shows three types of mosaicked around view.

NARROW The state of concentration, that is, user does not want to be bothered by others. Only the well selected awareness information, such as the colleagues next to the user or the one who walks behind the user, could be transmitted. Around view is mosaicked much.

NORMAL The state of normal working condition. The awareness information of colleagues in comparably near place could be transmitted.

WIDE The state of trying to feel the atmosphere of the entire office. All of the awareness information could be transmitted. Around view is not mosaicked.

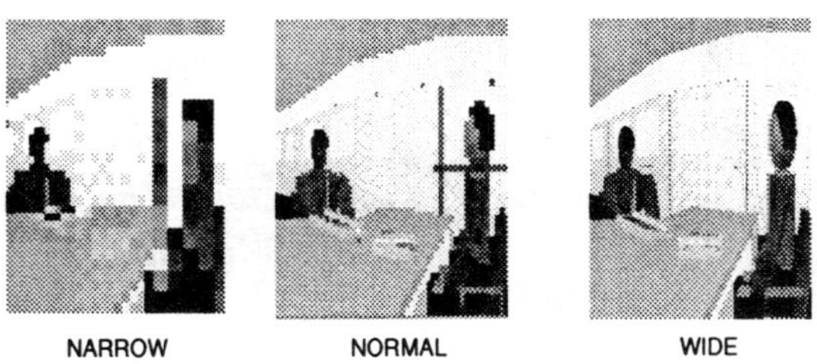

Figure 5: Three Types of Mosaicked View

In addition, the amount of the awareness information transmitted depends on the distance in 3D virtual space, so as the distance gets farther, the information decreases.

5.2 The Parameters for Deciding the Awareness Space

When user is concentrating on his/her project, there is no need of grasping the surrounding information. Giving too much information will lead to the bothering of user's work. In case of working in a project with multiple numbers, even when not working together, some factors such as chatting, knowing other members' mood, or feeling the team's atmosphere are thought to be important. Therefore, we have developed the idea of "Degree of Concentration", about which we talk the details in the later section, to change the awareness space.

In this system, the degree of concentration is provided 9 levels, when it is between 1 and 3, his/her awareness space becomes WIDE, when between 4 and 6, becomes NORMAL, between 7 and 9, becomes NARROW(Figure6). In this way, the awareness space has continuity and doesn't change so frequently. The initial level is 1 because users are disconcentrated when they arrive at office.

Initial Value ↓ (at 1)

Degree of Concentration	1	2	3	4	5	6	7	8	9
Awareness Space		WIDE			NORMAL			NARROW	

Figure 6: Degree of Concentration

5.3 Elements to Determine the Degreee of Concentration

To detect one's degree of concentration from the usual computer work, we applied two elements itemized below.

- the frequency of key typing and mouse movement
- the frequency of chair movement

The reason why these elements are selected is that an interface between computer and human is only keyboard and mouse. So we suppose it is only way to detect one's degree of concentration from the frequency of key typing and mouse movement. In addition, we expect that user do not move chair when he/she concentrate his/her work. Chair movement is easy to detect by simple device, so the frequency of chair movement is chosen. To determine one's degree of concentration from this two elements, we must know which situation of key typing and chair movement indicates concentration.

To derive the relevance between human concentration and these two elements, we have experimented as below.

5.4 Experiment

Each of the 25 subjects sat down in laboratory's workstation at a time to work on the menus such as programming, mailing, netscaping, or playing game.

While they are working on the menu, we took the measure of the frequency of typing and moving of the chair. At the same time, we observed the brain wave and took the video of the subjects to know whether the subject is concentrating or not. We use IBVA system[12] for measuring brain wave. A subject wears a band with an instrument around his/her head. The information from the instrument is send to Macintosh, analyzed and shown as Figure7.

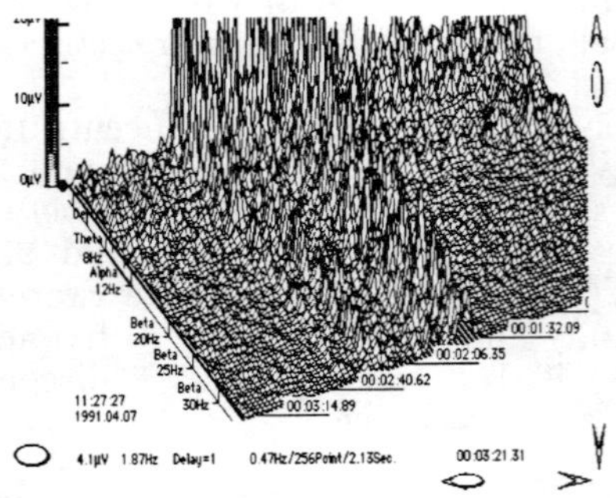

Figure 7: An Example of Brain Wave on Macintosh

The next two sections explain how to define the period of concentration from the brain wave and video of subjects.

5.4.1 Determining the Period of Concentration Using Brain Wave

As brain wave for a adult, when he/she is awake, and if the eyes are closed or the mental condition is stable, the alpha wave comes out. Coresponding to the mental activity or the opened eyes, the alpha wave is heldback, and the beta wave comes out. In detail, the alpha wave comes out when the eyes are closed and not talking to anyone, and the beta wave comes out when doing a logical, rational thinking like listening deeply into someone's story or solving test questions.

We have defined "the period of concentration" as the situation when the alpha wave is heldback, and the beta wave comes out.

Nevertheless, the beta wave also comes out when in anxiety or in tension. Some subjects had the beta wave at the beginning of the experiment. For these subjects, we did not start the experiment untill he/she has relaxed and the beta wave is heldback.

5.4.2 Determining the Period of Concentration Using Video

We can only determine whether subjects concentrate by using brain wave, but we cannot determine from the brain wave whether the subject is concentrating on his works, or other unrelated materials(e.g. playing games, chatting, etc). We only considered the concentration of users who engaged in their work. For this reason, the video of subjects and the workstation display were taken.

5.5 Standardizing the Degree of Concentration from the Experimental Results

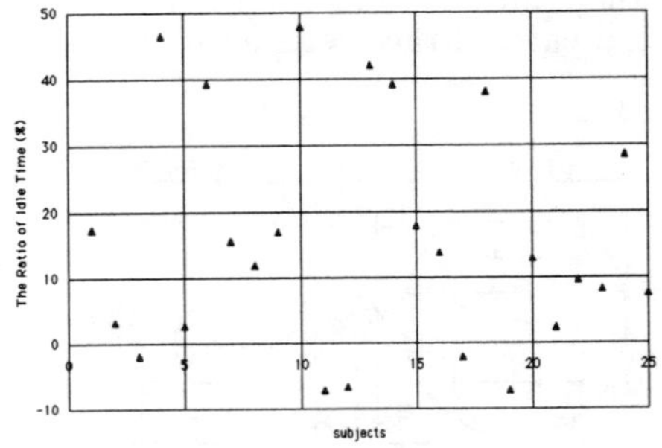

Figure 8: The Ratio of Idle Time(disconcentrating period–concentrating period)

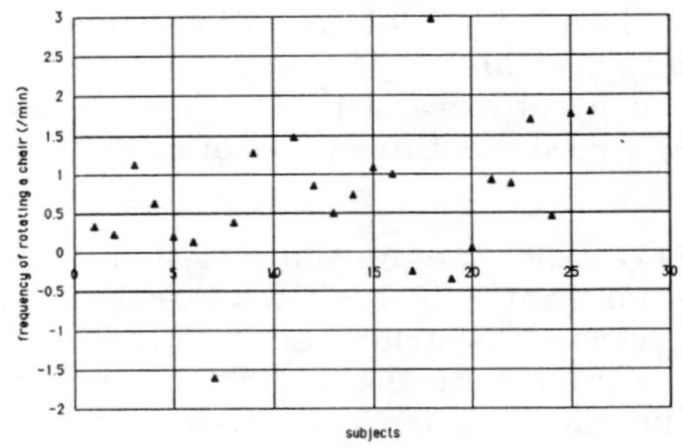

Figure 9: The Frequency of Rotating A Chair (disconcentrating period–concentrating period)

Figure 10: Headphone Metaphor

Figure8 shows the difference of the rate of idle time between concentrating period and disconcentrating period. Most subjects' idle rate of disconcentrating period is greater than that of concentrating period. Figure9 shows the difference of the frequency of rotating a chair between concentrating period and disconcentrating period. This also shows most subjects' chair movement of disconcentrating period is greater than that of concentrating period. From the result, compared to concentrating period, disconcentrating period has more idle time and more frequency of moving a chair.

Based on these results of experiments, we define algorithm to change the degree of concentration. First, two threshold(A, B) is defined for idle time and chair movement, and the value is larger than A or lesser than B, the degree of concentration is changed. The system measures the idle time and the chair movement every minute, and for the idle time when the value is greater than A, the degree of concentration of the user decreases by 1 level. When the value is smaller than B, the degree of concentration increases by 1 level. For the chair movement, the same.

By calculating the mean value of idle time and frequency of moving a chair, 63% and 1.5 count/min in concentrating period, 47% and 0.8 count/min respectively. The default value of A is 63%(keytyping) and 1.5 count/min(chair), B is 47% and 0.8 count/min. For the idle time, if more than 63%, or for the chair, if more than 1.5 count/min, the degree of concentration decreases by 1 level. And for the idle time, if less than 47%, or for the chair, if more than 0.8 count/min, the degree of concentration increases by 1 level. The parameter is variable and can be set by each user.

The Table1 shows the rate of more than 10 seconds of an idle. From this, compared to disconcentrating period, the concentrating period consists mostly of the idle of 10 to 20 seconds. The idle of more than 1 minute were rare. When the idle of more than 1 minute was detected, the system decreases the degree of concentration by 1 level.

Idle time(sec)	Concentrating(%)	Disconcentrating(%)
10-19	64	48
20-29	19	18
30-39	5	10
40-49	5	7
50-59	1	3
60-	6	14

Table 1: The Ratio of Idle Time

5.6 The Degree of Concentration Detected by Other Members

The member who is concentrating might not be able to answer others for he/she holds less information of surrounding. Therefore, there is a need of knowing other member's degree of concentration.

In our laboratory, some people put headphone and are listening to music, when he/she don't need others' awareness. This system utilizes "headphone metaphor" to solve this problem by putting the headphone to the member who has the awareness space level of NARROW. Now, the others are able to recognize that this member is concentrating. To talk with the member with the headphone, others have to walk closer to him/her(Figure10).

6 IMPLEMENTATION

6.1 System Overview

This system is implemented on SGI Indy, O2 and Sun SparcStation20. The user interfaces are implemented using C, Motif, and OpenGL. Figure11 shows the system overview. This system

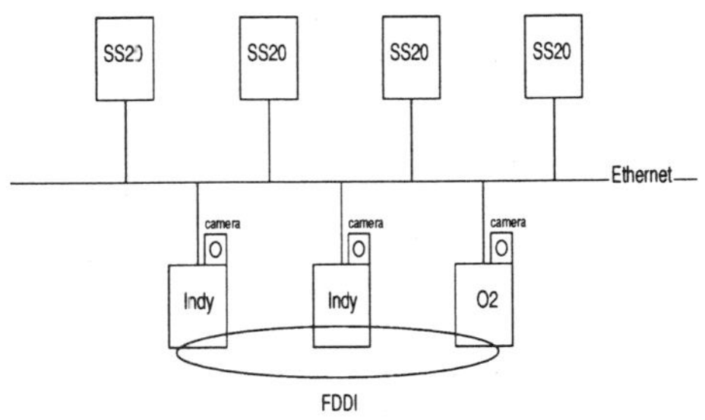

Figure 11: System Overview

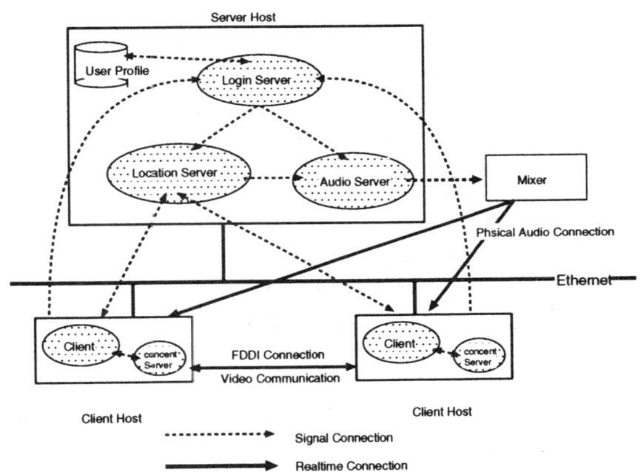

Figure 12: Software Architecture

uses Ethernet(TCP/IP) for signal connection and FDDI(UDP/IP) for continuous media(i.e., realtime audio/video streams). All workstations are connected by Ethernet. Two sets of Indy and one O2 have video equipment(camera, videoboard) for video communication and connected by FDDI.

Figure12 shows the software architecture. The role of servers and a client are described below.

loginServer It administrates each members' login and logout. By connecting to this server, each client is able to get all the informations of other members.

locationServer It notices the rest of the members' position, direction, and degree of concentration which changes dynamically.

audioServer It controls audio and sound effect by receiving the positional information from locationServer.

Client It displays the virtual office implemented by OpenGL, and the precise location of other members by positional information from locationServer. It also transfers video image with other clients through FDDI, if it requires.

concentServer It is run for every clients to calculate the degree of concentration of members every minute, and it informs the result to the client.

6.2 User Interface

Figure13 shows the office view of this system and the member(the second from right) is sitting and wearing headphone (which indicates his concentration is narrow). When two of the members look straight at each other, they can communicate in realtime video, by using FDDI. Figure14 shows video communication with the member who is walking to talk to the user and look straight at each other. The quadrilateral area at the center of the view is video window. User can select "GO TO OFFICE" from the dialogbox at the top of the view to enter the office. As we have stated our concept as "A virtual office environment" that the user can go to the office virtually via network, it is important to convince the user that he/she is really going there. When the user goes to a virtual office, there is a simulation of going through the hall and moving across the shared room until he/she sits down. If user wants to go by the other member, he/she can select the other member's name from the dialogbox. This system provides him/her the office view animation of going there. The member who is talked to can see the member's movememt(standing up and walking) by CG animation in the virtual office view.

User can change Awareness Space by selecting from the dialogbox if he/she prefer manual change to automatical change.

6.2.1 Providing the Image of Members

Each member who participates in a virtual office is provided with images and audio of other members which are defined according to relationships of their positions. In this system, user's body is represented in CG and the face picture is attached. Requiring face images of various directions, we use both the continuous video images and the still pictures; the system usually uses the still picture taken from 12 directions(Figure15), and uses the continuous video images when members face each other.

6.2.2 Providing Audio According to Distance and Direction

To localize the members' voice in real time, the following general and simple methods are used for localization[11].

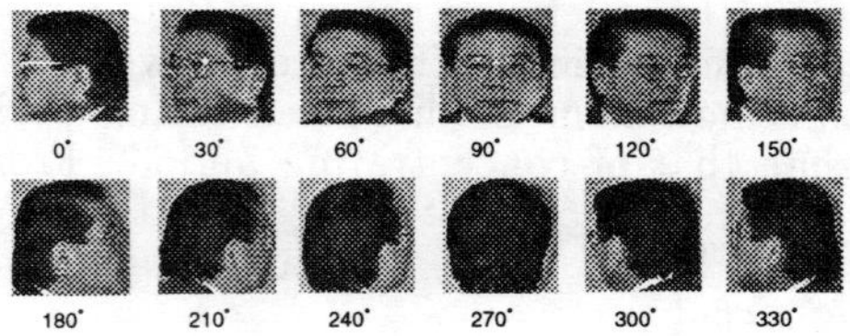

Figure 15: Still Pictures of User Taken from 12 Directions

Direction Attribute The most simple and effective way to give a sound source a direction attribute (i.e., left-right and back-front) is to use stereo speakers or headphones. Stereo-output mixers use differences in amplitude to generate a uni-dimensional spatial distribution for sound sources. This is so called "panning" of the sound source.

On the other hand, according to the analysis of HRTF(Head Related Transfer Function), we feel that sound from behind is muffled. To give a sound source a back-front attribute, a low-pass filter is employed.

Distance Attribute This system uses reverberation to give a sound source a distance attribute. The level and duration of reverberation of the sound source increases in proportion to the distance between the user and the sound source.

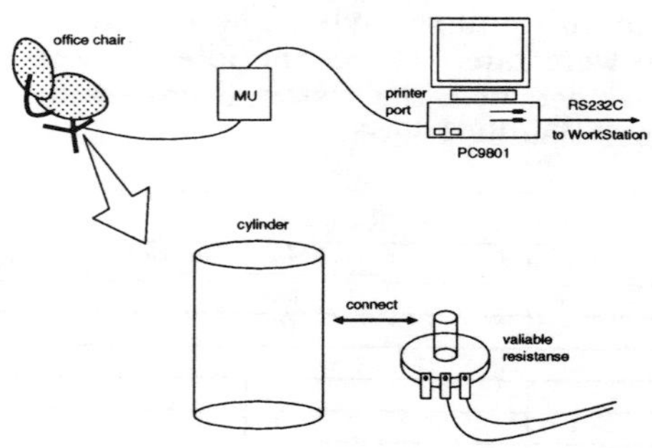

Figure 16: View Chair

6.2.3 View Chair Interface

In real world, when people look around, they usually turn their head or body. If the user uses mouse or keyboard to control it, the user might feel different. So we have developed the chair interface named "View Chair" which enables user to turn the virtual chair by turning the real chair.

We added the variable resistance to the shaft of the chair, and by reading the resistance, we calculate the rotating angle. If the user rotates the chair more than 30 degrees to the right, the view of an office rotates to the right, also. This gives a feeling of turning right

Figure 13: Office View

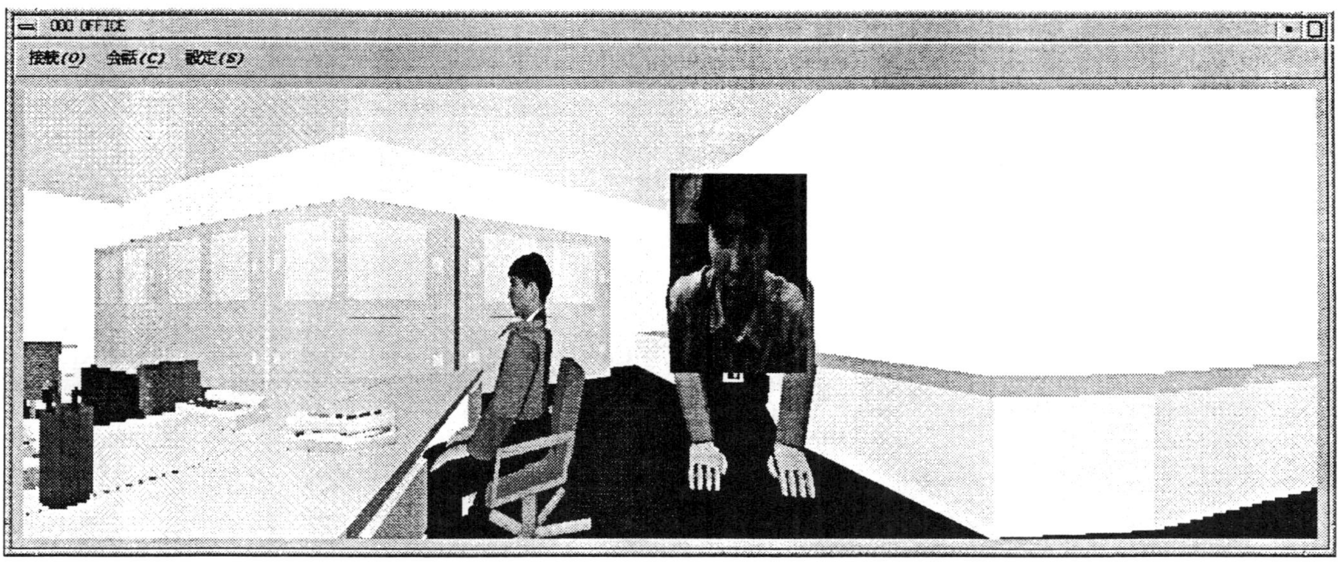

Figure 14: The Office View With Realtime Video

No.	Question	CaseA	CaseB
1.	I could be well aware of whether there sits a person next to me.	3.85	6.19
2.	I could easily look aroud the office.	5.77	4.41
3.	I could at once nocite the companion who was talking.	3.11	4.41
4.	I could at once nocite other persons who were talking.	5.00	6.11
5.	I could at once feel that other persons were walking in the office.	5.75	5.89
6.	I could at once feel that other persons were walking near to me.	5.00	5.33
7.	I could know well that other persons came to work.	4.77	5.76
8.	I could know well that other persons in front of me came to work.	5.46	6.06
9.	I could talk to other person without feeling of incompatibility.	5.89	6.38
10.	There was no feeling of incongruity on the talking gesture.	5.00	5.12
11.	There was no feeling of incongruity on the picture size.	5.33	6.00
12.	I could know well that person next to me came to work.	3.77	4.94
13.	I felt that I were in office.	5.31	5.63
14.	I wanted to greet or greeted.	5.62	5.00
15.	I felt that I went to office.	5.54	6.06
16.	I felt no incongruity on the 3D office.	5.23	5.12
17.	I knew well that other persons were talking to each other.	4.00	4.94
18.	I felt no incongruity on the video.	5.08	5.00
19.	I knew well who the person next to me was.	4.69	4.94
20.	I knew well what the person next to me did.	3.23	3.82
21.	I knew well where every person sat.	5.46	5.53
22.	he smooth communication was possible.	4.92	5.06
23.	I knew well which direction to which other person faced.	5.31	5.47
24.	I at once knew when other person was sitting down.	5.38	5.53

Table 2: Results of the Questionnaire Data from the Comparative Experiment

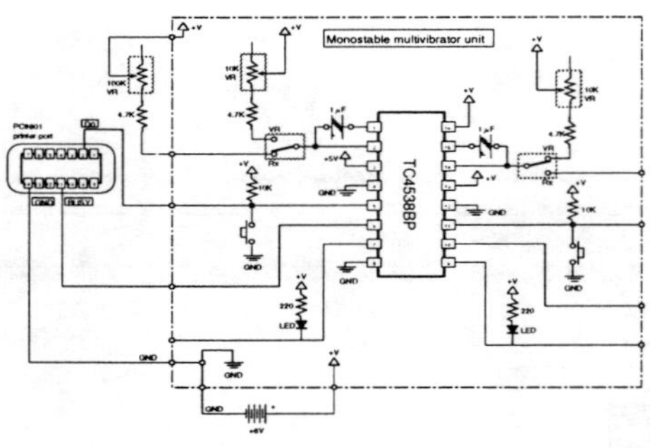

Figure 17: Multivibrator Unit

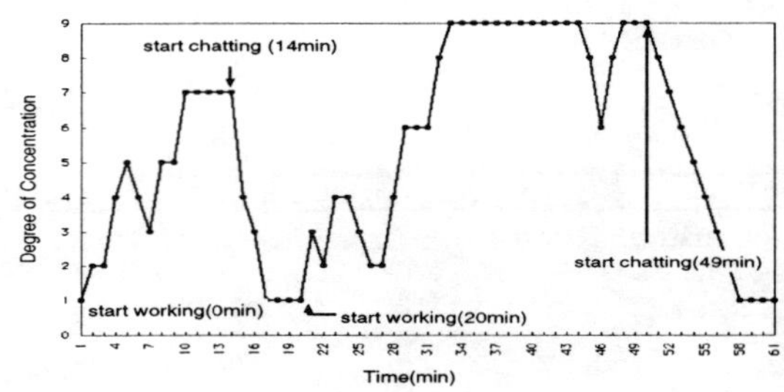

Figure 18: Degree of Concentration Change

in virtual office. The same thing happens if the user turns left. User can turn the view by clicking left/right button of a mouse if do not want to use View Chair.

This chair is also used for measuring the degree of concentraton.

Figure16 shows the architecture of View Chair. View Chair is connected to PC9801(NEC) via Multivibrator Unit(MU). Figure17 shows the circuit of MU. MU changes the value of variable resistance to digital signal and send it to PC. PC and workstation is connected by RS232C and communicate information about chair.

7 EVALUATION

We have evaluated this system by a comparative experiment. 18 subjects used two types of systems. Table2 shows the results of the questionnaire data from the comparative experiment. CaseA stands for the system without Around View and Sound Effect. CaseB stands for our complete system with Around View and Sound Effect. The scores are the mean value of respondents. The value has 7 steps from 1(bad) to 7(good).

The questions in the questionnaire have been selected to evaluate the influence of the effects of "Around View" and "Sound Effect" on providing awareness. And some questions are for evaluating the user interface of this system.

Our system scores higher than the system of CaseA on most of questions. Especially, providing awareness of the person next to the user is remarkable(question1, 12, 19, 20). This result indicates that Around View and Sound Effect are effective for transmitting awareness information. In addition, many subjects felt the sense of going to office on both CaseA and CaseB(question15). This shows the effect of office view animation of going through the hall and moving across the shared room until he/she sits down.

We also evaluate Awareness Space by taking video of user and make a comparison between the degree of concentration and the condition of user. Figure18 shows the typical result of changing degree of concentration. This result shows that the degree of concentration detected by our system almost corresponds to the condition of the subject.

8 CONCLUSION

In this paper, we describe a system that provides a "work-at-home" environment based on a virtual shared room built on a 3D graphics workstation. We realize "Awareness Space" on the system to avoid the tradeoff between providing facility of informal communication and keeping one's workspace from others' awareness information. Also, this system provides the feeling of the ownself presence at virtual office by using "around view" and "sound effect".

ACKNOWLEDGEMENTS

Special thanks to Dr.Jiying Zhao and Mr.Junya Noda for giving so much advice about writing this paper.

References

[1] Stefik, M., et al, "Beyoud the Chalk board: Computer Support for Collaboration and Problem Solving in Meetings.", Communications of the ACM, Vol.30, No.1, Jan. 1987.

[2] M. Sohlenkamp, G. Chwelos, "Integrating Communication, Cooperation, an Awareness: The DIVA Virtual Office Environment", Proc. ACM CSCW'94, 1994.

[3] N. Matsuura, G. Fujino, K. Okada, and Y. Matsushita, "VENUS:A Tele-Communicaation Environment to Support Awareness for Informal Interactions", Proc. 12th Scharding Int. Workshop-Design of Computer Supported Cooperative Work and Groupware Systems, 1993.

[4] H. Nakanishi, C. Yoshida, T. Nishimura, and T. Ishida, "FreeWalk:Supporting Casual Meetings in a Network", Proc. ACM CSCW'96, 1996.

[5] T. Inoue, K. Okada, and Y. Matsushita, "Learnign from TV Programs : Application of TV presentation to a videoconferencing system", Proc. ACM UIST'95, 1995.

[6] K.Okada, F.Maeda, Y.Ichikawa,and Y.Matsushita, "Multiparty videoconferencing at virtual social distance:MAJIC design", Proc. ACM CSCW'94, Chapel Hill, NC, USA, pp385-393, 1994.

[7] C. Greenhalgh and S. Benford, "MASSIVE: A Collaborative Virtual Environment for Teleconferencing", ACM Transactions on Computer-Human Interaction, Vol.2, No.3 Sep. 1995.

[8] J. C. Tang and M. Rua, "Montage: Providing Teleproximity for Distributed Groups", Proc. ACM CHI'94, 1994.

[9] P. Dourish, S. Bly, "Portholes: Supporting Awareness in a Distributed work Group", Proc. ACM CHI'92, 1992.

[10] S. E. Hudson and I. Smith, "Techniques for Addressing Fundamental Privacy and Disruption Tradeoffs in Awareness Support Systems", Proc. ACM CSCW'96, 1996.

[11] K. Teramoto, N. Oki, K. Okada, and Y. Matsushita, "VCP:Communication System Using Spatial Auditory Interface", Proc. Multimedia Japan'96, pp126-131, 1996.

[12] http://www.opendoor.com/pagoda/IBVA/

Modeling and Rendering for Virtual Environments

Sensor Based Creation of Indoor Virtual Environment Models

S. F. El-Hakim, P. Boulanger, F. Blais, and J.-A. Beraldin
Institute for Information Technology, National Research Council, Canada

Abstract

A system that can rapidly, reliably, remotely and accurately create a photo realistic three-dimensional model of indoor environments is needed for many applications. In this paper, we present a mobile mapping system that is designed to generate such models automatically from various sensors. Surfaces and features can be accurately mapped from images acquired by a unique configuration of different types of optical imaging sensor and dead reckoning positioning device. This configuration guarantees that all the information required to create the three-dimensional model of the environment is included in the collected data. The same general design concept can be used for environments ranging from simple office hallways to long winding underground mine tunnels. This paper describes the hardware systems and processing procedures. We also present test results and describe our virtual environment facility to display such models.

1: Introduction

Virtual exploration of remote places and environments, either for leisure, engineering design, simulations, or tasks in hazardous environments, is more effective and useful if geometrical relationships and dimensions in the virtual model are accurate [1-3]. The accuracy requirements of the virtual model will widely vary with applications. Even within an application the accuracy requirements may vary. For example, the accuracy of the spatial location and orientation of doors and openings through which the viewer or a vehicle navigates is higher than other details. On the other hand, some surfaces may need high-resolution texture maps rather than high geometric accuracy. For several reasons such as availability and cost, most models are built by using either standard geometric primitives, libraries of pre-modeled objects, or manual digitizing of every point. Building such a model graphically for a detailed environment takes enormous efforts and time. This model creation process is not suitable for applications requiring accurate representation of existing objects and sites. Thus, real-world image-based virtual environments (VE) can advantageously complement or replace artificially created VE in many endeavors. Currently, creating such models remains a challenge and is a limitation to implementing the technology in a wide range of useful applications [3].

There are many different sensor technologies that can be used to generate 3-D data, either directly such as range sensors [4,5], or indirectly such as video cameras [6,7]. A single type of sensor may not provide sufficient data to completely reconstruct an entire environment. The 3-D data captured by the different types of sensor are usually complementary; each can accurately provide data on only certain types of surface or scene subsets. For example, range data from a laser scanner can be accurate and complete over a continuous surface but may produce erroneous results on surface discontinuities such as edges or specular surfaces. By contrast, intensity images produced by photometric sensors cannot provide complete or accurate 3-D measurements on unmarked continuous surfaces but can provide high accuracy on features and edges. Since geometric properties required by VE applications include all surfaces and edges or features, both types of data should be integrated to provide these geometric properties completely and accurately. Requirement vs. cost is also a major factor when selecting the most appropriate sensor or a combination of sensors.

Except for small environments, a mobile platform is required to collect data for 3-D mapping. Mapping systems require precise calibration and must produce geometric models in one global reference system. In those systems the data processing is usually not required to be in real-time. In the following sections, a review of various mobile mapping systems will be given and the limitations for accurate indoor mapping will be pointed out. The proposed solution will then be presented.

1.1: Mobile mapping

Mobile mapping combines absolute and relative positioning devices and imaging sensors to locate features in a global reference system [8]. The absolute positioning sensors provide the framework for all other data collected

0-8186-8150-0/97 $10.00

by the relative positioning sensors. A global positioning system (GPS) is used in most mobile mapping systems that claim high absolute accuracy. Other positioning sensors such as an inertial navigation system (INS) and/or dead-reckoning devices are also required for positioning and orientation to fill in the gaps when GPS signal is interrupted or temporarily obstructed [9]. When the data from these sensors are integrated properly, a continuous and accurate tracking of the absolute position of the sensors becomes possible. In order to determine the position of the features and the details to be mapped, imaging sensors such as CCD cameras are used. These cameras will determine the feature position relative to the camera. Since the camera absolute position in a global coordinate system is known from the absolute positioning sensors, any mapped feature relative to the camera can be transferred to this global system. The final accuracy is a function of the accuracy of each of the individual sensors, the calibration and registration of the sensor positions relative to each other, and the method of processing and integration of data. Currently the best achievable accuracy reported from existing systems, using state-of-the-art GPS, INS, and digital CCD cameras, is 0.4 m to 1.0 m (RMS) in the global framework and much better for relative position between features [8-12]. The main application areas of these systems are road mapping, structural clearance measurements along railways, and aerial topographic mapping. In those applications, the data collection must be performed at the normal vehicle speed, while most of the data processing is carried out off-line. There is normally an operator on board who not only operates the vehicle but also performs interactive functions related to data collection. Since most of the existing prototypes for mobile mapping system do not use laser scanners, many surface details will not be mapped.

1.2: A sample of mobile mapping systems

The literature reports a spectrum of mobile mapping systems, the majority of which are either in prototype stage or still in a design/simulation stage. It is beyond the scope of this paper to evaluate all existing systems, thus only a representative sample will be mentioned. We will restrict those to land systems (i.e. excluding air and underwater systems) which are at least at the prototype stage and were tested in realistic settings.

Table 1 displays the properties of four mapping systems. It is obvious that these mapping systems are designed mainly for outdoor mapping and not useful for indoor applications since they rely on GPS for the global positioning. They also use stereo vision alone to obtain the relative position of features, thus only partial 3-D map can be constructed. We argue in the next section that the proposed solution solves the main problems of the existing mapping systems for indoor applications.

System Name	Sensors
GPSVan [8]	GPS, INS, wheel counter, CCD & color cameras
VISAT [10]	GPS, INS, CCD & color cameras.
KiSS [11]	GPS, INS, odometer, altimeter, CCD & color cameras.
Surveying Van [12]	GPS, wheel sensors, barometer, stereo CCDs

Table 1: Sample of mobile mapping systems

1.3: Problem statement and the NRC solution

One of the main problems in indoor mapping, particularly for large sites, is error propagation in the absence of GPS or landmarks of known global position. All measurements are made relative to the mobile platform while the absolute position is not accurately known because of the loss of accuracy of dead-reckoning devices or inertial navigation systems due to drift (error rapidly increasing over time.) Our solution is specifically designed to solve this error propagation problem. It has the following features:

1. It uses all data simultaneously in the solution, rather than sequentially, with dead-reckoning data only as initial approximation and range sensor data as constraints to reduce error propagation.
2. It employs sufficient number of cameras, the relationships between which, in one position, are known from a calibration procedure. This will be used as additional constraints.
3. It configures the relative position and orientation of the cameras to provide a strong geometric solution thus further reducing error propagation.

2: System Components and Lab Facilities

The proposed system [13] has been designed to implement the features mentioned above. Figure 1 shows the design of the mobile system. The sensor configuration is designed for coverage of the walls and ceiling of an indoor site. Modifications can be easily made to cover other views, such as the floor. In addition to the mobile system, other components are required: a calibration structure, a workstation, and a VE display facility. A relatively large site has been constructed to test the system. Each component will be described in some detail in the following sections.

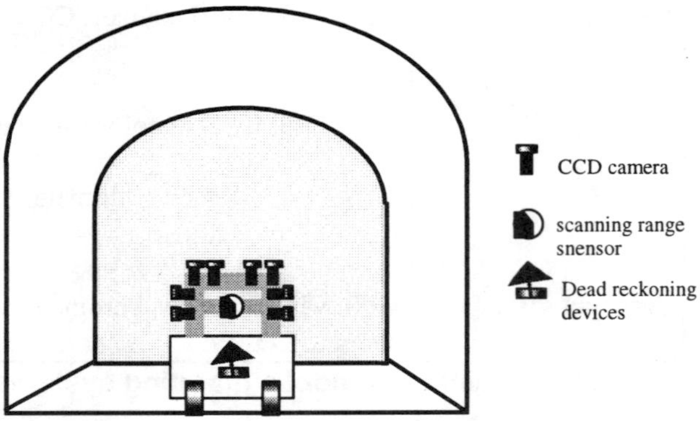

Figure 1: Design of the mobile mapping system

2.1: The Data Acquisition Platform -DAP

Figure 2 shows the mobile data acquisition platform (DAP) and the mounted cameras

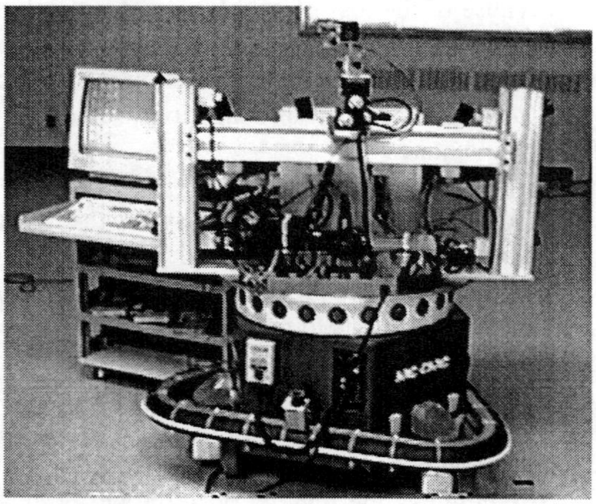

Figure 2: The DAP

The DAP consists of:

- A mobile platform with a dead reckoning system that provides relative position (X, Y), and a yaw (rotation angle about its vertical axis) feedback as calculated from wheel encoders. The mobile platform can be operated remotely via the computer network or manually using a joystick.
- Eight RS-170-standard analogue CCD cameras. Each camera is equipped with 8-mm C-mount lens.
- A 3-D range sensor: Biris model CHIN/S. It is designed and calibrated for ranges between 0.5 m and 4.0 m. The head is mounted on a pan and tilt unit. In any vehicle position, the pan and tilt unit will move the Biris head so that two slightly overlapped scans are taken in each side of the vehicle. These scenes cover approximately the same views as the CCD cameras.
- A Pentium PC, referred to as the acquisition PC, for controlling sensors acquisition and storing the data.
- Two Matrox-Pulsar image acquisition boards installed on the PCI bus on the PC. Each board has inputs for four video cameras.
- Software modules to control all the data acquisition devices. They acquire images from the CCD cameras and Biris, control pan and tilt unit, acquire data from the dead reckoning system, and store data on the PC. The acquisition and categorized data storage are completely automated.
- Sturdy mounts for the cameras, the pan and tilt unit, and the PC.
- Ethernet link for direct access between the acquisition PC and other processing and display computers.

2.1.1: The 3-D range sensor - Biris. One of the unique components of this system is the range sensor, Biris (named for bi-iris), which is specifically designed to acquire accurate 3-D data at a wide variation of ranges (between 0.5 m and 4.0 m for the model used in the tests described in this paper.) The basic optical principle of the range sensor, based on a modified Biris principle [14, 15] is shown in Figure 3. The range is obtained by either measuring the average position, $p=p_1+p_2$, of the two laser spot images p_1 and p_2 on the CCD photo-detector (plane of light method), or their separation, $b=p_2 - p_1$, (Biris method). Two very important properties of this sensor are worth mentioning for virtual environment mapping:

- The combination of range data obtained by the Biris and the plane of light methods are used to validate the range measurements. This enables the range sensor to automatically remove outliers and spurious peaks that may be created by ambient light such as sun interference or other light sources or from laser reflections on a highly reflective surface [15].
- The intensity of the laser light reflected from the scene directly provides an intensity image of the scene in perfect registration with the range measurement. The intensity image corresponds to the laser color (red) of the scene and is usually represented by a gray-scale picture [14, 16].

The intensity image can be directly used to create low-resolution realistic virtual environment of the scene. For increased resolution or to obtain a colored representation of the environment, range data can be combined with conventional photometric images, the intensity image provided by the range sensor can then be used to compensate for local perspective errors.

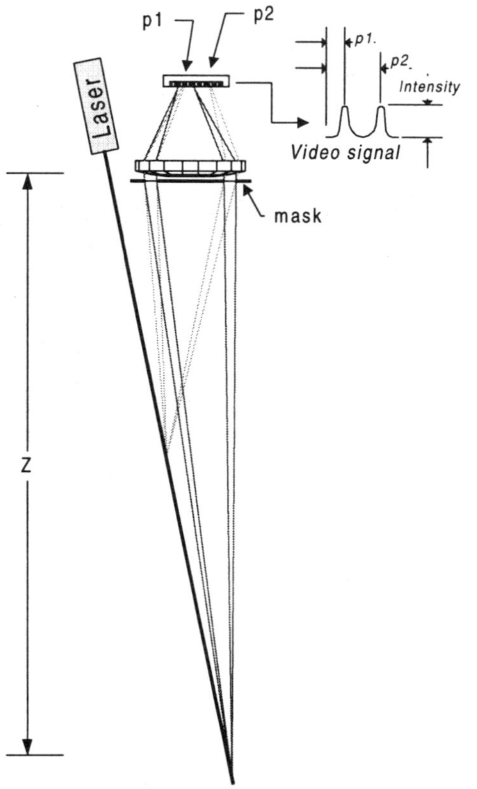

Figure 3: Optical principle of the Biris/Plane of Light method.

2.1.2: The pan-tilt scanning unit. To completely cover the surroundings of the vehicle, the range sensor was mounted on a pan-tilt unit. The unit (Figure 4 and 5) is used to scan the 3-D laser profile around a 360° pan angle and an 85° tilt angle. The scanning parameters as well as the image resolution are computer controlled and therefore fully programmable. Different modes of low resolution and high-resolution images can be preprogrammed to completely cover the surroundings of the vehicle.

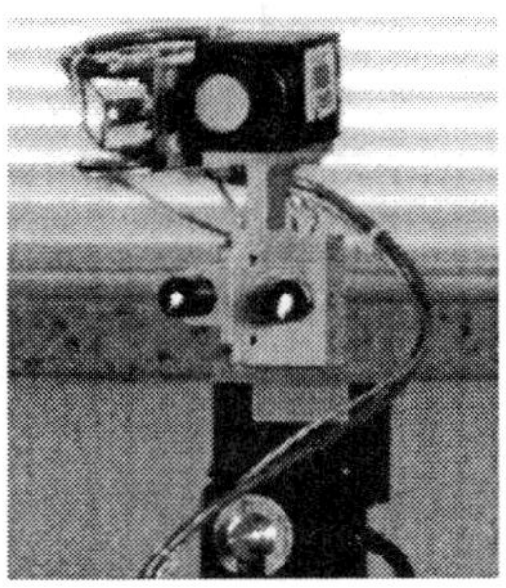

Figure 4. The Biris sensor and its pan-tilt unit.

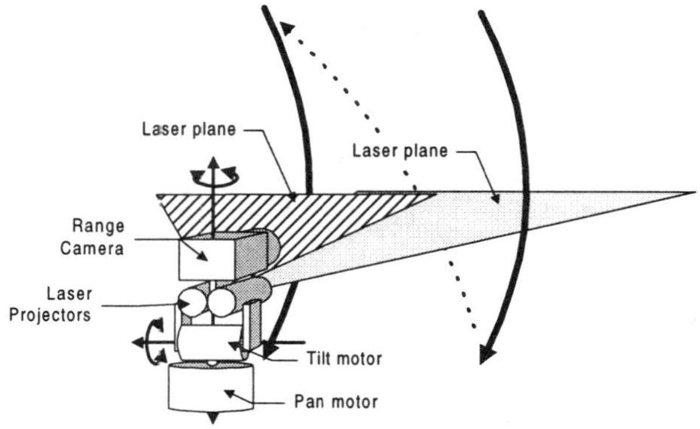

Figure 5. Description of the 3-D scanning unit

2.2: The calibration / registration structure -CRS

One of the most critical steps in the mapping procedure is the calibration of the sensors. The aim is to find the parameters defining the relationship between sensor measurements, in its local coordinate system in image space, and the desired measurements in the global coordinate system in the object space. The calibration parameters are determined using sensor measurements on targets of known positions in the global coordinate system (Figure 6). These targets are also used to register the data from all the different sensors in a single coordinate system. The calibration targets are chosen to be spherical in shape. This allows them to be viewed from any direction without being geometrically distorted. The targets were surveyed with 3"-theodolite to a positioning accuracy of 0.08 mm. The CRS is used to calibrate the 8-CCD cameras and the Biris scans as taken from a single vehicle position. The calibration parameters for the cameras and Biris scans are in the same coordinate system defined by the theodolite measurements of the targets.

Figure 6: Sensor calibration using the CRS.

2.3: The VE display facility

A facility dedicated to VE research and application has been established at the Institute for Information Technology of NRC. The goal is to develop a 3-D electronic visualization test bed that will integrate technologies in the fields of VE, real-time imaging, and 3-D range sensing to create, display, and interact with a digital model of an environment in a realistic manner (Figure 7). The current objectives of this facility are:

1. to demonstrate, in a virtual environment, the realism of the reconstruction of real environments from sensor-based digital models;
2. to facilitate the development of new digital modeling schemes to improve realism;
3. to experiment with and develop various devices to interact with the virtual environment;
4. to assess the usefulness of the VE technology in realistic applications,
5. to solve the visual latency problem associated with large models; and
6. to acquire experiences in the field of VE and 3-D interactive graphic systems.

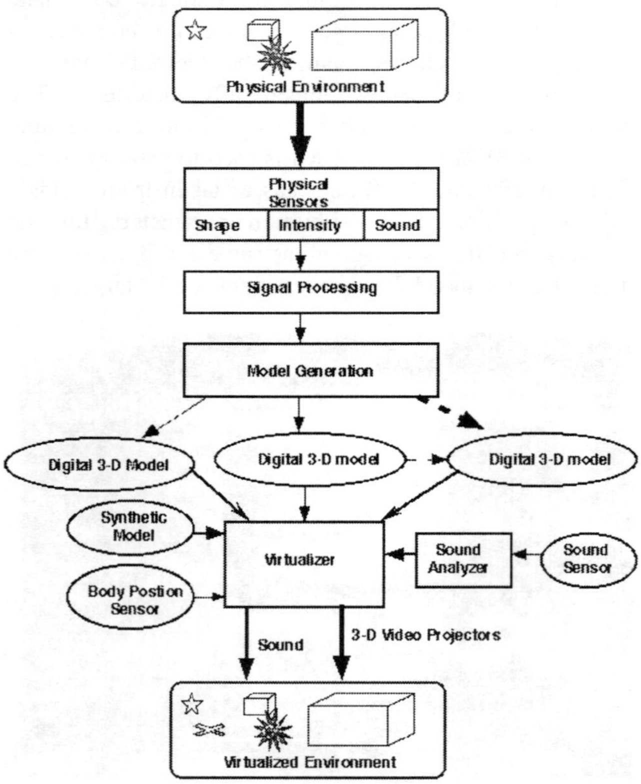

Figure 7: System design from real to VE

The facility (Figure 8), which measures 10 m x 6 m x 3 m, includes the following equipment:

- A high speed rear projector.
- A 2.25 m by 3 m rear projection screen.
- Liquid crystal glasses and a controller for large rooms.
- SGI graphic workstation- Infinite Reality and PC.
- Electromagnetic hand and head trackers.

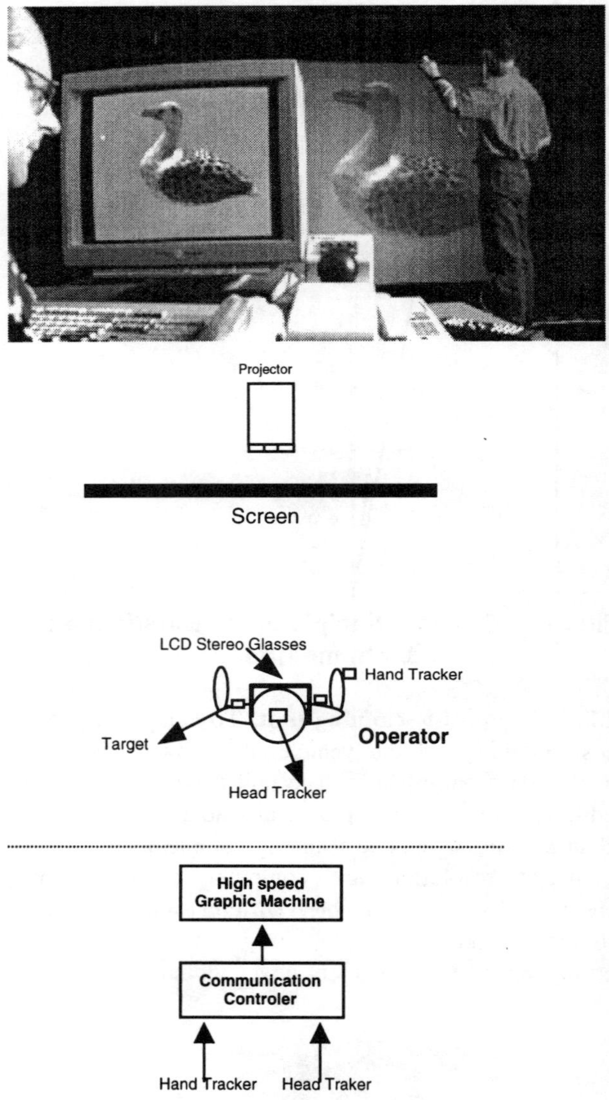

Figure 7. Components of the VE facility at NRC [ViEW (Virtual Environment Wall)].

2.4: The test site

A test site was constructed to evaluate the accuracy of the 3-D model produced by the mobile system and also assess its performance, mainly speed and reliability.

The dimensions of the test site are 12-m (L) by 5-m (W) by 3-m (H). It includes:

- *Reference* targets measured by theodolites to be used for the geometric accuracy evaluation.
- Various surface types to evaluate the range-sensor ability to detect different surface details.
- Various features and edges, such as lines, writing, holes and corners, to resemble those that may be found in an application site.

3: The 3-D Mapping Procedure

The computational mapping paradigm consists of the following steps:

1- Data collection and processing (Figure 9).
2- Building of the geometric 3-D model.
3- Texture mapping.
4- Display and manipulation of the model in VE.

Each of the above steps is described next.

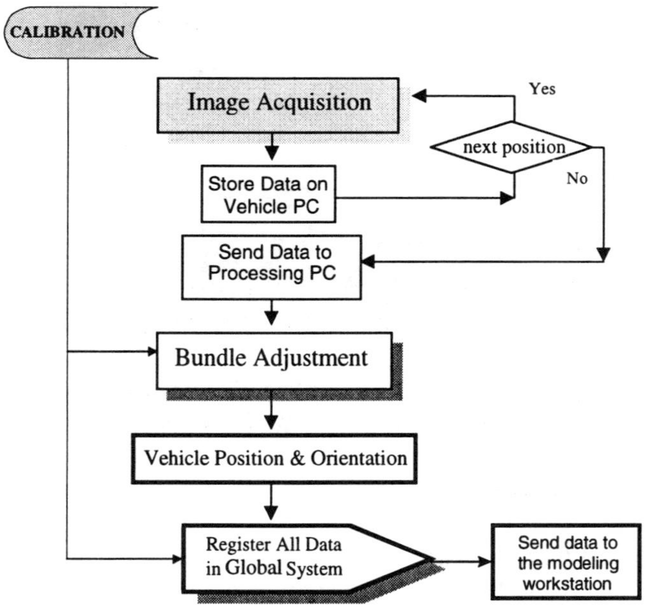

Figure 9: Simplified block diagram of the data collection and processing steps.

3.1: Data collection and processing

The eight images within one strip (one vehicle position) are pre-calibrated, i.e. their parameters relative to each other are known. Images in different strips (different vehicle positions) have unknown location parameters relative to each other. These parameters are computed from the well-known photogrammetric bundle adjustment approach [18] (simultaneous triangulation of all data from all images). Additional constraints in the form of the known relationships between the images in each strip are utilized to strengthen the bundle solution. Each point *p*, extracted from an image i, has two image coordinate, x and y, and contributes two equations (called the collinearity equations):

$$\begin{aligned} x_p &= f_x(X_p, Y_p, Z_p, X_i, Y_i, Z_i, pitch_i, yaw_i, roll_i) \\ y_p &= f_y(X_p, Y_p, Z_p, X_i, Y_i, Z_i, pitch_i, yaw_i, roll_i) \end{aligned} \qquad (1)$$

The parameters on the right-hand-side of the above equations are the XYZ coordinates of the point *p* in the required 3-D coordinate system, and the camera position and orientation (six parameters) in the same coordinate system. Those six camera parameters are the same for all points measured in the same image, however each point adds three unknown XYZ coordinates. Since each point contributes only two new equations, the solution for all the unknown parameters is not possible. If some of these points appear in another image, they will not add new XYZ coordinates, but six new camera parameters are added. When there is a sufficient number of overlapped images with sufficient number of common points so that the number of equations is larger than the total number of unknowns, a solution will be possible. This is the main principle of the photogrammetric triangulation approach known as bundle adjustment [18]. The system of equations to be solved is an over-determined nonlinear system that requires least-squares iterative solution. In the first iteration, initial values for the unknowns must be pre-computed or provided. If these values are too far off from the correct values and the geometric configuration of the cameras is poorly suited for triangulation, this iterative solution will break down. In outdoor mapping systems, GPS and INS combination determines the vehicle position, and thus the camera positions are considered known. In indoor mapping, however, since the GPS can not be used, significant error propagation may cause the solution to fail or at least deteriorates the accuracy. The proposed solution overcomes those problems associated with the bundle adjustment. The procedure steps are:

1. A dead reckoning system, such as wheel encoders, provides initial approximate values for the vehicle location, thus the 8-cameras position and orientation.
2. In order to strengthen the geometry of triangulation, data from the range sensor are used. It adds constraints in the form of geometric relationships between the same extracted points from the range sensor image and the video image as follows:

$$f(X_{p1},Y_{p1},Z_{p1},\ldots\ldots,X_{pn},Y_{pn},Z_{pn},A,B,\ldots)=0 \quad (2)$$

Equation (2) describes the relationship between the coordinates of the above mentioned points, where the constants A, B, ... are known from the range sensor data (for example a distance between two points or parameters of a plane). Equation (2) will be combined with (1) to strengthen the bundle adjustment solution.

3. The relationships between the images of the eight CCD cameras are accurately pre-determined by the calibration procedure. This results in another set of constraints:

$$f(X_{i1},Y_{i1},Z_{i1},pitch_{i1},yaw_{i1},roll_{i1},\ldots. \\ ,X_{i8},Y_{i8},Z_{i8},pitch_{i8},yaw_{i8},roll_{i8},a,b,c,..)=0 \quad (3)$$

The constants a, b, c,... are known from the calibration step. Again, sets of equation (3) are combined with sets of equation (1) and (2) to provide a strong bundle adjustment.

The shown sensor types and configuration and the simultaneous solution of equations (1), (2), and (3) to obtain reliable and accurate vehicle positions and absolute coordinates of object and site points are the main novel elements of this system [13].

In the registration procedure, the sensors take images of sufficient number of targets of precisely known positions. The known positions of the targets are used to solve for the CCD-camera parameters and establish the relationship between the range sensor coordinate system and the CCD-cameras. It also establishes the relationship between a reference coordinate system and that of the CCD-cameras and the range sensor. The result of this procedure is that all data have a common reference system defined by the coordinates of the calibration targets.

3.2: Building and displaying the 3-D VE model

The registered images generated from the previous steps contain a huge number of points each of which has XYZ coordinates in the global coordinate system. Even for a relatively small volume, for example a few meters of space, the size of data may become unmanageable. Therefore, a more suitable geometric representation of the data is required in order to display and interact with it. The most suitable representation is a non-redundant triangular mesh [19]. The registered 3-D images, from the Biris sensor, will now be converted from XYZ points into a single triangular mesh that can be efficiently rendered on any graphics system. Since there will be an overlap between the successive images, it is required that the redundant data be first removed. An algorithm for building a non-redundant mesh-model from a large number of overlapped 3-D images has been developed at NRC and was applied to all the 3-D image points generated of the test site [19]. The model (Figure 10) can be displayed using software that has the basic visualization tools, which include; loading, transforming, rendering, and controlling data. Using the SGI workstation at VIT's ViEW facility, the model can be visualized at high resolution and manipulated in real time.

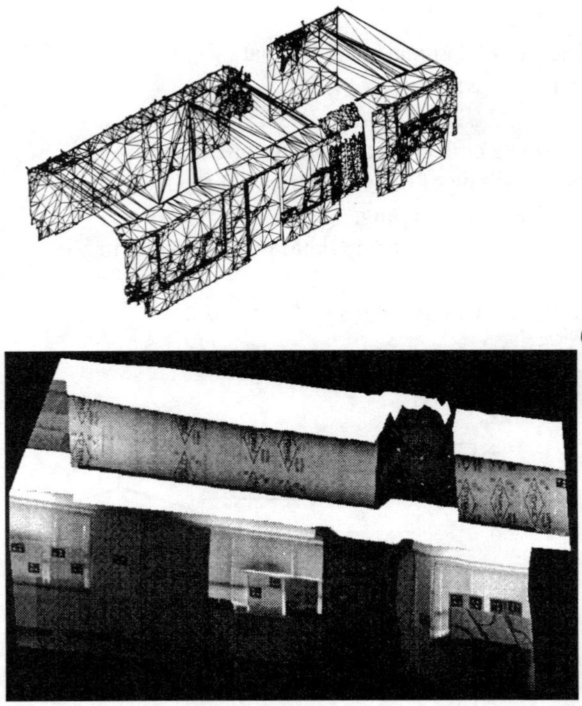

(a)

(b)

Figure 10: 3-D model of the site. (a) Geometric model. (b) Geometric model plus texture.

3.3: Texture Mapping

While the generated geometric model is useful for managing the 3-D construction of the site, many details can only be viewed from light intensity data. This requires that texture be mapped onto the geometric model. High resolution gray-scale or color images from a photometric camera can be precisely mapped into the geometric model provided that the camera position and orientation is known in the coordinate system of the geometric model. In this system, this data is available since the parameters for each video image are computed in the bundle adjustment procedure. Given the 3-D coordinates of the vertices of a polygon, the corresponding projections of these vertices in a video image can be located. The light intensity values within the area defined by these projected vertices are stretched and rotated to fit into its counterpart 3-D polygon. This procedure has been implemented and tested in this experiment and the results, applied to the full model, are shown in Figure 10-b.

Because of many errors such as: range measurement uncertainty, perspective transformation tolerance, uncompensated camera lens distortions, image resolution, blurring, or simply quantification errors, a direct image projection can create undesired and extremely disturbing errors that appear as textured image projected on the wrong object. As exemplified in Figure 11, the white texture image of the spherical calibration target can be projected on the black background, which is obviously wrong.

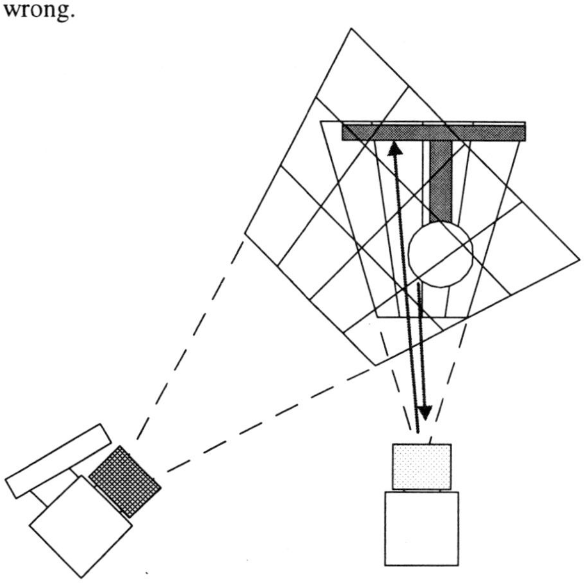

Figure 11. Projection uncertainty grid of photometric and range data.

We are proposing to use the perfectly registered intensity image provided by the range sensor to locally compensate for these small but disturbing effects. This will be accomplished by warping the projected photometric high-resolution image using the lower resolution intensity image from the range sensor and the system "uncertainty" grid.

4: Test Results and Analysis

The test site described in section 2.4 (Figure 12) was used for the accuracy evaluation and assessment of system performance (mainly the speed of operations). Some of the test results are presented.

4.1: Geometric accuracy of the 3-D model

All the results shown below are based on two data sets. The first is acquired with the vehicle moving from the west side of the room to the east (direction A in Figure 12) and the second is acquired with the vehicle moving in the opposite direction and along a different path (direction B in Figure 12). The accuracy is computed as the difference between coordinates obtained from the mapping system and the known coordinates of reference targets obtained from theodolite measurements. Using the absolute mean on all the points (none rejected for poor quality), the accuracy was about 0.6 mm, or one part in 20,000. When poorly defined features were removed (about 5% of the points), the accuracy numbers improved by a factor of two. The achieved accuracy, particularly on well-defined points, is close to what can be achieved using one strip of images (next section). This shows that error propagation has been limited.

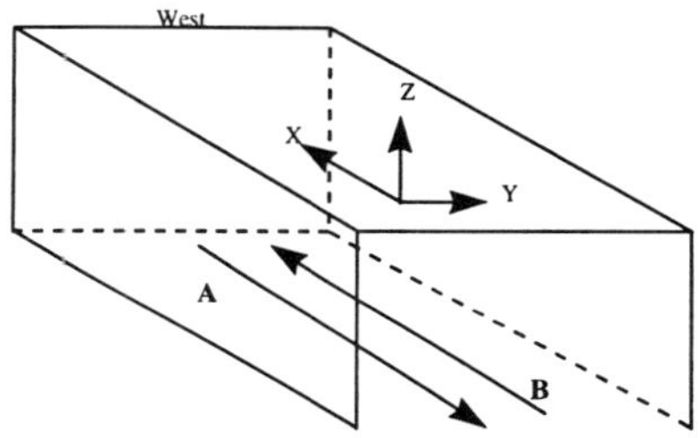

Figure 12: Test site and paths of data collection

4.2: Calibration accuracy

This is an indication of the accuracy of the XYZ coordinates at one vehicle location, before error propagation from registration with other locations, thus it depends on calibration quality. The estimated accuracy numbers for the sensors arranged in the configuration shown in Figures 1 and 2, using the targets on the calibration structure as reference, are shown in table 2. RMS values are obtained from the differences between known and computed coordinates. The results are close to theory-of-error expectations as computed from sensor resolution and the mathematical model (equation 1).

	CCD-Pairs	BIRIS
X-mm	0.10 mm	2.27 mm
Y-mm	0.25 mm	2.44 mm
Z-mm	0.21 mm	1.87 mm

Table 2: RMS values for calibration accuracy

4.3: Speed of various operations

The processing times on the stated hardware are:

- For data acquisition from all sensors and disk storage, on Pentium-150 PC, the time at one vehicle position is about 1.5 minute. The time for Biris scans is affected by the speed of the pan and tilt unit. The Biris scans alone take only 1/60 seconds per line.
- About 8 hours were needed for all operations, from target extraction (on PC) to model generation (on SGI), for 216 video images and 108 Biris images. The time is mostly consumed by interactive point extraction and is expected to be drastically shorter when this is fully automated.

5: Conclusion and future work

The results of the testing and a proof-of-concept demonstration of the system in the laboratory have shown that it can be very useful for mapping in an indoor environment. We feel that this technology would be most valuable where other technologies can not be used indoors (such as GPS) or do not have the required accuracy over the entire volume (such as dead reckoning). Based on the experience gained from this experiment, further development of the system will be required in order to guarantee consistent high accuracy, improve speed, and increase the level of automation. The proper integration of texture from high-resolution photometric cameras with the geometric model is also being developed, as suggested in this paper. Development is also under way to use multi-resolution hierarchical data structure to represent in an efficient manner the large models produced by such system. This issue is critical for real time performance.

Acknowledgements

Louis-Guy Dicaire and Mike New developed some of the software components. Gerhard Roth provided the mesh triangulation modeling software. David Green and Doug Taylor assisted with the hardware throughout the experiments.

References

1. J.C. Goble, K. Hinckley, R. Pausch, J.W. Snell, and N.F. Kassel, "Two-handed spatial interface tools for neurosurgical planning." IEEE Computer, 28(7), pp. 20-26, July 1995.
2. S.R. Hedberg, "Virtual reality at Boeing: Pushing the envelope." Virtual Reality Special Report, 3(1), pp. 51-55, Jan.-Feb., 1996.
3. M.F. Polis, S.J. Gifford, and D.M. McKeown Jr., "Automating the construction of large-scale virtual worlds." IEEE Computer, 28(7) July, pp. 57-65, July 1995.
4. S.F. El-Hakim and J.-A. Beraldin, F. Blais, P. Boulanger, and G. Godin, "Two 3-D sensors for environment modeling and virtual reality: calibration and multi-view registration" ISPRS Highlights, 2(1), pp 13-21, Nan, 1997.
5. V. Sequeira, J.G.M. Gonçalves, and M.I. Ribeiro, "Construction of a 3D Model of an Unknown Environment using Range Data", in "Modelling and Graphics in Science and Technology", edited by Teixeira J.C. and Rix J., pp.164-172, Springer Verlag, 1996
6. M. Hirose, "Image based virtual world generation", IEEE Multimedia, 4 (1), pp. 27-33, Jan-Mar, 1997.
7. T. Kanade, P. Rander, and P.J. Narayanan, "Virtualized reality: constructing virtual worlds from real scenes", IEEE Multimedia, 4(1), pp. 34-47, Jan-Mar, 1997.
8. K. Novak, "Mobile mapping technology for GIS data collection." Photogrammetric Engineering & Remote Sensing, 61(5), pp. 493-501, May 1995.
9. K.P. Schwarz, M.A.Chapman, M.W.Cannon, and P.Gong, "An integrated INS/GPS approach to the georeferencing of remotely sensed data." Photogrammetric Engineering & Remote Sensing, 59(11), pp. 1667-1674, Nov. 1993.
10. N. El-Sheimy, "A unified approach to multi-sensor integration in Photogrammetry." Integrated Acquisition and Interpretation of Photogrammetric Data Workshop, Stuttgart, Nov. 1995.
11. H. Heister, W. Caspary, Chr. Hock, H. Klemm, and H. Sternberg, "The mobile mapping system - KiSS - ."Integrated Acquisition and Interpretation of Photogrammetric Data Workshop, Stuttgart, Nov. 1995.
12. T. Aussems, and M. Braess, "Mobile mapping using a surveying vehicle integrating GPS, wheel sensors and digital video cameras." Integrated Acquisition and Interpretation of Photogrammetric Data Workshop, Stuttgart, Nov 1995.
13. S.F. El-Hakim and P. Boulanger, "Mobile system for indoor 3-D mapping and creating virtual environments." US patent pending, 1996.
14. F. Blais, M. Rioux and J. Domey, "Optical Range Image Acquisition for the navigation of a mobile robot", IEEE Conf. On Robotics and Automation, Sacramento, California, April 9-11, 1991.
15. F. Blais, M. Lecavalier, J. Bisson, "Real-time Processing and Validation of Optical Ranging in a Cluttered Environment", ICSPAT, Boston, MA, p.1066-1070, Oct. 7-10 1996.
16. M. Rioux and F. Blais, "Compact Three-dimensional camera for robotic applications", Optical Society of America A., Vol. 3. 1518-1521, Sept 1986.
17. M. Rioux, US Patent 5,075,561, Dec. 24, 1991.
18. D.C. Brown, "The bundle adjustment - Progress and prospective." International Archives of Photogrammetry, 21(3): paper no. 3-03-041, 33 pages, ISP Congress, Helsinki, Finland, 1976.
19. G. Roth and E. Wibowo, "A fast algorithm for making mesh models from multi-view range data." In Proceedings of the DND/CSA Robotics and Knowledge Based Systems Workshop, St. Hubert, Quebec, October 1995.

Ray-Based Creation of Photo-Realistic Virtual World

Takeshi Naemura Takahide Takano †Masahide Kaneko Hiroshi Harashima

Dept. of Inform. & Commun. Eng., The Univ. of Tokyo
7-3-1, Hongo, Bunkyo-ku, Tokyo 113, JAPAN
e-mail : naemura@hc.t.u-tokyo.ac.jp, URL : http://www.hc.t.u-tokyo.ac.jp/naemura
(† Currently with KDD R&D Laboratories)

Abstract

This paper introduces the concept of ray-based representation of spatial data and proposes a new method for creating the photo-realistic virtual world. In this method, the whole ray data of the world are treated as a set of orthogonal views of scene objects. The advantage of this approach is to allow the synthesis of any perspective view by gathering appropriate ray data from the set of orthogonal views independently of any geometric representation. First, several perspective views of the real world are taken as a set of real ray data, and orthogonal views of the world are synthesized from the captured real ray data. Then, structural models corresponding to each perspective view are locally estimated and adaptively stitched each other in order to interpolate the cracks on the orthogonal views. This approach can avoid the difficulty in estimating a unique structural model of the world.

1 Introduction

It is our dream to see and experience what is going on in distant places as natural and real as possible. It is clear, however, that the two-dimensional (2-D) imaging system, currently used widely, is not enough to give observers the illusion that they are physically placed in a distant scene. As the real world information which we obtain with our eyes is three-dimensional (3-D), a 3-D imaging system is a very promising approach expected to revolutionize the visual communication system. To date, 3-D image communication has not been discussed at a comprehensive level because several kinds of 3-D display technologies are still making rapid progress. From this point of view, most of the works on 3-D image processing can be regarded as specialized methods for limited combination of input and output technologies.

Considering such a situation, the authors proposed the concept of the "Integrated 3-D Visual Communication System" [1, 2] illustrated in Figure 1. The key feature in this new concept is a display-independent representation of visual data; all the differences of representation between input and output methods will be absorbed by the neutrality of the representation for any format of visual data.

In this paper, the ray-based approach, first developed by Fujii [3, 4] aiming to realize the neutral representation of visual data, is introduced. Since the visual sensation is excited by rays of light incident on the retina, each of these rays can be seen as a primitive element of visual data. So, any format of visual data can be decomposed into a set of such light ray data. Conversely, arbitrary visual data suitable for displaying technology can be synthesized from a set of appropriate light ray data.

Perspective views of a real scene can be regarded as a set of real ray data. The transmission of the captured real ray data is the fundamental aim of a 3-D image communication system. The quality of 3-D visual effect derived just from the real ray data is, however, not enough to give observers the illusion that they are physically placed in a distant scene. This is because viewpoint locations at the receivers are restricted to the camera arrangement at the transmitter, and observers perceive the discontinuity of their visual zone.

In order to enhance the 3-D visual effects by providing a perceptually continuous visual zone, this paper introduces a new concept of the "ray interpolation". First, a multi-dimensional data space is defined to store ray data. Secondly, perspective views of a real scene are decomposed into a set of real ray data, and each of the data is mapped onto its appropriate position in the data space. Thirdly, virtual ray data are interpolated to fill up the cracks in the data space. Thus, the data space is filled with both of the captured real ray data and the synthesized virtual ray data. Fourthly, we can synthesize any perspective view by gathering appropriate ray data stored in the data space. In this context, virtual views are interpolated as a consequence of the ray interpolation process. One of the advantages of this method is that once the data space is filled with ray data, any virtual views can be synthesized independently of any geometric representation. It is also the advantage of this

0-8186-8150-0/97 $10.00 © 1997 IEEE

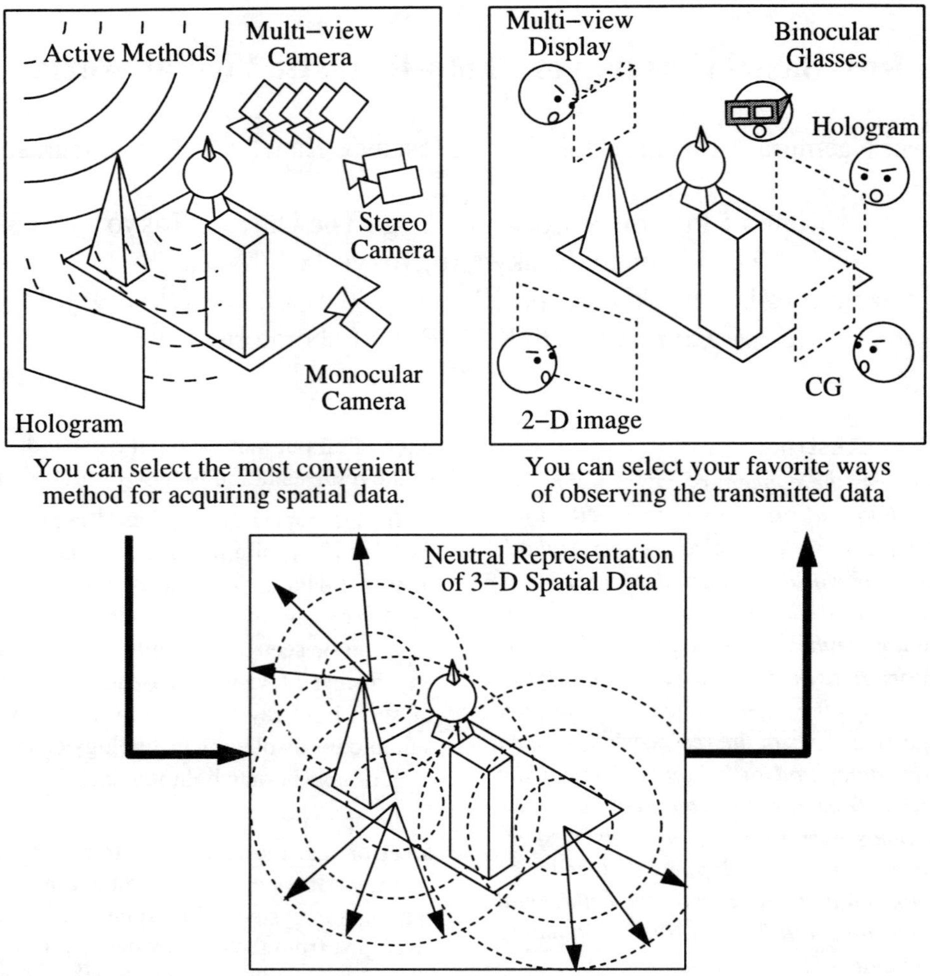

Figure 1: Basic concept of the "Integrated 3-D Visual Communication System".

method that the real views, which are decomposed into a set of real ray data in the second step, are embedded in the virtual world without any distortion.

This paper investigates and examines how the photo-realistic virtual world can be created from the light ray data of the real world.

2 Ray-Based Representation

A set of rays passing through any point in 3-D space is called a pencil. Pencils are distinguished by their positions (X,Y,Z) in the 3-D space. And light rays which constitute a pencil can be also identified by their directions (θ,ϕ) representing their azimuth and elevation angle of propagation. Therefore, light ray data at any point in any direction (should it be power or wavelength) can be stored separately in a five-dimensional data space (X,Y,Z,θ,ϕ). This data space is called "Ray-Space" [3, 4, 5, 6, 2] or "Plenoptic Function" [7, 8, 9, 10] and is represented in the form of $f(X,Y,Z,\theta,\phi)$.

The concept of the "Ray-Space" was proposed in the field of visual communication in order to realize the neutral representation of any format of visual data including hologram [3, 4]. The concept of the "Plenoptic Function" was proposed in the field of computer vision as the elements of early vision model [7], and it has affected a relatively new technical field called "image-based rendering" [8, 9, 10].

In the 5-D data space, 2-D image data, captured from the viewpoint (X_a,Y_a,Z_a), can be represented as follows (See Figure 2) :

$$f(\theta,\phi)|_{X=X_a,Y=Y_a,Z=Z_a}.$$

This means that a 2-D image corresponds to a 2-D subspace of a 5-D data space [4]. Thus, any kind of visual data can be embedded in the 5-D data space. Conversely, we can synthesize arbitrary visual data by gathering appropriate ray data stored in the 5-D data space.

Since the epipolar plane image [11, 12], synthesized from a set of 2-D images, is embedded in the 5-D data

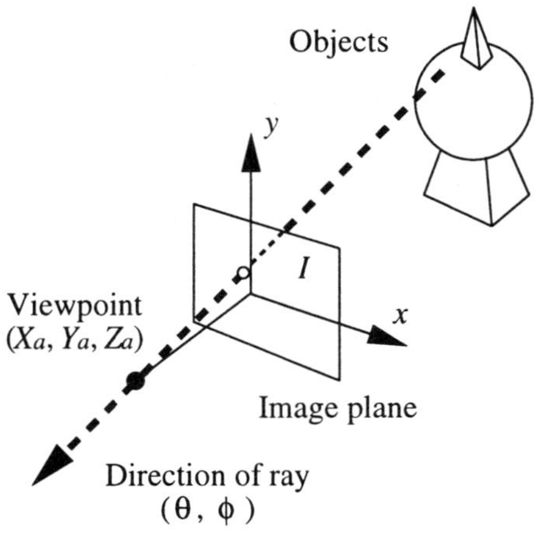

Figure 2: Light rays as primitive elements of visual data.

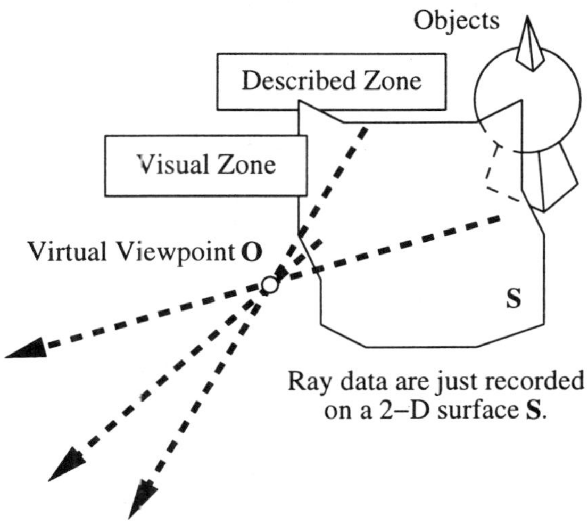

Figure 3: The 3-D space is divided into two zones.

space, proposed concept is also useful for structure recovery from a set of views. This fact can be exploited to fill up the cracks in the data space.

3 Ray-Space Projection

Any visual data can be synthesized from the ray data stored in the 5-D data space. This representation, however, requires a huge amount of apparently redundant data. An effective data compression method of the data space, aimed to save all the previously described necessary data, is strongly required.

3.1 From 5-D to 4-D Data Space

In this paper, we consider the case where ray data are just recorded on a surface **S** (See Figure 3).

The 3-D space is divided by **S** into two zones; visual zone and described zone. Since each of the ray data intersecting *bvecS* can be identified by two parameters P and Q, which represent the position of intersection on *bvecS*, all the ray data can be mapped onto a 4-D sub-space $f(P,Q,\theta,\phi)$. Thus, the set of rays intersecting **S** is stored in a reduced 4-D data space. By assuming that rays go straight on without any variation in the direction of propagation, we can even synthesize a virtual view at a viewpoint **O** which is not located on **S**.

Figure 4 illustrates two types of applications of the surface **S**. If the rays, going out of the bounded region, are recorded, we can observe the objects placed within this region from any direction with a natural depth feeling. Conversely, if rays, concentrating into this region, are recorded, we can enjoy this stereoscopic effect all around us. The conclusion is that, in many cases (such as watching an object from outside of the bounded surface or walking around within the bounded region), a 4-D data space is enough to describe 3-D images efficiently.

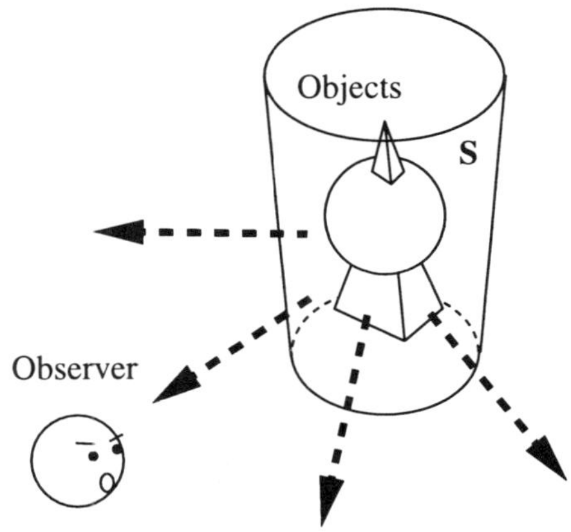

(a) 3-D object representation

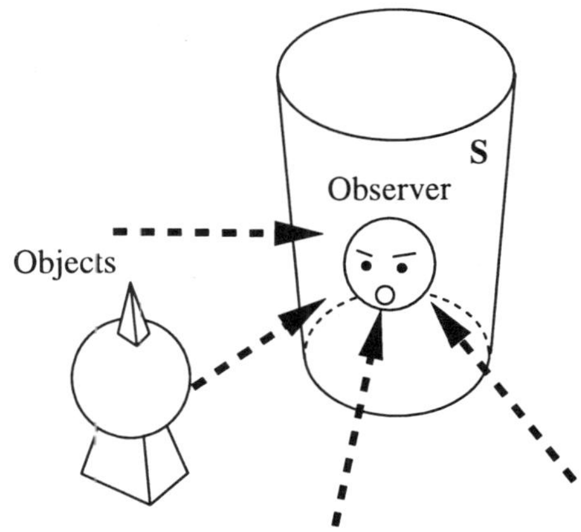

(b) 3-D surroundings representation

Figure 4: Applications of the surface **S**.

3.2 Direction-Uniform Projection

It is required for the sake of the neutrality, that the projection from a 5-D data space onto a 4-D one should be independent of the shape of the surface **S**. In this section, such a "direction-uniform" projection [5, 2] is explained.

Considering that the 3-D vectors **p**, **q** and **r** are linearly independent, any arbitrary vector $[X,Y,Z]^T$ can be represented by the linear combination

$$[X,Y,Z]^T = P\,\mathbf{p} + Q\,\mathbf{q} + R\,\mathbf{r}. \tag{1}$$

From this equation, we can derive an equation to transform the coordinate system (X,Y,Z) into the other coordinate system (P,Q,R).

Figure 5 illustrates some examples of *PQR* coordinate systems with various definition of 3-D vectors **p**, **q** and **r**. In all the examples, a 3-D vector **r**, which represents the direction or ray-axis *R*, is defined as follows :

$$\mathbf{r} = [\,\sin\theta\cos\phi,\ \sin\phi,\ \cos\theta\cos\phi\,]^T. \tag{2}$$

This means that the new coordinate system (P,Q,R) is defined for each direction of rays.

In the transformed 5-D data space $f(P,Q,R,\theta,\phi)$, variations of rays (such as attenuation or interference in the direction of propagation) are recorded along the ray-axis *R*. By assuming that rays go straight on without any variation along the direction of propagation, a 5-D data space $f(P,Q,R,\theta,\phi)$ can be projected onto a 4-D one $f(P,Q,\theta,\phi)$ by the following equation.

$$f(P,Q,\theta,\phi) = f(P,Q,R_o,\theta,\phi)$$

where, the *R* coordinate R_o represents the shape of the surface **S**. Thus, the 5-D data space can be projected onto a 4-D one without losing any data of the individual rays. The advantage of this method is that the *P* and *Q* coordinates are independent of the shape of the surface **S**.

Some possible variation in the projection methods are provided by the redefinition of the other axes *P* and *Q*.

3.2.1 Planer Coordinate System

A simple example illustrated in Figure 5(a) is to define two 3-D vectors **p** and **q** as follows :

$$\begin{aligned} \mathbf{p} &= [\,1,\,0,\,0\,]^T, \\ \mathbf{q} &= [\,0,\,1,\,0\,]^T. \end{aligned} \tag{3}$$

In this case, one *PQ*-plane is provided for all directions of rays. Ignoring the *R* coordinate, the following equations can be derived from the Equations (1), (2) and (3).

$$\begin{aligned} P &= X - Z\tan\theta, \\ Q &= Y - Z\tfrac{\tan\phi}{\cos\theta} \end{aligned} \tag{4}$$

Using these equations, the 5-D data space $f(X,Y,Z,\theta,\phi)$ is converted into a 4-D data space $f(P,Q,\theta,\phi)$. The merit of this type of projection is that calculation cost is lower than that of other projection methods. This method, however, cannot equally treat all the directions of rays; it can not store, for example, such rays that do not intersect with the defined *PQ*-plane (i.e. those are parallel to *X* or *Y* axis).

3.2.2 Cylindrical Coordinate System

In the same way, when we define **p** and **q** to be such as :

$$\begin{aligned} \mathbf{p} &= [\,\cos\theta,\ 0,\ -\sin\theta\,]^T, \\ \mathbf{q} &= [\,0,\ 1,\ 0\,]^T \end{aligned} \tag{5}$$

the following equations are derived for Figure 5(b).

$$\begin{aligned} P &= X\cos\theta - Z\sin\theta, \\ Q &= -X\sin\theta\tan\phi + Y - Z\cos\theta\tan\phi. \end{aligned} \tag{6}$$

Using these equations, a 5-D data space $f(X,Y,Z,\theta,\phi)$ is converted into a 4-D data space $f(P,Q,\theta,\phi)$. As a *PQ*-plane is provided for each θ, this method can store rays parallel to *X* axis. It is, however, still unable to cope with rays parallel to *Y* axis.

3.2.3 Spherical Coordinate System

Finally, when **p** and **q** are as follows :

$$\begin{aligned} \mathbf{p} &= [\,\cos\theta,\ 0,\ -\sin\theta\,]^T, \\ \mathbf{q} &= [\,-\sin\theta\sin\phi,\ \cos\phi,\ -\cos\theta\sin\phi\,]^T \end{aligned} \tag{7}$$

the equations bellow are derived for Figure 5(c).

$$\begin{aligned} P &= X\cos\theta - Z\sin\theta, \\ Q &= -X\sin\theta\sin\phi + Y\cos\phi - Z\cos\theta\sin\phi. \end{aligned} \tag{8}$$

In this case, a ray-axis *R* parallel to the ray direction and a *PQ*-plane normal to the *R*-axis are defined for each direction (θ,ϕ) of rays. Therefore, all the visual data are equally treated by this method. Using these equations, the 5-D data space $f(X,Y,Z,\theta,\phi)$ is converted into a 4-D data space $f(P,Q,\theta,\phi)$ without losing any data of the individual rays.

Since **p**, **q** and **r** are orthogonal, the *PQ*-plane defined for each direction (θ,ϕ) of rays as a 2-D subspace of the 4-D data space $f(P,Q,\theta,\phi)$ is an orthogonal view of the scene. Thus, $f(P,Q,\theta,\phi)$ can be thought as a set of orthogonal views (*PQ*-planes) for each direction of rays (θ,ϕ). This is the key feature of this method. Hence, though 3-D image representations based on a collection of perspective views heavily depends on the viewpoint locations of input data, proposed method is viewpoint-independent thanks to the use of a collection of orthogonal views. The following discussions will concentrate on this type of 4-D data space.

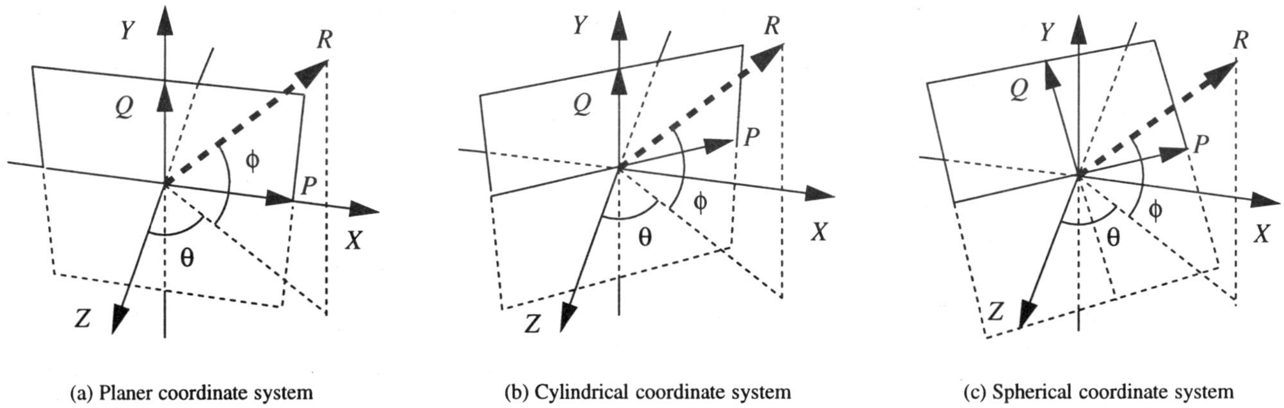

Figure 5: Examples of *PQR* coordinate systems.

4 4-D Ray-Space System

Based on the equations introduced in the previous section, a 4-D data space system can be constructed. Framework of this system consists of following four steps;

(a) Capture of real ray data

(b) Interpolation of virtual ray data

(c) Compression and transmission of ray data

(d) Display and handling of ray data.

4.1 Capture of Real Ray Data

In step (a), real image data are decomposed into real ray data. For this purpose, information about the positions of cameras (X,Y,Z) is utilized, and the image coordinates (x,y) are converted to the parameters (θ,ϕ) representing the direction of rays. In this paper, a computer-controlled camera gantry is constructed to capture real image data with camera parameters.

Figure 6 illustrates the special case in which the image plane is parallel to the XY plane. From this figure, the following equations can be derived.

$$x = -F\tan\theta, \quad y = -F\frac{\tan\phi}{\cos\theta} \tag{9}$$

where (x,y) denotes the image coordinate, and F focal length. These equations allow us to convert the direction (θ,ϕ) of a ray into its recorded position (x,y). Even if the image plane is not parallel to XY plane, we can formulate the relationship between the direction of rays (θ,ϕ) and the image coordinates (x,y), and can decompose image data into ray data.

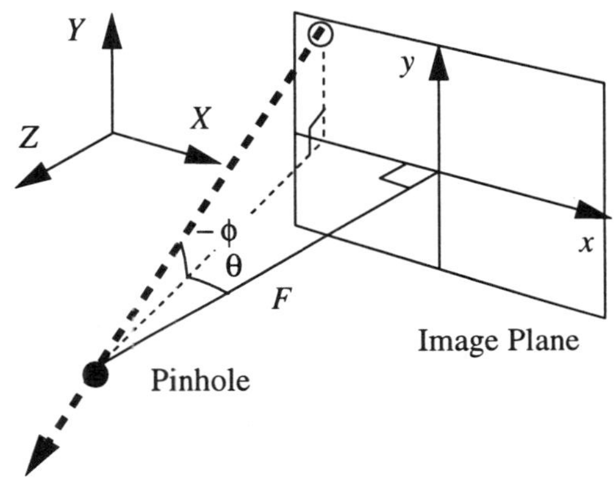

Figure 6: Relationship between the image coordinate (x,y) and the ray direction (θ,ϕ).

4.2 Interpolation of Virtual Ray Data

In many cases, the number of real ray data samples directly provided by the input data is not enough. As a consequence, sparsely sampled data space is constructed. In order to create a dense data space, virtual ray data is interpolated in step (b).

In this process, large number of orthogonal views are synthesized from a set of input perspective views, because a 4-D data space can be regarded as a set of orthogonal views. Once a 4-D data space is filled with ray data, arbitrary perspective views can be synthesized in step (d). So, we can evaluate the performance of the method as a real-time virtual reality system by the calculation time in step (d). This means that we can apply any complex and time-consuming method for the synthesis of orthogonal views (virtual ray data) in order to construct the photo-realistic virtual world. This feature of the method allows us to synthesize more natural and real views than conventional methods in which any perspective views are synthesized directly from a set of input views within a limited span for a real-time system.

In this paper, the following algorithm is applied to fill up each *PQ*-plane (orthogonal view) corresponding to a given direction of rays (See Figure 7).

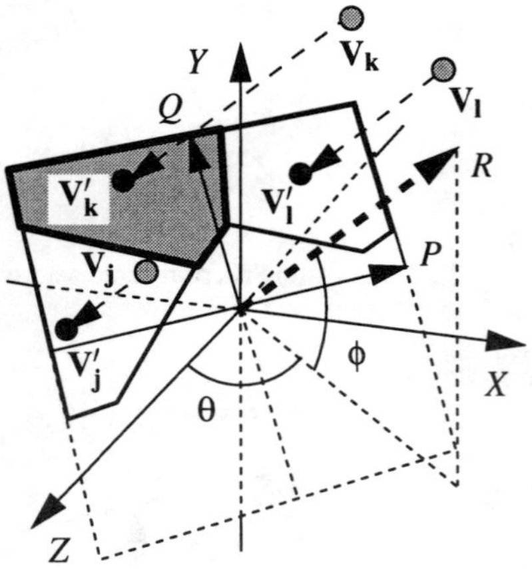

Figure 7: Synthesis of a *PQ*-plane (orthogonal view) from a set of perspective views.

1. A *PQ*-plane is divided into some regions using Voronoi diagrams whose center points are shadows of viewpoints from which the real ray data are captured. In Figure 7, the viewpoint locations of input data and shadows of them are denoted by $\mathbf{V_j}, \mathbf{V_k}, \mathbf{V_l}$, and $\mathbf{V'_j}, \mathbf{V'_k}, \mathbf{V'_l}$, respectively.

2. Each perspective view is warped to form an orthogonal view and pasted on the corresponding region on the *PQ*-plane. This warping is performed according to the results of disparity estimation between perspective views. This means that local structural models are prepared for each perspective view, and shadows of them are stitched on the *PQ*-plane.

3. Cracks on the *PQ*-plane are filled by the structural models of the neighboring regions.

4. Cracks on the *PQ*-plane are filled by median filters and boundaries of regions are blurred by average filters.

Since many structural models, resulting from disparity estimation at each view, are adaptively stitched to interpolate virtual ray data, this approach can avoid the difficulties in estimating a unique structure model of the world. Furthermore, even if the disparity estimation failed, median filters are utilized to fill up the 4-D data space. Thus, the 4-D data space is filled with both of the captured real ray data and the synthesized virtual ray data. It can be said that a virtual world synthesized from real ray data is represented in the data space.

4.3 Compression and Transmission of Ray Data

Since the data space, even though its dimension is effectively reduced to four, still contains a huge amount of data, an efficient compression method is strongly required in step (c). Waveform [13], structure-based [14] as well as fractal-based [15] methods, can be examined. The authors will report the practical data compression method in the other article [13]. In this paper, the application of 4-D DCT (discrete cosine transform) is examined. First, the 4-D data space $f(P,Q,\theta,\phi)$ is divided into subblocks, each of which consists of $8 \times 8 \times 8 \times 8$ ray data samples. Then, 4-D DCT coefficients of each subblock are encoded. The majority of non-null coefficients are at low frequency. Consequently, it is important to address primarily, or solely, this part in the transformed domain. In order to do this, we can carry out a 4-D zig-zag scanning of the coefficients. The scanned coefficients are entropy-encoded.

4.4 Display and Handling of Ray Data

Finally, in step (d), the transmitted ray data is converted into appropriate format for a 3-D display at the receiver. When the location of an observer (X,Y,Z) is given, the positions of the corresponding ray data in the 4-D data space are calculated from Equation (8). Then, the sampled ray data is converted into an appropriate view. We can also add some kinds of optical effects and merge several data spaces to give the observers some more enhanced visual effects.

5 Experimental Results

First of all, the 4-D DCT-based compression of a 4-D data space is examined. Three types of 4-D data spaces whose total amount of data is fixed to 74 MB are synthesized from polygonal models. The difference between them is the resolution of each axis P, Q, θ and ϕ. Configuration of each data space is as follows :

- $d\theta$ is coarser than dP/D,
- $d\theta$ is equal to dP/D,
- $d\theta$ is finer than dP/D,

where dP and $d\theta$ denote the quantization step size of each axes and D is calculated as follows:

$$D^2 = X_o^2 + Z_o^2,$$

where X_o and Z_o denote the position of the scene object in the XZ-plane.

Experimental results are listed in Table 1. These results show that the amount of data is most effectively compressed when $D\,d\theta$ is equal to dP. It can be said that the

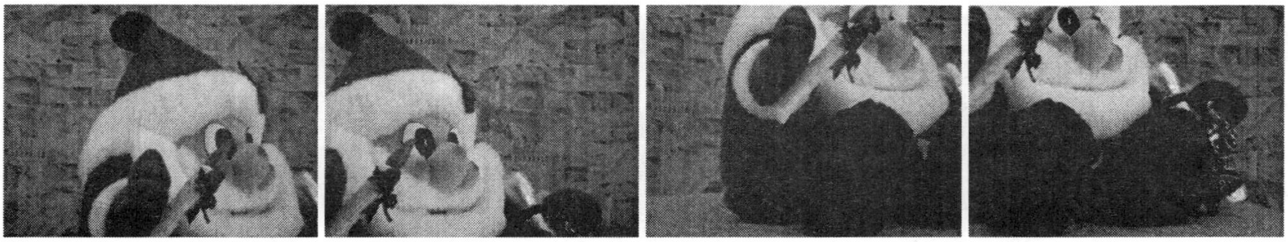

Figure 8: Parts of original multi-view images presented by University of Tsukuba, JAPAN.

quantization step size of each axis should be configured according to the distance D for the purpose of efficient compression of the data space, when the 4-D zig-zag scanning technique is applied. Alternatively, we can select the most effective 4-D scanning technique among a certain number of predetermined types of scanning (for example, zig-zag, $\theta\phi$-oriented and PQ-oriented).

Table 1: Results of the 4-D DCT with the 4-D zig-zag scanning.

configuration	$D\,d\theta > dP$	$D\,d\theta = dP$	$D\,d\theta < dP$
data size	3.6 [MB]	3.1 [MB]	3.8 [MB]
SNR	44.8 [dB]	45.1 [dB]	44.8 [dB]

The multi-view image database, presented by University of Tsukuba, is used as input perspective views for the other experiments. This image set consists of 81 views of a toy Santa Claus, parts of them are illustrated in Figure 8. Their camera parameters are given by University of Tsukuba.

For each direction of rays, a corresponding PQ-plane is synthesized by the above-mentioned method. Figure 9 shows some of the results. The resolution of each PQ-plane is 182×182 samples and the number of such PQ-planes is equal to the resolution of the $\theta\phi$-plane; 300×220 samples. The details of experimental configurations such as the resolution and the quantization step size of each axis are determined according to the results of the 4-D DCT experiment, and listed in Table 2. Thanks to the adaptive use of input views, we can see that the synthesized orthogonal views are visually natural.

Once a 4-D data space is created, we can select our viewpoint locations and the viewing angles to observe the described scene. Figure 10 shows virtual perspective views synthesized from the PQ-planes shown in Figure 9. Between these two views, both of the horizontal and the vertical disparities are realized. Thanks to the proposed ray interpolation technique, visually natural views are synthesized.

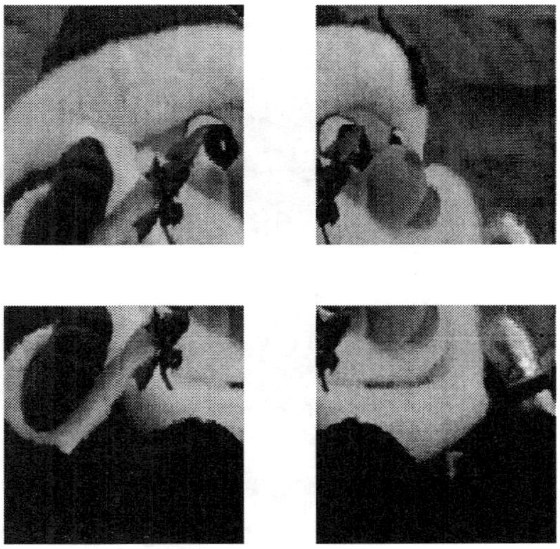

Figure 9: Examples of synthesized PQ-planes as orthogonal views of the scene.

Figure 11 illustrates the effect of the ray interpolation based on disparity estimation. The virtual view in Figure 11(a) is synthesized from the PQ-planes shown in Figure 9. If ray data is interpolated on the assumption of a unique disparity for each pixel on the inupt views, discontinuity between stitched views will appear on the synthesized virtual views (See Figure 11(b)). It can be said that the ray interpolation, based on the disparity estimation, succeeded in avoiding this discontinuity artifact.

Figure 12 shows our prototype camera gantry. As a CCD camera is mounted on a turn-table which is located on an XY-plotter, the horizontal position (X, Y) and the direction θ of the camera are controllable. By giving camera parameters, we can take pictures on the favorite condition. Figure 13 shows the resulted pictures of a toy town.

Since the camera parameters are given, input views shown in Figures 8 and 13 can be mapped onto each 4-D data space, respectively. By superimposing the PQ-planes as the orthogonal views of objects and surroundings, the

Table 2: Experimental configurations.

Range of P axis	$-70.2mm < P < 70.2mm$
Range of Q axis	$-70.2mm < Q < 70.2mm$
Quantization step size of P and Q axes	$0.77mm$
Number of sample points of $P \times Q$	182×182
Range of θ axis	$-13.0° < \theta < 13.0°$
Range of ϕ axis	$-9.6° < \phi < 9.6°$
Quantization step size of θ, ϕ axes	$0.0866°$
Number of sample points of $\theta \times \phi$	300×220
Total number of sample points	2.2×10^9
Total amount of data ($3bytes/sample$)	6.6 GB

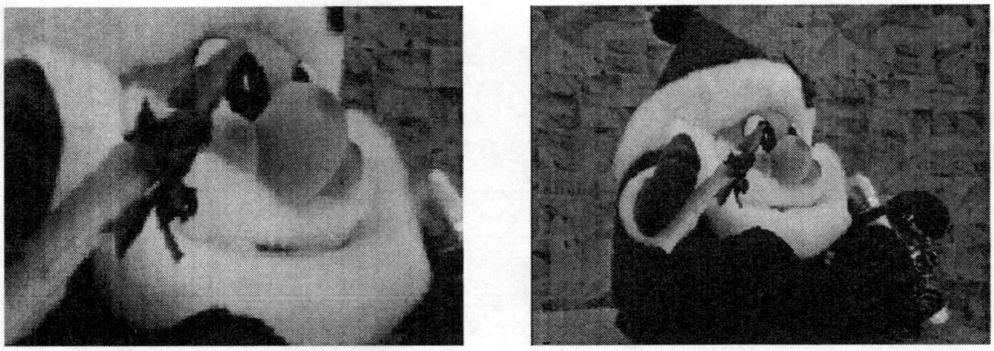

Figure 10: Synthesized virtual views from the dense data space.

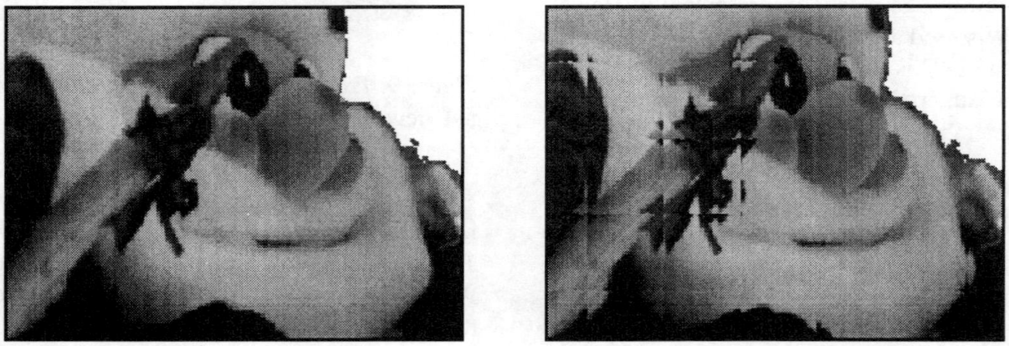

(a) Utilizing estimated disparity.

(b) Without disparity estimation.

Figure 11: Effect of the ray interpolation method.

photo-realistic virtual world can be created. Figure 14 shows the experimental results of the photo-realistic virtual world in which a toy Santa Claus is flying through the toy town. From the superimposed 4-D data space, we can synthesize any perspective views. As the stereopair shown in Figure 14 gives us the natural depth sensation, it can be said that the present method is useful and powerful for the creation of the photo-realistic virtual world.

6 Conclusions

In this paper, the concepts of the "Integrated 3-D Visual Communication System" and the "Ray-Space" are introduced, and an efficient data compression method based on the data space projection is proposed. The method how the 5-D data space is projected on a space of fewer dimension is formulated. By this method, the data space can be treated systematically.

Figure 12: Camera gantry and the surroundings model.

To clarify the applicability of the method, some experimental results are illustrated. We can synthesize a 4-D data space by decomposing input views into real ray data and can fill up the 4-D data space by interpolating virtual ray data. From this data space, any perspective view of the described scene can be synthesized. As they are visually natural, it can be said that the method is useful for the representation of autostereoscopic 3-D images. The photo-realistic virtual world is also created by superimposing *PQ*-planes of the input scenes. The fact that the resulting views give us the natural depth sensation proves the applicability of the method to the next-generation virtual reality system. One of the advantages of the method is that once the data space is filled with ray data, any virtual views can be synthesized independently of any geometric representation. This means that we can apply any complex and time-consuming method for the ray interpolation process. This feature of the method allows us to synthesize more natural and real views than conventional methods in which perspective views are synthesized directly from a set of input views within a limited span for a real-time system.

The authors will continue to investigate the effective data compression method for the reduced 4-D data space and develop various kinds of applications of the ray-based representation : virtual reality, computer graphics, computer vision and so on. Our method is useful and powerful for flexible 3-D image communication systems and virtual reality systems because of its neutrality and scalability.

References

[1] H.Harashima, "Three-dimensional image coding, future prospect," in *Proc. PCSJ'92*, pp. 9 – 12, Oct. 1992. (in Japanese).

[2] T.Naemura, M.Kaneko, and H.Harashima, "3-D visual data compression based on ray-space projection," in *Proc. SPIE VCIP'97*, vol. 3024, pp. 413 – 424, Feb. 1997.

[3] T.Fujii and H.Harashima, "Coding of an autostereoscopic 3-D image sequence," in *Proc. SPIE VCIP'94*, vol. 2308, pp. 930 – 941, Sep. 1994.

[4] T.Fujii, *A Basic Study on the Integrated 3-D Visual Communication*. PhD thesis, Course of Elec. Eng., School of Eng., The Univ. of Tokyo, Dec. 1994. (in Japanese).

[5] T. Naemura, T. Yanagisawa, M. Kaneko, and H. Harashima, "Efficient projection of ray space for a ray based description fo 3-D real world," Tech. Report IE95-119, IEICE, Feb. 1996. (in Japanese).

[6] T.Fujii, T.Kimoto, and M.Tanimoto, "Ray space coding for 3D visual communication," in *Proc. PCS'96*, pp. 447 – 451, Mar. 1996.

[7] E.Adelson and J.Bergen, "The plenoptic function and the elements of early vision," in *Computer Models of Visual Processing* (M.Landy and J.Movshon, eds.), ch. 1, MIT Press, 1991.

[8] L.McMillan and G.Bishop, "Plenoptic modeling : An image-based rendering system," in *Proc. ACM SIGGRAPH'95*, pp. 39 – 46, 1995.

[9] M. Levoy and P. Hanrahan, "Light field rendering," in *Proc. ACM SIGGRAPH'96*, pp. 31 – 42, 1996.

[10] S. Gortler, R. Grzeszczuk, R. Szeliski, and M. Cohen, "The lumigraph," in *Proc. ACM SIGGRAPH'96*, pp. 43 – 54, 1996.

[11] R. C. Bolles, H. H. Baker, and D. H. Marimont, "Epipolar-plane image analysis : An approach to determining structure from motion," *Int. Journ. of Computer Vision*, vol. 1, pp. 7 – 55, 1987.

[12] H.H.Baker and R.C.Bolles, "Generalizing epipolar-plane image analysis on the spatiotemporal surface," *Int. Journ. of Computer Vision*, vol. 3, pp. 33 – 49, 1989.

[13] T.Takano, T.Naemura, M.Kaneko, and H.Harashima, "DCT-based coding of ray data for 3-D image communication," in *Proc. 1997 ITE Annual Convention*, July 1997. (in Japanese) to appear.

[14] T.Naemura, M.Kaneko, and H.Harashima, "3-D object based coding of multi-view images," in *Proc. PCS'96*, pp. 459 – 464, Mar. 1996.

[15] T. Naemura and H. Harashima, "Fractal coding of a multi-view 3-D image," in *Proc. IEEE ICIP'94*, vol. III, pp. 107 – 111, Nov. 1994.

Figure 13: Original views of surroundings.

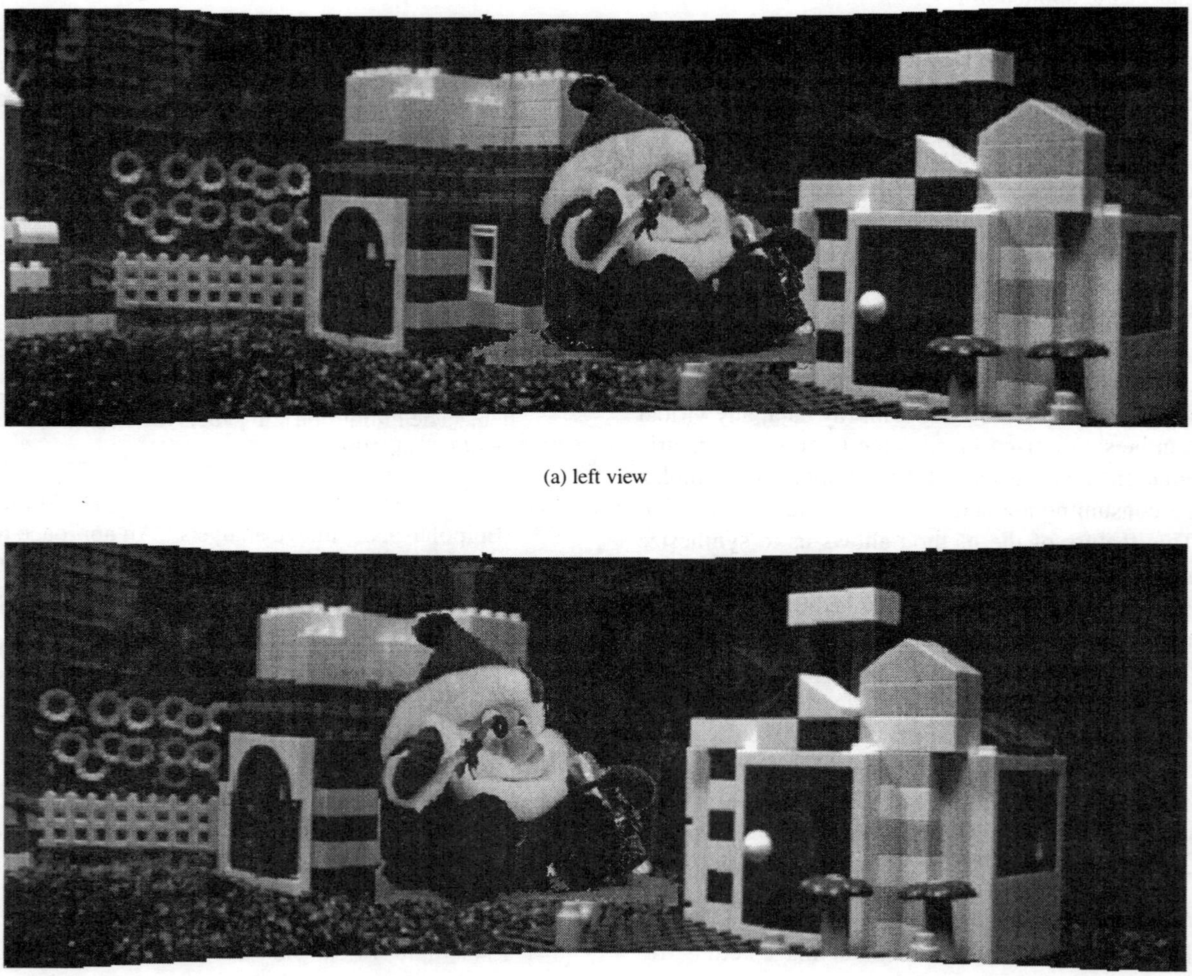

(a) left view

(b) right view

Figure 14: Stereopair of the synthesized virtual world.

Free-Form 3D Object Reconstruction from Range Images

C. Schütz, T. Jost, H. Hügli
Institute for Microtechnology, Neuchatel, Switzerland
schutz@imt.unine.ch

Abstract

The increasing use of virtual object representations for several applications creates a need for fast and simple object digitizing systems. Range finders provide a convenient way to digitize solid objects and permit the accurate and fast scanning of an object shape without any probe contact. However, only one view of an object can be captured at once and therefore for most objects several views have to be combined in order to obtain a description of the complete surface. We consider a digitizing system which captures and triangulates views of a real world 3D object and finally registers and integrates them. An interactive 3D environment allows the operator to enter an estimate of the relative pose of the different views which are then aligned automatically by geometric matching. A new fusion algorithm is proposed which takes advantage of the previous view matching to remove the redundant overlap area of two views and to fuse together their respective meshes by a gap filling algorithm.

1. Introduction

There exists a high demand for digitizing systems which allow to generate a virtual model from a real world object. Applications such as teleshopping, rapid prototyping and 3D object recognition [5] need a virtual representation of the 3D geometry of an object. Therefore, 3D surface digitizers get used more and more since the model construction with a standard modeler is a quite tedious task especially for objects of arbitrary shape.

Range images provide a direct access to the 3D geometric information of object surfaces. Current range finders allow an accurate digitizing of an object surface at low cost and high speed. Since most objects self occlude one acquisition captures only a subpart of the entire object surface. Therefore, there exists a need to combine several object views into one unique object representation.

The registration of such views becomes straightforward if the object is placed for instance on a turn table where the relative transformation between the views is well defined by the rotation angle of the turn table. However, especially for objects with concave surface regions, additional views are needed to scan the complete object surface. To access self occluded regions, a more sophisticated mechanical system or visual markers may help to measure the transformations between the different object poses.

To avoid such measuring systems, several authors [1] [6] proposed to use the object surface geometry to register two surfaces. An iterative closest point matching algorithm establishes the correspondence between the common parts of the two surfaces and minimizes a distance error. This geometric matching algorithm needs a good initial estimate in order to converge towards the best solution [3]. Therefore, we consider an interactive interface based on stereo display and space mouse that allows the user to roughly align the two surfaces before the automatic matching is started.

Once the surfaces are matched, the next step is the surface fusion. Several systems have been proposed to integrate range data from different object acquisitions. Early approaches triangulate the measured point set in 3D space and iteratively sculpt the surface polyhedron [2]. More recent approaches (see [4] for an overview) avoid the expensive 3D space triangulation and integrate meshes obtained from triangulation in 2.5D using the range image neighborhood relationships. They mainly differ in how they treat the redundant overlapping zone of the registered surfaces from two different acquisitions. Different methods for the erosion of the overlapping area and the fusion of the remaining triangle meshes have been proposed [4] [6].

This paper proposes a new mesh fusion algorithm which differs from other approaches by that it uses the closest point information from the geometric matching to detect the frontiers of the overlapping surface areas. The redundant part of one surface is removed and the remaining mesh is attached to the second surface mesh. Compared to others, the algorithm is simpler and integrates well in the complete reconstruction process.

2. View acquisition and matching

The scanned data points of each object view is organized in a range image. The 2.5D triangulation algorithm benefits from the neighborhood relations ships defined by the array structure of the range image. Discontinuity

0-8186-8150-0/97 $10.00 © 1997 IEEE

constraints avoid the covering of invisible object parts. The different surfaces represented by a triangle mesh are then registered using a geometric matching algorithm used in similar systems [6]. In our implementation, vertices of one surface are coupled with points on the triangles of the other surface. This results in a more accurate matching compared to a matching limited to vertices which needs a high surface sampling rate in order to find corresponding points at close distance.

3. View fusion

The proposed mesh fusion algorithm benefits a maximum from the closest point relationships established during the geometric matching. There is no need to run an extra routine to erode overlapping surfaces and to detect the surface frontiers as done in other work [4] [6].

It is characterized by the following features. Given P and X the meshes to be fused, the steps are:
1) overlap detection: The registration algorithm calculates for the vertices on surface P the closest points on the triangles of the surface X. Closest points pairs with a maximal distance are coupled. During the geometric matching iterations the coupled points on P converge to the overlapping area of the two surfaces P and X.
2) overlap remove: The redundant part of the surface P is deleted by removing the triangles with one or more coupled vertex. The remaining meshes are separated by a gap defined by a frontier on P and X.
3) frontier detection: Triangles where the geometric matching coupled only one vertex are connected to the frontier on P. Actually, the two non-coupled vertices build an edge of the frontier on P. The frontier on X is detected by a closest point search.
4) gap filling: The gap enclosed by the two frontiers is filled iteratively with triangles. Vertices on the two frontiers are used as candidates to build a filling triangle. The triangulation does not need projection into tangential planes. Triangles with a maximal opening angle are constructed in order to have the best surface approximation.

4. Results

The digitizing system has been successfully tested with several objects. A typical digitized object is shown in Fig. 1. Ten acquisitions are registered and fused which results in a surface of about 15000 vertices and 30000 triangles. Since our range finder uses white light to code the object space, the color information is available for every measured vertex.

5. Conclusions

The presented 3D object digitizing system successfully registers and integrates object views acquired by a range finder. It combines interactive and automatic modules in order to provide maximal flexibility. Several object views are acquired with a range finder and triangulated using the range image data structure. Geometric matching registers the roughly aligned surfaces at high precision since it establishes point to triangle correspondences. The integration uses an algorithm which is easy to implement and which integrates well in the context of the whole digitizing system. It consists of a new overlap remove and a gap fill module. Several objects have been successfully digitized with the presented system.

6. Acknowledgments

This research has been funded by the Swiss national science foundation under project number 2100-43530.

7. References

[1] P.J. Besl and N.D. McKay, "A Method for Registration of 3-D Shapes," Proceedings of IEEE Transactions on Pattern Analysis and Machine Intelligence (PAMI), vol. 14, no. 2, pp. 239-256, 1992.
[2] J.-D. Boissonnat, "Geometric Structures for Three-Dimensional Shape Representation," ACM Transactions on Graphics, vol. 3, no. 4, pp. 266-286, 1984.
[3] H. Hugli, C. Schutz, "Geometric Matching of 3D Objects: Assessing the Range of Successful Initial Configurations," Int. Conf. on Recent Advances in 3-D Digital Imaging and Modeling, pp. 101-106, 1997.
[4] R. Pito, "Mesh Integration Based on Co-Measurements," IEEE International Conference on Image Processing, Lausanne, vol. 2, 1996, pp. 397-400.
[5] Ch. Schutz, N. Natonek, Ch. Baur, H. Hugli, "3D Vision in a Virtual Reality Robotics Environment," Proceedings of SPIE Telemanipulator and Telepresence Technologies, Boston, vol. 2901, 1996.
[6] G. Turk, M. Levoy, "Zippered Polygon Meshes from Range Images," Proceedings ACM Siggraph, Orlando, 1994, pp. 311-318.

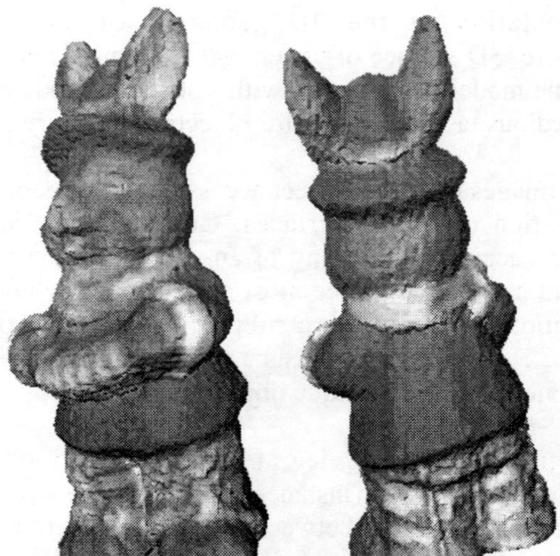

Figure 1. Views of a digitized free-form object

A Distributed Task Delegation Framework for Walkthrough Computations

S. P. Mudur, Deepraj S. Dixit, Shirish H. Shanbhag
Graphics and CAD Division,
National Centre for Software Technology, Juhu, Mumbai 400 049, India.
email: {mudur,dixit,shirish}@ncst.ernet.in

Abstract

VISPAR is a research project partially funded by the Commission of European Countries (CEC) at the National Centre for Software Technology in India for investigating the use of parallel computing in global illumination and visualization of 3D environments. A task delegation framework has been evolved based on the notion of distributed agents, which take both the responsibilities of suitably delegating tasks to other agents and of executing tasks delegated to them, based on their core competencies. The paper describes this framework and the distributed multi-agent architecture designed specifically, for obtaining high performance in interactive manipulation and walkthrough computations of very large virtual environments.

1. Introduction

The design of high performance software systems for interactive manipulation and visual walkthroughs in large virtual environments is a challenging problem and is being currently addressed by many research groups around the world [6]. It is not uncommon to see special hardware architectures being proposed and used for many of the subtasks involved. [1], [5]. The concern of this paper is specifically the computation of realistic images of the virtual world and to some extent the interactive manipulation of the 3D geometry describing the virtual world. In particular, we present the task-delegation framework that we have evolved as part of the VISPAR research project, the multi-agent architecture for walk-through computations and some implementation results.

2. The VISPAR Project

The VISPAR project is partially supported through grants from the CEC. It is a collaborative project between M/s BULL Overseas Limited (European partner) and NCST. VISPAR is a parallel processing system for interactive visualization of complex configurations with realistic illumination effects. Illumination effects, like shadows and reflections, are a must to construct photo-realistic images of complex virtual environments. NCST has earlier developed a specific technique known as the *Particle Tracing Method*, which can be used to produce realistic renderings of illuminated interiors with complex optical behaviour[4]. The particle tracing technique is based on a Monte Carlo simulation of the particle model of light In this model of light, particles denoting (packets of photons) quanta of light energy, are emitted and propagated from the emitting surface and volume elements and their interaction with the environment is simulated. The main objective of the VISPAR project is to suitably enhance the implementation of the particle tracing method and produce a system for facilitating the user/designer to walk-through in real time in computer modeled environments, rendered in a physically realistic manner.

3. The Task Delegation Framework

The task delegation framework is based on the concept of an agent. An *agent* is a component in the computing environment having abilities to communicate with other agents in the environment, accomplish a well-defined *task*, know about other (related) agents in the environment, and delegate tasks to other agents. Agents together achieve the goal of the application by sending triggers to other agents. A *trigger* is a combination of event and associated task. An *event* in the environment can be self generated by agents or can occur due to the user actions through the interface devices. The interested reader is referred to [2] for details of the design and implementation of this framework.

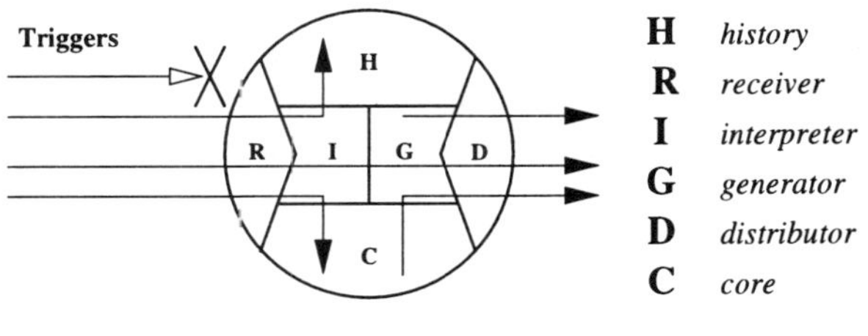

Figure 1. Agent and Triggers

Figure 1 shows the different parts making up an agent and the flow of triggers through them.

As an example, consider a Virtual Reality Walkthrough system, which allows the user to navigate through a model scene. Now if the user changes the camera position, an event corresponding to view-change will be generated by the agent interfacing with the user. The task associated with view-change event will be to update the display on the screen. The interface agent then forwards this event-task combination i.e., trigger to other agent(s) which are capable of and willing to undertake the task requested.

4. VISPAR's multi-agent architecture

We have designed the agents for VISPAR based on the functionality expected from a typical VR system.

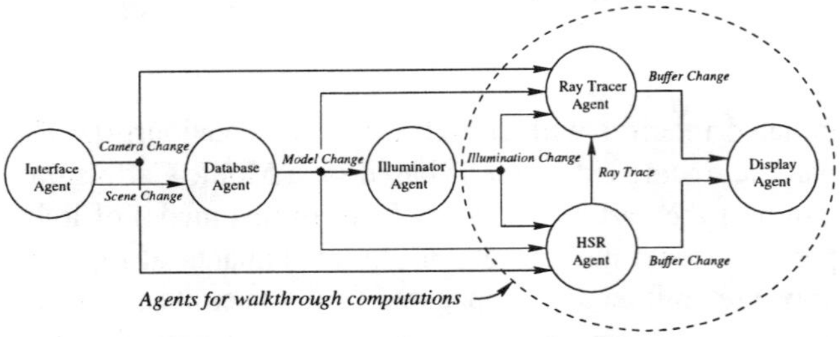

Figure 2. Agents in VISPAR

Figure 3. Scene Rendered for Walkthrough

The basic agents which make up the VISPAR system are shown in Figure 2. The types of events, these agents accept and generate in response are also shown.

The illuminator agent and the ray-tracing agent, whose core competencies are based on the use of computationally intensive algorithms have been implemented on a parallel machine. Multi-threading is used to exploit the full capabilities of the high performance computing machine. The interface agent, HSR agent and the display agent all of which make use of the special hardware capabilities are implemented on Silicon Graphics workstations. The illuminator agent performs global illumination computation once at the start and needs to be invoked again only when the environment changes. The HSR agent uses the depth buffer hardware based rendering capabilities of the machine to provide interactive walkthroughs.

Figure 3 shows an interior scene with a reflecting mirror surface rendered by the combined effort of the HSR agent and the ray-tracing agent. The multi-agent architecture based on the task delegation framework has resulted in substantive improvements in performance. For many of the subtasks we have obtained linear speed ups with increase in processing elements.

5. Conclusions

A primary goal when designing VISPAR architecture was to ensure optimal use of specialised graphics or massively parallel systems that will be available in the near future. Based on our implementation, and on the performance improvements obtained for a variety of virtual worlds, that we have experimented with, the task delegation framework and the multi-agent architecture seem to be well suited for use in interactive applications requiring voluminous data, extensive graphics and raw computing capabilities. VISPAR would improve its performance, both in interactivity and in capabilities to provide realism with the availability of more parallel machines or better graphics hardware systems. Unlike generic distributed object frameworks [3], specific tasks needed for virtual walk-throughs have been assigned to the agents.

Acknowledgments

We would like to thank CEC and M/s BULL Overseas Limited (France) for their contribution in creating the computing infrastructure. We would also like to thank scientists of the graphics division of NCST for their contributions and support.

References

[1] K. Akeley. Reality engine graphics. *Computer Graphics (SIGGRAPH '93)*, 27:109–116, August 1993.

[2] S. P. Mudur, D. S. Dixit, and S. H. Shanbhag. A distributed task delegation framework for walkthrough computations. Technical report, National Center for Software Technology, 1997.

[3] Object Management Group, Inc. *The common Object Request Broker Architecture and Specifications; Revision 2*, July 1995.

[4] S. N. Pattanaik and S. P. Mudur. Computation of global illumination by monte carlo simulation of particle model of light. *Proceedings of the Third Eurographics Workshop on Rendering*, pages 71–83, May 1992. Bristol, UK.

[5] J. Rohlf and J. Helman. Iris performer: A high performance multiprocessing toolkit for real-time 3d graphics. *Computer Graphics (SIGGRAPH '94)*, pages 381–394, July 1994.

[6] N. M. Thalmann and D. Thalmann, editors. *Virtual Worlds and Multimedia*. John Wiley & Sons, October 1992.

Virtual Heritage

Towards Greater Reality in Virtual Heritage — Modelling the Frigate HMS Unicorn

John N Sutherland
Visiting Researcher in Virtual Reality (1996-97), Gifu University, Japan
Lecturer in Software Engineering, University of Abertay Dundee, Scotland
j.sutherland@tay.ac.uk

Takeo Ojika
Virtual Reality Laboratory, Gifu University, Japan
ojika@ojk.info.gifu-u.ac.jp

keywords: virtual reality, virtual heritage, maritime history

This is a much reduced version of the full paper.

Much of the work in virtual heritage to date has been of a similar type of object: castles, stone circles, temples, ancient cities, etc. These have been variously successful, providing the viewer with a realistic insight into what lost structures would perhaps have looked like when they stood complete. The team in Scotland had been involved in the modelling of two ancient Scots castles: St Andrews and Dudhope. However, the Japanese team wanted a look into further aspects of realism. It was decided to model a sailing ship, the Frigate Unicorn, whose hull lies in Dundee Harbour.

This model proved a much more difficult task than a simple building. A mediaeval European castle doesn't move, is made up of simple surfaces and reflects a build designed for defence rather than artistic statements. It is relatively simple to construct a 3D building from a plan and wallpaper this with pictures of suitable stonework or harling.

However, a sailing ship has no flat surfaces, all are curved: decks rise towards the centreline, the hull follows a curved shape, masts taper, sails billow, etc. To achieve realism in real-time movement involving the extensive of nurbs is difficult. Further a ship's deck is naturally cluttered with ropes, poles, sails and other paraphernalia occupying much of the deck space. These add to the polygon count, adding further to the problems associated with real-time movement.

Even once rigged and completed to the satisfaction of the eye, the ship still does not look realistic. It needs to move against a backdrop of land, sky and sea. The sea is particularly difficult to model as it interacts with wind and the ship's hull. Lastly, the ship looks wrong with no people on board - a type of *Marie Celeste* - and these people should probably move to give full realism.

The team also considered moving the viewer using a 6dof platform. This added to the realism, suppressing mental consideration of the model's limitations. There was concern that such movement might induce motion sickness.

In conclusion, the modelling task was incomplete, but laid down certain criteria that future types of virtual heritage modelling need to consider if they are to break past the world of building modelling:

- the need for motion
- the need to model the object's surroundings
- the need for populating a model with moving humans
- alternative sensory inputs in addition to 2d/3d sight and 1d/2d sound

Using Multiple Data Sources within VR at Urquhart Castle

Jonathan Kelly - Managing Director - VirTech Software
Andrew Bishop - CAD Director - VirTech Software

Abstract:

The effective use of multiple data sets with different export/import requirements has become a necessity, as the scope and complexity of models becomes greater so the ability to manage effectively becomes increasingly important. The continued viability of any VR management tool is judged solely upon it's ability to allow free movement between the data collation methods i.e. CAD, survey data, photographs, Ordnance Survey data etc. and the final visualisation. The integration of different data types within an individual model is illustrated in the VR model of Urquhart Castle.

1. Introduction

In 1995 VirTech were asked to asses the viability of creating a VR computer model of the proposed car park that was planned for Urquhart Castle, Loch Ness. The model should be accessible using a standard desktop PC and be viewable in real-time. Given the size of the site and it's geographical position it was quickly recognised that the immediate surroundings would not suffice to give the true impact of any future developments on the site. Therefore the incorporation of Ordnance Survey data to give the topography of the surrounding terrain was also included.

After initial consultation with the client, Historic Scotland, we decided to select an area of 20 kilometres square with Urquhart Castle at the centre. We then identified the available existing data and broke the proposed site into component areas :- new car park/roads, proposed vegetation, castle ground model/walls and tower, proposed upper/lower visitor centres, surrounding site approx. 1 sq. kilometre, surrounding site approx. 400 sq. kilometres, relevant features and structures, surface textures and materials.

The project is still on-going with additional data-sets being introduced.

2. Background

The castle sits on the banks of Loch Ness and is visible from the village of Drumnadrochit. It can only be reached by the A82 which follows the shore around Loch Ness. The castle has had a chequered history with a variety of occupants, some welcome some not. It played an important part in the Jacobite troubles of the 1690s and was eventually laid to ruin by the retreating English army.

3. Project Management

a. New car park and road system

This was the only aspect of the site that had any previous data capture information. We were supplied with engineering drawings showing proposed developments. The data was edited using a survey/engineering package to create specific geometry for the site i.e. DTM information.

b. Proposed vegetation

We were supplied with comprehensive drawing plans.

c. Castle ground model, walls and tower

We carried a thorough ground survey using total stations and tunnel lasers to create a comprehensive model of the site. It was then taken into Microstation were it was processed into various types of geometry.

d. Introduction and application of *RealiScape*

While the various sections of the model were being processed, as described above, we were desperately

0-8186-8150-0/97 $10.00 © 1997 IEEE

trying to find a software environment that would first bring all of the sections into an efficient model and, secondly, provide the runtime environment for presentation of the model.

After a few weeks of trying every known branded tool-kit on the market we realised that there was nothing available that could deliver the results we, and the client, required. At that point we found a 3D programming library, RealiMation, that a British company, Datapath, were just starting to test in Beta. After testing the libraries with our data sets we knew that, using this underlying technology, we could write the applications that would build the models we needed.

We then set about designing and writing *RealiScape* to do the following:

- Build accurate, efficient, ground models using survey data from various sources.
- Automatically apply surface textures to the ground model.
- Automatically place features on the terrain such as trees and fence lines etc.
- Automatically produce level of detail sections of the terrain models.
- Provide project management tools to manage multiple data sets, model and object/texture libraries.

We first wrote the raw translators that would generate the VR terrain models from the survey data. This then gave us a base ground model upon which the buildings and structures could simply be dropped into. While the software was being written the basic libraries of landscape features and surface materials were being developed.

How to manage changes being made to original design drawings and having to manually rebuild the interactive models has always been an expensive and emotive issue. Our design philosophy has always been make the generation of the models an automatic process using the design drawings as input. This eliminates dumb transfer files, such DXF, and eliminates all of the usual rework.

RealiScape has now been developed into a Windows 95/NT application that allows end users to build their own models from survey data.

Telerobotics and VR Devices

CABIN - A MultiScreen Display for Computer Experiments

Michitaka Hirose
Department of Mechano-Informatics,
University of Tokyo

Abstract : This paper introduces the CABIN (Computer Augmented Booth for Image Navigation) multiscreen display system which was designed and developed at the Intelligent Modeling Laboratory (IML) at the University of Tokyo. Firstly, the features of the CABIN system, such as its glass floor screen, its capability for real image projection, and its parallel computer graphics workstation configuration, are discussed. Next, the introduction of several applications which will be based on CABIN technology are discussed briefly.

Keywords : Virtual Reality, Super-Computing, Five Screen Multi Projection System

1. Introduction

8 years have been passed since the word "Virtual Reality" was born. At the very beginning, this technology became popular just because its framework was new. However, it is now considered much more seriously. In this new developmental stage, the 'quality' of this technology has become a major focus for many research efforts.

In 1992, one of the most famous multi screen projection systems, CAVE (Cave Automatic Virtual Environment) was introduced into the field of virtual reality technology by EVL at the University of Illinois.[1] This system was demonstrated at SIGGRAPH'92 held in Chicago. One of the advantages of the system is that most of the hardware components are commercially available and use 'proven' technologies. Consequently, the quality of the virtual worlds generated by this display are much more sophisticated than those generated by other displays at the 'experimental' stage, such as the HMD (Head Mounted Display). For example, although current HMD resolutions are still around NTSC quality, which is 500 by 500 or so, the resolutions of projectors are more than an HDTV, which is 1000 by 1000.

2. CABIN MultiScreen Stereo Display

Our laboratory has been quite interested in CAVE technology, too. Five years after the first introduction of CAVE, a similar display was implemented in the IML (Intelligent Modeling Laboratory) at the University of Tokyo this spring (Fig. 1). We named this system CABIN. The objective of CABIN was to provide an advanced display system for supercomputers in this laboratory. One of the features of this new multiscreen system is that it has five screens which correspond to front, right, left, top, and bottom respectively (the original CAVE had four screens of front, right, left and bottom). The reason that we decided to implement a top and bottom screen was to support up and downward vision at the same time. By having 5 screens, the vertical field of view of users located at the center of floor increases from 158.9 deg. to 273.7 deg. (as shown in Fig. 2). This wide field of view is essential in several applications which require spatial simulation to be discussed later.

One of the technical difficulties involved in implementing a five screen system concerns the implementation of the bottom screen. Whereas the bottom screen of the original CAVE is a front projection, the bottom screen of our display needs to be projected from the back because the top screen will shield the light from the projector for the bottom screen. We used a reinforced glass floor for the bottom screen. Its dimensions were 2.5m by 2.5m and double 1.5cm thick. This glass floor's maximum load was designed to be safe when 700kgw (approx. ten people) is loaded on the central 20cm by 20cm area. Calculated displacement under the maximum load condition is about 9 mm (under worst assumptions). Considering this specification, we decided the maximum number of passengers for the operation of the system to be three.

The most difficult design problem encountered was with the structure of the edges of the bottom and top screen. The bottom screen and the side (front, left and

Fig. 1

0-8186-8150-0/97 $10.00

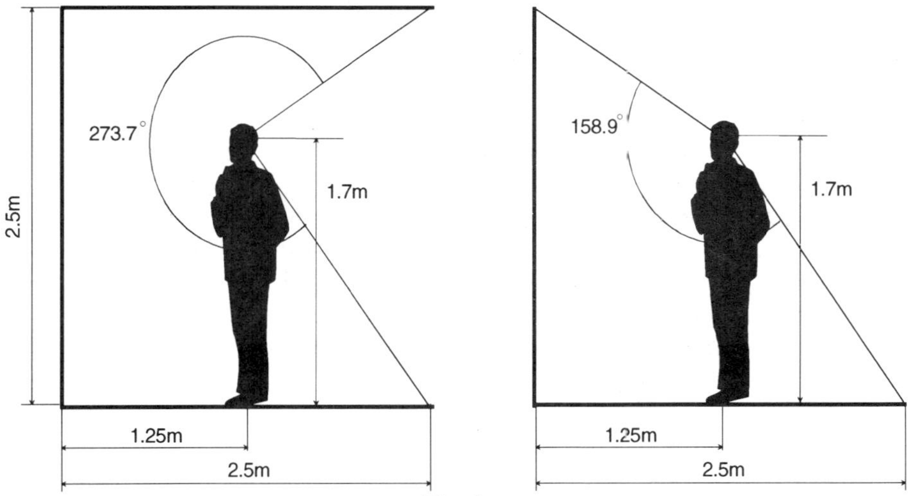

Fig.2

right) screens are connected as shown in Fig. 3. Even by using this structure, the existence of the 5 cm wide border lines is inevitable because a certain size of fringe is required for safety support of the glass floor.

When virtual objects are displayed outside of the cubic space surrounded by screens, these border lines will look like a kind of window frame, and will not cause wrong occlusion and there should be no disturbance of our 3D vision in this case. However, in contrast, when objects are displayed inside of the cubic space, the border lines will hide the virtual objects nearer than themselves and may cause depth cue confusion. According to a simple experiment however, the effect of the 5cm border line is still within a permissible limit.

The border between top and side screens has similar problems. However, the width of border lines is about 1.5cm for this case. The connection structure between the top and side screens is shown in Fig. 4.

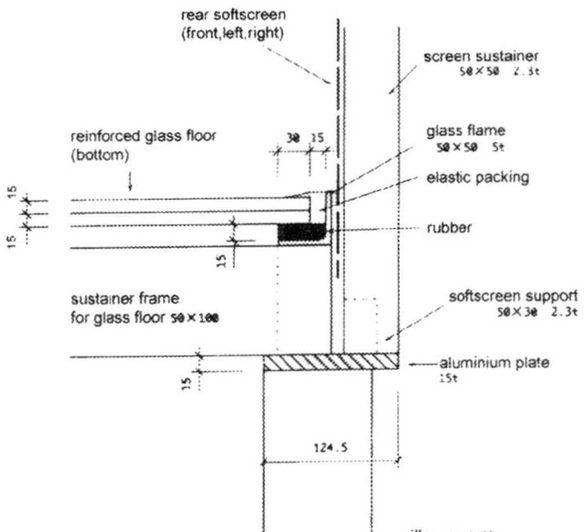

Fig. 3

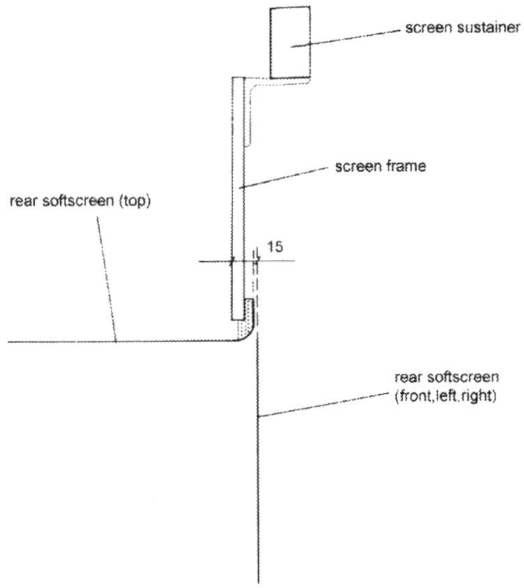

Fig. 4

3. Image Generation System

The image generation system for CABIN display consisted of graphics workstations (SGI i-station), video tape recorders, file servers, and a communication network to synchronize each graphics workstation (Fig. 5). One graphics workstation was assigned for each screen. LC (Liquid Crystal) shutter glasses (StereoGraphics CrystalEyes) are used for stereo image generation (left and right images are supplied successively and separated for each eye via shuttering).

The advantage of this configuration is that all of the workstations can be equally treated. However, of course, a synchronization system should be added to the workstation complex. First, in order to see stereo images from five screens by using one pair of stereo glasses, video signals should be completely synchronized. Use of the GENLOCK signal and SwapReady signal of i-station will provide this scan line level synchronization. Frame by frame drawing should also be synchronized. For this purpose, a high speed communication link called SCRAMNET was used. This network functions as a kind of shared memory. Several synchronization mechanisms such as semaphore can be implemented by using this network.

Another feature of our CABIN is that it can display 'real' stereo images taken by a special multi-lens camera. As shown in Fig. 5, ten synchronized VCRs are the image source. Scan line based synchronization is realized by using the GENLOCK signal, and the frame level synchronization is controlled by video controller (Sony V-box) using time code as reference.

Fig. 6 shows the special camera with ten lenses. Several mirrors are carefully positioned in order to minimize dead angles caused by the physical volume of CCD cameras as shown in Fig. 7. Besides the camera itself, camera operation techniques should also be developed. For example, microphones should be arranged out of the camera's field of view. The camera crew should also be hidden from the scene.

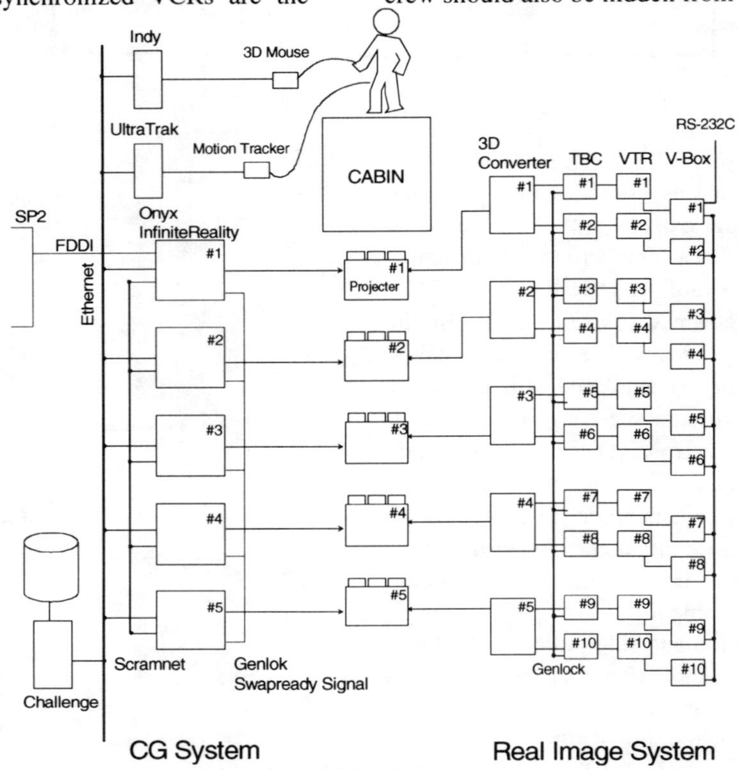

Fig. 5

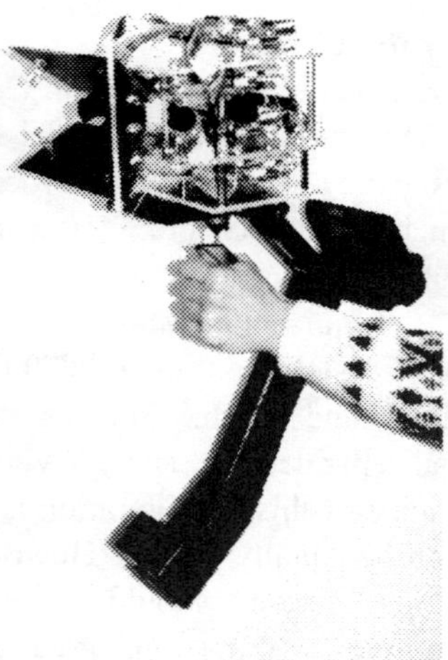

Fig. 6

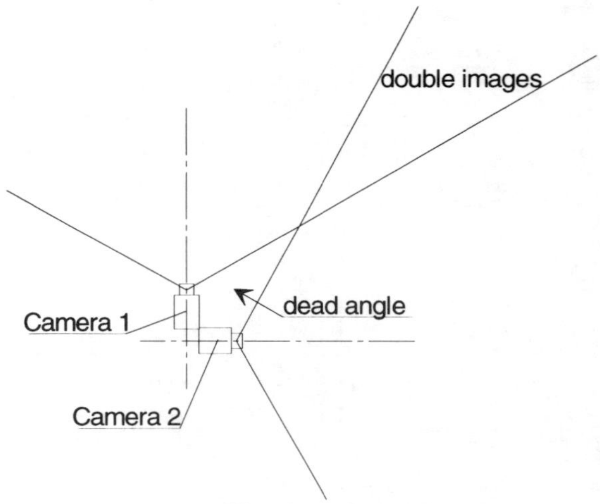

Fig. 7

4. Contents and Application

In order to understand the potential advantages of the multi screen display, we have developed several application software contents as shown below.

(1) Virtual Einstein World

The objective of this application is to give an environment where Einstein's theory can be experienced. This content is a kind of walk through, but the computer simulates a world which has a different light speed from the existing real world. If you lower the light speed as much as several m/s, we can experience various phenomena typical in Einstein's world such as the Doppler color shift, or distortion of space and time which we cannot experience directly (Fig. 8).

By using these types of contents, the user can understand the theory of relativity very intuitively. Usually, the strange phenomena caused by Lorenz transformations can be understood by looking at or solving the necessary equations. This application can provide us with other ways of obtaining an understanding of worlds which exist only in theory.

(2) Environmental Simulation Lab.

The aim of this project is to provide a new intuitive methodology for urban design. Unlike conventional urban design methodologies, virtual reality technology can generate sensations associated with being present on a city street which is going to be designed. Various design parameters can be checked and discussed based on experience by going inside of a design plan. Without this kind of methodology, it is often difficult to reach an agreement.

Technical problems with this application involve the generation of the often complex landscape of city streets. If we use a conventional 3D CG model, it is impossible to generate realistic landscapes in real time. Currently, two methodologies are being considered in our laboratory.

One method is to use 'image based rendering' which is a methodology for generating scenes from an arbitrary viewpoint by interpolating already recorded photographs from viewpoints near by.[3]

An automobile with a special multi-lens camera as shown in Fig. 9 is being developed to obtain photographs from broader areas. For this wide-range position data acquisition, we should use a positioning sensor with a wider measurement range such as GPS(Global Positioning System). The image data are transmitted to the graphics workstation and arranged as an image database. Using image interpolation greatly reduces the required number of prerecorded images because we are able to estimate images from arbitrary viewpoints.

The other method is to use conventional miniature models and a very small snorkel camera driven by the user interactively. Fig. 10 shows the principle of this methodology. This methodology is also user-friendly for urban designers having only general knowledge about computers.

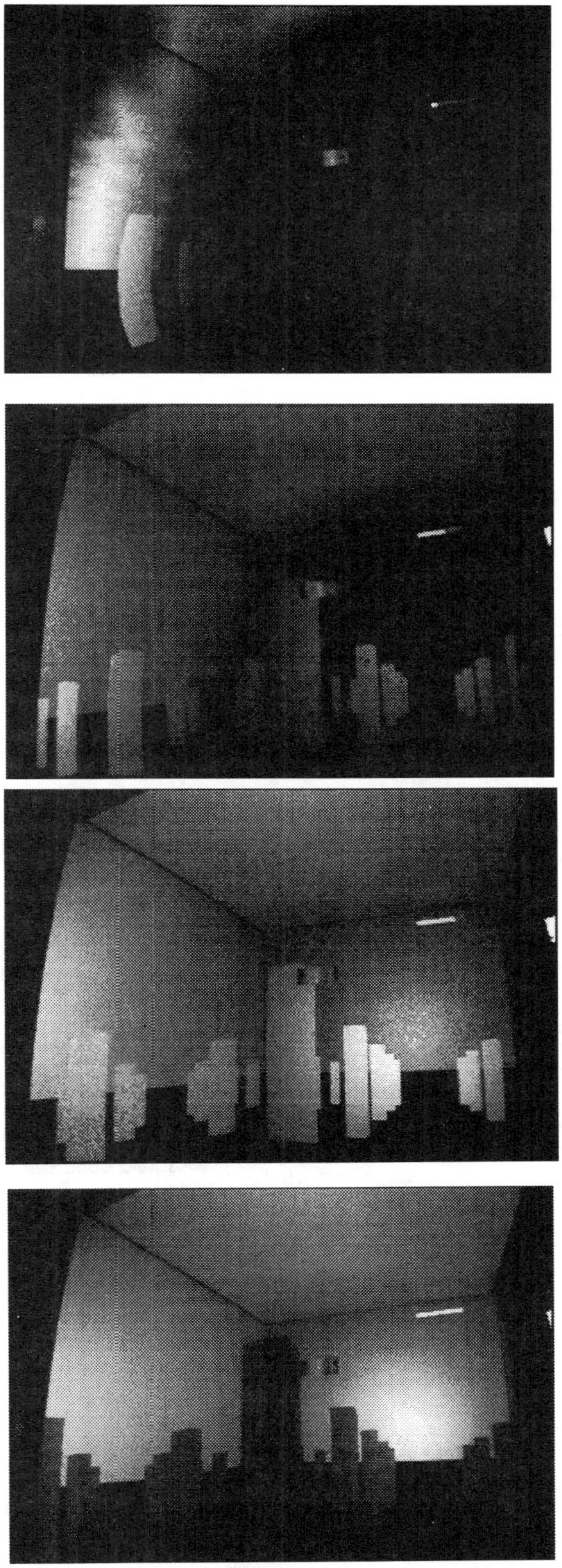

Fig. 8

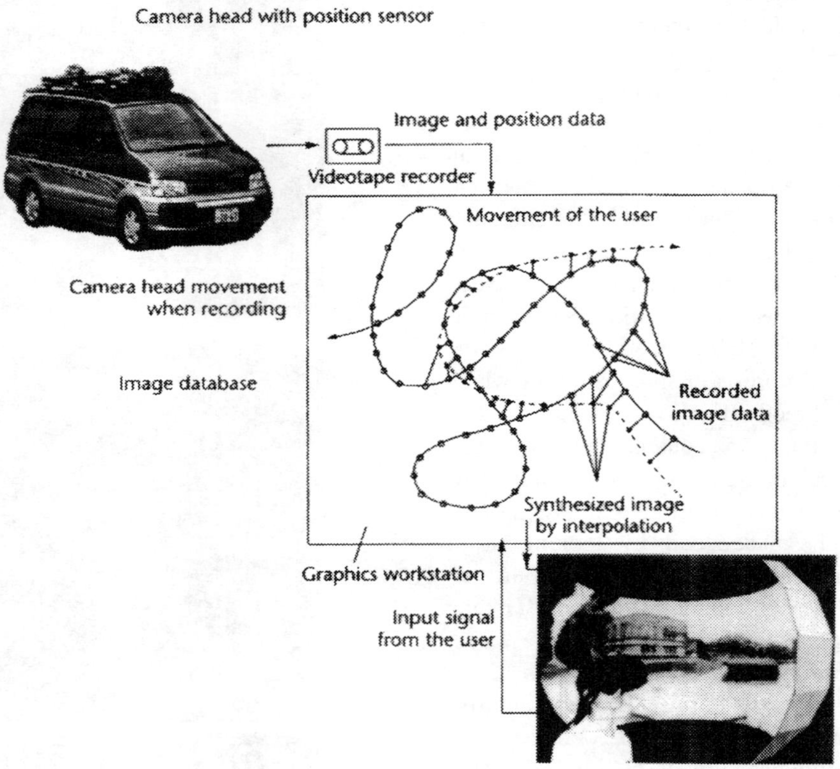

Fig. 9

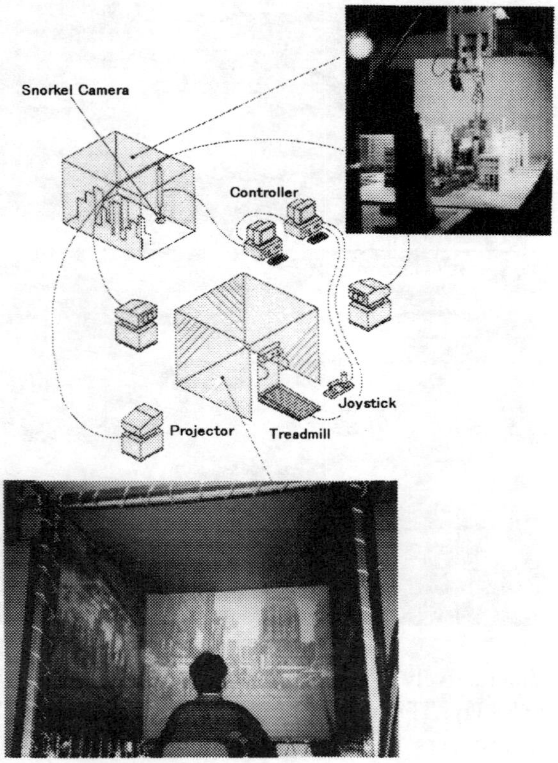

Fig. 10

(3) Computer Experiment Environments

This project is a kind of generalization of the virtual Einstein world application and an inter-disciplinary area between virtual reality and supercomputing. Our multi screen system has a high speed connection to the outside of our own system. For example, it is connected to a parallel computer (IBM SP2 / 48 CPUs) via FDDI.

Several computational mechanics programs such as FEM can be calculated almost in real time by using the parallel computer. For example, as shown in Fig. 11, distortion of virtual objects, when force is applied, can be calculated in real-time FEM on the super computer.[2] For this real-time FEM project, a haptic display is also being prepared so that the user can touch the virtual

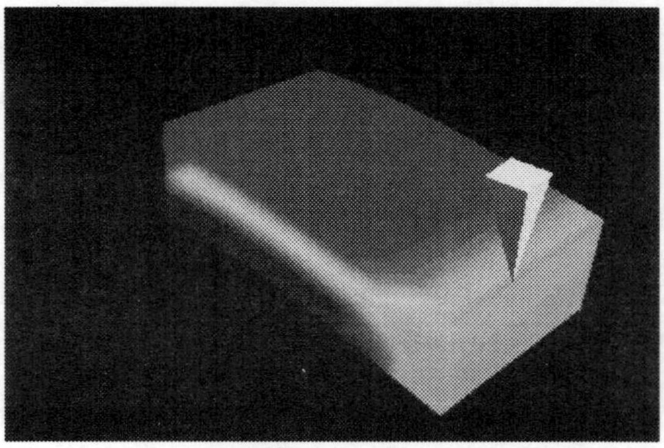

Fig. 11

object. This means that our multi screen system is going to have the capability to display haptic sensations and not only visual sensations, which will be one of the features of our system.

CABIN display system will provide us with a very powerful visualization capability to display the results of super-computing. Computer Experimental Environments such as the Virtual Wind Tunnel, Virtual Water Channel, and Virtual Material Testing Machine can be developed.

5. Conclusion

Recently, wide screen technology is becoming one of the eye-catching topics in the field of Virtual Reality. We will have various related research topics such as spatial distortion of virtual space displayed in the system or haptic displays for such a large display volume, etc.. The first workshop was held in Stuttgart this July. This technology provides virtual worlds with better quality. Consequently, various "real" applications can now be considered.

Acknowledgment

Our multi screen system, which has been rated as one of the more advanced and sophisticated system in Japan, has become possible under the support of various individuals. Especially, I would like to thank Prof. Tetsuro Ogi, Dr. Hiroshi Watanabe, Mr. Toshio Yamada, Mr. Yoshiyuki Nakagaki, Mr. Toshio Itou, Mr. Yasutomi Kakegawa, Mr. Eiichi Kawakita and the students in my laboratory group at the University of Tokyo.

References

(1) Calorina Cruz-Neira, et al. : "Surround-Screen Projection-Based Virtual Reality: The Design and Implementation of the CAVE", Computer Graphics (SIGGRAPH 93 Conference Proc.), pp.135-142 (1993)

(2) Tetsurou Ogi, et al. :"Real-time numerical simulation in haptic environment", Proc. of HCI'97

(3) Michitaka Hirose : "Image-Based Virtual World Generation", IEEE MultiMedia , Vol.4, No.1, pp.27-33 (1997)

Allowable Delay Between Images and Tactile Information in a Haptic Interface

Tsutomu Miyasato   Ryohei Nakatsu

ATR Media Integration & Communications Research Laboratories
2-2 Hikaridai, Seika-cho, Soraku-gun, Kyoto 619-02 Japan
miyasato@mic.atr.co.jp
Fax. +81-774-95-1408

Abstract

In a virtual environment, it is very important for users to directly manipulate the virtual objects, and we are researching ways to implement force feedback devices in VR environments. In order to provide good interaction, interactive systems must respond to the reactions of users as quickly as possible. However, due to the properties of input devices, output devices and software, lag is inevitable. There is a trade-off between generating highly realistic images and having them synchronize with other information in VR environments.

It is necessary to measure allowable delay and how it effects a user's sensation of realism. There is a lack of information concerning perceptional studies on the delay between visual information and tactile information when force feedback devices are employed. Accordingly, this paper describes the results of tests that measured the allowable delay between images and tactile information via a force feedback device. Two experiments were performed: 1) subjective evaluation in real space and 2) subjective evaluation in a virtual space using a force feedback device.

***Keywords**: Virtual reality, virtual environments, lag, human perception, force feedback, haptic interface.*

1. Introduction

In the near future, visual communication technologies are expected to provide real world sensations, and this requires that 3-dimensional surroundings be realistically reproduced. Recently, virtual reality (VR) technology that gives humans the sensation of being involved in a virtual environment, has been progressing worldwide. Applications of a virtual world generated by VR techniques are expected in many area, e.g., teleconferencing, cooperative work spaces, remote control, and CAD. Generally, such a system provides a directly manipulated interface for participants, and they can handle virtual objects generated by computer graphics.

As an application of virtual reality, we are developing a system that through the generation of computer graphics (CG) provides realistic sensations and can provide participants with a suitable environment for better communication and cooperative work. Figure 1 shows a prototype system called the "Virtual Space Teleconferencing System (VSTS), " which was built to study the feasibility and usability of teleconferencing with realistic sensations [1-6]. As is shown, the VSTS creates an image of a conference room (virtual conference room) by using computer graphics in real time. In this system, a human image is a 3-D model generated by CG and is reconstructed by processing 2-D images acquired through TV cameras. The system enables participants to view a screen and see what they want to see from the angle of their choice, just as in the real world. Users of the system can talk to each other or proceed with a conference and have the sensation of sharing the same space.

Through the VSTS, we are researching ways to implement a haptic interface using a force feedback device. In Fig. 2, two persons are using force feedback devices to cooperatively manipulate a virtual object. Haptic interfaces have been recognized as important input/output channels in a virtual environment [7-10]. We have developed and evaluated the usability of a force feedback device that uses a 3-joint master manipulator [9]. It is controlled such that users can feel the weight of virtual objects.

Since force feedback devices are mechanical devices, smooth operation is limited. A haptic interface is usually implemented with a visual display interface such as a head-mounted display or a stereoscopic display screen. When using pictures, sounds, and force feedback or tactile-feedback devices, the synchronization of stimuli is important. Poor visual/haptic registration could result in inconsistent situations where the user feels reaction forces from the haptic device before or after the user's hand actually reaches the virtual object in the visual display. If synchronization is not maintained, there may be illusions or unnaturalness for the users. However, there is a trade-off between generating highly realistic images and having them synchronize with other information in a VR environment. Therefore, it is necessary to measure the allowable delay and its effects on the user's sensation of realism. At present, there is a lack of information concerning perceptional studies on the delay between visual information and tactile information when feedback devices are employed. In this paper, we describe the results of tests that measured the allowable delay between images and tactile information via a force feedback device.

2. Influence of delay

In order to provide good interaction, interactive systems must respond to the reactions of users as quickly as possible. However, due to the properties of input devices, output devices and software, lag is inevitable. The presence of lag in an interactive environment increases the time needed to complete the motor-sensory tasks that we experience when using a pointing device with a slow response. Error rates also increase due to lag.

Communication mode, network configuration, software configuration, etc. all contribute to a system's slow response. Lag will dramatically increase when an output requires substantial computation for image or graphics processing in VR. In addition, mechanical linkages will especially cause delays.

If the delay time is too long in the Virtual Space Teleconferencing System, the computer generated room image will not be realistic and it will be difficult for the participants to take part in the teleconference. Although the lag in VR is only on the order of a few hundred milliseconds, its affect on human performance is considerable and can be a major bottleneck to usability. The shorter the delay, the easier it is to achieve a highly realistic image space. The VSTS displays images by using motion parallax, allowing the scene to change with the position of the participant's eyes. However, the time required to detect eye position decreases the time available to generate CG images, so CG images are restricted to simple, unrealistic objects.

Although reducing lag is a very important part of VR research, experimental measurements of lag and evaluating its effect on human performance have not been widely reported. In the field of TV picture transmission or TV conferencing via communication satellites, subjective evaluation of delay perception between picture and voice was done in the 1980s [11]. In an experiment using force feedback, Brooks et al. [8] reported that screen updates are needed a minimum

Figure 1. Scene of a virtual room in which three participants are cooperatively working

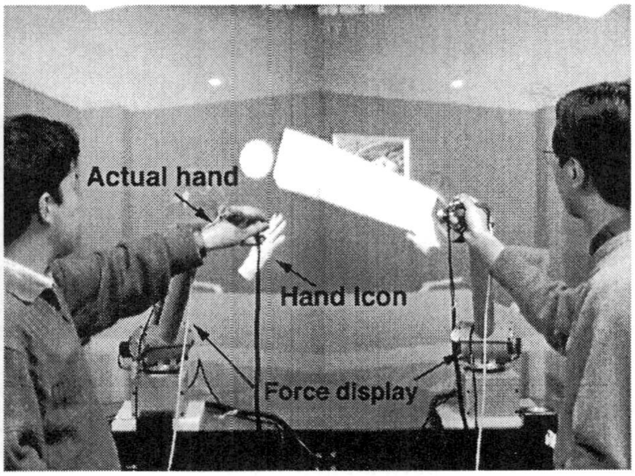

Figure 2. Cooperative work using force feedback display devices

of 15 times per second in order to maintain the illusion of a continuous change in the force sensed. In our previous research, Satoh et al. [12] showed the allowable range of lag without image degradation for images that have motion parallax in a 3-D display. We also subjectively evaluated the allowable transmission delay in a real-time CG eye-movement synthesis for the Virtual Space Teleconferencing System [13-14].

3. Experiments on allowable delay

We measured the allowable lag between images and tactile information by using two methods. The first experiment was conducted in a real environment, and the second one was done in a VR environment, i.e., a CG picture and a force feedback device were used in the experiment.

In the two experiments, randomly chosen 0-500 msec delays were set up at 30 msec intervals. Subjects were asked to evaluate the degree of unnatural lag using the five categories shown in Table 1. The number of the subjects is six, four females and two males. They are in their thirties, and have normal visual acuity of more than 1.0. They are not familiar with a force display device. We conducted the experiment twenty-five times for each subject and calculated average scores.

3.1. Subjective evaluation in real space

Figure 3 shows the experimental set up for the actual tactile stimulus. The subjects were asked to watch their hand on a 13-inch monitor that also displayed the stick that gave the tactile stimulus. The size of hand in the monitor is made to be equal to that of user's real hand. The images on the monitor is black and white due to the lack of memory size to store and display the images with time lag. A subject was located about one meter away from the monitor, and a TV camera was positioned about 50 cm behind the subject to shoot his hand.

In this experiment, only the picture was delayed against the tactile stimulus. Although it is easy to display a picture with lag, it is difficult to display a tactile stimulus with lag. The stick used for tactile stimulus was moved at about 60 cm/sec. The subject received the tactile stimulus on one of his palms, and on the monitor with controlled delay, he watched his palm being touched by the stick.

Table 1. Evaluation scores

Score	Category
5	Cannot feel lag
4	Can slightly feel lag
3	Intermediate
2	Lag is unnatural
1	Lag is very unnatural

Figure 3. Experimental setup for evaluating delayed feedback of visual information from tactile stimulus

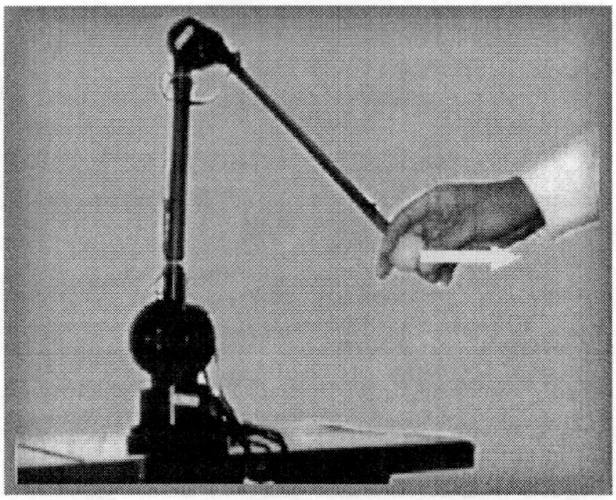

Figure 4. Force feedback display device

3.2. Subjective evaluation in virtual space

Figure 4 and Figure 5 respectively show a force feedback device using a 3-joint master manipulation [9] and experimental set up to evaluate the lag.

The subject watched an image of a free-falling ball that was generated by a graphic workstation and displayed on a 70-inch screen. The ball is red and has a diameter of 10 cm. The distance between a subject and the screen is about one meter.

The ball started falling at the height of 50 cm on the screen and bounced after it touched the surface of the palm on the screen. In the first experiment, the relative delay could only be set one way, but here the delay was set both ways; the image was shown before and after the tactile stimulus was given.

4. Results and discussion

Figures 6 and 7 show the relationship between delay and the subjects' evaluation. The horizontal axis shows delay and the vertical axis represents the mean opinion score (MOS) for the subjects. In the figures, the mean and 90% confidence interval of scores that all subjects reported are plotted. "0" on the horizontal axis in the figure means no lag between images and tactile information. A positive value of lag means the image is delayed from the tactile information, and a negative value means the opposite.

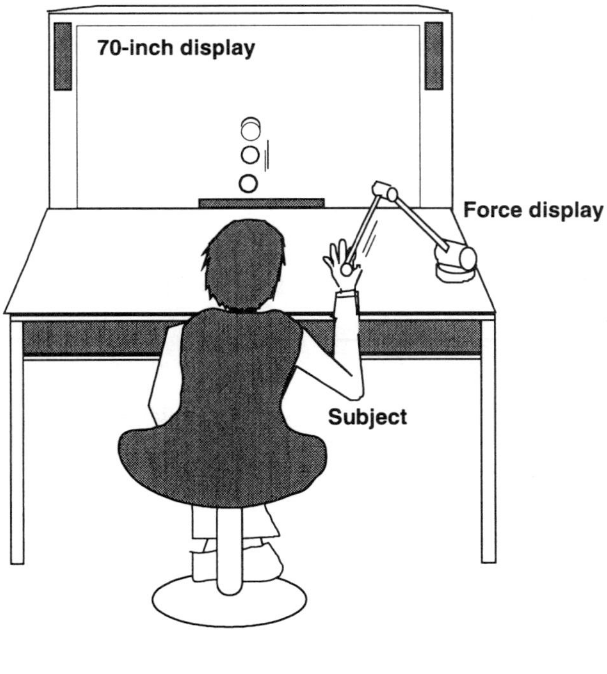

Figure 5. Force feedback display device

Experimental results for evaluating the actual stimulus are shown in Fig. 6. According to the evaluation based on the MOS, the allowable limit is 3.5. We can see that when visual information is delayed after tactile information, the maximum delay in which the MOS is higher than 3.5 is about 100 msec.

Similarly, as shown in Fig. 7, using the force feedback device results in shown in a delay of 100 msec. when visual information is delayed after tactile information and 120 msec. when tactile information is delayed after visual information.

Therefore, it can be deducted from the experimental results that allowable maximum delay between visual stimulus and tactile stimulus is between 100-120 msec.

The allowable delay, 100 msec., is nearly equal to the results of subjective evaluations in previous studies; 120 msec. was reported in a study on unnaturalness due to delay between picture and voice in TV picture transmission via communication satellites [11], and 100 msec. was shown to be the allowable delay for images with motion parallax in a 3-D display [12]. There may be some relations among those results with regard to the basic perceptional functions of humans. We need to further study this matter.

As for the experiments, the force feedback was passive feedback, i.e., a subject did not move his arm. With passive feedback, no muscles of the subject change. Therefore, differences may result when we measure the allowable delay using force feedback with active arm movements.

Furthermore, human perception of movement differs with direction. For example, if an object moves vertically or horizontally at the same speed, vertical movement will seem faster than horizontal movement due to an optical illusion. In the same way, the perception of delay could be effected by picture movement direction.

In Figures 6 and 7, the subject's impression resulted in the MOS score 4.5, not the score 5.0 for 'cannot feel lag', but instead at a level slightly below the score even when there is no delay. It may be due to the moderation effect by subjects that they avoid the extreme scoring. This can be the reason why the MOS score is not 1.0 but slightly above 1.0 'lag is very unnatural' for the delay of 0.5 seconds. There is another possibility that visual acuity degrades against a moving object. The stick used for tactile stimulus and the falling ball were moving objects, then it could be possible that the subjects did

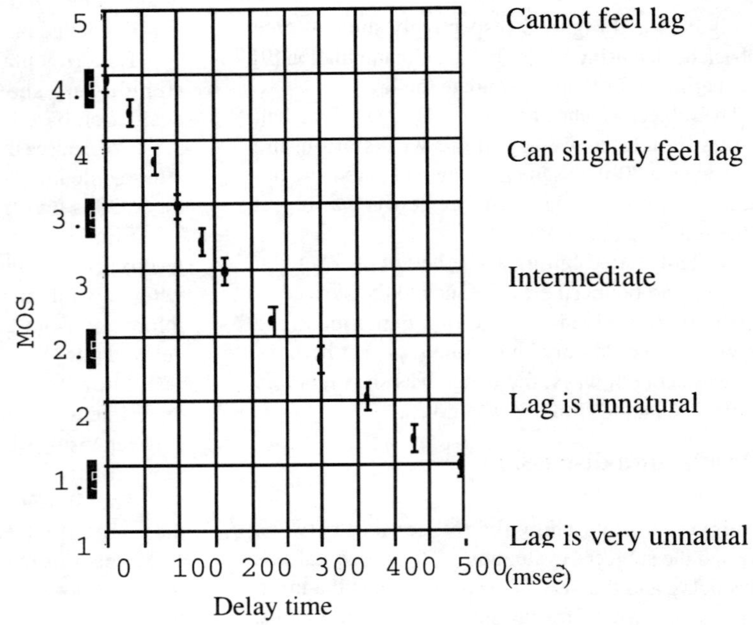

Figure 6. Results for subjective evaluation of delay perception between visual stimulus and tactile stimulus (actual stimulus). Delay 0 msec means when the tactile stimulus is given.

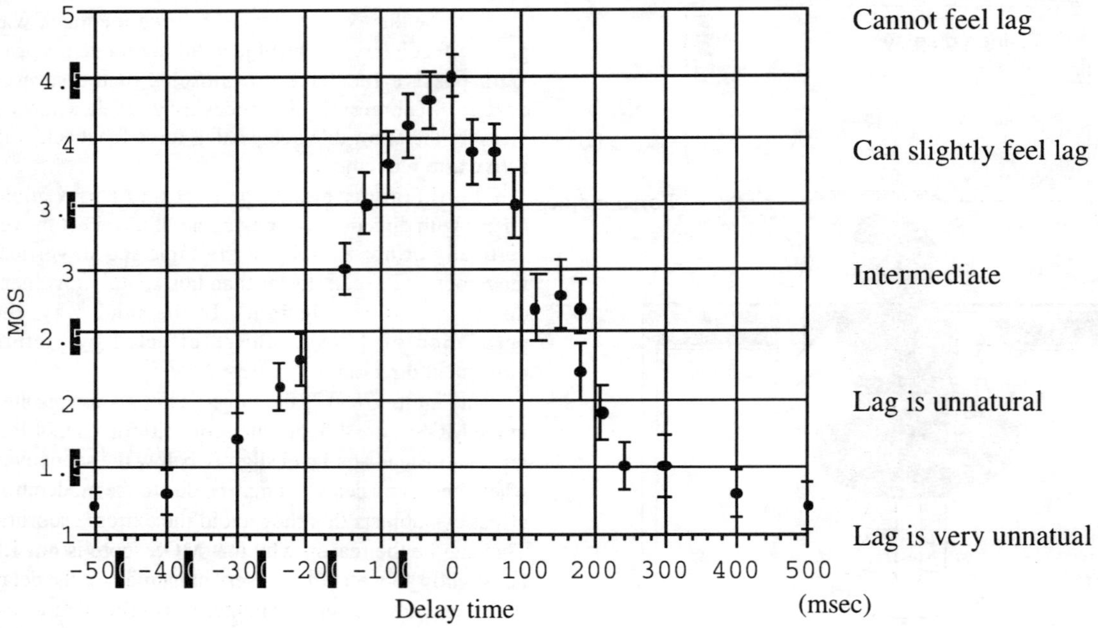

Figure 7. Results for subjective evaluation of delay perception between visual stimulus and tactile stimulus (stimulus via a force feedback device). Delay 0 msec means when the tactile stimulus is given.

not detect the visual instant precisely. We will study further on this matter with more sample of subjects used in the experiments.

5. Conclusion

Force feedback techniques will be implemented in many VR environments. However, force feedback devices are mechanical devices and inherent lag limits smooth operation. In this paper, we have described the results of tests that measured the allowable delay between images and tactile information. The results showed that the allowable maximum delay between visual stimulus and tactile stimulus is between 100-120 msec.

The present study is only a first step because we only investigated under passive touch conditions, but the results will be useful for research concerning manipulating objects in a virtual world. We plan to study in the case of "active touch", and based on those results, we will develop a new haptic interface in VR environments [15-16].

Acknowledgments

The authors would like to thank Dr. Yasuyoshi Sakai, Executive Vice President of ATR Institute International (Chairman of the Board of ATR Media Integration & Communications Research Laboratories), for his thoughtful advice and encouragement regarding this research. The authors also wish to thank Dr. Haruo Noma and the colleagues who voluntarily took part in discussing this study, and all the subjects for their cooperation during the experiments.

References

[1] Kishino, F.: "Communication with realistic sensations through Integrated Multi-media Environment", US-Japan Workshop on Integrated Comprehension and Generation System (Dec. 1991).

[2] Kishino, F., Miyasato, T., and Terashima, N.: "Virtual Space Teleconferencing "Communication with Realistic Sensations", Proc. 4th IEEE International Workshop on Robot and Human Communication (RO-MAN'95), pp. 205-210 (July 1995).

[3] Miyasato, T., Kishino, F., and Terashima, N.: "Evaluation of a Virtual Space Teleconferencing System with Eye Contact during Meetings with Position Movements" (In Japanese), IEICE Trans. vol. J79-A, no. 2, pp. 518-526 (Feb. 1996).

[4] De Silva, L. C., Miyasato, T., and Kishino, F.: "Emotion Enhanced Face to Face Meetings Using the concept of Virtual Space Teleconferencing", IEEE Proc. of International Conference on Multimedia Computing and Systems, MUTIMEDIA '96, pp. 128-33 (June 1996).

[5] Miyasato, T., Kishino, F., and Terashima, N.: "Evaluation of a Virtual Space Teleconferencing System with Eye Contact", Electronics and Communications in Japan, Part 3, vol. 80, no. 3, pp. 64-72 (1997).

[6] Miyasato, T., Kishino, F.: "An Evaluation of Detection of Objects Pointed through a Video Screen", VSMM '96, pp. 323-328 (Sep. 1996).

[7] Iwata, H.: "Artificial Reality with Force-Feedback: Development of Desktop Virtual Space with Compact Master Manipulator", Computer Graphics, vol. 24, no. 4, pp. 165-170 (1990).

[8] Brooks, F. P., Jr., Ouh-Young, M., Batter, J. J., and Kilpatrick, P. J.: "Project GROPE: Haptic displays for scientific visualization", Computer Graphics, vol. 24, no. 4, pp. 177-185 (Aug. 1990).

[9] Takemura, H., Tomono, A., and Kishino, F.: "A Study of Force Feedback in Virtual Workspace" (In Japanese), Proceedings of IEICE Conference 1991 (Spr. 1991).

[10] Kotoku, T., Komoriya, K., and Tanie, K.: "A Force Display System for Virtual Environments", Proceedings of IEEE International Workshop on Robot and Human Communication, pp. 1-3 (Sept. 1992).

[11] Yoroizawa, I., Takikawa, K., Okubo, S., and Watanabe, Y.: "Subjective Effects of Talker Echo and Transmission Delay in Video Conferencing via Communication Satellite" (In Japanese), IEICE Trans. vol. J64-B, no. 11, pp. 1281-1288, (Nov. 1981).

[12] Satoh, T., Tomono, A., and Kishino, F.: "Allowable Delay Time of Images with Motion Parallax, and High Speed Image Generation", SPIE vol. 1606 Visual Communications and Image Processing '91, Image Processing, pp. 1014-1021 (1991).

[13] Morii, K., Kishino, F., and Tetsutani, N.: "Evaluation of a gaze using real-time CG eye-animation combined with eye movement detector", HCI international '93, pp. 1103-1108 (1993).

[14] Morii, K., Kishino, F., and Tetsutani, N.: "A Study on CG Eye-Animation and the Feeling of a Gaze" (In Japanese), IEICE Trans. vol. J78-A, no. 4, pp. 512-522 (Apr. 1995).

[15] Noma H., Miyasato T., and Kishino F. : "A palmtop display for dextrous manipulation with haptic sensation", Proceedings of CHI '96, pp. 126-133 (1996)

[16] Noma, H., Kitamura, Y., Miyasato, T., and Kishino, F.: "Haptic and Visual Feedback for Manipulation Aid in a Virtual Environment", ASME International, DSC-Vol. 58, Proceedings of the Dynamic Systems and Control Division, pp. 469-476 (Nov. 1996).

"KhepOnTheWeb" : An Experimental Demonstrator in Telerobotics and Virtual Reality

Olivier Michel, Patrick Saucy and Francesco Mondada
Laboratory of Microcomputing
Swiss Federal Institute of Technology
Lausanne, Switzerland
Fax: ++41 21 693 5264
Olivier.Michel, Patrick.Saucy or Francesco.Mondada@di.epfl.ch
http://diwww.epfl.ch/lami/team/michel, saucy or mondada

Abstract

Research in mobile robotics often requires heavy investments in time and money. Mobile robots are still quite expensive and complex. Moreover, experimental set-ups need important preparations. Despite the fact that the number of researchers using real robots is growing, a good robot is still an important investment that many research groups cannot afford. For those groups that can afford a such equipment, the comparison of the results with other researchers is quite impossible due to the impact of the environment and the type of robot on the results. The goal of our work is to make complex mobile robots and environments available from a computer network, like Internet or ATM, for instance. This remote access could help in doing less expensive experiments and comparative benchmarks on a unique set-up. This paper presents a first set-up installed on Internet and used to demonstrate some possibilities of remote control of a Khepera mobile robot. Moreover, a virtual reality model of this experimental set-up has been developed in order to allow distant experimenters to get familiar with the system and to prepare experiments in virtual reality before accessing the real robot. The observation of the first users and the feedback on the development give important indications about the usability and the relevance of such a new tool for mobile robotics.

1 Introduction

In the scientific community, researchers are used since years to remotely access, via standard communication networks, unique or expensive structures, like supercomputers, important databases, unique information resources or the World Wide Web (shorlty, the Web), the email box or the ftp servers full of software.

Some experiments have been made to check the possibility to remotely access to unique or expensive physical devices using actual information networks [1]. The final goal of a such development has been, for instance, the creation of virtual laboratories, physically distributed over several countries, but having communications facilities that make them very near each to each other [6]. Despite the growing number of such experiments, we are still in a phase where those environments are made to test the actual possibilities, without a real use as a working tool. We know some Swiss projects in this field that have failed to move to the operational phase, due to a large number of limitations, spanning from the network possibilities to the kind of user interface.

In a similar way, some experiments have been carried out to make physical devices available on the Web. A very famous example is the "Mercury project" [4]. This kind of experiment is also very useful in the sense that it gives important information about the reactions of the users, the kind of equipment needed and the constrains that both have to deal with.

Due to the recent advances in computer horsepower, especially applied to computer graphics, simulations in robotics are becoming more and more used. On one hand, robotics companies are getting more and more interested by the new technologies available in the fields of virtual reality and computer networking. For example, Robot Simluation Ltd. provides a robot library of VRML models for more than 150 industrial robots. This library is available for free on the Web [5]. On the other hand, some software companies are currently developing new tools for animating and controlling vitual reality environments, making use of the recently approved VRML2 standard [2]. A demonstration of a robot arm controlled by a Java applet is available on the Web site of VRUniverse [9].

0-8186-8150-0/97 $10.00 © 1997 IEEE

2 Aims of the project

The goal of our project[1] is very similar to the first group of experiments described in the Introduction: our aim is to provide, through network communication facilities, one or more complex and unique mobile robotics set-up to the scientific community.

The main motivations are both economic and scientific. On one side, this kind of equipment is very expensive and could be shared between several research laboratories to reduces the expenses. On the other side, the comparison between different approaches in the field of mobile robotics can be made only on equipments where all conditions are perfectly identical. This do not only means that the robot has to be the exactly the same, but also that the environment has to be identical, in all details like light conditions or colour and type of floor.

The fact to have a common shared environment could be scientifically a great advantage for the understanding of the actual control approaches. Moreover, the availability of a virtual model of the experimental set-up provide an easy-to-use approach to the real set-up and can be used to prepare real experiments.

The goal and the motivation of this project fit very well with the activity of our lab, which is specialised in the development of mobile robots and tools for the research in control algorithms. The commercialisation of the miniature mobile robot Khepera, developed in our laboratory, is one of our major results in this direction. More than 170 universities and research centres in the world are equipped with this miniature mobile robot at the moment. The remote experimentation is the logic extension of this activity.

In a first exploratory phase, the goal or our work is to understand the possibilities available with the actual technology, the reaction of potential users and the requirement for the equipment used in this kind of set-up. For this reason we have chosen to make a first set-up available on the Web. In comparison with other similar projects, our set-up want to have some additional features:

- The device controlled has to be a mobile robot equipped with a on-board camera. This is already the case of some other set-up that are partially available [8][3].
- Unlike all other mobile robots set-up, KhepOnTheWeb run continuously, all the day and night, without the need of external support.

[1] This project, called "Sharing of Unique or Expensive Equipment for Research and Education: The Remote Manipulation Paradigm" is part of the Swiss Priority Programme SPP ICS of the Swiss National Foundation.

Figure 1: Khepera equipped with a video camera and looking into a mirror.

- The interface has to have a life video feedback and run in a standard Web environment.
- A virtual reality model of the experimental set-up is available, so that the user can get familiar with the user interface and the controls of the mobile robot.

3 KhepOnTheWeb Description

For this experiment, the choice has been made to use our miniature mobile robot Khepera equipped with an on-board CCD camera. The robot is placed in a maze and connected to a PC through a wired link. An additional camera is set on the ceiling, looking at the maze. The PC controlling the robot is equipped with a frame grabber for the image acquisition and is connected to Internet. A server provide "real-time" visual feedback to the user, who access to the information from Netscape. The user can switch between the robot camera and the external camera using the user interface. The virtual model of the robot features the same user interface as the real one, and hence the user can select a view from one of the two cameras.

3.1 Khepera: a miniature mobile robot

Khepera is a cylindrical robot 55 mm in diameter and of variable height. This miniature mobile robot has been developed by E. Franzi, A. Guignard, and

F. Mondada [7]. The size of Khepera lets the experimenter to realize a large environment on a limited surface. For this robot, indeed, a normal table of 0.9 x 1.8 m represents the same relative working surface of a tennis court for a standard size robot (55 cm in diameter). The space available over the table corresponds to a 6-floor-high building for a standard robot, which lets us to employ a suspended cable for power supply without disturbing the robot movements; we can also place a camera observing the environment without need of large-angle lenses.

In its basic configuration (two lower layers of figure 1) Khepera is made up of two layers corresponding to two main boards: the sensory-motor board and the CPU board.

The motor system consists of two lateral wheels and two pivots in front and back. This configuration is very good for facing complex geometric obstacles because the robot can turn in place without displacement.

The sensor system of the basic robot, also placed in the lower board, is composed by 8 infrared proximity sensors. These sensors can also be used as simple passive infrared light sensors.

The CPU board encloses the robot's processor, a Motorola MC68331. An RS232 serial line make it possible to communicate with an host computer. On the same cable, a wire provides power supply from an external power supply.

In our configuration, the basic Khepera has been extended with a CCD video camera. The video signal is send, by two additional wires, to the host computer equipped with a frame grabber.

3.2 Physical set-up

The robot has been placed in the maze shown in figure 2. The maze is made in such a way that the visitor can see various effects. In a general way, the walls are higher than the robot, so that the visitor has to move around to visit the maze. Just some walls in the middle of figure 2 are lower that the others. The wall placed on the left in figure 2 is a mirror, so that the visitor can see the robot in it. On the top right in figure 2, a ramp allow to the visitor to look outside the maze.

For an user coming for the first time in the maze, it is quite difficult to understand the geography of the environment. For this reason, and also because of the general interest to have an external view of the experiments, we have added, on the top of the environment, a mobile camera that can look to the maze. The complete set-up is shown in figure 3.

A flexible cable fixed over the maze connects the

Figure 2: Maze where Khepera can move. The size of the maze is 65 x 90 cm.

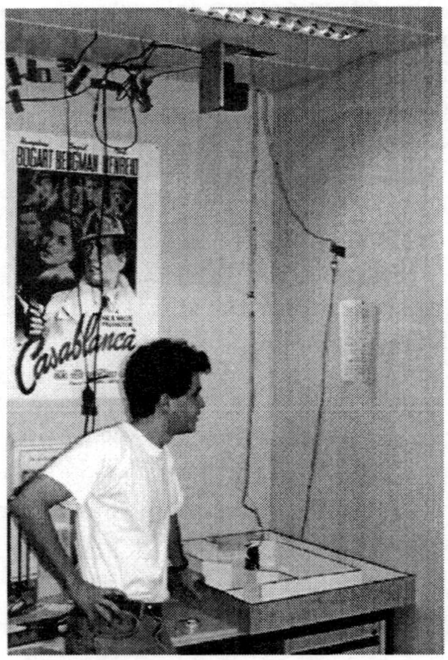

Figure 3: The complete set-up is composed by the robot placed in the maze (bottom right) and connected to a PC through a wired link. On the top of the maze, an external camera (black) can give a global view to the visitor.

Khepera robot to a PC computer equipped with a frame grabber. The cable supports the RS232 serial line for the communication between robot and PC, the power supply for the robot and the video signal coming from the camera placed on the robot.

The external camera mounted on the top of the maze is also connected to the PC by an RS232 serial line for the control of the position and the zoom of the camera. The video signal coming from this second camera is also placed as input of the same frame grabber, using an analogue multiplexer. By switching this multiplexer, the user can choose between the robot view and the external view.

The PC runs a Web server and some software which performs the several tasks necessary for the control of the set-up:

- A program grabs continuously the images and put them in the memory of the PC in JPEG format.
- The Web server gives the access to all pages required by clients that connect to it.

  As soon as a client access to the control page, the server starts a program that sends continously the images stored in memory, using the server-push mode, supported by Netscape. The stream of JPEG images makes the video flow for the visual feedback of the visitor.

  When the visitor clicks on a command, the server starts a program that analyses and executes the command. Three types of commands are available:

  - Commands to control the movement of the robot. In this case the program called by the server just send the orders to the robot using the RS232 serial line connected to the robot.
  - Commands to control the movement of the external camera. Also in this case, the program called by the server just send the orders to the camera using the RS232 serial line connected to the camera.
  - Commands to switch the camera. In this case the program called by the server acts on the multiplexer present at the input of the frame grabber.
- A Java script running on the client sends some requests of information about the state of the robot. A program on the server answers to these requests and get the information, if needed, from the robot, using the RS232 serial line.

To allow only one user to control the robot, a mechanism of exclusion is implemented. A timout disconnects the user after a given amount of time.

3.3 Graphical User Interface

The interface at the level of the client includes all possible operations that can be made on the robot, on the external camera and on the multiplexer. The complete window available under Netscape is shown in figure 4. The interface is composed by three columns, corresponding to the three types of commands that the user can perform: Video control and feedback, camera control (orientation and zoom) and robot control (position and speed).

The column in the middle includes the visual feedback, the control of the camera switch and the display of the status of the robot.

On the right column, two different control panels allow to send commands to the robot. The upper control panel allows to give displacement commands. By clicking on the graduation, it is possible to control the amplitude of the movement or of the rotation. The same type of interaction is used in the lower part, but to control the speed of the robot.

On the left column it is possible to control the orientation (pan and tilt) and the zoom of the external camera. Also in this case, the value is given by clicking on the graduation.

4 Virtual model

4.1 Overview

The virtual model of KhepOnTheWeb uses the same graphical user interface as the real KhepOnTheWeb. The images appearing in the camera view area look synthetic comparing to the ones coming from the real camera (see figures 4 and 5). The Khepera status is not reported since the interaction between the simulated robot and the user is very fast.

The HTML page contains a VRML scene (namely, `KhepOnTheWeb.wrl`) appearing on the center of the page and three Java applets: one on the left hand side (external camera control), one on the right hand side (robot control) and one in the middle below the VRML scene (switch between cameras). The applets display the same images as the ones displayed in the real KhepOnTheWeb, so that the user interface is very similar to the first one.

4.2 VRML scene

The VRML scene was written in VRML2 using a simple text editor and the specification manual of VRML2. It includes the mobile robot Khepera defined as a VRML `Transform` and the maze featuring textured shapes like the logo plates set on its walls

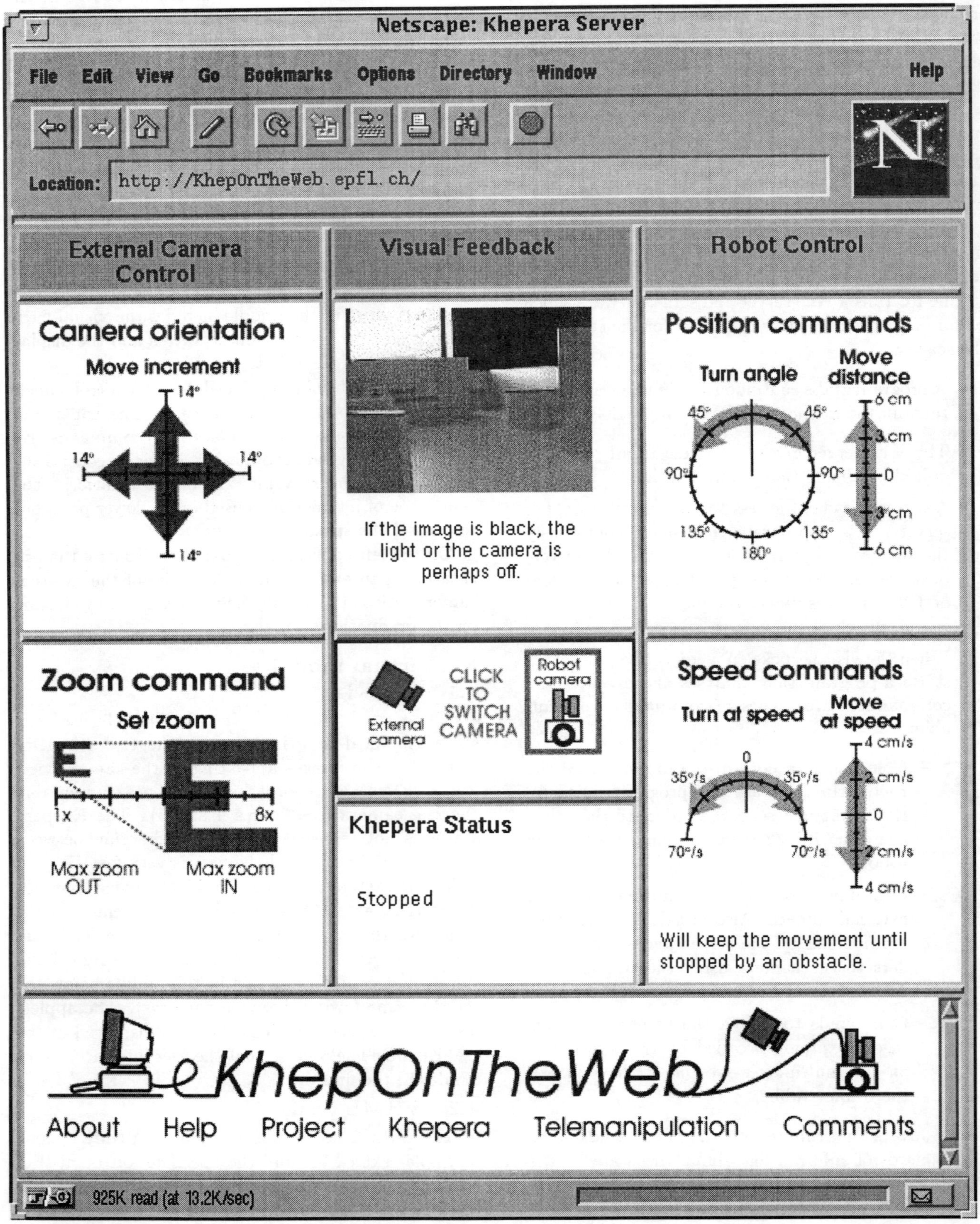

Figure 4: The remote control interface for the real robot under Netscape Navigator.

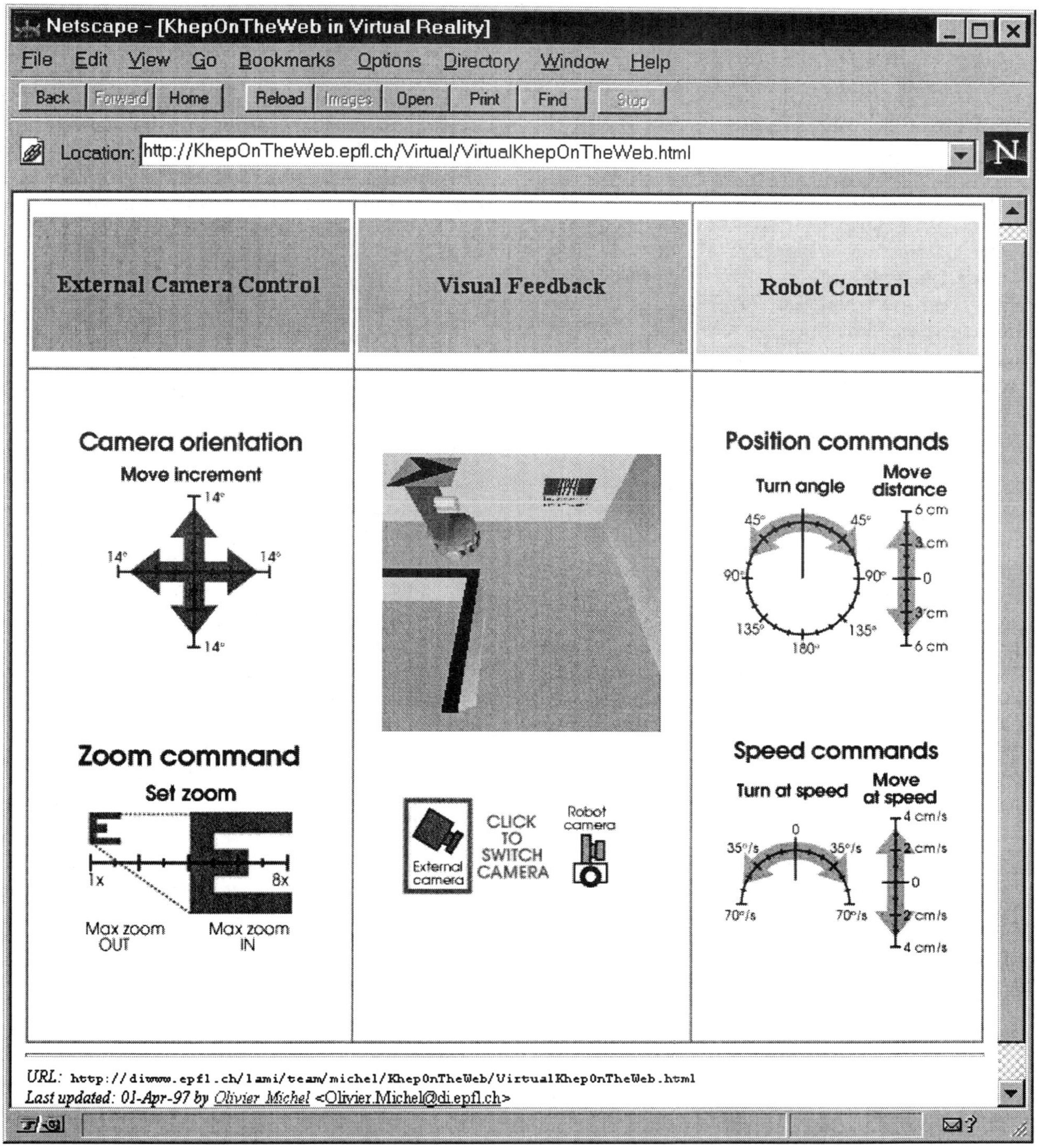

Figure 5: The remote control interface for the virtual robot under Netscape Navigator on a PC with Windows'95.

(LAMI, EPFL, IA and Khepera logos) as well as red arrows lying on the ground and indicating the inclination. Two view points are defined: one on the top of the scene corresponding to the camera above the maze and the other inside the robot itself, corresponding to the robot's onboard camera.

4.3 Java applets

Each applet receives click events from the user and sends VRML events to the VRML scene. Such an interaction between VRML and Java was made possible by a using a special Java package (vrml external interface) available from the Silicon Graphics since January 21, 1997 at `http://vrml.sgi.com/moving-worlds/spec/ExternalInterface.html`. This package allows Java applets to send events to VRML nodes and also to receive events from VRML nodes. It works only with VRML2. Hence, to move the robot on the scene, the Java applet needs to send a `set_translation` event to the Group node corresponding to the mobile robot. Rotation is achieved by sending `set_rotation` events to the robot Camera choices were made possible by sending a `set_bind` event to the View node corresponding to the camera the user wants to select.

Moreover, the use of a VRML2 time sensor allowed the simulated robot to run in real time. Such a time sensor is included in the VRML scene and sends events each simulation tick to the applet controlling the robot movement. Each event passes the current time with a high precision to the applet so that the applet can compute the new position of the mobile robot according to this time value. This approach provides a interesting advantage: the mobile robot runs on real time. In other words, a speed of 4 cm/s chosen by the user makes the robot actually move at four centimers per second in its simulated environment, independently from the horsepower of the host computer. Of course powerful computer will provide a better image quality mainly due to a better frame rate. Some tests performed on a Pentium 166 showed a very nice fluidity in the animation.

In order to prevent the mobile robot from running through the walls of the maze, it was necessary to implement a series of tests. These tests check continuously whether the coordinates of the robot enter the forbidden areas corresponding to the neighboorhood of the walls. Although VRML2 provide a number of sensors for the navigation into VRML scenes, we could not use them because they are relative to the current view: if the onboard camera is selected, the robot can detect collisions but if the external camera is selected, collision detection becomes impossible.

4.4 Implementation

Since VRML2 specifications were approved recently, very few VRML2 plugins and browsers are available at the time we developed the virtual KhepOnTheWeb. We used a beta version of the Silicon Graphics CosmoPlayer available for WindowsNT and Windows95. The vrml external interface package (also very recent) is only supported by Netscape Navigator. Hence, the only systems on which the virtual KhepOnTheWeb can be experienced are WindowsNT and Windows95 (and possibly Silicon Graphics Irix, but we didn't test it) running Netscape Navigator with the CosmoPlayer plugin. Since all components are available for free and Windows systems are widely used, a large public can access the virtual KhepOnTheWeb. Anyway, it is expected in the near future that the new technologies we used are going to be supported by an increasing number of systems.

5 Early feedback

This interface and this set-up are not really the first we have tried. We have started in 1995 developing a control interface based on a videoconferencing software. This first attempt gave interesting results, but the software was running only on Macintosh, and this was a major disadvantage. We tried some other solutions before coming to a pure Web interface, and this last solution seems to have many advantages:

- Netscape is a very standard software available on many machines. At the moment of writing this article, Explorer do not support the push server necessary to send the video feedback.
- The graphic possibilities and the interactivity on an HTML page are good, and the use of Java remove all limitations.
- Despite the heavy approach of continously sending complete images to the client, the performances are interesting.
- The availability of a virtual reality model makes the set-up easier to understand by novice users and allows experiments to be prepared in virtual reality before accessing the real robot.

Once decided to have a pure Web interface we have started to program and build the environment. The first results where interesting at the technical level, but the reactions of the first users have been very bad, due to the interface available in this first prototype. Many experiments on new users have been made at this stage to understand their needs and to define a better interface. The result of this definition, merged

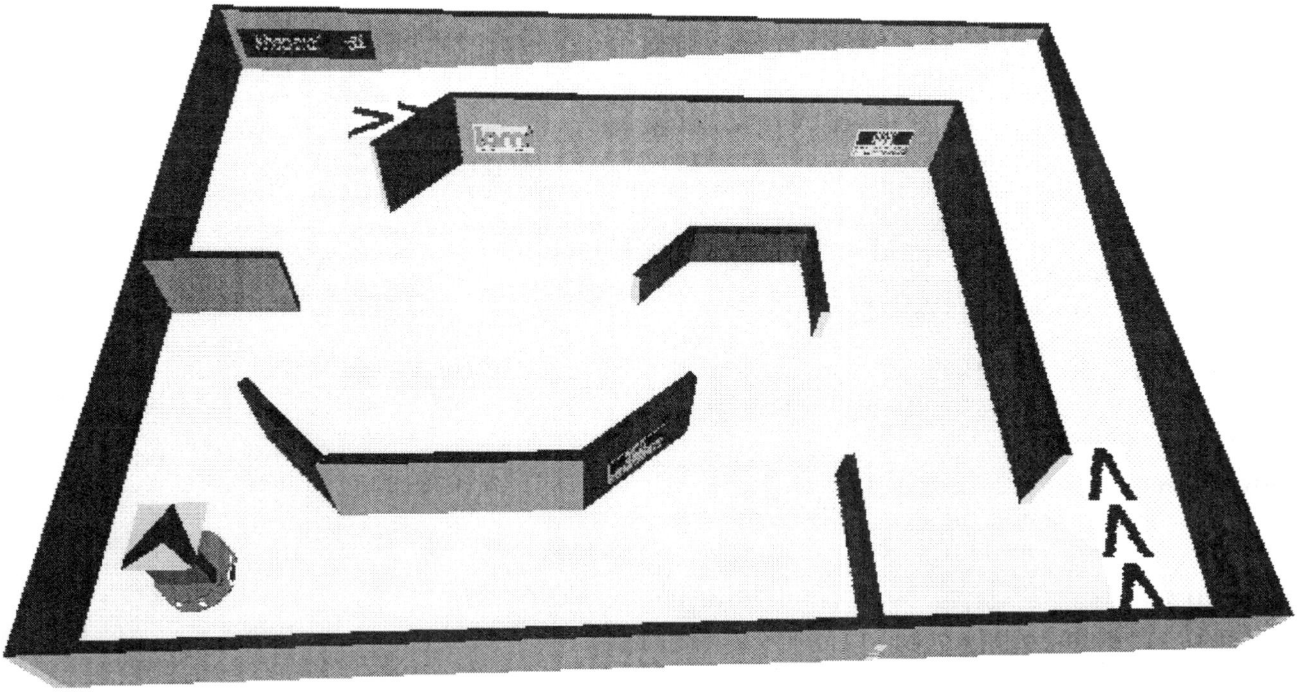

Figure 6: A view of the VRML scene including the robot and the maze.

with some technical limitations, has given the interface presented in figure 4. The use of colours, not visible in this paper, helps also to associate the right control panel with the right operation. Finally we have spent more time on the design of the interface than in all other engineering parts. In order to simplify the understanding of the system, the same user interface was choosen to develop the virtual reality model of KhepOnTheWeb.

Although the virtual implementation of KhepOnTheWeb could never replace the real experimentation, it turned out to be much more interactive than the real one. This property comes from the fact that every component of the virtual KhepOnTheWeb is downloaded and executed on the local host. Hence, once everything is donwloaded (i.e., Web page, Java applets and VRML scene), the user gets a very high execution speed depending only upon its computer horsepower and not upon the network performance. This very high interactivity makes it easier for novice users to discover the features of KhepOnTheWeb. Moreover, it also provides a powerful tool for preparing real experiments.

6 Conclusion

The server is open to public access on the Web at the following address: `http://KhepOnTheWeb.epfl.ch/`. Both the real and the virtual set-ups are available from this site.

The experience accumulated in our first tests shown some important aspects. Such a physical environment is technically feasible with commercial parts. Everything, from the robot to the camera, from the server to the frame grabber, are very standard commercial products. Moreover, it is very likely that the virtual reality technology used here is going to become increasingly widespread on the Web and hence very accessible. The real problem comes from the fact that Web surfers often prefer to "click and wait" than to "read and click" ; hence, it is very difficult to introduce a complex set-up. A great effort has to be made to build a user friendly interface, very intuitive and without the need of complex explanations. Nowadays, the software engineers must be able to create good quality control panels and visualisation tool, but also to provide simple interfaces and strong interactivities in order to make their softwares appreciated by the end users and finally used! The Web is going to be more and more used by industrial designers looking for productivity and demanding more and more interactivity. This is an important aspect that we will take into account in our further developments.

In addition to the features presented here, the next set-up will allow to program and monitor every action of the robot. Moreover new simulation tools allowing an easy circulation of robot controllers over the Internet could serve as a basis for designing a standard protocol for networked mobile robotics.

Acknowledgements

We would like to thank Edo Franzi and André Guignard for important work in the design of Khepera. We thank very much also Jean-Daniel Nicoud and all the LAMI assistants that have tested our interfaces for their useful comments.

References

[1] *Robotics and Machine Perception*, 5, 1996. Special Issues (1 and 2): Networked Robotics.

[2] ISO/IEC CD 14772. The Virtual Reality Modeling Language Specification Version 2.0. `http://vag.vrml.org/VRML2.0/FINAL/`.

[3] J. A. Fryer. Remote-control experiments using a networked robot. *Robotics and Machine Perception*, 5, issue 1:12, 1996. Special Issue: Networked Robotics.

[4] Goldberg K. A telerobotic garden on the world wide web. *Robotics and Machine Perception*, 5, issue 1:4, 1996. Special Issue: Networked Robotics.

[5] Robot Simulation Ltd. `http://www.rosl.com`.

[6] M. Mitsuishi, T. Hori, T. Hikita, M. Teratani, T. Watanabe, H. Nakanishi, and B. Kramer. Experiments in tele-handling and tele-machining at the macro and micro scales, using the internet for operational environment transmission. In *Proceedings of the 1995 IEEE/RSJ Int. Conf. on Intelligent Robots and Systems*, pages 13–20, Pittsburg, USA, 1995.

[7] F. Mondada, E. Franzi, and P. Ienne. Mobile robot miniaturization: A tool for investigation in control algorithms. In *Proceedings of the Third International Symposium on Experimental Robotics*, Kyoto, Japan, 1993.

[8] R. Simmons. Where in the world is xavier, the robot? *Robotics and Machine Perception*, 5, issue 1:5–9, 1996. Special Issue: Networked Robotics.

[9] VR Universe. `http://www.vruniverse.com`.

VR and Virtual Humans

Animated Interactive Fiction: Storytelling by a Conversational Virtual Actor

J. Piesk, G. Trogemann
Department of Computer Science, Academy of Media Arts Cologne, Germany
piesk@khm.de, trogemann@khm.de

Abstract

This paper presents an architecture for interactive storytelling using state-of-the-art-technology in natural language processing, speech synthesis and 3D-character animation. A conversational 3D-character is used to tell nonlinear stories interactively. Our research focuses on multimodal conversation that combines verbal-vocal with nonverbal-nonvocal natural language. We present a framework for synchronizing speech with facial movements, gesture and body posture by combining findings from linguistics and psychology. The interaction process incorporates the parsing of a textual natural language utterance, the emotion-based triggering of a textual response and its vocal and visual performance - speech synthesis linked with lip-synchronous generation of facial expressions and gestures.

Keywords: virtual actor, natural language processing, real-time 3D-character animation, autonomous agents, facial animation, nonverbal communication, nonlinear storytelling.

1 Introduction

Autonomous 3D-characters have been developed for two purposes: In multimodal user interfaces [1] [2] the computer becomes an anthropomorphic personal assistant. The second purpose is entertainment. Synthetic characters inhabit virtual worlds and interact with each other and the user [3] [4].

Nonlinear storytelling using conversational 3D-characters is a new approach to interactive entertainment. Our framework merges *autonomous 3D-character animation* with *nonlinear storytelling* incorporating selected principles from *computer linguistics* and *psychology*.

The characteristics of the system presented in this paper are:

- The interactive story emerges from the semi-autonomous behaviour of a virtual actor during the dialogue with a user. The autonomy is constrained by a nonlinear plot structure that is extended by a chatting mode.
- The virtual storyteller acts the way he does because he follows a script. There are however degrees of freedom in choosing different paths in the nonlinear story structure and taking minor detours while chatting about specific topics.
- The plot structure, chat topics and the 3D-character are designed by professional authors.
- The user participates as the interlocutor of the semi-autonomous character that tells the story.
- The user is guided by the utterances of the virtual actor in the dialogue.

A powerful approach to the problem of animation is demonstrated in [5] by providing tools for scripting complex behaviours. However, coming up with the appropriate communicative behaviours and synchronizing them with an actual conversation still remains a challenge. This paper focuses on the conjunction of verbal natural languages with nonverbal behaviour in the context of storytelling using an *autonomous 3D-character*. The intermediate textual representation is enacted by the 3D-character using both verbal-vocal and nonverbal-nonvocal natural language. The spoken language output is produced by a voice synthesizer. The nonverbal behaviour comprises lip-movements, facial expressions, gesture and body posture.

This concept has been designed for future *interactive television*. Virtual actors performing live in television shows should be able to interact autonomously with individuals of the target group. The scenario includes an author writing stories that are produced and performed automatically by an autonomous 3D-character during the conversation with the user. At periodic intervals (e.g. each week) a new story is written by one or more authors.

We implemented our ideas in a protype system called AIF-system (Animated Interactive Fiction). The AIF-system works with a conversational cactus (figure 7) who tells "Alice's Adventures in Wonderland" [6]. The 3D-character has been designed for live performances in german youth television. The story has been rewritten as an *interactive dialogue script* by the authors focusing on representing nonlinear narrative structures[1] in the hypertextual structure of the dialogue script.

This paper is organized as follows: Chapter 2 describes the way our approach combines principles of hypertext fiction with techniques from chat programs. In chapter 3 the story is integrated in a framework for audiovisual performance of individual sections of text using the virtual actors verbal and nonverbal communication skills. Chapter 4 describes the implementation of the AIF-system. An overview of future directions is shown in chapter 5. Chapter 6 gives a summary and concluding remarks.

2 Textbased Human Computer Conversation: Chatting in Hypertext

Most *natural language parsing systems* have been developed for special purposes such as natural language interfaces for databases inquiries (e.g. railway information desks, question answering systems). Dialogue systems [7] [8] have been developed as descendants of the ELIZA program [9]. These *chatterbots* use word pattern matching and answer templates for conducting dialogues about a special domain, which remains unchanged throughout the conversation. The textbased part of our approach to natural language interaction with virtual actors combines methods used by chatterbots with the principles of hypertext fiction.

In *hypertext fiction*, links between paragraphs offer the user freedom to choose between different paths, in most systems by clicking on marked words or icons. Some of them incorporate a keyword parser that matches keywords against the user input [10]. A successful match displays the text of the connected paragraph. The story structures have different degrees of nonlinearities. The approach of writing hypertext scripts allows the addition of high quality literature to natural language interaction with autonomous virtual actors.

2.1 Expectation Driven Natural Language Analysis

Nonlinear storytelling systems based on hypertext implicitly make use of changing story levels. The story level has an impact on the word patterns that are to be matched against the input string and the possible hyperlinks that are activated by a matched word pattern. Each story level has its own set of word pattern. The principle of word pattern matching has been introduced by [9] and adopted by [7] [8]. This dynamic adaptation of word patterns caused by the advancing story level extends the principle of word pattern matching by an *expectation based parsing algorithm.* In the highest level of our analysis we consider only word patterns that are likely to be used by a potential user. The search space is reduced to context-relevant utterances. Using an efficient hashing algorithm the production of an appropriate answer is not time critical.

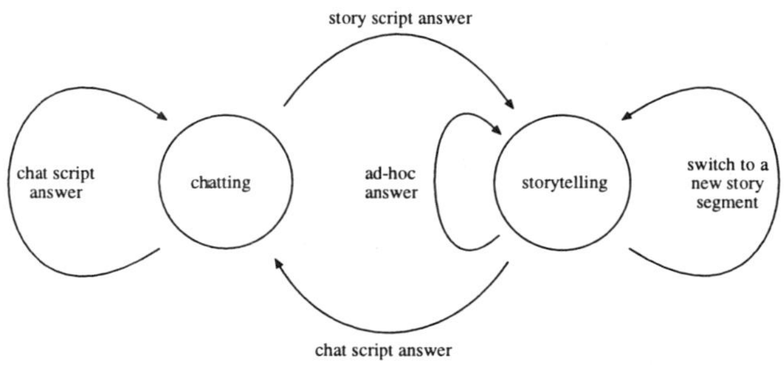

Figure 1: Two global states of the AIF-system: chatting and storytelling.

2.2 Strategy for Natural Language Understanding

It is the author's task to write an *interactive dialogue script.* An interactive dialogue script contains a dialogue with the part of one of the interlocutors being unknown during script writing. The unknown role is anticipated by the author and fulfilled by the recipient of the story at run-time. The author writes an utterance for his character and anticipates possible reactions. Assuming that the recipient is immersed in the story by the convincing nature of the character they will react in one of the anticipated ways. The author classifies the anticipated answers into semantic categories and identifies a common word pattern (the invariant part) for each category. The author has to discover what the recipient of the story (a typical member of the target group) is likely to ask or say. The key is to identify a common word pattern for each group of utterances that should lead to the same system reaction. By doing this he unifies a variety of possible user utterances to one semantic representa-

[1] The written version of Carrolls fary tail are based on conversations of Lewis Carroll with his niece Alice, a nonliear dialogue structure.

tion. This approach of identifying the invariant part of a group of utterances dealing with the same meaning has been termed *computational behaviourism* by [11]. The invariant part of a semantic category is the word pattern used for analyzing the user's textual input. The author specifies a reaction rule for each semantic category.

If the user does not react with an anticipated utterance we consider small *chatting detours* as an appropriate handling mechanism.

2.3 Storytelling with minor chatting detours

Our approach involves a script interface. This enables an author to write an interactive dialogue script without having specific programming skills. There are two kinds of scripts - one for *nonlinear story structures* and the second for *chatting*. In case of a communicational mismatch in the process of interactive narration, the virtual actor starts a small chatting sequence to bring the user back to the story context (figure 1).

The program performs a prewritten script by a professional author, who writes both the story's macro structure (narrative structure) and its micro structure (contents of single story segments). This allows interactive fiction to be of literary quality. Stories for this framework should have a nonlinear narrative structure.

2.4 Emotion-based Control of Text Generation and Animation

We propose the implementation of an emotional state E that influences the performance of a story segment. The emotional state E should be created out of the path taken in the nonlinear story structure. The psychologist Izard [12] identified nine basic emotions (interest, joy, surprise, sorrow, anger, disgust, contempt, fear, and shame). All emotional nuances can be represented by combinations of these basic emotions. While writing the story segment the author specifies a numerical value imp_i for each basic emotion i that is provoked by the presented narrative situation. Each emotional value specified for a story segment is a contributing factor in the calculation of the virtual actor's emotional state E as he tells that story segment. The actual intensity em_i of basic emotion i is computed at run-time by summing up all emotional impulses imp_i of previously activated segments:

$$em_i = \sum_{j=0}^{n} g(j, imp_i) \qquad \forall em_i \in E, j \in \mathbb{N}_0^+$$

j specifies the temporal distance between the previously activated segment and the current segment measured by the number of intervening segments. n is the number of basic emotions. $g(j, imp_i)$ delivers the contribution to em_i of an impulse imp_i from a distance of j segments. With a greater distance the contribution should be reduced:

$$g(j, imp_i) > g(k, imp_i) \qquad \forall j, k \in \{\mathbb{N}_0^+ | j < k \leq n\}$$

The emotional state E influences the way in which the storytelling character presents the content of the story segment in terms of text, speech, facial expression, gesture and posture.

3 Synchronizing verbal and nonverbal behaviour

We study animation of autonomous 3D-characters from the point of view of the animator. This means that we formalize the rules which an animator uses implicitly while telling a story by means of a 3D-character using both verbal and nonverbal language.

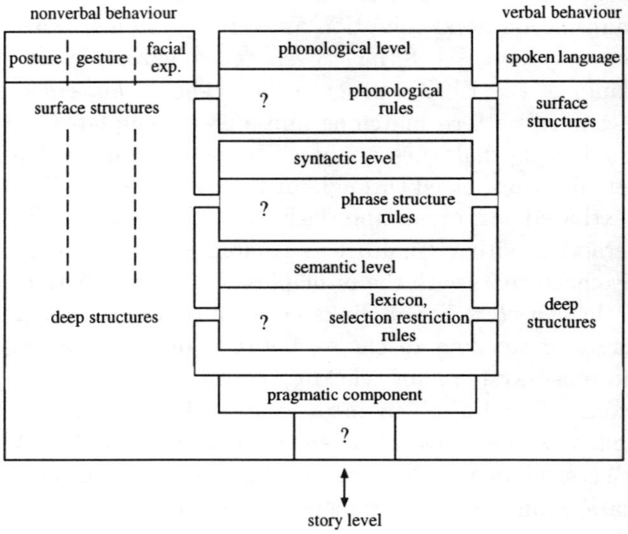

Figure 2: A theoretical model for establishing synchronization rules for verbal-vocal language and nonverbal behaviour.

3.1 Nonverbal Behaviour

The rules of verbal natural language are motivated by implicit syntactic and semantic agreements of a cultural group. Nonverbal behaviour is much more bound to and influenced by personal traits instead. Current research in communication psychology [13] tries to discover that part of nonverbal behaviour which is independent of personality. So far rules for the implicit psychological semantics of nonverbal behaviour have not been formulated. Although there are gestures and facial expressions that are understood nationally or worldwide (waving hello, a happy/sad face) most subtle semantic nuances of nonverbal behaviour are only interpreted in the right way if one knows the expressing person quite well. For cartoon characters idiosyncratic communicational signals are especially important. Some of these signals are modelled on animal behaviour (e.g. ear wiggling), others are purely fantasized by the cartoonist or animator. Our approach to autonomous animation of virtual actors views the characters as a whole: commonly understood nonverbal behaviour is combined with behaviour peculiar to the character. We aim to formalize the rules an animator uses implicitly during the process of animating a character.

3.2 Multimodal Dialogue

Verbal and nonverbal natural languages have been studied in linguistics and psychology. Verbal languages have evolved as the preferred intracultural communication medium. The use of the analytical levels *syntax*, *semantics* and *pragmatics* proposed by [14] are common in linguistics. Computer linguists use the sophisticated grammatical and lexical rules for developing natural language understanding and generation systems. Many psychologists, e.g. [15], [16], [17], use (explicitly or implicitly) the same analytical levels for the study of nonverbal behaviour. Our approach to autonomous character animation is based on the assumption that verbal and nonverbal behaviour can be synchronized on phonological, syntactic, semantic and pragmatic levels.

Chomsky's theory of transformational grammars distinguishes between *surface structure* and *deep structure* of sentences. The latter contains the information necessary for interpreting the sentence correctly. The surface structure defines the right word order of a sentence. *Transformational rules* map the surface structures bidirectionally onto the deep structures. Following Chomsky's theory of generative transformational grammars [18], figure 2 shows a theoretical model for establishing rules for the synchronization of speech with nonverbal behaviour. The pragmatic component deals with story segment, hypertextual links, mental concepts, ideas, etc. Confronted with new input from its environment (e.g. the user)

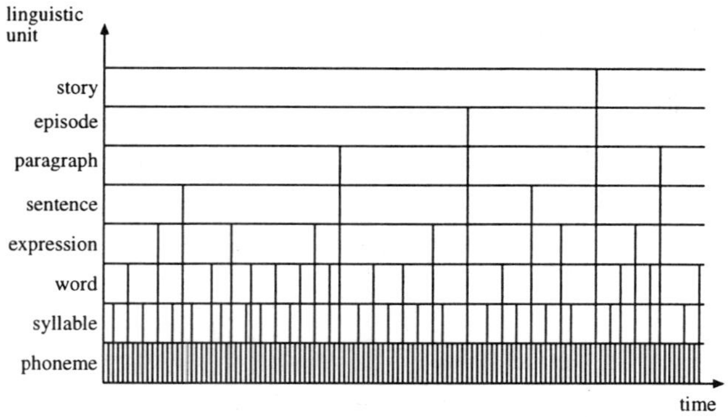

Figure 3: Linguistic units with different cycles of change.

the character selects a story segment with appropriate structures of verbal and nonverbal behaviour. For performing spoken language, gesture and facial movements, these deep structures have to be transformed into synchronized surface structures - the audiovisual output perceived by the user. This synchronization is performed on phonological, syntactic, semantic and pragmatic levels.

The question marks in figure 2 mark our research focus. Known strategies for natural language processing have to be linked to their equivalents for gesture and facial expression. Those linkage rules involve decisions such as "Should a semantic content be expressed verbally, use gesture or facial expression, or a combination of these?"; "Should meaningful words be stressed vocally and accentuated by gestures?", etc. Some rules are known from disciplines such as phonology, psychology, and cartoon animation. Some examples taken from [17]: raising the eyebrows or nodding the head on an accented syllable or a pause (syntactic functions); wrinkling the nose while talking about something disgusting or smiling while remembering a happy event can substitute for a word or refer to an emotion (semantic functions). The pragmatic level unifies body language with verbal natural language and connects the communication aspect with the story level. The emotional state E proposed in this paper synchronizes the nonverbal behaviour of the 3D-character with the content of the spoken language.

3.3 Synchronizing Speech with Gesture and Facial Expression

The first step for establishing a rule system for synchronized verbal and nonverbal behaviour of autonomous 3D-characters is to study the translation

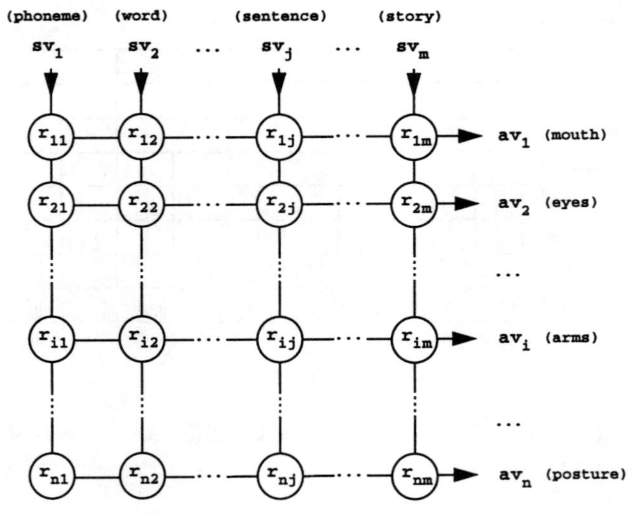

Figure 4: Translation system from text to animated speech.

from the textual representation into vocal language and nonverbal behaviour. We assume that body movements and voice intonation are determined at each point of time by the current phoneme, syllable, morpheme, word, linguistic expression, sentence, paragraph, episode, and story. Each linguistic unit influences verbal and nonverbal surface structure to a different degree. The linguistic units change their value at different frequencies (figure 3). The challenge is to formalize the influence of each linguistic unit on each physical movement of the character and to discover linkages between these influences that can be mathematically defined. Figure 4 shows these translation from text to animated speech. We implement lexica that assign animation rules to each control variable sv_j. These rules translate the input values into abstract values for $rule_{ij}$. The animation rule for $sv_{phoneme}$ = "a", e.g., is:

$$rule_{mouth,phoneme} = \text{``}open''$$
$$rule_{i,phoneme} = \text{``}neutral'' \; \forall i \in \{\mathbb{N}^{+} | av_i \neq mouth\}$$

Each animation variable av_i interpretes the abstract value of the animation rule $rule_{ij}$ individually. If the value r_{ij} is connected additively, the $rule_{ij}$ = "neutral" is translated into $r_{ij} = 0$. If the connecting operation is multiplication $r_{ij} = 1$ would be appropriate. The animation function for the mouth opening is e.g.:

$$av_{mouth} = r_{mouth,phoneme} * (r_{mouth,syllable} + r_{mouth,word} + r_{mouth,episode} + r_{mouth,story})$$

4 Current Implementation

The architecture of the current implementation (figure 6) comprises three modules. The *text module* translates the textual input into an output string. The *animation module* generates appropriate movements and synchronizes the *visualization module* and the *voice synthesizer* "Hadifix" [19].

4.1 Text Module

Viewed as a black box the text module seems like most systems for hyperfiction or chatterbots: a small textfield for the user input and a larger text area for output. The text module in itself can not show the emotional state that is being computed after each interaction. The representation of emotions is the task of the animation and visualization modules on a later processing level. The text module uses the emotions to choose between different ways of expressing the content of a paragraph textually.

The *script parser* of the AIF-System creates a nested structure of objects containing the textual strings and word patterns specified in the parsed scripts.

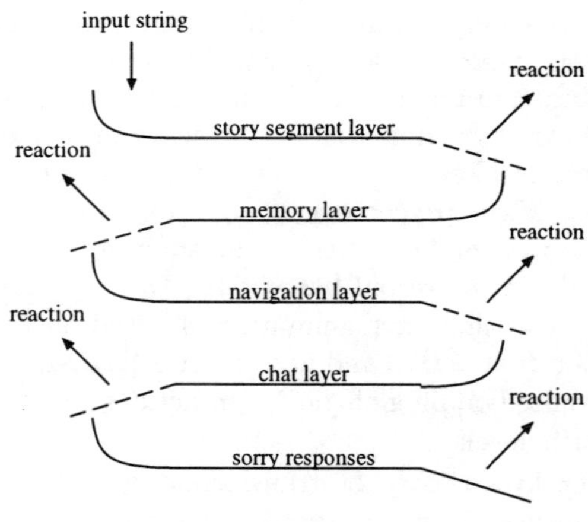

Figure 5: Miniexperts organized in prioritized layers.

The object structure is organized so that a group of objects form a "miniexpert", a small expert system for a special limited knowledge domain of the corresponding paragraph. These miniexperts are organized in prioritized layers (figure 5). The principle of a prioritized layer system of miniexperts is known from [7].

The *story segment layer* tries to find a matching word pattern and its corresponding segment in the current context of the story, as described above. AIF

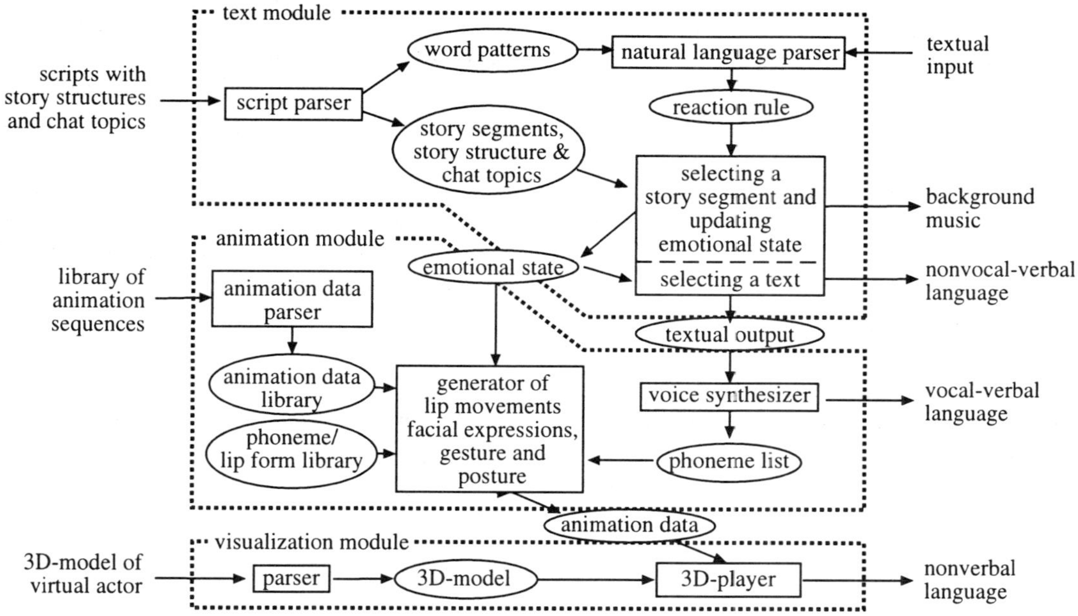

Figure 6: Architecture of the AIF-system.

analyses the textual input in the context of the current paragraph. Each paragraph has its own set of keywords and word patterns that are matched against the input string. *Priority stacks* are used in case of multiple matches. A successful match delivers a *reaction rule* that specifies one of the following:

(a) a simple text (spontaneous remark, additional explanations, etc.) that is recited without switching to a new segment,

(b) a text template that is filled with appropriate parts of the user's input string,

(c) a label that activates a new story segment, or

(d) a sequence of labels that invokes the corresponding segments without expecting an utterance in between.

The simple text contains for example less important but entertaining remarks or additional information referring to the current paragraph. It does not link to a new segment, nor does it update the emotional state E; the text is simply displayed. Reaction rule (d) activates the specified segments without waiting for a reaction from the user. Each activation has the same effect as reaction rule (c). As a new segment is activated, the system adds the emotional impulses imp_i of the new situation to the emotions that remain from the previous segments. The current emotional state E is computed by a weighted summing of all experienced emotions. The older the emotions are the less they contribute to the emotional state. For each basic emotion a numerical value is computed seperately using $g(j) = e^{-j}$:

$$em_i = \sum_{j=0}^{n} imp_i * e^{-j} \qquad \forall em_i \in E, j \geq 0$$

The emotion with the highest value determines the output text that is given together with the emotional state E to the animation module.

If the analysis in the context of the story segment fails, the input string is passed on to the *memory layer*. Here the path of previously activated segments is searched. The word patterns used for matching in the memory layer are different from the ones in the story layer. They are taken from different word pattern lexica and have different effects in the case of a positive match: the corresponding segment of a matched word pattern in the memory layer is not activated, a short summary of this segment is given and the activation stays at the current segment.

If the memory layer can not match the input string, it is passed on to the *navigation layer* that reacts on utterances intended as commands e.g. "tell the whole story from the beginning", "repeat the last paragraph" or simply "go on".

A matching word pattern in the *chat layer* leads to a switch to chatting mode (figure 1). In this case the analysis of the next interaction cycle does not start with the story layer but directly with the chat layer.

The system stays in this mode randomly for n interaction cycles. The value of n depends on the mood of the character. Frequent values are "n=2", "n=3" and "n=4".

A synonym lexicon is used to improve the method of word pattern matching. Furthermore the generation of answer sentences from templates requires word transformations to meet grammatical rules of the german language.

4.2 Animation Module

The text is synthesized and the spoken output is written to an audiofile. The sequence of phonemes is used to add the corresponding lipforms to the facial expressions that are generated together with body movements using libraries of animation data. The generator is based on the translation system shown in figure 4.

The generation of body movements is based on preproduced animation sequences stored in an *animation data library*. The methods and tools used to produce animation sequences for the library involve real-time recording with datagloves, a motion-capture-system and a modelling editor. This method of real time animation of 3D-characters has been developed by [20] [21] [22] for the purpose of live performances.

The movement generation module assembles an appropriate animation putting together sequences taken from the animation data library. The assembly rules stem from semantic and syntactic synchronization levels (figure 2). In the resulting sequence, adjustments are made to specific regions of the 3D-model to meet criteria of the phonological level, like synchronous lip movements or sudden movements of the hands. Emotional facial expressions are produced by a subsystem developed by [23].

The animation data produced by the animation module is used by the visualization module to animate the figure on the display. Both modules communicate by means of a shared memory area.

4.3 Visualization Module

The visualization module has read the data of the three-dimensional static appearance of the virtual actor during the start-up-phase of the AIF-system. The 3D-character used in the prototype system has 36 motion effectors (e.g. head up, mouth open, left arm up, etc.) that are controlled by the animation data. Each value is updated 25 times per second. A motion effector influences a group of triangles on the figures surface mesh, that defines the shape in three dimensional space. The mapping between 3D-data-points and each motion effector has been defined by the animator while designing the figure.

The virtual actor used in the current implementation is composed of approximately 4000 polygons. It is controlled via 36 motion effectors that in turn are connected to 178 basic expressions. Figure 7 shows the 3D-character of the current implementation - the conversational cactus telling the story of "Alice's Adventures in Wonderland".

Figure 7: Selected nonverbal behaviour of the conversational cactus.

5 Future Directions

We are continuously extending the script system and analyzing the degree of complexity required for improved conversational abilities. One question is to what extent a highly complex script system can be maintained by one author. Known Strategies from computer supported cooperative work (CSCW) can be used for distributed script authoring in teams of writers. Current work involves the development of graphical tools that enable the author to write non-linear story scripts more easily. These should incorporate facilities for grouping nodes and distinguishing between macro and micro structures in the linkage on different levels. We will try to feed the virtual actor with more than one story for developing strategies for domain switching.

The semantic classification into categories with a common invariant part is to be replaced by automated unification. A syntactic and semantic analysis that translates the textual surface structure into a meaning representation will be deployed as the unification algorithm. [24] is considered to be appropriate for the development of the meaning representation language.

The unknown implicit rules of an animator are formalized heuristically as yet. The *analytic approach* is based on the analysis of motion-frequencies. The changes of different linguistic units occur at different periodic intervals (figure 3). The influences of each linguistic unit on each motion effector can be separated using multi-resolution filtering methods and fourier transformation. For each motion effector the animator intuitively produces a text-synchronous animation curve. A fourier transformation of the data allows the separation of movements that stem from periodical changes occuring at different frequencies. The reverse fourier transformation delivers functional descriptions of influences that change at the specified separation frequencies. The frequencies with which a phoneme, syllable, word, etc. change are chosen as separation frequencies. The functional descriptions that are delivered by the reverse fourier transformation can be assigned to the linguistic units.

6 Summary and Conclusions

In our work, selected principles of natural language processing and hypertext fiction have been combined with methods from 3D-character animation to form a framework for interactive storytelling. Rules for the synchronization of verbal and nonverbal behaviour on phonological, syntactic, semantic and pragmatic levels have been implemented in the AIF-system. On the pragmatic level the character's emotional state connects the synchronized speech and body movements with the story level. The emotional state is influenced by previously experienced situations and adapts the behaviour of the virtual actor to the current path in the nonlinear story structure. The story is presented in a multimodal dialogue. The utterances of the user influence the path in the nonlinear story structure at each point of interaction. This approach allows the active participation of the user in the storytelling process.

References

[1] G. Ball et al. "Lifelike Computer Characters: the Persona Project at Microsoft Research", to be published in *Software Agents*, MIT Press, 1997, http://www.research.microsoft.com/research/ui/persona/home.htm.

[2] K. Nagao and A. Takeuchi, "Social Interaction: Multimodal Conversation With Social Agents", *12th National Conference on Artificial Intelligence (AAAI)*, 1994, pp. 22–28.

[3] J. Bates, A. Loyall, and W. Reilly, "Broad Agents", *Proceedings of AAAI Spring Symposium on Integrated Intelligent Architectures*, March 1991.

[4] B. Hayes-Roth, R. van Gent, and D. Huber, "Acting in Character", *Proceedings of AAAI Workshop on AI and Entertainment*, 1996, http://www-ksl.stanford.edu/projects/CAIT/publicity.html.

[5] K. Perlin and A. Goldberg, "Improv: A System for Scripting Interactive Actors in Virtual Worlds", *Computer Graphics Proceedings*, vol. 29, no. 3, ACM SIGGRAPH, August 1996, http://www.cat.nyu.edu/perlin/ publications.html.

[6] L. Carroll, *Alice im Wunderland*, Cecilie Dressler Verlag, Hamburg, 1989.

[7] M. Mauldin, "Chatterbots, Tinymuds, and the Turing Test: Entering the Loebner Prize Competition", *Presented at AAAI-94*, 1994, http://fuzine.mt.cs.cmu.edu/mlm/aaai94.html.

[8] K. Colby, *Artificial Paranoia: A Computer Simulation of Paranoid Process*, Pergamon Press, New York, 1975.

[9] J. Weizenbaum, "Eliza - a Computer Program for the Study of Natural Language Communication between Man and Machine", *Communications of ACM*, vol. 9, no. 1, 1966, pp. 36–45.

[10] M. Joyce, "Afternoon, a Story", Eastgate, 1987.

[11] T. Whalen, "Computational Behaviourism Applied to Natural Language", April 1996, http://debra.dgbt.doc.ca/chat/.

[12] C. Izard, *The Psychology of Emotions*, Plenum Press, New York, 1991.

[13] G. Bente and I. Otto, "Virtuelle Realität und parasoziale Interaktion: Zur Analyse sozio-emotionaler Wirkungen computer-simulierten nonverbalen Kommunikationsverhaltens", *Medienpsychologie: Zeitschrift für Individual- und Massenkommunikation*, vol. 3, Westdeutscher Verlag, Opladen, September 1996, pp. 217–242.

[14] C. W. Morris, "Foundation of the Theory of Signs", *International Encyclopedia of Unified Science*, vol. 1, University of Chicago Press, Chicago, 1938, pp. 77–137.

[15] P. Watzlawik, J. Beavin, and D. D. Jackson, *Menschliche Kommunikation*, Verlag Hans Huber, Bern, 1996.

[16] G. Bente, "Computersimulation nonverbalen Interaktionsverhaltens", *37. Kongreß der Deutschen Gesellschaft für Psychologie in Kiel*, 1990, http://www.uni-koeln.de/phil-fak/psych/diff/texte/comp1.html.

[17] J. Cassell et al. "Animated Conversation: Rule–Based Generation of Facial Expression, Gesture and Spoken Intonation for Multiple Conversational Agents", *Computer Graphics Proceedings*, ACM SIGGRAPH, July 1994, pp. 413–420.

[18] N. Chomsky, *Aspects of the Theory of Syntax*, MIT press, 1965.

[19] T. Portele, J. Krämer, and D. Stock, "A New High Quality Speech Synthesis System for German", *Proceedings of the CRIM/FORWISS-Workshop on Speech Research and Technology*, Munich, 1994, pp. 284–287, http://asl1.ikp.uni-bonn.de/ tpo/Hadifix.html.

[20] G. Fleischmann, R. Opalla, and A. Mähler, "Real-Time Animation of 3D-Characters", *Proceedings of the 96 European SMPTE Conference on Imaging Media*, Cologne, 1996.

[21] G. Fleischmann, "Performance animation: Über die Entfernung des Animators vom Einzelbild", *Formdiskurs: Zeitschrift für Design und Theorie*, vol. 2, January 1997, pp. 96 – 107.

[22] P. Kattwinkel, *Entwicklung eines visuell programmierbaren Bewegungstransformationssystems für die Performance Animation*, Diplomarbeit, Kunsthochschule für Medien Köln, Universität Dortmund, 1996.

[23] S. Bauckmann, *Emotionale Steuerung virtueller Charaktere*, Diplomarbeit, Kunsthochschule für Medien Köln, Universität Dortmund, 1996.

[24] E. König, "Lexgram - a Practical Categorial Grammar Formalism", *Proceedings of the Workshop on Computational Logic for Natural Language Processing*, Edinburgh, April 1995.

Developing Simulation Techniques for an Interactive Clothing System

Pascal VOLINO and Nadia Magnenat THALMANN
MIRALab, C.U.I., University of Geneva
CH-1211, Switzerland
Email : [thalmann|pascal]@cui.unige.ch

Abstract

In this contribution towards creating interactive environments for garment design and simulation, we present a powerful mechanically based cloth simulation system. It is based on an optimized way to compute elastic forces between vertices of an irregular triangle mesh, which combines the precision of elasticity modelisation with the speed of a simple spring-mass particle system. Efficient numerical integration error management keeps computation speed efficient by allowing high computation timesteps and also maintains very good stability, suitable for interactive applications. Constraints, such as collisions or "elastics", are integrated in a unified way that preserves robustness and computation speed. We illustrate the potentialities of our new system through examples showing its efficiency and interactivity.

Keywords : *cloth animation, mechanical simulation, particle systems, collision response, constraints, stability, interaction, garment design tools*

1. Introduction

In a step towards unifying cloth simulation to the wonderful universe of Virtual Reality and dreaming about a world where virtual humans could manipulate cloth in real time and in a way that seems so natural for us, real humans, we present a contribution for a fast and robust cloth model suited for interactive virtual cloth design and simulation system.

Literature now brings us several techniques for cloth simulation. Many of them present physically based models for simulating in a realistic way fabric pieces based on elastic deformation and collision response. The first of them used simple mechanically-based models, such as relaxation schemes, for simulating objects such as flags or curtains ([WEI 86], [HAU 88]). More general elastic models were developed for simulating a wide range of deformable objects, including cloth ([TER 87], [TER 88]). Recently, several particle system based models attempted to simulate simple cloth object realistically using experimental fabric deformation data ([BRE 94], [EBE 96]). These models claim to be fast and flexible, as opposed to finite element models ([COL 91], [KAN 95], [EIS 96]), which are very accurate, but slow and complex to use in situations where behavior models are complicated and where collisions create non-linearities and complex boundary conditions, thus not suited for interactive applications.

Dressing a virtual body is a complex application for these models. It involves the ability to design complex garment shapes, as well as a complex simulation system able to detect and to handle multiple collisions generated between the cloth and the body. Our work contributed to the development and evolution of this topic through several contributions ([LAF 91], [THA 91], [YAN 91], [CAR 92], [YAN 93]). More recently, we studied how to consider cloth as being an object that could be considered independently from the body which wears it, involving the issues of folding, wrinkling and crumpling, with all the associated problems related to collision detection and response ([VOL 95]). Our work was materialized by several garment design and dressing systems for animated virtual actors ([WER 93], [THA 96]).

On the other hand, new V.R. technologies and efficient hardware open a very attractive perspective for developing interactive systems where virtual actors would interact autonomously with mechanically animated objects, such as the garment they themselves wear. In a nearer goal, we could take advantage of these new tools for interactively designing garments and dressing virtual actors in ways that are much more natural and close to the "real" way of manipulating fabric.

With this article, we provide simulation tools to take a step towards the requirements defined above. Of course, the main problems for interactive or real time mechanical

0-8186-8150-0/97 $10.00 © 1997 IEEE

simulation are related to computation speed issues. We should not however trade away design flexibility and mechanical modelisation accuracy that would lead to unrealistic cloth simulation. Thus, we describe here a mechanical model that allows to modelise elastic behavior of cloth surfaces discretized into irregular triangle meshes, and which is not much more complicated to a simple spring-mass modelisation. This approach combines the flexibility obtained in [VOL 95] with simulation speeds aimed in [EBE 96] and [HUT 96] which are restricted to regular meshes. Furthermore, a suited integration method has been associated to this model to maximize simulation timesteps and computation speeds without trading away mechanical stability, which is ensured in a very robust way, compatible with all the inaccuracies resulting from most tracking devices used in 3D positioning and V.R. devices.

Beside this, a new approach for handling geometrical and kinematical constraints (such as collision effects or "elastics"), generalization of the collision response process described in [VOL 95], ensures collision response as well as integration of different manipulation tools in a robust way that does not alter simulation efficiency and thus makes this system efficient for interactive purposes.

We illustrate the achievements brought by these techniques with the help of examples concerning cloth manipulation, dressing and realtime interactive manipulation.

2. A mechanical model suited for interaction

The mechanical simulation system is the core of a physically based cloth animation system, and also the most time consuming part. Our main contribution has been to improve the speed and robustness of the associated computation, first on the mechanical model itself (2.1), then on the integration algorithm and the associated numerical error managements (2.2), and finally on the constraint management, including collision response (2.3).

2.1. A fast and robust, yet realistic elastic model

The first problem of particle-system based models is to compute accurately the forces deriving from internal elasticity applied on each vertex.

2.1.1. What has been done until now

The simplest, and fastest method is to consider the surface as being a mesh of vertices, each one linked to its neighbors by a damped spring, forming a structure usually called "mass-spring" structure. Such models have already extensively been used for simple and fast cloth simulation ([PRO 95], [HUT 96]).

Most of these models rely on a regular grid. In [BRE 94] and [EBE 96], a square grid is used to compute tension, shear and bending. Internal forces are then computed using precise models resulting from experimental data. Mesh regularity is extensively used to keep geometrical properties easily computed in an accurate way. In [PRO 95] and [HUT 96], bending and shear effects are simply modeled by extra diagonal springs. However, our goals require non regular meshes as a basis for cloth structure. We need to be able to model complicated cloth shapes that may contain high curvature with as few elements as possible, and our interactive design process (cutting, seaming, local topology or size modifications) highly relies on a very general and multi-purpose triangular mesh structure.

In [VOL 95] and [THA 96], we have proposed a model derived from particle system models which computes the mechanical deformation state in each triangle elements of such an irregular mesh. By computing contributions from the edge elongations, compression and shear strains of the triangle material are found in local coordinates by solving a linear system, in a way similar to a stress rosette computation [TIM 82]. This model allowed a precise modelisation of an elastic material, taking into account the Young modulus and the Poisson coefficient, along with other parameters concerning viscosity and plasticity. However, this computation was quite expensive, as it required complex geometrical evaluations with the construction of local coordinates in each triangle element. At the opposite, the simplest spring and mass system, in which the forces applied on each vertex directly derives from the elongation of each edge connected to it, is very simple to compute, but would merely modelise more than a simple elastic material with a Poisson coefficient unrealistically high, unsuitable for any realistic cloth deformation.

Thus, our contribution is to define a new way to compute the forces applied on the vertices, comparably simple to the basic spring-mass system, but which allows precise modelisation of the Young modulus and the Poisson coefficient, which are the basic parameters of an elastic material.

2.1.2. The proposed elastic model

Let's consider a triangle $(\mathbf{P_a}, \mathbf{P_b}, \mathbf{P_c})$ in which deformations have elongated its edges from rest length $(\mathbf{L_a}, \mathbf{L_b}, \mathbf{L_c})$ to the current length $(\mathbf{l_a}, \mathbf{l_b}, \mathbf{l_c})$ (Fig. 1). In a simple elastic spring-mass model, each edge would attract its vertices to reach its rest length, and impose a displacement along its main direction, proportionally to the amount of elongation from the rest length. Please refer to the Annex for detailed formulas.

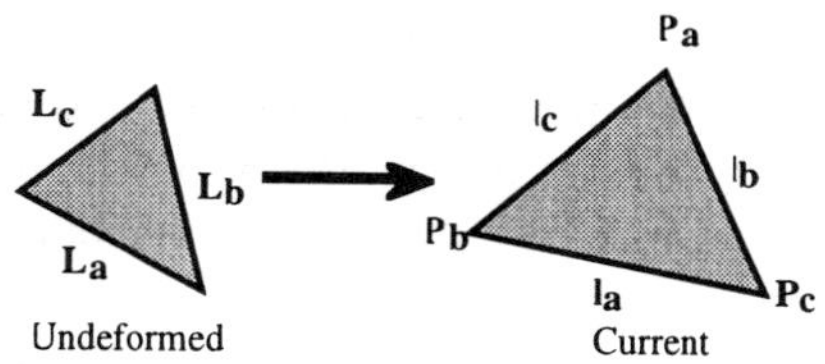

Fig. 1: Deforming a triangle element.

Quite easy to compute, this model does not however reflect the actual forces when a "full material" triangle gets deformed. Each deformed edge will produce a force component along its direction, which is usually not the deformation direction, as in the example shown in Fig. 2. The resulting effect is an extra orthogonal deformation similar to the one produced by the Poisson coefficient, but which produces unrealistic effects especially when the triangles are not equilateral (irregular meshes or high deformations).

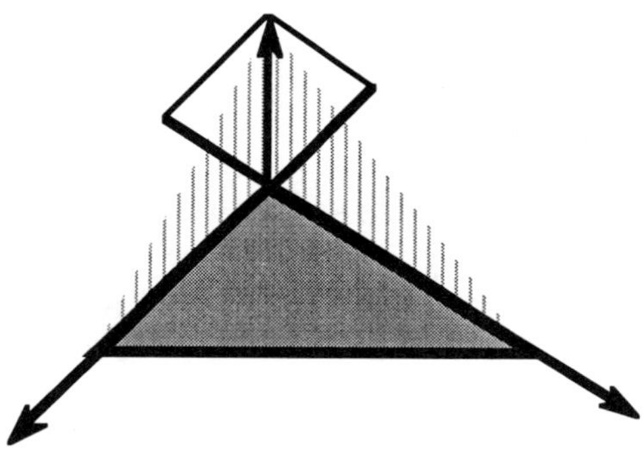

Fig. 2 : Vertical compression stretches the triangle horizontally.

The main idea of our new model is to recompute the individual elongation contribution of each edge of the triangle by taking into account the interdependence of the displacements that would be generated by each of them in their respective directions. Thus, the combined effect of the edge forces based on these corrected displacements will produce a more accurate constraint situation.

In the situation shown in Fig. 3, if we suppose that the length of the edge **J** varies an amount of $\mathbf{d_j}$, its extremity points $\mathbf{P_i}$ and $\mathbf{P_k}$ will be displaced in its direction by a amount proportional to $\mathbf{d_j}$, weighted in function of the values $\mathbf{M_i}$ and $\mathbf{M_k}$, the *inverse* mass of $\mathbf{P_i}$ and $\mathbf{P_k}$. The elongation contribution on edge **I** is then the displacement of the point $\mathbf{P_k}$ multiplied by the cosine of the angle between the two edges, $\mathbf{c_k}$. We linearize the problem by supposing that the edge angles do not vary significantly. **(i, j, k)** are all the permutations of **(a, b, c)**.

As we would like the final length variation of the edge **I** to be the value $\mathbf{l_i\text{-}L_i}$, we equal this to the sum of the elongation contributions of the three edges **I, J** and **K** individually would elongate at an amount of $\mathbf{d_i}$, $\mathbf{d_j}$ and $\mathbf{d_k}$. Doing this on the three edges simultaneously yields a linear system of three equations with three unknowns ($\mathbf{d_a}$, $\mathbf{d_b}$, $\mathbf{d_c}$), shown in Annex B (4).

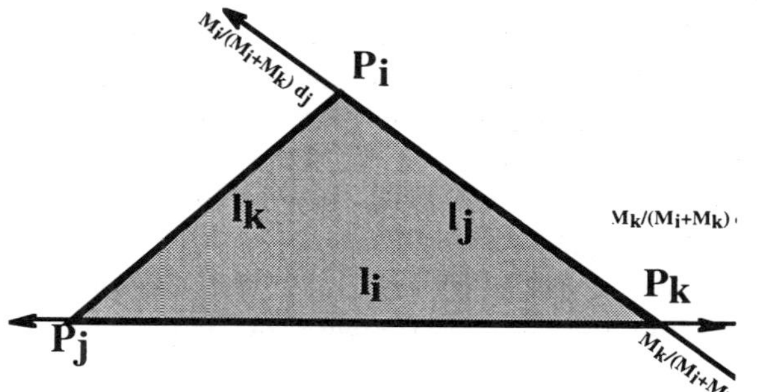

Fig. 3: Computing the elongation effect of the edge **J** on the direction of the edge **I.**

Solving the system leads to values of ($\mathbf{d_a}$, $\mathbf{d_b}$, $\mathbf{d_c}$), that, if applied altogether, would contribute to deform the triangle to its equilibrium state. After some variable substitutions, we obtain the force values shown in Annex B (7).

When working with almost regular meshes, we can make the approximation that all the vertices of the mesh have approximately the same mass. This yields the force values shown in Annex B (10). This assumption has proved experimentally not to alter much the behavior of the simulated elastic material in most usual situations dealing with cloth simulation.

The main positive aspect of this model is its simplicity, as it is yet able to compute realistic elastic forces in irregular triangle meshes. It involves very few vector operations, by directly computing force contributions along the edge direction without the need of any local coordinate system. Experimental tests have shown that, included in a resolution system such as the one discussed later, iterations are about twice as slow as the most basic spring-mass system (which was implemented for comparison), but it yet provides a realism similar to what was obtained in our previous work ([VOL 95]) which involved much more complicated geometrical evaluations.

2.1.3. Dealing with robustness and simulating the Poisson coefficient

A realistic elastic model should compute forces depending on the material deformations as similar as possible to the actual constraints that would be produced in a real material. However, it is impossible to guarantee that the imposed deformations are themselves realistic, depending on how they were previously computed (inaccurate modeling, inaccurate simulation, imprecise input devices,...). A robust model should deal with all situations whatever unrealistic they are, without leading to situations where the computed forces become infinite or still worsen the deformations.

In order to prevent any "infinite force" configuration, we introduce the α coefficient, which indeed represents a linear interpolation factor between a simple spring-mass system ($\alpha = 0$) and the model described above ($\alpha = 1$) (see Annex B (1)). Setting $|\alpha| < 1$ prevents any position configuration to lead to infinite forces. Furthermore, the forces remain continuous functions of the vertex positions, which increases the simulation quality.

With $\alpha = 1$, our model simulates a fabric material with a null Poisson coefficient. The simple spring-mass model simulates a material with an unrealistically high Poisson coefficient, which highly depends on the shape of the triangles. In addition to stability, the α coefficient allows us to keep control on the Poisson coefficient of the simulated fabric, as shown in Fig. 4, which would require more calculations if it had to be integrated explicitely in the force computation formulas.

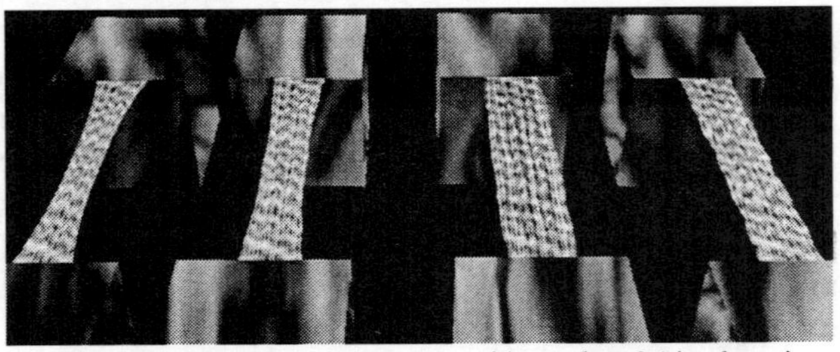

Fig. 4: A 400% stretched fabric square, with α values 0 (simple spring-mass system), 0.6, 1, 1.2 (transversal buckling).

2.2. Integrating motion equations

The dynamic system can be thought of as a huge ordinary second order differential equation system, where the variables are the positions for all vertices upon time. We may consider it as a first order system by taking as variables positions and speeds for all vertices. A numerical integration method is required for computing the evolution of the system with time.

In our previous work ([VOL 95], [THA 96]), we used an adapted midpoint method derived from the Euler formula that provided simple and quick calculation, while being adaptable enough to cope with highly nonlinear behaviors and direct handling of geometrical constraints, such as collisions. However, this method was not accurate enough, and could lead to numerical instabilities when dealing with important constraints and deformations. In order to increase numerical precision, we implemented a 4th order Runge-Kutta integration algorithm, adapted to the one described in [PRE 92]. The choice of this algorithm was motivated by several facts:

A) It only requires evaluation of the forces on the vertices depending on their positions and speeds at a given time, without any gradient evaluation, and the computation remains simple by implementing directly the formulas of part 2.1.

B) Current positions and speeds of all vertices are enough to describe the kinematical state of the system, as the integration procedure does not require any data from the previous system evolution. Position and speed may then be altered without disturbing the motion integration procedure.

C) With some adaptations, it offers an evaluation of the numerical error for the computed step, enabling efficient motion corrections and time step control.

A comparison of several integration methods has been presented in [EBE 96], showing the superiority of the Runge-Kutta method compared to more complex algorithms.

An adaptation of the Runge-Kutta method described in [PRE 92] yields the kinematical state of all the vertices of the simulated object along with an estimation of the error on this state.

This error may be used for adaptative timestep control, as done in [EBE 96]. However, for interactive applications where computation time is sensitive and where the timestep should be kept as high as possible, we would rather trade away precision for computation speed.

Whatever approximations we allow, we should ensure that the model keeps being stable and does not "explode" when becoming too imprecise. Our idea is to use the error estimations as a damping factor that would put the model in the lowest deformation energy state within the error range. Thus, we perform a kinematical correction on the position and velocity of the vertices accordingly, out of and after the dynamical computation process. This correction is performed on each edge by comparing and correcting the kinematical state of its extremity vertices.

A) The error on position values are compensated by modifying the vertex positions according to mechanical conservation laws to lead to the minimum deformation potential energy of the considered edge within the position error range.

B) The error on velocity values are compensated damping the vertex speed difference to lead with the minimum deformation kinetic energy of the considered edge within the velocity error range.

This correction technique ensures stability of the model even if mechanical damping parameters are very low, as mechanical deformation energy decrease is guaranteed by the corrections.

Obviously, if the error becomes too high and when it cannot be compensated by corrections, more standard timestep control schemes have to be implemented: The timestep is reduced and the dynamical process is recomputed if the error exceeds a given threshold, and the timestep is increased when the error becomes small.

As a result, we get a very robust simulation system that prevents deformation energy to increase because of numerical imprecision. Implemented using our mechanical model described in 2.1., which guarantees no singular situations where the forces become infinite, our model is almost impossible to break because of instability. This is particularly important when using inaccurate tracking devices for object manipulation in interactive or V.R. applications.

2.3. Handling dissipative forces, collisions and other constraints

In an approach introduced in [VOL 95], we handled geometrical constraints, such as those generated by collisions, using kinematical correction on the constrained elements: Positions and velocities were corrected according to the mechanical conservation laws to fit the constraints precisely. This approach permitted to skip the use of "potential walls" to enforce the constraints, which produced intense and discontinuous forces that could perturb the dynamical simulation. More recently, [EBE 96] used a similar way to handle friction effects.

Our new system generalizes this approach by giving a procedure for dealing with several types of constraints, such as collisions, but also seaming elastics described in 3., or some types of dissipative forces such as friction or high damping.

As mentioned earlier, the first motivation is to limit the value of the forces that are enforcing these constraints. These forces may be intense, thus participating to important energy transfer, and their discontinuity may lead to important simulation errors concerning their effects.

Constraint effects are split into three components:

A) An immediate correction on the position and velocities of the relevant vertices, taken into account before the dynamical simulation process, aimed to reflect the immediate effects of the constraint. Though less accurately simulated, damping effects integrated here are ensured to be perfectly dissipative, whatever their intensity, without altering the simulation.

B) A force correction in the dynamic simulation, that will attenuate or cancel the acceleration difference between the constrained vertices, in order to maintain the imposed kinematical constraints.

C) A force contribution in the dynamic simulation, when long-range constraints participate actively in the dynamics with continuous forces and durable effects. Along with force correction, it may be used for modeling an imposed acceleration constraint.

Our system implements several types of constraints:

Collision response is mainly a geometrical constraint imposing a minimum distance between two surface elements in contact. Position and velocity immediate correction (A) is performed in order to put the elements in an acceptable position and prevent their speeds to push them further together. Force correction (B) then enforces the maintaining of collision distances between iterations. Friction effects, which are usually intense, are simulated by velocity correction (A) and force correction (B) to simulate solid Coulombian friction. The collision detection aspect has been developed in our previous work [VOL 94] and [VOL 95].

Elastics are interaction tools introduced in [VOL 95] to permit seaming of cloth panels in a garment simulation system. An elastic attracts two vertices together and produces an attach point holding two elements together. In our previous work, they were simulated by adaptive forces that pulled the vertices together. However, their behavior were thus difficult to control and could lead to unpredictable results when interacting with collisions. Simulating them as kinematical constraints is the main improvement of our work. We use a combination of force correction and contribution (B) (C) to handle them as speed constraints producing a smooth acceleration toward the goal, parametrized by only one user defined time constant. They produce predictable results whatever the kind of objects they are attached to, and handling them along with collisions in an unique system makes them interact smoothly.

Damping is usually modeled by a force contribution (C) that opposes a speed difference. However, if damping is high (for example when dealing with non-linear models or solid friction), its effect will have time constants that may become much smaller than the simulation timestep, perturbing the simulation efficiency and accuracy.

Purely dissipative effects may then be simulated directly by a velocity damping (A) that is guaranteed to be dissipative whatever its intensity.

3. Results: Interactive tools for cloth design

Through the following examples, we illustrate the advances brought by our new system and the new potentialities concerning interactive cloth applications.

3.1. Interactive fabric manipulation

With our new model, interactive cloth manipulation is now possible, as shown by the following example. Here, we illustrate basic manipulations that are performed on a cloth element discretized to about 400 triangles. The display frame rate varies from 8 to 20 frames per second on a 250MHz R4400 SGI Indigo II, which is quite a comfortable speed for motion perception. Most of the time, the numerical approximation correction scheme allows us to perform the simulation with only one iteration per frame. The following figures are a sample of the system's interactive possibilities, the user performing actions that affect immediately and continuously the objects.

3.2. An improved clothing system

We take advantage of the new advances brought by algorithms in our software described in [VOL 95] and [THA 96], by highly improving the garment generation and simulation speed.

The following example illustrates how garments are assembled around the body and seamed together.

Fig. 5: Interactive cloth manipulation:

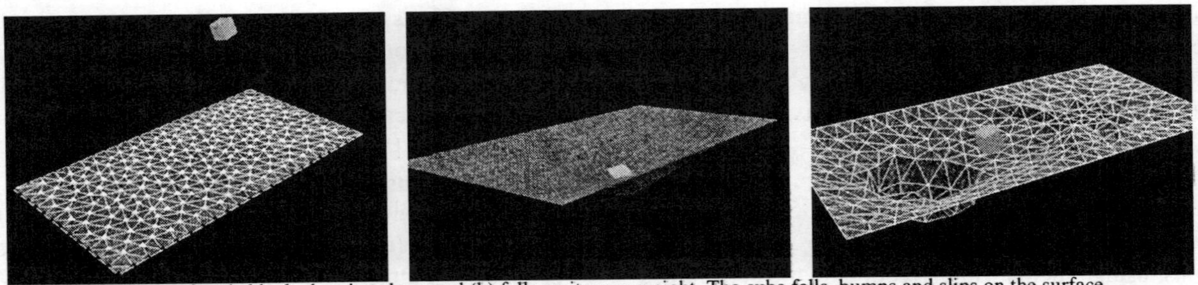

(a) The surface is blocked on its edges, and (b) falls on its own weight. The cube falls, bumps and slips on the surface.

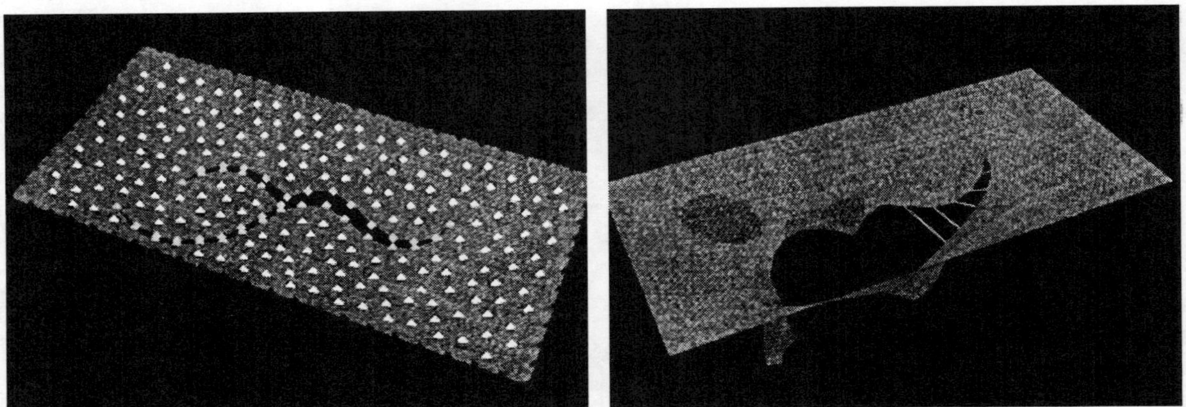

(c) The surface may be locally expanded or shrunk. (d) Cuts can then be performed. (e) Extra material can be removed.

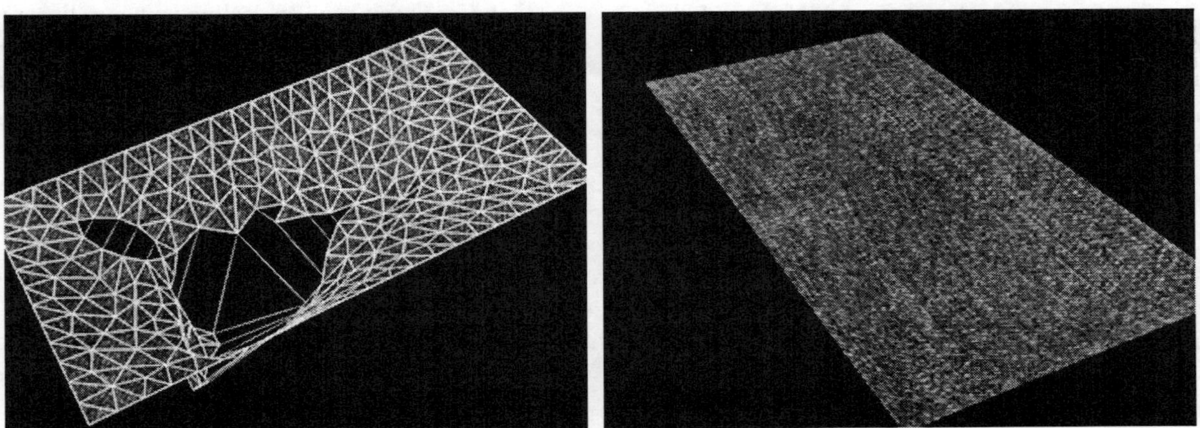

Elastics pull the surface borders together (f) and finally (g) seaming fills the holes.

Fig. 6: Dressing a virtual actor:

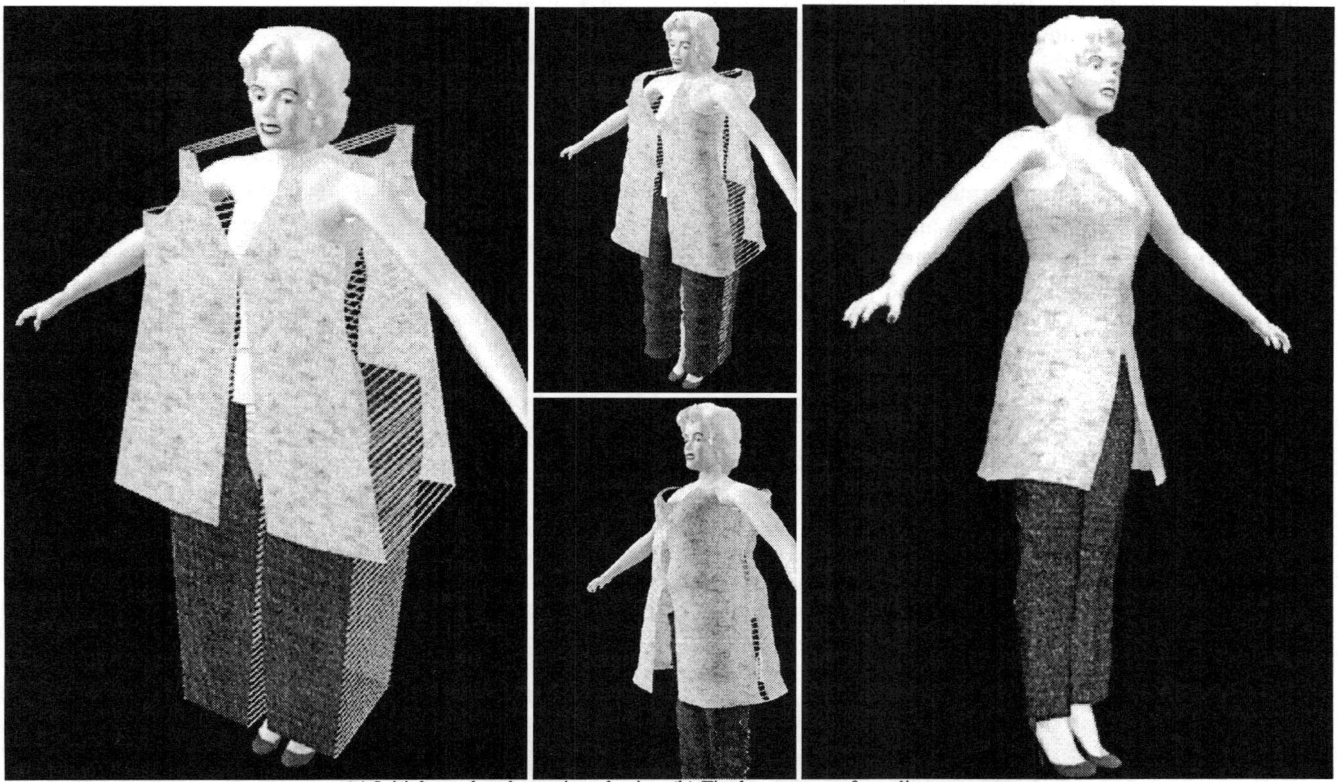

(a) Initial panel and seaming elastics. (b) Final garments, after adjustments.
Intermediate steps: after 5 seconds computation and after 20 seconds, ready for panel seaming.

The main improvements from the results of our previous work is the computation time. The results above were obtained on a 150MHz R5000 SGI Indy, and take into account mechanical simulation computation as well as full collision detection and self-collision detection. As soon as the cloth begins to fit the body, collision detection becomes the major computation weight, which reached more than 70% in this example. Implementing incremental collision detection algorithms could reduce this.

3.3. Using tracking devices for cloth manipulation

In a first attempt to use our clothing system with Virtual Reality devices, we adapted a Flock-of-Bird type tracking system to move cloth object held by some of its vertices. Direct manipulation of the object is then possible in real time, with the six degrees of freedom. Several trackers may be used simultaneously to manipulate several objects or several parts of a same object, enabling for example two-hand manipulation.

On a 250MHz R4400 SGI Indigo II, the "feeling" of interactive manipulation remains very good with objects of less than 300 triangles for which the display rate is about 10 frames per second, and a good quality realtime simulation is reached with objects of less than 100 triangles, where the display rate exceeds 40 frames per second. These computation times include full collision handling.

Yet, the system accomodates very well to noisy tracking signals and remains stable even when the noise becomes too high for interaction use. The system is robust enough to cope with a few erroneous values which would send the object far away during a few frames.

We are now developing more natural manipulation tools using for example datagloves. A grasping system is being implemented, enabling two-hand cloth manipulation, and therefore many new and exiting new possibilities for an interactive clothing system.

4. Conclusion

Interactive cloth applications represent a wide subject on the crossroad of image synthesis, human animation, cloth design and Virtual Reality. We brought a contribution by providing through this work a fast and robust mechanical simulation system. Not really more complicated than a simple spring-mass particle system, it however simulates quite accurately an elastic material discretized into any irregular triangle mesh. Associated with Runge-Kutta integration and using numerical error evaluations as damping position and speed corrections, our model is robust, and yet performant by keeping computation timesteps high. A powerful constraint integration scheme also provides a powerful way of handling collisions, as well as a general support for extra interaction and manipulation tools.

Suited for complicated garment simulations as well as for interactive clothing tools, applications may be extended in any direction of the crossroad. We demonstrated the model's efficiency by some simple examples showing the speed, robustness, flexibility, and adaptability for tracking devices and Virtual Reality applications.

We would now like to take advantage of these potentialities to push further in the direction of interactive clothing applications. First, a powerful set of virtual tools would allow us to design, assemble and manipulate garments in a very natural way, enabling us to visually "feel" the fabric material in the 3D space. Then, using our VLNET system [CAP 97], we are preparing tools and techniques for a collaborative interactive system where distant partners together design and fit a common dress on a virtual being.

Acknowledgements

We are grateful to the Swiss National Research Foundation (FNRS) for funding this project, as well as Stéphane Carion who is developing the V.R. tools and interface.

Fig. 7: Cloth manipulation with Virtual Reality tools.

Bibliography

[BRE 92] : **D.E. Breen, D.H. House, P.H. Getto**, *"A Physical-Based Particle Model of Woven Cloth"*, Visual Computer, 8(5-6), pp 264-277, 1992.

[BRE 94] : **D.E. Breen, D.H. House, M.J. Wozny**, *"Predicting the Drap of Woven Cloth Using Interacting Particles"*, Computer Graphics (SIGGRAPH proceedings 1994), Orlando, USA, pp 365-272, July 1994.

[CAP 97] : **T.K. Capin, I.S. Pandzic, H. Noser, N. Magnenat-Thalmann , D. Thalmann**, *"Virtual Human Representation and Communication in VLNET Networked Virtual Environments"*, IEEE Computer Graphics and Applications, Special Issue on Multimedia Highways, 1997 (to appear).

[CAR 92] : **M. Carignan, Y. Yang, N. Magnenat-Thalmann, D. Thalmann**, *"Dressing Animated Synthetic Actors with Complex Deformable Clothes"*, Computer Graphics (SIGGRAPH proceedings 1992), 26(2), pp 99-104, 1992.

[COL 91] : **J.R. Collier et al**, *"Drape Prediction by Means, of Finite-Element Analysis"*, Journal of the Textile Institute, 82 (1), pp 96-107, 1991.

[EBE 96] : **B. Eberhardt, A. Weber, W. Strasser**, *"A Fast, Flexible, Particle-System Model for Cloth Draping"*, Computer Graphics in Textiles and Apparel (IEEE Computer Graphics and Applications), pp 52-59, Sept. 1996.

[EIS 96] : **J.W. Eischen, S. Deng, T.G. Clapp**, *"Finite-Element Modeling and Control of Flexible Fabric Parts"*, Computer Graphics in Textiles and Apparel (IEEE Computer Graphics and Applications), pp 71-80, Sept. 1996.

[HAU 88] : **D.R. Haumann, R.E. Parent**, *"The Behavioral Test-Bed: Obtaining Complex Bevavior with Simple Rules"*, The Visual Computer, Springer-Verlag, 4, pp 332-347, 1988.

[HUT 96] : **D. Hutchinson, M. Preston, T. Hewitt**, *"Adaptative Refinement for Mass-Spring Simulations"*, Eurographics Workshop on Animation and Simulation, Poitiers, France, pp 31-45, Aug. 1996.

[KAN 95] : **T.J. Kang, W.R. Yu**, *"Drape Simulation of Wowen Fabric Using the Finite-Element Method"*, Journal of the Textile Institute, 86 (4), pp 635-648, 1995.

[LAF 91] : **B. Lafleur, N. Magnenat-Thalmann, D. Thalmann**, *"Cloth Animation with Self-Collision Detection"*, IFIP conference on Modeling in Computer Graphics proceedings, Springer, pp 179-197, 1991.

[PRE 92] : **W.H. Press, W.T. Vetterling, S.A. Teukolsky, B.P. Flannery**, "Numerical Recipes in C", Second edition, Cambridge University Press, 1992.

[PRO 95] : **X. Provot**, *"Deformation Constraints in a Mass-Spring Model to Describe Rigide Cloth Behaviour"*, Graphics Interface proceedings 1995, Quebec City, Canada, pp 147-154, May 1995.

[PRO 96] : **E. Promayon, P. Baconnier, C. Puech**, *"Physically-Based Deformations Constrained in Displacements and Volume"*, Computer Graphics Forum (Eurographics proceedings 1996), Poitiers, France, 15 (3), pp 155-164, Aug. 1996.

[TER 87] : **D. Terzopoulos, J.C. Platt, H. Barr**, *"Elastically Deformable Models"*, Computer Graphics (SIGGRAPH proceedings 1997), 21, pp 205-214, 1987.

[TER 88] : **D. Terzopoulos, K. Fleischer**, *"Modeling Inelastic Deformation: Viscoelasticity, Plasticity, Fracture"*, Computer Graphics (SIGGRAPH proceedings 1988), 22, pp 269-278, 1988.

[TIM 82] : **S.P. Timoshenko, J.N. Goodier**, "Theory of Elasticity", Third edition, McGraw-Hill Int. Editions.

[THA 91] : **N. Magnenat-Thalmann, D. Thalmann**, *"Complex Models for Visualizing Synthetic Actors"*, IEEE Computer Graphics and Applications, 11 (5), pp 32-44, 1991.

[THA 96] : **P. Volino, N. Magnenat-Thalmann, J. Shen, D. Thalmann**, *"An Evolving System for Simulating Clothes on Virtual Actors"*, Computer Graphics in Textiles and Apparel (IEEE Computer Graphics and Applications), pp 42-51, Sept. 1996.

[VOL 94] : **P. Volino, N. Magnenat-Thalmann**, *"Efficient Self-Collision Detection on Smoothly Discretised Surface Animation Using Geometrical Shape Regularity"*, Computer Graphics Forum (Eurographics proceedings 1994) Oslo, Norway, 13 (3), pp 155-166, Sept. 1994.

[VOL 95] : **P. Volino, M. Courchesne, N. Magnenat-Thalmann,** *"Versatile and Efficient Techniques for Simulating Cloth and Other Deformable Objects"*, Computer Graphics (SIGGRAPH proceedings 1995), Los Angeles, USA, pp 137-144, Aug. 1995.

[WEI 86] : **J. Weil**, *"The Synthesis of Cloth Objects"*, Computer Graphics (SIGGRAPH precoeedings 1986) 24, pp 243-252, 1986.

[WER 93] : **H.M. Werner, N. Magnenat-Thalmann, D. Thalmann,** *"User Interface for Fashion Design"*, IFIP trans. on Graphic Design and Visualisation, pp 197-204, 1993.

[YAN 91] : **Y. Yang, N.Magnenat-Thalmann**, *"Techniques for Cloth Animation"*, New trends in Animation and Visualisation, John Wiley & Sons Ltd, pp 243-256, 1991.

[YAN 93] : **Y. Yang, N.Magnenat-Thalmann**, *"An Improved Algorithm for Collision Detection in Cloth Animation with Human Body"*, Computer Graphics and Applications (Pacific Graphics proceedings 1993), 1, pp 237-251, 1993.

Annex: Detailed formulas for the proposed model

Considering a triangle ($\mathbf{P_a}$, $\mathbf{P_b}$, $\mathbf{P_c}$) in which in-plane deformations have elongated its edges from rest length ($\mathbf{L_a}$, $\mathbf{L_b}$, $\mathbf{L_c}$) to the current length ($\mathbf{l_a}$, $\mathbf{l_b}$, $\mathbf{l_c}$):

$$l_i = \left\| \overrightarrow{P_j P_k} \right\| \qquad \begin{matrix} i \\ j \\ k \end{matrix} = \begin{pmatrix} a & b & c \\ b, & c, & a \\ c & a & b \end{pmatrix} \tag{0}$$

The current angle cosine ($\mathbf{c_a}$, $\mathbf{c_b}$, $\mathbf{c_c}$) is also computed (taking $\boldsymbol{\alpha} = \mathbf{1}$):

$$c_i = \alpha \frac{l_j^2 + l_k^2 - l_i^2}{2 l_j l_k} \tag{1}$$

A. Simple spring-mass model

Computing the elongation of the edge springs:

$$d_i = l_i - L_i \qquad i = (a, b, c) \tag{2}$$

Computing the spring forces from the elongation:

$$F_i = \frac{R_i}{L_i} d_i = \frac{R_i}{L_i}(l_i - L_i) \tag{3}$$

$\mathbf{R_i}$ is a strength factor linked to the surface elasticity as well as a "shape factor" of this edge in the triangle (quite often, the rest length of the associated height).

B. The proposed model

Computing the desired elongation of each edge as sum of displacement contributions generated by all edge spring forces, $\mathbf{M_i}$ being the *inverse* mass of the vertex $\mathbf{P_i}$:

$$d_i + c_k \frac{M_k}{M_k + M_i} d_j + c_j \frac{M_j}{M_j + M_i} d_k = l_i - L_i \qquad \begin{matrix} i \\ j \\ k \end{matrix} = \begin{pmatrix} a & b & c \\ b, & c, & a \\ c & a & b \end{pmatrix} \tag{4}$$

Simplifying calculus by computing the following intermediate values:

$$u_i = c_i M_i \qquad N_i = M_j + M_k \tag{5}$$

The system (4) is then simplified to:

$$d_i + \frac{u_k}{N_j} d_j + \frac{u_j}{N_k} d_k = l_i - L_i \qquad \begin{matrix} i \\ j \\ k \end{matrix} = \begin{pmatrix} a & b & c \\ b, & c, & a \\ c & a & b \end{pmatrix} \tag{6}$$

Computing the forces from displacement contributions by solving the system (6):

$$F_i = \frac{R_i}{L_i} d_i = \frac{R_i}{L_i} N_i \frac{(u_i^2 - N_j N_k)(l_i - L_i) - (u_i u_j - N_k u_k)(l_j - L_j) - (u_i u_k - N_j u_j)(l_k - L_k)}{u_i^2 N_i + u_j^2 N_j + u_k^2 N_k - 2 u_i u_j u_k - N_i N_j N_k} \tag{7}$$

Taking the assumption that all vertices have comparable mass:

$$M_i = M_j = M_k \tag{8}$$

The system (4) is simplified as follows:

$$d_i + \frac{1}{2} c_k d_j + \frac{1}{2} c_j d_k = l_i - L_i \qquad \begin{matrix} i \\ j \\ k \end{matrix} = \begin{pmatrix} a & b & c \\ b, & c, & a \\ c & a & b \end{pmatrix} \tag{9}$$

Computing the forces by solving the system (9):

$$F_i = \frac{R_i}{L_i} d_i = \frac{R_i}{L_i} \frac{(c_i^2 - 4)(l_i - L_i) - (c_i c_j - 2c_k)(l_j - L_j) - (c_i c_k - 2c_j)(l_k - L_k)}{c_i^2 + c_j^2 + c_k^2 - c_i c_j c_k - 4} \tag{10}$$

The acceleration contribution from the triangle applied on the vertices are finally computed from (1), (7) or (10) by:

$$\overrightarrow{A_i} = M_i \left(\frac{F_j}{l_j} \overrightarrow{P_i P_k} + \frac{F_k}{l_k} \overrightarrow{P_i P_j} \right) \qquad \begin{matrix} i \\ j \\ k \end{matrix} = \begin{pmatrix} a & b & c \\ b, & c, & a \\ c & a & b \end{pmatrix} \tag{11}$$

Multilevel Deformation Model Applied to Hand Simulation for Virtual Actors

Laurent Moccozet, Nadia Magnenat Thalmann
MIRALab - CUI
University of Geneva
24 Rue du Général Dufour
CH 1211 Geneva 4, Switzerland
{Laurent.Moccozet, Nadia.Thalmann}@cui.unige.ch
http://miralabwww.unige.ch/

Abstract

Until now, real-time environments have focused on optimizing the speed of the display, mainly by managing various levels of details of the scene's objects. These approaches are generally aimed at virtual scenes with rigid objects. If we consider that objects can be deformed trough time, another process has to be considered in the scene building pipeline: each object must be deformed prior to its display in a given frame. Similarly to other processes of the pipeline, the control of the display speed must be made by balancing between visual quality and time cost. This requires either to combine various deformable models, sorted by their cost in time, or to use a single deformable model able to work at various levels of details. Our purpose is to propose such a multilevel deformable model that we illustrate by its application to human hands simulation.

1. Introduction and background

In VR environments, the main objective in rendering a virtual scene is to reach a pseudo real time display speed (as near as possible to the 25 frames per second), and to maintain a constant frame rate. In such environments, objects are modelled using triangular meshes. The main reason for that is that graphics hardware have the best performance with that type of geometric representations. Level of details (LODs) modelling is one of the main approaches developed to optimize the display of VR huge and complex scenes. This technique consists in providing each object of the scene with a set of geometric representation sorted by their number of vertices. The underlying idea is that depending on the relative situation of a given object in the scene, its visual aspect can be depreciated against saving computation time. Such environments are focused on rigid objects. The next challenging step in VR environment is to involve deformable objects[SHAD96], such as virtual humans and human-like avatars[PAND97, CAPI97]. Introducing deformable components into real time environments requires to take them into account with the scene rendering pipeline. The scene rendering pipeline involves all activities needed to construct a 2 dimensional view of the scene updated at a given frame. In order to incorporate the deformation process, we will rather talk about the scene building pipeline. By scene building pipeline, we mean all the processes that are involved in generating a 2 dimensional display of the scene at a given frame from either a default scene or from the scene at the previous frame situation. With such a definition, the deformation and rendering processes are parts of the building pipeline. In [FUNK93], Funkhauser et al. only consider the visual rendering pipeline and subdivide it into two steps: first is the per-primitive process, including applying coordinate transformations, lighting calculations, etc.; then comes the per-pixel process, including z-buffering, texture mapping, etc.. . In figure 1 which describes the scene building pipeline, both are combined into the display process, which occurs after the deformation and transformation process. This process is aimed at determining the global transformation (translation, rotation, etc.) to be applied to the objects, either rigid or deformable, and at determining and applying the deformations to the deformable objects. Whereas global transformations can be stored in a single transformation matrix for each object, deformations have to be applied to each vertex of the deformed object, as the deformation function is changing for each vertex. Figure 1 shows the whole scene building pipeline. The scene database can describe the scene either at frame i-1 or at a default status.

0-8186-8150-0/97 $10.00 © 1997 IEEE

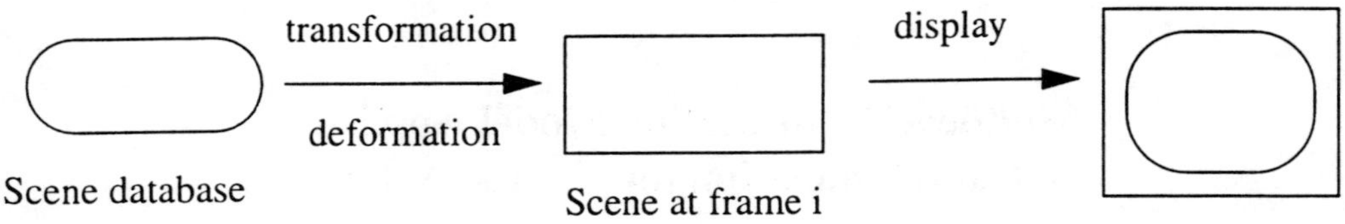

Fig. 1: scene building pipeline

Current researches in geometric LODs involves two aspects. The first one is focused on getting LODs for a given representation of an object[SCHR92, TURK92, HOPP93, ROSS93, ECK95, HOPP96]. The second one is focused on proposing strategies to choose the LOD to display for a given object at a given frame, and handle the swap from a given LOD to another one[FUNK93,ROHL94]. Similarly to the geometric LODs, Funkhauser and Sequin[FUNK93]propose to parametrize the choice of the rendering algorithm for an object. The various rendering algorithms are sorted by time cost. The set of sorted rendering algorithms can be considered as defining rendering LODs. The strategy will then choose, for a given frame, the best geometric LOD with the best rendering LOD. In this context best means the best visual quality for a given time constraint. We propose here to define deformation LODs in order to further incorporate them inside LODs choice strategies that would control geometric, rendering and deformation LODs.

The rest of the paper is articulated into 2 main sections. We first describe the basic approach used to model and simulate virtual human hands. The model is based on a 3-layers model where muscles and hands lines are modelled using a generalized Free-Form Deformation model. The next section is dedicated to the description of the deformation LODs we have defined from the basic model. We describe how the deformation process can be optimized, and at which levels.

2. Hand modelling approach

Deformable models for articulated characters are traditionally based on a multi-layer approach[CHAD88]. We propose here a 3-layer model where the intermediate muscular layer between the skeleton and skin is modelled using a generalized Free-Form Deformation[SEDER86].

2.1 Dirichlet based FFD model

Free-Form Deformations(FFD)[SEDER86] belong to a wider class of geometric deformation tools. An extended survey of existing models with comparisons included can be found in [BECH95]. We propose a generalized Free-Form Deformation model. Our main goal is to overcome their basic limitations concerning the design of muscle layers in a multi-layer realistic animation model. These limitations are partially addressed by further extensions : EFFDs by Coquillart in [COQU90], Direct FFD manipulation by Hsu in [HSU92] and NFFDs by Lamousin in [LAMO94]. The main cause for these limitations is the use of rectangular local coordinates to express any point of the surface to deform relatively to the control points box. The main resulting constraint is that control points boxes have to be rectangular. In [COQU90], Coquillart et al. propose an Extended FFD model that allows other shapes of control boxes, but as they do not reconsider the problem of the local coordinates, restrictions still exist. Even in [MACC96] the model proposed by MacCracken and Joy, where the deformation approach is based on a recursive subdivision of the control lattice, the model still requires the explicit construction of the topology of the control lattice. The topology construction can be quite tedious for a complex control lattice, and it is almost impossible to evaluate the influence of a given topology on the resulting deformations. We may conclude that, most FFDs extensions aim to overcome limitations, but instead of reconsidering the geometric tools on which FFDs are based, they keep the initial FFD method and extend its possibilities by using approximation methods. This way, each extension solves only one specific limitation, but does not generalize the FFD concept. Local coordinates is a general problem extensively addressed in visualization [WATS92], especially in the area of data interpolation. FFDs are close to data interpolation if viewed as the interpolation of displacements of given control points at given locations. The most general of all the systems is the natural neighbors or Sibson coordinates system[SIBS80], from which Sibson derived a scattered data interpolant. Sibson coordinates computation is based on Voronoi/Dirichlet and Delaunay diagrams [AURE91] In [FARI90], Farin extends the natural neighbors interpolant based on the natural neighbors coordinates, by using the natural neighbors as the support for a multivariate Bézier simplex[DERO88], in which any point can be expressed relative to a set of data nodes with a similar relation as the deformation function in FFD's. Farin defines a new type of surfaces defined with this extended interpolant called Dirichlet surfaces. Combining FFD's and Dirichlet surfaces leads to a generalized model of FFD's : Dirichlet FFD's or DFFD's. The deformation function also can be seen as an interpolation of the displacements of the control points. In the Dirichlet based FFD approach, any point of the surface to deform located in the convex hull of a set of control points in general position, is expressed relative to a subset of the control points set with the Sibson coordinate system. Control points of this subset are called Sibson or influencing control points. One major advantage of this technique is that it removes any constraint on the position and topology of control points. It also removes the need to specify the control lattice topology. The deformation process is similar to the one developed by Coquillart for EFFD in [COQU90]: the control points set can be edited, then frozen on the top of a surface by computing the Sibson coordinates of each point of the surface relative to the control points set. The deformation function can then transmit the displacements applied to the control points to the surface. The complete deformation model is extensively described in [MOCC96].

2.2 DFFD extensions

Most of standard FFD extensions can be applied to DFFD. We review here the main ones, that are used in the hand deformation model:

- *Rational DFFD:* As in [KARL92], we can assign weights to the control points. DFFDs are then special cases of rational DFFDs where the weights are all given a value of 1.0. By varying the weight, deformations can be introduced without moving the control points. When the weight of a control point increases, the deformations behave as if the control point was attracting the surface towards itself.
- *Direct point manipulation:* As in [HSU92], direct manipulation consists in applying FFDs not by moving one or more control points, but by directly moving one or more points on the surface to be deformed. This feature can be directly added to DFFDs by inserting the points to move as control points of the lattice. A control point is defined at the same position as the surface point, so that any displacement applied to the control point will be completely applied to the surface point. This relation can be expressed like the general relation by assigning a Sibson coordinate of 1.0 to the surface point relative to its associated control point. These control points are called constraint control points.

2.3 Hand simulation model

We combine the approaches of Chadwick et al. in [CHAD89] and Delingette et al. in [DELI93] to design a multi-layered deformation model for hand animation. The muscle layer will be modeled by a DFFD control point set that will correspond to a simplified surface hand topography. From the observation of a hand, especially its topography[KAPA80], we can derive the following simplified observations :

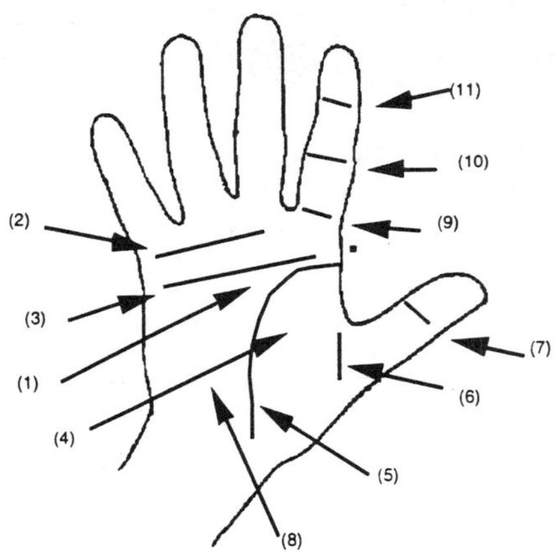

(1) palm
(2) upper transversal line
(3) lower transversal line
(4) thenar eminence
(5) thenar line
(6) thumb first line
(7) thumb second line
(8) hypothenar eminence
(9) finger first line
(10) finger second line
(11) finger third line

Figure 2: Topography of the hand

- each joint of the skeleton is associated with a hand line on the surface of the hand.
- each hand line can be seen as a closed line, and has almost no change in its shape.
- rotation at the joint creates an inflation of the part delimited by the hand line associated with the rotating joint and the hand line just above.
- hand lines stop the propagation of the skin inflation.

These observations lead us to define the basic data structure for our hand model, that we call wrinkle, as we want to keep that data structure general enough to be used forthe animation of other human parts:

- the wrinkle itself, which is a set of constraint control points, that are generally selected around the joint and form a closed 3D line. We call such points wrinkle control points.

- - two points among the wrinkle control points, that are used to define the axis on which the associated skeleton joint should lie. In this way, a skeleton model can be easily adapted to the hand's skin. This data allows an easy and realistic hand-skeleton mapping by defining an implicit skeleton to which the skeleton can be fitted.

- - a mixed set of control points and constraint control points that surround the upper part of the hand surface that will be affected by the rotation of the joint associated with the current wrinkle. We call these points influenced wrinkle control points, as they are influenced by the rotation of the wrinkle itself.
- - one control point, called an inflation control point, which will be used to simulate inflation at the upper limb associated with the joint.

For each wrinkle, the muscle layer gets the joint angle variation from the skeleton layer. If the rotation angle is α, the wrinkle itself is rotated atan angle of $\alpha/2$, and the set of influenced control points is rotated by α. At the rest position, all control points have a weight of 1. When the joint angles vary, the weights of the inflation control points vary accordingly, such that weight(P) = $f(\alpha)$, where P is an inflation control point and α an angle of rotation at the joint. This point is placed on the mesh so that when its weight increases, it attracts the mesh.

One unclosed wrinkle exists at the base of each of the four fingers. The union of these four wrinkles defines a closed composite wrinkle which simulates the transversal line going through the palm, and each distinct wrinkle will simulate the line at the first joint of the finger. The topography is then simplified without altering the visual aspect of the deformed hand.

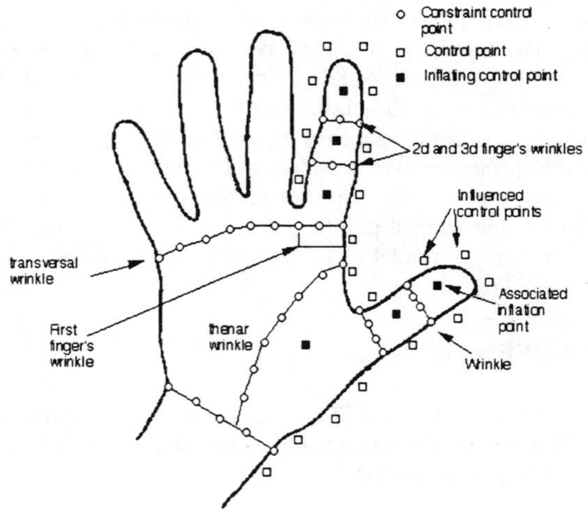

Figure 3: Control points set and wrinkles design

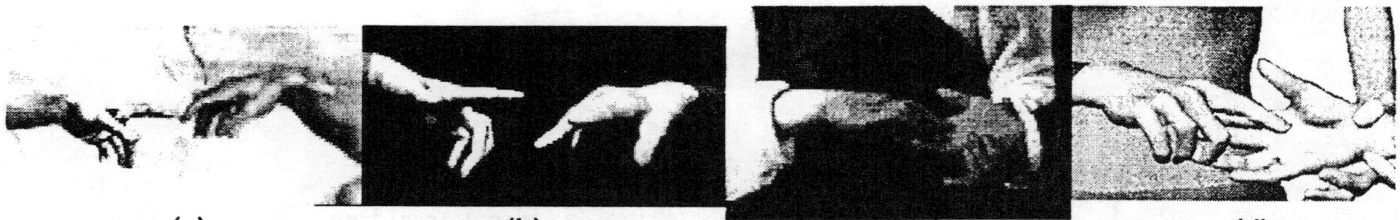

(a) (b) (c) (d)

Figure 4: Hands postures reproductions from famous painting details
(a) is a detail from 'La Genèse. Création d'Adam' from Michaelangelo, reproduced in (b).
(c) is a detail from 'La diseuse de bonne aventure' from Caravage, reproduced in (d).

Figure 2 shows the simplified surface hand topography we want to model with the important hand lines associated with the underlying skeleton joints. Figure 3 shows how control points, constraint control points and inflation control points are designed around the surface of the hand to build the control points set and the different wrinkles. Normal control points approximate the shape of the hand, and embed the hand surface in a deformable space. Constraint control points are used to define the hand lines. The resulting hand topography can be compared with figure 2 that represents the 'real' hand topographyFigure 4 shows some hands postures produced with the described approach

3. Multilevel deformable model

After the description of our basic approach for hand modelling, we now wantto show how we can define deformation LODs. According to the multilayer approach, there are two levels on which we can work. The first one is the general deformation function involved in the deformable model. We are going to show that DFFDs allow to express deformations at various levels. Another approach is to skip layers in the model. The most direct approach would be to skip directly from the skeleton layer to the skin layer without going through intermediate layers. In the humans simulation context, deformations are constrained by the skeleton's degrees of freedom. Based on this assumption, it is possible not to optimize the muscular layer, but to skip it, using interpolation of extremal hands postures.

3.1 Deformation function level

It is possible to define different levels of details at the deformation functions level. The first option is to control the complexity of the deformation function. In our context it can be performed at two levels. The deformation function complexity depends on:

- the degree of the function.
- the number of Sibson control points involved.

3.1.1 deformation function degree

As for basic FFDs, the deformation function is a cubic function of the local coordinates. The use of Sibson coordinates, and particularly the resulting continuity properties they offer makes it possible to use deformation functions of lower degrees. Figure 5 shows the effect of the different degrees used for the deformation functions. A cylinder is embedded inside a cubic control points set, similar to the one used in FFDs. The control box is then bent. The two bent cylinders at the bottom of the pictures show the resulting deformations using a deformation function of degree 1 (linear) at the bottom left, and the same deformation using a deformation function of degree 3 at the bottom right. For the cubic deformation function, intermediate control points have to be inserted to construct a multivariate Bézier simplex of the corresponding degree. The displacement of these intermediate control points can be controlled, either by directly assigning their displacement or by constraining their displacements to the displacements of the basic control points (as it is done in the deformation applied to the cylinder). Such as shown in figure 4, a deformation function of degree 3 allows to control the smoothness of the deformed surface.The properties of Sibson interpolant and extended interpolant are also valid in the DFFD context if we consider the deformation process as interpolating a displacement function whose values are known for control points, playing the role of data nodes in scattered data interpolation[FARI90,WATS92]. The interpolant properties are widely described in [SIBS80,FARI90,SAMB95]. Among all these properties the ones related to the interpolation function continuity are of particular interest regarding the optimization of the deformation function. Sibson coordinates are continuously differentiable at all points except at control points/data nodes, and the Sibson interpolant(corresponding to linear DFFDs) guarantees continuity in first and second derivatives except at control points/data nodes. The continuity properties of the interpolant function is a result of the continuity of the local coordinates, which is not the case for the local coordinates used in FFDs. The result for FFDs is that constraints have to be defined to ensure continuity between adjacent control boxes.. This is another interesting result of our approach to generalize FFDs by reconsidering the underlying local coordinates system. Farin's work in extended Sibson interpolant allows to extend the continuity properties to control point/data nodes. In our context, this implies that we can expect a good deformation result with linear deformations. Table 1 at the end of this section shows time costs for different degrees of the deformation function: linear, quadratic and cubic.

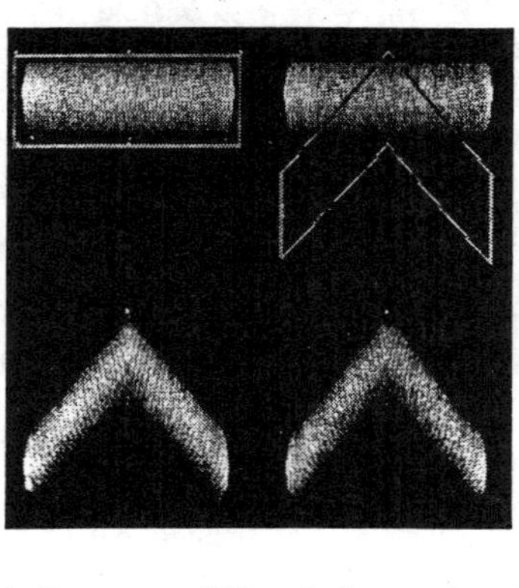

Figure 5: influence of the deformation function degree

3.1.2 control points number

The dimension of the Sibson coordinate system is not predefined and depends on the local configuration of the set of control points at any location inside the control points convex hull. The subset of Sibson control points for a given location is the set of control points that have a non-zero Sibson coordinate relative to this location. The value of a Sibson coordinate for a given location P relative to a control point is a measure of the control point influence. When the value is close to 1, P is near the control point, and the value decreases when P is moved away from the control point. It reaches 0 when P is outside the area of influence of the control point. Sibson coordinates for a given point P then give a way to sort Sibson control points. On the other hand, the function cost is linked to the number of control points that influence the points of a given surface. The number of control points can be controlled and constrained between four control points (this corresponds to using Bézier tetrahedrons) up to the number of Sibson control points. The same surface and control lattice can be associated to a set of local coordinates. The set of natural neighbours is first defined, then natural neighbours control points are sorted by decreasing value of their associated Sibson coordinate. The n first are kept, and for these n control points, subset of the set of natural neighbours, the Sibson coordinates are recomputed. It must be pointed out that the four first control points are the points defining the Delaunay tetrahedron in which the point lies. If the number of control points influencing a surface point is restricted to 4, then the Sibson coordinates are the barycentric coordinates of the surface point in the tetrahedron defined by the 4 control points. In the example shown in figure 6, limited to 2 dimension for clarity, there are 5 Sibson neighbours related to p. These 5 control points, from p2 to p6, will have a non zero Sibson coordinate relative to p. The control points are determined by inserting p in the Voronoi diagram of the set of control points.This results in the insertion of a new Voronoi tile related to p. All control points sharing a common Voronoi edge with the p's Voronoi tiles are p's Sibson control points (from p2 to p6; p1 is not a Sibson control point). The Sibson coordinate value relative to each of the Sibson control point is the normalized size of the intersection between the Voronoi tile of p and the Voronoi tile of the Sibson control point in the Voronoi diagram of the Sibson control points without p. The figure shows intuitively that the three control points p5, p4 and p2 have the biggest Sibson coordinates relative to p, and so will have the maximum influence on p's displacements . We can reduce the Sibson control points subset of p to a minimum of 3 points (4 in 3 dimensions). These 3 points are the corners of the Delaunay triangle in which p lies. This approach requires to compute Sibson coordinates twice. The first time one must first select the Sibson control points, then choose among them the ones with the biggest influence (i.e., the biggest Sibson coordinates). The second time is required to get Sibson coordinates related to the subset of Sibson control points chosen at the first step.It must be noticed that limiting the number of control points to 4 results in continuity problem between adjacent Delaunay tetrahedrons of the Delaunay diagram of the control points set.This has to be considered as the price to pay for the gain in speed. Figure 6 shows, for the same hand posture, 3 different results with various constrained Sibson control points. Figure 7.a shows the basic DFFD function, whereas Sibson control points are constrained to be at maximum 9 in 7.b and 4 in 7.c.

As conclusion to this first level of optimization, we have shown that the complexity of the deformation function can be controlled and parametrized according to the degree of the function and the maximum number of control points to use. If the deformation function name is DFFD, LODs can be defined by setting the two parameters Degree, and MaxControl of the DFFD function: DFFD(Degree, MaxControl). Degree can take its values between 1, 2 and 3, and MaxControl takes values higher than 4. Table 2 at the end of this section gives time costs for different maximum number of Sibson control points: normal, 4and 9, and for different degrees of the deformation function.CPU time costs are given for one hand in seconds. The hand's figure contains around 1500 vertices.

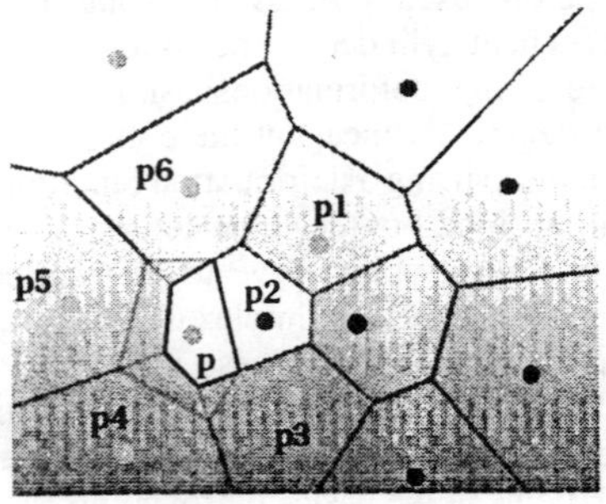

Figure 6: Sibson control points (in 2 dimensions).

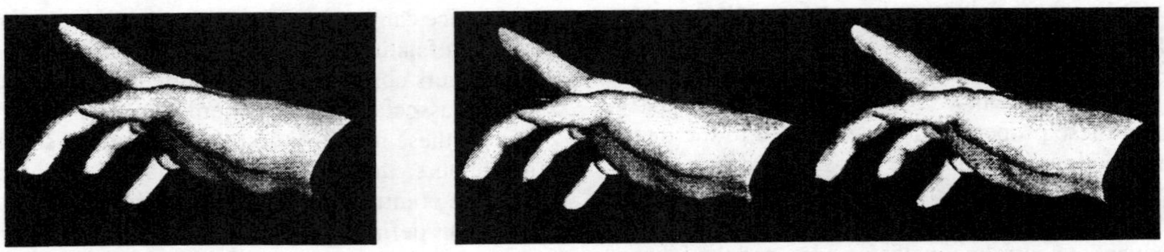

(a) Unconstrained **(b) 9 control points** **(c) 4 control points**

Figure 7: Hand posture with various constrained Sibson control points

3.2 Deformable model layers level

The complete deformable articulated model is defined in multi-layers. The complete deformation process is in fact divided into sub-processes. Each sub-process, that we call a procedural layer, has to use the outputs of the previous layer to transform the next structural layer, as shown in figure 8. Our deformable model can be subdivided into two main sub-processes.

1 - pre-process: the control lattice (muscular layer) is updated according to the current skeleton posture.

2 - deformation: the geometric skin is warped according to the current control lattice status.

The deformation function only affects the second step, and so it allows to control the second procedural layer (muscle mapping). If we want to optimize the time cost, we must be able to control also the first sub-process. Unfortunately, this sub-process cannot be optimized: all control points have to be moved to mirror the current skeleton posture.The only optimization option is to restrict the number of the skeleton's Degrees of Freedom (DOFs). The number of rotation to apply to control points would then be reduced, and as a consequence, would reduce the time cost of the procedural layer. We can consider for example that some DOFs, such as metacarpi flexion or finger twists,defined in the skeleton model we use, are very rarely activated. There is anyway a minimum number of DOFs to keep and once this number is reached the muscular operators layer cannot be optimized further with this approach. As the minimum number of DOFs is high , there is a strong limitation to the gain we can expect.Whatever level of the deformation function we will use, the cost of the pre-process will finally remain constant. As hand movements are constrained by the predefined DOFs of the underlying skeleton, we can use interpolation between extreme postures. The interpolation is not performed at the global hand surface level, but by regions.

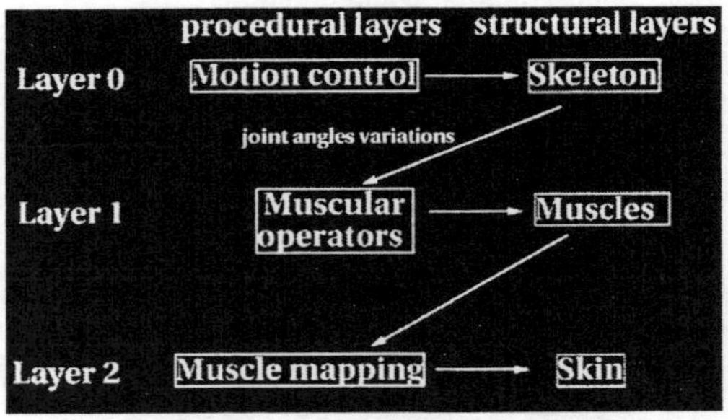

Figure 8: deformable model layers

A region of the surface is associated to each skeleton segment. If we consider any point of the region, we can make the approximation that for a given Degree of Free-

dom(DOF) and its location in the deformed surface for the maximal and minimal value of the DOF, the point varies between these two extreme locations and is subject to a rotation, or more generally a homotethy around the joint's rotation axis. Figure 9.a shows the basic interpolation approach. O is the joint, at the intersection of segments S0 and S. The default joint posture is defined by S0,O,S. P0 is a point of the skin linked to segment S. The segment S is rotated at an angle a1. The joint posture is then defined by S0,O,S'. P1 is the new location of point P0 in this new configuration. The angle a1 is given by S,O,S'. We want to determine point P, location of point P0 for a rotation angle of value a, with a between 0 and a1. The angle a is defined by S,O,S", S" being the location of segment S for an angle value of a.
P is defined with the following relations:
We first define an intermediate P' point on segment POP1,

$$\overrightarrow{OP'} = \overrightarrow{OP_0} + d\overrightarrow{P_0P_1}, \text{ with } d=\alpha/\alpha_1$$

A scaling factor is then determined,

$$r = \|\overrightarrow{OP}\| = r_0 + d(r_1 - r_0),$$

$$\text{with } r_0 = \|\overrightarrow{OP_0}\| \text{ and } r_1 = \|\overrightarrow{OP_1}\|$$

P' is then scaled to the interpolated final location P,

$$\overrightarrow{OP} = \frac{r}{r'}\overrightarrow{OP'}, \text{ with } r' = \|\overrightarrow{OP'}\|$$

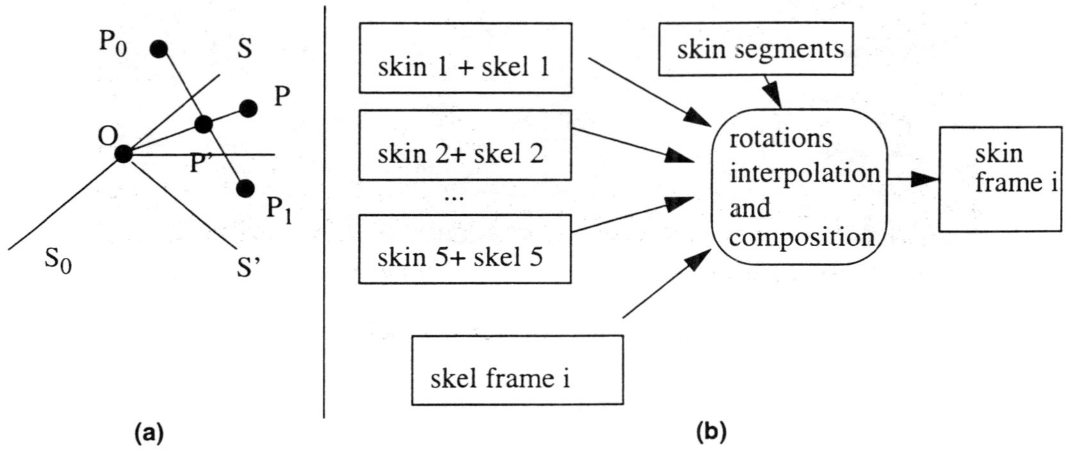

Figure 9:Hand skin segments interpolation process

Figure 9.b shows the animation process for a given frame i. There are three different types of inputs. First a set of hand skins together with their corresponding skeleton postures, then a list of regions of triangles on the geometric skin. Each region corresponds to a skeleton segment. The last input is the skeleton posture at frame i. The rotations interpolation and composition process outputs the hand's skin at frame i. Particular care has to be taken when many DOFs are geometrically located at the same joint place, such as the thumb. We propose a simple way to interpolate all the possible hand postures from a predefined set of extreme hand postures. These hand postures are pre-computed using the basic hand simulation model described above. Figure 10 describes the set of pre-defined extremal postures. Figure 10.a is the default posture, figure 10.b defines the maximal flexions for the 3 flexions of the five fingers, figure 10.b defines the maximal pivot for the four fingers, index, middle, ring and pinky. Finally figure 10.d and e define respectively the maximal abduction and pivot for the thumb. Figure 11 shows a hand posture (the same as in figure). For figure 11.b, the hand surface is generated using an interpolation of the set of predefined hand skin in extreme postures. In figure 11.a, the same hand posture is shown but created with the DFFD based model. In order to be complete, a last low level is to be added, where the complete hands are divided into rigid pieces associated with each skeleton segments. Such pieces are generally cylinders, and spheres are placed at joints in order to smooth the connection between two incident cylinders. This is the approach usually used in real-time environments for human body simulation. Table 3 shows the different time costs for the different layers of the basic model and compares it to the interpolation approach.

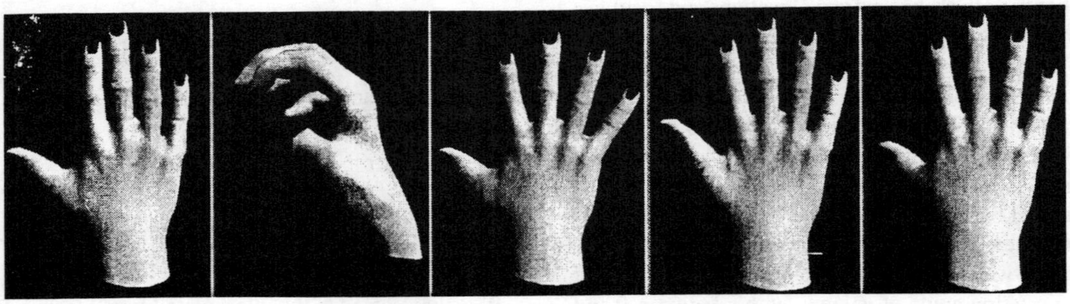

(a) initial posture | (b) flexions | (c) pivots | (d) thumb abduct | (e) thumb pivot

Figure 10:Initial set of extremal postures

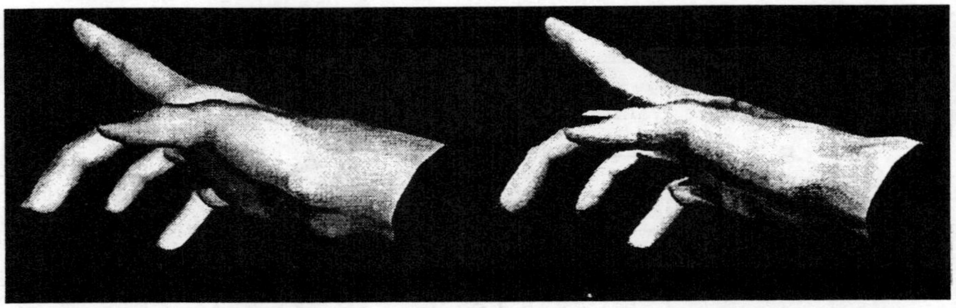

(a) DFFD approach | (b) interpolation approach

Figure 11: comparison of results

degree	linear	quadratic	cubic
cpu time (sec.)	0.024200	0.182800	1.616800

Table 1: Deformation function time cost for different degrees

number of Sibson control points	4	9	unconstrained
linear	0.013400 sec.	0.018800 sec.	0.024200 sec.
quadratic	0.034200 sec.	0.090400 sec.	0.182800 sec.
cubic	0.206400 sec.	1.176000 sec.	1.616800 sec.

Table 2: Deformation function time cost for different Sibson control points numbers

	interpolation	DFFD (linear, 4 Sibson control points)
preprocess	0.000000 sec.	0.009500 sec.
deformation	0.004200 sec.	0.013400 sec.
total	0.004200 sec.	0.022900 sec.

Table 3: Total deformation time cost for the model layers optimization

All these time cost evaluations have been performed on a Indigo II Impact, R4400-250MHZ Time costs are the total CPU time cost and are given in seconds. For each estimation, the deformation process has been applied on one hand with the same skeleton's animation. The hand's geometric skin contains around 1500 vertices.

5. Conclusion

We have proposed a multi-level deformation model with the aim of being inserted into VR real-time environments involving deformable objects. Such a model is designed to be used in various types of contexts, from off-line raytraced animation to real-time environments. For the latter, the different levels of deformations can provide a set of Level Of Details for the deformation process. The main motivation is that handling deformable models requires the capacity to control the time cost of the deformation process. Similarly to geometric LODs, widely used in VR environments to control the object display in the scene, deformation LODs can be developed and inserted into the scene building pipeline. This approach is illustrated and applied to a human hand simulation model. Our choice is based on the fact that this part of the body is generally under-treated despite its great importance in terms of visual realism of human-like avatars and of human communication.The hand multi-layers model is based on a general geometric deformation model, that generalizes the traditional FFDs approach: DFFDs. The properties of DFFDs make the model flexible enough to work at various levels, with a minimal loss in the visual results. We have shown at which levels of a multi-layer deformable model optimization can be performed: deformation function, intermediate layers. The resulting multilevel deformation proposes a set of compromises between a low time cost and a high level of deformation quality. The deformation LODs can be further integrated into a LODs management strategies in order to keep a high and constant frame rate for virtual scenes involving rigid and deformable objects.

6. Acknowledgments

This work has been funded by the Swiss National Research Foundation.

7. References

[AURE91] Aurenhammer F., Voronoi Diagrams - A Survey of a Fundamental Geometric Data Structure, ACM Computing Survey, 23, 3, September 1991.

[BECH95] Bechmann D., Space Deformation Models Survey, Computers and Graphics, 18, 4, Pergamon, pp. 571-586, 1995.

[BOUL95a] Boulic R., Capin T., Huang Z., Kalra P., Lintermann B., Magnenat-Thalmann N., Moccozet L., Molet T, Pandzic I., Saar K., Schmitt A., Shen J., Thalmann D., The HUMANOID Environment for Interactive Animation of Multiple Deformable Human Characters, Proceedings Eurographic's 95, 1995.

[CAPI97] Virtual Human Representation and Communication in VLNET Networked Virtual Environments, T. K. Capin, I. S. Pandzic, H. Noser, N. Magnenat Thalmann, D. Thalmann, IEEE Computer Graphics and Applications, Special Issue on Multimedia Highways, March-April 1997.

[CHAD89] Chadwick J. E., Hauman D., Parent R. E., Layered Construction for Deformable Animated Character, Proceedings Siggraph'89, PP 243-252, 1989.

[COQU90] Coquillart S., Extended Free-Form Deformation : A Sculpting Tools For 3D Geometric Modeling, Proceedings Siggraph'90, pp. 187-196, 1990.

[DELI93] Delingette H., Watanabe Y., Suenaga Y., Simplex Based Animation, proceedings Computer Animation'93, Eds Magnenat-Thalmann N. Thalmann D., Springer Verlag, pp. 13-28, 1993.

[DERO88] DeRose T.D., Composing Bezier Simplexes, ACM Transactions on Graphics, 7(3), pp. 198-221, 1988.

[ECK95] Multiresolution analysis of arbitrary meshes. M. Eck, T. DeRose, T. Duchamp, H. Hoppe, M. Lounsbery, and W. Stuetzle, Proceedings Siggraph'95, pp. 173-182, 1995.

[FARI90] Farin G., Surface Over Dirichlet Tessellations, Computer Aided Geometric Design, 7, pp. 281-292, North-Holland, 1990.

[FUNK93] Funkhauser T. A., Sequin C.H.,Adaptative Display Algorithm for Interactive Frame Rates During Visualization of Complex Virtual Environments, Proceedings Siggraph'93, pp247-254, 1993.

[GOUR89] Gourret J.-P., Magnenat-Thalmann N., Thalmann D., Simulation of Object Grasping and Human Skin Deformations in a Grasping Task, proceedings Siggraph'89, pp. 21-30, 1989.

[HOPP93] Mesh optimization, H. Hoppe, T. DeRose, T. Duchamp, J. McDonal and W. Stuetzle, Proceedings Siggraph'93, pp. 19-26, 1993.

[HOPP96] Progressive meshes, H. Hoppe, Proceedings Siggraph'96, pp. 99-108, 1996.

[HSU92] Hsu W., Hugues J. F., Kaufman H., Direct Manipulation of Free-Form Deformations, Proceedings Siggraph'92, pp. 177-184, 1992.

[ISAA87] Kalra P., Mangili A., Magnenat-Thalmann N., Thalmann D., Simulation of Facial Muscle Actions Based on Rational Free-Form Deformations, Computer Graphics Forum, 2, 3, Blackwell Publishers, pp. 65-69, 1992.

[KAPA] Kapandji I. A., Physiologie Articulaire, Tome 1, Maloine SA Edtions., pp45-58.

[LAMO94] Lamousin H. J., Waggenspack W. N., Nurbs-based Free-Form Deformations, IEEE Computer Graphics and Appli-

cations, 14, 16, pp 59-65, 1994.
[LEE95] Lee Y., Terzopoulos D., Waters K., Realistic Face Modeling for Animation, Proceedings of Siggraph'95, pp. 55-62, 1995.
[MACC96] MacCracken R., Joy K.I., Free-Form Deformations with Lattices of Arbitrary Topology, Proceedings Siggraph'96, pp. -, 1996..
[MAGN88] Magnenat-Thalmann N., Laperrière R., Thalmann D., Joint-Dependent Local Deformations for Hand Animation and Object Grasping, Proceedings Graphics Interface'88, Canadian Man-Computer Communication Society, pp. 26-33, 1988.
[MOCC96] Moccozet L., Hands Modeling and Animation for Virtual Humans, Thesis report, University of Geneva, 1996.
[PAND97] A flexible architecture for Virtual Humans in Networked Collaborative Virtual Environments, I. S. Pandzic, T. K. Capin, E. Lee, N. Magnenat Thalmann, D. Thalmann, Proceedings Eurographics 97, Budapest, Hungary, 1997. (to appear)
[ROHL94] IRIS Performer: A High Performance Multiprocessing Toolkit for Real-Time 3D Graphics, Rohlf J., Helman J., Proceedings Siggraph'94, pp. 381-394, 1994.
[ROSS93] Multi-resolution 3D approximations for rendering complex scenes, J Rossignac, P. Borrel, Modeling in Computer Graphics, pp. 455-465, 1993.
[SEDE86] Sederberg T. W., Parry S. R., Free-Form Deformation of Solid Geometric Models, Proceedings Siggraph'86, pp. 151-160, 1986.
[SHAD96] Shade J., Lischinski D., Salesin D.H., DeRose T., Snyder J., Hierarchical Image Caching for Accelerated Walkthroughs of COmplex Environments, Proceedings Siggraph'96, pp. 75-82, 1996.
[SIBS80] Sibson R., A Vector Identity for the Dirichlet Tesselation, Math. Proc. Cambridge Philos. Soc., 87, pp. 151-155, 1980.
[TURK92] Re-tiling polygonal surfaces, Greg Turk, Proceedings Siggraph'92, pp. 55-64, 1992.
[SCHR92] Decimation of triangle meshes, W. Schroeder, J. Zarge, W. Lorensen, Proceedings Siggraph'92, pp. 65-70, 1992.
[UDA93] Uda N., Kimura F., Tsuruoka S., Miyake Y., Shunlin S., Tsuda M., Expansion of the Solid Modeler's Functions for Use in Designing a Model of the Human Body, New Advances in Computer Aided Design & Computer Graphics, (Eds Zesheng Tang), International Academic Publishers, pp. 357-363, 1993.
[UNUM95] Unuma M., Anjyo K., Takeuchi R., Fourier Principle of Emotion-based Human Figure Animation, Proceedings of Siggraph'95, pp. 91-96, 1995.
[WATS92] Watson D. F., Contouring - A Guide to the Analysis and Display of Spatial Data, Computer Methods in the Geosciences, Volume 10, Pergamon, 1992.

Face Recognition Using Range Images

Bernard Achermann, Xiaoyi Jiang, Horst Bunke
Institute of Computer Science and Applied Mathematics
University of Bern, Neubrückstrasse 10, CH-3012 Bern
email: {ackerman,jiang,bunke}@iam.unibe.ch
phone: +41 31 631 48 65, fax: +41 31 631 39 65

Abstract

A system for face recognition using range images as input data is described. The range data acquisition procedure is based on the coded light approach, merging range images that are recorded by two separate sensors. Two approaches, which are known from face recognition based on grey level images, have been extended to dealing with range images. These approaches are based on eigenfaces and hidden Markov models, respectively. Experimental results on a database with various range images from 24 persons show very promising results for both recognition methods.

1 Introduction

Analysis of human faces is a very challenging research area which has gained much attention during the last years. Most of the works, however, are focused on intensity or color images of faces, and only few approaches deal with range images. But there is evidence that range images have the potential to overcome some problems of intensity and color images. Some advantages of range images are the explicit representation of 3D shape, invariance under change of illumination, and invariance under change of color and reflectance properties of the objects. An example of the last type of invariance are images of a person with and without makeup. While the basic biometric properties of the face represented by a range image remain the same, the visual appearance of a person can be altered with makeup in such a way that not even humans are able to recognize the person anymore. In the present paper we present our experiences with applying eigenfaces and hidden Markov models (HMMs) to range images of human faces for the purpose of person identification.

One of the first works based on 3D images of human faces was proposed by Lapresté et al. [5]. The authors analyzed the curvature on a human face in order to extract feature points on the profile line. The recognition of the face was then based on the characteristics of the profile. Lee/Milios [6] extracted the convex regions in range images of human faces. These regions form the set of features of a face. For all these convex regions the Extended Gaussian image is calculated. The matching of facial features of two face images is based on these Extended Gaussian images. Gordon [3, 4] presented a detailed study of range images in face recognition. She computed the curvatures on a face in order to find face specific descriptors (e.g., nose ridge and eye features). These descriptors were used in the recognition stage. Yacoob/Davies [12] proposed a method for labeling the regions of a human face with the help of range images. Again, convex and concave points are calculated, but with a different method, namely a multistage diffusion process. The resulting regions are then labeled using a qualitative reasoning procedure. Lengagne et al. [7] created a depth map of the face with the help of a stereo pair of images. This depth map is improved by various processing steps, and, finally, feature extraction and segmentation is performed on the depth map. A recognition step is obviously planned by the authors, but not yet described.

The present paper describes two recognition procedures for images of human faces. One is based on the eigenface method [11], and the other on hidden Markov models [8]. We describe the processing steps and present some experimental results. The paper is structured in the following manner. In Section 2 we describe the data acquisition and range sensor setup. In Section 3 we present the preprocessing and the merging steps. After the description of the recognition procedures in Section 4, we show experimental results in Section 5. Finally, we discuss them and present future developments in Section 6.

2 Data Acquisition

The acquisition of range images of human faces is not trivial. Very good images are provided by the range scanner of Cyberware (e.g., used in the work of Gordon [3, 4]). The system is based on a laser range finder and a rotation platform. Generally, the scanner yields data of very high accuracy and provides a panoramic, 360° view of the object. Disadvantages are the high cost and the long scan time which is not suitable for the acquisition of face images.

For our system, we decided to use the coded light approach for acquiring range images. The disadvantages are missing data points due to occlusion or improperly reflected regions (e.g., dark regions such as eyebrows or beards, and specular regions such as the eyes). But the advantages of this method are its relatively high speed and the low cost of the equipment.

The acquisition of range information with the coded light approach [1] requires a setup as depicted in Figure 1. A sequence of stripe patterns is projected onto the scene, and for each projection an image is taken

0-8186-8150-0/97 $10.00

with the camera. This sequence of images results in a code for each pixel seen by the camera. But the code also corresponds to one projection plane of the projector. If the parameters of the projector and the camera are known, it is possible to compute the 3D position of a given image point by triangulation. The camera and projector parameters are calculated in a calibration step. However, for any shadow region as well as regions that do not properly reflect the projected light (e.g., dark regions), no 3D data can be computed. Thus, the coded light approach results in range images with missing data.

First experiments with the sensor configuration given in Figure 1 showed that the number of missing data points due to occlusion was rather large, which had a negative effect on the recognition performance. Therefore, we choose a multi-sensor setup in order to get a better quality of the data. This setup is depicted in Figure 2. We use two fully equipped range sensors which are sensing the object under different views. Both sensors operate in the same coordinate system. By merging the data of these two range images into one, we can reduce the problem of missing data significantly. The merging procedure will be described in detail in Section 3. Images generated in the merging step will be referred to as "merged images", whereas the original range images of a single sensor will be called "base images".

We acquired a collection of range images from 24 persons. For each person we have ten images, each resulting from two base images. The direction of the head was restricted to five standard directions. We took two images with the person looking straight ahead, two looking to the right, two looking to the left, two looking upwards, and two images looking downwards. Our database includes images of 21 men and three women; 15 wearer of glasses; three men with moustache; two man with beard; 21 Europeans; three Asians. In Figures 3 (range) and 4 (grey level) the images of one person from our database are shown. The images in Figure 3 are visualized by applying a triangulation procedure and graphical rendering to the range data.

3 Merging and Preprocessing of Range Images

An essential step in our system is the merging of two range images (base images) that were simultaneously taken from different positions. As mentioned above, by merging two range images from different viewing points we get a higher data density, and thus a better range image quality.

Our merging procedure aims at constructing a new range image out of an arbitrary collection of 3D points. Note that in our case we merge the data of only two base images. But the procedure can be easily expanded to merging data from any number of base images.

The basic idea in merging is to compute images as they might be seen by a virtual sensor. In our case the best position for the virtual sensor – i.e., the one that leads to the highest data density – is the center point between the two real sensors (see Figure 2). For this virtual sensor position a range image is computed out of the collection of 3D points. The procedure consists of the following steps:

1. **Initialization:** The input images and some user-defined parameters are read. After this step a set of range data, i.e., 3D coordinates, from both sensor systems are available.

2. **Positioning the virtual sensor:** The positioning of the virtual sensor is based on the set of 3D data points. First, the center of gravity $\vec{g} = (g_x, g_y, g_z)$ of the points is computed. The virtual sensor is then positioned at $\vec{s} = (g_x, g_y, g_z + d)$ where d is the displacement in z-direction; d is a parameter to be specified by the user. The view direction is given by $\vec{g} - \vec{s}$ (see Figure 2).

3. **Rotation of the object:** The user may specify rotation angles for the x, y and z axis in order to rotate the face into a canonical position. If such an angle is specified, the object is rotated around the center of gravity by the specified angles. If no rotation is specified, this step is skipped.

4. **Computation of the virtual sensor parameters:** Based on positioning information, the parameters of the virtual sensor (e.g., projection matrix, projection center in the new image, camera direction) are computed.

5. **Computation of the merged images:** For every original 3D data point, the coordinates in the merged range image are calculated based on the parameters of the virtual sensor. Since we are merging data from two different view points, it might happen that 3D points of two different surfaces are mapped onto the same pixel in the new range image. In this case we apply a sort of z-buffering [2]. If the distance between the two competing points is beyond a predefined threshold, the point further away from the virtual sensor is discarded. If the distance is lower than the threshold, the range values of the points involved are averaged and taken for the range image.

In Figure 5 the results of the merging procedure for the base images shown in Figure 3 are presented. Again, a triangulation procedure and graphical rendering were applied for the purpose of visualization.

After the merging procedure no further preprocessing of the data is done except a smoothing step, which was applied in some of our experiments. Smoothing is done with a standard Gaussian filter.

4 Recognition

A standard procedure for the analysis and recognition of faces is the so-called eigenface method described by Turk/Pentland [11]. Basically, a template matching is done after all images have been transformed into the so-called face space, which contains much less redundancy than the original image space.

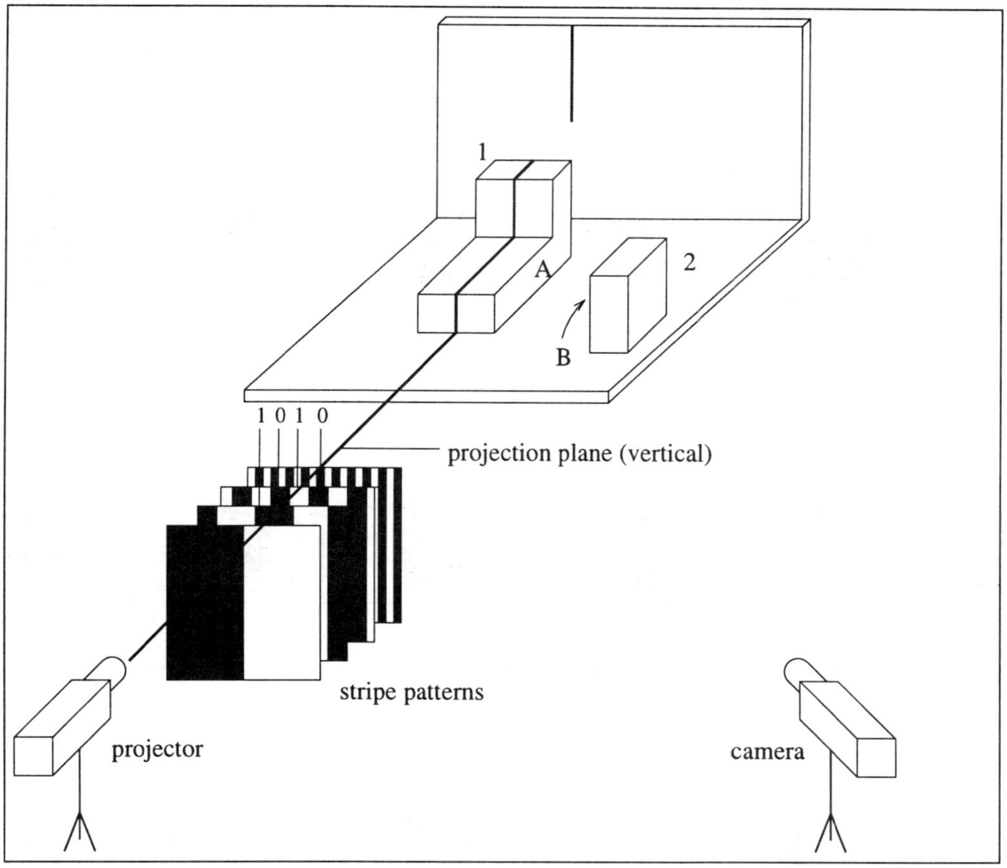

Figure 1: Range acquisition with the coded light approach

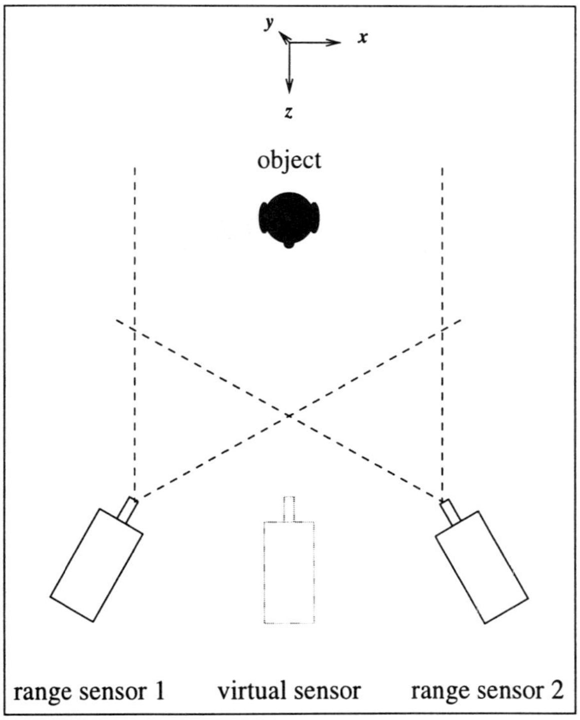

Figure 2: Setup of range sensor (as seen from above)

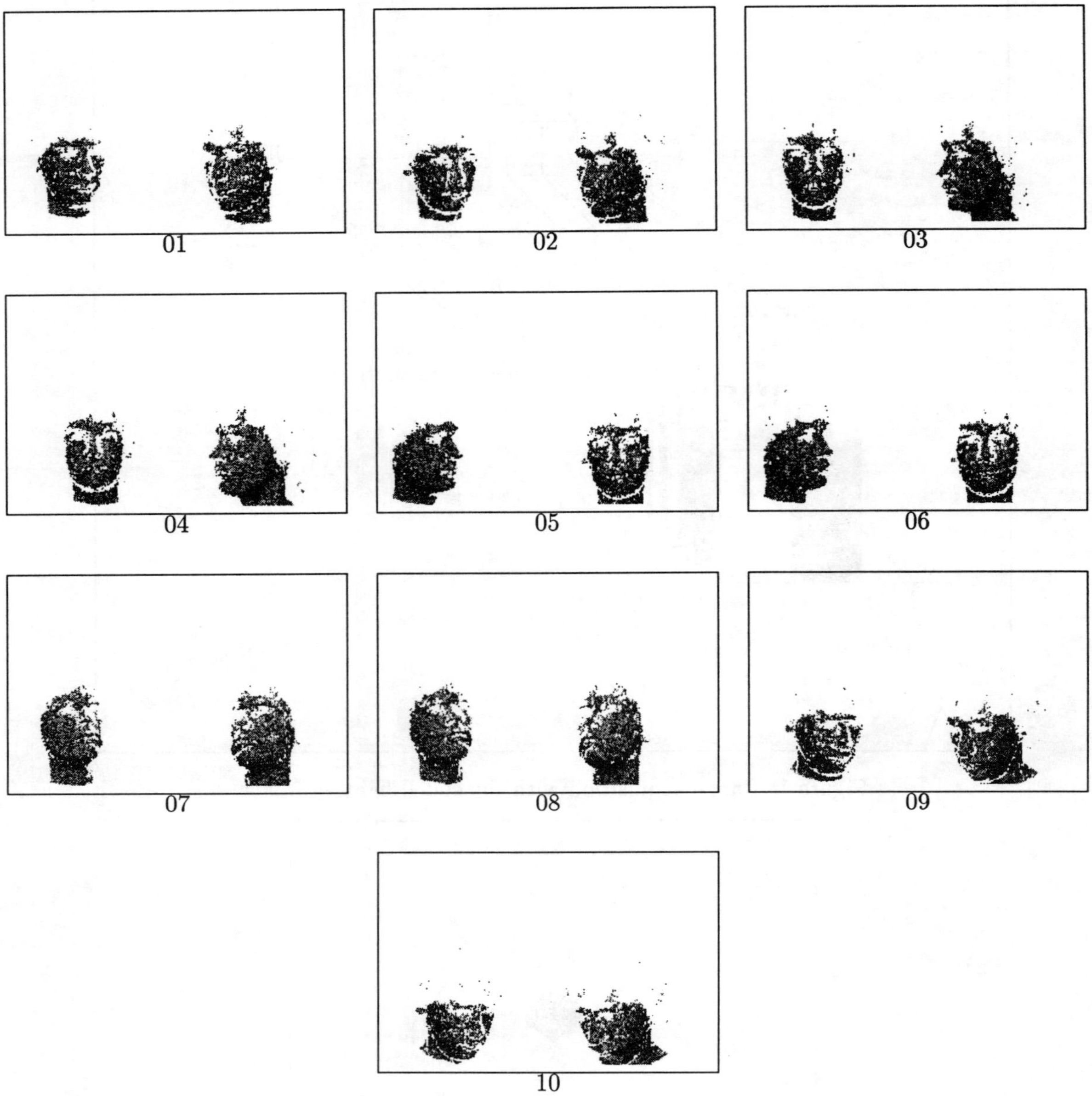

Figure 3: Ten range images (base images) of the same person. The white does represent missing data.

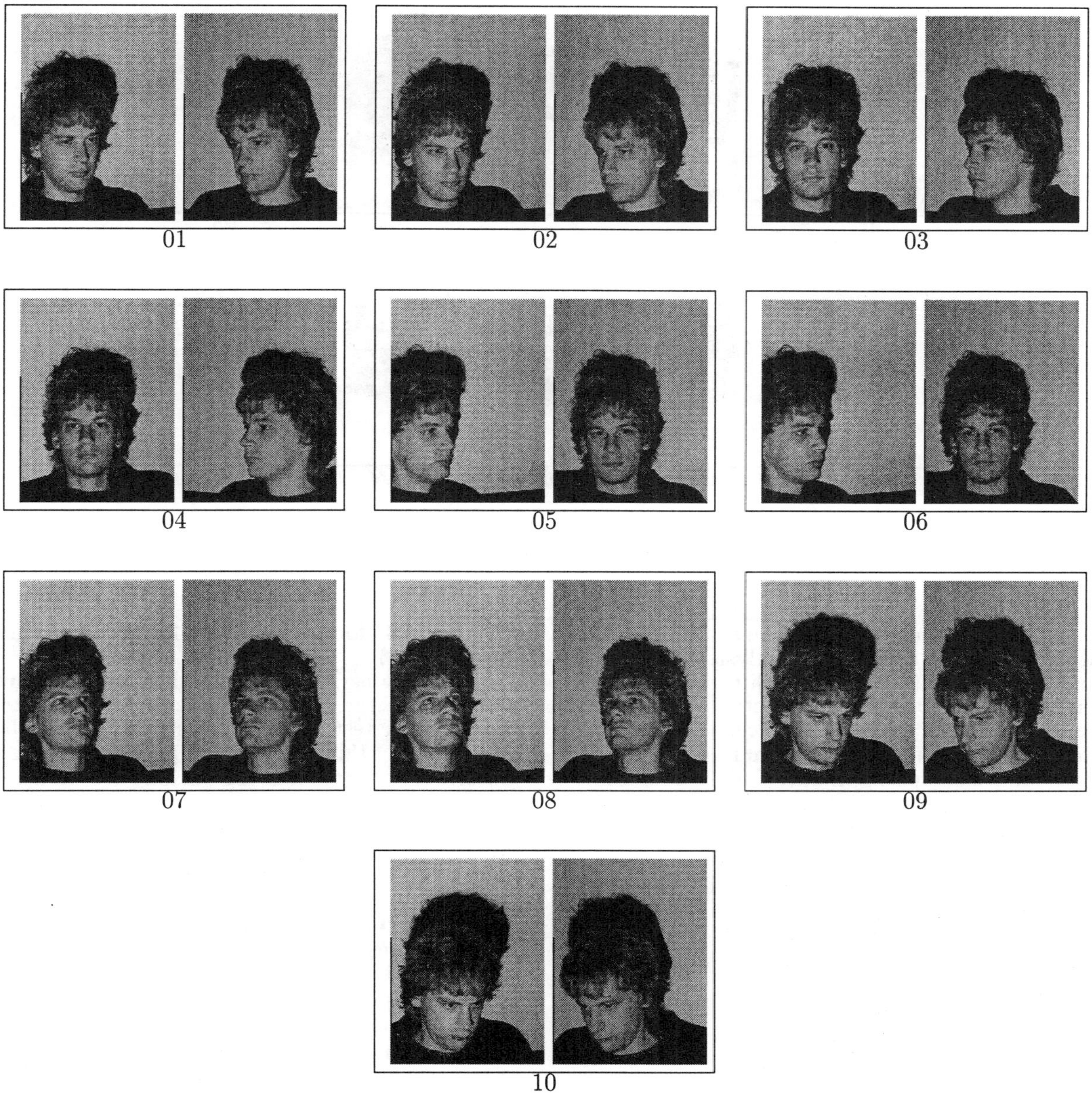

Figure 4: Grey level images of one person, corresponding to Figure 3.

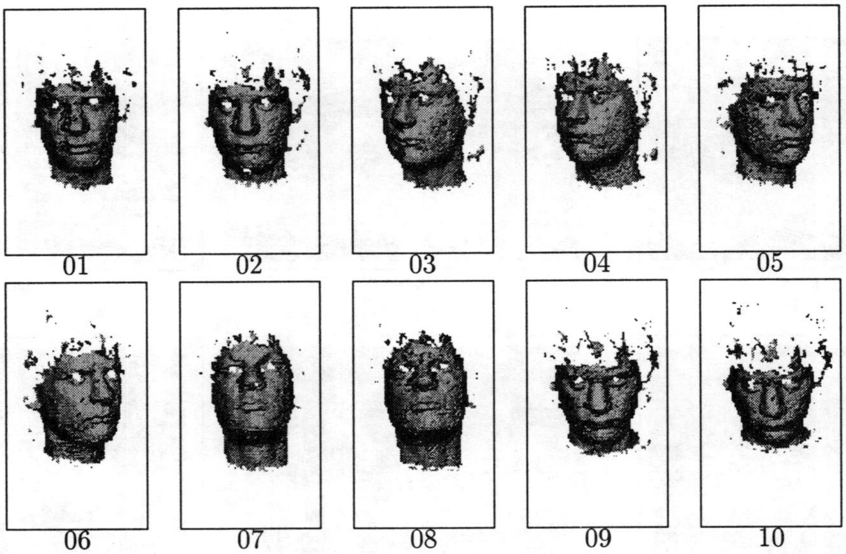

Figure 5: Merged range images

The base vectors which span the face space are determined by a principal component analysis of a series of training images, and the vectors with the most significant eigenvalues are taken as base vectors. Test images are first projected into the face space, and then it is determined which person's training image is the most similar in the face space. If the similarity is above a certain threshold, this yields the recognition result. Otherwise, the test image is rejected as unknown.

A second method which has gained some attention recently is face recognition based on hidden Markov models. It has been described by Samaria/Fallside [9, 10]. For a detailed description of HMMs see Rabiner [8]. Generally, HMMs are working on one-dimensional signals, or feature vectors. Images, however, contain two-dimensional information. In order to make HMMs applicable to images, we reduce the image information to one-dimensional vectors by applying a sliding window. This window is moving from the top of the image to the bottom and covers the whole width of the image. The step size is chosen so that two successive windows have a certain overlap. The reason for the overlap is to avoid the cutting of significant face features and bring some context information into the process. The pixel values in the sliding window are given as feature vector to the HMM.

The idea underlying this method is the following. Intuitively, a human face consists of a number of regions, for example, forehead, eyes, nose, mouth, chin and so on. These regions remain identifiable for a human observer, even when the face image is cut into sliding windows as described above. With the HMM we try to make use of this property. A human face is represented by a linear left-right model consisting of five states as shown in Figure 6. These states correspond to the face parts ("1" for the forehead, "2" for the eyes, "3" for the nose, "4" for the mouth and "5" for the chin).

For every person in the database the parameters of the hidden Markov model are calculated in a training phase. If a test image is presented, the probability of producing this image is computed by means of the Viterbi algorithm for every person (i.e., model) in the database. The classifier returns a ranking of the persons in the database in ascending order of the score for each model. The score s is computed dependent on the probabilities p of the models, i.e., $s = -2 \cdot \log p$.

5 Experimental Results

All images in our database have a size of 75 x 150 pixels. Since hidden Markov models and the eigenface method require training, we had to divide our data set into a test and a training set. For every head direction we used one image as a training and one as a test image. E.g., the images "01", "03", "05", "07", and "09" of the person shown in Figure 5 were used as training images, the other five images belonged to the test set. Totally, the database contains 120 training and 120 test images.

The tests for the eigenface method were done with the program facerec,[1] which was adapted for dealing with range images. The dimension of the eigenface space is 119. The computations involving the hidden Markov models, i.e., training and testing, were done with the ISADORA package[2].

The HMMs are linear left-right models consisting of five states as explained in Section 4. A sliding win-

[1]facerec was written by M. Turk at the Massachusetts Institute of Technology in Boston, USA.

[2]ISADORA was developed by E.G. Schukat-Talamazzini at the Friedrich-Alexander-Universität in Erlangen-Nürnberg, Germany.

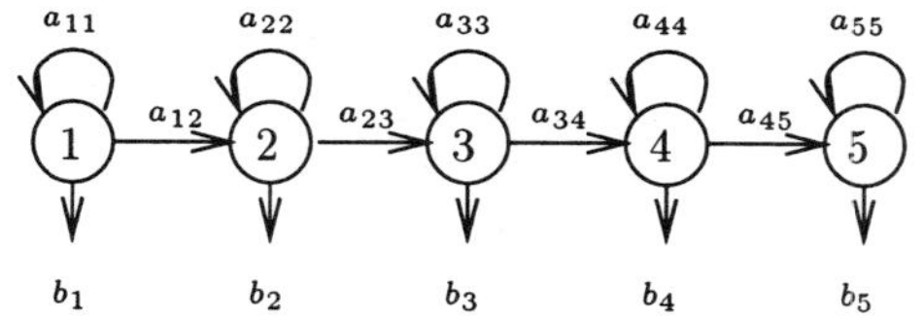

Figure 6: Linear left-right human face model

dow of 4 pixels height was moved from the top to the bottom of the images, and the data within the window were fed to the HMMs. The window overlap for the slide operation was 3 pixels.

The results of our experiments are shown in Table 1. For the experiments of the category "no preprocessing", no smoothing and no rotation are applied to the input images. Therefore, we have images of five different head directions. For each direction and each person, we have one image belonging to the training and one belonging to the test set. For the experiments reported under the category "smoothing", no rotation was done, but an additional smoothing step was applied. A Gaussian filter with $\sigma = 0.5$ and $\sigma = 1.5$ was used at this stage. Since the directions of the head were controlled to some degree, a rotation was applied in the experiments of the last category in order to bring the faces more or less in a canonical position (looking straight ahead). The rotation around the y axis was constantly 30° (head direction to the left or to the right side), and the rotation around the x axis 20° (head direction upwards or downwards).

The results for both recognition procedures are very promising. It seems that the eigenface strategy outperforms the HMM procedure. Since the database is rather small, however, we are not yet able to definitely conclude which of these procedures is superior to the other.

We additionally ran some tests with ten states instead of five in the HMM in order to check the influence of the number of states on the recognition rate. We did not notice any significant differences in the results, however.

The results for a smoothing step in the preprocessing are not as we expected for the HMM-based method. Since the data acquired with the range sensor are affected by white noise, it was hoped to get rid of the effects of noise by applying a smoothing procedure. The experiments, however, showed that the smoothing obviously removes characteristics of the facial surface which are important for the recognition (oversmoothing).

A similar effect was observed for rotation. The recognition rate for the eigenfaces is getting higher, whereas the rate for the hidden Markov models slightly drops.

6 Conclusions and Future Work

In the present paper, a low-cost and fast acquisition method for 3D facial data is described. Furthermore, two methods that are known for face recognition with grey level images have been extended to range images. These techniques are based on eigenfaces and on hidden Markov models, respectively. Though the data collection is not large (24 persons), we believe that the results are very promising. The eigenface approach outperforms the HMM strategy in our experiments.

The results of our experiments show clearly that face recognition with range images is a challenging and promising alternative to techniques based on intensity and color images. Procedures originally designed for grey level images work very well on range images, and the recognition rates are in a similar range. There is clear evidence that range images have some advantages over intensity images, for example availability of explicit 3D information and invariance properties. The explicit 3D information is useful for the transformation of a face image into a canonical position, since the pose of the object can be determined more accurately. And the invariance properties under change of color and illumination potentially lead to more robustness and stability. Another area which offers a large number of applications for range images is virtual reality. Our acquisition method is very well suited for the modeling of objects in VR systems, since in addition to the range image we also get an intensity image of the scene from our sensor. The combination of these two information sources by means of texture mapping yields object models that can be incorporated into virtual worlds.

In our future work, we plan to enlarge our collection of range images of human faces. We also plan to enhance the preprocessing of the images and incorporate additional recognition techniques in our system. Furthermore, we shall work on the combination of the classifiers involved, especially on the combination of range image and grey level image classification.

Acknowledgments

The software for the range image acquisition was originally provided by the ETH Zürich, Switzerland, and has been adapted to our sensor setup. The visualization of the 3D data was done with BOOGA (Bern's Object Oriented Graphics Architecture) which was developed by the Research Group for Computational Geometry at the University of Bern, Switzerland, headed by Prof. H. Bieri.

References

[1] P.J. Besl. Active, Optical Range Imaging Sensors. *Machine Vision and Applications*, 1:127–152, 1988.

[2] J.D. Foley, A. van Dam, S.K. Feiner, and J.F. Hughes. *Computer Graphics. Principles and*

preprocessing	eigenface procedure	HMM procedure
no preprocessing	97.50%	90.83%
smoothing ($\sigma = 0.5$)	98.33%	90.00%
smoothing ($\sigma = 1.5$)	98.33%	76.67%
rotation	100.00%	89.17%

Table 1: Results of the experiments

Practice. Addison-Wesley Publishing Company, 2nd edition, 1990.

[3] G.G. Gordon. Face Recognition Based on Depth Maps and Surface Curvature. In *SPIE Proceedings: Geometric Methods in Computer Vision, San Diego, CA*, volume 1570 of *SPIE Proceedings*, July 1991.

[4] G.G. Gordon. Face Recognition Based on Depth and Curvature Features. In *Proceedings IEEE Computer Society Conference on Computer Vision and Pattern Recognition (CVPR), Champaign, IL*, pages 808–810. IEEE Computer Society Press, June 1992.

[5] J.T. Lapresté, J.Y. Cartoux, and M. Richetin. Face Recognition from Range Data by Structural Analysis. In G. Ferrate, T. Pavlidis, A. Sanfeliu, and H. Bunke, editors, *Syntactic and Structural Pattern Recognition*, NATO ASI Series, pages 303–314. 1988.

[6] J.C. Lee and E. Milios. Matching Range Images of Human Faces. In *Third International Conference on Computer Vision (ICCV), Osaka, Japan*, pages 722–726, December 1990.

[7] R. Lengagne, J.-P. Tarel, and O. Monga. From 2D Images to 3D Face Geometry. In *Proceedings 2nd International Conference on Automatic Face and Gesture Recognition (ICAFGR), Killington, Vermont*, pages 301–306, October 1996.

[8] L.R. Rabiner. A Tutorial on Hidden Markov Models and Selected Applications in Speech Recognition. *Proceedings of the IEEE*, 77(2):257–286, February 1989.

[9] F. Samaria and F. Fallside. Face Identification and Feature Extraction Using Hidden Markov Models. In G. Vernazza, A.N. Venetsanopoulos, and C. Braccini, editors, *Image Processing: Theory and Applications*, pages 295–298. Elsevier Science Publishers, 1993.

[10] F. Samaria and S. Young. HMM-Based Architecture for Face Identification. *Image and Vision Computing*, 12(8):537–543, October 1994.

[11] M.A. Turk and A.P. Pentland. Eigenfaces for Recognition. *Journal of Cognitive Neuroscience*, 3(1):71–86, 1991.

[12] Y. Yacoob and L.S. Davis. Labeling of Human Face Components from Range Data. *CVGIP: Image Understanding*, 60(2):168–178, September 1994.

System Architecture and Techniques for Gesture Recognition in Unconstraint Environments

M. R. J. Kohler
Informatik VII (Computer Graphics)
University of Dortmund
44221 Dortmund, Germany
e-mail: Markus.Kohler@cs.uni-dortmund.de
http://ls7-www.informatik.uni-dortmund.de/~kohler

Abstract

Controlling appliances in home environments by gestures is a step towards more intuitive and natural human computer interfaces. A brief overview on an existing vision based gesture recognition system and its architecture and details on ergonomic remote control of devices by gestures are clarified. The focus is on the motion detection, object normalization and identification, the modelling and the prediction of motion by the Kalman Filter. The initialization problem of the Kalman Filter of a vision based system for human motion tracking differs from initialization for physical systems, where manuals report measurement errors. A main interest was to develop the initialization and adequate Kalman model for human motion. Most aspects mentioned in this report were implemented in the ARGUS prototype.

1 Introduction

Human computer interfaces based on visual input (video) have found growing interest during the last few years. One reason may be the continuously falling expense of hardware for image grabbing and processing. Even colour image processing is now available and fast enough for pattern recognition.

There are several examples of gesture recognition systems and tracking systems (survey [20]). A motion recognition system was presented by Darrell and Pentland [6] using special hardware. "Digit Eyes" [21] models hand postures with 27 degrees of freedom and tracks the motion of the fingers. Ahmad [1] describes a real time tracking system where 19 degrees of freedom are available. Maggioni [17, 18] enumerates several useful applications of a vision based interface. A colour look-up table is determined considering both, the object's and background colours. It is used for segmentation. Bröckl-Fox [3] considers ergonomic and anatomic aspects concerning the gesture based interaction between user and computer. An ergonomically remarkable "Television control by hand gestures" war presented by Freeman [10]. The problem of perspective distortion also affecting ARGUS was already discussed in [19, 7]. All these systems implement different input techniques and several aspects in gesture recognition in constraint environments.

This report discusses the research and underlying problems and solutions of the project ARGUS [13]. The goal of the prototype system ARGUS is to apply visual input in home environment without the need of markers attached to the user's body. The user may communicate with the devices in his home environment in a natural way. There are no constraints on the position from where he communicates through gestures as long as he is within the *interaction area*[1]. ARGUS shows that gestural input can be realized on low cost personal computers. This makes ARGUS available for disabled (e. g. speech impaired) and elderly people. The remote control in this prototype is done completely by gesture input, and it is a challenge to evaluate the usefulness of gestural input. In the near future, ARGUS will be combined with speech input because the combination of speech and visual input is the most natural way of communication: "Open that window" when pointing towards a window. Neither remote control by gesture recognition itself nor by mere speech recognition will work. Speech recognition fails in noisy environments (if the TV or audio devices are switched on) and gesture recognition can not be used in dark environments to switch on the light, for ex-

[1] Assuming that a finger appearing with two pixel thickness is good enough to be recognized continuously and a real finger has a thickness of 18 mm, an interaction area of 3.45 m diameter is derived with a maximum x resolution of the camera's colour channels U/V of 384 pixel. This is based on the assumption, that 5 fingers with 4 spaces between must be recognized.

0-8186-8150-0/97 $10.00 © 1997 IEEE

Figure 1: The above gesture sequence is called *pointer click*. The very left hand posture shows the *pointer gesture*.

ample. Visual and speech input will complete each other. The output of ARGUS is speech.

The following Section 2 describes the assembly, functionality and architecture of the ARGUS system. Section 3 explains details about motion detection, tracking and object identification and Section 4 outlines the results and future investigation.

2 Assembly and Functionality of ARGUS in an Home Environment

This Section shows briefly the overall assembly, functionality and system architecture of ARGUS. In the calibrated ARGUS system (see [13] for calibration) two cameras observing the user are installed close to the wall above the devices (Fig. 3). The user points towards a device with straddled thumb and forefinger. The system reports the aimed device by speech feedback. The selection is done by bowing the thumb (called *pointer-click*, Fig. 1). Further control is according to Table 1, where one gesture is used for each line. Every gesture is mapped to several similar tasks from different devices[2], which reduces the number of gestures and makes the dialogue more intuitive. Additional functionality is achieved by gesture sequences. Devices like a VCR, TV, CD player, lamps or coffee maker etc. (Fig. 3) may be connected to the computer either through a home bus system (separate cables, power supplies, radio waves — bidirectional), or they may be controlled with infrared signals (unidirectional) by the computer [13].

The ARGUS system architecture consists of the four recognition systems (Fig. 2), *Motion Recognition, Colour Recognition, Gesture Recognition and Sequence/Trajectory Recognition*, and the *Dialogue Control System.* For each *object* (hands or head) detected by the subsystem *Object Recognition and Tracking* (Section 3), one instance of the modules *Segmentation, ZYKLOP* and *Motion Interpreter* is generated.

The subsystem *Segmentation* separates the foreground from the background for each *object* separately in an almost natural environment based on a V channel histogram [13, 2, 14]. In a future step the prom-

[2] The user will communicate with one device at a time, only.

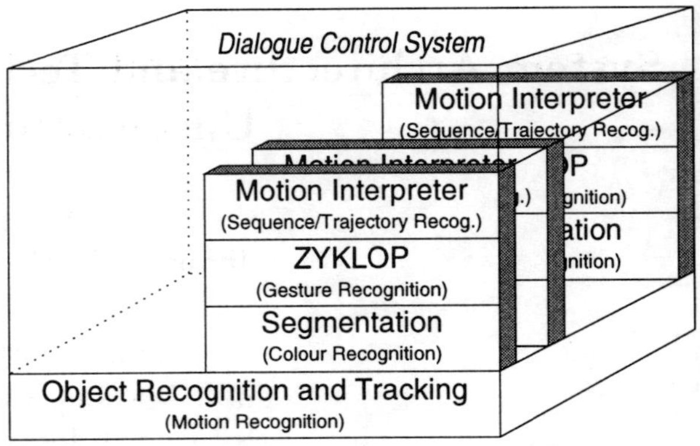

Figure 2: System architecture of the Integrated Gesture Recognition System

ising colour recognition from Schröter[3] [23] and further edge and motion based methods will be included, as the independence of variation in colour and brightness still needs to be improved in ARGUS.

A further segmentation step, called *automatic cutting*, separates or normalizes the hand objects. If the forearm is partly covered by clothes, it generally confuses gesture recognition. The resulting boundary adulteration is similar to the problem of recognizing occluded or overlapping objects. Hence, the referenced solutions proposed in literature [25, 11, 12, 16] will be further examined. Another method is to use a code sequence recognition like that implemented in ZYKLOP [24]. It may be applied to Chain Codes [5, 9] to recognize the relevant part of the contour (invariant to rotation, scaling and to a high degree to perspective distortion). Another promising method is to fit a growing circle (tracked by Kalman Filter) — called bubble —, that completely lies within the hand, (Fig. 5), which is similar to search for crossings in the skeleton. The search direction for this bubble may be forced by a potential function.

As a hand mainly "rotates" around the elbow the centrifugal force is an appropriate potential function to shift the bubble towards the end of the arm. The potential function and bubble shape depend on the object that needs to be separated. If a head needs to be separated from the body, a head detecting bubble should be driven by impetus forces and should be an ellipse, as a head is generally upright. Bubbles with search-object specific attributes may be used to separate body parts. If one of the above automatic cutting

[3] Schröter includes a survey of the available contributions concerning colour and brightness constancy.

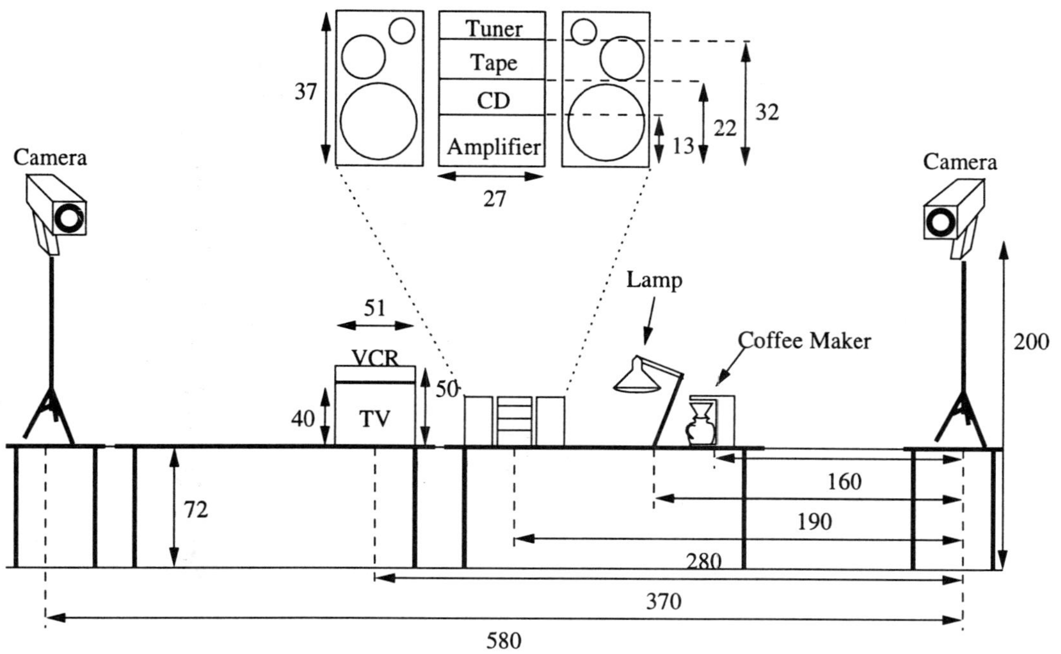

Figure 3: Test environment: Vision based remote control in intelligent home environments: (The measurement is in *cm*).

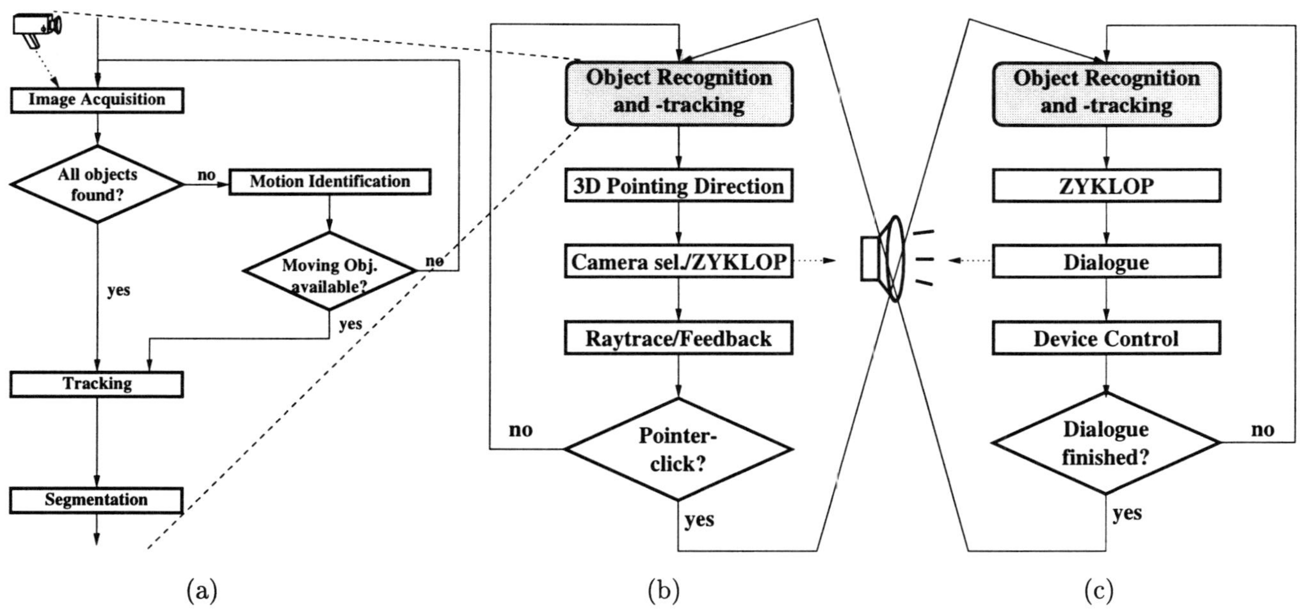

Figure 4: Control flow of the *Object Recognition and Tracking* (a), device selection by pointing including feedback *(Determine Direction and Device)* (b) and dialogue with one device *(Dialogue, Device Control)* (c).

Function	amplifier	compact disk player	tuner	compact cassette system	video cassette recorder	television	gesture
Volume +	⋆					⋆	
Volume −	⋆					⋆	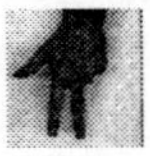
Play		⋆		⋆	⋆		
Stop		⋆		⋆	⋆		
Source	⋆						
Power off	⋆				⋆	⋆	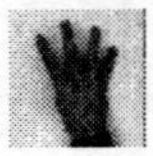
		title	program	wind	wind	program	
+ function		⋆	⋆	⋆	⋆	⋆	
− function		⋆	⋆	⋆	⋆	⋆	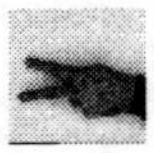

Table 1: Example of common functions of devices: Same functions are mapped to the same gesture; similar functions may be mapped to the same gesture if this is intuitive and no other function is overloaded.

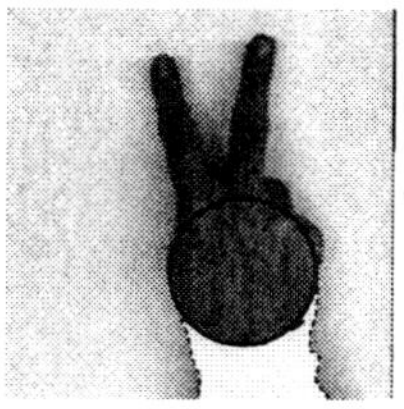

Figure 5: Automatic cutting: Separating the hand from the forearm by potential driven search bubbles.

methods is used, the "cut" gestures must be taught to the gesture recognition system.

Next, the pure gesture recognition [24] evaluates only the hand's bounding box of that camera, whose cosine of the angle between the optical axis and the pointing direction is minimal. This saves computing time. A meaningful gesture is further processed by the *Motion Interpreter* together with position parameters delivering the final gesture number. The subsystem Motion Interpreter includes the *Sequence and Trajectory Recognition* for each object. This was already included in ZYKLOP [24]. The sequence recognition may further be improved by using HMMs [26].

Finally, the Dialogue Control System combines a final gesture of the multiple output of the recognition process instances and decides, which task to complete and which device to control. The stereo view is used to estimate 3D pointing directions [13] and determining the selected device by a ray tracing step. Speech feedback compensates the inaccurate human pointing. Exchanging the Dialogue Control System by a simple interpreter table, that serves to translate gesture codes to commands, enables to use ARGUS as a single camera gesture recognition system for controlling desktop applications through ASCII commands (see project ZYKLOP [24]) or X events.

Fig. 4 shows the detailed, self explaining control flows of ARGUS for the main system states: (a) object recognition and tracking (continues during both processes (b) and (c)), (b) device selection by pointing and (c) dialogue with one device — either (b) or (c) is active.

3 Object Recognition and Tracking

The subsystem *Object Recognition and Tracking* is able to handle up to three cameras with arbitrary moving objects and includes the basic modules *Image Acquisition, Image Management* and *Bounding Box Management* [13]. In the following subsections we discuss the special topics: an improved *Motion Detection* compared to [22], *Tracking* including the initialization and the *object identification.*

3.1 Motion Detection

The module *Motion Detection* uses the difference images for each camera and each channel. Due to noise of the camera, only differences exceeding a certain threshold are considered. A fast filter algorithm detects the relevant motion according to the ideas of the *Motion to Shape Sensor* [22]. It first operates on lines of the difference image. Each finger must appear at least as one pixel to be available for hand gesture recognition. Further, gesture recognition requires that spaces between straddled fingers are visible. Hence, hand objects must result in run lengths with at least five pixels, where longer run lengths may contain up to approximately 45 % non-set pixels. All the run lengths of that format are accepted and otherwise rejected. This rule already eliminates most of the noisy motion. Next coherence is examined by a scan line algorithm. Bounding boxes are generated for the detected domains. A sequence of the following heuristic filters may be configured in ARGUS and the order is essential to the result. Filters may be called several times. Some filters are (see also [13]): If bounding boxes are not tall enough (at least five pixel), they are removed. Boxes with less distance, than a certain percentage of the average distance between all the boxes, are melted together. Too large, too small and very eccentric boxes are eliminated. Experiments showed that these filters mostly eliminate all the noise but no relevant objects. The resulting sensor is very sensitive to motion. An advantage is the speed up, because subsampling of the image can easily be applied. All the detected moving objects (resp. labeled bounding boxes) are tracked according to the next section.

3.2 Tracking

The control flow of ARGUS object recognition and tracking is shown in the self explaining Fig. 4 (a). Motion Detection is called interchangeably with Tracking. Hence, once a visible object is detected it will not get lost even when it stops moving. The *Tracking Module* uses the *Discrete Kalman Filter* [4]. The filter predicts the position of each object's bounding box in the two dimensional image.

The physical law of motion $\mathbf{s}(t) = \mathbf{s}(0) + \mathbf{v}(0) \cdot t + 1/2 \cdot \mathbf{a}(0) \cdot t^2$ results from truncating the Taylor Series of a time variant motion. If acceleration is constant, it exactly models the motion. If velocity is constant, then $\ddot{\mathbf{s}}(t) = \dot{\mathbf{v}}(t) = \mathbf{a}(t)$ is zero and the constant velocity model follows $\mathbf{s}(t) = \mathbf{s}(0) + \mathbf{v}(0) \cdot t$. However, if neither $\mathbf{v}(t)$ nor $\mathbf{a}(t)$ is constant, both laws only hold for very small t, due to generally bad convergence of

Taylor Series. What does it mean, that the acceleration is constant? It means that the force F driving the object of mass m is constant, because $F = m \cdot a$, with acceleration a. This may be true for vehicles and missiles after some startup time. But in human motion forces keep changing continuously.

Thus, the motion is considered to be the superposition of an ideal basic motion of constant velocity, for example, and the acceleration as white noise. For further information about "white noise" signals we refer to [15].

3.2.1 Discrete Time Model of the Kalman Filter

We start to model a motion of a single point with the Kalman Filter (e. g. the lower left, upper right corner of a bounding box or the center of gravity)[4].

Experiments with ARGUS showed that modelling human motion with constant velocity and considering acceleration as white noise is sufficient. If we idealize the human motion to the constant velocity model, i. e. we assume the velocity is constant in the time interval $[t_k, t_{k+1}]$, we can transform it to a description with linear equations. More generally, let $\mathbf{s}_j := \mathbf{s}(t_j)$ be a position of an object at time t_j and $\mathbf{v}_j := \mathbf{v}(t_j)$ its velocity. Then it is $\mathbf{s}_{k+1} = \mathbf{s}_k + \mathbf{v}_k \cdot (t_{k+1} - t_k)$ and $\mathbf{v}_{k+1} = \mathbf{v}_k$, which is equivalent to

$$\begin{pmatrix} \mathbf{s}_{k+1} \\ \mathbf{v}_{k+1} \end{pmatrix} = \mathbf{\Phi_k} \cdot \begin{pmatrix} \mathbf{s}_k \\ \mathbf{v}_k \end{pmatrix}, \; \mathbf{\Phi_k} := \begin{pmatrix} 1 & \Delta t \\ 0 & 1 \end{pmatrix} \quad (1)$$

and $\Delta t := t_{k+1} - t_k$. The vector $\mathbf{x}_k := (\mathbf{s}_k, \mathbf{v}_k)^T$ is called the *process state vector* at time t_k. The matrix $\mathbf{\Phi_k}$ is the *transition matrix* that relates $\mathbf{x}_k$ to $\mathbf{x}_{k+1}$ in absence of a forcing function. However, human motion is not constant at all. It is driven by arbitrary forces and the acceleration seems to be random. Therefore we model this aspect by a random noise $\mathbf{w}_k$, which is added to the left side of Equation (1) yielding

$$\mathbf{x}_{k+1} = \mathbf{\Phi_k} \cdot \mathbf{x_k} + \mathbf{w_k} \,. \quad (2)$$

For detailed explanation see [15]. The time between two images is assumed to be constantly Δt.

During the recursion of the Kalman Filter each prediction will be followed by a measurement. Putting this measurement into the recursion will influence the next prediction. This is best described in [8, 15]. So the Kalman Filter "learns" the data included by the measurement. The measurement of the random process occurs in time at discrete points in accordance with the linear relationship

$$\mathbf{z}_k = \mathbf{H}_k \mathbf{x}_k + \mathbf{e}_k \quad (3)$$

where $\mathbf{z}_k$ is the *vector measurement* and $\mathbf{H}_k$ gives the ideal (noiseless) connection between the measurement and the state vector at time t_k. Hence, the Kalman Recursion considers that the internal state vector of the model may not directly be measured.

In our case, we can only measure positions on the screen in two dimensions. We cannot measure velocity but only calculate it roughly from several positions. But therefore we use the Kalman Filter. The state vector is modelled to have a position and a velocity. The matrix $\mathbf{H}_k$ shall only extract the position from the state vector which is done by $\mathbf{H}_k = (1, 0)$. Further, $\mathbf{e}_k$ is the *measurement error* and also should have white characteristic. Let $\mathbf{z}_k$ be the measurement, then $\mathbf{z}_k = \mathbf{s}_k + \mathbf{e}_k$, i. e. the measurement $\mathbf{z}_k$ is identical to the position $\mathbf{s}_k$ of the process state vector plus a measurement error $\mathbf{e}_k$.

Physically, forces that induce acceleration and velocities do not influence each other, if they are perpendicular (superposition of orthogonal forces). Any translational force, acceleration and velocity in 2D or 3D space is a superposition of two resp. three orthogonal forces, accelerations or velocities. Hence, the Kalman Model (2) and the measurement relation (3) may be written for each dimension separately [15]. Thus, for two dimensional prediction as in the ARGUS case two separate Kalman recursions are evaluated. If several objects in the plane are tracked, it is highly recommended to split up the system for reasons of time efficiency of matrix inversion.

3.2.2 Initialization of the Filter Covariance Matrices

The Kalman Recursion requires some covariance matrices, that must be determined and initialized: the covariance matrix of the measurement error $\mathbf{R}_k$, the covariance matrix of the white acceleration $\mathbf{Q}_k$ and the covariance matrix of the estimation error $\mathbf{P}_k$. Further, the a priori estimate $\hat{\mathbf{x}}_0^-$ must be set to an initial value. This initialization is discussed in detail in [15]. Here the results are summarized. Because gesture recognition is driven near the lower resolution boundary to achieve a bigger interaction area, it is a prerequisite,

[4] As motion prediction is applied to images, the positions, velocities etc. will have two dimensions. But let us abstract from our special situation. The values $\mathbf{s}(t), \mathbf{v}(t), \mathbf{a}(t)$ might be a vector or a scalar. The fact, that $\mathbf{s}(t)$ might be a vector, is marked by bold letters. All matrices and vectors are also marked bold and matrices are, in contrary to vectors, in capitals. All equations should be regarded carefully, as they might imply tensor products.

that the measurement error should be below one pixel. Further, the x and y measurement error are independent. According to [15], this leads to the initialization of the *measurement error covariance matrix*

$$\mathbf{R}_k = \frac{2}{3} \cdot \begin{pmatrix} 1 & 0 \\ 0 & 1 \end{pmatrix} \quad \forall k \, ,$$

Note, that this matrix is related on the unit "pixel", because measurement is done in pixels. With $\Delta t = t_{k+1} - t_k$ as previously defined, [15] inspires to initialize the covariance matrix of the white acceleration to

$$\mathbf{Q}_k = \frac{a^2 \Delta t}{6} \begin{pmatrix} 2\mathbf{I}\Delta^2 t & 3\mathbf{I}\Delta t \\ 3\mathbf{I}\Delta t & 6\mathbf{I} \end{pmatrix} s$$

while a is the spectral amplitude of the white noise and $\mathbf{I}$ is the 2×2 identity (s is the unit seconds). As the acceleration is identified as white noise, a is the amplitude of the acceleration frequencies. According to experiments we estimate the spectral amplitude to a value smaller than $a \approx 1225 \frac{pixel}{s^2}$ for fast hand movements (the assumption was, that the motion mainly takes place in the maximum interaction area of 3,45 m), which is the same as $a = 49$ pixel/frame^2 at 5 frames per second, $a = 12$ pixel/frame^2 at 10 frames per second or $a =$ 5pixel/frame^2 at 15 frames per second.

At this point we assume that we have an initial estimate of the process at some point in time t_k, and that this estimate is based on all of our knowledge about the process prior to t_k. This prior (or *a priori*) estimate will be denoted as $\hat{\mathbf{x}}_k^-$ where the "hat" denotes estimate, and the "super minus" is a reminder that this is our best estimate prior to assimilating the measurement at t_k. The estimation error is then $\mathbf{x}_k - \hat{\mathbf{x}}_k^-$ and the associated error covariance matrix $\mathbf{P}_k^- = E[(\mathbf{x}_k - \hat{\mathbf{x}}_k^-)(\mathbf{x}_k - \hat{\mathbf{x}}_k^-)^T]$. According to [15] we take the covariance matrix of the estimation error as

$$\mathbf{P}_0^- = \frac{1}{16} \cdot \begin{pmatrix} s^2 & 0 \\ 0 & v^2 \end{pmatrix} .$$

The report [15] suggests to take the distance $s =$ 25 pixel at 5 frames per second, $s = 6$ pixel at 10 frames per second and $s = 3$ pixel at 15 frames per second and the maximal velocity $v = 49$ pixel/frame at 5 frames per second, $v = 12$ pixel/frame at 10 frames per second or $v = 5$ pixelframe at 15 frames per second. Again this suggestion was made under the assumption that the action mostly takes place such that the hands appear near the resolution boundary. The initial value of the process state vector is set to $\hat{\mathbf{x}}_0^- = (\mathbf{s}_0^-, 0)^T$, where $\mathbf{s}_0^-$ is the center of gravity of the (two!) domains of an object detected by the motion detection.

3.2.3 The Kalman Recursion

The matrices $\mathbf{P}_0^-, \mathbf{R}_0$ and $\mathbf{Q}_0$ must be initialized previously as well as the $\hat{\mathbf{x}}_0^-$. It is important to find good values for $\mathbf{R}_0$ and $\mathbf{Q}_0$. If the values $\hat{\mathbf{x}}_0^-$ or $\mathbf{P}_0^-$ are poor they will mostly converge towards the expected values. Next the *Kalman Recursion* is evaluated (see also [4, pages 195–200] and [15])

1. Compute gain (blending factor) $\mathbf{K}_k = \mathbf{P}_k^- \mathbf{H}_k^T (\mathbf{H}_k \mathbf{P}_k^- \mathbf{H}_k^T + \mathbf{R}_k)^{-1}$
2. Update estimate $\hat{\mathbf{x}}_k = \hat{\mathbf{x}}_k^- + \mathbf{K}_k(\mathbf{z}_k - \mathbf{H}_k \cdot \hat{\mathbf{x}}_k^-)$
3. Update *error covariance matrix* $\mathbf{P}_k = (\mathbf{I} - \mathbf{K}_k \mathbf{H}_k)\mathbf{P}_k^-$
4. Project ahead $\hat{\mathbf{x}}_{k+1}^- = \mathbf{\Phi_k \hat{x}_k}$
5. Update *error covariance matrix* $\mathbf{P}_{k+1}^- = \mathbf{\Phi_k P_k \Phi_k^T} + \mathbf{Q_k}$.

The blending factor and the update estimate is discussed in [15]. For each relevant bounding box a new position is estimated with the Kalman Filter. The main advantage of Kalman Filtering is that tracking speeds up the image processing and improves the independence of varying illumination. Further advantages are reported in [13].

To make sure that a tracked, fast moving object (like the hand) completely lies within the predicted bounding box of the Kalman Filter, this box is increased by a certain factor. Further, if two objects partly overlap, the bounding boxes may coincide after segmentation, as the objects appear as a single object. In this case if two objects are detected within one box that emerged from previously two boxes, the estimated box must be split to two boxes surrounding the two detected objects.

3.3 Object Identification

Another part of the Object Recognition and Tracking subsystem is the *Object Identification.* It is important to gradually identify the objects. If an object (motion) is detected, it will be tracked immediately and it is first identified to a certain confidence by its absolute and relative position to the other objects, by its size, eccentricity, colour and further heuristics. For further stabilization or correction of the identification, the process state vector of the tracking process is used, which includes motion parameters as the position and velocity and may be extended by the acceleration and further derivatives. Various features are extracted from the process state vector. These features are compared to previously learned ordinary human motion parameters of hands and heads. As head movements are generally of slower translational acceleration compared to hand movement, it is possible to identify objects by motion parameters.

As the reliability of the identification increases with the amount of time an object is tracked, the confidence attribute of the object's identifier must be increased. The object must be continuously compared against other objects in all camera views: firstly, to skip it as soon as possible, if it is identical to another tracked object in the same camera view[5], and secondly, to recognize equal objects in different camera views and give them the same identifier. Thus even the left and the right hand may be distinguished as they will have similar motion characteristic in both projections. In case of uncertainty the heuristics (like relative/absolute position, size etc.) should further be considered.

4 Results and Future Improvements

ARGUS showed that it is possible to use gestures for remote controlling devices in a home environment. The functionality was evaluated in a test environment illustrated in Fig. 3 and Fig. 6. In the ARGUS project a PC Pentium 133 MHz with 16 MByte was used. The performance was ranging from 5 to 15 frames per second and camera [13]. It turned out that rates below 10 frames per second and camera appear to slow for a natural and comfortable dialogue. The angular resolution is below one degree.

Figure 6: ARGUS labs: Remote controlling audio and video devices by gestures.

Further improvements will be the inclusion of colour recognition according [23] to be more independent from illumination, the use of rotatable cameras to increase the interaction area and the forearm segmentation. ARGUS must further be improved with respect to ergonomic aspects. The gesture dialogue must be improved by selecting easily performable gestures, by adapting timeouts and latency timers to the user needs and by an overall intelligent speech and gesture dialogue interface.

[5]This might occur, because Tracking and Motion Detection are called interchangeably. So Motion Detection will also find the tracked objects.

Acknowledgments

I appreciate the great work that was done by the graduate students M. Breig, D. Dechow, M. Fellenberg, R. Jaeschke, M. Jedamzik, T. Kuleßa, D. Pukropski, D. Rief, D. Rosemann, A. Thümmler, J. Albrecht, D. Aust, L. Cleff, B. Deimel, C. Esken, C. Kirstein, M. Kukuk, S. Mork, S. Schewe, S. Schröter, G. Veltmann, C. Wenger and my colleagues M. Stark and M. Wittner. Thanks to Prof. Dr. H. Müller who supported both projects.

References

[1] Subutai Ahmad. A usable real-time 3D hand tracker. In *Proceedings 28th Asilomar Conference on Signals, Systems and Computers*, pages 1257–1261. IEEE Computer Society Press, 1995.

[2] Projektgruppe 277: ARGUS. Ein ergonomisches Dialogsystem zur Steuerung von technischen Systemen in Wohnbereichen mittels Gestenerkennung — Abschlußbericht. Technical report, Informatik VII, University of Dortmund, 1997.

[3] Ulrich Bröckl-Fox. *Untersuchung neuer, gestenbasierter Methoden für die 3D-Interaktion.* PhD thesis, University of Karlsruhe, February 1995. Shaker-Verlag, ISBN 3-8265-0620-0.

[4] Robert G. Brown. *Introduction to random signal analysis and Kalman filtering.* Wiley, New York [u.a.], 1983.

[5] Mo Dai, Pierre Baylou, and Mohamed Najim. An efficient algorithm for computation of shape moments from run-length codes or chain codes. *Pattern Recognition*, 25(10):1119 - 1128, February 1992.

[6] T.J. Darrell and A.P. Pentland. Space-time gestures. In *Proc. Conf. on Computer Vision and Pattern Recognition*, pages 335–340, New York, NY, June 15-17 1993.

[7] A. Drees, F. Kummert, E. Littmann, S. Posch, H. Ritter, and G. Sagerer. A hybrid system to detect hand orientation in stereo images. In E.S.

Gelsema and L.N. Kanal, editors, *Pattern Recognition in Practice IV: Multiple Paradigms, Comparative Studies and Hybrid Systems*, pages 551–562. Elsevier, Amsterdam, 1994.

[8] Roger M. du Plessis. Poor Man's Explanation of Kalman Filtering or how I stopped worrying and learned to love Matrix Inversion. Technical report, Autonetics Division, Rockwell International, 3370 Miraloma Avenue, Anaheim, California 92803, June 1967.

[9] H. Freeman. Computer processing of line drawing images. *Computing Surveys*, 6:57–98, 1974.

[10] W. T. Freeman and C. Weissman. Television control by hand gestures. In M. Bichsel, editor, *Proc. Intl. Workshop on Automatic Face- and Gesture-Recognition*, IEEE Computer Society, pages 179–183, Zürich, Switzerland, June 1995. http://www.merl.com/TR/TR94-24.

[11] W. Haettich. Recognition of overlapping workpieces by model directed construction of object contours. *DSIA*, 1(2–3), 1982.

[12] M. H. Han and D. Jang. The use of maximum curvature points for the recognition of partially occluded objects. *Pattern Recognition*, 23:21–33, 1990.

[13] Markus Kohler. Vision Based Remote Control in Intelligent Home Environments. In B. Girod, H. Niemann, and H.-P. Seidel, editors, *3D Image Analysis and Synthesis'96*, pages 147–154, University of Erlangen-Nuremberg/Germany, November 18–19 1996. infix Verlag. ISBN 3-89601-000-X; see also *Ein ergonomisches Dialogsystem zur Steuerung von technischen Systemen in Wohnbereichen mittels Gestenerkennung — Abschlußbericht* at Dep. f. CG/University of Dortmund.

[14] Markus Kohler. Technical details and ergonomical aspects of gesture recognition applied in intelligent home environments. Technical Report 638, Informatik VII, University of Dortmund, January 1997.

[15] Markus Kohler. Using the Kalman Filter to track human interactive motion — Modelling and initialization of the Kalman Filter for translational motion —. Technical Report 629, Informatik VII, University of Dortmund, January 1997.

[16] H. C. Liu and M. D. Srinath. Partial shape classification using contour matching in distance transformation. *IEEE Trans. Pattern Analysis Mach. Intell. PAMI-12*, 11:1072–1079, 1990.

[17] Ch. Maggioni. GestureComputer: New ways of operating a computer. In M. Bichsel, editor, *Proc. Intl. Workshop on Automatic Face- and Gesture-Recognition*, IEEE Computer Society, pages 166–171, Zürich, Switzerland, June 1995.

[18] Ch. Maggioni and B. Kämmerer. GestureComputer – history, design and applications. In Ed. R. Cippola and A. Pentland, editors, *ECCV '96 Workshop on Computer Vision in Man-Machine Interfaces*. Cambridge University Press, to appear in June 1996.

[19] Andrea Meyering and Helge Ritter. Learning to recognize 3d-hand postures from perspective pixel images. *Artificial Neural networks*, pages 821–824, 1992. Elsevier Science Publishers B.V.

[20] Thomas S. Huang Vladimir I. Pavlovic. Hand gesture modeling, analysis and synthesis. In M. Bichsel, editor, *Proc. Intl. Workshop on Automatic Face- and Gesture-Recognition*, IEEE Computer Society, pages 73–79, Zürich, Switzerland, June 1995.

[21] James M. Rehg and Takeo Kanade. DigitEyes: Vision-based human hand tracking. Technical report, School of Computer Science, Carnegie Mellon University, December 1993.

[22] Hans Röttger. Echtzeit-Interaktion auf Basis visueller Bewegungserfassung. Master's thesis, University of Dortmund, July 1995.

[23] Sven Schröter. Entwicklung von Verfahren zur automatischen Kalibration eines farbbasierten Objekterkennungssystems. Master's thesis, University of Dortmund, August 1996.

[24] Michael Stark and Markus Kohler. Videobasierte Mensch-Maschine-Interaktion. *Informationstechnik und Technische Informatik*, 38(3):15–20, June 1996. More Details in english *Video Based Gesture Recognition for Human Computer Interaction*, TR 593 and *Projektgruppe 247: ZYKLOP — Visueller Mensch-Rechner-Dialog — Abschlußbericht (1995)* at Dep. f. CG/University of Dortmund.

[25] Peter W.M. Tsang, P.C. Yuen, and F.K. Lam. Recognition of occluded objects. *Pattern Recognition*, 25(10):1107–1117, 1992.

[26] Junji Yamato, Jun Ohya, and Kenichiro Ishii. Recognizing human action in time-sequential images using hidden markov model. *IEEE*, pages 379–385, 1992. ISBN or ISSN 0-8186-2855-3/92.

Distributed Multimedia

What We Want from WWW as a Distributed Multimedia System

Hermann Maurer
IICM, Graz University of Technology,
A-8010 Graz, Austria
hmaurer@iicm.edu

Abstract

WWW is used increasingly for dealing with large amounts of multimedia data. Unfortunately early WWW concepts are not particularly supportive of such kinds of applications. The simple link paradigm of ordinary WWW does not handle links in arbitrary document types, or multiple views of the same document space and does not support automatic link maintenance. Nor is the link concept powerful enough to handle complex structural requirements in distributed databases. In this paper we define the scope of multimedia. We then discuss features needed in a distributed multimedia system and why some of them are difficult to implement in ordinary WWW systems. We finally show that WWW systems that generalise the link concept and introduce additional structuring mechanisms to handle the problems discussed can be and have indeed been developed: we explain some of the relevant points using as an example the most prominent such system, Hyperwave.

1. Multimedia

Multimedia is often defined as combining traditional "media" such as text, graphics, pictures, animation sequences, and video- and audioclips in digital form . This is the truth, but only half of it: digital multimedia includes a host of other elements such a panoramic views in one or two dimensions, two dimensional animation sequences, 3D models and 3D scenes including animation in such environments [26],[27],[25], interactive movies [8], abstract mixed mode representations such as in MUSLI [15], interactive components in all media, and down-to-earth but often overlooked elements such as technical drawings, cartographic material, electronic courseware, provisions of multilinguality, etc.

Observe that clearly any such media element if represented by a certain data-type, i.e. using some special coding, can be stored in any WWW server and viewed with appropriate plug-ins or helper applications; however, this is not enough: techniques to introduce links in such media elements and proper navigational features have to be available, together with facilities to search for and locate media elements easily, to support the maintenance of dynamically changing repositories of such media elements, possibly in a distributed environment, and - maybe most important of all - to "customise" material to allow different "views" of the document space for varying user groups or environments. It should be clear after a moment's thought that the only structuring element available in ordinary WWW - a single type of unidirectional link with anchors embedded in the document - cannot provide the flexibility that is needed.

The analysis in the next section will show how weaknesses of ordinary WWW links can be overcome by using a more flexible model, and how this naturally leads also to other features necessary to handle the situations described.

2. What is needed for multimedia repositories

Assuming that we have a large set of different multimedia objects and we want to use links as known from WWW as part of our navigational tools (i.e. we are considering "hypermedia" systems) we immediately note a basic problem with the ordinary WWW link concept. In this concept the source anchors of links are embedded in a static way in the documents. However, if we have specific document formats that are interpreted with special viewers then anchors inserted destroy this format, hence requiring a re-write of all viewers involved. A more elegant way to solve the problem is to treat anchors (source and destination) not as parts of the document but as separate objects in a separate database. Doing so immediately also offers another big advantage: by assigning attributes to the link objects many important other uses become possible. E.g, access rights to links can be made different from the access rights of the underlying document. Thus, the document may be visible

0-8186-8150-0/97 $10.00 © 1997 IEEE

in the same way for a certain group of persons, but some links may only be visible to designated persons or groups of persons: this means that links for "private" or "group-use" are possible. This is a first important step towards being able to customise an information space for special purposes without object replication. Since links and underlying documents may have different access rights it is possible to e.g. "freeze" documents, yet allow changes or additions of links, of paramount importance, e.g. for electronic journals[19]. Note that links in ordinary WWW are unidirectional. If three documents X,Y,Z have a link to a document A, and A is removed, three "broken" links remain in X,Y,Z and can only be corrected by the owners of the documents X,Y,Z. Storing links in a separate database with separate attributes allows to follow the links from A back to X,Y,Z (i.e. introduces bi-directionality) and allows to deactivate the links in X,Y,Z without having access rights to X,Y,Z: thus, using the technique described automatic link maintenance becomes possible.

We thus see that our basic requirements for links in all media documents, for easy link maintenance and for customisation automatically leads to the need for non-embedded, bi-directional, typed links.

Note that already [28] has pointed out the analogy between goto's and links. Indeed, goto's in programming languages, explicit pointers in data structures and links are very similar concepts. We have learnt in programming and data structures that explicit goto's and pointers should be replaced by structure wherever possible. The same clearly applies to WWW: explicit links should be replaced by introducing structural constructs. The most obvious way to define structure is to use hierarchies similar to the directories we know from computers. A closer look reveals that a somewhat more general structure that allows multiple classification of objects and groups of objects is more desirable and - together with customised links - eases the customisation of the information space. We will return to this aspect later. For now, it suffices to realise that grouping documents in "collections" and collections again into collections, etc., not only will help to reduce explicit links, it will also help searching (by allowing to restrict attention to a specifically defined set of collections) and - as by-product - allows a systematic distribution of documents to physically different servers, easing the problem of handling distributed multimedia databases.

We have seen that is it necessary to assign attributes to links to make them more flexible. In analogy it should be clear that such attributes are also valuable for documents or collections of documents e.g. for searching purposes.

Above considerations have shown that a number of obvious wishes (handling a variety of media types, customisation and search facilities, automatic link maintenance and distributed databases) naturally lead to certain extensions of WWW.

Now we turn around: by analysing weaknesses of WWW we also derive a number of necessary extensions. We will note that they largely coincide with the ones obtained above. Hence modern WWW servers - and we use Hyperwave as an example - are bound to incorporate the features mentioned.

3. The Need for Advanced WWW Systems

In this section we explain that the navigational and structural tools currently available in ordinary WWW are not sufficient to fully exploit the tremendous power of the largest information and communication resource mankind has ever had. Most current hypermedia systems and the most widely spread WWW servers do not have enough functionality to provide the power that is needed.

Ordinary WWW servers are easy to install and clients are available on all major platforms. Much software is free and sources are sometimes available. The node-link technique for navigating and finding information is quite appealing at least for small to medium amounts of data, and the mix of media makes the use of WWW aesthetically pleasing. All this has contributed to the proliferation of WWW. Indeed there is no doubt that WWW is not only the first widespread hypermedia system available through the Internet, but that WWW has actually replaced some earlier more traditional information systems. The success of WWW, the number of WWW proponents and freaks, and its publicity even in non-scientific publications may create the impression that WWW, as it now exists, is the solution for most information needs and defines the dominating technology for the foreseeable future.

The reality is different, however. Whilst WWW is undoubtedly a big step forward compared to pre-WWW times, experience shows that much functionality required for sizeable applications is missing from ordinary WWW. In this sense, ordinary WWW should be considered a first generation networked hypermedia system. More advanced hypermedia systems are required to cope with the problems currently being encountered in WWW. Just to give one example, while pure node-link navigation is satisfactory in small systems it tends to lead to confusion and disorientation, if not chaos, when applied to large amounts of data[3]. For substantial applications, some additional structuring and searching facilities are clearly required. That links may actually be more harmful than useful has been already pointed out in [28] and elaborated in [18]. Similarly, the necessity to keep links separate from rather than embedded in documents as is the case in most current WWW systems as explained in the previous section has already been demonstrated in the pioneering work on Intermedia at Brown University [6]. HyperWave [17] and Microcosm[7] are the only two major systems that support this important feature at the moment.

In what follows, we concentrate on features that are desirable in advanced WWW multimedia information systems. We compare the features found in "first generation" (i.e. ordinary) WWW systems with those found in the more advanced WWW system Hyperwave. This is not to belittle early WWW systems or to glorify the advanced WWW system Hyperwave, but rather to clarify why certain facilities are needed. We also briefly look at communicational and co-operational features that will have to be integrated in hypermedia systems if they are to be successful: such features are currently scarcely supported by any hypermedia system. They are often dealt with in the context of computer supported co-operative work, rather than hypermedia. Although we look in a little more detail at Hyperwave in this section and how it allows a smooth transition from first generation WWW systems to second generation versions like Hyperwave, we consider two of the most important aspects of Hyperwave in a separate Section 4.

Information in a hypermedia system is usually stored in "chunks". Chunks consist of individual documents which may themselves consist of various types of "media". Typically, a document may be a piece of text containing a picture or other multimedia objects. Each document may contain links leading to (parts of) other documents in the same or in different chunks. Typical navigation through the information space is based on these links: the user follows a sequence of links until all relevant information has hopefully been encountered.

In ordinary WWW, a chunk consists of a single document. Documents may consist of a combination of arbitrary multimedia elements. To give a simple example, a document may consist of textual information and may include pictures and the (source) anchors of links. Pictures and links are an integral part of this document. Pictures are thus placed in fixed locations within the text ("inline images"). Links may lead to audio- or videoclips or other multimedia elements which can be activated. The textual component of a document is stored in so-called HTML format, a derivative of SGML.

In Hyperwave the setting is considerably more general: chunks, called "clusters" in HyperWave terminology consist of a number of documents. A typical cluster may, for example, consist of five documents: a piece of text (potentially with inline images), a second piece of text (for example in another language, or a different version of the same text, or an entirely different text), a third piece of text (the same text in a third language perhaps), an image and a film clip. Anchors can be attached to textual information, to parts of images, and even to regions in a film clip, a 3D scene, etc. Links are not part of the document but are stored in a separate database. They are both typed and bi-directional: they can be followed forward (as on any WWW server) but also backwards.

The support for multiple pieces of text within a cluster allows Hyperwave to handle multiple languages in a very natural way. It also elegantly handles the case where a document comes in multiple versions: e.g., a more technical (or advanced) one and one more suitable for the novice reader. Or different versions for different bandwidth, for different drivers, like offering the choice of picture, video or 3D scene depending on the user's environment.

Text can be stored in Hyperwave in a variety of formats including PostScript and PDF. In addition to the "usual" types of documents found in any modern hypermedia system, Hyperwave also supports arbitrary other types of information such as 3D objects and scenes [25] or electronic courseware and animations [21].

One of the most crucial differences between simple WWW and Hyperwave is the treatment of links. In simple WWW systems links are unidirectional, have no type and are embedded in documents. In Hyperwave they are bi-directional, can have types and are stored in a link database separate from the actual documents. This difference is very significant as we have hinted at earlier, but we will present further details in Section 4.

Navigation in ordinary WWW is performed solely using the hypertext paradigm of anchors and links. It has become a well accepted fact that structuring large amounts of data using only hyperlinks in a way that users don't get "lost in hyperspace" is difficult to say the least. Ordinary WWW databases are large, flat networks of chunks of data and resemble more an impenetrable maze than well- structured information. Indeed every simple WWW server acknowledges this fact tacitly, by offering pages that look like menus in a hierarchically structured database: items are listed in an orderly fashion, each with an anchor leading to a subchapter (subdirectory). If links in WWW had types, such links could be distinguished from others. But as it is, all links look the same: whether they are "continue" links, "hierarchical" links, "referential" links, "footnote links", or whatever else cannot be distinguished.

In Hyperwave not only can have links a type, links are by no means the only way to access information.

Clusters of documents can be grouped into collections, and collections again into collections in a pseudo-hierarchical fashion. We use the term "pseudo-hierarchical" since, technically speaking, the collection structure is not a tree, but a DAG. I.e., one collection can have more than one parent: an impressionist picture X may belong to the collection "Impressionist Art", as well as to the collection "Pictures by Manet", as well as to the collection "Museum of Modern Art". The collection "hierarchy" is a powerful way of introducing structure into the database. Indeed many links can be avoided this way [18], making the system much more transparent for the user and allowing a more modular approach to systems creation and maintenance. Collections, clusters and documents have titles and attributes. These may be used in Boolean queries to find documents of current interest. Finally, Hyperwave provides sophisticated full-text search facilities. Most importantly, the scope of any of such searches can be defined to be the union of arbitrary collections, even if the collections reside on different servers. We will return to this important aspect of Hyperwave as a distributed database in Section 5. The concept of collections has one other very significant advantage: it allows insertion and deletion of documents into a Hyperwave database without any link adjustment, a luxury unknown in ordinary WWW systems. We return to this aspect in the second half of Section 4.

Note that some WWW servers also permit full-text searches. However, no full-text search engine is part of "standard" WWW. Thus, the functionality of full text search is bolted "on top" of most WWW servers: adding functionality on top of WWW leads to the fragmentation of WWW, since different sites will implement missing functionality in different ways. Thus, to stick to the example of the full text search engine, the fuzzy search employed by organisation X may yield entirely different results from the fuzzy search employed by organisation Y, much to the bewilderment of users. Actually, the situation concerning searches on most WWW servers is even more serious: since documents in such WWW servers do not have attributes, no search is possible on attributes; even if such a search or a full text search is artificially implemented, it is not possible to allow users to define the scope for the search, due to the lack of structure in most WWW databases. Hence full-text searches on most WWW servers always work in a fixed, designated part of the database residing on one particular server.

Hyperwave provides various types of access rights and the definition of arbitrarily overlapping user groups. Hyperwave is also a genuine distributed database: servers (independent of geographical location) can be grouped into "tribes" that act as one logical system. Thus, users can define the scope of searches by defining arbitrary sets of collections on arbitrary servers. We will return to this in more detail in the separate Section 5. Note further that proper authorisation schemes allow different groups to work with the same server without fear of interfering with each other's data.

Ordinary WWW systems have traditionally been seen mainly as (simple) information systems. Most applications currently visible support this view: very often WWW servers offer some pleasantly designed general information on the server-institution, but only rarely does the information go much deeper. If it does, usually a "hybrid" system is used, WWW with some add-ons or a database in the background using the scripting interface of WWW.

It is our belief that hypermedia systems acting as simple information systems, where someone inputs information to be read by other users, do not offer much potential: they will disappear into obscurity sooner rather than later. To ensure the success of a hypermedia system, it must allow users also to act as authors, allow them to change the database, create new entries for themselves or other users, create a personal view of the database as they need it, and, above all, allow the system to be used also for communication and co-operation.

Ordinary WWW systems almost entirely lack support for such features. Emerging more advanced hypermedia systems are bound to incorporate more and more features of the kind mentioned; Hyperwave provides a start.

Hyperwave supports annotations (with user-definable access rights): Hyperwave annotations become part of the database, i.e., are also available when working with other clients, or from another user account or machine. Annotations can themselves be annotated; the network of annotations can be graphically displayed using local map functions. Thus, the annotation mechanism can be used as the basis of (asynchronous) computer-conferencing, and has been successfully employed in this fashion.

We believe that many of the features discussed in the area of computer supported co-operative work (for a compact survey see [4]) will eventually be incorporated into advanced hypermedia systems.

As has become clear from the above discussion, ordinary WWW servers do not have enough functionality to be a solid and unified basis for substantial multi-user multimedia repositories with a strong communicational component.

Hyperwave is a first attempt to offer much more basic functionality, yet to continue to work as WWW system: every WWW client can be used to access every Hyperwave server.

4. Linking and Data Structuring

The WWW system Hyperwave differs in its design significantly from ordinary WWW systems by adding much functionality for both users and information providers.

In this section we discuss two important points in more detail: the link concept and the notion of collections.

As has been mentioned earlier, ordinary WWW uses unidirectional links that are embedded in the documents and cannot be typed. In Hyperwave WWW links are bi-directional, can have a type and attributes and are handled not as part of the document but in a separate database. These extensions of the link concept have far-reaching consequences. We mention a few of the most important ones in what follows.

When viewing a document it is clearly always necessary to know which other documents can be reached from it: this is after all what links are all about, and such "out-links" are of course supported in all WWW systems including Hyperwave. However, it is equally important to also know which documents are pointing to the current one, i.e., to know the "in-links"; this is what bi-directional links are all about. There are many reasons why also the knowledge of "in-links" is important:

First, it gives users (and information providers) the valuable information who is pointing to a particular document for "information only" reason: the context of the document becomes clearer, its "popularity" can be determined, etc. To be specific, suppose you are interested in impressionist art and you have located a picture in the (virtual) gallery of the Museum of Modern Art in Vienna; by examining all "in-links" you are bound to find valuable information about the painting that would have escaped your attention otherwise.

Second, having bi-directional links allows to generate a graphic representation of the "local surroundings" of the current document (the "local map" of Harmony, see [5] and available in Hyperwave Versions 2.5 and higher for arbitrary clients!).

This local map will show you an iconized version of your current document, plus all those that (via one or more steps) lead to it or can be reached from it: this is a very powerful support for navigation and helps to avoid the "lost in hyperspace" syndrome mentioned earlier.

Third, and still more important, it is the only way towards better link maintenance to avoid "dangling links", a phenomenon that is a problem on all large WWW servers. Again, to be specific, suppose an important document X is pointed to by documents A(1), A(2), ..., A(n). If X is removed and only unidirectional links are used there is no way to know that A(1), A(2), ..., (A)n point to X, particularly if the A(i)'s reside on different servers. Hence the links in all A(i)'s when activated by users will all yield the very frustrating message "document cannot be found" or such, a phenomenon well-known to every WWW user. However, if bi-directional links are used then the removal of X can at least result in notifying the owners of the documents A(1), A(2), ..., A(n) that X has disappeared so that the links in the A(i)'s can be adjusted. Indeed, if the links in A(1), A(2), ..., A(n) are not embedded within the A(i)'s rather than just notifying the A(i)'s the links in the A(i)'s leading to X can be deactivated automatically.

This, then, is a first step towards automatic link maintenance, a feature imperative for large systems and addressed in Hyperwave for the first time: to be able to carry it out it is necessary to have bi-directional, not-embedded links and to be able to assign rights and attributes to links that differ from those assigned to the document at issue. Typically, you may permit automatic link deletion of a link to X in a document A(i) you have authored although you are unlikely to permit any change of the contents of A(i). This is one reason why keeping links separate from the documents is very important! Automatic link maintenance does not stop at deleting links that are no longer valid, it can also be used to automatically generate links. Suppose you have a contribution about St. Stephen's Cathedral in Vienna and you have activated automatic link generation for documents of type picture. Then, in a properly working hypermedia system, when a picture of St. Stephen's Cathedral is inserted with "Title: St. Stephen's Cathedral; Type: Picture" an automatic link can be generated from your essay about the cathedral to that picture ... again, of course, only if non-embedded links are available.

Links are usually attached to pieces of text or to pictures. However, one may also want to attach them to parts of a picture, to a moving object in a movie, a 3D object in a 3D scene, etc. In all such cases it is clearly impossible to embed the link information in the document (how would you embed such information in an MPEG film without destroying the MPEG coding?). I.e., links in "unorthodox documents" are only feasible if non-embedded links are used or, if explicitly allowed such as in VRML2. Note that in such cases all drawbacks of embedded links will again re-surface.

Another reason why it is of paramount importance to keep links and documents separate and to be able to differentiate between the rights of links and documents and to add attributes to the links ("typed links") is that only in this way can hypermedia systems be "personalised" and "customised". Suppose teachers want to prepare multimedia presentations based on existing material for a particular class without (e.g., for copyright reasons) being allowed to copy the material. The teachers can connect various bits and pieces of information using links with the name of the class at issue as attribute. Students of the class are identified as such when they log-in and hence only the links generated for that class become visible. Thus, the concept of being allowed to add "private" links to arbitrary documents combined with link filtering based on some link attribute allows to customise a hypermedia system arbitrarily without copying any information. This is basically the original "transclusion" idea of Ted Nelson, see [22]. See [20] and [14] for applications to teaching support, and [2], [16] and [19] for applications to electronic journals and digital libraries. For electronic journals see also in particular the beautiful "classic" papers by Odlyzko, [23] and [24].

To be able to type links offers a tremendous additional potential: it is possible to display different links differently (indicating that one is a footnote, the other one a reference, the next one a link back to a table of contents), to filter out links (e.g., to only show links created by certain authors within a certain time period), or to perform even more complex computations based on the link types.

Hyperwave allows annotations, another feature that requires non-embedded, typed links: an arbitrary document can be attached as annotation to another one by you (even if you have no editing privileges for either of the two documents) and the link to the document attached is shown as annotation. This can be generalised to computer conferencing where link types can be used to show that for a particular thesis a certain number of counter-examples, supporting arguments, generalisations, etc. have been proposed.

Typed links are also convenient tools for version control! Summarising, the original link concept of WWW works well for small amounts of data (say 50 documents) but just does not support larger amounts of data, multi-person co-operation, customisation and other desirable features: more powerful additional features as available in Hyperwave are essential.

There is still another twist to links: without additional structure, using links in a large system becomes very confusing, much like "spaghetti-programming" in first generation high level programming languages such as FORTRAN or Basic. It is desirable to organise and structure information in a way going beyond having a "flat database with myriad's of links". In Hyperwave one crucial concept in this direction is the notion of collection mentioned earlier. Documents are gathered into collections, collections may belong to other collections, etc. with a DAG-like structure.

Not only does this allow to structure material better so that it is easier to find; not only does it allow to define the scope for searches, or for the material to be packaged on a CD-ROM, or printed out, or whatever. It is also a powerful tool to replace links to some extent. To be specific, suppose we have defined a collection "pictures of Graz". Once this has been done adding a picture to this collection does not require the creation of any links (nor would the removal of a picture necessitate adjustment of links): when the collection is accessed the titles of all pictures are shown and the relevant ones can be selected. If the collection has the attribute sequence one can automatically step forwards and backwards in the sequence of pictures, again requiring no links at all.

To quote Dieter Fellner from the University of Bonn, Germany: "The collection concept alone is enough reason to choose Hyperwave as WWW server".

In this section we have just mentioned two of the important advanced concepts of Hyperwave, features that go beyond ordinary WWW.

It is our contention that ordinary WWW and HTML should be seen as "thin interface layers" (and this is how Hyperwave treats them) but that more powerful tools must be used as further underpinning (and this is what Hyperwave does). For detailed information see the "HyperWave" book [17]. An electronic version of this book is available under http://www.iicm.edu/hgbook. Additional information on Hyperwave can also be found in [1], [10], [11], [12], [13] and up-to-date manuals on http://www.hyperwave.com.

5. (Distributed) Database Facilities

In ordinary WWW servers HTML pages or other documents are stored as such, without any "meta-information", i.e. without any information about the documents. In contrast, in Hyperwave every document has some standard attributes and arbitrary further ones as defined by the user. Standard attributes include author, creation date, date when the data is to be made public, expiration data, keywords, etc.

Note that such attributes are invaluable for searching and for administration. Typically, if a document concerns an event on a particular date, clearly the document should be removed (and links pointing to it deactivated) after this date. In ordinary WWW systems this has to be done manually. This requires much effort, tends to lead to many documents whose removal has been forgotten and hence are obsolete, and adds to links whose activation results in a message "object not found" or such, since when the document was removed the deactivation of some link in some document (invisible due the unidirectionality of links in ordinary WWW systems!) was forgotten. In Hyperwave a document as mentioned would be entered with an appropriate expiration date. The removal of the document and the deactivation of links pointing to it (or at least the notification of owners of links pointing to it) can be handled without manual intervention by Hyperwave.

Consider as further example some server that wants to present a new joke every day. In an ordinary WWW server some person has to manually (even on Sundays and holidays!) replace the current joke by the new one...and if possible at 00:00 hours, so that early risers find a new joke and won't be disappointed. Using Hyperwave an arbitrary set of jokes can be entered into the system, successive jokes with successive opening and expiration dates. The system will do the rest!

Of course creation/modification dates are also valuable in other contexts. It may be a good idea for the Webmaster to have the system show all documents that have not been modified for (say) 2 years: the likelihood that such documents are not of interest any more is very high. In ordinary WWW systems it is impossible to even determine if a document has not been modified for a long time or not. The author attribute of a document is also helpful for administrative purposes. Consider again a specific example: if the presentation of an organisation, as becomes more and more usual, includes a presentation of the persons in the company including some WWW pages edited by the persons at issue it might be wise to check once in a while whether the server contains information on persons no longer associated with the organisation. Again, this is virtually impossible with ordinary WWW servers, but is easy to handle with Hyperwave.

Thus, document (and collection) attributes in Hyperwave are just one other feature supporting system administration. Remember that structuring information (see Section 4) was one other such helpful feature, and turned out not only to be convenient for the system administrator, but also for users: it allowed users to e.g. search for information within certain scopes (unions of collections) eliminating many useless "hits" when applying a search engine. The same holds for attributes: they can be used for searching. Hence searching within a certain scope and e.g. only for documents created after a certain date, or by a certain author, allows much more specific queries than would otherwise be feasible.

As has been mentioned before, Hyperwave is a distributed database system in the sense that the databases in physically different servers can be seen as one logical database. Users may e.g. decide to perform a full-text search for a word like "butterfly" in three collections that reside on separate servers (and potentially in completely different corners of the world), and indeed restrict the search to documents that have been created after a certain date...all this with a single command!

Hyperwave supports link consistency within a "tribe" of servers: a highlighting that indicates a link from document X to document Y is automatically deactivated if the document Y is removed. This is very valuable in its own right, yet becomes particularly interesting since Hyperwave preserves link consistency beyond the boundaries of servers: if the document Y is removed on one server, all (Hyperwave) servers within a "tribe" of Hyperwave servers having links pointing to Y are notified of this fact (and the link highlighting is deactivated). To avoid that the maintenance of such "surface links" (links from a document in one server to a document in another server) causes undue traffic on the net an ingenious algorithm ("p-flood", see [9]) can be used in large tribes that propagates the information to only some servers "in the vicinity" that propagate the information to others, etc. The problem that has to be addressed by the algorithm at issue is that all servers must be notified "fast", even if many of the servers are currently "down" and unable to receive, let alone propagate information.

Summarising, much of the power of Hyperwave and a power that will be required by all future distributed hypermedia systems is that much coherence of data can be assured across physical server boundaries.

It should also be clear, however, that Hyperwave is just a first step in a necessary direction for large multimedia repositories and that further steps will be unavoidable. Only the actual use of very large WWW multimedia databases will show what new features or concepts will be needed. However, sizeable multimedia databases like the AEIOU Project http://www.aeiou.at (an 8 Gbyte presentation of Austria!) or the picture collection of the National Library of Newzealand (http://timeframes.natlib.govt.nz) do demonstrate that techniques such as the ones explained and realised in Hyperwave work well, and replace much manual work while insuring consistency of the database.

References

[1] Andrews, K., Kappe, F., Maurer, H., Schmaranz, K.: On Second Generation Hypermedia Systems; *Proc.ED-MEDIA'95, Graz (June 1995)*, 75-80. See also J.UCS 0,0 (1994),127-136 at http:///www.iicm.edu/jucs.

[2] Calude, C., Maurer, H., Salomaa, A.: J.UCS: The Journal of Universal Computer Science; *J.UCS 0,0 (1994)* 109-117 at http://www.iicm.edu/jucs.

[3] Conklin, E.J.: Hypertext: an Introduction and Survey; *IEEE Computer 20 (1987)*, 17-41.

[4] Dewan, P.: A Survey of Applications of CSCW Including Some in Educational Settings; *Proc. ED-MEDIA'93, Orlando (1993)*, 147-152.

[5] Fenn, B., Maurer, H.: Harmony on an Expanding Net; *ACM Interactions 1,3 (1994)*, 26-38.

[6] Haan, B.J., Kahn, P., Riley, V.A., Coombs, J.H., Meyrowitz, N.K.: IRIS Hypermedia Services; *Communications of the ACM 35,1 (1992)*, 36-51.

[7] Hall, W., Davis, H., Hurtchings, G.: *Rethinking Hypermedia*; Kluwer Academic Pub., Boston/London (1996).

[8] Jayasinha, C. Lennon, J., Maurer, H.: *Interactive and Annotated Movies*; *Proc. ED-MEDIA'95, Graz (1995*), 366-371.

[9] Kappe, F.: A Scalable Architecture for Maintaining Referential Integrity in Distributed Information Systems; *J.UCS 1,2 (1995),* 84-104.

[10] Kappe, F., Maurer, H., Scherbakov, N.: Hyper-G - a Universal Hypermedia System; *Journal of Educational Multimedia and Hypermedia 2,1 (1993),* 39-66.

[11] Kappe, F., Maurer, H.: Hyper-G: A Large Universal Hypermedia System and Some Spin-offs; *IIG Report 364,* Graz, Austria (1993); also appeared as electronic version, anonymous FTP siggraph.org, in publications/May-93-online/Kappe.Maurer.

[12] Kappe, F., Maurer, H.: From Hypertext to Active Communication/Information Systems; *J.MCA 17,4 (1994*), 333-344.

[13] Kappe, F., Andrews, K., Faschingbauer, J., Gaisbauer, M., Maurer, H., Pichler, M., Schipflinger, J.: Hyper-G: A New Tool for Distributed Multimedia; *Proc. Conf. on Open Hypermedia Systems, Honolulu (1994),* 209-214.

[14] Lennon, J., Maurer, H.: Lecturing Technology: A Future With Hypermedia; *Educational Technology 34,4 (1994),* 5-14.

[15] Lennon, J., Maurer, H.: *MUSLI -- A MUlti-Sensory Language Interface*; Proc. ED-MEDIA' 94 (best paper award), AACE, Virginia (1994), 341-348.

[16] Marchionini, G., Maurer, H.: The Role of Digital Libraries in Teaching and Learning; *Communications of the ACM 38,4 (April 1995),* 67-75.

[13] Maurer, H.: *HyperWave: The Next Generation Web Solution*; Addison Wesley Pub.Co., UK (1996).

[14] Maurer, H., Philpott, A, Scherbakov, N.: Hypermedia Systems Without Links; *Journal of Microcomputer Applications 17, 4 (1994),* 321-332.

[15] Maurer, H., Schmaranz, K.: J.UCS -- The Next Generation in Electronic Journal Publishing; Proc. Electronic Publ. Conference, London (November 1994), in: *Computer Networks for Research in Europe 26, Supplement 2-3 (1994*), 63-69.

[16] Maurer, H., Lennon, J.: Digital Libraries as Learning and Teaching Support; *Proc. ICCE'95, Singapore (December 1995),* AACE, Charlottesville, USA (1995), 28-33

[17] Maurer, H., Scherbakov, N.: *Multimedia Authoring for Presentation and Education: The Official Guide to HM-Card.* Addison Wesley Pub.Co. Germany (1996).

[18] Nelson, T.H.: *Literary machines*; Edition 87.1, 702 South Michigan, South Bend, IN 46618, USA (1987)

[19] Odlyzko, A.M.: Tragic Loss or Good Riddance? The Impending Demise of Traditional Scholarly Journals; to appear in: Electronic Publishing Confronts Academia:The Agenda for the Year 2000; (Peek., R.P., Newby, G.B., eds.) MIT Press (1995); see also *J.UCS 0,0 (1994),* 3-53 at http://www.iicm.edu/jucs.

[20] Odlyzko, A.M.: On the Road to Electronic Publishing; *Euromath Bulletin (1996)*; see also *J.UCS 2,11 (Nov. 1996)* at http://www.iicm.edu/jucs.

[21] Pichler, M., Orasche, G., Andrews, K., Grossmann, E., McCahill, M.: VRweb: A Multi-System VRML Viewer; *Proc. VRML 95,* San Diego, CA (December 1995),77-85.

[22] Thalmann D., Magnenat-Thalmann, N. (Eds): *New Trends in Animation and Visualization*; Wiley (1991)

[23] Thalmann, D., Magnenat-Thalmann, N. (Eds.): *Virtual Worlds and Multimedia*; Wiley (1993).

[24] Van Dam, A.: Hypertext'87 Keynote Address; *Communications of the ACM 31, 7 (1988),* 887-895.

Design and Implementation of a System for Multimedial Distributed Teaching and Scientific Conferences *

Jens Deponte, Heinrich Müller, Georg Pietrek
Stefan Schlosser, Bernd Stoltefuß
Informatik VII (Computer Graphics)
University of Dortmund, D-44221 Dortmund, Germany
http://ls7-www.informatik.uni-dortmund.de/

Abstract

Computer-based telecommunication technology together with audio and video technology may help to improve the quality of teaching and scientific conferences. Examples are the use of PC- or notebook-based presentations in talks and courses, teleteaching via ISDN- or ATM-lines, and self-learning based on CD-ROM courseware. In this paper, a more comprehensive scenario for the application of multimedial telecommunication to teaching and scientific conferences is presented. The scenario is illuminated from the view of application and from the view of technical implementation. As new aspects, it includes the possibilities of remote control of devices and signal processing, in particular of image processing. A part of the ideas was implemented into a first prototype. The software HS113 outlined in this contribution allows to control the devices as well as the transmission of video, audio and whiteboard streams from any location in the network. This flexibility is achieved by combining the possibilities of the programming language Java and the MBone video conferencing tools.

1 Introduction

Computer-based telecommunication technology together with audio and video technology may help to improve the quality of teaching and scientific conferences. Although most of its functionality could also be implemented with classical studio and telecommunication facilities before, the costs were high, and thus the application was restricted to special centers. Now standard computing, audio, and video devices, as well as local networks, the Internet, or ISDN, can be combined and are widely accessible, at reasonable prices. Thus multimedial telecommunication can be installed at many sites, and new aspects are opended for teaching and conferences.

*supported by a NRW MWF grant within the NRW-Forschungsverbund "Die virtuelle Wissensfabrik"

Currently three main streams of application of multimedia technology to teaching and conferences can be observed. The first one is to use computers, in particular portable notebooks, combined with projection, as *presentation media*. Often, these presentations resemble traditional, transparencies-based talks. However, it is now possible to include high-quality pictures, animations, and short movies without switching between different devices like slide projector, video player, and computer. Computer-integrated multmedia makes the presentation for the lecturer more comfortable, however, at the expense of the considerable time required for the preparation of the material.

The second stream is *transmission of lectures and talks*. The most simple and well established possibility is the tv-like transmission of the event to other, external sites. This sort of teleteaching can be improved by interaction. A typical scenario consists of two lecture rooms. In one of the rooms, a traditional lecture is given which is transmitted to the second room. The audience in the second room can be seen by the lecturer in the first room via video transmission, and they can ask questions to the lecturer. ISDN- or ATM-lines are often used for that purpose. Besides audio- and video-transmission, data lines and remotely installed software may be used for purposes of textual and pictural presentation. There are quite a few examples of such activities world-wide, and it is practically impossible to give a complete survey. Lists of projects concerned with multimedial teaching can be found under [22]. In Germany we know, besides of ours, of activities at universities and institutes at Darmstadt [6, 10], Dresden [7], Erlangen [8], Freiburg [13], and Mannheim [17], and Sankt Augustin [19].

The third stream is *computer-based self-learning*. Using computers in this field is not new. Also here, multimedia technology brings up new qualities, cf. e.g. [20]. The educational software can be distributed on media like CD-ROM, but also through network-based access to servers. The latter may have the advantage of a closer feedback

0-8186-8150-0/97 $10.00 © 1997 IEEE

between the consumer and the producer of the courseware which simplifies, for instance, updating. While much is published about teaching software, little can be found in literature on these aspects in relation to scientific conferences. One example is the paper of Cheyney et al. [5] who report on the experience gained with the production of CD-ROM-based conference proceedings.

In this paper, we develop a more comprehensive scenario for the application of multimedial telecommunication to teaching and conferencing (section 1). As traditional lectures and talks given on conferences and workshops are closely related to each other with respect to the media and techniques of presentation, multimedial telecommunication facilities can also be used in quite similar manner in both fields. The scenario is illuminated from the view of application and from the view of technical implementation. As new aspects, it includes the possibilities of remote control of devices and signal processing, in particular of image processing.

A part of the ideas was implemented into a first prototype. As a reference installation for other locations, audio, video, computing and networking equipment useful for that purpose was installed in the lecture room HS 113 of the University of Dortmund. Based on standard software tools, in particular tools available with and written in the programming language Java [1], Web servers and browsers, and the MBone tools for video conferencing [9], the necessary operating software was developed. The complex combination of analogue and digital data streams and the remote control of several devices, paired with the necessity of a user-friendly interface that does not burden the speaker, makes this a non-trivial task. A particular feature of the HS113 software is that the event can be controlled from everywhere in the network. The possibilities supported by the HS113 software and the underlying hardware are outlined in the sections 3 and 4. A further section, 5, is devoted to the user interfaces to the system which takes in a major part of HS113.

Using existing tools limited the efforts necessary for the implementation of the system. Furthermore, to some extent this guarantees the portability to other environments. Portability and adaptability to different configurations at other sites was a key issue that was considered in the design of the HS113 software. The design and implementation which follow the philosophy of object-orientation are described in sections 6. Finally, experiences with the current implementation are compiled in section 7.

2 A Scenario of Computer Supported Cooperative Teaching and Conferences

Scientific conferences as practiced today have several disadvantages: time consuming and expensive traveling, the preparation of different, but overlapping documents like transparencies and printed contributions to the proceedings, and limited possibilities to demonstrate experiments on-line. On the other hand, the classical conference offers the possibility of spontaneous and personal contacts to other researchers, and a creative atmosphere which should not be given up.

A solution may be *locally distributed conferences*. This means that the conference simultaneously takes place at different locations. In fact, at each location a sub-conference is organized which is quite similar to a usual conference. In this manner, the participants still come together at a conference site, but now they can choose the place which is most convenient for them, for instance which is closest. The different sites are linked through a network which allows interactive communication. The communication comprehends audio, video, and data channels.

The interaction between the sites may be of different form. A traditional talk may be given which is transmitted to the other places, including the material of presentation used. People may ask questions by either interrupting the speaker, or at the end of the talk. Another possibility are distributed discussions and workshops in which a panels as well as the whole audience can be involved.

The infra-structure necessary for this scenario can also be used for transmission from external sites which have to do with the subject of a talk. For example, an on-line experiment can be transmitted in live from a laboratory, a technical plant, or an operating room.

The infra-structure also may allow single participants at home or in their offices to attend, thus, however, giving up the stimulating atmosphere of the conference.

Up to now, we have focussed on interaction between people. Another dimension of electronic telecommunication is that data and programs can be transferred. The speaker of a conference gives his presentation using material and software directly transmitted from his own computer in his office or institute.

Everything going on at the conference may be documented by recording the streams of audio, video, and data communication. The material may be post-processed into electronic conference proceedings.

The scenario just outlined, translated to teaching, means distributed classes. Distributed classes are particular interesting for advanced studies. They may bring together a critical mass of students from different universities interested in a special subject which otherwise could not be offered. Education in humanities and social sciences live from presentations jointly prepared by students and professors, paired with extensive discussions of the pros and cons of assertions. To our experience, this is particularly interesting if students of different countries or even continents can be brought together in such a virtual class. In engineering and science, distributed tutorial classes may be helpful to get experienced with special techniques and experiments possibly not available at each place. For example in engineering, remote insight into installations in industrial plants can be given. The quality of advanced teaching can also be improved by inviting specialists or famous scientists to a class which can be implemented easier by interactive telecommunication than by a journey. A key issue in all cases is interaction between the different locations.

With the implementation of this scenario, several *boundary conditions* have to be regarded which are important for the acceptance of the system by the users, and which imply considerable technical and didactical challenges.

A first one is the *smooth and flexible transition between classical forms of medial presentation*, like blackboard and overhead transparencies, and modern computer-based multimedial documents presented on screen. Cameras can be used to record the contents of blackboards and projected transparencies. Remotely controllable swivel and zoom cameras are useful for this purpose. Digital image enhancement [14] may be necessary to improve the quality of the digitized pictures. The transmission of still pictures instead of video may allow a better image quality because the bandwidth constraints of the transmission channel are less severe than for motion pictures. Still pictures, however, exclude the typical interaction of the speaker with the blackboard and the transparencies.

A second boundary condition is that *the presentation has to be kept interseting and exciting*. This is a matter of didactics, and a lot of didactical and educational research accompanying the introduction of multimedial telecommunication in education still has to be done, cf. e.g. [11]. As noticed before, the personal contact between attendees, and between attendees and speakers is of equal importance. One implication of this observation for distributed teaching is that the number of students attending a distributed course has to still allow personal feedback. Otherwise the same negative consequences can be expected as with classical lectures attended by several hundreds of students.

A third boundary condition is sufficient *audio and image quality*. Audio is central, and good acoustics of the room and suppression of echo caused by re-transmission over the communication line must be garanteed. A key problem of video is projection. Projection implies that the room has to be darkened, a fact that is particularly annoying for teaching. Although of less quality, backprojection may be preferred from this point of view. Audio and video compression for transmission reduces the quality further. However, experience shows that attendees are more tolerant towards low quality video than towards low quality audio. Also, video is often not really required. Exceptions are personal discussions, and interaction of the speaker with the media or subject of presentation, for example with the blackboard or with an experiment.

A fourth boundary condition is *user-friendly, intuitive interaction with the system*. A first aspect of interaction is *control of the audio, video, and data streams*. It is almost impossible that the speaker can be made responsible for that. A solution may be be to introduce a further person taking over the role of a director. The director may be located at the place of the speaker. This means if speakers are allowed at different locations of a distributed conference, that the particular interface to the system has to be available at all places. The director should have control over the equipment (audio, video, swivel cameras, video players and recorders) at all sites. Alternatively, one director might be located at each site, and communication between them has to be established. Of course, there is also the need of communication between the speaker and the director(s).

Attempts are necessary to lighten the director's burden. Possibilites are automatic tracking of the speakers by the cameras, automatic camera motions, recognition of activities in the audience which are worth to be transmitted, and automatic selection of the channels that are delivered to the different places. Image- and audio-based pattern recognition methods may be applied for that purpose, similar to those described in [16].

A second aspect is *interaction of the speaker with the presentation media*. For computer demonstrations during a talk, sitting in front of a screen and operating with the mouse is not a satisfying solution for the speaker. A good way would be if he could freely interact with the projection, that is moving the mouse cursor and selecting menu items by pointing to the screen.

A fifth boundary condition is *efficient preparation and post-processing of multimedial presentation documents*. The preparation of electronic teaching material and post-processing of the recorded material is time consuming. The goal of post-processing can be quite different, reaching from a sequential film up to an interactive hypermedial course. This requires particular time-consuming efforts if multiple and traditional media were used for the presentation. If the presentation is purely computer-based, "authoring on the fly" proposed in [2, 3] is an efficient solution. In that case work has to be invested in preparing the electronic teaching materials (text and drawings) not in common use up to now. This, however, will change in the future.

One issue in preparation of presentations is on-line demonstration of software. The goal is that the demonstration can be followed by participants of the event. Often, however, the software is not available at all places, due to limited performance of external systems or missing license. Even if the demonstrated software is installed at all sites, time synchronization between the sites is not necessarily given. One solution may be to transmit the screen of the computer on which the demonstration takes place, as a video. Disadvantages of that approach might be low quality because of limited bandwidth of transmission, resampling to video resolution, and compression.

3 The System HS113

The main goal of the remainder of this contribution is to give an example of a technical solution for a part of the operating requirements of the scenario of the previous section.

The system HS113 reported on allows to transmit presentations from a lecture room to external participants. The range of external participants reaches from single attendees up to an audience which comes together in a lecture room. In contrast to TV-like broadcasting, transmission is bi-directional, that is, external participants can pose questions to the speaker and enter into a dialogue with him. Transmission is based on MBone-multicasting.

The speaker can use the traditional media, like the blackboard and overhead transparencies. This means that no special preparation is required. The contents of the blackboard and the transparencies are captured by video cameras and transmitted over the computer network to the external participants. The same holds for voice and audio. Documents available electronically can also be transmitted in a whiteboard which can be used for discussion with external participants, too.

The event can be recorded on-line. Because of the huge amount of memory required for digital video, video is recorded on traditional S-VHS video tape. Several recorders may be used, dependent on the number of interesting video streams (eg. a video stream from the blackboard camera, a video stream from a camera observing the speaker and the audience). The sound track of the video tape is used for recording the sound in the lecture room. The use of the whiteboard and communication with external participants are recorded digitally. The recorded material may be used for later post-processing which, however, is out of scope of the current system.

Control of the HS113 system is taken over by a director. The director controls the cameras, recorders, and transmission of video, audio, and whiteboard streams. He decides what can be seen by the participants. Interaction with external participants is controlled by the speaker.

In the following, the hardware and software components of the current implementation of the HS113 system are described.

4 The Hardware Components

Figure 1 shows the hardware configuration of the installed HS113 system in use. Most of the components are located in the central lecture room.

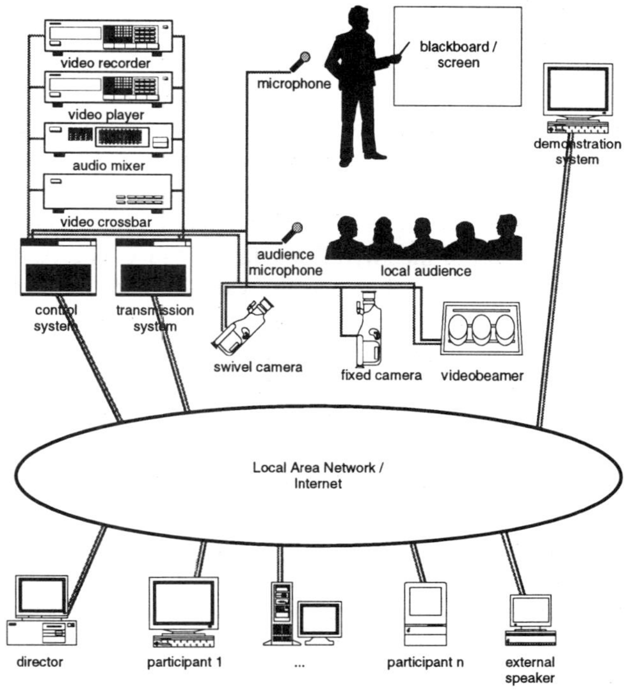

Figure 1: The hardware components of the current installation of the HS113 system.

Up to three *cameras* can be used. The first one is fixed and is directed to the screen on which transparencies are projected. The second one is a motor-driven swivel-mounted camera. This camera is installed so that it can capture the blackboard, the area in which the speaker is located, and part of the audience in the lecture room. Pan and zoom is computer-controlled through a serial interface, too. The third camera is a camcorder which is operated manually.

Two *video recorders* controlled through a serial interface can be used for recording, but also for playing videos which are projected with a *video beamer*.

Video sources (camera, video players) and sinks (video beamer, video recorders, frame grabbing computers) are connected by a *video crossbar switch* which is controlled through a serial interface, too.

Audio is captured by two microphones, one for the speaker and one for the audience. The audio signals (microphones, sound from video player, sound from external participant) are sent through an audio mixer to an amplifier and a loudspeaker in the lecture room and to audio-digitizing computers.

For video/audio digitizing, transmission and control two computers are installed in the lecture room. According to their roles they are called *transmission system* and *control system*, respectively. The *transmission system* (Sun Sparc 20) is equipped with a Parallax video board. It grabs the video and audio signals and transmits the digitized streams into the local network. The *transmission system* also receives the sound from the external participant (via local network) who is in discussion with the speaker. The *control system* (Sun Sparc 5) has a standard frame grabbing board and a large number of serial interfaces. It is responsible for control of the swivel camera, the video recorders, the video crossbar switch and the video beamer through the serial interfaces. The frame grabbing board is used to grab one of the output streams of the crossbar switch. This video stream is sent to a computer in the network from which the whole event is controlled. The computer needs not necessarily be located in the lecture room. This follows the philosophy of the HS113 software that processes performing user interaction can be located anywhere in the network. The whole event is controlled by an interactive process which is supplied by the *director subsystem* of the HS113 software. Usually, an additional person besides the speaker, the director, is responsible for the overall control. Details are explained in section 5.1.

The two other major interactive subsystems of the HS113 software are the *participant subsystem* and the *speaker subsystem*. While the participant subsystem of course runs on external hardware, a further computer (Sun Ultra 1), the *demonstration system* is in the lecture room. In the current version of the HS113 software, the speaker has to be in the lecture room. The process initiated by the speaker subsystem is running on the demonstration system. Beside that, the demonstration system can be used as a platform for software demonstrations being a part of the speaker's presentation. The demonstration system is connected to the video beamer so that the local audience can follow the software demonstration. The speaker and the participant's interface are explained in sections 5.2 and 5.3, respectively.

The computers are connected to a *local area network* based on 100 Mbit/s Fast Ethernet technology. All computers having access to this network can be used as external computers. Currently, the implementation works for Unix systems (Sun-Solaris 2 and SGI Irix systems were used up to now) but it can be basically extended, cf. section 6.

5 The User Interface

The user interface of the HS113 software is implemented on the basis of the Netscape HTML Browser (Version 3.0). The particular interfaces of the director, the speaker and an external participant can be selected from a HTML Document. As a reaction, the corresponding entry page is loaded. It is divided into three main areas, a welcome area which also can be used for HTML based presentations, a help index, and a current help page. Furthermore, windows of interaction are opened which can be placed arbitrarily on the screen by the user.

5.1 User Interface of the Director

The director is responsible for the control of the devices in the lecture room, and for the information that is transmitted to the external participants. The director's interface offers access to all components of the system. It consists of the following parts (see figure 2):

control of the video sources. A control panel for each of the video recorders and a control panel for the swivel camera are offered by the system. They offer menu buttons for the different functions of these devices. The panel of the swivel camera allows to store up to eight camera positions. They can be arbitrarily defined and then selected from a list offered on the panel.

selection of the transmitted video/audio stream. A panel allows to select the video (cameras, video player) and audio source that is transmitted to the external participants (this is the video stream grabbed by the transmission system). Independent of transmission, the director can browse through all possible video sources in a separate window (this is the video/audio stream grabbed by the control system), in order to choose the source most interesting for the external audience, even if he is not in the lecture room. For example, the director might be located in an external lecture room, and he decides from there what is of interest for his audience.

observation of the whiteboard. If a whiteboard is used by the speaker, the director is able to get it on his screen in order to follow what is going on. He cannot interact with the whiteboard.

audio connection to the lecture room. The director can establish a two-way audio communication with the lecture room. This allows him to give operational hints to the speaker, for instance to dim the lights or open the microphone.

control of the video beamer. The director also controls the video beamer in the lecture room. The tasks are switching on or off, and selecting the video source (video player, demonstration computer).

The director's Web page can only be accessed by authorized people who identify themselves by a password. After initialization, the director is asked whether he uses the system on this computer for the first time. If so, a software archive is downloaded and the HTML browser displays an installation manual.

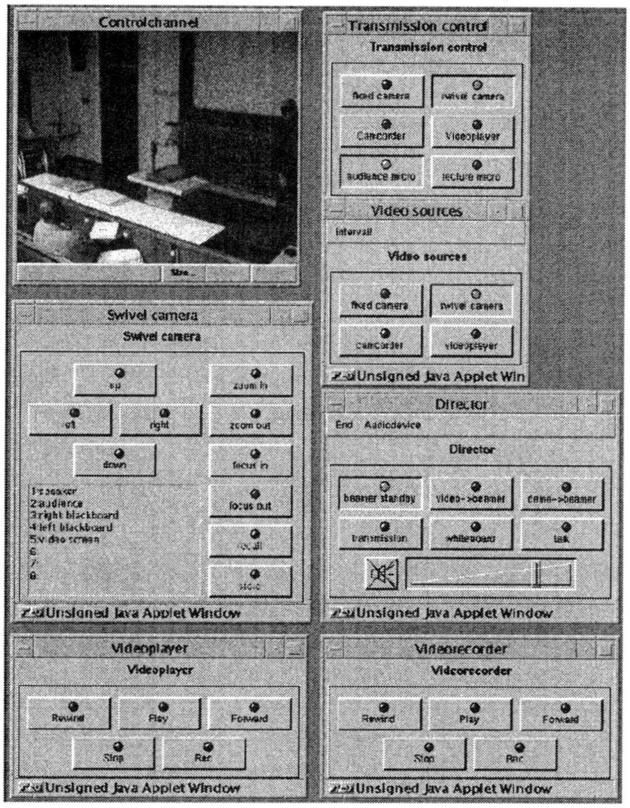

Figure 2: The user interface of the director.

5.2 User Interface of External Participants

An external participant also enters the system through a Web page. If it is his first access, he has to download the required software and to install it. In these actions he is guided by the system. After initialization, the participant's interaction is based on the following items:

selection of the level of communication. The level of interaction of the external participant with the system depends on the equipment of his computer system. The participant communicates his level through a panel offering the menu items "video and audio", "audio" and "none". The first one means that the participant's system has a camera and a microphone, the second one that there is only a microphone and the last one that there is neither.

registration. Participants have to register themselves before they can use the system. After pressing the *"register" button*, the system asks the user for the necessary data. The data are stored in an individual configuration file of the user. The system returns a user identifier which allows the participant to enter into a session by pressing the *"open" button*.

session control panel. After entering a session, the user gets a session control panel. A video button allows to switch on or off the reception of the video/audio channel transmitted from the lecture room. A whiteboard button does the same with the whiteboard transmission.

The question button opens a window into which the user can type a question to the speaker. The question is transmitted to the speaker where it is appended to a list of posed questions displayed on the screen of the speaker. The speaker may select questions from this list. If the participant's side is equipped with audio or video, a connection is established to the participant who had the question. The audience in the lecture room can follow the discussion on the video projection of the demonstration systems screen. Otherwise, the speaker will reply to the question without interaction with the questioner.

A help text exists for each button and menu point which can be accessed by pressing the right mouse button.

5.3 User Interface of the Speaker

The speaker also enters the system through a special Web page. Then he gets an interaction panel offering the following functionality:

response to external questions. The speaker's interface to the reply mechanism for external questions, as described in section 5.2, contains a list with the names of all questioners, a *"reject"* and a *"reply" button*. By selecting a name from this list the text of the question is displayed. The entry can be removed by using the *"reject" button* without responding to it. This is useful if not all questions can be answered and a selection becomes necessary. The *"reply" button* establishes a connection to the selected questioner. The type of this connection depends on the level of communication possible with the external system.

whiteboard presentation. The speaker can use a whiteboard for his presentation. The material of presentation consisting of text (ASCII, Postscript) and graphics can be loaded in the whiteboard. The drawing facilities of the whiteboard allow the user to annotate the text interactively in the same way as it is often done with transparencies. The whiteboard content is transmitted to the external participants. They usually have only read access, but by using a particular button, the speaker can give write access to that participant whose question is currently answered.

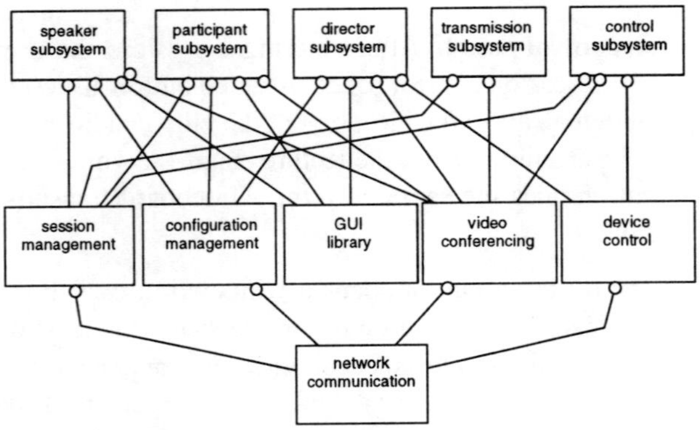

Figure 3: The subsystems of HS113.

HTML presentation. Another possibility is to use presentation material in HTML. A menu button allows to load a HTML file in the main window of the Web browser. Simultaneously, the document is displayed in the main window of the browsers of the participants. If the speaker branches through a link to another HTML page, this page is automatically transmitted to the external participants. This mechanism of *joint browsing* allows each participant to follow the presentation.

Help is organized in the same way as before.

6 The Software Architecture of HS113

The software system HS113 is designed according to the object-oriented approach, following [4]. From the statical point of view, HS113 is split into three levels, cf. figure 3. The levels are induced by the functional dependency ("uses" relation) of the subsystems. Access to subsystems goes through well defined interfaces, the implementation details are transparent to the higher level.

6.1 The Basic Level 1

The basic level 1 consists of only one subsystem, *network communication*. This subsystem offers the functionality of TCP/IP based communication. It is based on an *object-request broker* which allows transparent access to methods of classes whose instances exist on remote computers, by remote procedure calls [15].

6.2 The Intermediate Level 2

The intermediate level 2 consists of the following five subsystems.

session management. The session management contains classes which are responsible for the administration of the actors (speaker, director, external participants) during a session and for the communication between the respective programs. The class "session manager" runs a static process within the server of the object-request broker so that all processes (speaker, director, and participant process) which execute remote procedure calls over a proxy instance of the session manager work on the same instance of the implementation. This ensures synchronization of the calls and allows exchange of information between these processes.

configuration management. The classes of this subsystem are responsible for the administration of the configuration data on local and remote computers. Communication with external computers is based on the object-request broker.

GUI library. In this subsystem, classes of the graphical user interface are collected which are the basis of all implemented user interfaces.

video conferencing. The classes of this subsystem are used for initialization and control of the video, audio and whiteboard transmission. Because of different locations, server classes running on a remote computer, and client classes which are integrated in a user interface, are distinguished.

Video conferencing is based on available products (the MBone Tools). They are completely encapsulated into classes so that they are not visible to the user. Encapsulation also simplifies a possible exchange of these tools in that only the re-implementation of the defined interface is required.

device control. These classes define the interface to and implement the control of the devices installed in the lecture room (cameras, recorders, video crossbar switch).

6.3 The Top Level 3

The top level 3 defines the following self-contained components which together offer the high-level functionality of the HS113 software. Figure 4 shows the process view of these components.

speaker subsystem. The speaker subsystem implements the user interface to the speaker. It is based on the session management, the video conferencing clients and the configuration management classes of level 2. These components are controlled by corresponding elements of the user interface.

participant subsystem. The participant subsystem implements the user interface to an external participant.

director subsystem. The director subsystem implements the user interface to the speaker. It is split into the

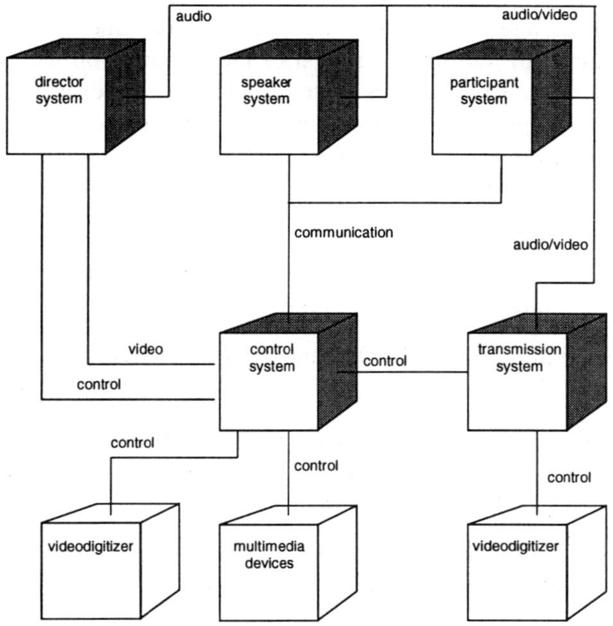

Figure 4: The process view of the HS113 system. The processes are implemented on the top level 3 of the system.

five subsystems *direction panel*, *transmission panel*, *video sources panel*, *recorder panel* and *camera control panel*. By using the GUI library of level 2, the user interface is guaranteed to have a uniform look.

transmission subsystem. The transmission subsystem does not have a user interface. It essentially consists of the class "broadcast video server" and "broadcast audio server", which are implemented using the video and audio conferencing servers of level 2. During runtime, instances of these classes exist within the object-request broker so that all control commands which are transmitted to these objects by the session manager are forwarded to the same instance of the conference classes. This ensures a synchronization of the commands.

control subsystem. This subsystem does not need a user interface, too. It uses the device control class of level 2 for its purpose. Furthermore it implements the separate video transmission to the director, analogously to the transmission subsystem.

6.4 Implementation

The HS113 software was implemented in the programming language Java [1], based on Sun's Java Development Kit (JDK), version 1.0.2, and Netscape 3.0. Java was chosen because of its advantage of installation-free and automatic availability on different platforms which is favorable for the implementation of distributed systems with different categories of users like in our application. Furthermore, the network and GUI libraries allow easy implementation of complex graphics application with networking functionality without knowledge about hardware and operating system. Since Java is part of almost all Web browsers, Java programs can be loaded and executed in a familiar environment.

A disadvantage of the choice of Java were the security restrictions of Java applets in Web browsers. These restrictions aggravates the realization of hardware specific functions and the integration of other software products. This problem was coped with using native-C-functions which can be accessed from Java and by running the object request broker in a separate Java virtual machine.

The use of Java applets made it necessary to install a Web server on one of the computers in the lecture room. For this purpose, the pd server *Apache*, version 1.1.3, was used.

For the implementation of network communication the pd Java library *HORB*, version 1.3b1, was used [15]. It is a Java implementation of an object-request broker.

The GUI library on level 2 was implemented based on the *Abstract Window Toolkit* (*AWT*) of Java using inheritance. On a high level of abstraction, AWT hides the differences between different window systems, but contains only a few GUI classes which are quite rudimentary. Thus a couple of new GUI elements were derived from the existing elements of AWT.

For conferencing, the HS113 software uses the *MBone tools VIC*, version 2.8, for video communication [18], *VAT*, version 4.0beta, for audio communication [23], and *WB*, version 1.60, for whiteboard communication [24]. These tools were chosen because of the availability on different platforms and the possibility of multicast transmission.

7 Experiences and Possible Extensions

Up to now, the HS113 environment was only used locally within the department of computer science for talks of up to one hour on specific topics. The lecture room and the external workstation are located in different buildings which are connected by an ATM line. Transmission in the local network, a part of which is still 10 MBit/s Ethernet technology, achieves a quality which allows to read transparencies and blackboard contents on the receiving screens. Transmission is stable, with exceptional stops of transmission for a few seconds which seem to correlate with loading particularly long Postscript files into the whiteboard.

We have good experience with point-to-point connections for jointly held classes of the University of Dortmund and the University of Pennsylvania at Philadelphia. Students of American studies at Dortmund and students of nursing from Philadelphia discussed the different cultures of health care in the two countries and the role of "emotional intelligence" in education and everydays human interaction. Initally, both instructors and students were awed by the technology provided for their exchange and experience a few awkward moments. After a while, however, the medium became less intrusive and the arguments picked up speed as the two classes established a pattern of dialogue and learned that is vitally important to listen to the other side. Technically, the transmission was based on ISDN video conferencing. ISDN is not integrated in our system up to now, but will be done in the near future.

We are currently working on the application of the system with external participants at the University of Bonn based on the 34 MBit/s network connecting the universities of the country. First experiments show promising results.

Within this project, two extensions are under work. The first one is to give up the restriction that the speaker has to be in a specific lecture room. The second one is to experiment with an external, remotely controlled mobile roboter, as an implementation of the idea of a distributed experiment which can be interactively followed by a distributed audience.

A further step can be to experiment with more than one lecture room with remotely controllable equipment.

An important condition for acceptance of a system is user-friendliness. Our user-interfaces are menu- and mouse-based. For computer demonstrations during a talk, sitting in front of a screen and operating with the mouse is not a satisfying solution for the speaker. A good way would be if he could freely interact with the projection, that is moving the mouse cursor and selecting menu items by pointing to the screen. Furthermore, the director's burden may be lightened by automatic tracking of the speaker by the camera. We are working on image-processing based solutions of these problems.

A further question is how to post-process the material recorded on-line (audio, video, whiteboard). The goal of post-processing can be quite different, reaching from a sequential film up to an interactive hypermedial course. This requires particular time-consuming efforts if multiple and traditional media were used for the presentation. If the presentation is purely computer-based, "authoring on the fly" proposed in [2, 3] is an efficient solution. In that case work has to be invested in preparing the electronic teaching materials (text and drawings) not in common use up to now. This, however, will change in the future.

A last point is on-line demonstration of software. The goal is that the demonstration can be followed by participants of the event. Often, however, the software is not available at all places, due to limited performance of external systems or missing license. Even if the demonstrated software is installed at all sites, time synchronization between the sites is not necessarily given. One solution may be to transmit the screen of the computer on which the demonstration takes place, as a video. Disadvantages of that approach might be low quality because of limited bandwidth of transmission, resampling to video resolution, and compression.

References

[1] K. Arnold, J. Gosling (1996). *The Java Programming Language,* Addison-Wesley

[2] Ch. Bacher, Th. Ottmann (1995). *Authoring on the Fly,* Journal of Universal Computer Science 1(10) 706

[3] Ch. Bacher, Th. Ottmann (1996). *Tools and Services for Authoring on the Fly,* in: Proceedings of the ED-MEDIA, Boston, 1996

[4] G. Booch (1994). *Object-Oriented Analysis and Design With Applications,* Addison-Wesley

[5] M. Cheyney, P. Gloor, D.R. Johnson, F. Makedon, J. Matthews, P.T. Metaxas. *Towards Multimedia Conference Proceedings,* Communication of the ACM 39(1) 50–59

[6] *CO-LEARN – Cooperation in Learning,* University of Darmstadt
http://ben.pu.informatik.th-darmstadt.de/Projekte/Co-Learn/co-learn.html

[7] *Teleteaching Dresden-Freiberg,* University of Dresden/ University of Freiberg
http://www.telematik.tu-freiberg.de/teleteaching/index_telet.html

[8] *Multimedial teleteaching,* University of Erlangen
http://teleteaching.wi2.uni-erlangen.de/

[9] H. Eriksson (1994). *MBone: The Multicast Backbone,* Communication of the ACM 37(8) 54–60

[10] *Teleteaching and -training,* Fraunhofer-Institut für Graphische Datenverarbeitung
http://www.igd.fhg.de/www/igd-a3/a3home/projects/ttt-e.html

[11] A. Eckert, W. Geyer, W. Effelsberg. *A Distance Learning System for Higher Education Based on Telecommunications and Multimedia – A Compund Organisational, Pedagogical, and Technical Approach,* accepted for ED-MEDIA/ED-TELECOM'97, Calgary, Canada, June 1997, cf. [17]

[12] M.R. Macedonia, D.P. Brutzman, *Mbone Provides Audio and Video Access Accross the Internet,* IEEE Computer 27(4) 1994

[13] *Multimedia, Teleteaching and Electronic Publishing,* University of Freiburg http://rom.informatik.uni-freiburg.de/mmgroup

[14] R.C. Gonzalez, R.E. Woods. *Digital Image Processing,* Addison-Wesley, 1992

[15] HORB: http://ring.etl.go.jp/openlab/horb/

[16] M. Kohler (1996). *Vision Based Remote Control in Intelligent Home Environments,* 3D Image Analysis and Synthesis'96, infix Verlag, pp. 147–154

[17] *Teleteaching,* University of Mannheim/University of Heidelberg http://www.informatik.uni-mannheim.de/informatik/pi4/projects/teleTeaching/

[18] S. McCanne, Van Jacobson (1995). *vic: A Flexible Framework for Packet Video,* ACM Multimedia '95, San Francisco, CA, pp. 511-522

[19] *HSN provides ATM Connectivity for TeleTeaching: GMD Sankt Augustin – University of Geneva* http://www.gmd.de/IMK/NW/HSN/GENEVA

[20] R.C. Schank. *Active Learning through Multimedia,* IEEE Multimedia, Spring 1994, 69–78

[21] J.A. Schnepf, D.H.C. Du, E. Ritenour, A. Fahrmann (1995). *Building Future Medical Education Environments Over ATM Networks,* Comm. ACM 38, pp. 55–69

[22] YAHOO: *Education:Distance Learning:On-line Teaching and Learning:* http://www.yahoo.com/education/on_line_teaching_and_learning

[23] VAT: http://www-nrg.ee.lbl.gov/vat/

[24] WB: http://www-nrg.ee.lbl.gov/wb/

The Modular Training System (MTS)

A System Architecture for Internet-Based Learning and Training

Taofen Wang, Christoph Hornung
Fraunhofer-Institute for Computer Graphics (Fh-IGD)
Rundeturmstraße 6
D-64283 Darmstadt, Germany
eMail: {twang, hornung}@igd.fhg.de

Abstract

Based on the results of and experience gathered during several national and international training and teaching projects, this paper proposes a new style of learning in the upcoming information age and addresses an open framework for internet-based learning and training using WWW technology. After the introduction of the virtual learning and training environment as the modern CBT infrastructure, the courseware concepts based on the modularity with separation of the course framework from the course contents and with the separation of the course material from the course material description are discussed in this paper. The concept virtual references is introduced to support the late binding of courseware components. User adaptation is supported by using special exploration and examination components. In order to realize the concepts, a system architecture of an internet-based CBT system „Modular Training System (MTS)" and its functionality including courseware production, courseware presentation and administration are presented.

1: Introduction

1.1: CBT-Applications

Traditional training focuses on teaching in classroom-like settings at fixed times and places or individual learning lacking teacher guidance, feedback and the opportunity to apply the presented information. The upcoming information age demands new training concepts and infrastructures for livelong high quality training. The learners need to access on-demand and goal-oriented training from their workplace or at home. Training should be adapted to individual knowledge and learning style of the user. Even within a high quality learning environment the human factor will remain vital to allow expert consultation, teacher guidance and user cooperation [Horn96].

Such environments themselves introduce additional requirements. Training providers need applications for efficient multimedia courseware production by teams of experts, pedagogues and media designers. The accumulation of knowledge in such environments demands efficient management concepts to enable the multiple use of existing courseware.

Computer based distance learning satisfies this need because of the flexibility at place and time. Today we can identify steps towards integrated solutions based on the Internet which enable access to the learning material independent of the learning's time and place. In contrast to the stand-alone learning the distance learning led to a trend to merge the whole world together into one global network where the learners can study virtually and access multimedia courseware combined with adapted traditional learning approaches [Dimi94].

1.2: CBT-Systems

The Internet is the almost important global network and is growing exponentially. It's now not only used in the original scientific and military branches but also in the private and commercial branches. The "World Wide Web" (WWW) is the often seen as just a tool to navigate through hyper-documents across the Internet but more sophisticated uses are however possible. Even though the WWW technologies are still young, they are already being used for a lot of application scenarios specially in multimedia distance learning to transport the courseware from the WWW server to the clients. But after our analyses of some commercial products and services, the almost WAN-based CBT systems realized with WWW technologies like Oracle OLA [Orac96] or Global Learning Platform provided by German Telecom [Glob] focus on the courseware management and organization or they integrated only their courseware results into the WWW using built-in tools or external applications such as Macromedia Director [Beyd96], Asymetrix Multimedia-WWW-PC [Logu95] and LATE [Maur97]. The educational and pedagogical requirements, especially in the fields like user adaptation and re-using of the course material have not been considered in the most Web-based learning system. The courseware structure in these systems are still pure fixed hyper-linked document.

To solve these problems the Fraunhofer-Institute for Computer Graphics, in co-operation with various development partners, has developed a Modular Training System (MTS) [Horn96] to support the internet-based lifelong learning. The concepts and realization of MTS are described as follows.

2: Concepts

2.1: Virtual Learning and Training Environment

The Integration of various learning aspects is the goal of the Modular Training System (MTS). From the user's points of view the MTS is like a virtual classroom or virtual training center which offers a complete multimedia distance learning environment including course presentation, course production, user and course administration, group learning and online tutoring (*figure 1*).

Learning and training takes place in MTS according to the following model. Two main types of sites should be distinguished: the Local Training Center (LTC) and the user's workplace. Local Training Center is composed of standard WWW server, MTS server and MTS database server and provides management functionality for distributed courseware and administration functionality for users.

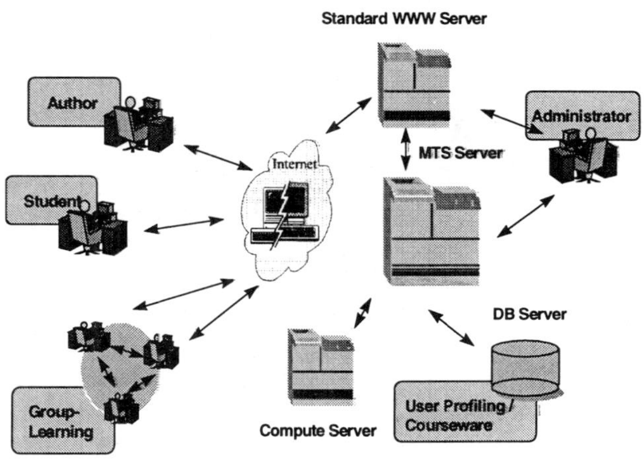

Figure 1: Learning and Training Environments

The LTC is the central infrastructure element as access points to training facility. Each LTC offers their training facility to registered users. It administrates access rights to courseware, assigns experts for consultation and aid the formation of virtual learning groups. The LTC is responsible for guaranteeing the quality of new courseware made available to the entire Virtual LTCs by their local authors and it is the owner of a distinct subset of the distributed courseware domain. On the client site the main component of the MTS are the WWW browser and its add-ons. The client is running as course front-end at the trainee's and author's workplaces to handle the user's input, edit, download and display the course framework and the different kind of courseware material.

Since the material is stored in the Local Training Center, each LTC must run a WWW server to connect the WWW client. The MTS server which provides all the necessary functionality to control the course, and the database provides the multimedia courseware and user information. Physically LTCs are interconnected via terrestrial and satellite links to form a global Virtual LTC that provides transparent access to all courseware for users from arbitrary locations with different networking bandwidth and client configurations (*figure 2*). The courseware material and user information stored in the local LTCs are shared for all the users and authors within entire Virtual LTCs using distributed database.

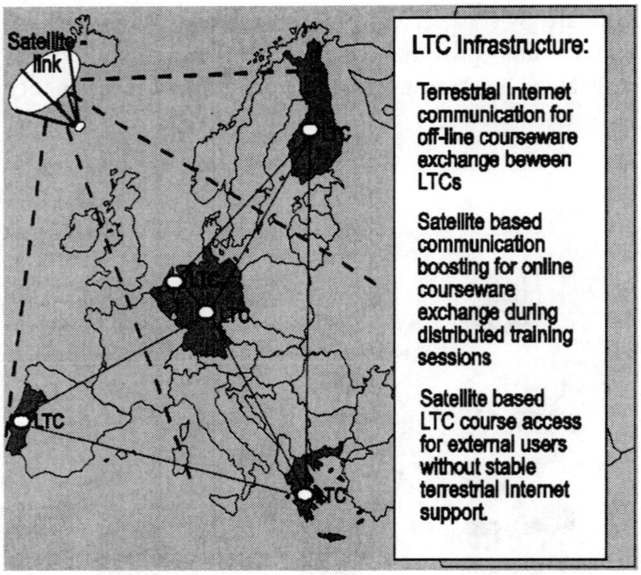

Figure 2: Virtual Local Training Centers

2.2: Operation Modes

The MTS integrates course presentation, course production and administration into one system using the different operation modes: the course runtime mode, the course authoring mode and the administration mode. The operation modes are used by the different kinds of users such as learner, author and administrator to support the different kinds of the MTS usage. In the course runtime mode and the course authoring mode the users use the remote client to connect the LTC , while in the administration mode the LTC administrator use the administration tool locally to manage the course configuration and the user data stored in the MTS database (*figure 1*). For the different kinds of usage the MTS offers the responsible modules and tools both at the client site and the LTC site which are integrated smoothly to a complete MTS system.

2.3: Courseware Concepts

MTS strictly applies the concept of modularity and reusability to courseware. This leads to two design concepts: a modularity concept composing courses out of different, clearly separated components, and the strict separation of the content of these components from their description using metadata.

Structuring Courseware. Courseware is broken down into three different categories (*figure 3*):

- Course Nodes (CN), defining the contents and structure of the course
- Course Units (CU), implementation (layout, interaction) of specific steps in the training process (e.g. presentation, exploration, testing)
- Course Material (CM). Basic material includes standard multimedia formats as well as material with complex internal behavior and interaction, such as simulations and microworlds

Course Nodes are solutions to the question "what to learn?". They define the learning goals. It should be noted, that a course node does not contain any information about *how* this learning goal can be reached. Courses are arranged as networks of course nodes. Each course node delivers a return value indicating the learner's success. Dependent on this value, the appropriate "next" course node can be chosen. The content of a course node is a script in the special language CDL (course definition language) [Enca93]. This script describes the implementation of the course node and may reference either other nodes or units. It never references material herewith supporting the clear separation of structure and content.

Course Units are solutions to the question "how to learn?". Course units either may be presentation units, exploration units or test units. Each of these unit types can be implemented using characteristic templates. Course units are self contained. They contain only references to course material, but neither references to other units or to nodes. In this sense, course units form containers of course material. They are implemented as an extension of HTML, the so-called HTML-M (for MTS-HTML). This extension includes special tags for referencing (see the next section). Course Units deliver a return value indicating the learner's success when traversing this unit.

Course Material describes the material used in the course units and, herewith, the visible parts of a course. The course material consists of internet standard formats like Text, Audio, Video. Course material is elementary; currently there is no composite course material yet.

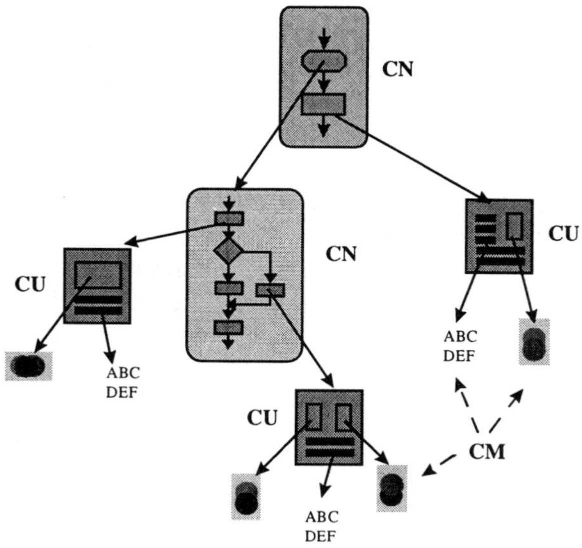

Figure 3 Modular Structure of Courseware

In order to enable re- and multiple use of courseware on a large scale, each module is stored as a separate entity, is self-contained and implements a common interface. This also allows course adaptation to the individual needs of the trainee by using the best fitting modules.

The three different module categories reflect the different kinds of experts involved in courseware production. Since an intuitive graphical authoring environment is integrated into MTS, even teachers and course creators without programming skills can directly work with the system to bring in their expertise.

The flexible linking between the documents of course requests the separation of the course framework and the course contents. The MTS server controls the structure of course independent of the WWW documents which represent the course content. Herewith way the reuse of the course material in different courses is possible. For the special user group the course can be produced with special course framework and available course material. In this context the database server plays an important role: In order to use the existing course contents the domain must be efficiently browsed to retrieve the suitable material. For the domain browsing the self-description of material and catalogues must be stored in the MTS multimedia distributed database.

Referencing of Courseware. An orthogonal concept of the MTS courseware is the *referencing* of courseware. The different courseware components introduced above are never embedded directly, but always referenced instead. Moreover, to every courseware components there exists a separate *description* containing metadata of this component in the form of characteristic attributes, value pairs. Even more, constraints on the attribute, value pairs can be defined. Herewith, the following hierarchy of references exists in the MTS system:

- direct references, pointing to a course component's data and metadata directly
- virtual references, describing a constraint set of direct references

While a direct reference points to single component, a virtual reference defines an open set of characteristics, and herewith a set of course components.

This design principle allows to the concept of *late binding* to be introduced in courseware. While a direct reference is bound at authoring time, virtual references are late bound. They either can be bound at a special configuration step before course delivery, or they can be bound at runtime. The binding at run time allows to choose the best fit course component depending on the user's learning progress.

3: The Modular Training System (MTS)

3.1: Overall Architecture of the MTS

Components of the MTS. The MTS System combines both, a classical WWW-System with a 3 tier architecture and consists of the following layers (*figure 4*):

- client layer, containing the user interface
- application server layer, containing the application logic
- resource server layer, containing remote data and compute resources

The *Client Layer* containing the WWW browser and the MTS client. It defines the top level of a virtual learning environment and offers graphical user interfaces to learner. While the WWW browser is used for the presentation and interaction of the course material, the MTS client is implemented as a Java-based extension (plug in). The MTS client supports the functionality like graphical authoring and interactive group management, and as add-ons of the WWW client the MTS client is implemented with Java to complete the learning environment, for example to start the video conference software to support the online tutoring.

The *Application Layer* contains the WWW server and the MTS server (CBT server). While the WWW server is the standard components for the network connection between client and server side, the MTS server contains the application logic to steer learning and training sessions, mainly the course control, but also components for session management and group work.

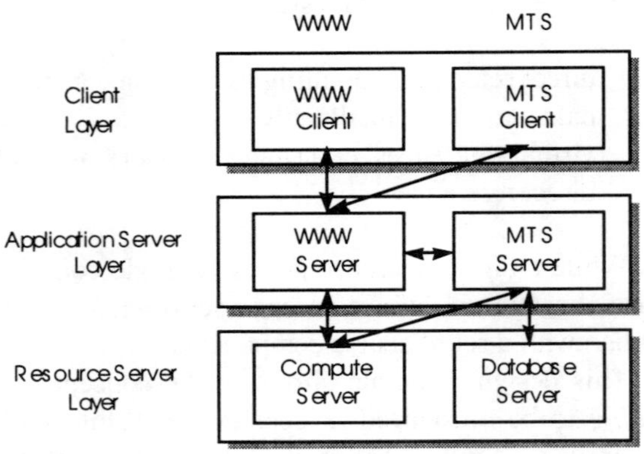

Figure 4: Overall Architecture of the MTS System

The *Resource Layer* consists of database and compute servers. A database server contains material and user data, a computer server executes applications (simulations and microwords) to support training applications effectively. Both the database as well as the compute servers can be distributed themselves.

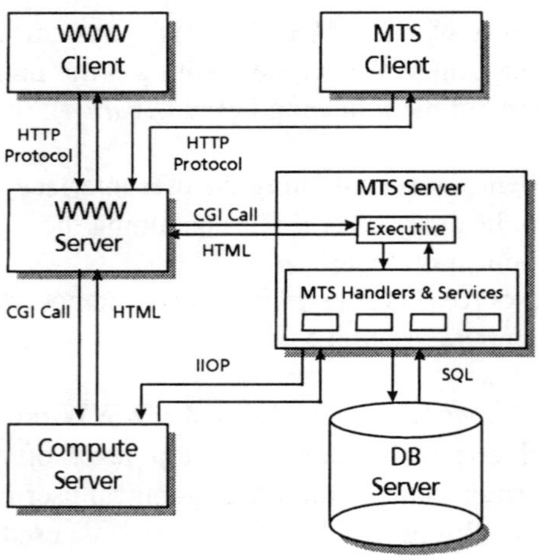

Figure 5: Functional Architecture of the MTS Server

Functionality of the MTS. The MTS server is a CBT server which communicates on the one hand with the WWW server to exchange the WWW-based information and on the other hand with database server to get and store the course material and user data. The user sends requests through the WWW browser to the WWW server using HTTP protocol. The WWW server redirects this request to MTS server via CGI program. The MTS server preserves the different information from permanent user data to user interaction, from course contents to individual course flow and exchanges this information with the MTS database (*figure 5*).

Every request from a client can be identified with the cookies mechanism. The behavior of learners will be stored in the user profile. During the operation of a client request the user profile is used to determine the course flow individually for every user. Herewith the fixed 'links' of normal WWW documents are replaced by the flexible course structure with the consideration of the interaction made by users up to now and the knowledge state of users.

The compute server is connected by CGI call, if a course unit contains such requests. The results from compute server like graphical images or video stream are sent back to the WWW server and presented in the course online. The other possibility to connect the compute server is IIOP (Internet Inter-ORB Protocol) architecture. The figure 6 shows an exploration unit which calls a ray-tracing tele-service with different parameters to get the illumination effects online.

3.2: The Architecture of the MTS Server

Components. The MTS server consist of three types of components (*figure 7*):

- the Executive
- the Message Handlers
- the Services Modules

The executive serves as the central dispatcher in the MTS server, while the message handlers implement the different application functions. The service modules define an underlying layer of tools which are commonly used by the different handlers. Dependent on the operation mode (see 2.2), the executive creates the message handlers or instances of the message handlers concerned and passes the user requests to them. The results produced by the message handlers will be then sent back to the WWW server by the executive.

The Executive is the central component of the MTS server. It is connected to the WWW server via a CGI program and acts as the main demon process. It receives the incoming user requests and sends them out as *messages* to the message handlers. This design leads to a very simple and flexible structure of the MTS server: all handlers register their interest at the executive. The executive itself does not need to know about the specifics of the different handlers. Moreover, the executive is responsible for the creation of instances of the different handlers.

The Message-Handlers provide the application logic of the MTS system. Currently, the following handlers are implemented:

- session management
- group management
- course runtime
- course authoring

applets to create, modify and save the course interactively. Again, there is a separate instance of the course authoring handler for every session.

The *Group Work* handler provides the tutor administration service and the group management service to construct tutor office and configure the communication and co-operation utilities. Standard Internet components (Mbone-Tools) as conferencing software are smoothly integrated into the MTS client.

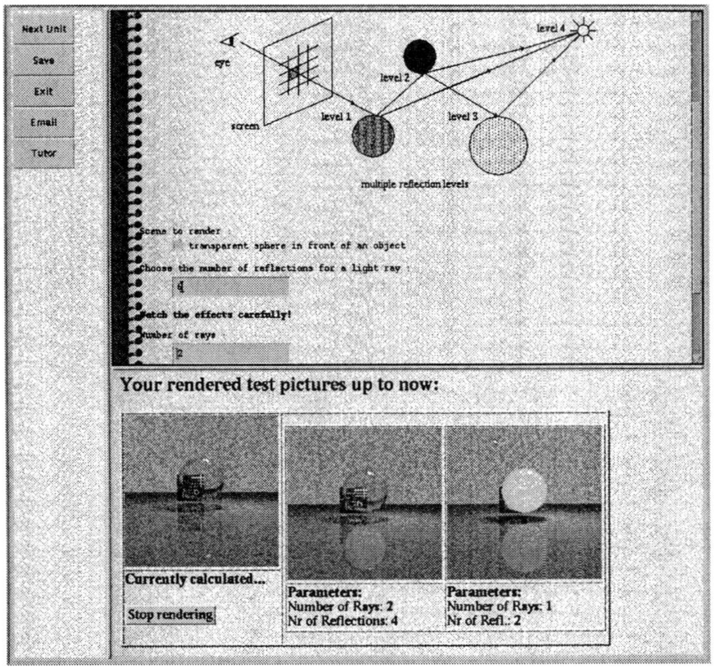

Figure 6: Exploration Unit Using Compute Server

The *Session Management* handler provides specific mechanisms to transparently distinguish the requests from different learners or authors and thus allows handling multiple users and learning groups simultaneously. There is only a single session management handler instance at the MTS server.

The *Course* Runtime handler interprets the course structure and determines the next unit of course with the aid of user profile. For the user adaptation the executive creates an instance of the course runtime handler module for each user and sends the user input to the responsible instance. It means every user has an individual course flow control. There is a separate course runtime handler instance for every session.

The *Course Authoring* handler produces the MTS courseware with the aid of the course authoring environment at the WWW client side. The authors can use the graphical authoring tool implemented with Java

The application sharing software is used to support the co-operative work. The group work handler has only a single instance.

The MTS services are responsible for accessing the reference-based courseware components from the data base. These services consist of the following modules:

- Mapper
- Converter
- Component Management

The *Mapper* service will be used for mapping virtual references onto direct references. As mentioned in chapter 2, a virtual reference consists of a constraint set of key, value pairs. By accessing the Component DB directly, the mapper retrieves a set direct references to components fulfilling the given virtual reference. It should be noted, that this mechanism can be applied uniformly to nodes, units and material.

The *Converter* service converts the HTML-M format into plain HTML. This service is used for resolving direct references to course units into the corresponding course material.

The *Component Management* module retrieves direct references to course components and returns the content of this component. The component management includes authorization and accounting services to check whether to access to the component is allowed.

server. All subsequent requests are then processed by the according handlers.

Course Authoring. In the authoring mode, the authors selects a course. Then, the authoring environment is started and the authoring client, implemented in Java, is downloaded. This tool supports the interactive graphical design of course nodes and units, while course material will be produced by standard editors. In authoring mode, both virtual and direct references can be created. The authoring client send messages describing the creation, modification and deletion of nodes and units, which are passed via the executive to the course authoring handler. The authoring handler then uses the mapper for mapping virtual references onto direct references and the component management services for accessing the database.

The author can preview the course using the course runtime handler.

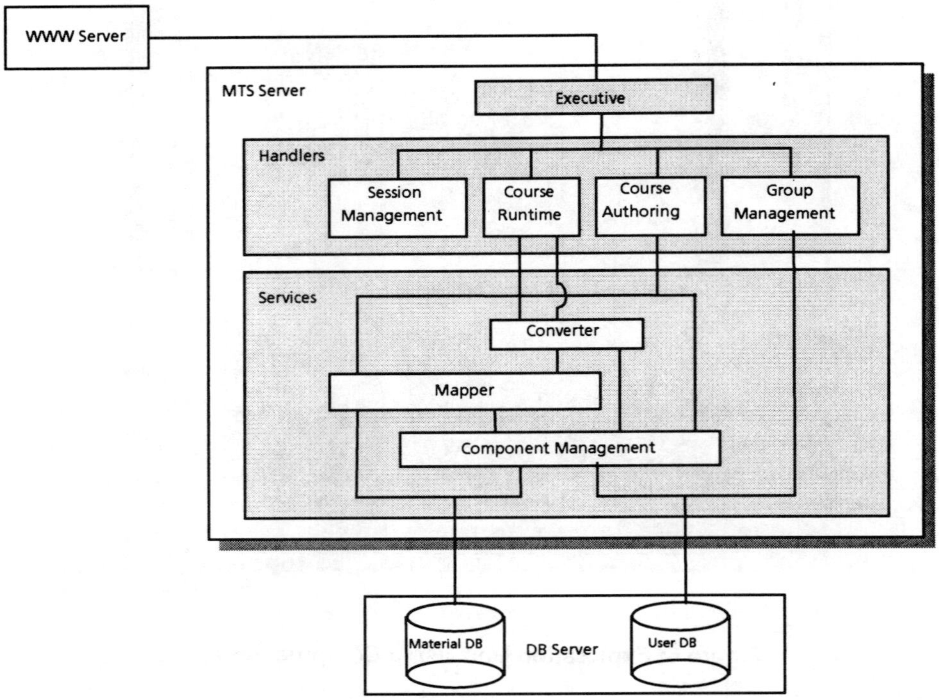

Figure 7: Detailed Architecture of the MTS Server

3.3: Functionality of the MTS Server

Login and Session Creation. The user of the MTS system always start with a login message. This message identifies the user and its role: administrator, author or learner. The session management handler checks the input with user data stored in the User DB. Dependent on the role, the executive then creates a new instance of the course runtime handler or the course authoring handler. Next, a session ID is created which uniquely identifies this session. The executive uses this ID for passing further requests. The session ID is passed back to the WWW client using the "cookies" mechanism. This gives a unique identification of the WWW client to the MTS server.

Course Runtime. The course runtime handler is used either in learner mode or in authoring preview mode. The user starts the course runtime when selecting a course node. This node is loaded and the course runtime executes it by the interpretation of the CDL script (see 2.3).

The course runtime distinguishes between virtual and direct references and between references to nodes and references to units. All virtual references are passed over to the mapper service which returns a set of direct references. Next, direct references to units are passed to the converter which, by means of the component management service, returns an HTML page. Direct references to nodes are accessed directly via the component management service. This node is then interpreted directly in a recursive manner.

The actual course component (node or unit) may return a value via a Java applet. This value is passed via the executive to the course runtime which, updates the user profile and, based on the actual value of the user profile, determines the next course component to execute.

Group Management. The group management functionality is available after the user is logged in, but besides the session management. A user can watch at active user groups, join user groups, communicate with other users e.g. via email. Moreover, synchronous communication and teletutoring are supported using the teleconferencing systems [Marc95].

4: Application and Demonstration

MTS is used and enhanced in two major projects: IDEALS [Bor96b] and COBRA-3 [Bor96a]. The IDEALS (Integration of DEDICATED for Advanced Training Linked to Small and Medium Enterprises and Institutes of Higher Education) project, which is sponsored by the EU Telematics Application Programme, anticipates tomorrow's learning scenarios with distributed, user adapted, on-demand, co-operative training environments to support authoring and learning. In this project, the MTS system is demonstrated in different scenarios in small and medium enterprises as well as in institutes of higher education.

The project COBRA-3 (Co-operation within Bureau, Research and Administration), co-sponsored by the German Telekom, evaluates telecommunication services for small- and medium-sized enterprises. In this project, the MTS system is used as the backbone for a network of Fraunhofer Institutes developing advanced multimedia courseware in such different areas as logistics, CAD and ASIC design.

5: Conclusions

Compared with other distance learning systems the MTS concatenated the up-to-date CBT features to the internet to satisfy the important pedagogical and didactic demands with his concepts of multi and re-usability, modularity and adaptability. MTS is open for new media types and running in a heterogeneous computer environment. Its modular, scaleable, open system architecture is designed to support reuse of courseware and to meet the increasing upcoming demands.

6: References

[Beyd96] Beyer D.: *CBT-Spezialist*, c't, magazin für computer technik, 11/96.

[Borg96a] Borgmeier E., Beyer M.: *COBRA-3 STI. Online Teaching, Training and Information in Heterogeneous Environments*, Computer Graphics Topics, Darmstadt, 1996.

[Borg96b] Borgmeier E., Graf F., Brisson Lopez J.M., Mengel M.: *IDEALS, a Telematics Based Training Environment for the Future*, EAEEIE '96 Conference, Oulu, 1996.

[Dimi94] Dimitroyannis D. A: *Virtual Classroom: A Case Study*, Advance Proceedings of the First World-Wide-Web conference, Geneva, Switzerland, May 25-27, 1994, pp 325-329.

[Enca93] Encarnação J.L., Tritsch B., Hornung Ch.: DEDICATED - Learning on Networked Multimedia Platforms, Visualization in Scientific Computing: Uses in University Education, Elsevier Science Publisher B.V., 1993.

[Glob] German Telecom: http://www.global-learning.de/

[Horn96] Hornung Ch., Borgmeier E., Wang T.: *Teaching and Training in Intra- and Internet*, Online Educa, Berlin, 1996.

[Logu95] Logue S., Tosolini P.: *Web based Toolbook Applications in the Educational Environment*, Third International WWW Conference '95, Darmstadt, Germany.

[Marc95] Marcos A.: *Cooperative Multimedia Support for Software Development and Distributed Training of X-Windows Applications*, IGD-FhG Technical Report 95i004-FIGD, 1995.

[Maur97] Maurer H.: *Late: A Unified Concept for a Learning And Teaching Environment*, Graz University of Technology, Austria, 1997.

[Orac96] Oracle Corporation : *Oracle Learning Architecture: Bringing Education On-line and Into the Next Century*, Oracle White Paper, October 1996.

Multimedia Education, Distance Learning and Electronic Commerce Applications

Jürgen Vaupel, Manfred Sommer
University of Marburg - Computer Science Department -
vaupel@informatik.uni-marburg.de, sommer@informatik.uni-marburg.de

Abstract

Beginning with a description of an actual teaching and learning situation at an University this article deals with a possible further evolution of university education. Motivation is the discussion how to integrate new technologies like the Internet and Multimedia in university education. Therefore the second part of this article reviews the question what happens when these technologies are simply applied to an university education system. These reflections lead to a second framework of an "electronic lecture". Because of imperative additions to this application scenario the resulting framework of a "virtual lecture" extremely differs from the first approach. The last step reviewed is the export and import of educational units to and from other universities or companies. The extension of the second framework to a "virtual university" is more a conclusion than a real extension. Adding some new centralized services and institutions like a payment service and an "education broker" will lead to an electronic commerce framework for education. This article concludes with some statements about the influence of information technology to university education and the way of learning. A further conclusion is a possible use of the last framework as a classification scheme for educational multimedia applications. This application could lead to an efficiency evaluation or design of such systems.

First Framework: The Actual Situation

Since hundreds of years students are sitting in lecture halls, using pen and paper to note what their professors are saying and writing down on the blackboard. Many lectures consist of hundreds of electronic slides and a projection unit copies the contents of the PC display onto an electronic board in front of the audience. Even this first implementation of an "electronic lecture" changes the preparations of a lecturer in many ways. The actual situation at many University can be described with the following application scenario:

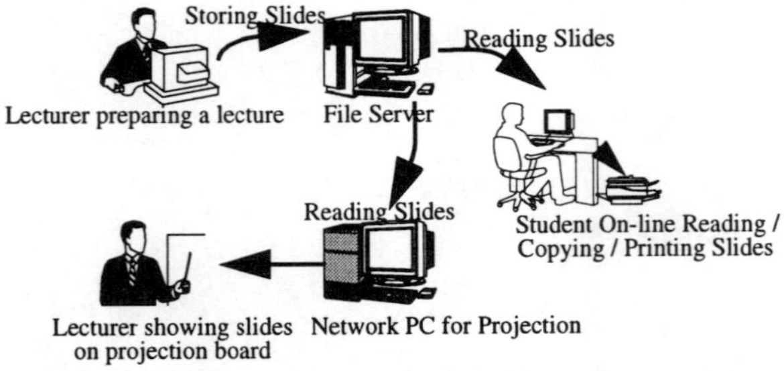

Figure 1. Implementation of an "Electronic" Lecture

Transforming this application scenario into a framework leads to:

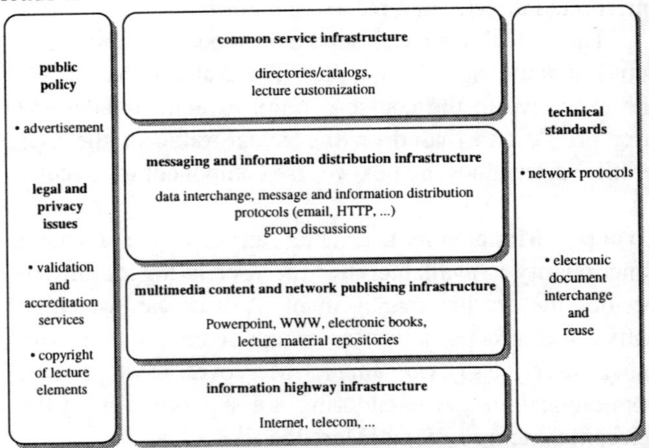

Figure 2. First Framework for an Electronic Lecture

The first main column of this framework deals with public, private and legal issues, which can be described as organizational. The topics mentioned in this context are the problems of advertisement, validation and accreditation services and the general problem of copyright protection. The second column concerns different infrastructural subjects, which are varying in a wide range from a common service down to an information highway infrastructure. Neither one component nor the other can be changed without paying attention to the crossrelations in this framework.

Second Framework: "Electronic Lecture"

The emerging technologies that make up the biggest difference in education fall into three broad categories: networking, multimedia, mobility. Integration of these technologies in the first implementation of an "electronic" lecture seems to be easy and straightforward, but reasoning a little bit about this approach will raise many fundamental questions. For example: What's about the advertisement of these lectures? Who validates the learning material? Are the objectives of the lecture achieved? Is the reading of some electronic slides all that makes a good lecture?

It is in the interest of both, the lecturers (producer) and the students (consumer), to establish standards and quality requirements that apply to the education unit and define procedures for the certification and assessment of the learners progress. Security and authentification mechanisms are also high-priority issues. Accreditation is another major concern in any education-related endeavour. Applying these ideas will lead to a scenario and a framework which

0-8186-8150-0/97 $10.00 © 1997 IEEE

we can call a "virtual lecture":

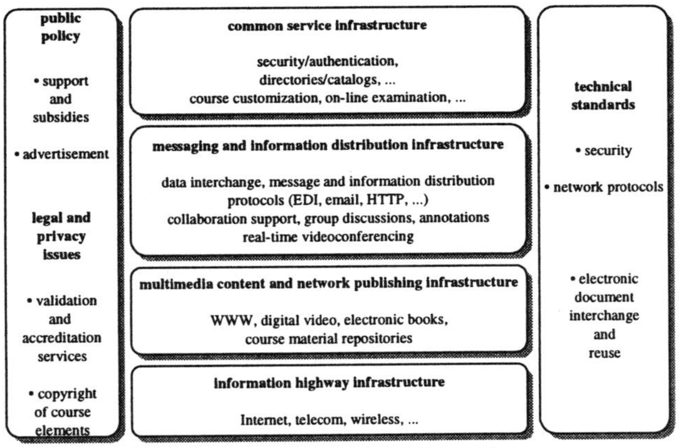

Figure 3. Framework of an Virtual Lecture

But the ultimate goal is to create a "virtual university" by adding more universities to the application scenario and offer lectures and programs to other locations.

Third Framework: "Virtual University - Education Brokerage"

In this new application scenario an "education broker" has to fulfil some of the tasks formerly done by the university like a validation and accreditation service. But the main task for them is to provide product marketing and advertisement for education suppliers. The existing framework for an electronic lecture has also to be extended by an electronic payment system. With this additions we can review our framework for an electronic lecture as an electronic commerce application: ([[1]])

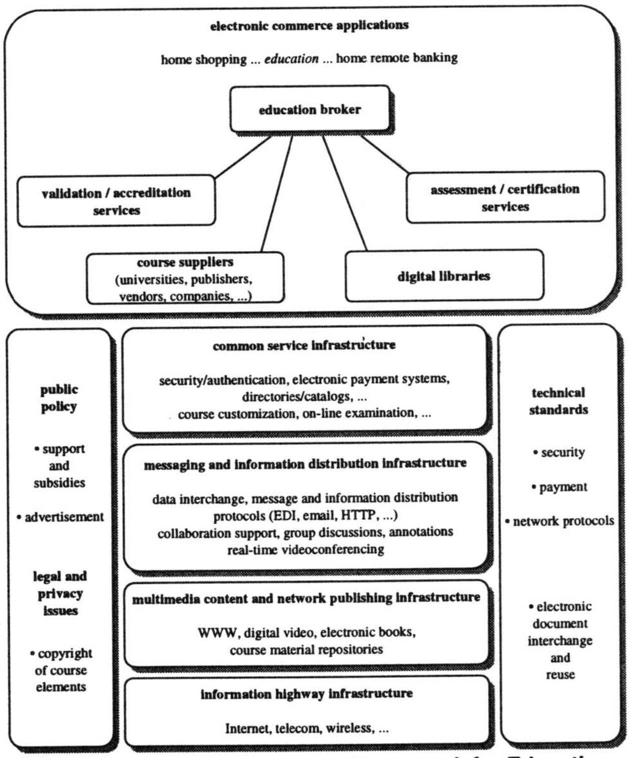

Figure 4. Electronic Commerce Framework for Education

All these concepts of distance and distributed learning are applicable to education in industries. The paradigm of training and learning as a separate activity or centralized department is dead. The new paradigm is "just-in-time learning" rather than "in-advance learning".

Conclusions

A further discussion of the conclusions of this work will lead us to two main topics: its usability as a classification scheme and the consequences of this evolution for University education. Using the third framework as a classification scheme for multimedia applications and especially for educational applications leads to an efficiency evaluation of these systems. For given systems it can help to find out the pros and cons of a system usage in case of a specific application scenario. During the design of new systems it supports the analysis of the needs and specification of the system requirements in order to produce a complete and satisfactory system. This means on one hand that someone can use the framework to evaluate interesting systems for a given specific application scenario and generate a priority list of abilities which are necessary for his specific scenario. On the other hand it is possible to generate general schemes for systems and produce classes of applications depending on their strength in the different fields of the framework. The second topic mainly deals with didactic issues in such a way that possible new ways to learn and teach also imply new ways for university education. These new ways are founded in new relationships between teacher and student as well as in new learning paradigms. The representation of education in an electronic commerce framework also establishs new strong relations to other fields with the necessity for education and will raise up many fundamental questions about the quality, sense and contents of university education. Since the development described with the third framework is more a conclusion than a decision, there is a need to answer these questions and depending on this the answer of the question is given, whether the emerging new technologies are a challenge or a menace for future education. The convergence discussion of multimedia education and electronic commerce applications will work out the peculiarities of multimedia education in context of specific application scenarios and lead to a more objective discussion of how to use multimedia for university education and establish the developed multimedia techniques as an integrated part of it.

References:

[1] Hämäläinen M., Whinston A.B., Vishik S.: Electronic Markets for Learning, Communication of the ACM Vol. 39, No. 6, p. 51-58

[2] Kalakota R., Whinston A.: Frontiers of Electronic Commerce, Addison-Wesley, Reading, Mass., 1996

[3] Reinhardt A.: New Ways to Lear, Byte 20, 3, p. 50-72

[4] Vaupel J., Sommer M.: Electronic Slides and Books, Proc. of the 2. Russian-German Symposium: "New Media for Education and Training in Computer Science", Infix 1996

Image/Video Processing for Multimedia

An Image Expression Room

Seiki Inoue Michitoshi Ishiwaka Shoji Tanaka Jong-Il Park
Media Integration & Communications Research Laboratories, ATR
2-2, Hikaridai, Seika-cho, Soraku-gun, Kyoto, 619-02, Japan
Tel: +81-774-95-1460, Fax: +81-774-95-1408
Email: {sinoue, ishiwaka, gon, pji}@mic.atr.co.jp

ABSTRACT

Studies on techniques for multimedia works production and imagination expression have been insufficient. Developments in computer graphics and synthesis technologies, however, have resulted in new types of methods and systems for creating video scenes, that is, virtual reality and virtual systems such as virtual studio.

We are engaged in research on tools and an environment using technologies for virtual systems that can help non-specialists effectively create and present the images they wish to convey.

In this paper, we propose a new image expression environment called IER (the Image Expression Room) which consists of two parts: a virtual studio with a large display and a new and integrated media handling system called COMI&CS (Computer Organized Media Integration & Communication System). IER allows people that do not have expert knowledge on the manipulation of media or techniques to express their images, to do so with a high degree of freedom. Moreover, we introduce a new type of media handling technique that uses impressions. It is called KANSEI processing in Japan.

1. Introduction

Advances in communications technologies and audio-video compression technologies have made it easy to transmit high-volume video data, which was previously very difficult to achieve. In addition, with advances in computer-related technologies and video technologies, it has become easy to process and edit video images and sound, that is to say, multimedia, and various types of processed multimedia data are being made and transmitted via electronic media.

Nevertheless, there has been insufficient study on techniques for multimedia works production [1][2]. Currently, high-quality multimedia production requires special knowledge on the techniques involved in the individual media. Therefore, only experts in broadcasting studios or video production companies can assist. Yet, the development of communications environments, such as the Internet, has led to a growing need for environments that make it possible for individuals to make content easily and express their imagination.

Developments in computer graphics (CG) and synthesis technologies have led to the creation of new types of methods and systems for creating video scenes. In the field of broadcasting, Virtual Studios are being developed in which actors can act in virtual worlds [3]. These actors, however, are treated merely as tools. A user of Virtual Reality (VR), on the other hand, can act subjectively in a virtual world.

Recently, a new type of VR system has been eagerly studied, i.e., a small room is surrounded by screens [4][5]. The user can experience and feel a virtual world even if he or she does not wear a Head Mounted Display (HMD). The intent is to offer the user a tool to experience a virtual world and not to create new scenes.

We are engaged in research on tools and an environment, using technologies of the above virtual systems so that even non-specialists can effectively and freely create and present the images they wish to convey [6][7].

In this paper, we propose a new image expression environment called IER (the Image Expression Room) which consists of two parts: a virtual studio with a large display and a new and integrated media handling system called COMI&CS (Computer Organized Media Integration & Communication System). The large display with a half mirror provides an environment in which the user can see himself/herself in some scene on a screen (like a real mirror). COMI&CS provides a free connection between all input and output media. This allows people that do not have expert knowledge on how to manipulate media or techniques to express their images, to do so interactively.

Moreover, we introduce a new type of media handling technique that uses impressions. We call it KANSEI

0-8186-8150-0/97 $10.00 © 1997 IEEE

processing. Examples of scene manipulation using impression words are also introduced.

2. Image Expression Room

In communications, we often have a desire to express ourselves differently. For example, to our friends we try to show ourselves casually but to our bosses we try to be more professional. Sometimes we may even want to imagine ourselves in a gorgeous palace. For such desires of expression, we are now developing a special room. It consists of a virtual studio and a large screen with a half mirror. Figure 1 shows its configuration. Figure 2 and Fig. 3 show an operating scene and an output.

(1) Studio

The main part is a chroma-key studio and there is also a large display with a half mirror in front of the user. The user can see himself/herself in a virtual scene. Although it is not possible to add the camerawork at the current stage, we do have a plan to do so, to make the setup like a typical virtual studio. Moreover, the lighting conditions will be controlled by a computer and operate according to the scenario.

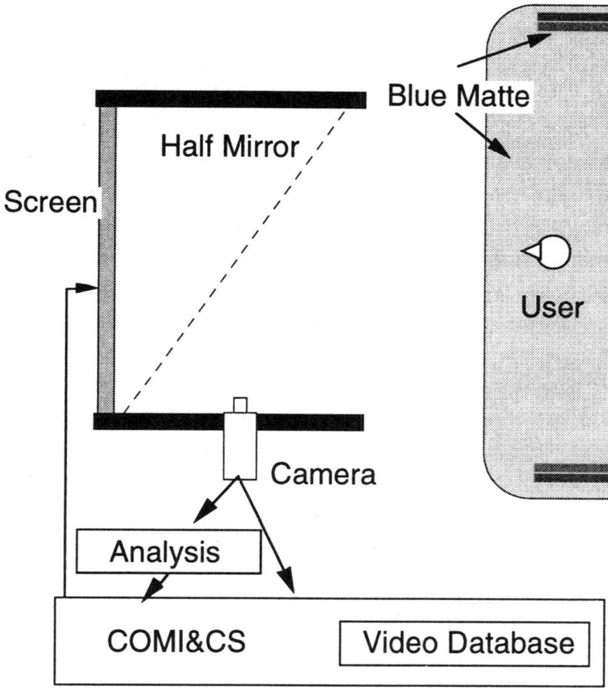

Figure 1: System configuration

Figure 2: An operating scene

Figure 3: An output video

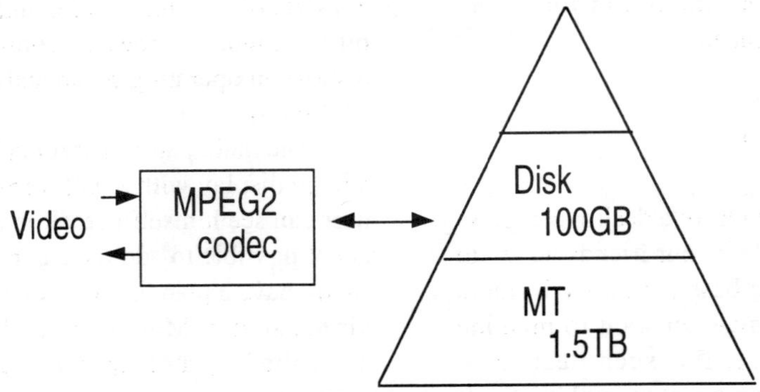

Figure 4: A hierarchical storage system

The analysis part will extract video features from the camera, such as the motion of the user. These features will be input to COMI&CS as input media components.

(2) COMI&CS

In COMI&CS, various kinds of media components can be freely connected. Such media components includes not only segmented video and audio parts but also their attributes such as motion, shape and depth which can contribute toward a better expression of images. COMI&CS is described in detail in chapter 3.

(3) Database

The database can store media components. Because video requires an especially large amount of data, we are developing a hierarchical storage system for video sequences as shown in Fig. 4.

Virtual studios have recently become very popular in the field of broadcasting. In typical virtual studios, however, actors facing a camera cannot see the monitor in which their actions are displayed. Therefore, we have added a large screen with a half mirror to the virtual studio. Users can use the screen, and view the output of the virtual studio, like a mirror. But this mirror is not a usual mirror in that the users can see themselves in special scenes and change scenes interactively. We think this is very important and effective for non-experts.

3. COMI&CS

3.1 The Concept of COMI&CS

Looking at current video production environments, video products are generally created by teams of experts that have specialized knowledge and lots of experience. COMI&CS, on the other hand, provides an environment in which media manipulation devices are managed in an integrated fashion under the control of a computer, so even non-specialists can easily manipulate and freely combine various media to express the images they have in mind. The concept of COMI&CS is shown in Fig. 5.

A database stores video and audio material (components) for combination into images. Although in most cases only video and audio clips are considered to be media components, with COMI&CS each element in the composition of video and audio material, such as the shape or motion of an object, the camera operation, and the lighting condition in a video scene, is also stored as a component. By linking and outputting these components, a single image can be expressed. The linked information is, as you would expect, in the form of a script that is also stored in the database.

In computer music, i.e., a MIDI (Musical Instrument Digital Interface) system, we assume the input device to be a musical instrument such as a MIDI keyboard and the output device to be a speaker. The system has a digital interface MIDI which can control sound resources.

As a complement to computer music, we would like to develop computer video. The input device for computer video will likely be a camera and the output device will be a video monitor. The system will also have a digital video interface VIDI (Video Instrument Digital Interface) which can control video resources such as CG or video components. In addition, there will be video effects just as there are sound effects.

If we were to combine computer music, computer video and other computer media and change the input and output devices, the range of expressions would be expanded drastically. In COMI&CS, users could connect each input to each output freely and, for example, play video instruments like musical instruments. For example, lighting information or motions could be connected to sound. Note that an input device does not always mean a hardware device, and can sometimes be information extracted from ordinary video images or sound.

A multimedia creation is output by controlling various audio and video input sources, e.g., music input from a

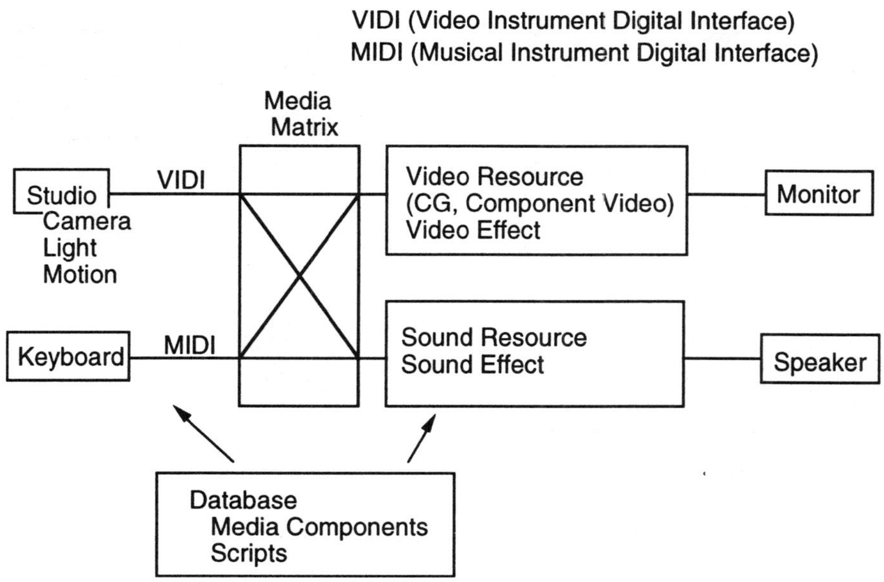

Figure 5: The concept of COMI&CS

keyboard and sound output by a sound generator. The input media is not ordinary video or sound, but the constituent elements of video or sound; for example, the shapes or movements of objects in the video.

It is not simply the case for video-related input media to be controlled as video sources and sound-related input media to be controlled as audio sources; video-related input media are also controlled as audio sources and sound-related input media are also controlled as video sources by a media matrix. In this way, the motion that goes with a piece of sound and the piece of sound that goes with a motion can be expressed.

3.2 Examples of Synthesis using Media Components

As we described before, COMI&CS can store depth and motion data as media components. Figure 6 shows a piece of video and its depth information. Depth here means the distance between a viewpoint and an object. The brightness of the depth image represents the distance. Although it is easy to get the depth information of CG images, it is not easy to get the depth information of real images shot by cameras. The depth image of Fig. 6 could be obtained by a technique we developed; the technique uses multiple cameras and stereo matching [8]. Figure 7 shows an example of synthesis using depth information. If depth information were used like in Fig. 7, the video of a user could be inserted into any layer of a scene. We are developing the technique to get more accurate depth image.

Figure 8 shows another example in which a video effect, that is, the position of a highlighted area, is controlled by the motion of the user. The area of her face can be tracked using color information in real time.

4. KANSEI Processing

4.1 Overview of Research on KANSEI Processing

If media components could be handled and new scenes created freely, that would still not be enough. Created scenes must satisfy user demands. In addition, the system must show proper examples when demands to do so are made. Therefore, we must study rules and determine which combinations of media components are better and which media components are proper for scenes or images. For this purpose, we are now beginning studies on KANSEI processing which is now actively being studied in Japan [9][10].

KANSEI is a very vague Japanese word which cannot be defined exactly. Many Japanese often use it in a unique context. KANSEI is like an emotion, feeling or sense but not exactly. Although there has been a lot of research on KANSEI, there is still no clear definition of what is meant by KANSEI or by KANSEI processing. The research itself ranges very widely from work on music to the processing of facial images and psychology. Research on industrial designs has included practical works and has a long history.

For example, some people have a greater impression on their audience than others, even though both parties use the same set of video and sound material. In cases like this, we often say that the former has KANSEI. We define

(a) Video information

(b) Depth information

Figure 6: Video with depth information

Figure 7: Synthesis using depth information

(a) Tracking of face region

(b) An output video

Figure 8: Video effect using motion information

KANSEI as some kind of ability or knowledge experts have to express their images. They know well what is effective in giving a special feeling or impression to an audience. The KANSEI processing we seek is a matter of extracting as KANSEI data the special knowledge and expertise of image expression specialists such as professional cameramen, TV program directors, and artists, and creating a database of that data. In other words, this is knowledge about what kinds of impressions can be made on viewers by taking pictures and recording pictures in different ways and by combining media elements in different ways.

Even simple word impressions involve a number of levels, as shown in Fig. 9. The closer an impression is to the left in Fig. 9, the more it corresponds to a physical quantity; the more it is to the right in the figure, the more abstract the impression is. Impressions that have a high level of abstraction can be considered to be complex combinations of less abstract impressions. Furthermore, impressions naturally vary with the person, the place, and the generation. On the other hand, it is a fact that there are works that invoke common feelings in humans that span locations and generations.

One of our research objectives is to clarify the correspondence between impressions (psychological quantities) that are common to some groups such as ordinary Japanese people (distinguishing males and females) and the factors (physical quantities) that give rise to those impressions. Another objective is to organize those correspondences into a database as KANSEI data and provide a means of using it to create new images. Taking a visual image as an example, this concept is illustrated in Fig. 10. By means of the database, the system can present expert knowledge on image expression and make suggestions to non-specialist users.

Further research is needed on how to change the method of presenting knowledge and content existing at this time according to the expressive capabilities of users.

4.2 Creating Scenes using Impression Words

In the IE Room, we would like to implement tools that create scenes using impression words such as refreshing or pretty, based on KANSEI processing. For that purpose, we are now studying the relationship between impressions and scenes.

Simply speaking, let's suppose that a scene consists of a still image. The impression a person gets from viewing the image depends greatly on how he/she views the image and on the points drawing his/her attention. Judging from the current state of image recognition technology, the automatic recognition of the subject of a photograph and the acquisition of the impression it gives are nearly impossible. Nevertheless, when looking at an image casually, we often form an impression of the overall image from our impressions of the color tone and composition. Color in particular sometimes greatly governs the impression made by an image. Therefore, we first began with studies concerning impressions and image feature quantities that focused on color.

Color is important in a wide range of applications, and has long been studied in various fields, such as design [11][12]. There are many references in literature concerning color and impressions. There is also ongoing research on determining the impressions made by paintings on the basis of the impressions given by color, but there has been relatively little work done on natural images. What is important at this time is to establish a technology for extracting representative colors from a color image.

We referred to reference [13] for information on

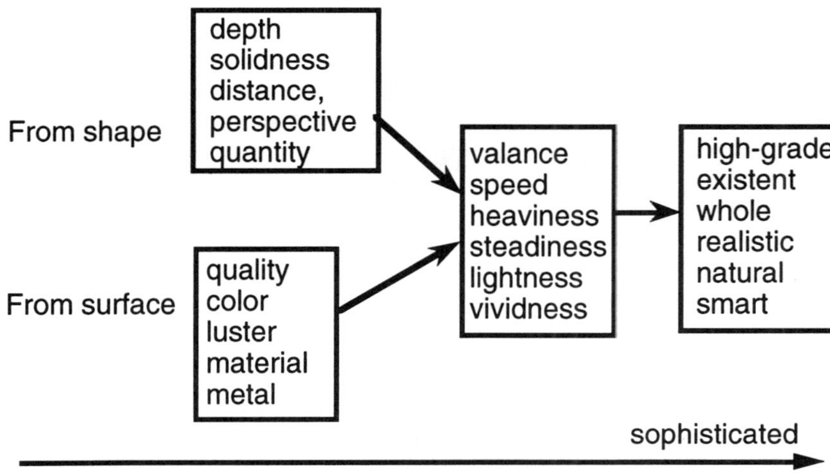

Figure 9: Examples of impressions

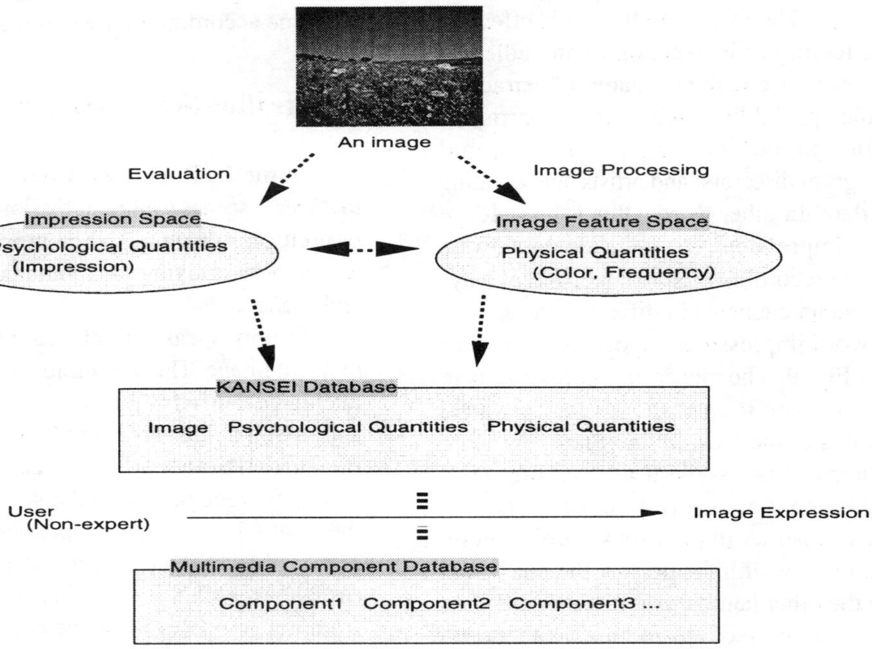

Figure 10: KANSEI processing for image expression

impression data concerning color. At present, we are obtaining impressions from three-color color schemes (a color scheme database). Figure 11 shows several examples. The usual use of this kind of data is to determine the colors to use when making a new design. When this data is applied to natural images, it is necessary to extract three particular colors from a color image; many techniques are available for doing that. We conceived of several color extraction methods giving consideration to how people focus their attention on images. We combined and used them in performing color extraction experiments. After extracting three colors from an image, we obtained the color scheme that was closest to those three colors from the color scheme database and output the corresponding impression [14].

Using this technique, we retrieved an image or a video sequence for a background scene by impression words from a database. Figure 12 shows results of the retrieval; three-color and retrieved images. Figure 13 shows an output with the retrieved background scene on the display in the IE Room . It also shows an overlapped cloth; the color of the cloth could be changed by impression words using the same technique.

We have also developed an interface for inputting impression words. Figure 14 shows a KANSEI space as an

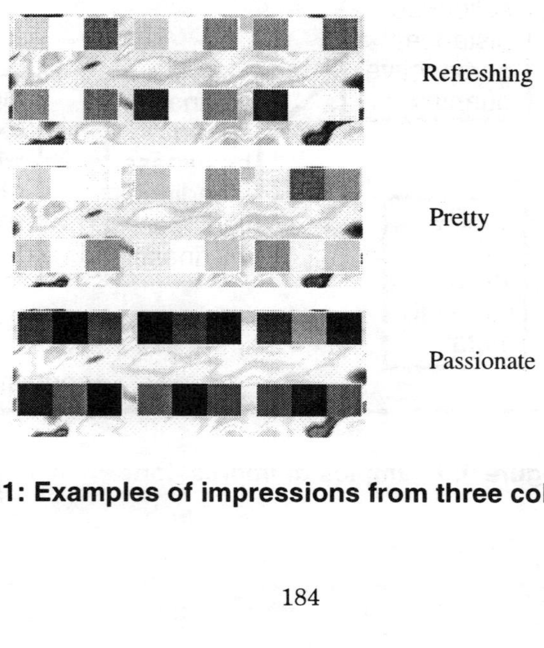

Figure 11: Examples of impressions from three colors

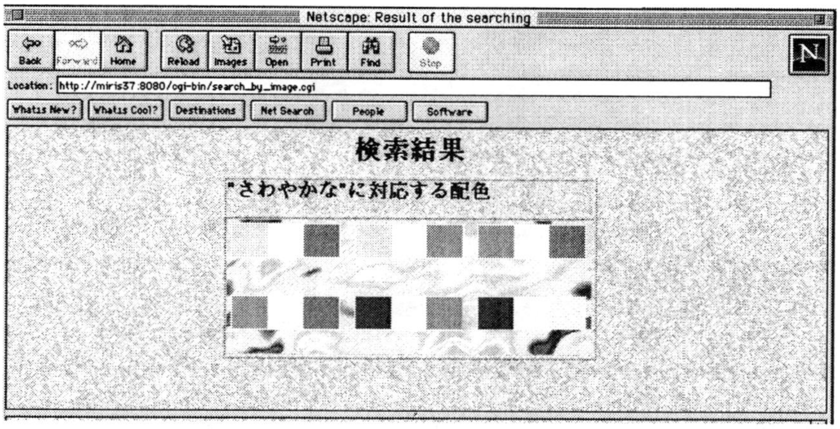

(a) Three colors corresponding to an input impression

(b) Retrieved images

Figure 12: Retrieval by impression words

interface. Impression words are already scattered about in the KANSEI space. The distances among those words are evaluated by SD (Semantic Differential) and PCA (Principal Component Analysis) methods. The user does not have to type in impression words. It is sufficient for him/her to point out words on a screen. The system can show corresponding three-color sets and retrieved background videos. The user selects or changes one from among them.

5. Conclusion

We have described IER as an image expression environment. We are now expanding it and are also studying KANSEI processing. KANSEI processing is a very important factor of IER, because we expect IER to help non-experts express themselves. We define KANSEI as the ability for expression which is held in artists or special persons. If we can extract them and store into a KANSEI

Figure 13: A created scene with a background and a cloth

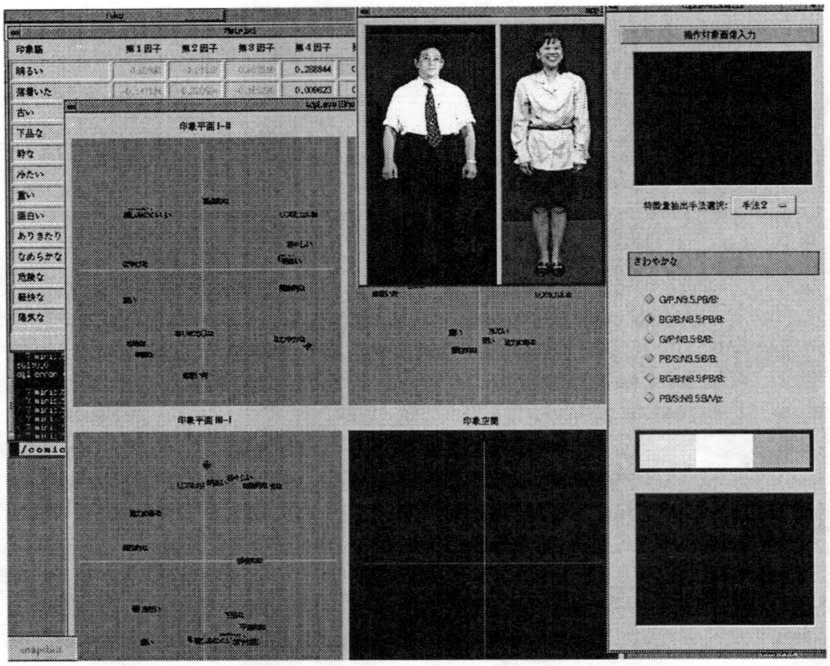

Figure 14: An interface for inputting impression words

database, IER can support non-experts using them from the viewpoint of expression technique.

On the other hand, COMI&CS can offer simplicity of handling media by media integration. Non-experts don't have to study media equipments or processes of media handling from the viewpoint of hardware. They only study the feature or behavior of media components and connect them.

We would like to combine KANSEI processing and COMI&CS, and finally develop a total environment where users can create images freely using KANSEI data.

References

[1] K. Enami, "Desk Top Program Production (DTPP) -A Scenario of Studio Digitization-", 18th International Television Symposium, June 1993.

[2] H. Sumiyoshi, et al., "Network-based Cooperative TV Program Production System", IEEE Trans. on Broadcasting, Vol. 42, No. 3, pp. 229-236, Sept. 1996.

[3] M. Hayashi, et. al., "Desktop Virtual Studio System", IEEE Trans. on Broadcasting, Vol. 42, No. 3, pp. 278-284, Sept. 1996.

[4] C. Cruz-Neira, D. J. Sandin T. A. Defanti, "Surround-Screen Projection-Based Virtual Reality: The Design and Implementation of CAVE", Proc. of SIGGRAPH '93, ACM SIGGRAPH, pp. 135-142, 1993.

[5] M. Nakajima, H. Takahashi, "Multi-Screen Virtual Reality

System: VROOM", International Workshop on New Video Media Technology, pp. 95-100, Jan. 1997.
[6] S. Inoue: "Mental Image Expression by Media Integration ~COMICS (Computer Organized Media Integration & Communication System)~", Proc. of International Workshop on New Media Technology, pp. 122-127, March 1996.
[7] M. Ishiwaka, et al., "A Framework and a Prototype of Integrated Media Handling Environment COMICS" Conv. IPS Japan, March 1996.
[8] J. Il. Park, S. Inoue, "Toward Occlusion-Free Depth Estimation for Video Production", International Workshop on New Video Media Technology, pp. 131-136, Jan. 1997.
[9] Y. Matsubara, M. Nagamachi, "Hybrid Kansei Engineering System and Design Support", Proc. of HCI International '95, pp. 161-166, July 1995.
[10] K. Imamura J. Nomura, "KANSEI Structural Modeling for Virtual Kitchen Design System", VSMM '96, pp. 317-322 Sept. 1996.
[11] Shigenobu Kobayashi, "Color Image Encyclopedia", Nihon Color Design Laboratory, 1983.
[12] Shigenobu Kobayashi, "Color Image Scale", 1995.
[13] The Color Science Association of Japan, "Color Science Handbook", 1991.
[14] S. Tanaka et. al., "A Study Concerning Automatic Addition of Impression Keywords to Natural Images", Technical Report of IEICE Japan, Oct. 1996.

3D-DCT Quantization as a Compression Technique for Video Sequences

Raymond K.W. Chan and M.C. Lee
Department of Computer Science and Engineering,
The Chinese University of Hong Kong, Shatin, Hong Kong

Abstract

This paper proposes a novel method to generate quantization values for 3D-DCT coefficients. Such quantization values are important as they would affect significantly the extent of the compression achieved by any 3D-DCT based video compression scheme. It was found that the distribution of the dominant AC coefficients spread along the major axes of the 3D-DCT cube. The coefficient distribution can be modeled by dividing the cube into two regions, one for most of the significant coefficients and the other for the high frequency coefficients which can be discarded. The quantization values are computed by using an exponential function. The same function is also used to determine a scan order of the 3D-DCT coefficients, which is better than a three dimensional zig-zag scan method in general. Experimental results show that the proposed method can produce good visual quality videos and can achieve an attractive compression ratio of 16:1 by quantization alone.

1. Introduction

A video sequence, often visualized as a volume of data, can be conceived as a 3-dimemsional signal. Extending the 2D-DCT[7] to three dimensional Discrete Cosine Transform (3D-DCT) has some advantages [1,2,6]. Such a 3D-DCT based compression scheme eliminates some of the problems caused by motion estimation, which is a time-consuming and lossy operation in MPEG[4] video coding. For a video sequence involving fast moving objects, motion estimation cannot yield a good output since it is not feasible to carry out a full search. Further, motion estimation cannot perform well in the presence of non-translational motions, for instance, rotation, zoom, and shearing of objects. A 3D-DCT based codec is symmetric. Moreover, it can give high video quality, with only a moderate loss in the compression ratio. Like the 2D-DCT based compression, the 3D-DCT based video compression scheme also consists of the usual components for transform coding[3], including *transformation*, *quantization* and *coding*.

This paper focuses on the quantization of the 3D-DCT coefficients. There are two reasons for having the quantization step. The first is to reduce the bit rate by reducing the magnitude of the coefficients. Less bits are required for each coefficient as each coefficient is divided by a constant relating to the location concerned. The second reason is that usually the high-frequency coefficients of the transform domain are insensitive to the visual quality and thus can be discarded during transmission. For the 2D-DCT, we have the quantization matrix (or table), and various methods for designing the table have been proposed [4,10]. However, so far little effort has been made on providing a corresponding table for the 3D-DCT coefficients. In fact, for the 3D-DCT, the quantization matrix is referred to as *quantization volume* since the matrix here actually consists of a volume of constants. This paper proposes a method to construct such a quantization volume for 3D-DCT coefficients.

There are three problems to be solved if we use a 3D-DCT compression scheme. Firstly, we need a fast algorithm for computing both forward and inverse 3D-DCT. A three dimensional fast discrete cosine transform (3D-FCT) has been proposed in order to eliminate the high complexity problem in calculating the 3D-DCT coefficients. Secondly, we need to quantize the resulting coefficients. Quantization tables are used for 2D-DCT based compression schemes, such as JPEG and MPEG. However, in 3D-DCT, such quantization tables cannot be used. Instead a new quantization volume has been constructed by using some statistical properties [8] of the coefficients such as their dynamic range and the periodicity of their magnitudes. Thirdly, we need to encode the quantized coefficients by using some encoder. It will be further probed for 3D-DCT in our on going research.

In section 2 the dynamic range [3] of the 3D-DCT AC and DC coefficients will be discussed. In section 3, we analyze the probability distribution of the AC coefficients and determine some statistical model to fit the empirical distribution of the AC coefficients. A quantization volume is proposed in section 4. Section 5

0-8186-8150-0/97 $10.00 © 1997 IEEE

presents our *shifted complement hyperboloid* method for selection of the coefficients. The task here is to collect the coefficients from the quantization volume according to our proposed scan order to form a linear vector for encoding. Finally a vector of coefficients will contain a lot of consecutive zeros which can be encoded by run length encoding followed by an entropy coding. Some preliminary results and the interpretations from our experiments using the proposed quantization volume generation method are presented in section 6 Concluding remarks are presented in section 7.

2. Dynamic Range of 3D-DCT Coefficients

In the most general case, the transform operation consists of point-wise multiplication of a set of sample data values by a set of weighting coefficients, and subsequent summation of the products so formed. The sample data values may take on any value between zero and the maximum allowable within the system. Once the cube size has been selected, the maximum possible value of the transform coefficient may easily be calculated. In our 3D-DCT compression scheme, the theoretical range of the coefficients can be derived as follows:

Consider the basic equations of a 3D-DCT

The forward 3-D discrete cosine transform (3-D DCT) is given by

$$Y_{u,v,w} = \sqrt{\frac{8}{MNP}} E_u E_v E_w \sum_{m=0}^{M-1}\sum_{n=0}^{N-1}\sum_{p=0}^{P-1} y_{m,n,p} \times Cs_{2M}^{(2m+1)u} Cs_{2N}^{(2n+1)v} Cs_{2P}^{(2p+1)w}$$

where $E_u, E_v, E_w = \begin{cases} \frac{1}{\sqrt{2}} & \text{for } m,n,p=0 \\ 1 & \text{otherwise} \end{cases}$ and

$$Cs_J^i = \cos(\frac{i\pi}{J}) \quad (1)$$

$y_{m,n,p}$ is the 3D spatio-temporal data element of the mth row, n^{th} column and p^{th} frame

$Y_{u,v,w}$ is the 3D transform domain data element at position u,v,w in the 3-D transform space.

We normalize $Y_{u,v,w}$ as $\tilde{Y}_{u,v,w} = \sqrt{\frac{MNP}{8}} \frac{1}{E_u E_v E_w} Y_{u,v,w}$;

Thus equation (1) becomes

$$\tilde{Y}_{u,v,w} = \sum_{m=0}^{M-1}\sum_{n=0}^{N-1}\sum_{p=0}^{P-1} y_{m,n,p} Cs_{2M}^{(2m+1)u} Cs_{2N}^{(2n+1)v} Cs_{2P}^{(2p+1)w} \quad (2)$$

The inverse 3-D DCT (IDCT) for spatio-temporal data points can be represented by :

$$y_{m,n,p} = \sqrt{\frac{8}{MNP}} \sum_{u=0}^{M-1}\sum_{v=0}^{N-1}\sum_{w=0}^{P-1} E_u E_v E_w Y_{u,v,w} \times Cs_{2M}^{(2m+1)u} Cs_{2N}^{(2n+1)v} Cs_{2P}^{(2p+1)w} \quad (3)$$

We normalize $Y_{u,v,w}$ as $\hat{Y}_{u,v,w} = \sqrt{\frac{8}{MNP}} E_u E_v E_w Y_{u,v,w}$

Then $y_{m,n,p} = \sum_{u=0}^{M-1}\sum_{v=0}^{N-1}\sum_{w=0}^{P-1} \hat{Y}_{u,v,w} Cs_{2M}^{(2m+1)u} Cs_{2N}^{(2n+1)v} Cs_{2P}^{(2p+1)w}$ (4)

For each cosine term, the range is from -1 to +1. Combining the range of these cosine terms with the range of values of $y_{m,n,p}$, (that is the intensity levels in the video) the theoretical dynamic range of the transform coefficients can be investigated. Let DR_{DC} be the dynamic range for DC and DR_{AC} be the dynamic range for AC coefficients. Then DR_{DC} is given by :

$$DR_{DC} = -\hat{y}_D \sum_{m=0}^{M-1} Cs_{2M}^{(2m+1)0} \sum_{n=0}^{N-1} Cs_{2N}^{(2n+1)0} \sum_{p=0}^{P-1} Cs_{2P}^{(2p+1)0} \quad (5)$$

where $\hat{y}_D = (\hat{y}_{max}+1)/(\hat{y}_{min}+1)$, $\hat{y}_{max}$ and $\hat{y}_{min}$ correspond to the maximum and minimum value of $\hat{y}$ respectively.

The dynamic range of the AC coefficients is:

$$DR_{AC_{u,v,w}} = \frac{\hat{y}_D \sum_{m=0}^{M-1} \left|Cs_{2M}^{(2m+1)u}\right| \sum_{n=0}^{N-1} \left|Cs_{2N}^{(2n+1)v}\right| \sum_{p=0}^{P-1} \left|Cs_{2P}^{(2p+1)w}\right|}{\left|Cs_{2M(\min)}^{(2m+1)u}\right| \left|Cs_{2N(\min)}^{(2n+1)v}\right| \left|Cs_{2P(\min)}^{(2p+1)w}\right|} = \hat{y}_D \sum_{m=0}^{M-1} \left|Cs_{2M}^{(2m+1)u}\right| \sum_{n=0}^{N-1} \left|Cs_{2N}^{(2n+1)v}\right| \sum_{p=0}^{P-1} \left|Cs_{2P}^{(2p+1)w}\right| \quad (6)$$

We have conducted a number of experiments on testing the dynamic range of coefficients from some video sequences compressed through using 3D-DCT. Four raw test sequences were used in testing video; it is observed that the DC coefficients range from several hundreds to several thousands. For instance, the minimum and maximum DC values for the Tennis video sequence are 633.66 and 5374.88 respectively. Figure 1 presents the dynamic range of the DC coefficients. It shows two levels of DC values. For the upper level, there are DC lower values from the sequences 0-4 and 8, and higher DC values from the remaining sequences. A lower value corresponds to sequences with high activity, complex motion such as zooming, or video scene change. In Tennis test video, there is a scene change at frames 65-72, which correspond to sequence 8 and zooming at frame 0-32 which correspond to sequence 0-4. Such lower DC values are caused by the spread of energy in the AC coefficients. This implies that high activity scenes have larger AC values. If we need to encode a DC value with no more than 8 bits, the quantization value should be $(DC_{max}/255)\cong 25$, without significant loss of accuracy.

Tables 1 and 2 show the dynamic range of the coefficients from different test video sequences. The distributions of DC values from the test sequences are similar in some way; the DC coefficients vary between 700 and 6000. That is, the DC coefficients are bounded by two values for any video. The two values may vary, depending on the nature of the video. However, irrespective of the type of video, it is expected that DC coefficient values will still lie within these bounds. Such bounds could be found through some statistical techniques and extensive experiments.

We also analyzed the values of the AC coefficients and these are presented in the form of graphs for different video sequences. Figure 2 shows a plot of the AC coefficient values versus the coefficient numbers for some Football video frames. Note that the coefficient number is defined by $u\times 64+v\times 8+w$ for a 8x8x8 cube. The AC coefficients range between -1000 and +1000; most of them assume a small value, less than 100, and have a mean value of zero. In fact many of the AC coefficients are close to zero. Thus compared with the DC coefficient, AC coefficients contain little energy for the whole 3D-DCT cube. There are periodic high peaks from the 511 coefficients for an 8x8x8 data cube. The period is 8. It is expected that more energy is concentrated on the major axes of the cube and is decreased as the locations concern are away from the *u*, *v* and *w* directions of the cube. For a scene change or higher activity taking place within a frame sequence, the AC values are much higher and are spread in the high frequency region, those locations far from the origin (0,0,0). Figure 3 shows the AC values distribution for a video sequence involving scene change. It is noted that AC peak values are higher for lower coefficient numbers, that is, for locations on the first plane of coefficients, or all (x,y,0) coordinates. Thus, if the ranges of most AC coefficients are from -500 to 500 (see figure 2), we want to limited to 4 bits allocation, then we expect that the quantization values for the 3D-DCT AC coefficient range would be around 20 to 80.

Figure 1. Dynamic Range of the DC coefficients of Tennis sequence

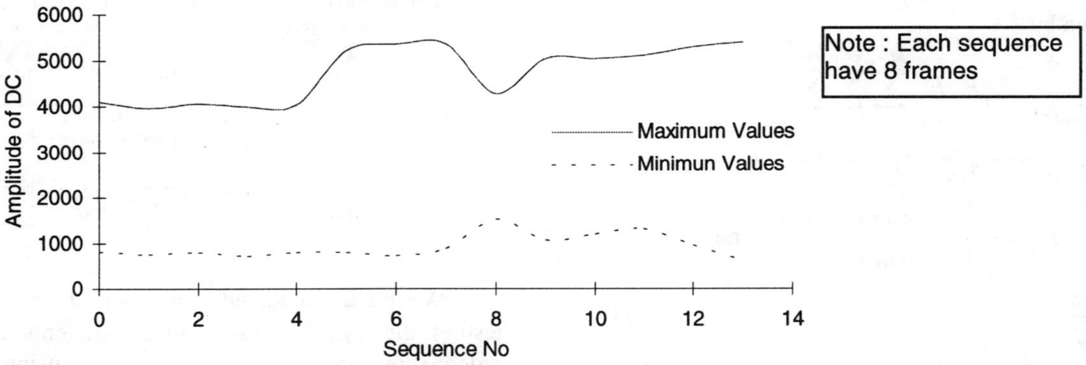

Table 1: The minimum values for DC coefficients for different video sequences.

Frame No.	1-8	9-16	17-24	25-32	33-40	41-48	49-56	57-64	65-72	73-80
Tennis	830	768	809	727	807	816	740	893	1517	1078
Football	954	1040	1001	887	956	869	902	924		
Garden	1342	1163	1169	1205	1201	1183	1205			

Table 2: The maximum values for DC coefficients for different video sequences.

Frame No.	1-8	9-16	17-24	25-32	33-40	41-48	49-56	57-64	65-72	73-80
Tennis	4098	3957	4067	3993	4037	5210	5350	5346	4267	5022
Football	4898	4561	5049	4980	4733	5192	5084	4991		
Garden	5525	5514	5510	5497	5480	5382	5394			

Figure 2: AC Distribution from Football Frame 9-16

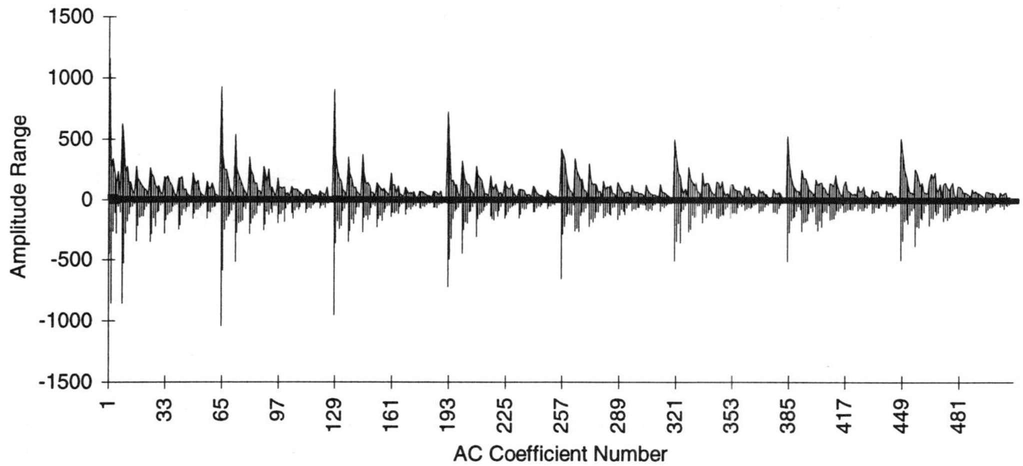

Figure 3: AC Distribution from Tennis Frame 65-72

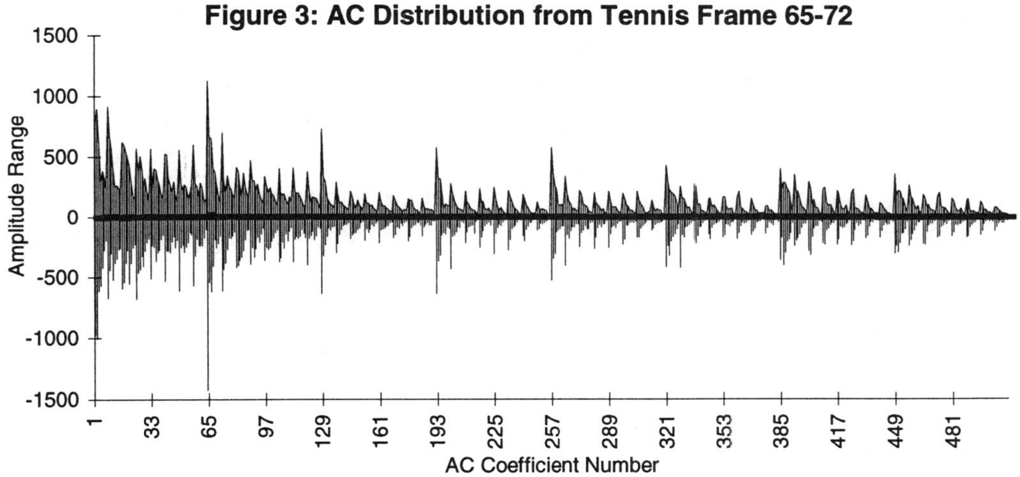

3. Distribution of 3D-DCT AC Coefficients

It is generally believed [9] that the distribution of the AC coefficients of the transformed image block for the 2D-DCT is Laplacian (double sided exponential). The Laplacian distribution

$$p(x) = \frac{\lambda}{2} e^{-\lambda|x|} \qquad (7)$$

is symmetrical about zero (x=0), and it can be readily matched to a sample distribution by finding appropriate value for the parameter λ. We need to know if the Laplacian distribution is equally suitable for the 3D-DCT AC coefficients. From figures 4 and 5, we note that the plot of Laplacian has shapes similar to the distribution for AC coefficients with λ=0.31 and λ=0.17 respectively for different sets of video sequences. The actual coefficient distribution is about three times the magnitude of the Laplacian distribution in both sequences.

These distributions give us the idea of the mean and variance of the AC coefficients and so we can estimate the number of coefficients to be included after quantization.

Figure 4: The pdf of the AC Coefficients of Tennis sequence

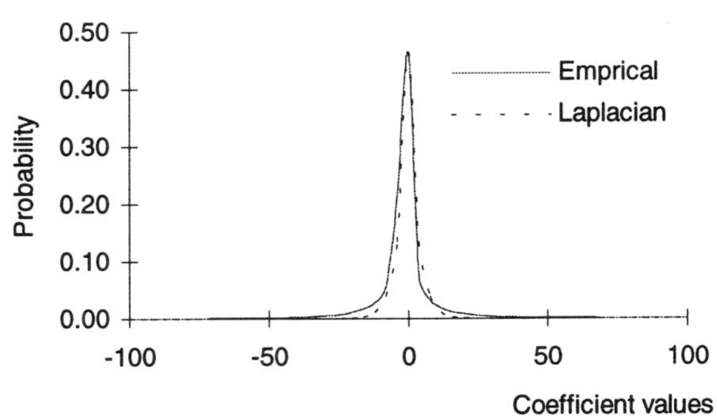

Figure 5: The pdf of the AC coefficients of Football Sequence

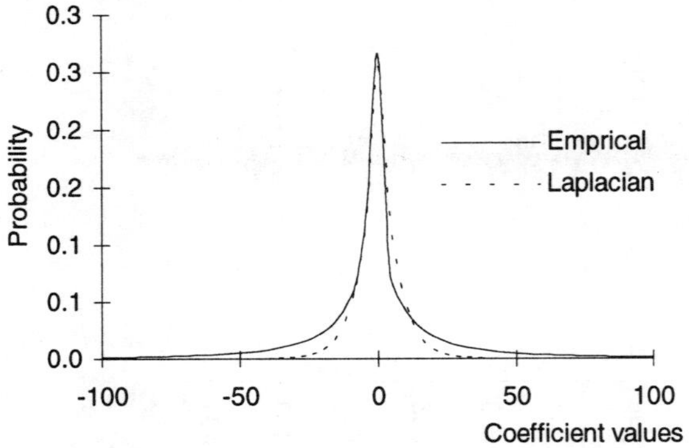

4. The Quantization Volume

The quantization step plays an important role in the compression scheme because it reduces the magnitude of the coefficients by dividing them with some constants. However it is a lossy step in the whole compression scheme since a portion of the coefficients are being quantized to a zero level which cannot be restored by the decompressor. It is important to design a universal optimal quantizer for all data sets. Lloyd and Max[5] suggested methods to design an optimal quantizer for a given data set by using the statistical characteristics of the data set. In JPEG and MPEG, the quantiation values are often given by some 'de facto' standard quantization table. This table is based on the 2D-DCT characteristics and the AC and DC coefficient distributions for some standard test data. Nevertheless, it is quite different when using 3D-DCT which gives a 'volume' of coefficients rather than a matrix as described in the previous sections. Our goal is to provide a general quantization 'volume' for the 3D-DCT since we cannot use the values for the 2-D DCT case.

In the previous section, we confirmed the distribution of the AC coefficients as a Laplacian. It is also observed that the dominant coefficients are spread along the major axes of the coefficient cube, constituting over 80% of the total energy. (Also see figures 2 and 3) Mathematically, this dominant coefficients are described by $Y_{u,v,0}, Y_{u,0,w}$ and $Y_{0,v,w}$. The probability of occurrence of the coefficients or the number of coefficients decrease exponentially as the indices increase. Thus, the approach we take in determining the values for the quantization volume is to generate a solid representing the coefficients to be selected. We called the solid the *shifted complement hyperboloid*, since it actually represents a complement of the hyperboloid formed by the non-selected coefficients. The idea of *shifted complement hyperboloid* is depicted in Figure 6 below.

Figure 6 : The 3D-DCT coefficients are concentrated along the major axes. This is captured by a *shifted complement hyperboloid*.

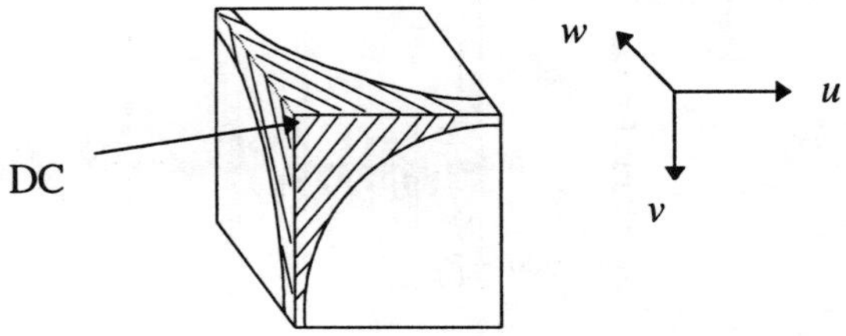

To model the solid as shown in Figure 6. We first consider the first u-v plane ($w = 0$). Assuming the solid lies on the first octane, that is $u \geq 0$, $v \geq 0$ and $w \geq 0$. Let us consider 2-D case. The shaded area can be treated as a hyperbola such that

$uv \leq C_1$ where C_1 is an arbitrary constant (8)

Similarly, the shaded areas in the v-w and w-u planes can be respectively represented by

$vw \leq C_2$ and $wu \leq C_3$ (9)

where C_2 and C_3 are constants.

Combining (8) and (9), we have

$$g(u,v,w) = uvw \leq \sqrt{C_1 C_2 C_3} = C' \quad (10)$$

This function $g(u,v,w) \leq C'$ defines the solid under the shaded area as shown in Figure 7

Figure 7: The region defined by $uvw \leq C'$

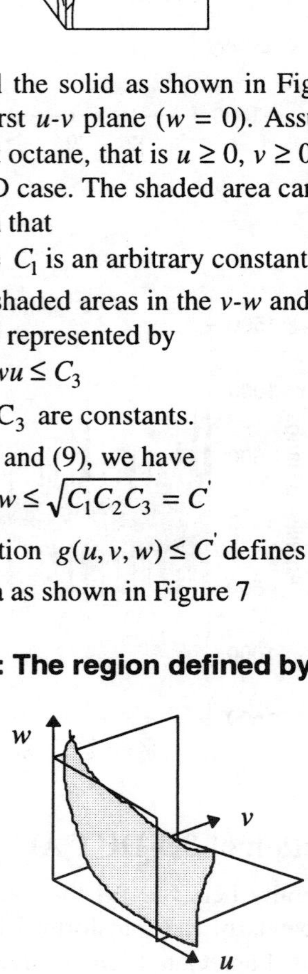

Note that the region includes the three planes $u = 0$, $v = 0$ and $w = 0$ and it is not actual description of the region shown in figure 6. To avoid the effect of u, v and w being zero, we can shifted the region by 1 if we use $f(u,v,w) = g(u+1, v+1, w+1) \leq C$, that is

$$(u+1)(v+1)(w+1) \leq C \quad (11)$$

Expanding equation (11), we have

$$uvw + uv + vw + wu + u + v + w + 1 \leq C \quad (12)$$

where $C' = C - (uv + vw + wu + u + v + w + 1)$,

the upper-bounds defined by (10) & (11) being assumed to assure uvw=C'. Equation (12) defines our *shifted complement hyperboloid* solid.

The solid or region defined by equation (12) can be used to select the dominant coefficients. We can vary the value of C in order to include various number of coefficients within the region. Experimental results, which will be discussed in a later section, show that for some values of C, we can discard the coefficients outside the region, (that is $f(u,v,w) > C$), without any adverse effect on the visual quality of the video after reconstruction.

The quantization volume should have an entry for each coefficient. Using the dynamic range of the coefficients and the coefficient distribution, we can design the quantization volume based on the following criteria.

1. The quantizaton values should have range from 20-80 within the solid.
2. The quantization values should facilitate the quantizer to discard the high frequency components outside the region.
3. The quantization values should have values that match with the exponential (Laplacian) distribution.
4. Base on the dynamic range of the coefficients and the coefficient distribution, the quantization values should have lower values along the major axes and higher values in the remaining part of the cube.
5. The quantization values should increase as we go down the scan order of the coefficients

A function with different parameters for defining the values for the inside and the outside of the region is used so that an appropriate value for any position in the quantization volume can be assigned. A candidate function that can generate quantization values meeting the criteria stated above is given by:

$$q'(u,v,w) = \begin{cases} A_i(1 - \dfrac{e^{-\beta_i(uvw)}}{e^{-\beta_i}}) & \text{for } f(u,v,w) \le C \\ A_o(1 - e^{-\beta_o(uvw)}) & \text{for } f(u,v,w) > C \end{cases} \quad (13)$$

where (A_i, β_i) and (A_o, β_o) are constants for inside and outside the region respectively and $u,v,w \ge 0$

We attempt to determine experimentally values of $A_i, A_o, \beta_i, \beta_o$ and C in order to find an optimal set of parameters for different types of video. The function defined is a general exponential function with its initial amplitudes determined by A_i and A_o, and the rate of the decay (or the rate at which if approach the maximum of function q') can be controlled by the parameters β_i and β_o. Therefore, by adjusting the parameters, different shapes of the solid can be obtained. We can make the parameter A_o to a high value so it can filter out the high frequency coefficients. Again for the case $u = 0$, $v = 0$ and $w = 0$, to avoid the effect of making the exponent part zero, we thus modify the equation as follows:

$$q(u,v,w) = \begin{cases} A_i(1 - \dfrac{e^{-\beta_i((u+1)(v+1)(w+1))}}{e^{-\beta_i}}) + 1 & \text{for } f(u,v,w) \le C \\ A_o(1 - e^{-\beta_o((u+1)(v+1)(w+1))}) & \text{for } f(u,v,w) > C \end{cases} \quad (14)$$

It is also possible to define different solids by using different values of C, and thus make use of different sets of A's,β's and Cs to obtain the desired result. However, to demonstrate the idea proposed, we only use one solid for simplicity.

5. Scan Order for the 3D-DCT Coefficients

Another important issue is to collect the coefficients to a linear array in order to perform encoding as a last step in the compression scheme. There are many ways to collect the coefficients. Yeo and Liu [12] suggested the use of isoplane, $u + v + w = K$ to be the scan order, where K is a constant. However, this method cannot effectively include the coefficients that lie on the major axes and it will include more zeros inside the cube for some $K > 3$. Moreover, the periodic nature and the distribution of the coefficients make this approach inappropriate.

A better method is proposed here by making use of the quantization function (14) to collect the coefficients inside a cube of 3D-DCT. Based on experimental results from some sample video sequences, we notice that if the magnitudes of the coefficients are sorted by descending order before quantization, the large coefficients would be within the solid defined in the previous section. It is also noted that the first few tens of coefficients have small indices u,v,w or $uvw \le C'$ as described by equation (10). This implies that we should collect the coefficients within the solid first, before those outside the solid. The reason is that more consecutive zeros of the coefficients can be grouped together for more efficient encoding. As describe below, the quantization values may also be used to define the scan order for the coefficients. This ordering method gives better result because it collects more dominant coefficients inside the solid.

Below is defined a procedure to determine the scan order for the coefficients in a cube. We assign values to the quantization volume by varying u,v,w in equation (14) by setting $A_i < A_o$, to ensure the values inside the region are smaller than that outside the region. These values are then sorted in ascending order which actually corresponds to the order of the coefficients being collected since the coefficients inside the solid will be collected before those outside the region. There may be some equal values. An algorithm for collecting the coefficients can then be made to select coefficients along the u direction first, then along the v direction, and finally along the w direction. By scanning u,v direction first is important because in most cases the coefficients are spread over the smaller values of w. The order of u and v is immaterial. This algorithm defines the whole scanning sequence.

6. Experimental Results

Four sequences of video have been tested with different parameters of A, β and C. We first adjust the parameter C so that we can define a region to include the coefficients with minimum distortion. The distortion can be described in two ways. One is based on some statistical methods and the other is on the perceptual observation [11] of the reconstructed sequences. In the statistical method, we can use the mean square error (MSE) from the reconstructed video which is given by:

$$MSE = \frac{1}{MNP} \sum_{m=0}^{M-1} \sum_{n=0}^{N-1} \sum_{p=0}^{P-1} (y_{m,n,p} - \tilde{y}_{m,n,p})^2 \qquad (15)$$

where $y_{m,n,p}$ is the original data cube and $\tilde{y}_{m,n,p}$ is the creconstructed data cube.

We can also find the peak signal to noise ratio (PSNR) by the following equation:

$$PSNR = 10\log_{10}\left(\frac{255^2}{MSE}\right) \qquad (16)$$

The lower the distortion, the lower the value of MSE or the higher the value of PSNR.

A good set of parameters for equation (14) can be found by using the perceptual method to view the reconstructed videos and to find the just-noticeable-difference threshold by comparing with the original video. Besides, we can also determine parameters for a just-acceptable quality for the worse case. This measure is quite subjective and vary from person to person but it is more sensible for human's perception.

We try to determine the parameters by both methods. To ensure the values in the quantization volume are not more than 8 bits, we fix the parameters A_i and A_o to be 255 so that the maximum value in the quantization volume will not be greater than 255. Then, we try to tune the parameter C which will affect the boundary of the two solids in the quantization volume. By varying the parameter C, different number of coefficients can be included. To exclude the effect of the β, we set β_i=0.00001 and β_o=10 which makes the values inside the region to be 1, those outside the boundary to be 255. That means we want to see the effect of varying the number of selected coefficients on quality degradation. The coefficients inside the region will not be quantized since they are divided by 1 but the coefficients outside the region will be discarded since they are divided by 255.

Figure 8 shows the first reconstructed frame of Tennis sequence with different values of C. We notice that the image quality for $C > 12$ is indistinguishable from the original. When $C = 10$, it would be just-acceptable in quality. Figure 9 shows the average MSE versus different values of C for different video sequences.

Figure 8 : Reconstructed video frame for different values of *C*

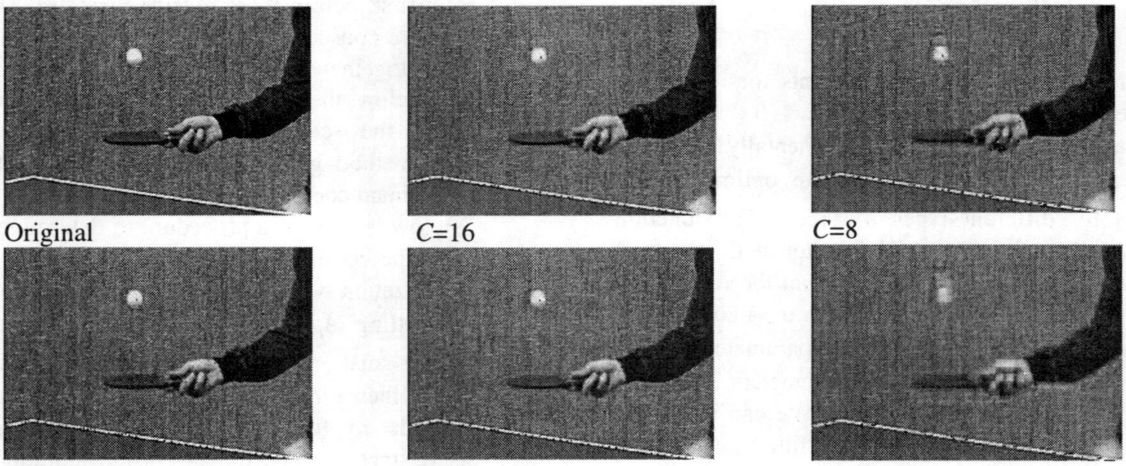

Figure 9: Average MSE versus the value of Parameter C

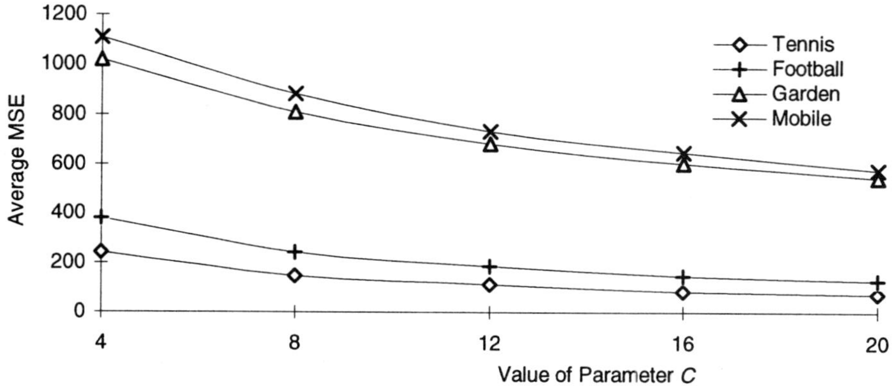

The next step is to fix the parameter C = 10, and adjust the value for β_i . Figure 10 shows the plot of PSNR versus β_i for values from 0.0001 to 0.1 while Figure 11 shows the plot with β_i values ranging from 0.01 to 0.05 for the first 8 frames of Tennis sequence. The PSNR is inversely proportional to β_i. For the best visual quality, the value of β_i is around 0.04. Fixing β_i = 0.04, we vary β_o from 0.0001 to 0.1. The results are shown in Figure 12. For best performance for rate-distortion or visual quality, the value of β_o should be around 0.1. Figure 13 shows the video frame with parameter C=10, β_i=0.04 and β_o=0.1.

Figure 10: PSNR versus beta(i)

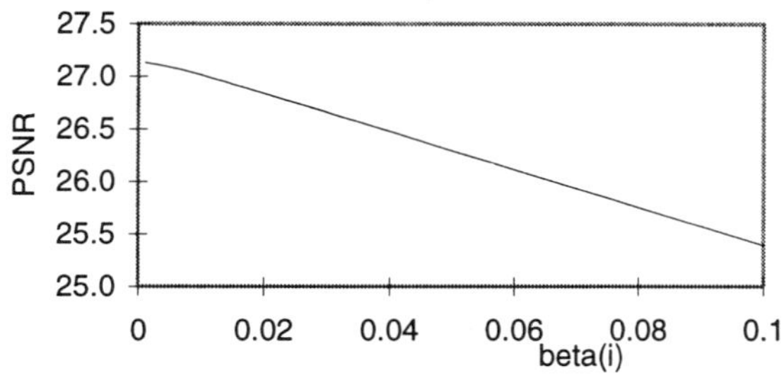

Figure 11: PSNR versus beta(i)

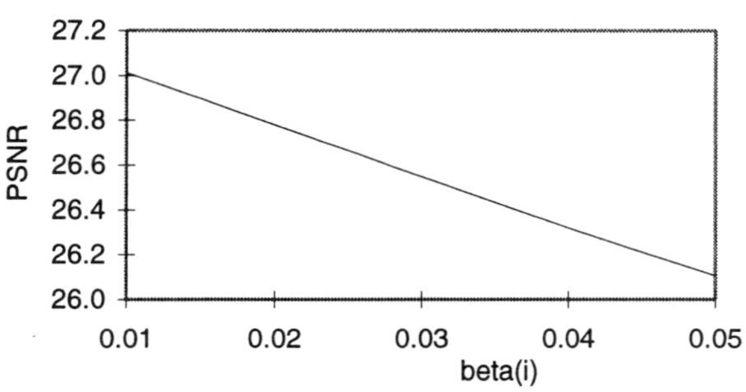

Figure 12: PSNR versus beta(o) with Beta(i)=0.04

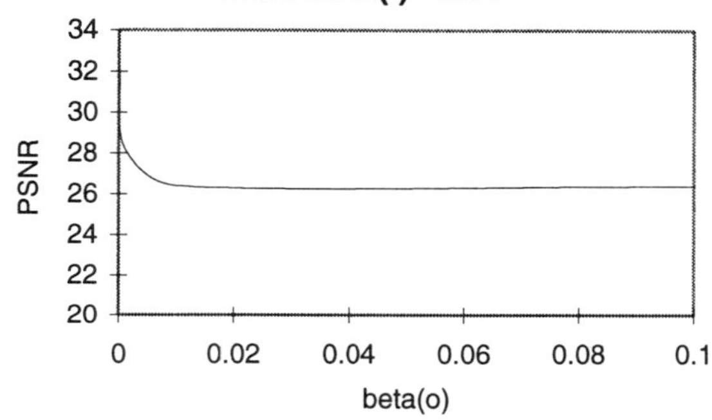

Figure 13: Tennis frame with C=10, β_i=0.04, β_o=0.1

7. Concluding Remarks

In this paper we have attempted to design quantization values for each coefficient in a 3D-DCT cube. We first studied the dynamic range of the DC and AC coefficients from several set of raw testing video sequences. It is concluded that the range of the DC is from several hundreds to several thousands depending on the distribution of the AC coefficients. High activity frames or frames with scene change will give lower values of DC but more spread in the AC terms. Homogenous cubes, the DC values are very high and which contain most of the energy. The range suggests that the values of the quantization volume should be around 25 for the DC with 8 bit allocation and below 100 for AC coefficients with 4 bit allocation.

From empirical observations, we also notice that the AC coefficients distribution can be modeled by Laplacian distribution. This suggests the quantization values according to an exponential function. We modeled the distribution by dividing the cube into two regions, one for containing most of the significant coefficients and the other for the high frequency coefficients which can be discarded. The parameters are determined by some experiments with different video sequences. If we want to limit 8 bits for DC coefficients and 4 bits for AC coefficients, we have $A_i = A_o \approx 255$, $\beta_i = 0.04$, $\beta_o = 0.01$ and $C = 10$. These values will give a PSNR of 25db without adverse deterioration in visual quality.

We are currently investigating how to encode the quantized coefficients. From the previous derivation, we have set the parameter with 8 bits for the DC and 4 bits for AC coefficients. For $C = 10$, less than 64 (that is one-eighth) of the coefficients will be collected, and the others will have zero magnitude after quantization. This implies that we have at least 16:1 in compression ratio by quantization alone. After encoding, the compression ratio is expected to be much higher than this value. So the compression scheme is expected to have good potential for very low bit-rate video transmission applications.

References

[1] G. P. Abousleman, M. W. Marcellin, B. R. Hunt, "Compression of hyperspectral imagery using the 3-D DCT and hybrid DPCM/DCT," *IEEE Transactions on Geoscience and Remote Sensing*, Vol **33(1)**, pp. 26-34, 1995.

[2] V. Bhaskaran, K. Konstantinides, *Image and Video Compression Standards, Algorithms and Architectures*, Kluwer Academic Publishers, pp. 88-91, 1995.

[3] R. J. Clarke, *Transform Coding of Images*, Academic Press, 1985.

[4] D. L. Gall, "MPEG: a video compression standard for multimedia applications," *Communication of the ACM*, Vol. 35, pp.46-58, April 1991.

[5] J. Max, "Quantizing for minimum distortion," *IEEE Transaction on Information Theory*, vol. **IT-6**, pp. 7-12 March, 1960.

[6] T.R. Natarajan, N. Ahmed, "On Interframe Transform Coding," IEEE Transactions On Communications, Vol. **COM-25(11),** pp. 1323-1329, November, 1977.

[7] K. R. Rao, and P. Yip, *Discrete Cosine Transform*, Academic Press, pp. 82, 1990.

[8] Randall C. Reininger and Jerry D. Gibson, "Distributions of the two-dimensional DCT coefficients for images," *IEEE Transactions on Communication*, Vol. **COM-31(6)**, pp. 835-839, June 1983.

[9] Stephen R. Smoot and Lawrence A. Rowe, "Laplacian Model for AC DCT Terms in Image and Video Coding," *Ninth Workshop on Image and Multidimensional Signal Processing*, 1996.

[10] G. K. Wallace, "The JPEG still picture compression standard," *Communication of the ACM*, Vol. **34(4)**, pp.30-44, April 1991.

[11] Andrew B. Watson, "Perceptual Optimization of DCT Color Quantization Matrices," *Proceedings of the IEEE International Conference on Image Processing*, Austin, TX, November, 1994.

[12] Boon-Lock Yeo and Bede Liu, "Volume Rendering of DCT-Based Compressed 3D Scalar Data," *IEEE Transactions on Visualization and Computer Graphics*, Vol. 1, No. 1, pp. 29-43, March 1995.

Segmentation of moving human body parts by a modified MAP-MRF algorithm

F. García-Ugalde
T.A. Furness III

J. Savage-Carmona
D. Gatica-Pérez
V. García-Garduño

Human Interface Technology Laboratory
University of Washington, Box 352142
Seattle, WA 98195

Depto. de Ing. Eléctrica-DEP
FI-UNAM, Apdo. Postal 70-256
04510 México, D.F., MEXICO

Abstract

Using a dense motion vector field as the main information we develop a region segmentation algorithm in which each region is matched to a four-parameter motion model. Based on Markov Random Fields the segmentation model detects moving parts of the human body with different apparent displacement such as the hands. The motion vector field has been estimated by a Baaziz pel-recursive method and considered together with others sources of information such as intensity contours, intensity values and non-compensated pixels as inputs of the Markov Random Field model. The maximum a posteriori criterion (MAP) is used for the optimization of the solution, and performed with a deterministic method: Iterated Conditional Modes (ICM). Results on segmenting and classifying real sequences are shown and based on a roughly defined directional dictionary one application is pursuing for using the segmented regions as commands for a virtual robot. The classification is based on the correlation coefficient (between the trained sequences and others) of wavelet coefficients, of the projected sum of the intensity of the segmentation field (in its binary version).

1 Introduction

The problem of segmenting moving regions was traditionally studied for coding video, in this work we are interested in a different application oriented to allow communication with a virtual robot using a very simple directional gesture dictionary. The idea behind this very simple dictionary is to permit us to communicate with the robot without cumbersome gloves and to consider this kind of communication as complementary of speech communication [13] into a multimodal interface. Accurate motion vector field estimation is crucial in this application as well as the segmentation and can be seen as interdependent problems, because one is needed to obtain the other with accuracy (estimation-segmentation ambiguity). Thus, motion-based segmentation is crucial for extracting high level information from the time-varying intensity of a sequence and for improving the motion measurement process [4], [6], [7], [11], it represents a qualitative change from a local motion description to a regional one. In this paper, we present an algorithm to segment image sequences that begins with a Baaziz [1] pel-recursive estimation of a motion vector field. Later, we model the image sequence using Markov Random Fields and pursue the optimization of the segmentation problem by a Bayesian estimation criterion (MAP) performed with a deterministic method: Iterated Conditional Modes (ICM) [2]. Our probabilistic approach takes into account the fact that an exact displacement field does not exist (errors usually occur at or around motion boundaries), and that better results can be attained if an indicator of the quality of the vector field is known, this indicator is obtained from the non-compensated pixels as well as the contours. The classification of the segmented areas has been developed by computing for the *trained sequences* and others, a correlation coefficient of wavelet coefficients, of the projected sum of the intensity (at 0^0 and 90^0) of the segmentation field (in its binary version).

2 Pel-recursive motion estimation

The mainly use of pel-recursive displacement estimation since it was proposed by Netravali and Robbins [12], has been on predictive motion-compensated image sequence coding. A dense motion field based on the spatio-temporal varying intensity of a sequence is produced, such a field can be considered as a low level information source. For its computing, in this

0-8186-8150-0/97 $10.00 © 1997 IEEE

work we have selected the Baaziz method which consist on two main steps: in the first one it uses the method proposed by Biemond et al. [3] and in a second step for reducing the number of non-compensated pixels the Walker and Rao method is used (on non-compensated sites only). We have applied it towards a higher level representation of an image sequence: a dense field will constitute the main clue to guide the pixel fusion process into regions of similar motion.

Displacement is computed along the scan direction according to a prediction-updating scheme until convergence is obtained. One proper criteria for convergence is the recursive minimization of the reconstruction error; this minimization can also be iterative. Thus, in the Wiener-based algorithm, the displacement is estimated for each pixel until the DFD has been minimized by

$$\hat{\mathbf{d}}^{\mathbf{i}} = \hat{\mathbf{d}}^{\mathbf{i-1}} - \begin{pmatrix} \sum_{j=1}^{N_n} (i_x^j)^2 + \mu & \sum_{j=1}^{N_n} i_x^j i_y^j \\ \sum_{j=1}^{N_n} i_x^j i_y^j & \sum_{j=1}^{N_n} (i_y^j)^2 + \mu \end{pmatrix}^{-1} \cdot \begin{pmatrix} \sum_{j=1}^{N_n} i_x^j \cdot DFD(\mathbf{z}_j, \hat{\mathbf{d}}^{\mathbf{i-1}}) \\ \sum_{j=1}^{N_n} i_y^j \cdot DFD(\mathbf{z}_j, \hat{\mathbf{d}}^{\mathbf{i-1}}) \end{pmatrix} \quad (1)$$

where

- $i(x, y, t)$ is the intensity of each pixel of the sequence
- $\mathbf{z} = (x, y)$ is the position of each pixel
- $\mathbf{d}(x, y, t) = (d_x(x, y, t), d_y(x, y, t))$ is the displacement vector of each pixel in the interval $(t - k\Delta t, t)$
- $\hat{\mathbf{d}}^{\mathbf{i-1}}$ is the initial displacement estimation (prediction) for each pixel. If estimation is iterative, it represents the displacement after $i-1$ iterations
- $\hat{\mathbf{d}}^{\mathbf{i}}$ is the final estimation for each pixel, (or after i iterations)
- DFD is the displaced-frame-difference (reconstruction error)

$$DFD(\mathbf{z}, \mathbf{d}) = i(\mathbf{z}, t) - i(\mathbf{z} - \mathbf{d}, t - k\Delta t) \quad (2)$$

- N_n represents the number of pixels in a small casual spatial neighborhood of each pixel
- i_x^j y i_y^j are the components of the intensity gradient vector ∇i on the displaced positions in frame $t - k\Delta t$

$$\begin{aligned} i_x^j &= i_x(\mathbf{z}_j - \hat{\mathbf{d}}^{\mathbf{i-1}}, t - k\Delta t) \\ i_y^j &= i_y(\mathbf{z}_j - \hat{\mathbf{d}}^{\mathbf{i-1}}, t - k\Delta t) \end{aligned} \quad (3)$$

- $\mu = \sigma_v^2 / \sigma_u^2$ is the ratio between linearizing error variance and actualization term variance respectively.

Figure 1: Sequence *hand # 1.* (a) Frame 1. (b) Frame 4.

Pel-recursive algorithms based on linear estimation includes local context information so its motion fields

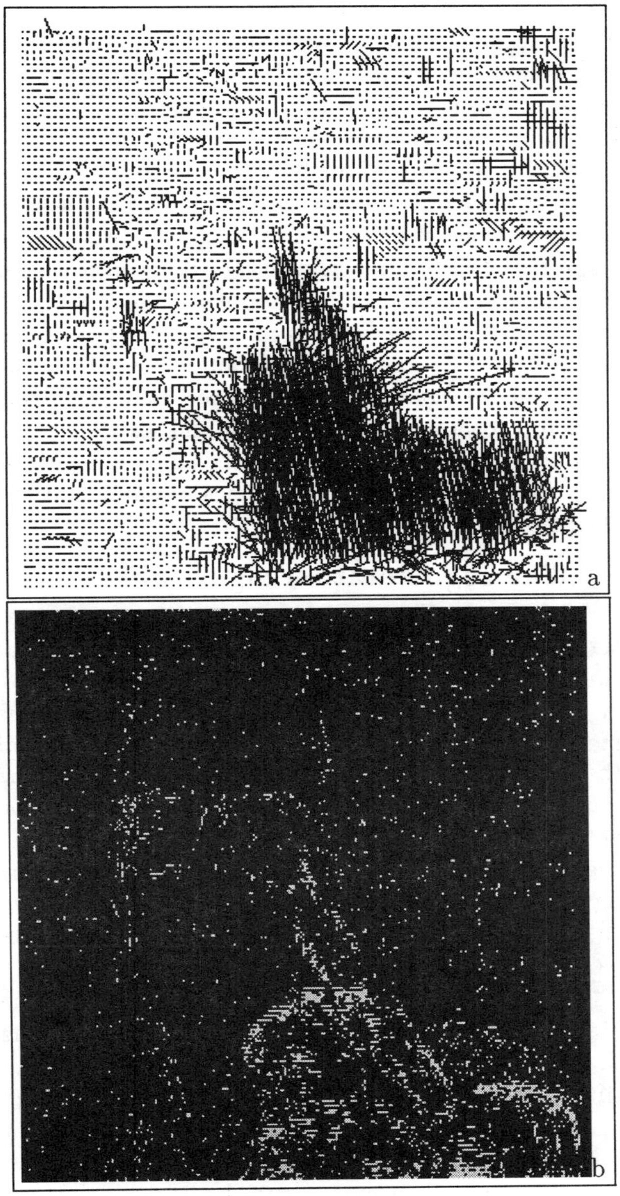

Figure 2: (a) Motion field obtained with the Baaziz method using *hand # 1*, frames 1 and 2. (b) Non-compensated pixel binary image (0 = compensated pixel, 1 = non-compensated pixel).

Figure 3: Sequence *hand # 2*. (a) Frame 1. (b) Frame 9.

are more immune to noise and quantitatively more accurate, but simple enough to compute. On those pixels in which the convergence criterion is not satisfied we had applied the Walker and Rao method and even if after this second step the pixel remains non-compensated (NC), this information will be useful during the segmentation process as a simple partial confidence measure of the motion estimation quality.

Figures 1a and 1b show frames 1 and 4 of the test sequence *hand # 1*. In figures 2a and 2b we present respectively the motion field and the non-compensated pixel image, obtained using frames 1 and 2 and the Baaziz method, the hand is moving from bottom to top. Figures 3a and 3b show frames 1 and 9 of the test sequence *hand # 2*, in which the hand is moving from top to bottom, in figures 4a and 4b we present respectively the motion field and the non-compensated pixel image, obtained using frames 6 and 7 and the Baaziz method.

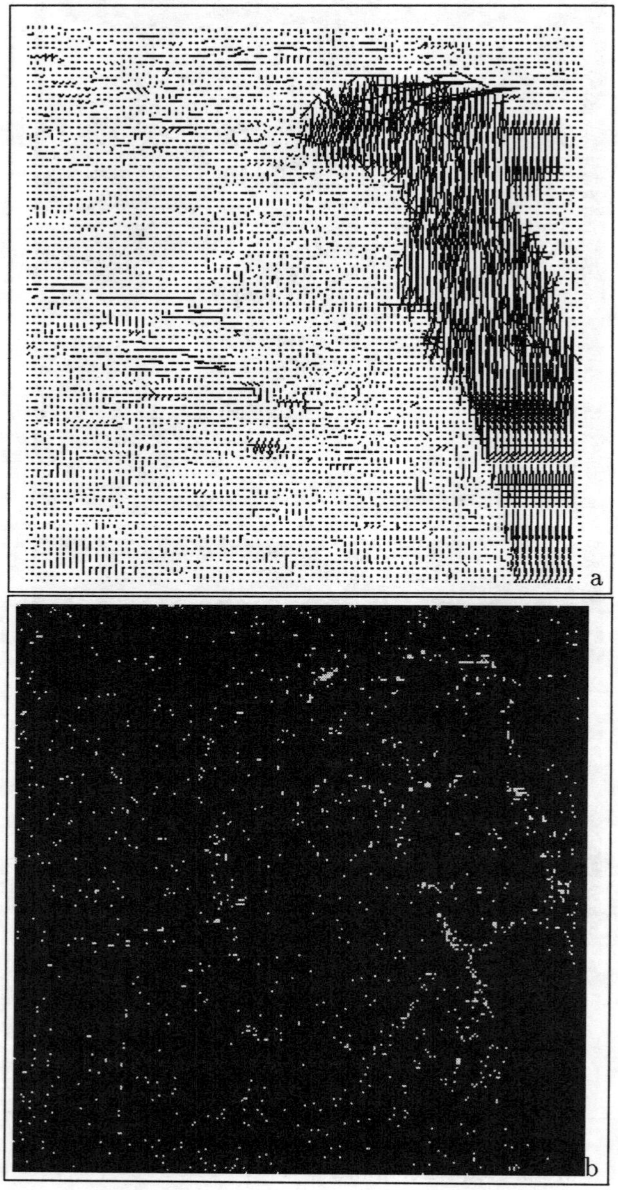

Figure 4: (a) Motion field obtained with the Baaziz method using *hand # 2*, frames 6 and 7. (b) Non-compensated pixel binary image (0 = compensated pixel, 1 = non-compensated pixel).

3 The segmentation algorithm

In presence of pure divergent motion, simple spatial clustering techniques for motion-based segmentation do not work well [7]. In this case, a model Θ_M of both the motion and the structure of the regions in the scene has to be introduced. Thus, the goal of the segmentation process is to assign each pixel in the image to one out of several regions, depending on the accuracy between each estimated motion vector and the assumed model. Each region is characterized by a motion parameter vector. The obtained regions can then be associated to different regions of the same object, or to different objects in the scene.

The proposed segmentation algorithm is based on Markov Random Fields and estimation theory, using the maximum a posteriori criterion as optimality principle. Such a combined approach provides a common framework in which we can introduce information sources of distinct nature, model their interactions, and incorporate expected properties on the solution.

Markov Random Fields modeling is appropriate for motion segmentation: we have a dense displacement vector field as the main information for separating an image into regions, but as we have discussed, motion information is not always correct, especially at movement discontinuities; in this case we may also include other data sources: intensity gray values, non-compensated pixels and intensity contours, as additional observations to improve the final solution. Furthermore, we add physical properties to the model: (a) a motion model Θ_M for each region in the scene to be segmented, (b) spatial continuity for the segmentation, (c) presence of motion boundaries only when strong intensity changes occur, and (d) expected geometrical shapes for the region boundaries. According to MRF theory, we will represent each information source as an *observation field*, and each expected result as a *label field*. In this case, observations are:

- the estimated horizontal and vertical components of the motion field $\mathbf{d}_x$ and $\mathbf{d}_y$
- the binary non-compensated pixel field $\mathbf{p}$. As we mentioned earlier, it can be considered as a simplified way of removing motion outliers, for it represents a way of switching between displacement and more reliable information (intensity values) when the motion field is not accurately estimated
- the image intensity gray values field $\mathbf{i}$
- the binary intensity contour field $\mathbf{g}$, that favors the coincidence of motion boundaries and strong spatial gradients: 0 means no contour; 1 means contour.

On the other hand, desired *label fields* are:

- the desired segmentation label field $\mathbf{e}$, which has associated a four-parameter simplified linear motion model $\Theta_{MLS} = (t_x, t_y, k, \theta)$, that can describe combined translational, rotational, and divergent motions of planar surfaces parallel to the image plane [7]

$$\begin{bmatrix} d_x \\ d_y \end{bmatrix} = \begin{bmatrix} t_x \\ t_y \end{bmatrix} + \begin{bmatrix} k & -\theta \\ \theta & k \end{bmatrix} \begin{bmatrix} x - x_g \\ y - y_g \end{bmatrix} \quad (4)$$

  where (x_g, y_g) is the center of gravity of each surface.

- To improve the segmentation process we introduce an auxiliary binary motion discontinuity line field $\mathbf{l}$ along with the segmentation label field: motion boundaries (0 means no motion discontinuity; 1 means motion discontinuity).

In Figure 5 we show the interaction model of observations, labels and physical assumptions.

Fields $\mathbf{e}$, $\mathbf{d}_x$, $\mathbf{d}_y$, $\mathbf{p}$ and $\mathbf{i}$ are defined over a lattice S of pixel sites s, and fields $\mathbf{l}$ and $\mathbf{g}$ are defined over a lattice S_l of line (interpixel) sites s_l (figure 6). We will assume that there are N pixels in the image.

We formulate the motion-based segmentation as an estimation problem: simultaneously find the *label* fields $(\hat{\mathbf{e}}, \hat{\mathbf{l}})$ that maximize the *a posteriori* probability density function (**pdf**) of the labels, given the *observed* data :

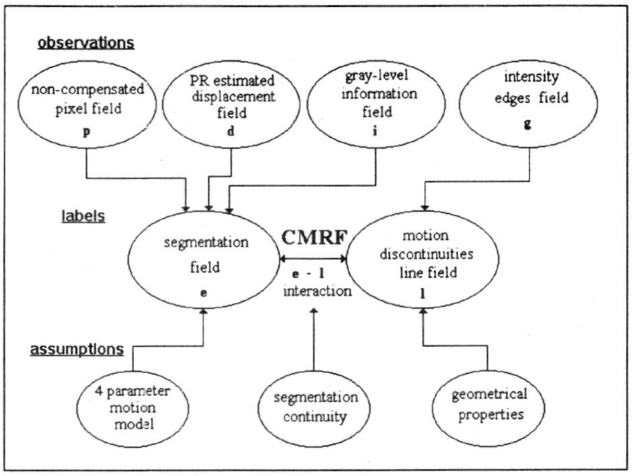

Figure 5: Interaction model for the motion-based segmentation algorithm.

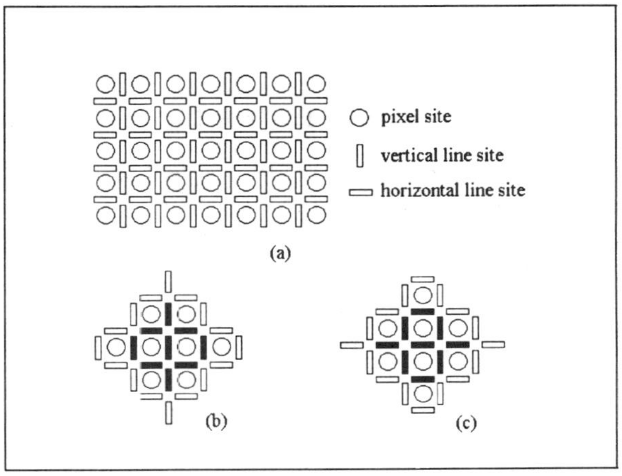

Figure 6: (a) Definition of pixel sites s and line sites s_l. MRF neighborhood system including pixel and line sites: (b) vertical; (c) horizontal.

$$(\hat{\mathbf{e}}, \hat{\mathbf{l}}) = argmax_{\mathbf{e},\mathbf{l}} \quad p(\mathbf{e}, \mathbf{l}/\mathbf{d}_x, \mathbf{d}_y, \mathbf{i}, \mathbf{p}, \mathbf{g}) \quad (5)$$

Reversing the problem using the Bayes rule, the last equation can be expressed as

$$(\hat{\mathbf{e}}, \hat{\mathbf{l}}) = argmax_{\mathbf{e},\mathbf{l}} \quad p(\mathbf{d}_x, \mathbf{d}_y, \mathbf{i}/\mathbf{e}, \mathbf{l}, \mathbf{p}, \mathbf{g}) p(\mathbf{e}, \mathbf{l}/\mathbf{p}, \mathbf{g}) \quad (6)$$

In [8] we have shown that maximizing the a posteriori **pdf** is equivalent to minimize a so-called *energy function* $U(\mathbf{e}, \mathbf{l}, \mathbf{d}_x, \mathbf{d}_y, \mathbf{i}, \mathbf{p}, \mathbf{g})$ which has the form

$$U(\mathbf{e}, \mathbf{l}, \mathbf{d}_x, \mathbf{d}_y, \mathbf{i}, \mathbf{p}, \mathbf{g}) = \alpha U_{\mathbf{d}}(\mathbf{d}_x, \mathbf{d}_y, \mathbf{e}, \mathbf{p}) + \beta U_{\mathbf{i}}(\mathbf{i}, \mathbf{e}, \mathbf{p}) + \gamma U_{\mathbf{e}}(\mathbf{e}, \mathbf{l}) + \kappa U_{\mathbf{l}}(\mathbf{l}, \mathbf{g}) \quad (7)$$

where α, β, γ y κ are weighting terms, all these energy terms has been also defined in [8].

3.1 Global optimization using Iterated Conditional Modes method

To overcome the great computational cost required by simulated annealing, the global optimization of the solution is reached by using an iterative deterministic relaxation procedure: a modified Iterated Conditional Modes (ICM) method based on an instability table [6]. ICM methods minimize the local energy ΔU_s in each pixel $s = (x, y)$ of the image. Our minimization scheme considers two phases in each iteration [7]: one for the optimization of the segmentation field through minimizing

$$U_1 = \alpha U_{\mathbf{d}}(\mathbf{d}_x, \mathbf{d}_y, \mathbf{e}, \mathbf{p}) + \beta U_{\mathbf{i}}(\mathbf{i}, \mathbf{e}, \mathbf{p}) + \gamma U_{\mathbf{e}}(\mathbf{e}, \mathbf{l}) \quad (8)$$

and the other for the optimization of the motion discontinuity line field, minimizing

$$U_2 = \gamma U_{\mathbf{e}}(\mathbf{e}, \mathbf{l}) + \kappa U_{\mathbf{l}}(\mathbf{l}, \mathbf{g}) \quad (9)$$

The term $U_{\mathbf{e}}(\mathbf{e}, \mathbf{l})$ represents a link term between the two stages of the optimization general process.

3.2 The complete motion-based segmentation algorithm

The complete motion-based segmentation algorithm includes four stages (a) initializing, (b) numbering and labeling of each region in the image, (c) motion model parameter estimation in each region, and (d) optimization of the label fields. These steps are repeated until the method reaches the maximum number of iterations allowed, or until the segmentation becomes stable. An advantage of our algorithm is that the number of regions in the image is not fixed through the segmentation process (Figure 7).

4 Segmentation Results

Results obtained on the test sequences *hand # 1* and *hand # 2* for segmenting the moving parts are presented in figures 8 and 9 respectively. The segmentation fields obtained using the proposed algorithm are shown in figures 8a and 9a. A superposition of *hand # 1* and *hand # 2* with their respective segmentation can be seen in figures 8b and 9b. From the results it can be observed that the *hands* in motion have been well segmented from the rest of the scene. This result is qualitatively correct and reached only after 2 iterations (for each case: *hand # 1* and *hand # 2*) of the segmentation algorithm, the tiny regions remaining in the background could be fused in posterior iterations.

No further processing has been done on the segmentation frontiers. The motion vector fields obtained

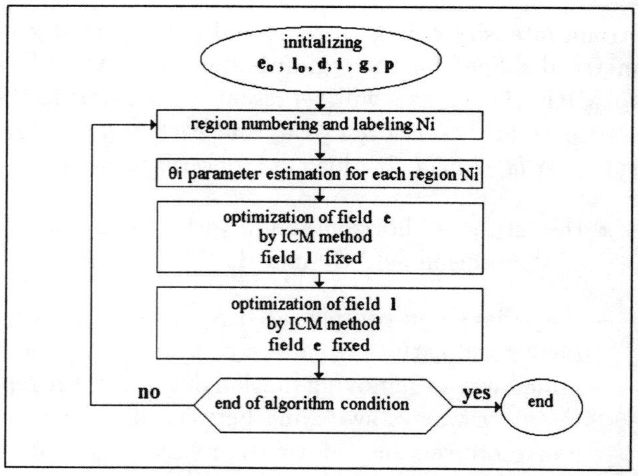

Figure 7: General diagram of the proposed motion-based segmentation algorithm.

with the Baaziz method, figures 2a and 4a, are somewhat homogeneous and properly adjusted to the moving areas. The non-compensated pixels shown in figures 2b and 4b, represent respectively only 4.65 % and 1.99 %. A very important input to the segmentation algorithm is the initial binary segmentation regions, this initialization was obtained by thresholding the difference between, respectively frames 1 and 2 for *hand # 1* and frames 6 and 7 for *hand # 2*, and passing the resulting difference through a median filter of window 3x3. When the segmentation of the *hands* has been completed, we have defined a very simple dictionary of movements for commanding a virtual robot in a two dimensional space. In a first phase this dictionary will permit the displacement of the virtual robot depending on the directional movement of the *hands* and in a second phase the interpretation of some signs or gestures of the *hands* will permit to realize more complicated actions.

5 Gesture Classification

For classifying the segmented fields $\mathbf{e}$ of *hand # 1* and *hand # 2* we have proceed first to obtain a binary version of these fields comparing them with a threshold, so rendering the classification faster. Then based on the Radon transform [9]

$$p(t) = \int_{u=-\infty}^{\infty} \mathbf{e}(t_1, t_2) \mid_{t_1 = t\cos\theta - u\sin\theta,\, t_2 = t\sin\theta + u\cos\theta} du \quad (10)$$

a computation of the projected sum of the intensity has been done at 0^0 and 90^0 and are shown in figures 10 and 13 for *hand # 1* and *hand # 2* respectively.

Then for reducing the number of data to be processed a wavelet decomposition of the projected sum of

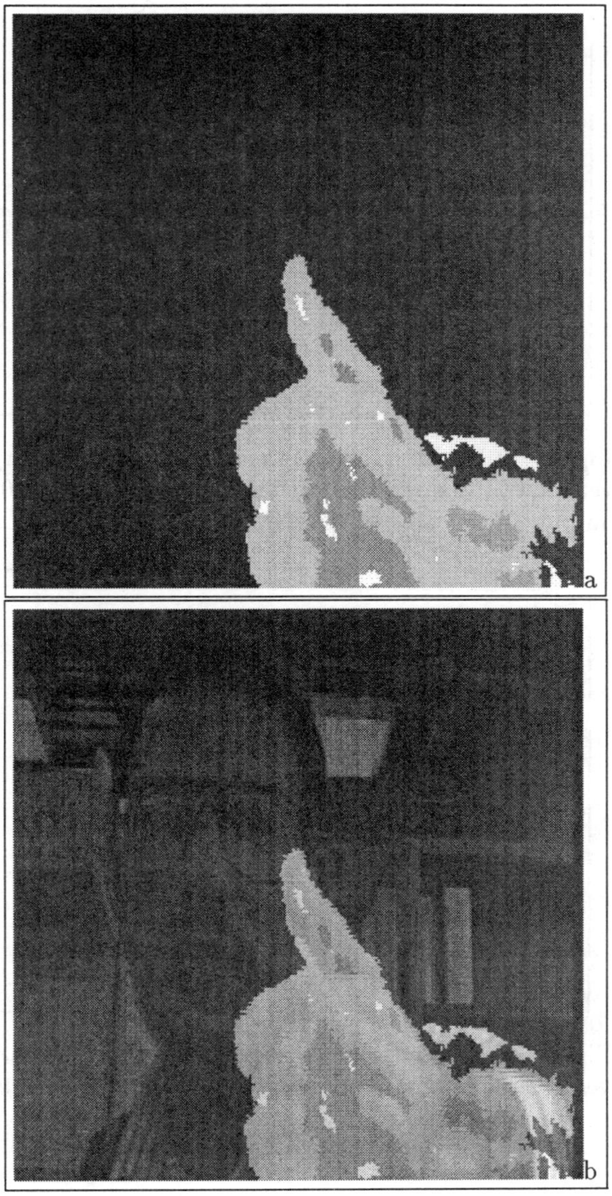

Figure 8: MAP motion-based segmentation algorithm. (a) Segmentation field e of ***hand # 1***. (b) Superposition of frame 3 of ***hand # 1*** and segmentation field e.

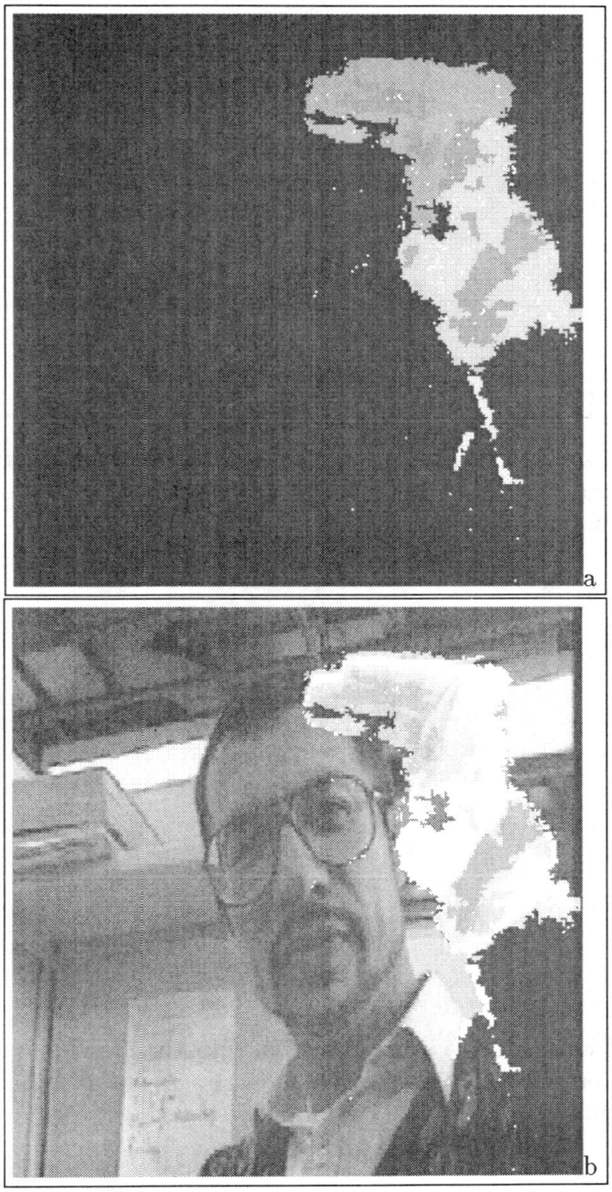

Figure 9: MAP motion-based segmentation algorithm. (a) Segmentation field e of ***hand # 2***. (b) Superposition of frame 7 of ***hand # 2*** and segmentation field e.

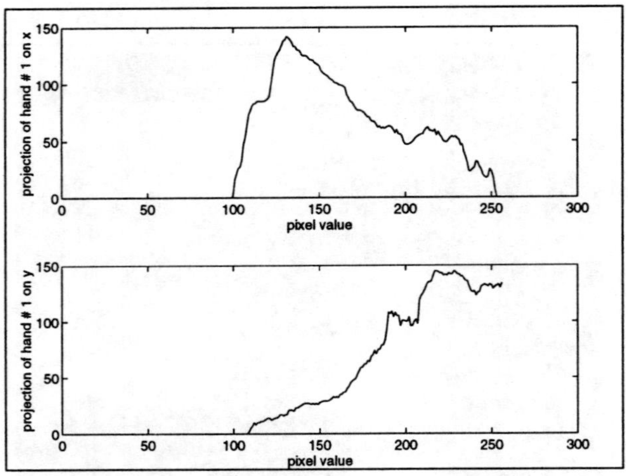

Figure 10: Projected sum of the intensity of the binary version of the segmentation field **e** of *hand # 1* at 0^0 and 90^0 respectively.

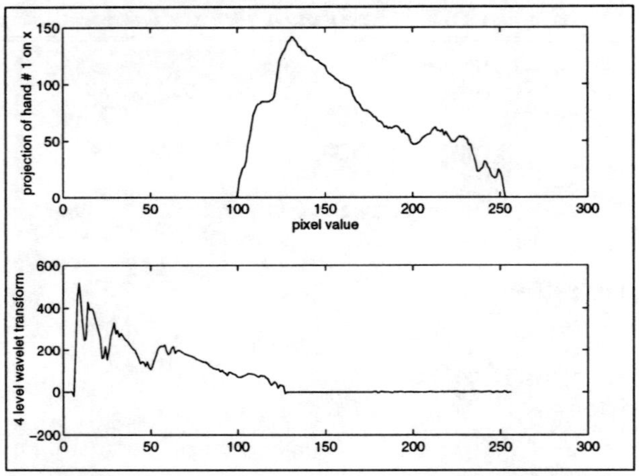

Figure 11: Projected sum of the intensity of the binary version of the segmentation field **e** of *hand # 1* at 0^0 and its 4 level wavelet transform respectively.

the intensity for each orientation (0^0 and 90^0) has been done using Daubechies filters: d4 [5]. The wavelet transform of $f(t)$ at scale 2^i is given by

$$WF_i(t) = f * \psi_i(t) = \int_{-\infty}^{\infty} f(\tau)\psi_i(t-\tau)d\tau \qquad (11)$$

Where from Mallat and Zhong [10] $\psi(t)$ is a wavelet function with average $\int \psi(t)dt = 0$ and $\psi_i(t) = 1/2^i\psi(t/2^i)$ is its dilation by a factor 2^i. The dyadic wavelet transform is the sequence of functions $WF[f()] = [WF_i(t)]i\epsilon Z$. Figures 11 and 12 show the four level wavelet decomposition for *hand # 1* at 0^0 and 90^0 respectively. And figures 14 and 15 show the four level wavelet decomposition for *hand # 2* at 0^0 and 90^0 respectively.

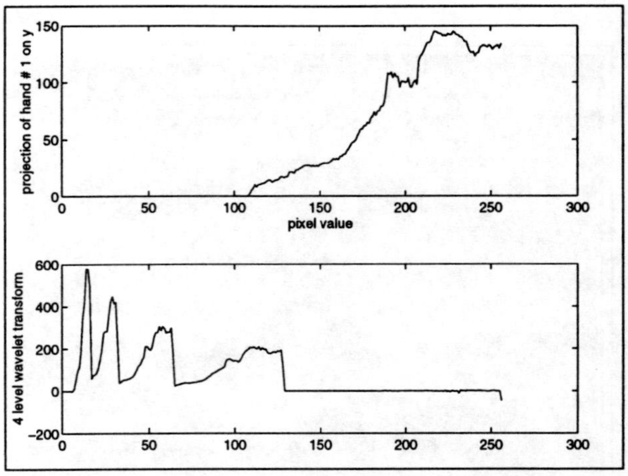

Figure 12: Projected sum of the intensity of the binary version of the segmentation field **e** of *hand # 1* at 90^0 and its 4 level wavelet transform respectively.

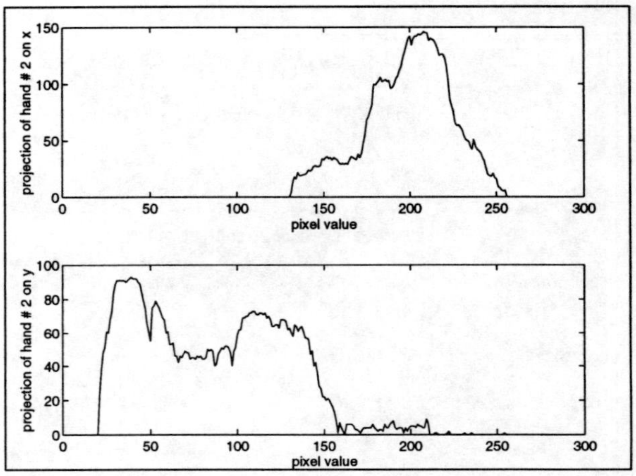

Figure 13: Projected sum of the intensity of the binary version of the segmentation field **e** of *hand # 2* at 0^0 and 90^0 respectively.

This projected and wavelet decomposed information has been used for classifying the gestures, training our system with our dictionary and computing the correlation coefficient between the wavelet coefficients corresponding to *trained sequences* and others.

6 Conclusions

For this particular application and even in this preliminary phase of the project the results of motion estimation, segmentation and classification of the segmented fields are very encouraging. The segmentation of moving regions has been well realized with this MAP-MRF algorithm. The classification of *hands* gestures are correctly and quickly realized with the combination of projected sum of intensities at 0^0 and 90^0,

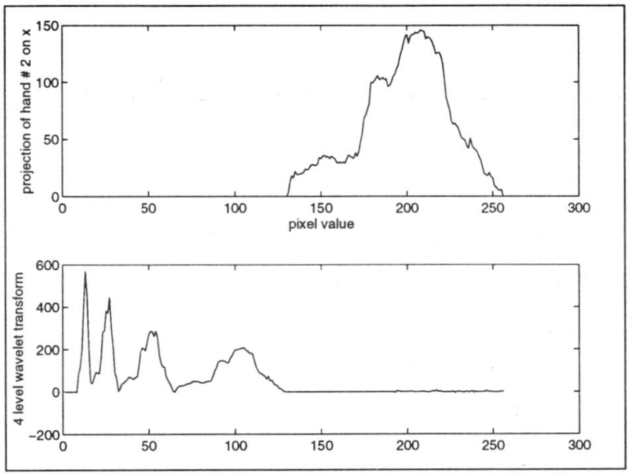

Figure 14: Projected sum of the intensity of the binary version of the segmentation field e of *hand # 2* at 0^0 and its 4 level wavelet transform respectively.

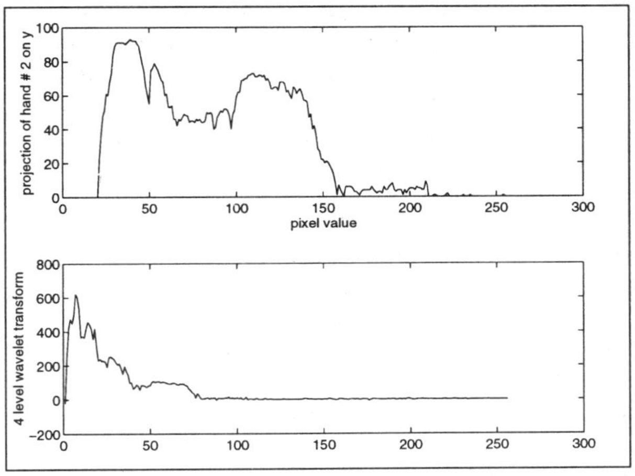

Figure 15: Projected sum of the intensity of the binary version of the segmentation field e of *hand # 2* at 90^0 and its 4 level wavelet transform respectively.

computing then the wavelet decomposition of these projections and finally the correlation coefficient between the wavelet coefficients corresponding to *trained sequences* and others. For this very simple dictionary we have obtained a 100 % successful hand gesture recognition system. Currently now we are integrating this processing to a general multimodal interface, in which others sources of information as speech will be taking into account for communicating with a virtual robot without cumbersome gloves.

Acknowledgments

This work was supported in part by "Universidad Nacional Autónoma de México" (UNAM) and "Consejo Nacional de Ciencia y Tecnología" (CONACyT) and realized during the sabbatical leave of the first author from 8/1/96 to 7/31/97 at Human Interface Technology Laboratory, University of Washington.

References

[1] N. Baaziz. *Approches d'estimation et de compensation de mouvement multiresolutions pour le codage de séquences d'images,* Ph. D. Thesis, Université de Rennes I, France, October 1991.

[2] J. Besag. "On the statistical analysis of dirty pictures." *Journal of the Royal Statistical Society B,* Vol. 48, No. 3, pp. 259-302, 1986.

[3] J. Biemond, L. Looijenga, D.E. Boekee and R. Plompen. "A pel-recursive Wiener-based displacement estimation algorithm." *Signal Processing,* Vol. 13, No. 4, pp. 399-412, December 1987.

[4] M. M. Chang, A. M. Tekalp and M. I. Sezan. "Motion-field segmentation using an adaptive MAP criterion," *Proc. of the ICASSP,* Vol. 5, pp. 33-36, 1993.

[5] I. Daubechies. "Orthonormal bases of compactly supported wavelets," *Comm. Pure and Applied Mathematics,* Vol. 41, pp. 909-996, 1988.

[6] E. Francois. *Interpretation qualitative du mouvement a partir d'une séquence d'images,* Ph. D. Thesis, Universite de Rennes I, France, June 1991.

[7] V. García-Garduño. *Une approche de compression orientée-objets par suivi de segmentation basée mouvement pour le codage de séquences d'images numeriques,* Ph. D. Thesis, Université de Rennes I, France, May 1995.

[8] D. Gatica-Pérez, F. García-Ugalde and V. García-Garduño. "Segmentation algorithm for image sequences from a pel-recursive motion field." *Proc. of the VCIP, SPIE,* Vol. 3024, pp. 1152-1163, 1997.

[9] J.S. Lim. *Two dimensional signal and image processing,* Englewood Cliffs, NJ: Prentice Hall, 1990.

[10] S. Mallat and S. Zhong. "Characterization of signals from multiscale edges," *Trans. Pattern Anal. Machine Intell.,* Vol. PAMI-14, No. 7, pp. 710-732, July 1992.

[11] D.W. Murray, and B.F. Buxton. "Scene segmentation from visual motion using global optimization," *IEEE Trans. Pattern Anal. Machine Intell.,* Vol. PAMI-9, No. 2, pp. 220-228, March 1987.

[12] A.N. Netravali and J.D. Robbins. "Motion-compensated television coding: part I," *The Bell System Technical Journal,* Vol. 58, No. 3, pp. 631-670, March 1979.

[13] J. Savage-Carmona. *A hybrid system with symbolic AI and statistical methods for speech recognition,* Ph. D. Dissertation, University of Washington, July 1995.

Extraction of Hand Region and Specification of Finger Tips from Color Image

Shinji Tsuruoka*, Akio Kinoshita*, Tetsushi Wakabayashi+, Yasuji Miyake+, Muneaki Ishida*
*Department of Electrical and Electronic Engineering, Faculty of Engineering,
Mie University, 1515 Kamihama, Tsu, Mie Japan 514
+Department of Information Engineering, Faculty of Engineering,
Mie University, 1515 Kamihama, Tsu, Mie Japan 514
E-mail: tsuruoka@ts.elec.mie-u.ac.jp

Abstract

In this paper, we propose a new method (Vision Point Out System (VPOS)) of the extraction of the hand region and the specification of the finger tips from color image. This algorithm uses the product of the skin color information and the brightness information. Even if the input image has the nail and the complex background, this method can extract the correct hand region. We evaluated the effectiveness of this method for some hand images with the complex background by the computer experiments. This algorithm can find the extended finger, and can classify "Janken (Japanese finger guessing game; Gu-Choki-Pa)". The string region pointed out by the finger on the background can be extracted.

1. Introduction

In the virtual reality system, the special pointing devices such as the data glove are used widely as the man machine interface. But the data glove has some problems. The data glove destroies easily and the feeling of the fitness for user's hands is not good, so that the action is not natural. Recently the new more natural man machine interfaces instead of the data glove are required by the virtual reality, virtual school, TV meeting and so on. The pointing method using vision system for the human hand has no stress, no attachment sensor and it's very natural and useful technique for the man machine interface [1],[2].

In the vision system, the marked hand or the marked glove is used for the simplification of the calculation [3],[4]. But the marked hand or marked glove is not natural for human life, it isn't suited for the unspecified users. Some researchers analyze the image of no marked hand by the template matching and the hand pose estimation using the 3D shape model [5],[6]. These approarch have a large calculation cost. We think that these methods are not appropriate for real time processing without a special hardware.

In this paper, we propose a new method (Vision Point Out System (VPOS)) of the extraction of the hand region and the specification of the finger tips from color image for small computer. This algorithm uses the product of the skin color information and the brightness information. Even if the input image has the nail and the complex background, this method can extract the correct hand region. We evaluate the effectiveness of this method for some hand images with the complex background by the computer experiments. This algorithm can fine the extend finger, and can classify " Janken (Japanese finger guessing game)", which has three categories (Gu, Choki, Pa)". The string region pointed by the finger on the background can be extracted. We hope that this method become one of the new pointing methods, and that this is very important approach for the human computer communication.

2. Hand Region Extraction from Color Image

2.1 Outline of the Hand Region Extraction

We set the following conditions for the input image.

(1) The hand is located horizontally for the camera, and the extended finger don't overlap.
(2) The light is white light, and the hand is natural skin color.
(3) The image can include the complex background, but the maximum skin color area in the image is the hand.
(4) The situation of the each finger is extended or bended, it doesn't include the situation of the half bended.

The hand picture taken by the camera is scanned to

0-8186-8150-0/97 $10.00 © 1997 IEEE

the digital color image by the 100 dpi color scanner, and the size of the image is 640 x 400 pixels, RGB 8 bits/pixel. The skin color image and the intensity image are made from the input color image. The skin color image is obtained by the skin color distribution table on the HVC (HVS) in the Munsell color space, which is learned by the pixels of the learning sample regions. The intensity image is obtained by the intensity function from the RGB color.

The skin color image and the intensity image are multiplied at each pixel, and the multiplied image is obtained. The multiplied image is binarized, and we find the region of the maximum area. We detect the hand region on the image.

2.2 Generation of the Skin Color Distribution Table

2.2.1 Skin color data for learning

In the learning process, the regions belonged to the skin on the learning images are extracted on the CRT by the mouse. The RGB color data on the sets of the pixels is used for the skin color data for learning. The RGB color of the pixel (r, g, b) is transferred to the HVC (H: Hue, V: Value, C: Chroma (S: Saturation)) (h, v, c) in Munsell color space. The transfer functions [7],[8] are given by

$$h = \begin{cases} \frac{\pi}{3}\cdot\frac{b-r}{\max(r,g,b)-\min(r,g,b)} & if \quad g=\max(r,g,b) \\ \frac{\pi}{3}\cdot\left\{2+\frac{r-g}{\max(r,g,b)-\min(r,g,b)}\right\} & if \quad b=\max(r,g,b) \\ \frac{\pi}{3}\cdot\left\{4+\frac{g-b}{\max(r,g,b)-\min(r,g,b)}\right\} & if \quad r=\max(r,g,b) \end{cases} \tag{1}$$

$$c = \frac{\max(r,g,b)-\min(r,g,b)}{\max(r,g,b)} \tag{2}$$

$$v = \max(r,g,b) \tag{3}$$

The range of the hue h is generally 0 - 2 π in Munsell color space, but we define that the range of h in this paper is 0-255 (0 (green) - (cyan) - (blue) - (magenta) - (red) - (yellow) - 255 (green)). The range of the value v is also between 0 (black) and 255 (white), and the range of the chroma c is also between 0 (no color, neutral color) and 255 (saturated color).

2.2.2 Skin color distribution table

All RGB color data are transferred to (h, v, c). The value v of the pixels belonged to the skin has a large variance by the amount of the lights and the individual difference, and we make the skin color histogram on HC plane. The 3-D skin color histogram is shown in Fig. 1. The vertical axis means the degree of the pixels, the right-left axis means the hue and the up-down axis means the chroma (the saturation). For the compensation of the short learning samples, we analyze this skin color histogram statistically. The mean μ and the covariance matrix K for HVC color vector at n-th pixel (h_n, s_n) are given by

$$\mu = \frac{1}{N}\sum_{n=1}^{N} h_n \tag{4}$$

$$K = \frac{1}{N}\sum (H_n-\mu)(H_n-\mu)' \tag{5}$$

where,

$H_n = [s_n \cdot \cos(2\pi h_n/255) \quad s_n \cdot \sin(2\pi h_n/255)]$

: skin color vector, N : the number of the learning pixels, and t means transpose.

The skin color function $S(h,s)$ [0-255] for color vector at an input pixel (h, v, c) is as follows.

$$S(h,s) = 255\cdot\exp\left\{-\frac{1}{2}(H-\mu)'K^{-1}(H-\mu)\right\} \tag{6}$$

The values obtained from the actual skin pixels for the learning images are given by

$$\mu = [218 \quad 126]' \qquad K = \begin{bmatrix} 408 & 151 \\ 151 & 1120 \end{bmatrix} \tag{7}$$

$$S(h,s) = 255\cdot\exp\left(-\frac{N}{869\times 10^3}\right) \tag{8}$$

where,

$$N = 1120(h_x+37)^2 - 301(h_y+37)(h_y+129) + 408(h_y+129)^2 \tag{9}$$

$$h_x = s\cdot\cos(2\pi h/255) \tag{10}$$

$$h_y = s\cdot\sin(2\pi h/255) \tag{11}$$

We make the skin color table (256×256, Fig. 2) from above functions for high speed processing, and save as the file in the disk. The skin degree for an input pixel is given by this table.

2.3 Hand Region Extraction Using Skin Degree and Intensity

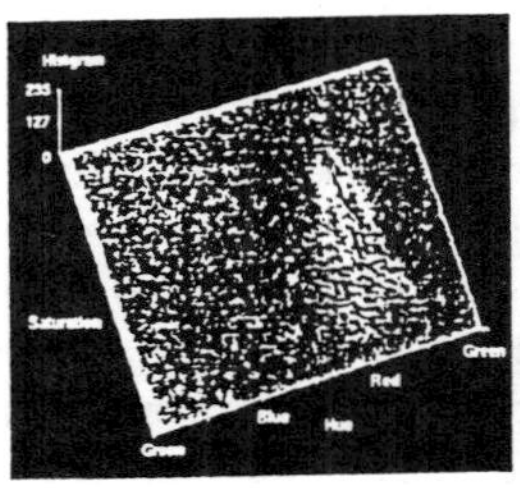

Fig. 1 Skin color histogram

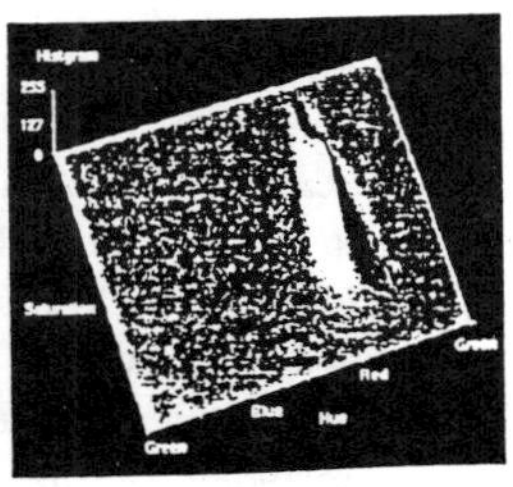

Fig. 2 Skin color table

2.3.1 Hand Region Extraction Using Skin Degree

All pixels belonged to an input RGB color hand figure (Fig. 3) are transferred to HVC color space, and the skin degree image is obtained by the skin color table (Fig. 4). The skin degree image is averaged by 5×5 pixels edge preserving smoothing filter [9] for noise reduction. The smoothed image is binarized by the threshold which is determined by Otsu's threshold selection method [10]. This algorithm seems that the maximum area region is the hand region shown in Fig. 5. In this figure, the background noise (arrow A in Fig. 5), which is the face region on the background paper, appears at the side of the little finger, and the lacks of the finger (arrow B in Fig. 5) appear for the highlight (specular reflection) at the nail.

The hand region extraction using skin degree is the efficient detection method of the specific objects with simple background and without the highlight. But this method is not adequate for the image with the complex background and the highlight. For this reason, the edge of the hand between the hand and the background can hardly find. And the intensity at the nail is very high as the specular reflection of the white light source. So that, the hue is approximately white. As the skin color areas for learning images don't include the white area, the skin degree at the nail area is low. The hand region with the holes is extracted by the skin color table.

2.3.2 Hand region extraction using skin degree and intensity

We propose the mixture of the skin degree and the intensity for resolving the above problems. The feature of the intensity is the high detection ability of the edge though the ability of the detection of the specific objects is low. This feature is the complement of the skin degree. The intensity Y is used in the TV broadcasting in Japan, it's given by the following equation.

$$Y = 0.30r + 0.59g + 0.11b \qquad (12)$$

The intensity image of the Fig. 3 is shown in Fig. 6(a), and the intensity distribution on the white line in this figure is shown in Fig. 6(b), where the edge between the hand and the background corresponds to the second large valley ($x \fallingdotseq 35$) from the left end. The multiplied image from the skin degree image (Fig. 4) and the intensity image is shown in Fig. 7. The extracted hand region by the previous process (edge preserving smoothing, Otsu's binarization and extraction of the maximum area) is shown in Fig. 8. At the edge between the background and the hand, the intensity is low, and the components of the hand and the background aren't connected in the multiplied image. The extracted image doesn't include the background noise. At the nail area, the skin degree is low, but the intensity is high. The multiplied value is medium over the threshold. The nail areas are included in the hand region. So that, the extracted hand region is natural.

Fig. 3 Input color hand image

Fig. 4 Skin degree image

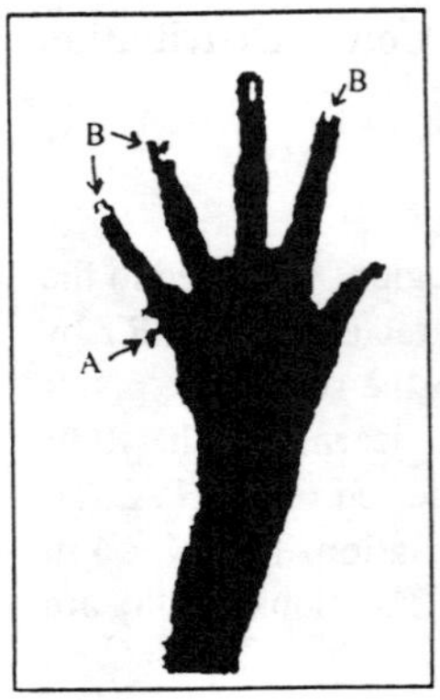

Fig. 5 Maximum area region

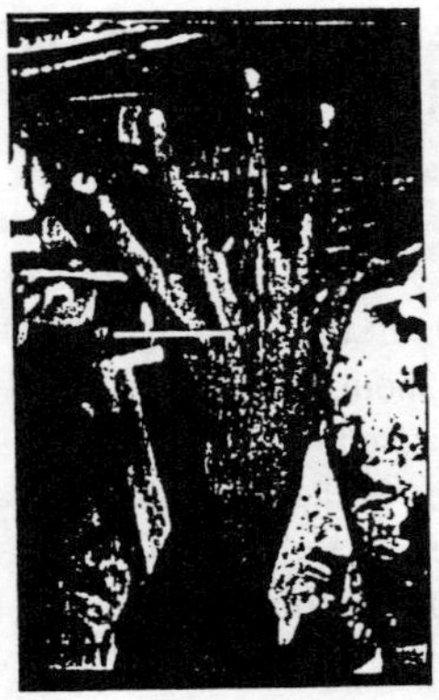

Fig. 6(a) Intensity image

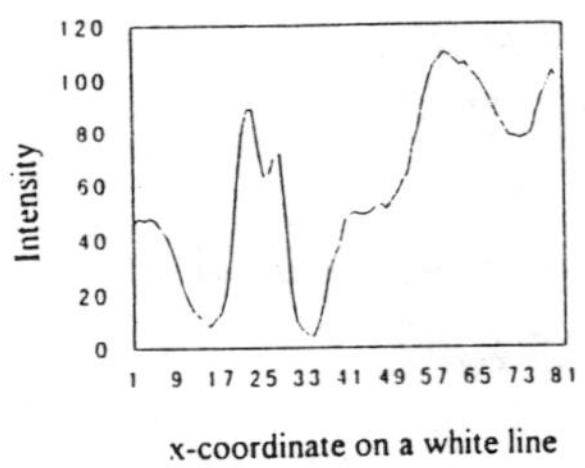

Fig. 6(b) Intensity distribution

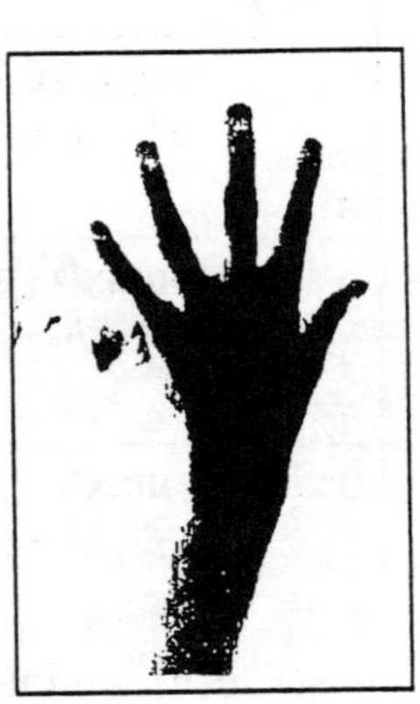

Fig. 7 Multiplied image

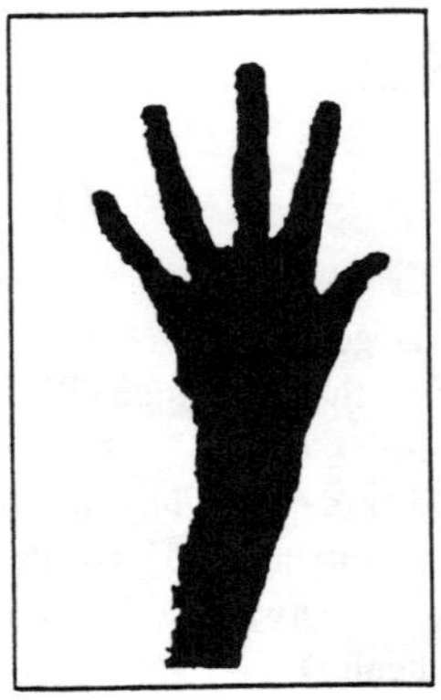

Fig. 8 Binary image

3. Specification of the finger tips

We extract the contour (Fig. 9) from the extracted hand region by the border following algorithm. The algorithm is the sequential type with clockwise, and the starting point is the top of the contour, that is, the minimum y-coordinate (point P in Fig. 9). We find the candidates of the finger tips as following geometrical process.

(1) We call the interesting contour point P_1 (Fig. 10), and the neighbor points P_2 and P_3 are the 10 dots away before and after P_1 . The neighbor points P_4 and P_5 are the 30 pixels away before and after P_1. In Fig. 10, the part of the finger tips is enlarged and display every five pixels for the simplification.

(2) The angle θ between the vector P_1P_4 and the vector P_1P_5 is calculated by the inner product of the vectors.

(3) If the continuous more than three points with the angle θ under the 90 degree exist on one contour, the center point in the neighbor of P_1 is the candidate of the finger tips (Fig. 11).

These candidates include the true finger tips and the valley points between the fingers. We eliminate the valley points between the fingers. A classification method is whether the gravity of the three points P_1, P_4, and P_5 is within the hand region or not. But this method has the problem where the concave region such as the nail area in Fig. 7. So that, we propose a new classification method about the candidate point P_1 given as follows.

(4) The translation and the rotation, which point P_2 is located at the origin and the point P_4 is on positive x-axis, are done for the coordinates of the five points P_1, P_2, P_3, P_4, and P_5 .

(5) The conditions of the finger tips are given as follows.
  (a) The y-coordinate of the point P_3 and the point P_5 are negative.
  (b) The x-coordinate of the point P_5 is larger than the x-coordinate of the point P_3.
  (c) The absolute of the gradient of the line P_3P_5 is small than 1.

The extracted points are shown in Fig. 13. The extracted points are all finger tips, and the number of the extracted points is five. It seems that all fingers are extended, which is the "Pa" in "Janken".

4. Some examples

We evaluated our algorithm by the other images. First examples are the images of "Janken (Japanese finger guessing game)", which include the three categories (Gu, Choki, Pa). Fig. 14(a) and Fig. 15(a) show the input color images in the "Choki", which has two extended fingers, and "Gu", which has no extended finger. Fig. 14(b) and Fig. 15(b) show the extracted hand

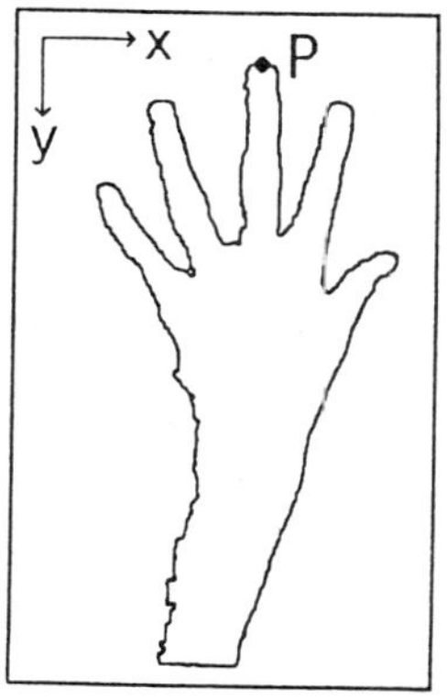

Fig. 9 Contour image

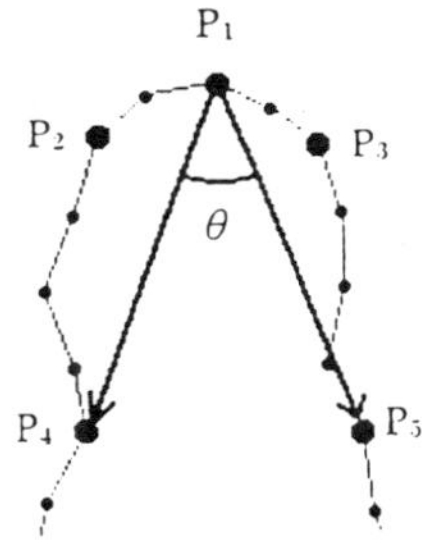

Fig. 10 Points of the finger tip

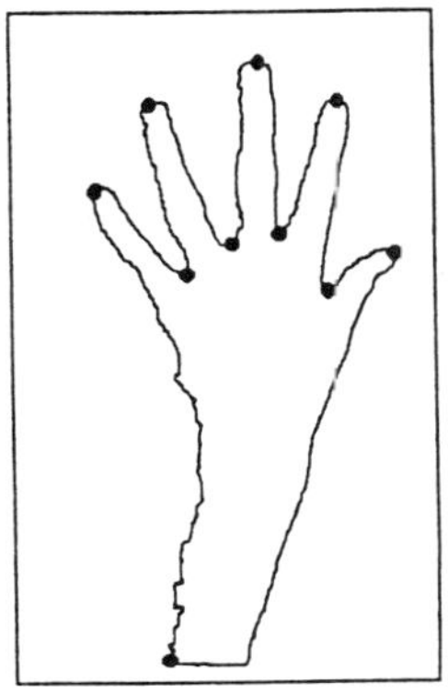
Fig. 11 Extracted points

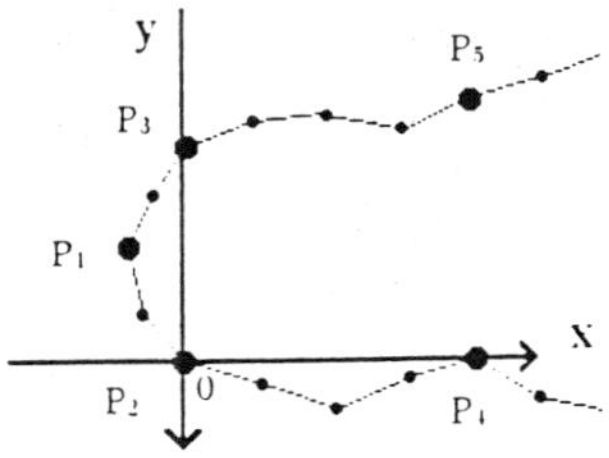

Fig. 12 New coordinate system

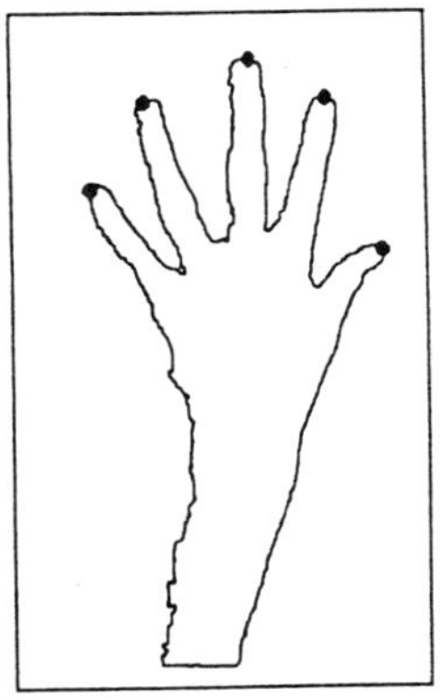
Fig. 13 Extracted finger tips

Fig. 14(a) Input color image Fig. 14(b) Extracted hand region Fig. 14(c) Extracted finger tips

region and Fig. 14(c) and Fig. 15(c) show the extracted finger tips. From these results we think that our conditions are adequate. We think that man and machine (computer) can play the "Janken" each other as the application of this algorithm.

Second example is the image of the string region pointed out by the finger. Fig. 16(a) and Fig. 16(b) are input color images. Fig. 16(c) is the contour of the extracted finger and the extracted finger tip. Fig. 16(d) shows the extracted string region. The detail of the this algorithm will be appeared at the next chance.

Fig. 15(a) Input color image

Fig. 15(b) Extracted hand region

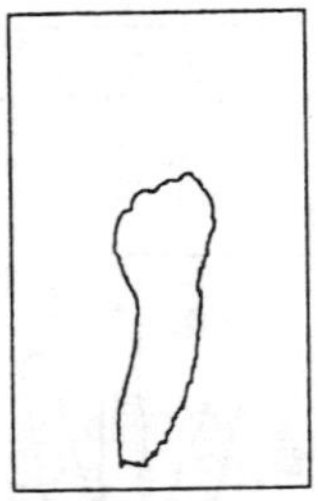

Fig. 15(c) Extracted finger tips

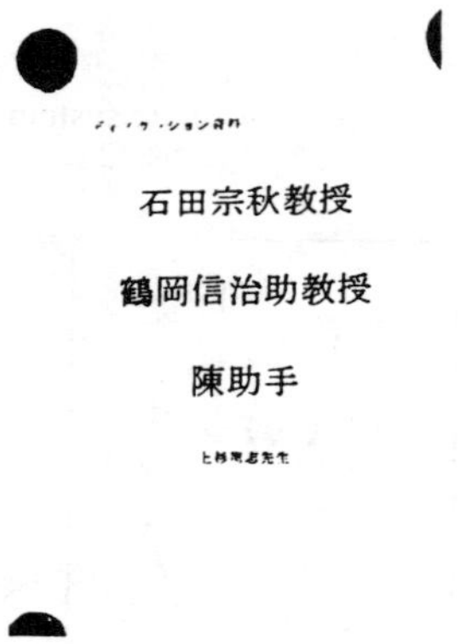

Fig. 16(a) Input color image

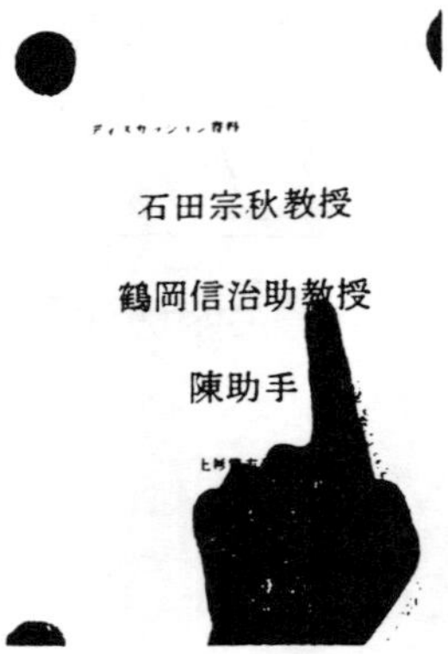

Fig. 16(b) Input color image

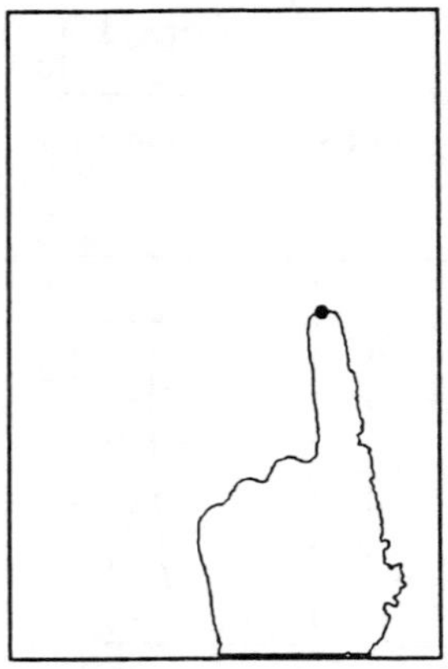

Fig. 16(c) Contour and finger tip

Fig. 16(d) Extracted string region

This algorithm can apply to the natural one hand image where the hand is setting horizontall for the camera without the glove , but can't apply to the image with more than two hands, the image with hand and face, or the image with large skin color objects except the hand. We are considering the extended algorithm for such images.

The total computational time / image is about 15 seconds on UNIX workstation SUN SPARCstation 10 / 40 (100 MIPS) with C language.

5. Conclusion

We proposed a new method Vision Point Out System (VPOS) of the extraction of the hand region and the specification of the finger tips from color image with complex background. This algorithm uses the product of the skin color information and the intensity information, and the geometrical analysis for finding the finger tips. The features of this method are given as follows.

(1) This algorithm is the simple method and low calculation cost.
(2) This algorithm can extract the hand region from the image with the complex background.

The remaining problems are as follows.

(1) Finding the high speed region extraction algorithm for real time processing.
(2) Comparison with the other color spaces [11],[12].

Acknowledgment

The authors would like to express their gratitude to previous Prof. Nariyasu Minamide and Prof. Takamasa Hori (Fac. of Eng., Mie University) for giving the chance of this research, suggestions and discussions, and Kurato Maeno (OKI Electric Industry Co., Ltd.) for the use of a part of the program.

References

[1] M.W. Kruger, "Artificial Reality II," Addison-Wesley, 1991
[2] Y.Suenaga, K.Mase, M.Fukumoto, and Y.Watanabe, "Human reader: An advanced human machine interface based on human images and speech," IEICE Trans.D-II, J75-D-II, 2, pp.190-202, 1992
[3] J.Davis and M.Shah, "Recognizing hand gestures," Proc. ECCV'94, pp.331-340, 1994
[4] K.Ishibuchi, H.Takemura, and F. Kishino, "Real time hand gesture recognition, " Proc. of IEEE Inter. Conference on Systems, Man and Cybernetics, pp.324-328, 1993
[5] R.Cipolla, Y.Okamoto and Y.Kuno, " Qualitative visual interpretation of 3D hand gestures using motion parallax. " IAPR Workshop on Machine Vision and Applications, pp.477-482, 1992
[6] N.Shimada and Y.Shirai, "3-D hand pose estimation and shape model refinement from a monocular image sequence," Proc. of VSMM'96, pp.423-428,

1996

[7] S.Tsuruoka, K.Maeno, N.Minamide, F.Kimura, Y.Miyake, "New region segmentation for corrected face image," Proc. of VSMM'96, pp.213-218, 1996

[8] S.Harrington, "Computer Graphics," McGraw Hill, pp.376-388, 1987

[9] M.Nagao and T.Matsuyama, "Edge preserving smoothing", Computer Graphics and Image Processing, 9, pp.394-407, 1979

[10] N.Otsu, "A threshold selection method from gray-level histogram," IEEE Trans. SMC, SMC-9, 1, pp.62-66, 1979

[11] Y.Ohta, T.Kanade, and T.Sakai,"Color information for region segmentation,"Comput. Graphics Image Process., Vol.13, pp.222-241, 1980

[12] E.Saber, A.M. Tekalp, R. Eschbach, and K. Knox," Automatic image annotation using adaptive color classificatioin," Graphical Models and Image Processing, Vol.58, no.2, pp-115-126, 1996

VR Systems and Applications
(medical, architectural, industrial, artistical)

VR Systems: Out from the Laboratory

Lawrence J. Rosenblum
Director, VR Systems and Research
Information Technology Division (Code 5580)
Naval Research Laboratory
Washington, DC 20375

Abstract

In spite of the large amount of "hype" that accompanied virtual reality (VR) earlier this decade, the field has produced only a few examples of demonstrably useful systems. Systems must be fielded and validated to show that VR is useful for purposes other than academic research. This paper discusses two VR systems developed at the Naval Research Laboratory that have received validation by statistical analysis or by user acceptance. One system focuses on experiments in shipboard firefighting to verify the effectiveness of VR as a mission planning tool. Using trained U.S. Navy firefighters, we conducted a shipboard experiment. The VR-trained firefighters performed significantly better on both navigation and firefighting tasks. The second system involved developing an application using NRL's VR Responsive Workbench to provide situational awareness inside a U.S. Marine Corps combat operations center (COC). This system has been called a major advance that is likely to eliminate paper maps in the COC.

1.0 Introduction

The concept of a natural and effective interaction between user and computer is compelling, but it has proven difficult to implement. To maintain a sense of presence (the illusion of "immersion"), frame rates must be kept high and system latency in responding to users' actions must be minimal. Interface designs to VR systems are still poorly understood and often are application specific. Disparate technologies must be integrated within the environment, often requiring an interdisciplinary team.

After a long gestation period that produced many interesting research results but few usable systems, VR is emerging as a valuable technology. User communities are accepting the value of VR, and formal testing and evaluation of VR systems are now taking place. This paper discusses experiences with two VR systems that were developed in the Virtual Reality Laboratory at the Naval Research Laboratory (NRL) and placed in the hands of a user community.

2.0 VR for Shipboard Firefighting and Damage Control

Shipboard fires are a more serious problem for the Navy than the risk of a ship sinking. Such fires can spread very rapidly and generate extremely high temperatures. Thus, shipboard survivability depends on effective firefighting when a few critical seconds determine success or failure.

2.1 Shipboard firefighting and the NRL test platform

Training Navy firefighters is expensive but, even worse, there are limited opportunities for such training, a task for which VR is well suited. Firefighters can familiarize themselves with areas of ships where they have little or no actual experience. By practicing navigation in VR, firefighters can concentrate on firefighting, rather than on navigational tasks. With virtual fire and smoke added, the virtual environment becomes sufficiently realistic so that firefighters can practice standard procedures and test tactics and strategies without endangering personnel or property.

0-8186-8150-0/97 $10.00 © 1997 IEEE

The ex-USS Shadwell is a decommissioned ship maintained by NRL off Mobile, Alabama and is used by NRL as a firefighting and damage control research, development, test, and evaluation platform. Real-life testing of firefighting personnel aboard the Shadwell has demonstrated that key elements in successful firefighting are familiarity with the neighboring compartments and operating effectively under limited visibility conditions.

2.2 An experiment on the Shadwell

Based on our earlier work in shipboard modeling for VR, where personnel with experience aboard the Shadwell felt it gave an accurate representation of "being there," an experiment was performed to evaluate the value of VR for shipboard firefighting. An area where a shipboard experiment with trained Navy firefighters would be performed was modeled. Terrain following and collision detection restricted users to pathways and generated collisions when they walked into a table, locker, wall, or other scene element. A glove avatar allowed users to look around while walking and navigation was performed using a "fly where you point" metaphor. Buttons on a 3D joystick interactively controlled the doors. Accurate 3D models represented many of the shipboard objects, although non-interactive objects such as fire hoses were texture mapped. A dynamically growing 2D texture-mapped fire simulation provided realistic behavior and the smoke model included distant and nearby effects.

A statistical analysis of these experiments was performed [1]. Firefighters who used VR for mission rehearsal experienced a measurable improvement in the performance. These firefighters performed, on average, thirty seconds faster over a two minute navigation task to reach a predetermined location. In addition, all members of the "Traditional Training" group, who were given directions to the fire using currently standard methods, made at least one wrong turn while only one member of the VR Training group did so. For this time-critical application, both traversal time and wrong turns contribute significantly to the final success or failure. The VR Training group also had better performance on firefighting tasks. While the number of personnel taking these tasks were limited, the combined results indicate that VR provides an environment in which firefighters can familiarize themselves with ships and, with fire, smoke, and physical realism added, practice tactics for firefighting without risking lives and property.

3.0 Situational Awareness

Ranging from disaster relief through air traffic control and military operations, there are a wide variety of crisis-oriented events that need the combination of 3D visualization, detailed interaction, and the integration of real-time data feeds and information. For this, we use NRL's version of the VR Responsive Workbench [2].

3.1 The VR Responsive Workbench

The Responsive Workbench [3] is an interactive VR environment designed to support a team of end users such as military and civilian command and control specialists, designers, engineers, and doctors. The Responsive Workbench creates a match for the "real" work environment of persons who would typically stand over a table or a workbench as part of their professional routine.

The Responsive Workbench operates by displaying computer-generated, stereoscopic images onto a table (i.e., workbench) surface that is viewed by a group of users around the table. Using stereoscopic shutter glasses, they observe a 3D image displayed above the tabletop. By tracking the group leader's head movements, the Workbench permits changing the view angle and interacting with the 3D scene. Other group members observe the scene as manipulated by the group leader, facilitating easy communication between observers about the scene and defining future actions by the group leader. Perhaps the greatest strength of the Responsive Workbench is the ease of natural interaction with virtual objects. Current interactive methods emphasize gesture recognition, speech recognition, and a simulated "laser" pointer to identify and manipulate objects.

3.2 The Workbench in the field

Even with the advent of computers and sophisticated decision-making software in Marine Corps Combat Operation Centers (COC), command and control is predominantly undertaken with paper maps and acetate overlays. This is a cumbersome, time-consuming process. In addition, detailed maps and overlays can take several hours to print and distribute. There currently exists no overall picture of the battlespace that provides a commander with a dynamic range of resolution sufficient to track units ranging from aircraft carriers to six-Marine fire teams.

As part of a U.S. Marine Corps experiment in March 1997, we displayed on the Workbench map-quality 3D terrain resolution of Twentynine Palms, California (62 by 72 Km) and inserted a virtual "ocean" outside a road network bordering Twentynine Palms [4]. The terrain was textured with line-drawing maps at a geographic resolution of 1:25,000. Both models and Intelligence Preparation of the Battlefield (IPB) icons were used to represent objects to be placed on the terrain. The models and IPB icons were selected and modified through discussions with the Marines.

Interactive methods for the Workbench include gesture recognition using a pinchglove, speech recognition, and a simulated laser pointer. The latter was used for this system because of its robustness when employed by a variety of users. When the laser intersects the terrain, it's as if the user's hand was attached. Lateral hand movements pan the terrain, while vertical movements zoom in and out. Rotating the laser pointer rotates the image. Additional modes use the simulated laser to pick up and move objects, to query objects, to measure distances and headings, and to perform several other tasks.

The next step for our situational awareness system will be the far more challenging case of an urban environment. Modeling, visualization, and interactions are significantly more difficult in the "urban canyon." Additional figures from the 1997 experiment and a CNN Headline News segment showing the Workbench in the "Blue Team" COC can be found on our homepage: www.ait.nrl.navy.mil/vrlab.

4.0 Other VR Systems

We briefly mention two other VR systems of interest that have undergone evaluation either through statistical testing or through user acceptance with additional analysis.

4.1 The acrophobia project at the Georgia Institute of Technology

This project used virtual reality to examine fear of heights, which is clinically defined by anxiety upon exposure to heights, avoidance of heights, and having the fear interfere with normal daily functions. In normal treatment, the psychologist will accompany the patient through a succession of tasks involving height with the task difficulty increasing. Thus, using VR offers several advantages: lower cost (less time spent by the psychologist who need not accompany the patient on tasks), a less intimidating environment, and safety. The virtual reality treatment comprises three stages: a virtual "see-out" elevator inside a 49-story virtual hotel, balconies of several different heights, and bridges over a river and through a canyon. This research included careful statistical evaluation that demonstrated its effectiveness [5].

4.2 The NASA Hubble space telescope repair mission

In 1990, following the launch of the Hubble Space Telescope, astronomers discovered flaws in its optical systems. Training for a repair mission became a major NASA effort, including the use of VR [6]. By using VR to immerse the repair team in their operating environment, they were provided with knowledge of both the telescope hardware and repair procedures. The training enhanced both cognitive and psychomotor skills, and the repair mission was successful. A post-flight survey was used to conduct an analysis demonstrating that members of the flight team judged, on average, that the VR training had a positive effect on their performance during the mission. Moreover, audio and visual cues were judged to have helped the participants. Discomfort in the virtual environment had a negative but acceptable impact on team members.

5.0 Conclusions

It has taken at least a half-decade longer than anticipated, but VR is moving out of the research laboratories and into the hands of users across many applications. Situational awareness and crisis planning, medicine, and engineering design are disciplines that are leading the way. We anticipate that the year 2000 will see VR truly benefiting society.

Acknowledgments

The NRL efforts described in this paper were sponsored by the U.S. Office of Naval Research, the MCWL, and OPNAV N86D. The efforts of the many VR Lab staff members who developed these projects are gratefully acknowledged. David Tate headed the shipboard damage control project and Jim Durbin has led the development of the Workbench for situational awareness.

References

[1] Tate, D., L. Sibert, and T. King, "Virtual Environments for Shipboard Firefighting Training," *IEEE Computer Graphics and Applications*, Vol. 17, No. 6, to appear Nov. 1997.

[2] Rosenblum, L., S. Bryson, and S. Feiner, "Virtual reality unbound," *IEEE Computer Graphics and Applications*, Vol. 15, No. 5, Sept. 1995, pp. 19-21.

[3] Krueger, W., C.A. Bohn, B. Froehlich, H. Schuth, W. Strauss, and Wesche, G., "The Responsive Workbench: A virtual work environment," *Computer*, Vol. 28, No. 7, July 1995, pp.42-48.

[4] Rosenblum, L.J., J. Durbin, and R. Doyle, "The Virtual Reality Responsive Workbench", to appear in *Virtual Worlds on the WWW, Internet, and Networks,* IEEE Computer Society Press.

[5] Hodges, L.F., B.O. Rothbaum, R. Kooper, D. Opdyke, T. Meyer, T. North, J.J. deGraff, and J. Williford, "Virtual Reality for exposure therapy," *Computer*, Vol. 28, No. 7, July 1995, pp. 27-34.

[6] Loftin, R.B. and P.J. Kenney, "Training the Hubble space telescope team," *IEEE Computer Graphics and Applications*, Vol. 15, No. 5, Sept. 1995, pp. 31-37.

A Virtual Environment for Learning to Pilot Remotely Operated Vehicles

Nicholas J. Pioch
npioch@bbn.com
BBN Corporation
70 Fawcett St.
Cambridge, MA 02138

Bruce Roberts
broberts@bbn.com
BBN Corporation
70 Fawcett St.
Cambridge, MA 02138

David Zeltzer
dzeltzer@sarnoff.com
David Sarnoff Research
CN 5300
Princeton, NJ 08543

Abstract

Remotely Operated Vehicles (ROVs) are used extensively for underwater search and salvage, inspection, surveying, scientific exploration, and mine countermeasures. ROV pilots must learn to rely on limited data from video and sonar displays and a few other positional indicators to maintain a sense of their vehicle, its tether, and its surroundings. Pilot training typically occurs on-the-job, where equipment is placed at risk, controlled learning situations are hard to create, and time for instruction is minimal. The TRANSoM project is developing a training environment that combines two emerging technologies to overcome these limitations. A Virtual Environment (VE) simulates the ROV and its surroundings as well as instructional enhancements such as external views of the ROV, directional cues, and alternate modes of interaction with the vehicle; e.g. a head-tracked head-mounted display (HMD). An Intelligent Tutoring System (ITS) monitors student pilot behavior and offers verbal and graphical feedback, mission review, and performance assessment. Near-transfer experiments comparing the utility of different artificial viewpoints have been completed, with full transfer experiments involving a real ROV to follow.

1. Introduction

Unmanned Remotely Operated Vehicles (ROVs) are used in industry and in the military for underwater tasks too dangerous or difficult for humans to perform; e.g., mine countermeasures or deep ocean search and salvage. They are also used extensively for more mundane but nevertheless vital tasks; e.g., inspecting ship hulls and underwater structures. A pilot controls the ROV from a shipboard console which supplies power and communicates with the vehicle via a tether. The vehicle's video camera and sonar serve as the low-resolution "eyes" through which the pilot views the ROV's immediate environment. A mechanical manipulator on the ROV often serves as the "hands." Despite the high cost and level of skill involved in ROV piloting, few formalized training procedures exist. In fact, most pilots learn on-the-job, putting expensive equipment at risk. A safer and more effective alternative using a Virtual Environment (VE) simulation is being developed under the TRANSoM (Training for Remote Sensing and Manipulation) project by a multi-disciplinary team of university and industry researchers from MIT, BBN Corporation, McDonnell-Douglas Aerospace, and Imetrix Inc.

A prototype system has been developed which combines VE technology with ITS techniques to create a curriculum for training ROV maneuvering skills. Very little formal research on VE training systems has been done, with the notable exception of R. Bowen Loftin's NASA-sponsored Hubble Repair and Maintenance training system [1] and the Virtual Environment Technology for Training (VETT) project's Officer of the Deck VE simulation [2]. TRANSoM augments a VE simulation with ITS-supported verbal coaching and graphical cues. The VE simulation is based on an actual ROV system specially constructed for this project — *Talon* — which will also be used to validate the effectiveness of the training curriculum. This paper describes the prototype implementation of the TRANSoM ROV trainer with special emphasis on the use of verbal and graphical techniques to promote skill learning.

Section 2 offers a brief analysis of ROV piloting skills. Section 3 summarizes the ITS techniques adopted for training maneuvering skills. Section 4 presents details

0-8186-8150-0/97 $10.00 © 1997 IEEE

of the VE implementation and discusses the impact of the ROV training domain on system design. The paper concludes with a summary of a recently completed experiment comparing alternative viewpoints and a description of future work planned for TRANSoM to extend the system to train additional piloting skills.

2. Task Analysis

The team invested significant effort in the early stages of the project in order to identify key piloting skills and to design situations in which these skills would be exercised. The researchers visited several ROV operations centers: the Woods Hole Oceanographic Institute in Woods Hole, MA, the home base of JASON, a large ROV used for undersea scientific exploration; the Navy's Unmanned Vehicle Detachment in San Diego, which uses ROVs for search and salvage operations; and the Naval Coastal Systems Station in Panama City, FL, where two TRANSoM members participated in a three-day course using an embedded computer graphics simulation of the Mine Neutralization System, an ROV specialized for disabling underwater mines. Although the full details of this task analysis phase are beyond the scope of this paper, surveys of experienced pilots and the TRANSoM project team's observations at ROV operations centers revealed the following three critical skills for ROV pilots:

- *Maneuvering* - Familiarity with the vehicle dynamics, including momentum, drag, and control effects, is the most basic piloting skill. Pilots say that getting sufficient practice time is the only way to develop maneuvering skills; however, those with good hand-eye coordination will be likely to learn faster. The best pilots can readily transfer their maneuvering skills from one vehicle system to another, after familiarizing themselves with the new controls and displays.

- *Situational Awareness* - This collection of skills encompasses a sense of the vehicle's spatial location and heading, the tether configuration, and any surrounding objects and terrain. Since the tether may easily become entangled on objects encountered earlier, or stretched to its capacity, tether awareness is particularly important. Expert pilots report that they mentally project themselves into the frame of reference of the ROV to help make accurate navigational decisions and control movements.

- *Sensor Integration* - ROV operators must be able to synthesize partial or degraded information from several different displays, such as sonar and video. Good pilots do not become overly dependent on one display but distribute their attention to all the displays. Sensor integration is important in dealing with equipment failures in that a good pilot will know which secondary sensors and displays to use as backup.

Of these three sets of skills, situational awareness is generally considered the most critical. However, since being able to drive an ROV effectively is a prerequisite to developing situational awareness, TRANSoM focused initially on training maneuvering skills, which require some sensor integration. The basic maneuvering skills taught by the TRANSoM system, such as orbiting or hovering in a current, are common across all ROVs. Other skills, like the proper launch and recovery of ROVs are beyond the scope of this project, since the procedures vary widely among different types of vehicles.

3. ITS for ROV Maneuvering

The prototype TRANSoM ROV trainer employs tutoring techniques derived from cognitive science and education research on the value of coached practice and apprenticeship learning [3] [4]. The general framework of a tutoring session is to demonstrate a mission, allow the student to practice the mission, and then review the student's performance. During the demonstration a simulated expert pilot flies the mission, talking through the control strategies and the proper use of the displays. During practice the student can solicit verbal help regarding the current mission phase and strategy or visual help in the form of a global view (see Section 4.4). Unsolicited coaching is triggered by monitors that track the student's progress and detect deviations from expert performance, such as drifting too far from a prescribed path. Since a pilot's hands and eyes are fully occupied flying the ROV, this feedback is delivered verbally. These warnings become increasingly specific the longer a violation goes uncorrected (e.g. "Watch your depth" is followed by "You are too low," followed by "Apply upward thrust to reach the target's depth."). The computer coach's verbal commentary must be carefully moderated to avoid becoming overly intrusive. For example, while several coaches may be simultaneously checking for different classes of mistakes, only the highest priority mistake is be coached at one time. There is also an enforced refractory period before any subsequent coach can be triggered. During the review phase, the student is presented with a summary of his or her performance compared against an expert and an overall view of the student's path. For each detected mistake, the student can replay the portion of the trial when the mistake occurred, view a demonstration of how to recover from that type of mistake, and retry that portion of the mission.

This Demonstrate-Practice-Review cycle occurs within the larger context of a maneuvering curriculum, which features a progression of increasingly challenging exercises. Most of these exercises include four subtasks, as illustrated in Figure 1:

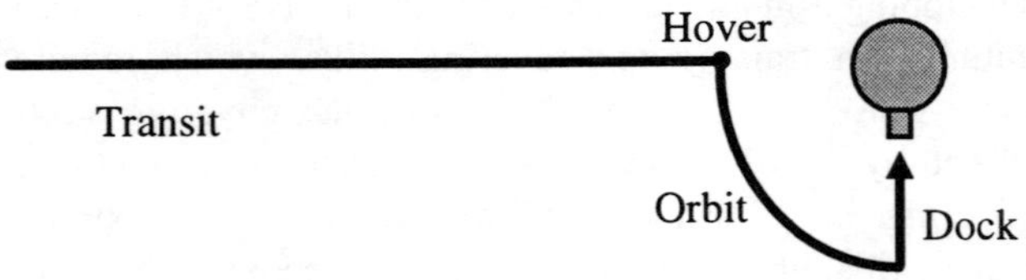

Figure 1. The canonical maneuvering exercise consists of four phases: *Transit* out to a target, *Hover* and take its picture, *Orbit* around the target to a porthole, *Dock* with it and take another picture of the interior.

These subtasks were chosen because they are all common ROV maneuvers and can be combined to produce a wide range of difficulty. The curriculum itself contains four skill levels: Beginner, Intermediate, Advanced, and Expert. Beginner problems abbreviate the difficult orbit subtask and feature high to fair visibility. The Intermediate level introduces mild water currents with a longer orbit subtask and good to poor visibility. The Advanced and Expert levels also feature good to poor visibility, but with moderate and strong currents respectively. At the end of each exercise review, the tutor presents a matrix of color-coded scores covering the following maneuvering skill factors: driving smoothly, facing the target, staying on course, making steady progress, avoiding collisions, and taking good snapshots. A separate color-grade of green, yellow, or red is given for these skill factors for each phase in which they are relevant. The tutor then synthesizes these scores into a recommendation either to repeat the exercise, try another exercise at the same skill level, or graduate to the next level in the curriculum.

The performance criteria and thresholds used to trigger verbal coaching and derive exercise scores were established by analyzing recorded data from professional ROV pilots. Each pilot ran through all of the curriculum exercises in increasing order of difficulty, but without verbal coaching or graphical aids. Their average scores in such skills as facing the target, staying on course, and smoothness of control have been incorporated into the maneuvering tutor as upper bounds on expected student performance.

After finishing the exercises in the curriculum, the experts were asked to role-play a novice pilot on certain exercises, revealing common beginner mistakes. New verbal coaching capabilities have been added to address these tendencies; e.g., warnings about overcorrections or control reversals. Verbal coaching, graphical aids, and review phase activities were turned on during these trials to get feedback from the experts about the intelligent tutoring components.

These expert pilots have been an invaluable source of constructive criticism about the fidelity of the VE and the utility of the coaching. At the end of the session, each expert filled out a written questionnaire rating their satisfaction with various components of the VE and tutor on a scale of one to five. The system received fours and fives across the board. Overall, their subjective comments about the system's potential to facilitate training new pilots have been overwhelmingly positive. While these informal asessments by expert pilots are encouraging, they do not take the place of formal evaluations of training effectiveness. Section 5 summarizes our plans for evaluating the tutor more objectively.

4. Virtual Environment

Any feature of a VE simulation can be classified as contributing to either the *baseline* or *enhanced* simulation. The *baseline* simulation refers to the task-essential objects and interactions comprising a realistic rendition of a given environment at a specified level of complexity. An *enhanced* simulation includes features or distortions not found in the modeled environment, but important for instruction [5]. Following a brief overview of the TRANSoM hardware and software architecture, this section describes both the baseline ROV environment and the enhanced visual features and interaction.

4.1 Hardware Architecture

The TRANSoM training system was developed on the MIT VETT testbed [6], a local-area network consisting of a Silicon Graphics Onyx workstation with Reality Engine2, several Silicon Graphics Indy desktop machines, and several commercial off-the-shelf devices, including a Virtual Research VR4 head-mounted display (HMD), a Polhemus Fastrak position sensor, and a Beachtron sound spatialization system hosted on a PC.

The base system performs satisfactorily on an Indy with R5000 processor and XZ graphics board. However, the Onyx's capability for real-time texture-mapping and support for head-tracked viewpoints in the HMD provide a more visually compelling sense of realism. This head-tracked viewpoint, coupled with the spatialized sound capabilities of the Beachtron, are currently being explored for their potential training value, as described in Section 4.5.

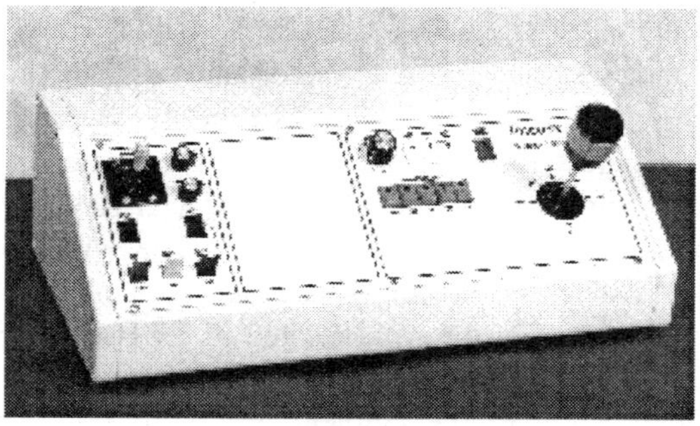

Figure 2. *Talon* vehicle control box.

To allow users to fly the simulated ROV with the same controls as the physical ROV, serial communication between the VE software and the *Talon* vehicle's control box has been enabled (see Figure 2). This was done mainly to ensure that trainees have identical control paradigms during transfer experiments comparing groups trained on the simulated ROV versus the actual ROV. Although the handbox itself is compatible only with the *Talon* vehicle, it is representative of the controls of most small ROV systems.

4.2 Software Architecture

The development of a graphics application is greatly facilitated by a dynamic language that supports rapid prototyping and object-oriented design. A number of languages — Python, Java, Guile, and Alice — were evaluated as front-ends for the Open Inventor software which controls graphical functions on the SGI platforms being used in TRANSoM. In the end, the Ivy system was selected, which is based on the language Scheme [7], a statically-scoped dialect of Lisp. Designed by Ken Russell of the MIT Media Lab, Ivy provides bindings to virtually all Inventor classes and has a documented method for compiling additional library modules into the language using a process called Header2Scheme. Ivy incorporates SCM, an extensible C implementation of Scheme. The ability to extend the language with C libraries has proved especially useful for TRANSoM. Computationally intensive C code, such as the vehicle dynamics, could be directly integrated into Ivy as well as third-party Scheme extensions such as Boston Software Works' Xscm, which provides bindings to Xwindows, the Xt toolkit, and Motif library. Xscm has been valuable for rapidly building conventional window- or text-based interaction such as curriculum menus, dialogs, and exercise review.

The TRANSoM training software consists of three main modules. The VE reads in the world configuration, loads the appropriate Inventor objects, and provides views that simulate the baseline ROV displays rendered in real-time. The ITS contains information about the maneuvering exercise curriculum, as well as performance sensors and coaches that provide verbal and graphical feedback to the student. The Experimenter Interface (EI) is a separate process which provides a unified GUI for monitoring the simulation, collecting data, and modifying environmental or ROV parameters such as water currents, visibility, or lighting. It was implemented using RapidApp, a native SGI interface-building tool. The VE uses SocketMan, an Ivy module with primitives for socket communication, to receive state-change commands from the EI.

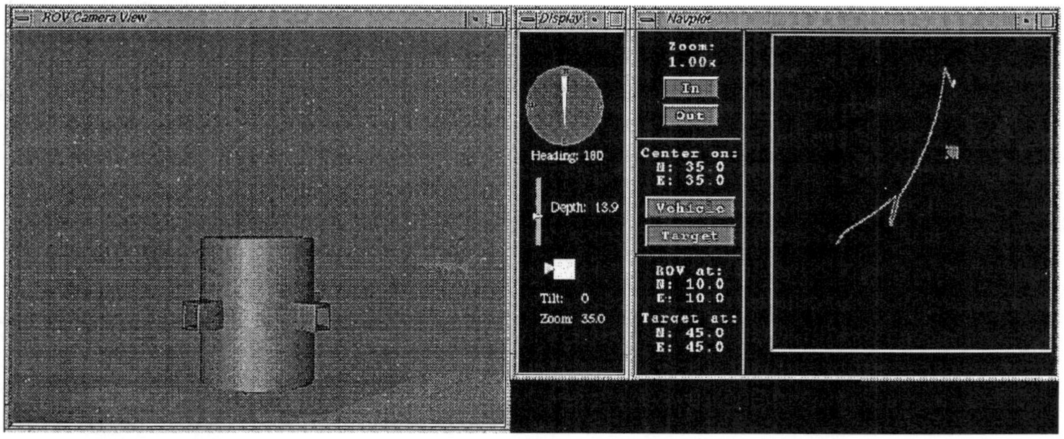

Figure 3. TRANSoM baseline displays. Left to right: ROV Camera View, Compass/Depth/Tilt, Nav Plot

4.3 Baseline Simulation

The upper half of the TRANSoM screen display is dedicated to graphical versions of the displays and indicators found in the *Talon* ROV. Although lacking a sonar display, which is currently under development, it is representative of the displays and indicators available to pilots of most commercial and military ROV systems. Figure 3 shows a Camera View, in the upper left corner, which simulates ROV underwater video. In the upper right a simplified plan view of the environment — the Nav Plot — is rendered in wireframe mode. It includes buttons for zooming in or out and centering on the ROV or target. The Nav Plot also indicates the ROV and target coordinates numerically to the left of the coordinate axes, and displays a trace of the ROV's path in yellow. The upper center screen region contains a compass, depth bar, and camera tilt indicator (the ROV camera can be tilted 90 degrees up or down via a switch on the control box).

As described in Section 4.1, the simulated ROV is controlled by a two-joystick handbox console. The main joystick on the handbox allows for simultaneous control of fore/aft thrust, left/right thrust, and left/right yaw, as shown in Figure 4. The depth joystick moves in one dimension only, controlling vertical ROV thrust. Other controls on the handbox include switches for tilting the camera up or down at a constant rate, as well as for zooming or focusing the camera. The handbox also controls vehicle power and light intensity and has a button for taking a snapshot of the current camera view.

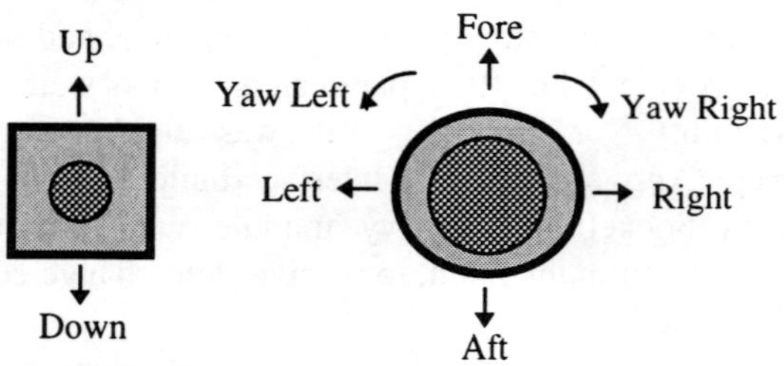

Figure 4a) Depth joystick b) Main joystick

The ROV dynamics module computes the response of the ROV to the current joystick input from the handbox. It is coupled with the graphics frame update; hence, it accepts variable timesteps based on the time elapsed since the last update. The dynamics module accounts for an ambient water current with a user-specified direction and magnitude, as well as a simple tether model based on a damped spring with user-specified length and spring constant. Although the dynamics are currently tuned to match the characteristics of the *Talon* ROV, relevant parameters such as mass, buoyancy, drag and inertial coefficients, and center of gravity are reconfigurable through a vehicle parameter file which is read during system initialization.

In the VE several important environmental factors are represented visually through the richness of the built-in Inventor class hierarchy. Fog is used to simulate the limited visibility encountered underwater. The distance at which objects become invisible can be controlled through a slider in the EI, and is typically decreased from 100 m. (near-perfect visibility) to 5 m. (more typical of ROV conditions) as a student progresses through the curriculum. Particulates are often visible in undersea environments and provide important cues about local currents. Rather than keep track of thousands of separate particle objects, the VE makes use of a single Inventor object comprised of a toroid-shaped star-field densely populated with pixel-sized squares. The width of the toroid is slightly greater than the size of the ROV environment. The toroid is rotated like a wheel through the environment to produce the effect of particulate flow in the direction of the ambient water current. The EI provides controls for other environmental conditions, such as vehicle light intensity, tether length and spring constant, and surrounding objects which may be loaded from scene description files.

Developers of real-time simulations must decide how to detect collisions in the simulated world. Although general techniques have been developed for collision detection among many independently moving objects [8] [9], the TRANSoM environment allows some useful simplifications due to the fact that the ROV is typically the only moving object in the scene, among a small number of other fixed objects. Furthermore, several objects in the VE scene graph represent intangible components for which collisions are not meaningful; e.g., the particle field and instructional cues like the vehicle's path (see Section 4.4). Our solution was to allow the modeler to control, by annotating the scene graph, whether an object should be "collidable," and if so, at what level of detail in its geometric decomposition collisions could occur. Modelers may place an "ignore" tag on a node in the scene graph to eliminate it from collision, or place a "boundingbox" tag on a node to signal that a minimal bounding box is used to test for a collision. Collisions with the seafloor are treated specially. Because the seafloor consists of a large Inventor triangle-mesh, mathematical checks for polygon intersection would be very time-consuming. Instead, a two-dimensional lookup-table of seafloor depths is generated at load-time from examination of the triangle-mesh polygon coordinates. Since the ROV is relatively stable in pitch and roll axes, the depth of its lower face can be used as a lower bound in Z. Thus, if the ROV is at location(x,y), one need only check if the ROV's lower face depth is greater than depth(x,y) in the table. This tradeoff of space for time was a success in that the time added to the main loop for the seafloor collision check was found to be insignificant.

4.4 VE Training Enhancements

One of the unique advantages to VE training is the ability to include instructional cues and interactions beyond what is possible in real situations. However, enhancements must be chosen carefully to avoid distracting or over-simplifying features, which can alter the underlying nature of the task being learned. Furthermore, a means of fading out these enhancements must be employed to prevent an over-dependence on features that are not available in the real task. TRANSoM is conducting a series of experiments to evaluate whether particular enhancements are indeed useful as training aids or simply as performance aids. Training aids produce better piloting of the real vehicle by students exposed to the VE training; performance aids produce better piloting only so long as they are available but do not transfer to the real vehicle.

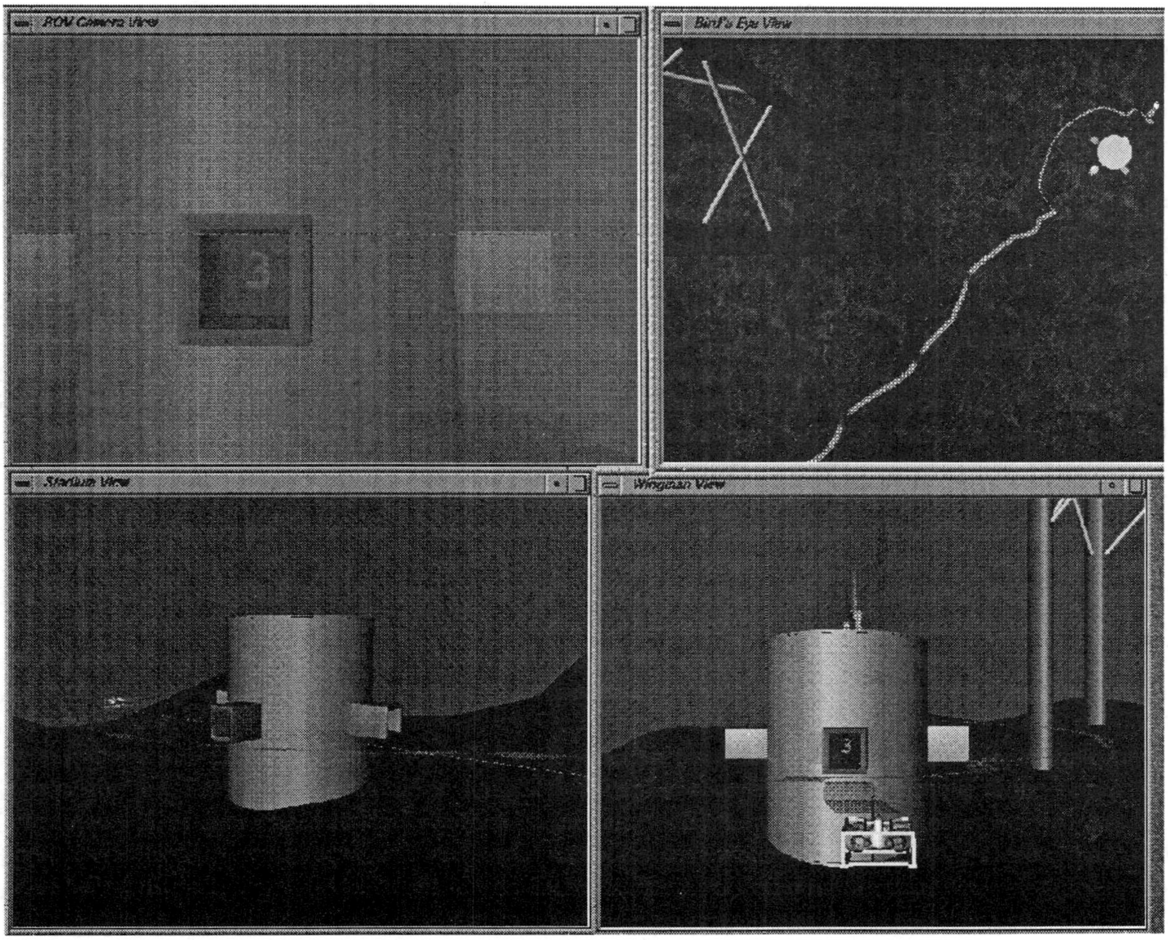

Figure 5. Clockwise from upper-left: ROV Camera, Overhead, Wingman, and Stadium Views.

When considering training enhancements it is important to remember that direct user control is not always the most productive style of human-computer interaction, especially when complex virtual worlds are involved. In particular, unconstrained, interactive navigation through large virtual worlds can be difficult and disorienting [10] [11]. Trainee interaction with a VE training system must be carefully designed to allow the trainee to focus on mission-related tasks. It is crucial not to distract the trainee with extraneous interaction tasks; for example, adjusting the viewpoint in VE displays.

To support these requirements, software interface agents have been designed that manage special external VE views of the ROV in the trainee interface. One of TRANSoM's most instructionally useful enhancements is called the "Stadium" view because, although stationary most of the time, it smoothly pans and zooms as needed to keep both the ROV and target within the viewport, much as a cameraman moves around a stadium to maintain a focus on the action. In fact, a similar method is used by many expert pilots during their first exposure to a new vehicle; they place the ROV in a clear pool and control it nearby so they can directly monitor its response. The Stadium view is currently used for short intervals, usually to help a student recover their bearings when lost. External views have also proved useful outside of practice, such as in reviewing a mission, in which an oblique overhead view shows the target, ROV path, and points highlighted on the path where notable mistakes were made. Another viewpoint, the "Wingman" view, was borrowed from an aircraft mission visualization system [12] and has been adapted for use in TRANSoM. The Wingman view positions the viewpoint a short, fixed distance above and behind the ROV but tracks the ROV's orientation. Hence it is a step toward a vehicle-centric view. Figure 5 shows these alternative views along with the ROV Camera View for comparison.

Figure 5 also shows several other VE instructional cues included in the maneuvering trainer. A semi-transparent ribbon trailing out behind the ROV denotes its path within the session. It approximates the tether's topology in that it shows where the tether could become wrapped around an object and how many twists it has accumulated (more than two constitute a hazard). Controls for clearing or turning the path history on or off are included in the EI. A directional cue found only in the Stadium view is presented as a red ray extending out forward from the ROV in the direction of the camera's aim. This is intended to help correlate the ROV Camera field of view with a specific region in the scene, and it serves as a reminder of the camera tilt status (which is often forgotten by novices). One directional cue not visible in Figure 5 is a compass rose "floating" underneath the ROV in the Wingman and Stadium views. This is intended to help correlate the information in the north-up Nav Plot display with the ROV-centric Wingman view and target-centric Stadium view. These cues are included to provide temporary support or "scaffolding" for beginners who show deficiencies in the relevant skill area [13]. Other cues were considered but then rejected either because they were too distracting or because they actually inhibited learning by unnaturally constraining the task. For example, we thought of adding "guard rails" around the prescribed path to help beginners learn to transit in a straight line while being buffeted by currents. However, this type of aid would lead to negative training effects since the ROV would behave differently than expected near the boundaries, and since it eliminates the opportunity to practice recovering from one's own mistakes. Another deceptively detrimental cue was revealed in early experiments; marking the target's location on the Nav Plot caused an over-reliance on the Nav Plot during close-in maneuvers such as orbiting, when the ROV camera view should be the primary focus. To promote better sensor integration skills, this marking has been replaced by numerical range and bearing readings in half of the curriculum's exercises.

To support demonstration and review, a record and playback mechanism allows the system to replay critical excerpts of a student's path to emphasize a mistake, and to demonstrate how to recover from that type of mistake. The Inventor substrate again proved useful in developing this facility. During a practice session, the ROV's position and orientation are saved as a stream of time-stamped Inventor nodes. To replay the sequence, the system resets the clock and the node pointer, waits until the next time-stamp in the node stream, and then sets the ROV position and orientation to that of the saved node for that time-stamp. The paths of expert pilots can be saved to a file and used later for demonstrations.

4.5 Alternate Modalities

As an alternative to conventional flat-panel CRT displays, an additional VE view, the "Cockpit" view has been implemented for use with a head-tracked HMD. Such a display allows the trainee to see the ROV's immediate surroundings in all directions as if the trainee were inside the ROV itself and is intended to promote the feeling of being in the ROV reported by most expert pilots. The VETT testbed includes two such HMD's: the LCD-based VR4 from Virtual Research and the Virtual i-glasses from Virtual i-O. While the VR4 has better resolution and image quality, the Virtual i-glasses have the advantage of an unobscured lower field of view, allowing the trainee wearing them to glance down at the baseline ROV displays or ROV control box. Spatialized sounds via the Beachtron device are being used to enhance learning of control effects. Thrust from the main joystick is played as a "white noise" sound emanating from the direction the ROV is being pushed by its thrusters. The volume of the sound is proportional to the magnitude of the thrust. Because of limitations in the human ear's ability to aurally resolve the fore/aft dimension, different frequency bands are used for forward thrust than for aft thrust. Although exercises for tether awareness are still under initial design, these sounds could also prove useful in detecting tether snags. The sounds would indicate that thrusters are working normally, so the ROV's failure to respond could be readily diagnosed as a tether problem.

5. Experimental Results

TRANSoM researchers at McDonnell Douglas Aerospace have carried out an experiment comparing the performance of subjects with varying exposure to two VE viewpoints: the Stadium view (see Section 4.4) and an ROV-Centered view with perfect visibility. The purpose of the experiment was to assess the contribution of alternative views to acquiring maneuvering skills. The training task was similar to the four-phase maneuvering task described in Section 3. The near-transfer task, also performed in the VE, was a slightly more difficult variation involving the same basic phases except with a downward spiraling orbit path and no indication of target location in the Nav Plot. Six groups of six subjects each were used. Two groups trained using the Stadium view for 50% or 100% of the missions, while two other groups used the ROV-Centered view 50% or 100% of the time. Two control groups were used, one which trained at 0% exposure (baseline displays only) and another which received no training (transfer condition only). The groups that trained with the Stadium view showed significantly better performance in transfer in the categories of depth control and adherence to an expert path. In almost all categories, the no-training group's deviations were significantly greater than the those of the other groups. Important subjective lessons have also been learned from this study. Subjects often exhibited "tunnel vision," focusing on one display such as the Nav Plot, while neglecting visual information in the camera view and other indicators. This occurred most frequently in the orbit phase. Moreover, a significant variability in performance across subjects was seen, with pilots of other classes of vehicles such as helicopters performing the worst.

Having completed this near-transfer study, TRANSoM is now turning its attention toward a full transfer study of the maneuvering trainer. This study will employ four groups of at least eight subjects, who receive varying degrees of exposure to the tutor. All subjects will undergo a pre-test and post-test of maneuvering exercises with the real ROV in a test tank. Between these tests, one "full-training" group will work through the curriculum of exercises with the verbal coaching and other artificial cues available. Another group will practice similar tasks but without the benefit of coaching or artificial cues. This "sim-only" group will help quantify the added value of the intelligent tutor over the simulation alone. A third group will spend a corresponding amount of time practicing the task with the real ROV in a test tank, for an "on-the-job" training benchmark. Finally, a control group will receive no practice whatsoever between the pre-test and post-test. In addition to variants on the transit-hover-orbit-dock task (see Section 3), the post-test also includes a pipe-following task for an indication of transfer to different classes of maneuvering tasks. To test out experimental procedures, a small-scale pilot study has been completed using three subjects per group, omitting the "on-the-job" group. As with the near-transfer study, a remarkable amount of individual differences in ability were seen throughout all groups, especially within the full training group. For example, one subject made it all the way through the curriculum in the time allotted while another got stuck on the first exercises in which currents were introduced. The pilot study hints that the effects of the training will be visible in the consistency of performance, not just the level of achievement. Another outcome of the pilot study was the decision to include much more challenging conditions in the transfer task to insure that it can reveal the full range of each pilot's abilities.

6. Concluding Remarks

Several important components will soon be added to the baseline VE simulation, including a side-scanning sonar display and a graphical tether based on a piecewise linear dynamic tether model. Speech recognition capability, already included in the VETT testbed, has been integrated as a preferable alternative to mouse-based help menus during practice, which require taking one's hand off the ROV controls. A Dynamic Positioning software package, which provides automated ROV control, will be incorporated as a new Ivy module. This will allow expert demonstrations to be generated on-the-fly from a set of waypoints, instead of using pre-recorded, manually-flown missions. In addition, validation and verification comparisons of simulated vehicle responses to those of the actual *Talon* vehicle have been performed as part of the preparation for the full transfer study [2][14][15]. TRANSoM is also investigating similar classes of vehicles to which this technology would be easily transferrable, such as Autonomous Underwater Vehicles (AUVs), Untethered Underwater Vehicles (UUVs), or remote-controlled aircraft.

7. Acknowledgments

The authors wish to acknowledge the contributions of the entire TRANSoM team: Stewart Harris and Barbara Fletcher (Imetrix); Richard Pew, Yvette Tenney, William Ferguson, and Jason Vantomme (BBN); Nat Durlach, Walt Aviles, Johnny Yoon, Fran Taylor, Jonathan Pfautz,

David Manowitz, and Dorrie Hall (MIT); Jim Curtin, Barbara Barnett, and Bruce Perrin (MacDonnell Douglas Training Systems); and Sandy Katz (Learning Research and Development Center, University of Pittsburgh). This work was sponsored under the Office of Naval Research contract N00014-95-C-0181. Terry Allard and Harold Hawkins deserve our special gratitude for their continuing support.

7. References

[1] R.B. Loftin and P. Kenney, "Training the Hubble Space Telescope Flight Team," *IEEE Computer Graphics & Applications,* 15 (5), pp. 31-37, September, 1995.

[2] N. J. Pioch. *Officer of the Deck: Validation and Verification of a Virtual Environment for Training*, RLE Technical Report No. 596, Massachusetts Institute of Technology, Cambridge, MA, June 1995.

[3] A. Collins, J. S. Brown, and S. E. Newman. "Cognitive Apprenticeship: Teaching the Craft of Reading, Writing, and Mathematics," in *Cognition and Instruction: Issues and Agendas*, L. B. Resnick, ed., Lawrence Erlbaum Associates, Hillsdale, NJ, 1987.

[4] A. Lesgold, S. LaJoie, M. Bunzo et al. *SHERLOCK: A Coached Practice Environment for an Electronics Troubleshooting Job*, University of Pittsburgh, Learning Research and Development Center, Pittsburgh, PA, 1988.

[5] D. Zeltzer and N. J. Pioch. "Validation and Verification of Virtual Environment Training Systems," *Proc. IEEE 1996 Virtual Reality Annual International Symposium*, pp. 123-130, IEEE Computer Society Press, Los Alamitos, CA, 1996.

[6] D. Zeltzer, W. A. Aviles, R. Gupta, et al. *Virtual Environment Technology for Training: Core Testbed*, Technical Report, Naval Air Warfare Center Training Systems Division, Orlando, FL, July 1995.

[7] G. Sussman, H. Abelson, J. Sussman. *Structure and Interpretation of Computer Programs*, MIT Press, Cambridge, MA, 1985.

[8] P. Dworkin and D. Zeltzer. "A New Model for Efficient Dynamic Simulation," *Proc. 4th Eurographics Animation and Simulation Workshop*, pp. 135-147, Barcelona, Spain, 1993.

[9] S. Gottschalk, M. C. Lin, and D. Manocha. "OBBTree: A Hierarchical Structure for Rapid Interference Detection, *Proc. ACM SIGGRAPH 1996*, Association for Computing Machinery, New York, NY, 1996.

[10] D. E. McGovern. "Experience and Results in Teleoperation of Land Vehicles," in *Pictorial Communication in Virtual and Real Environments*, pp. 182-185, S. R. Ellis, ed., Taylor & Francis, London, England, 1991.

[11] C. Esposito. "Virtual Reality: Perspectives, Applications, and Architecture," in *User Interface Software*, pp. 103-127, L. Bass and P. Dewan, eds., John Wiley & Sons, Chichester, England, 1993.

[12] D. Zeltzer and S. Drucker. "A Virtual Environment System for Mission Planning," *Proc. 1992 IMAGE VI Conference*, pp. 125-134, Phoenix, AZ, 1992.

[13] S. P. Gott. "Apprenticeship Instruction for Real-World Tasks: The Coordination of Procedures, Mental Models, and Strategies," in *Review of Research in Education*, 15, E. Z. Rothkopf, ed., American Educational Research Association, Washington, D.C., 1989.

[14] P. L. Knepell and D. C. Arangno. *Simulation Validation: A Confidence Assessment Methodology.* IEEE Computer Society Press, Washington, D.C., 1993.

[15] B. Fletcher. *ROV Simulation and Verification.* Proceedings of the OCEANS '97 Conference, 1997.

An Interactive 3D Interface for a Virtual Ceramic Art Work Environment

Kazuyoshi KORIDA[1] Hiroaki NISHINO[2] Kouichi UTSUMIYA[2]

[1]Dept. of Communication, Oita Prefectural College of Arts and Culture
1-11 Uenogaokahigashi, Oita 870, JAPAN
Tel : +81-975-45-0542, E-mail : korida@oita-pjc.ac.jp

[2]Dept. of Computer Science and Intelligent Systems, Oita University
700 Dannoharu, Oita 870-11, JAPAN
Tel : +81-975-54-7876, E-mail : {hn, utsumiya}@csis.oita-u.ac.jp

Abstract

This paper describes the design and implementation of a hands-on interface to support 3D object creation in a virtual environment (VE). This interface provides a 3D stereoscopic display facility. Virtual objects are presented stereoscopically just in front of users through LCD shutter glasses, enabling them to manipulate the objects directly by using their own real hands with two-handed instrumented gloves. It provides those functions such as dynamic gesture expressions, position and size indication of the 3D objects, spatial manipulations, and a stereoscopic display function to operate with the two-handed gloves. A method called quasi-force-feedback is designed to control the spatial tasks such as translations, rotations and deformations of the objects. It takes advantage of the objects' deformation speed to give the users a sense of force resistance from the objects visually without using any real force-feedback devices. Ceramic art is chosen as a target application and a prototype system for providing a realistic 3D virtual environment by simulating the pottery making space in the real world is under development to verify its usefulness and effectiveness.

Keywords : 3D interface, ceramic art, instrumented glove input, hand gesture, virtual environment.

1 Introduction

Because of its convenience and handiness, research on methods of human gesture input and its understanding using the image processing technology has been accelerated rapidly in recent years. It is an ideal solution to allow users to interact with 3D objects in a virtual environment (VE) through natural gestures performed by both hands in the same manner as they do in the real world. Although the vision-based method does not enforce the users to wear special equipment to measure human motions, the current technology can only treat relatively simple gestures and geometrical expressions in 2D. Some instrumented devices are required to deal with dynamic gestures and spatial tasks like 3D objects creation and deformation effectively.

While considering ultimate human-computer interfaces in the future, we have been designing and implementing an interactive 3D VE for creating ceramic art work targeted at supporting natural and intuitive human-computer communications. The system is characterized by the utilization of two-handed electronic gloves [1] and stereoscopic graphics drawings. It supports the process of 3D objects creation in the VE by providing those functions such as dynamic gesture expressions, position and size indication of the objects and spatial manipulations like translations, rotations and deformations by using the two-handed glove devices. Although the users are required to wear the two gloves, they are free to use their own hands to produce the objects. Thus, it makes possible to share their experiences in both real and virtual environments by simulating the real ceramic art production processes, realizing rapid and easy prototyping of potteries virtually with less time and efforts. Additionally, it cannot only use the system as a testbed to record and scientifically analyze experts' hand motions, but also be expected to apply it to the introductory education in ceramic art classes.

This paper describes the design and implementation of an interactive 3D interface, called ***CHINA*** (**C**yberglove-based two-**H**anded **IN**terface for virtual **A**rt work environment), being founded on our previous research work [2] to provide a virtual environment for ceramic art work creation by utilizing the two-handed gloves and the stereoscopic display techniques. Section 2 reviews the related research work briefly and points out our approach taken to resolve some problems discovered there. Section 3 presents the overview and design concepts of *CHINA*. After analyzing a potter's hands motions used in actual pottery making, section 4 explains its architecture and implementation details. Section

0-8186-8150-0/97 $10.00 © 1997 IEEE

5 describes the preliminary experiments and observations acquired from them. Finally, section 6 concludes the paper with the potential uses of the system and our future work.

2 Related work

As a non-instrumented approach without wearing any special equipment, Takahashi et al. developed a system for recognizing human gestures by analyzing motion pictures [3]. The target gestures are limited to generous 2D motions. Krueger implemented a system called VIDEODESK, facilitating users to manipulate objects by using their hand images displayed on a computer screen which are captured with a video camera [4]. Whereas the utilization of the users' real hands is a great advantage of the system, it is not possible for them to directly manipulate the objects.

There are many previous research activities using instrumented devices. Boulic and Thalmann invented a method to give users the awareness of force-feedback in a visually displayed information, reducing work load occurred in tedious object manipulation tasks by using an electronic glove [5]. A graphical virtual hand is used to control the manipulation tasks without stereoscopic vision in their method. Baudel et al. developed a system, called Charade, a presentation tool to control a remote computer display by performing free-hand gestures with a VPL DataGlove [6]. In spite of the effectiveness of the system discussed in the literature, it mainly deals with pointing gestures expressed by a single hand posture while it does not give any consideration on two-handed spatial gestures. Galyean et al. developed a virtual sculpture system by using a pair of an electromagnetic (EM) tracker (Polhemus Isotrack) and a force-feedback device to determine positions of sculpting tools in 3D virtual space [7]. While a method of expressing virtually sculpted objects has similarity of the ceramic art work, the sculpting processes to be simulated by using the virtual tools cannot be directly applied to the pottery making processes performed by two-handed operations. Kamei et al. proposed a deformable clay model to easily create virtual potteries [8]. Because their method only deals with rotationally symmetric objects, it cannot be available for free-form modeling with the two-handed manipulations.

As regards the methods of virtual objects expression, Arthur et al. showed some results obtained from their 3D task performance evaluations in the fish task virtual worlds [9]. They claim that "head-coupled & stereo" viewing is the best way to improve 3D task performance in the case of applications having great importance on the depth perception, while they show a result that "head-coupled binocular" is appraised as a better method than "head-coupled & stereo" by subjects in a simple stereo viewing test. The stereoscopic viewing is especially important in our ceramic art work environment which needs to display the objects being produced as well as to provide interactive manipulation functions in the virtual environment. Kruger et al. developed a system called Responsive Workbench for physicians, engineers and architects by utilizing commercially available 3D devices [10]. They point out the importance of tactile-feedback via the glove devices. Because our current implementation does not support this facility, it is an issue necessary to be considered in the near future.

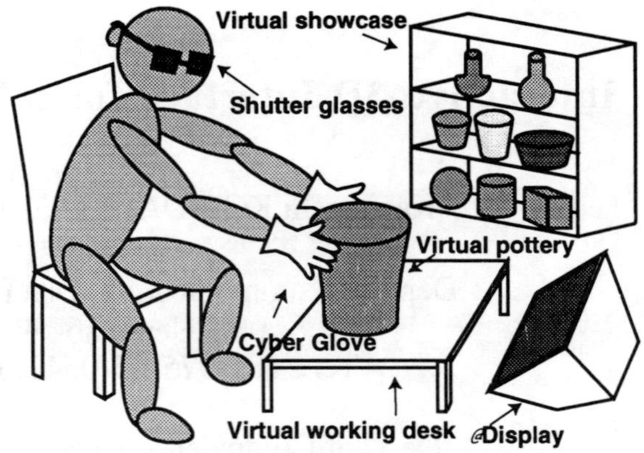

Figure 1: Concept of desirable VR ceramic art work

3 System concepts

3.1 Basic design concepts

CHINA provides two different kinds of simulated environments for ceramic art work creation. One is for appreciating completed virtual potteries, and the other is for enabling the users to experience the pottery making process which is then divided into several sub-processes such as basic design, kneading, forming, painting, and firing. This paper focuses on the forming process which requires two-handed spatial manipulations, targeting at designing virtual working space and a hands-on 3D interface to support the process.

Most conventional spatial tasks in the 3D virtual environments require to use mice and keyboards to specify dedicated coordinate values, enforcing the users to get expert skills of manipulations which are totally different from the actual motions performed in the pottery making. The users are not allowed to use their know-hows and experiences of the pottery making practically, wasting enormous time and efforts in forming object shapes. Additionally, it is difficult for them to concrete the images in their minds as formed objects intuitively by using the traditional methods of indirect manipulations, making hard to apply the methods to artistic productions.

Figure 1 illustrates our concept of *CHINA*. The users can manufacture virtual potteries through the two-handed manipulations with their own hands. The system provides those functions to support the efficient production such as replaying the forming process, restarting it in the middle of the production, and composing multiple objects. There is a virtual potter's wheel available for throwing and a showcase

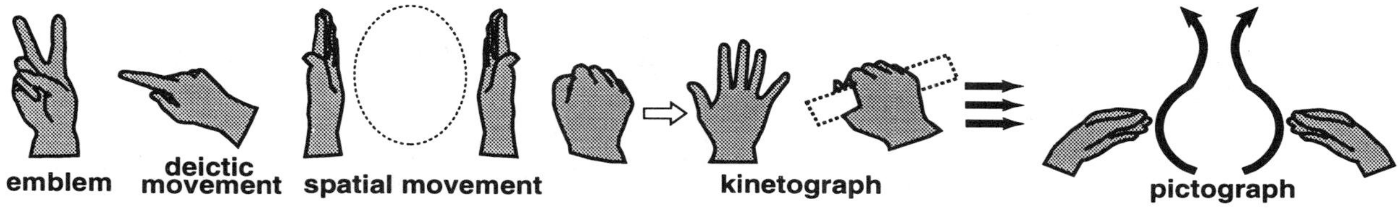

Figure 2: Hand motions used for non-verbal communication

for exhibiting the virtual potteries both finished and under production which are put back and taken out at any time. The pair of instrumented gloves (Virtual Technologies CyberGlove) and 6DOF EM sensors (Polhemus Fastrak) is introduced as an input method to measure the users' hand shapes, positions and orientations in 3D space. The output is displayed in stereo through LCD shutter glasses (Stereo Graphics CrystalEyes) to the users. The system is implemented by using IRIS GL (partially implemented by OpenGL) on an SGI Onyx/RE2.

The following design policies are set to make the sharing of the pottery making know-hows in both real and virtual worlds possible, allowing the users to easily use the system without any special awareness or knowledge.

(1) develop an interactive 3D interface to put the users' real hands and the virtual objects together in the same field of view,
(2) free forming operations for the 3D object modeling by using the two-handed spatial manipulations,
(3) stereoscopic vision and direct manipulations by hand gestures which are closer to the real motions performed in the pottery making, and
(4) enhanced visual feedback in place of tactile- and force-feedback.

The system under development based on these policies is used as a testbed to assess how human performance is influenced by the interface. Its application to the introductory ceramic art education and the collection of experts' skills and know-hows are other issues to be considered.

3.2 A virtual environment in CHINA

There are two important factors in implementing *CHINA*:

(1) the working space to hold the users' hands, viewpoints and virtual objects all together, and
(2) the hand gestures performed by the users.

To make the environment closer to the real pottery making workplace, the system allows the users to form the objects by using their hand motions and visually check the effects of operations in real time in the same field of view. This environment provides high degree of reality due to the sharing of the pottery making know-hows in the real and virtual worlds, enabling novice users to utilize the system easily. Additionally, it is expected to realize some distinctive features proper to the computer-based implementation such as record and replay of production processes, reuse of the products, and geometric processing.

In general, a working space with human hand operations tends to be limited within one to two meters away from the operator's position. The pottery making environment is further limited to a smaller rounded area within the radius of approximately thirty centimeters, keeping apart from thirty to forty centimeters away from the human body. Therefore, the following conditions are set to make the forming operations possible in such restricted space:

(1) virtual objects are put in the working space,
(2) a 3D interface is provided to realize interactions between the operator's real hands and the virtual objects, and
(3) the operator's hands and the virtual objects are kept in positional relations for easy viewing.

To satisfy these conditions, *CHINA* draws the virtual objects stereoscopically through shutter glasses which can be seen as if they are placed between the users' both hands from their viewpoints, allowing them to manipulate the objects directly by using their own real hands with instrumented gloves. Additionally, it provides the capability to adjust the users' hand positions and the points on the objects to be deformed interactively.

3.3 Hand gesture interface

Hand gesture is a method of nonverbal communication to complement or alternate specific words and sentences which are difficult to express by using verbal languages. The human hand movements useful for a human-computer interface can be classified into the following five categories [11]:

(1) *emblem* to be translated into a corresponding verbal word,
(2) *deictic movement* to point out a specific target,
(3) *spatial movement* to indicate spatial relationships,
(4) *kinetograph* to express human or object behaviors, and
(5) *pictograph* to show object shapes in a space.

While (1) to (3) are expressed by static postures, (4) and (5) are represented by dynamic gestures which tend to be excluded from the scope of human-computer interface (see figure 2). *CHINA* supports an environment very similar to the real world working space with the provision of dynamic hand movements and motions specific to the pottery making based on this classification. There are four basic glove operations supported to implement these five hand

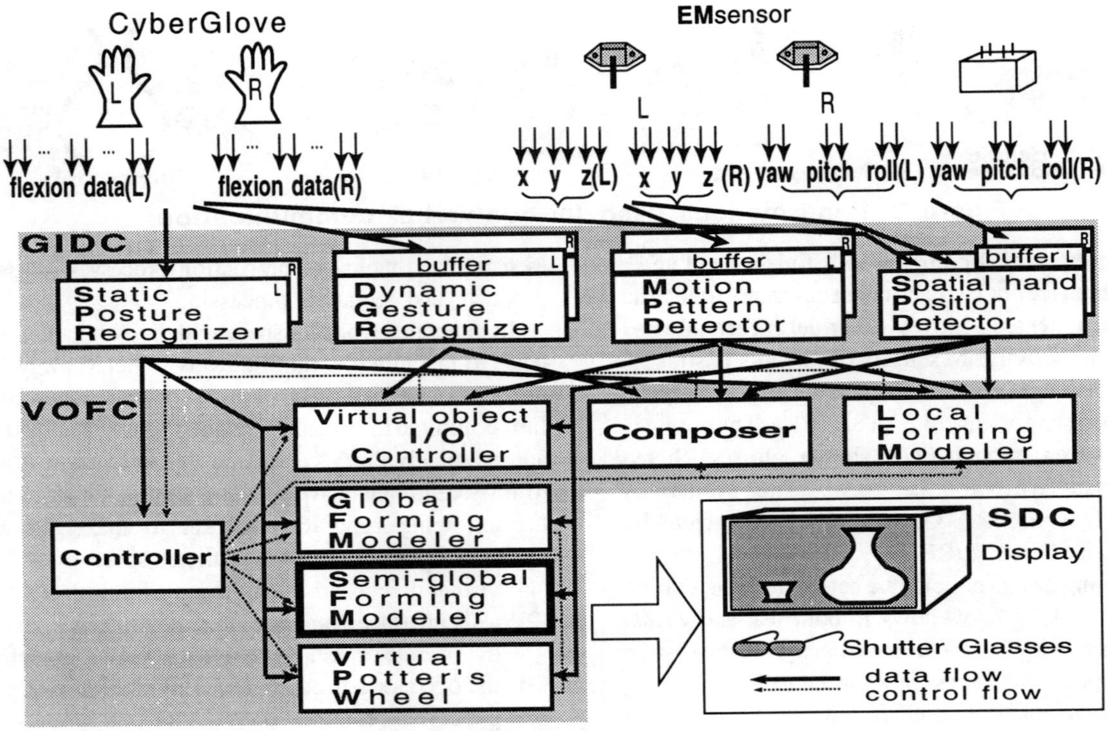

Figure 3: System organization of CHINA

movements as follows:
(a) static posture recognition (SPR),
(b) spatial hand position detection (SPD),
(c) dynamic gesture recognition (DGR), and
(d) motion pattern detection (MPD).

The emblem is used as an interpreter to manage the system's control flow and is supported by SPR. Table 1 shows the relationships between the five hand movements and the four glove operations.

Table 1: Relationships between hand motion and basic operator

Hand Motion	Basic Operator
Emblem	SPR
Deictic Movement	SPR, SPD
Spatial Movement	SPR, SPD
Kinetographic Movement	DGR, MPD, SPD
Pictographic Movement	SPR, MPD

The glove-based hand gesture allows the users to directly manipulate the virtual objects, providing an intuitive interface closer to the method of human communications in the real world. DGR and MPD are particularly important functions to support hand movements for object deformation which is a mandatory requirement in the ceramic art work environment. Thus, it is possible to implement a natural interface in the virtual environment with the employment of typical expressions used in the real world.

4 System organization and implementation

4.1 Gesture analysis in ceramic art

Because we think it is important to support hand gestures and motions closer to the real ones used in the actual pottery making, we recorded a potter's hands motions on videotapes to analyze at the beginning of system implementation. The following features are extracted from the analysis:

(1) each hand tends to have its own role in most gestures,
(2) there are significant differences in speed and preciseness between right and left hands,
(3) both hands are used symmetrically in the case of indicating size or width, and shape of the objects (a pair of thumbs and index fingers are used frequently),
(4) similar motions have sometimes different meanings with the usage of different tools,
(5) while visual information is effective to get rough positions and shapes of the object, tactile- and force-feedback is required for precise information.

(1) suggests a basic approach to the two-handed interface as described in [12]. (2) shows a need for a gesture understanding mechanism to recognize each hand's feature separately, being followed by combination of each result to get a final answer. (3) indicates the symmetrical use of both hands (especially thumbs and index fingers) is particularly important in the forming process of the ceramic art. According to (4), the system needs to support multiple modes of operations. Because the mouse and keyboard operations are not suitable for glove manipulations, finger

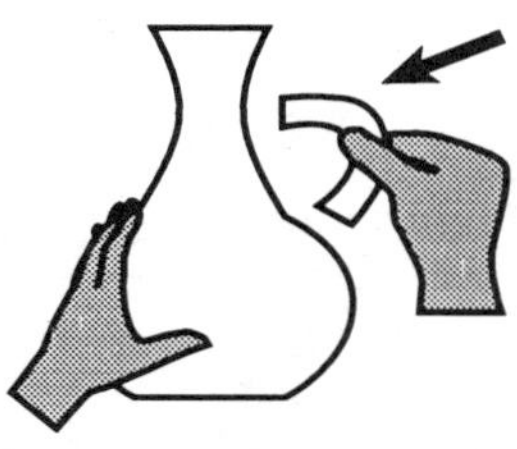

Figure 4: Composing

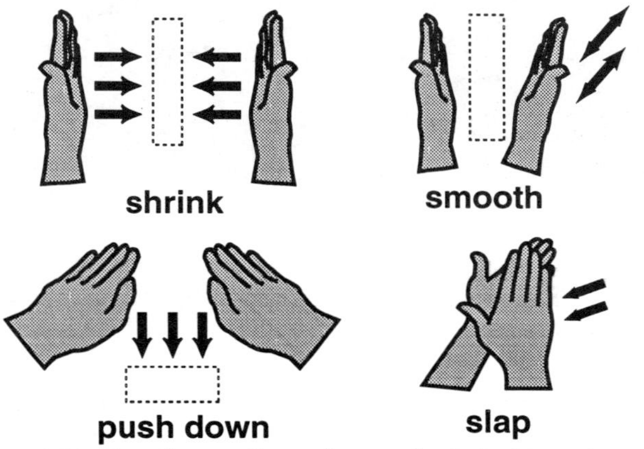

Figure 5: Hands motions in semi-global forming

alphabet character recognition is used to select a mode to make these operations the minimum. (5) points out a requirement to incorporate the tactile-feedback function into the collision detection between the objects and the hands. Additionally, the object deformation demands some type of force-feedback function strongly.

4.2 System organization

Figure 3 illustrates the organization of *CHINA*. It consists of a pair of CyberGloves and Fastrak EM sensors, glove information display controller (GIDC), virtual object forming controller (VOFC), stereoscopic display controller (SDC), and the LCD shutter glasses. GIDC is made up of four sub-components such as static posture recognizer (SPR) to recognize the hand postures according to the data sampled from the gloves, dynamic gesture recognizer (DGR) to recognize the temporally varied hand shapes according to the data stream sampled from the gloves, motion pattern detector (MPD) to extract the hand movement patterns using the data gathered from the tracker, and spatial hand position detector (SPD) to get the current hand position from the tracker. VOFC is controlled by the output from GIDC. All operations are performed by using the two-handed gloves. The inter- and intra-component control flow is managed by finger alphabet characters recognized by SPR. SDC displays the objects in front of the computer screen stereoscopically, providing an interactive calibration capability to adjust the positions of an EM sensor on each hand and displayed objects to give the users a feeling as if the objects are located at their

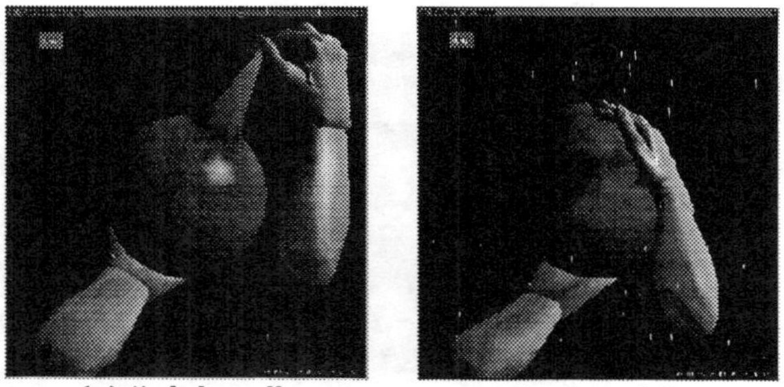

(a) "pick up" (b) "push"

Figure 6: Direct manipulations in LFM

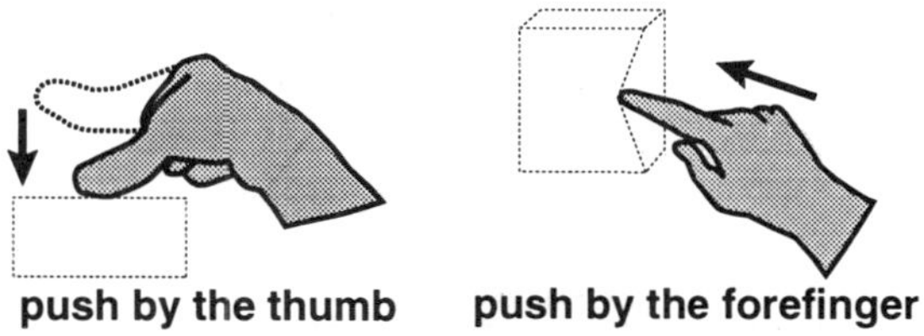

Figure 7: Hands motions in local forming

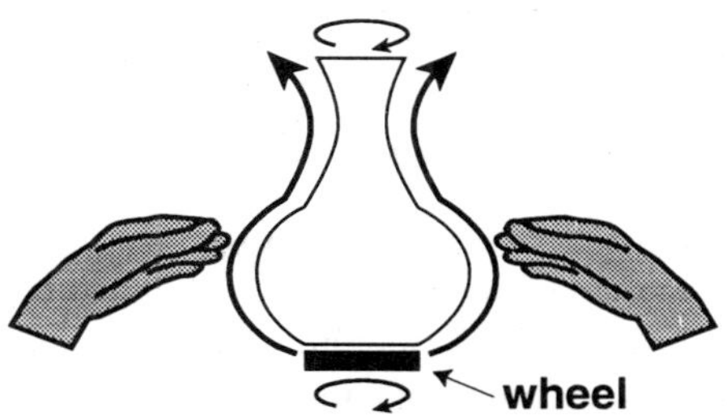

Figure 8: Throwing

hand positions.

SPR is implemented by using a feed-forward neural network to recognize the finger alphabet characters. It achieved 91.7% hit rate for the test with multiple subjects. DGR is also implemented by using a recurrent neural network which has feedback connections to hold the input history from the gloves and tracker, making the network possible to handle data streams varied temporally. The two-handed dynamic gestures showed better hit rate over the one-handed, indicating the potential powers to realize more stable and reliable recognition for complex gestures [13].

Virtual object I/O controller (VIOC) is used to load three primitive objects (sphere, cube, and cylinder) and existing objects created and stored previously onto a virtual working desk. The primitive objects are loaded by using the two-handed dynamic gestures. The existing objects can be selected by touching them with the right-hand index finger in the middle of production. Object composer (OC) is provided to unify multiple objects into a complex shape. DGR is used to grasp, move and release the objects to be composed as shown in figure 4. Any objects can be stored in a virtual showcase for later reuse by VIOC.

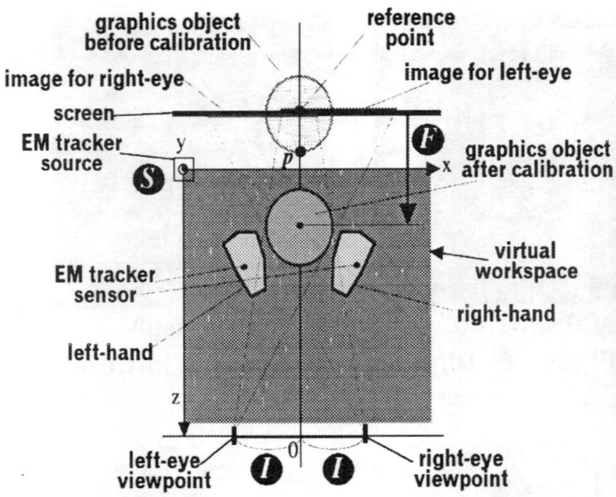

Figure 9: Interactive stereo calibration

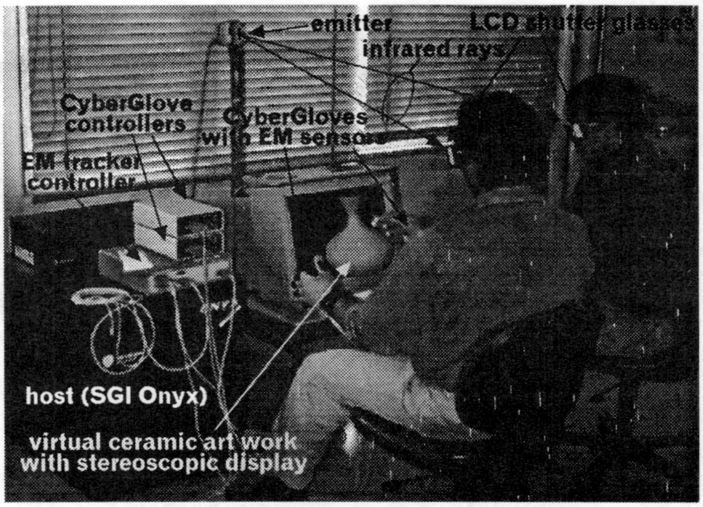

Figure 10: Operational environment of CHINA

Table 2 :Relationships between modeler and basic operator

Modeler	Basic Operator
Global Forming Modeler	SPR, SPD
Semi-global Forming Modeler	SPR, SPD, MPD
Local Forming Modeler	SPR, SPD
Virtual Potter's Wheel	SPR, SPD

Object forming operations are mainly performed with non-contact manipulations treated by semi-global forming modeler (SGFM). SGFM monitors the positions and movement patterns of both hands to scale the object size and make their surfaces smoother only for the portions of the objects surrounded by the hands. The effective degree of these operations can be controlled by the number of iterations of Figure 5 illustrates gestures used to control SGFM. Global forming modeler (GFM) is used to change the size of the whole object globally. The scale is determined by the distance between two hands. SPR and SPD are used for this function. Local forming modeler (LFM) is available to perform the detailed forming manipulations. An object is represented as a collection of polygons under the current implementation. LFM calculates the distances between the object's vertices and fingertips or palms in every graphics rendering cycles for collision detection. If the collision is detected, it changes the positions of the detected vertices according to the hand movements such as "picking up" and "pushing" as shown in figure 6. The opening and closing gestures are used to designate the start and end of each operation respectively. SPR and SPD are used for these operations. Figure 7 shows the examples of this function. Virtual potter's wheel (VPW) is provided to create rotationally symmetrical objects specific to the ceramic art. A horizontal circle made by thumbs and index fingers of both hands is used to roughly sketch the object shape as shown in figure 8. SPR and SPD are used for this function as well. It is also possible to replay, suspend, and resume the operations at any moment in each modeler. Table 2 shows the relationships between the modelers and the glove operations.

4.3 Stereoscopic vision and hand manipulation

We first implemented the system to control object manipulations by using virtual graphics hands drawn with the objects without stereoscopic display capability. A difficulty in recognizing the spatial relationship between the graphics hands and the objects became obvious. It was especially a serious problem of depth perception in the process of object deformation. Therefore, we enhanced the easiness of getting the depth perception in the environment by using stereoscopic display capability provided by Onyx Reality Engine2 processor. It supports quad buffering with high resolution (960 x 680 pixels) and frequency (108Hz), realizing flicker-less stereoscopic viewing of the objects.

In the standard graphics rendering methodologies, it is only possible for the users to look at the objects being manipulated and the graphics hands or tools representing their motions from distant viewpoints, making the direct object manipulation difficult to realize. On the contrary, *CHINA* displays the objects being manipulated closer to the users from the display screen, realizing the integrated real (hand) to virtual (object) working environment for giving the users a feeling as if they can reach the objects and manipulate them directly by their own hands. It enables the users to produce the potteries in an environment similar to the real world working space.

Figure 9 explains a method of calibration to realize the environment. First of all, the EM tracker source is moved to find the place where the position data sampled from both hands match with the actual hand positions on XY plane (fix "S" parameter in the figure). Then, the object displayed at the center of the screen is moved forward until it reaches the actual hand position (fix "F" parameter). The "F" parameter

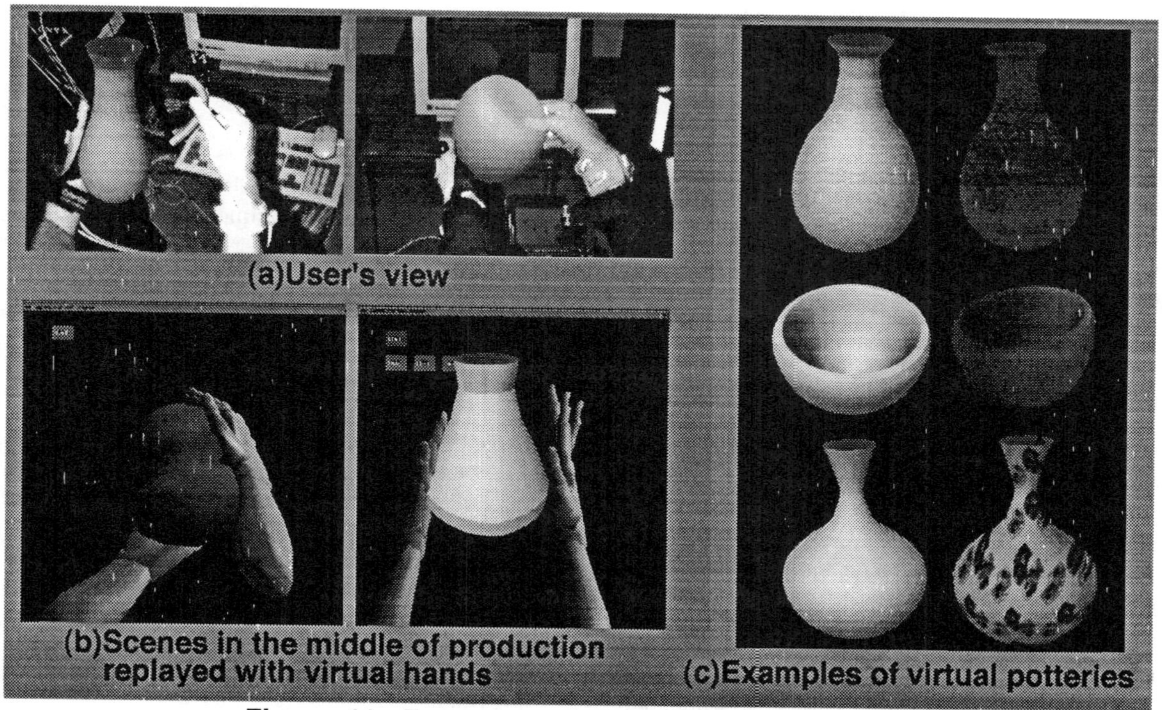

Figure 11: Examples of virtual ceramic art work

is determined by duplicating the EM sensor position on each hand and the point P on the object. This calibration procedure relies on the users' visual perception. The position information of each hand is indicated by a 3D marker on the screen. The binocular parallax is another variable to be adjusted to provide better stereoscopic images for different users (fix "I" parameter).

5 Preliminary experiments

We conducted some preliminary experiments by using *CHINA*. Figure 10 illustrates the operational environment of *CHINA*. Figure 11 shows the user's view, snapshots captured in the middle of object deformation, and some examples of virtual potteries produced by the system. According to the experiments, it is observed that *CHINA* is quite useful for the operations like intuitive 3D geometrical expressions, direct object manipulations and spontaneous deforming operations. On the other hand, detailed deforming operations tend to spend time longer than other 3D modelers.

There are some problems and issues observed through the experiments as follows:

(1) While semi-global forming operations based on the hand movement patterns tended to get good results generally, local forming operations fully dependent on the visual feedback turned to be difficult to manage. Whereas it requires to specify the detailed positions of objects to modify, the EM tracker was inaccurate due to its weakness in the noisy environment, making the local forming operation difficult to execute precisely. There are some methods under consideration to stabilize the tracker data such as excluding outranged data and supplementing current data with some previous values to make them linear.

(2) Because the current method of collision detection employed by LFM is based on the Euclidean metric, it tends to consume larger CPU cycles as the objects become more complex. The resultant time delay cannot be ignored for smooth and natural operations. Therefore, a more efficient method to detect the objects' vertices being deformed is required [12].

(3) The polygon based representation of the objects is good for real-time graphics rendering, but less intuitive for deforming the objects. The method based on parametric curves and surfaces is required to support better object deformation interface [14].

(4) Putting hands on the back of objects immediately obstructs the portions of visual feedback to the users. Using see-through HMD is an alternative method for this problem. However, the objects are drawn in front of the hands even if the objects are located behind the hands. In the ceramic art environment, stereoscopic vision with the shutter glasses is better because hand manipulations on the front side is the principal operations.

(5) As regards a tactile-feedback facility, an enhanced collision detection capability is under development to simulate contacts between the users' hands and the objects by using programmable vibrotactile options facilitated on our left-hand CyberGlove. Additionally, a method to give the users a feeling of force-feedback visually without using any special devices is also under

consideration. An idea is to present the objects' stiffness by controlling the deformation speed. For example, a harder object is modified slower than a soft one. Thus, the users are required to iterate more gestures to modify the shape of the harder one compared with the modification of the soft one. We call it as a vision-based quasi-force-feedback method.

(6) There are some additional enhancements to be planned such as the object surface smoothing and the object deformation methods with several properties of material (i.e. elasticity and plasticity).

6 Conclusions and future work

The traditional 3D interfaces with instrumented devices are required for users to manipulate virtual objects indirectly by using an electronic glove through a virtual hand drawn in a computer display, making systems very difficult to use, and enforcing the users to get expert skills to manipulate. On the other hand, the interface described in this paper allows the users to use two-handed instrumented gloves as their real hands and LCD shutter glasses as ordinal glasses to wear, treating virtual objects in recalling to their corresponding real objects. It makes the two-handed spatial manipulations effective to handle the virtual objects displayed in stereo directly. Thus, it is possible to deal with the objects in a similar manner to do in the real world. Predicting improvements in the glove and tracker devices in the future is not so difficult. If more cost-effective, easy-to-wear and codeless gloves and higher performance trackers will become available, it is expected for the system to be used more effectively with less discomfort to wear the equipment.

The system is considered to be useful as some applications in the following area:

(1) Art

It supports an environment to create handmade 3D objects other than artificial 3D CAD models by using two-handed direct manipulations.

(2) Education

It enables trainees to experience the production process of ceramic art work from the same viewpoint of experts and to compare their motions with the experts'.

(3) Augmentation of human sensation

It augments and alternates human sensation, especially for physically handicapped people, through computer supported two-handed motions and gestures.

We have plans to work on some further enhancements and assessments of the system as follows : developing a method to stabilize the data from the tracker, investigating the influence of stereoscopic vision upon the human eyes, implementing the vision-based quasi-force-feedback method, introducing the tactile-feedback option with instrumented gloves, supporting pottery making processes in addition to the forming process, and experimenting and evaluating the possibility of its application to the ceramic art education. We would like to verify the usefulness and effectiveness of the interface through these activities.

Acknowledgments

The authors would like to thank the VSMM'97 reviewers for their thoughtful comments. This work is partly supported by the Japan Society for the Promotion of Science, "Research for the Future" Program under Program No. JSPS-RFTF96P00603, and the Grant-in-Aid for Scientific Research under Grant No. 09680345 by Ministry of Education, Science, Sports and Culture.

References

[1] Sturman,D.J. and Zeltzer,D. : A Survey of Glove-based Input, IEEE Computer Graphics and Applications, Vol.14, No.1, pp.30-39, 1994.

[2] Nishino,H., Korida,K. and Utsumiya,K. : A Synthetic Virtual Environment for Collaborative Product Development, Proc. of VSMM'96, pp.69-74, 1996.

[3] Takahashi,K., Seki,S.,Kojima,H. and Oka,R.: Spotting Recognition of Human Gestures from Time-Varying Images, Trans.IECE, Vol.J77-D-II, No.8, pp.1552-1561, 1994.

[4] Krueger,M.W. : Environmental Technology : Making the Real World Virtual, Comm.ACM, Vol.36, No.7, pp.36-37, 1993.

[5] Boulic,R., Rezzomico,S. and Thalmann,D : Multi-finger Manipulation of Virtual Objects, Proc. of ACM VRST'96, pp.67-74, 1996.

[6] Baudel,T. and Beaudouin-Lafton,M. : CHARADE: Remote Control of Objects Using Free-hand Gestures, Comm.ACM, Vol.36, No.7, pp.28-35, 1993.

[7] Galyean,T.A. and Hughes,J.F. : Sculpting : An Interactive Volumetric Modeling Technique, Proc. of SIGGRAPH'91, pp.267-274, 1991.

[8] Kamei,K., Nakamura,Y. and ABE,S. : A Deformable Clay Model for Rotaionally Symmetric Objects, Trans. IECE, Vol.J76-D-II, No.8, pp.1772-1779, 1993.

[9] Arthur,K.W. and Booth,K.S. : Evaluating 3D Task Performance for Fish Tank Virtual Worlds, ACM Trans. on Information Systems, Vol.11, No.3, pp.239-265, 1993.

[10] Kruger,W., Bohn,C.A., Frohlich,B., Schuth,H., Strauss,W. and Wesche,G. : The Responsive Workbench: A Virtual Work Environment, IEEE Computer, Vol.28, No.7, pp.42-48, 1995.

[11] Ekman,P. and Friesen,W.V. : The Repertoire of Nonverbal Behavior, Semiotica 1, pp.49-98, 1969.

[12] Shaw,C. and Green.,M. : THREAD: A Two-Handed Design System, ACM Multimedia Systems, Vol.5, March, pp.126-139, 1997.

[13] Nishino,H., Utsumiya, K., Kuraoka, D., Yoshioka, K. and Korida, K. : Interactive Two-handed Gesture Interface in 3D Virtual Environments, Proc of the ACM VRST'97, 1997 (to be appeared).

[14] Watt,A. and Watt,M. : Advanced Animation and Rendering Techniques, Chapter 3 The Theory and Practice of Parametric Representation Techniques, Addison-Wesley, 1994.

Factory Animation by Self-Organization Principles

Jari Vaario[†], Nobutada Fujii[‡], Dirk Scheffter[*], Michael Mezger[*], and Kanji Ueda[‡]
[†]Nara Women's University, Kita-Uoya Nishi-machi, 630 Nara, JAPAN, [*]
[‡]Kobe University, Rokkodai Nada, Kobe 657, JAPAN
[*]Fraunhofer Institute for Factory Operation and Automation,
Steinfeldstrasse 3, 39179 Barleben, GERMANY

Abstract

In the paper a novel idea of combining a virtual reality with an automated action control based on self-organization simulation is introduced. The concept provides an intelligent control for entities in the virtual reality enabling the user to participate in real-time to the self-organization simulation through the virtual reality interface.

The concept is demonstrated with an implementation in a manufacturing domain, where a real world factory shop-floor is modeled in virtual reality, and factory operations are controlled based on self-organization simulation. The control provides a real time and continuous adaptation of the factory operations to the user interactions and other environmental disturbances.

The implementation is based on distributed programming, where the self-organization simulator and the virtual factory are running on a separate computers. Two programs interchange continuously information through a local area network. The first implementation have proved to provide sufficient respond times for real time user interactions.

1 Introduction

Recently the factory modeling in virtual reality has become popular. The motivation in these models is to provide a better visualization of factories. However, these models being static do not represent the actual situation of living factories. Being able to animate factory operations with the possibility of interactions would provide not only a more realistic visualization, but also the verification of the whole factory design with simulation results. This has been the main motivation in this work.

The work reported hereafter combines two independent works: a static virtual factory model and a dynamic simulation of factory operations by self-organization principles. The result suggests a new concept of how static virtual models could be converted into living models with an intelligent control.

The result is not only a better visualization of a factory, but a realistic simulation of factory operations with user interactions. This provides a tool for analyzing the material flows and the required personal participations. The animated factory provides a method to explain the planned factory for people not familiar with abstract descriptions, and help them to improve the quality of simulations. In addition, the system could be used in educational or remote control purposes.

This paper consists of chapters to describe the general concept as a new virtual reality technique (*Intelligent Animation Control*), the practical application to the manufacturing domain (*Interactive Factory Animation*), the remarks on the implementation (*Implementation Notes*), and, finally, the test case used to verify the concept (*Verification of the Concept*) with a discussion and conclusion.

2 Intelligent Animation Control

The combination of virtual reality and self-organization simulation has two major contributions. For virtual reality it provides a simple method to create animations, *ie.*, *intelligent animation control.* On the other hand, the virtual reality part enables the user participation to the process of self-organization, *ie.*, *interactive self-organization simulation.*

Both of these are remarkable advantages for each field and provide together a powerful tool for new applications. Later, in this paper an intelligent factory animation is presented. Other possible applications could include design of molecules, entertainment, architectural design, layout design, *etc.*

2.1 General concept

The general concept of combining a virtual reality model and the self-organization simulator is shown in

[*]From July 1, 1997, NTT Human Interface Laboratories, Hikarinooka 1-1, Yokosuka, 238, JAPAN

0-8186-8150-0/97 $10.00

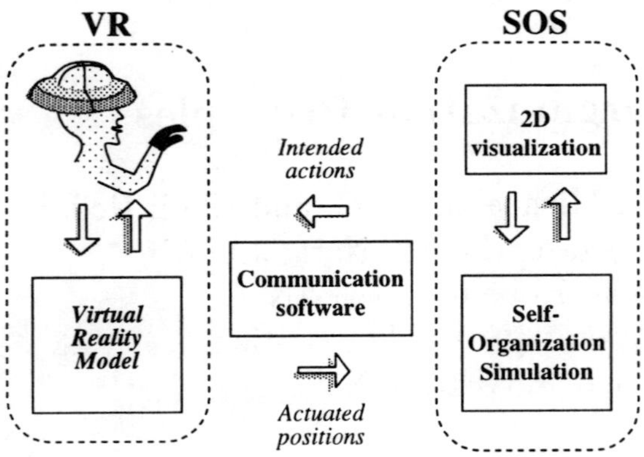

Figure 1: Combination of virtual reality model and self-organization simulator.

Figure 1.

The virtual reality model takes care of the user interactions with the model. The results of interactions, *ie.*, the actuated positions of virtual objects, are transfered via the communication software to the self-organization simulator. The changes in the model will take effect immediately, and the self-organization simulator will send updated versions of intended actions to the virtual reality to be actuated.

The intended actions could be thought like force vectors describing the direction and strength of virtual objects to move. These values are resulted in by the self-organization simulator. In the self-organization simulator each object is described by the capability to create attraction fields, and by the sensitivity for these attraction fields. This is explained in the following section.

It is worth of emphasis that the both parts are independently running programs. The merits and details of this are described within implementation section.

2.2 Simulating self-organization

The method is based on the potential fields, divided into attraction and repulsion fields, that describe the forces effecting autonomous entities in a function of distance between them. Each entity could generate several type of attraction fields, as well as each entity could locally decide its sensitiveness for the attraction fields generated by the other entities. As a result of a straightforward simulation, the effect of these forces emerges the global dynamics. Figure 2 illustrates how the basic concept from local dynamics to global dynamics. It is this virtual space where the user may interact with the entities through the virtual reality interface.

A simple form of the used attraction, repulsion and combined force fields as a function of the distance are

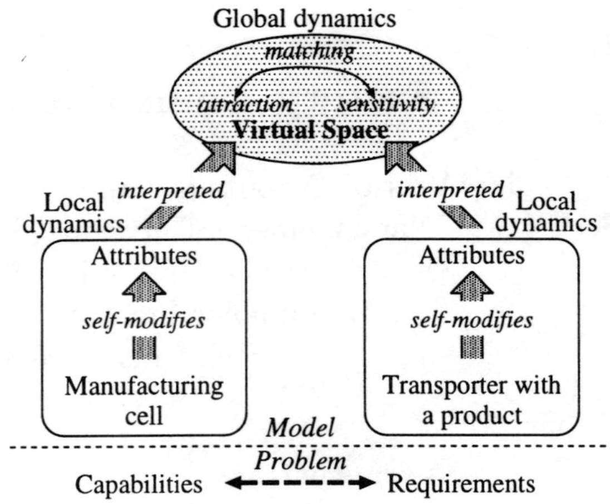

Figure 2: The general concept to create local and global dynamics.

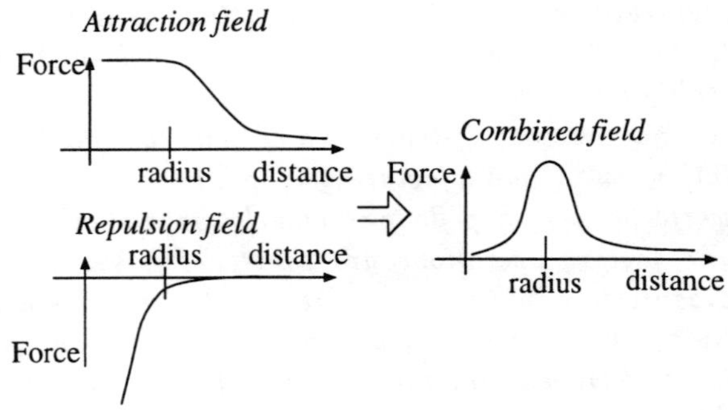

Figure 3: An example shape of potential fields.

shown in Figure 3.

3 Interactive Factory Animation

The traditional virtual factory models are static. There are usually no actions, or at most predefined sequences of actions, involved in the models. After all it is difficult to model intelligent factory operations even without virtual models. How to include the intelligent control of factory operations has been a difficult task. Various approach [2, 8] has been tried that all are characterized by the lack of adaptability to the non-predictable changes in the environment.

However, the latest results of biologically inspired manufacturing systems [3, 4, 5, 6] has not only provided a simulation of factory operations, but also a real-time animation of the operations. Adding here the virtual techniques enabling user interactions with the animation, results in the concept of *interactive factory animation.*

The new interactive direction is thus defined as follows: a virtual factory with its built-in automation and to allow users to work within this virtual environment like they would work in the real environment. This would not only produce the simulation results, but a conceptual verification of the designed factory environment and its working conditions. Later, the virtual factory could be replaced by a real factory, where the same automation system with the same people could work as they did in virtual reality. The virtual implementation would thus provide also an educational system for to-be-workers. The virtual factory could be also used for the remote control of dangerous operations.

The key concept in this kind vision is the combination of the intelligent control of factory operations with the interactive user participation. In this paper the intelligent control of factory operations means the control of material flows on the shop-floor level [1, 7].

The virtual factory is implemented using virtual reality techniques. The simulation part in the current implementation is based on the self-organization simulator (SOS), that has proved to be an efficient way to control the material flows in a factory.

The concept allows SOS to control all factory floor operations. In other words, SOS is continuously sending directions to materials directing their movement in the virtual factory. On the other hand, if there are any user interactions on the shop-floor through the virtual reality interface to the factory, these are sent to SOS effecting immediately the further directions.

For example, if an obstacle is put in the front of transporter, this could be immediately noticed by the controller, and the transporter avoids it. The obstacle could be also a moving object, like a human walking in the factory.

3.1 Factory model at the SOS side

In manufacturing domain, autonomous entities are manufacturing units, such as manufacturing cells and transporters with products. Each manufacturing cell generates attraction fields according to its attributes. The attributes are modified by itself according to its capabilities.

On the other hand, each product on a transporter also has attributes according to its sensitivity to attraction fields generated by manufacturing cells. These attributes being self-modifiable describes the processing requirements. When these two attributes, capability and requirements, are matched, the field forces are calculated and the movement of manufacturing units are simulated.

Figure 4 and 5 demonstrate how each machine and transporter are defined to generate attraction fields and to be sensitive for these fields.

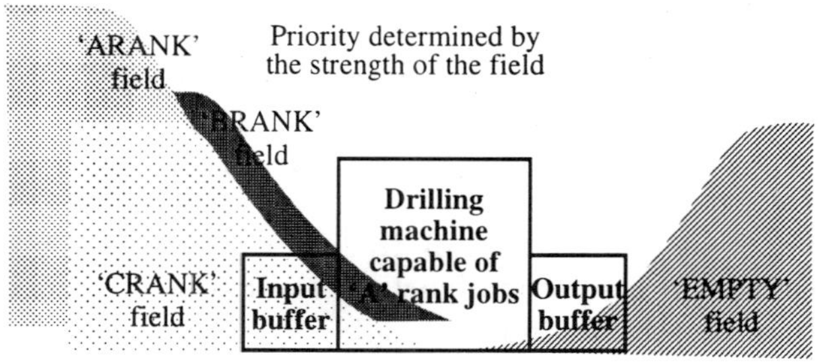

Figure 4: Definition of machines. The attraction fields are generated at input and output buffer locations. Priorities are expressed by large field values.

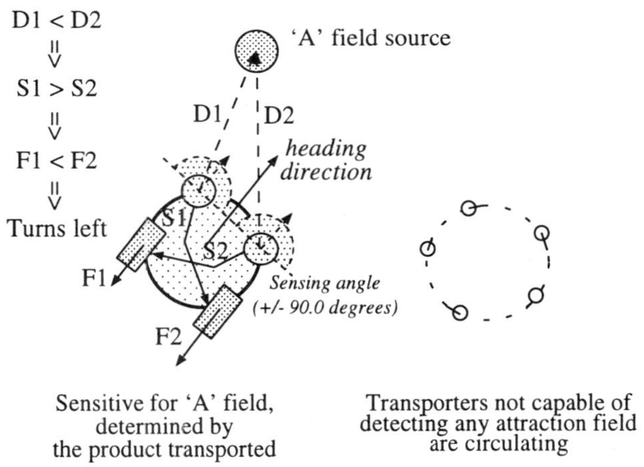

Figure 5: Definition of transporters. The attraction is calculated at two locations with a cross-connection to control the movement. The sensitivity is cut by 180 degrees. In the case of no attraction is detected, the transporter start to circulate.

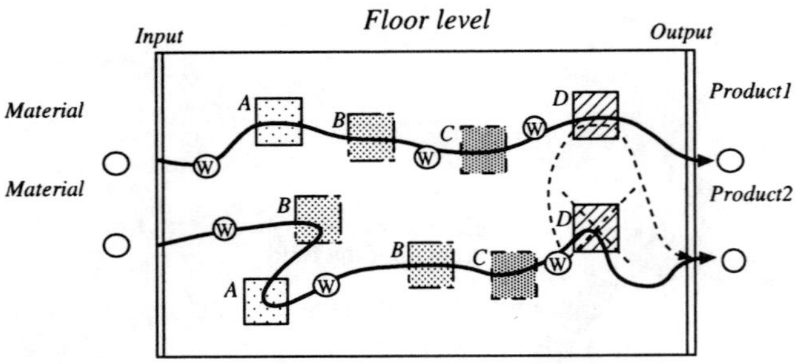

Figure 6: Navigation of transporters between machines. In case of malfunction, the re-routing occurs immediately and automatically.

When the machines are placed on the shop-floor the transporters with a product will navigate between machines finding a suitable machine for processing the product. This is shown in Figure 6.

While the simulation of the forces is continuous at any time a disturbance on the shop-floor will effect directly to the movement of transporters. Thus a malfunction in one machine will cause its attractions disappearing and the transporters will direct to another machine satisfying the conditions.

The method allows an abstract level matching of capabilities and requirements. Thus the method can be easily applied to various fields. Later in the case study an example of the matching possibilities will be given.

4 Implementation Notes

An overview of the implementation is shown in Figure 7.

The virtual reality part is implemented using Open Inventor graphics library. The self-organization simulator is based on C++ programming with LEDA (Library of Efficient Data structures and Algorithms). The communication software is a C++ class utilizing the MPI (Message Passing Interface) standard (LAM 6.1 implementation). In addition, a separate software is developed to collect and view the simulation results. This is also based on C++ programming with LEDA.

In the following, the main focus is on the concept of communication. Self-organization simulator is described in [7].

4.1 Distributed control

The connection between virtual factory and SOS controller is done in a distributed way. Both parts run as independent programs.

There are several merits for this approach.

- The software are kept separate from each others simplifying the work to development and modifications for further applications
- The performance is better on the low-end machines.
- With a heterogeneous network several kind of machines could be used. This is certainly an advantage in a project developed in collaboration on various platforms, but this could be also an advantage when the SOS part is put into the real factory environment and the virtual factory part is no more needed.

The communication interface consists of messages sent from the SOS controller to the virtual reality part, and vice versa. The messages are summarized in Figure 8.

The messages could be divided into two main groups: initialization messages and continuous messages. The former messages are used to establish initial configuration of the virtual factory.

The latter messages are sent continuously between virtual factory and SOS controller. Each object is identified by a unique label. This label is used to recognize the target object of each message. The objects are, obviously, transporters and machines.

Each object could have basically two kinds of messages including either position or status information. The position information could in addition be relative or absolute. In other words, the relative position as a movement from the current position, and the absolute position as a movement into a specific location. The position information are acknowledged by a message indicating the "actuated" positions, *ie.*, the absolute position.

The communication overhead causes some delay in the animation. In order to compensate this, the relative positions are interpreted as forces effecting to the objects in the virtual reality part until the next relative position is received. This causes a slight asynchronous situations that can be noticed best with the collision. On the other hand, a smoother movement is resulted.

5 Verification of the Concept

In the following a case study to verify the concept is given. The test case is a hall, where several drilling machines of printed circuit boards (PCBs) operate in parallel. Jobs arrive this hall in a more or less continuous flow, but in a non-predictable order.

It is assumed that the factory is not fully automated. The task is to distribute the jobs among

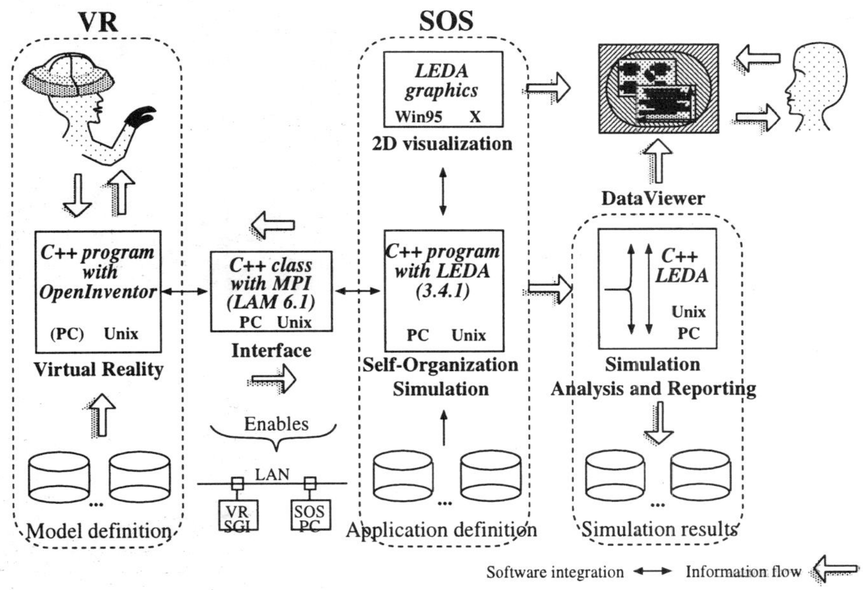

Figure 7: An overview of the implementation.

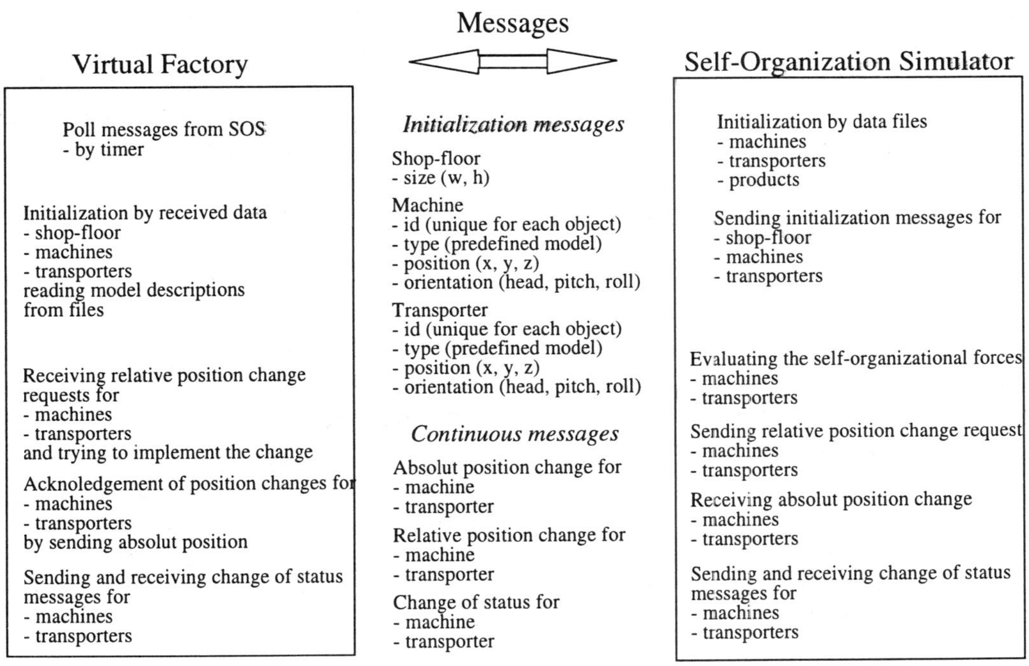

Figure 8: The communication messages.

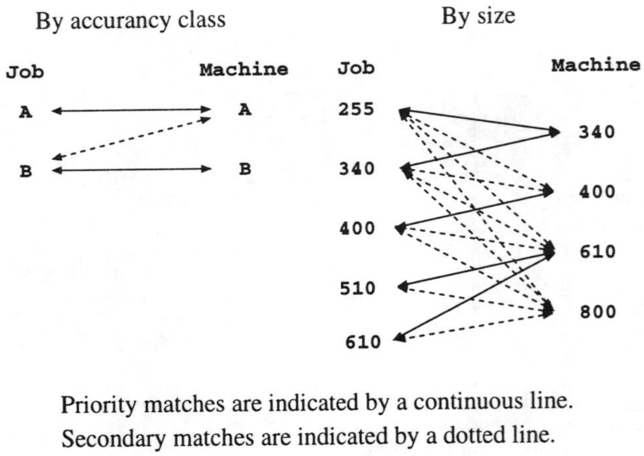

Figure 9: The matching rules between machines and jobs by the board/table sizes and the precision requirements/capabilities.

drilling machines as efficiently as possible using only the information of jobs currently in the input queue.

Note that it is impossible to determine the optimal allocation for this problem, because 1) there is no prior-information when a particular job arrives into the hall, 2) the number of operators is limited and load and unload times for machines varies depending on whether the operators are busy with other work, and 3) there are several restrictions on which machine a particular job could be processed.

The detail information of matching jobs to machines can be found in Figure 9.

The problem was solved using the self-organization simulator [7]. In the following a slightly updated model has been used. The major changes are as follows.

- Intelligent input queue: the order of picking up a next job for transportation is determined by calculating the attraction field for each job in the queue, and then simple selecting a job having the largest attraction field.

- Repulsion fields: Repulsion fields are used for collision avoidance. This provides a rudimentary way to handle collisions by calculating negative attractions.

- New shop-floor layout: A realistic shop-floor layout is used. Now the dispatching and collection point are located in the middle of the shop-floor, like in the real factory.

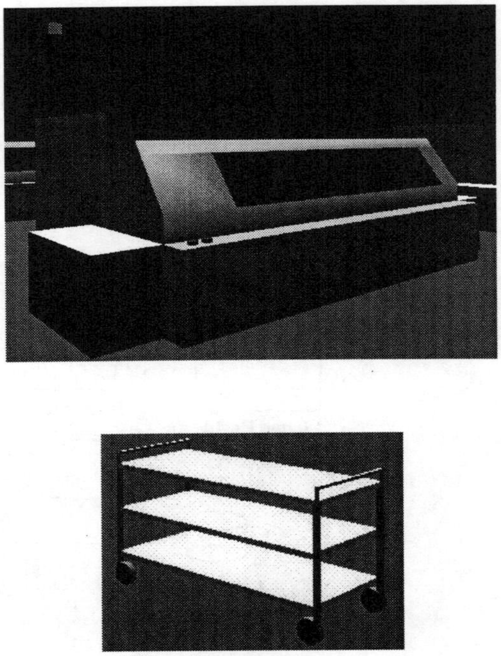

Figure 10: The virtual factory objects: machine and transporter.

5.1 Factory Model

Factory model consists of transporters and drilling machines. There are several type of machines varying in their size and properties. In the virtual factory the size and the color of machines are distinguished.

Transporters are modeled simple as trolleys with a relative size to the machines. In the real factory the transporters are very much same with a human operators. Figure 10 illustrates a machine and a transporter.

The initial positions and types of the machines are received from SOS. Based on these information the predefined models are retrieved and placed in the hall, that's size is also given by SOS.

5.2 Results

A snapshot of the actual simulation is given in Figure 11. The interactions include 1) movement of machines in virtual reality or in self-organization side, 2) stopping and starting the machines or transporters. and 3) generating new obstacles, also movable, on the shop-floor.

The respond time is reasonable depending on the hardware the system is running. There are some "jumpy" movement in transporters that has been smoothed by keeping the transporters moving in the previous defined direction even they do not receive new directions from the SOS part. This, however,

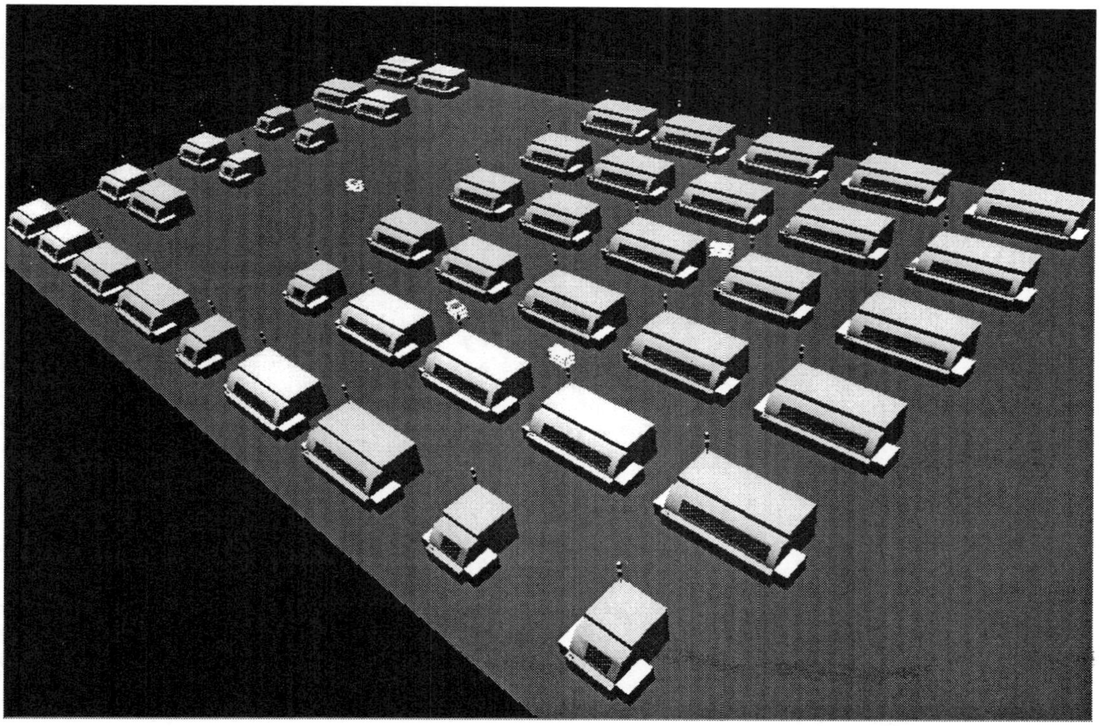

Figure 11: The layout of virtual factory.

causes slight overlap of objects, because the collision avoidance is implemented by repulsion fields, and now this respond is delayed.

6 Conclusion

We described in this paper a novel concept to combine the virtual implementation of factory model with a self-organization simulator. The combination was implemented in a distributed way having various merits, although causing also a slight communication overhead.

The results proved the concept feasible. It is assumed that the developed system could be applied with simple modifications in a wide range of other applications. Work is continuing to improve the presented application and to test it within a real factory environment. Other applications have also been started.

The work has conducted in a close collaboration between Fraunhofer Institute for Factory Operation and Automation and BMS (Biological Manufacturing Systems) group of IMS Japan's (Intelligent Manufacturing Systems) NGMS (Next Generation Manufacturing Systems) program.

References

[1] Nobutada Fujii, Jari Vaario, and Kanji Ueda. Potential field based simulation of self-organization in biological manufacturing systems. In *Proceedings of Manufacturing System Design'97, May 14-16, 1997, Magdeburg, Germany*, page Paper 5. LOGIS, Stuttgart, 1997.

[2] A. Tharumarajah, A.J. Wells, and L. Neems. Comparison of the bionic, fractal and holonic manufacturing system concepts. 9(3):217–226, 1996.

[3] K. Ueda and K. Ohkura. A biological approach to complexity in manufacturing systems. In *Proc. of the 27th CIRP International Seminar on Manufacturing Systems*, pages 69–78. Ann Arbor, 1995.

[4] Kanji Ueda. Intelligent manufacturing systems – from knowledge-base to emergence-type. *Journal of Advanced Automation Technology*, 6(3):143–149, 1994.

[5] Kanji Ueda and Jari Vaario. The biological manufacturing system: Adaptation to growing complexity and dynamics in manufacturing environment. pages 39–44. 29th CIRP International Seminar on Manufacturing Sytems, May, 1997, Osaka, Japan, 1997.

[6] Kanji Ueda, Jari Vaario, and Kazuhiro Ohkura. Modeling of biological manufacturing systems for

dynamic reconfiguration. 47th CIRP General Assembly, Tianjin, China, August 24-30, 1997, 1997. (to appear).

[7] Jari Vaario and Kanji Ueda. An emergent method for dynamic scheduling. pages 187–198. The Second World Congress on Intelligent Manufacturing Processes & Systems, June 10-13, 1997, Budapest, Hungary, 1997.

[8] H.P. Wiendahl and P. Scholtissek. Management and control of complexity in manufacturing. 43(2):533–540, 1994.

Evaluation of a virtual reality system for medicine

Hiroshi Oyama1), Fumihiko Wakao2)
1) Chief of MedVR Projects, Head of Neurosurgery, Dept. of Neurosurgery,
2) Dept. of Diagnostic Radiology, National Cancer Center Hospital,
5-1-1, Tsukiji, Chuo-ku, 104 Tokyo, Japan.
Tel:+81-3-3542-2511, Fax: +81-3-3542-1724.
E-mail: hoyama@ncc.go.jp.

Abstract

We are currently developing a virtual reality system for cancer diagnosis and treatment. The new technology of virtual reality will be applied to a surgical simulation system, a new diagnostic system, a palliative care support system and an informed consent support system. In the research and development of this virtual reality system, we need a method to evaluate it for practical use. For evaluating a medical virtual reality system, we propose the equation S (S: System factor = Sp: presentation factor, Sm: measurement and control factor, So: operation system factor)= $\alpha \cdot$ A/H (A: Application factor, H: Human factor, α : a coefficient). We think that the human factor is the most important consideration for the development of a medical virtual reality system.

Keywords: virtual reality system, methodology, equation, medicine, surgery.

1 Introduction

Research on the application of virtual reality (VR) to medical treatment began in the National Cancer Center in 1993. Five sub-projects on medical VR are currently underway. Three prototype applications for surgical support, medical education and informed consent being developed.[1,2] Thus, it is important to establish an objective method for evaluating such systems. In the present paper, we report a method for evaluating a VR system for medical treatment based on an analysis of the comments of medical students after they had experienced a surgical simulation system for removing a brain tumor. The purpose of this application was to teach an operation plan to medical students.

2 Method

Subjects: Eleven 3rd-year medical students who had not previously experienced VR participated in this study (8 men and 3 women). Outline of the study. Date: March 15, 1996. Place: National Cancer Center VR Development Room. System name: Surgical simulation support system. Application name: Brain tumor removal surgical simulation. Presentation system (Sp: presentation factor): The subject used a Head-Mounted Display (HMD). Shape data of the brain were displayed in virtual space using three-dimensional texture mapping by real-time rendering. The amount of data in virtual space was less than about 15000 polygons per frame, and more than seven or eight frames were displayed per second. The tactile system was not used. The auditory system presented the sound of both a skin incision and a drill used in the operation. The vestibule system and the system used to present the applied force were not used. The systems for olfaction, nociperception, and temperature were also not used. Measurement and control system (Sm: measurement and control factor): The Polhemus sense system was used to track position. The eye-, tactile- and force-measurement systems were not used. Operation

0-8186-8150-0/97 $10.00 © 1997 IEEE

system (So: operation factor): Command instruction method: A pen-type stylus was used to provide commands. VR session: All of the subjects were given a simple 10-min explanation concerning the use of the VR system for medical treatment at the National Cancer Center VR Development Room. In addition, all of the subjects were also given a brief overview of the equipment and about a 5-min explanation on the use of the stylus. The subjects were divided into two groups and briefly instructed how to select objects in virtual space; e.g., a virtual surgical knife and a drill. Each subject spent about 10 minutes in virtual space. The subject sat in a chair and wore an HMD. With the HMD in the see-through mode, a data glove was placed on the left hand, and a stylus was placed in the right hand. The subject was then instructed to look at the ceiling in the virtual world, then at the virtual floor, and finally at objects to the right and to the left. The purpose of this procedure was to orient the subject in the virtual world. The left hand with the data glove appeared in the virtual world, and opening and closing of the virtual hand in the virtual world could be seen with the HMD. (Photograph) Thereafter, a virtual surgical simulation was experienced. Afterwards, the subject completed a questionnaire.

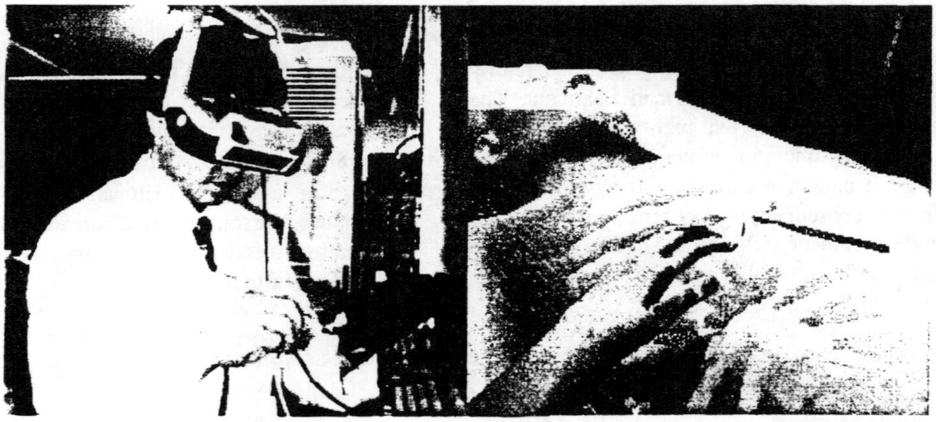

Photograph: VR surgical simulation environment and demonstration scene.

3. Evaluation

We evaluated the VR system for medical treatment using three indices: a human factor, a system factor, and an application factor. The subject's understanding of VR technology, computer literacy, and the content of the education were used as an index of the human factor. The subject evaluated both the experience of using the system and the value of its application.

4. Results

All of the subjects were familiar with the term "virtual reality" before experiencing this system; 73% had learned about it from television and 45% had learned about it from magazines. Only 27% knew that VR technology has been applied to medical treatment, and most of these had learned of this from more senior students who had experienced VR at the National Cancer Center the previous year. Evaluation of the subjects' level of education: The subjects had completed the phase of their instruction which involved lectures concerning basic and clinical medicine. They had not yet received training in a hospital ward or in an outpatient clinic, and had never seen an actual surgery. Evaluation of the system by the subjects: Presentation system: Visual system: Resolution is insufficient: 45%. The systems tires the eyes: 18%. The septum of the HMD is disturbing: 18%. The image does not appear to be three-dimensional: 36%. The difference between the right and left images is disturbing: 18%. Tactile system: The illusion of reality is impaired because the sense of touch is not experienced: 64%. Auditory system: (not evaluated). Position system: There is no sense of distance: 9%. Vestibule system: (not evaluated). Force system: The illusion of reality is impaired because force is not experienced: 55%. Olfaction system: (not evaluated). Temperature and nociperception system:(not evaluated). Measurement and control system: Visual system: The HMD is heavy and tires the neck: 18%. It is not easy to focus: 73%. The difference between movement in the virtual world and movement in reality is disturbing: 27%. Both responses and movement are slow in virtual space. Operation system: Command instruction method using a stylus: It is difficult to select a menu item: 36%. The arm becomes tired when the stylus is used for a long time (about 15 minutes in this study): 27%. It is difficult to select a menu item in the virtual world: 9%. Overview of the subjects' responses: The subjects noted that while this technology has the potential to revolutionize the field of medical training and treatment, the current state of the art, particularly with regard to the surgical simulation, does not provide either an adequate sense of reality, due in part to inadequate resolution, or adequate information to be a stand-alone system. Many students noted that the system's value could have been enhanced if their experience had been associated with a conventional lecture or a live demonstration of the surgical technique. However, even with its current limitations, some of the subjects thought that the system could be very useful for studying anatomy, and could be immediately used for patient education/ entertainment. Subjects recommended that the system be more portable, for use outside of the Development Room, and that costs could be kept down by using a pen-type pointing device. The subjects also recommended that training aids could be superimposed on the virtual image; e.g., navigation aids could be used to identify the location of an incision. Evaluation of the system's potential usefulness in the field of medicine: Operation simulation: 100%. Medical education: 91%. Radiation diagnosis study: 64%. Remote medical treatment: 45%. Relaxation: 36%. Patient support system (education/ entertainment): 36%, Rehabilitation: 27%. Radiation treatment plan support: 27%. Treatment of nervous disorders: 9%. Home medical treatment: 9%.

5. Summary

We think that VR is an important technology for the resolution of various problems in the medical field. Unfortunately, there is currently no established method for evaluating medical VR systems. In the present study, we analyzed our medical VR system by considering three levels: (subject level (Human factor: H factor), system level (System factor: S factor) and application level (Application factor: A factor)) by using our medical VR system. The medical VR system consists of three subsystems: a virtual-space presentation system: Sp ; a measurement and control system: Sm ; and an operation system: So. We developed the following formula as an evaluation tool: S (S: System factor = Sp: presentation factor, Sm: measurement and control factor, So: operation system factor)= $\alpha \cdot A/H$ (A: Application factor, H: Human factor, α : a coefficient).

The subject's computer literacy plays an important role in using VR technology, even though it is believed that VR currently represents the ultimate human/computer interface. In the present study, although all of the subjects had heard of the term "virtual reality", few knew that it has been applied to the field of medical training and treatment. As this technology matures, it will become increasingly important to evaluate medical VR systems in terms of a) the subject's experience of the system's ability to deal with measurement and control in the presentation, b) the subject's personal background, and c) the subject's experience of the operation system. Moreover, in the future it will be important to be able to recognize problems with VR technology in terms of the subject's VR experience. We are developing an improved medical VR system using this approach.

Acknowledgments: We are grateful to the students of the Hokkaido University Department of Medicine for their cooperation in this research during a training period at the National Cancer Center Hospital.

References:

[1] Oyama H., et al.: VR medical support system for cancer patients. Cancer edutainment VR theater (CEVRT)and psychooncological VR therapy (POVRT). Interactive Technology and Healthcare, 433-438: Edited by R. M. Satava et al., IOS Press and Ohmsha,1995.

[2] Oyama H., et al.: Surgical simulation support system. Interactive Technology and Healthcare, 439-444: Edited by R. M. Satava et al., IOS Press and Ohmsha,1995.

The Virtual and Real Environments: Symbiosis

Francis Pelletier, OAA
Digital Simulation Laboratory, RPS, Public Works and Government Services Canada
pelletif@pwgsc.gc.ca

Parliament Hill, West Block, Aerial View

Introduction

Traditionally, architects and engineers have used CAD systems to assist them in the development of construction drawings. This approach enables the professionals to produce drawings in a more cost efficient manner but, unfortunately, at this point it may also be too late to make any major changes to the original concept. Our goal is to find other alternatives to assist the decision makers in the initial stages of the project.

At the Digital Simulation Laboratory (hereafter referred to as DSL), we explore the possibility of using computers in the preliminary stages of the project in order to ensure a better integration of the project in its environment. The ultimate goal of this approach is to allow the design team to simulate in real time how each proposed design could meet the clients' demands. All this, without conflicting with an existing building or generating an environmental problem that could affect the viability of the project.

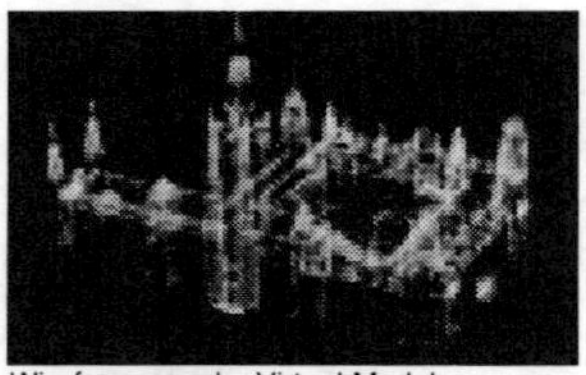

Wireframe mode, Virtual Model

Shade mode, Virtual Model

Texture mapped rendering, Virtual Model

Capturing our Environment

The architectural 3D modelling process involves three stages: Information Gathering, Modelling and Visualisation / Rendering. These steps must be repeated in sequence for each individual element in order for it to be digitally recreated.

The first step consists of gathering information from many different sources. A variety of information is required: plans, cross-sections, elevations, survey data, retouched photographs and aerial photographs. Using a file transfer format we are able to recover computer files from most software.

The modelling process begins with the manipulation of the information gathered to create a 3D digital model. This is the longest and most laborious part of the process. Photography is memory intensive, but essential in order to enrich the 3D model and make it realistic.

In the visualization stage, the camera is manipulated to produce images from many different angles. This task is critical in visually evaluating the quality of the modelling. The final rendering process then provides an image that precisely reflects the effect of the textures applied to the geometry. The image is further enhanced by shade and/or shadow.

Sun and Shadow Study
Congress Centre, Québec City

Interaction with "Virtuality"

Once the physical environment is captured, we have the ability to simulate various natural phenomenons such as "sun and shadow" or "wind and snow" within the virtual environment. These simulations provide a better evaluation of the potential performance of a proposal on a given site.

Generic Simulator, DSL

Generic Simulator

The ultimate goal of the Digital Simulation Laboratory has always been to immerse our clients in their project through the 3D virtual mode. This idea motivated the DSL team to develop a Generic Simulator that would fulfill this goal.

We adapted a "MicroSoft Sidewinder 3D Pro" joystick in order to facilite the navigation through the 3D digital model. This device provides total freedom and control to navigate the virtual space in real time. The dynamic module was conducted by adapting the Crystal Eyes technology and a Stereoscopic Electrohome Projector.

An additional function was incorporated to allow individuals to interact with the 3D digital model. An example of this feature allows the user to look at various alternative designs just by pressing a button on the joystick, all within the same simulation.

Since this walkthrough is performed in real-time, the software and hardware usually restrict the environment complexity and rendering quality. We are presently capable of simulating up to 12,000 polygons and 16 MB of texture with a refresh rate of 15 Mhz.

Closing the Loop

Parliament Hill, West Block, Physical Model

Since December 1995, we have been able to recreate all of the traditional tasks required in the development of an architectural or engineering project with digital technology. Even a physical model can now be produced directly from the 3D digital model.

To achieve this dramatic result, we chose to use a technology called Stereolithography. It allows us to produce physical models without any limitations, ensuring complete flexibility regardless of the building complexity.

With the help of the of the NRC Institute for Information Technology and the Softimage Special Project Team, production of a physical model from a digital model was achieved.

Before the construction of the physical model can begin, the computer file containing the 3D digital model must be converted. Stereolithography was designed to operate from a computer file that contains the topology of a solid, volumetric model. Our original files use a 3D polygonal format to model *surfaces*, as this is most convenient for rendering and animation purposes. To resolve this incompatibility, we then had to develop a file translator.

Once the file conversion was complete, the computer was able to read the data and direct an ultraviolet laser beam. The outline of the 3D object was traced in a photosensitive resin which hardens upon contact with the laser. Once the first layer is drawn, the platform holding the resin automatically lowers by one tenth of a millimetre. The laser then draws the next layer and thus, millimetre by millimetre, the model begins to take shape. A detailed model that would have taken a craftsman months to create, without ever achieving the same degree of accuracy, was constructed in a matter of hours.

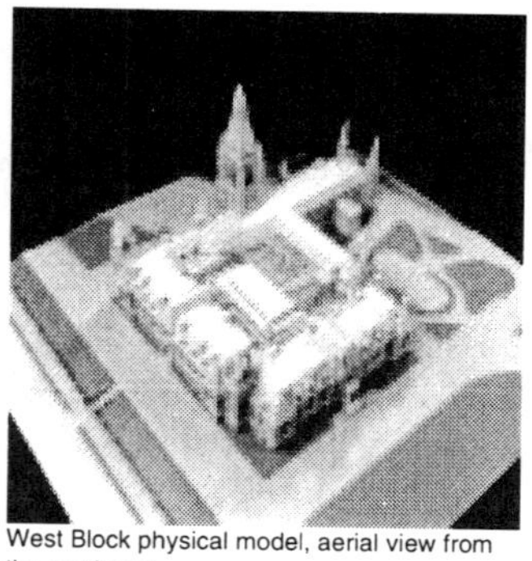
West Block physical model, aerial view from the southeast.

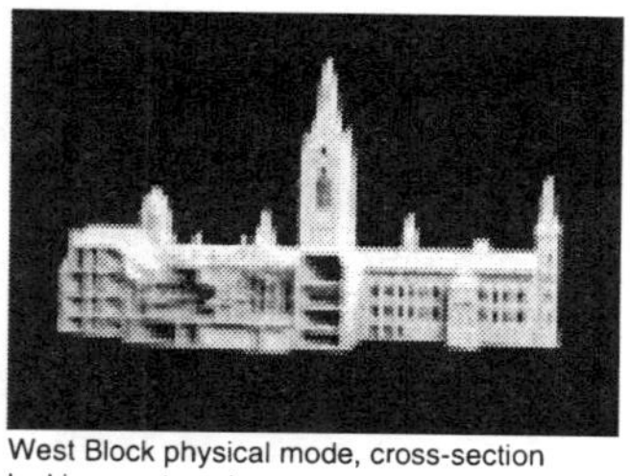
West Block physical mode, cross-section looking westward.

Conclusion

This research allowed us to break down even further the barriers between the virtual and real environments, achieving a state of symbiosis in exchanging information. The encouraging results demonstrated that we can bring digital information "back to life". We can now further investigate the many possibilities, extending the concept of building physical models to actual construction. We believe that as automation and technology have transformed the automobile industry, so could they also revolutionize building construction as we know it.

Web Sites

For additional information, we invite you to "surf" the net at the following addresses:

- www.sgi.com/International/Canada/success/parliament.html (produced by Silicon Graphics)
- www.softimage.com/default.htm?url=/EN-US/Projects/CustomerStories/DS.htm (produced by SoftImage)
- www.radio-canada.com/decouverte/d5_arch/1a.html (produced by Radio-Canada)

Any reference to any specific commercial product, service or firm, by trade name, trademark, manufacturer or otherwise, does not imply any endorsement or favoring by Public Works and Government Services Canada (PWGSC) or any of its components. PWGSC does not assume any responsibility for the contents of any third party product. Unless otherwise stated, the images in this document are from the Digital Simulation Laboratory.

This is an excerpt of a full-length paper.

Reviewers

Massimo Bergamasco, *Scuola Superiore S. Anna, Italy*
Tat-Seng Chua, *National Univ. of Singapore, Singapore*
Rae A. Earnshaw, *University of Bradford, UK*
Ole Henrik Ellestad, *Norsk Regnesentral, Norway*
Jose L. Encarnacao, *Fraunhofer-Institut fur Graphische Datenverarbeitung, Germany*
Scott S. Fisher, *Telepresence Research Corp., USA*
Eddy Flerackers, *Limburg University Center, Belgium*
Jean-Guy Fontaine, *Laboratoire de Robotique de Paris, France*
Mark W. Green, *University of Alberta, Canada*
Charles Grimsdale, *Division Group, Ltd, UK*
Chua Grim Guan, *National Univ. of Singapore, Singapore*
Hiroshi Harashima, *University of Tokyo, Japan*
Ng Hern, *National University of Singapore, Singapore*
Michitaka Hirose, *University of Tokyo, Japan*
Tohru Ifukube, *Hokkaido University, Japan*
Prem Kalra, *University of Geneva, Switzerland*
Takeo Kanade, *Carnegie Mellon University, USA*
Young Whan Kim, *Korean Telecom, South Korea*
Stanislav Klimenko, *Inst. for High Energy Physics, Russia*
Myron Krueger, *Artificial Reality Corp., USA*
Tosiyasu L. Kunii, *LDAT, Japan*
Yen H. Lee, *National Univ. of Singapore, Singapore*
Nadia Magnenat Thalmann, *Univ. of Geneva, Switzerland*
Hermann Maurer, *University of Graz, Austria*
Steffen Meschkat, *ART+COM, Germany*
Laurent Moccozet, *University of Geneva, Switzerland*
Makoto Nonaka, *FISA, USA*
Junji Nomura, *Matsusita Electric Works LTD, Japan*
Setsuo Ohsuga, *Waseda University, Japan*
Takeo Ojika, *Gifu University, Japan*
Alex Pentland, *MediaLab MIT, USA*
Werner Purgathofer, *Vienna Univ. of Technology, Austria*
Larry Rosenblum, *Naval Research Laboratory, USA*
Joachim Sauter, *ART+COM, Germany*
Hans-Peter Seidel, *Erlangen University, Germany*
Luis Serra, *National Univ. of Singapore, Singapore*
Sung Yong Shin, *KAIST, South Korea*
Mel Slater, *University College London, UK*
Robert J. Stone, *VR Solutions Ltd, UK*
Yasuhito Suenaga, *Nagoya University, Japan*
Susumu Tachi, *University of Tokyo, Japan*
Demetri Terzopoulos, *University of Toronto, Canada*
Daniel Thalmann, *Swiss Federal Institute of Technology, Switzerland*
Hal Thwaites, *Concordia University, Canada*
Junichiro Toriwaki, *Nagoya University, Japan*
Jiaxin Wang, *University of Tsinghua, China*
Kaye Wohn, *KAIST, South Korea*
Franz-Heinrich Wolter, *Univ. of Hannover, Germany*
Kazuhiko Yamamoto, *Gifu University, Gifu, Japan*
David Zeltzer, *David Sarnoff Research Center, USA*

Author Index

Notes

IEEE COMPUTER SOCIETY

4/15/97